D1294433

MYTH, LEGEND & ROMANCE

MYTH, LEGEND & ROMANCE

AN ENCYCLOPÆDIA OF THE IRISH FOLK TRADITION

DR DAITHI O HOGAIN

New York London Toronto Sydney Tokyo Singapore

PRENTICE HALL PRESS
15 Columbus Circle
New York, New York 10023

First Edition.

Published simultaneously in Great Britain by Ryan Publishing Company Ltd.

Library of Congress Cataloging in Publication Data

Ó hÓgáin, Dáithí, 1949-
Myth, legend, and romance: an encyclopaedia of Irish Folk tradition /Dáithí Ó hÓgáin.—
1st ed.
p. cm.
Includes bibliographical references.
ISBN 0-13-275959-4 : $29.95
1. Folklore—Ireland—Encyclopedias.
2. Folk literature. Irish—Encyclopedias.
I. Title.
GR153.5.016 1991 90-43107
415—dc20 CIP

Origination by Wenham Arts, Peterborough, England.
Printed on part recycled paper by
Martin's of Berwick Ltd, England.

do Chaitríona, ós í atá foighneach...

CONTENTS

CONTENTS

INTRODUCTION

The purpose of this work is to provide a comprehensive key to the rich tradition of storytelling in Ireland. The material ranges from the country's early literature to its late folklore, and the discussion covers all narratives of importance which have survived in either written or oral form. The general intention is to illustrate how diversity and unity can exist side by side and complement each other, and as such to place the material in its full context. The entries are arranged on the basis of designations which act as indicators to the great wealth of story. These designations are mostly names of celebrated characters, since narratives tend to cluster about personalities, but in order to present an integral picture some general entries were also deemed necessary. Within each entry the appropriate stories are summarised, and the pattern of development of these stories is described so as to show the chronology of their composition and of their elaboration. In this way, the author attempts to clarify the origins of different aspects of the lore, and the role played by various social and cultural factors as well as by simple motif-attraction. At the end of each entry is a list of the best editions of original texts and of the most significant discussions of them to appear in print. These lists provide detailed guidelines for the serious student and academic researcher, and the sources listed can be clearly identified by reference to the Bibliography at the end of the book. The attention of non-Irish users of this Encyclopaedia is drawn to the special Guide to Language and Pronunciation which is included, and such users are also reminded that most of the cited sources give translations of the original texts or references to where such can be found. In this book generally, bold print is used to indicate that a particular item is the subject of a separate entry.

For the author, the assembling of this material into one volume has been a life ambition, and he wishes to express gratitude to all those who rendered assistance - in particular Professor Bo Almqvist and the staff of the Department of Irish Folklore at University College Dublin - and to the publisher David Ryan for his vision and encouragement. A special thanks is due to those individuals and institutions who assisted in the provision of pictures and illustrations.

ACKNOWLEDGMENTS

Acknowledgment is gratefully made to the following for their generosity in providing illustrations and giving permission for reproduction. Plate numbers are indicated in brackets:-

Bord Fáilte (8, 15, 19, 21, 22, 29, 33, 34, 45, 50, 53, 63, 68, 74, 77)
British Museum (26, 27)
Cambridge University (23)
C. J. Fallon, Educational Publishers (47)
Dáithí Ó hÓgáin (28, 44)
Dan Cronin and Oifig an tSoláthair (32)
Dean and Chapter of the Cathedral Church of St. Patrick, Armagh (62)
Department of Irish Folklore, University College Dublin (12, 18, 39, 66)
Dr. H. Taylor of Keele University (91)
Educational Company of Ireland (83)
Franciscan Library, Killiney (85)
Green Studio, Dublin (24)
Hulton Picture Library (94)
Irish Horse Museum (2)
Malcolm Murray and Routledge & Kegan Paul (90)
Mary Bergin (3)
National Gallery of Ireland (67, 82, 89)
National Library of Ireland (6, 36, 54, 64, 65, 70, 71, 76, 88)
National Maritime Museum, Greenwich (72)
National Museum of Ireland (1, 10, 20, 30, 31, 41, 55, 61, 75, 80, 84)
National Museums of Scotland (11)
National Portrait Gallery, London (52)
Office of Public Works, Dublin (7, 35, 40, 48, 60, 73)
Oifig an tSoláthair, Dublin (43)
Oscar Marne (4)
Rheinisches Landesmuseum, Bonn (57)
Royal Irish Academy (79, 86)
The Hon. Grania O'Brien Weir and Oxford University Press (59)
The late Professor S. P. Ó Riordáin and Methuen & Co. (46)
Trinity College, Dublin (17, 38)
Ulster Museum, Welch Collection (25)

The sources of the other illustrations are:-

A. E. Brehm, *Tierleben* (42)
Anthologia Hibernica 2 (58)
Illustrated Sporting and Dramatic News (87)
James Graves / J. G. A. Prim, *History and Antiquities of St. Canice's Cathedral* (13)
J. C. Hall , *Ireland* (51, 69)
J. G. Millais, *Mammals of Great Britain and Ireland* (5)
J. H. Todd, *War of the Gaedhil with the Gaill* (9)
John Derricke, *Image of Ireland* (49, 81)
Joseph Strutt, *Sports and Pastimes of the People of England* (16)
P. D. Hardy, *Legends, Tales and Stories of Ireland* (56)
P. W. Joyce, *Social History of Ancient Ireland* (14)
Thomas Messingham, *Florilegium Insulae Sanctorum* (78)
Thomas Stafford, *Pacata Hibernia* (37)
Transactions of the Royal Irish Academy 18 (92)
William Carrigan, *History and Antiquities of the Diocese of Ossory* (93)

Thanks are also due to Herma Boyle and Margaret Delaney of the Audio-Visual Centre, University College Dublin, for their advice and assistance.

GUIDE TO LANGUAGE AND PRONUNCIATION

Irish is in origin a Celtic tongue, belonging to that family of languages once spoken in many areas of central and southern Europe. It seems to have first reached Ireland in or about the 5th century BC and to have gradually displaced whatever other languages were spoken by prehistoric inhabitants of the country. Primitive Irish must have remained comprehensible to speakers of other Celtic dialects for many centuries, and the ogham-inscriptions show that the integral Celtic word-forms had still not been forgotten in the 4th century AD. When the language was first committed to parchment at the end of the 6th century, however, many internal and final syllables had become syncopated, giving rise to a new morphology which clearly distinguished Irish from its Celtic sources. The language in texts from the 7th to the 9th century is referred to by researchers as Old Irish, and towards the end of that period a tendency to restructure the forms of nouns and verbs, and to re-arrange the syntax, gave rise to Middle Irish, which is the term employed for the language as it was written from the 10th to the 13th century. There is evidence that a wide range of sound-changes occurred at the end of this period, and this combined with the ongoing grammatical changes to produce Modern Irish.

The initial form of the modern language is often referred to as Classical Irish, which was promulgated by the literati as a standard literary system from the 14th to the early 17th century, after which political and social changes brought about the downfall of the native social and literary order. From that time onwards, new and less rigid literary forms developed, and the literature began to recognise divergencies in word-forms which reflect those found in modern dialects. A certain amount of variation must have always existed, but it is apparent that most of the regional differences in contemporary spoken Irish are of post-mediaeval provenance. The dialects can be generally divided into a northern one (known as 'Ulster Irish'), a central one ('Connacht Irish'), and a southern one ('Munster Irish'). All dialects graduated into each other on a geographical plane, and versions of all three were in fact spoken until recently in the appropriate areas of the fourth province, Leinster. For the benefit of some readers, it may be necessary to state that two other languages - Scottish Gaelic and Manx - originated in Old Irish, but in the post-mediaeval period diverged significantly from the language spoken in Ireland.

In ancient times a tendency had developed to soften intervocalic consonants, and this gave rise to the aspiration of several such consonants in Irish. It also gave rise to the peculiar feature - common to all surviving Celtic languages - of mutation of initial consonants, usually according to the grammatical context. Initial mutation took the form of aspiration ('softening', indicated in writing by a dot above the letter or by a succeeding 'h'), or of eclipsis ('hardening', indicated in writing by inserting a special consonant before the word). From the 12th century onwards some notable changes occurred. Eclipsis was dispensed with in some contexts, but it strongly maintained its position in others. Aspirated consonants, since they repesented special phonemes, remained constant, but some of them underwent modification in sound. For instance, the pronunciation of 'th' was assimilated to that of 'h', while the pronunciation of 'dh' was assimilated to that of 'gh'. Furthermore, intervocalic 'dh'/'gh' generally disappeared in pronunciation, leaving the preceding vowel either lengthened or diphthongised; while in final position 'dh'/'gh' was either muted or given other qualities according to dialect. In the southern and central dialects, medial 'bh'/'mh' was often silenced, causing the preceding vowel to be lengthened or diphthongised, and varying phonemic shifts also occurred due to final 'll', 'nn', and 'm' in monosyllables.

Stress is the most distinctive feature of differentiation between spoken dialects of Irish. The original practice of placing strong stress on the initial syllable of a word was a major contributory factor to historical change in the language, from the development of aspiration and the syncopation of syllables in primitive Irish to the restructuring of verbal forms in Middle Irish and the muting of secondary aspirated consonants in post-mediaeval times. It is apparent that penultimate stress was the norm in all parts of the country, and that it did not generally affect the lengthened forms which many secondary syllables had acquired. This remained the position until the beginning of the Modern Irish period, but thereafter it survived fully only in the central dialect -as in Galway and Mayo today. In the north, probably under Scottish influence, the strong penultimate stress began to cause the shortening of long syllables elsewhere in a word. The opposite occurred in the south, where long syllables often attracted the stress onto themselves and away from the penultimate. This southern development appears to have been accelerated by the influence of Anglo-French spoken by the Norman settlers.

It should be noted that, in Irish generally, each consonant is pronounced as either palatal or non-palatal. This sound contrast (often referred to as 'slender' and 'broad') sprang from the syncopation of syllables in early times. Standard orthography indicates the palatal quality of a consonant by placing the letter 'i' before it or either 'i' or 'e' after it. The letters 'a', 'o', or 'u' next to a consonant, or the letter 'e' before one, indicate that it is non-palatal. Furthermore, an initial 'r' in a word is almost always pronounced non-palatal. An acute accent over a vowel indicates lengthening, and long vowels affect consonants in the same manner as short ones.

The vocabulary of the Irish language has, through the centuries, been influenced by the several other languages and peoples which have played a part in the country's history - such as ecclesiastical Latin, and spoken Welsh, Norse, French, Scottish, and English. It therefore can be said to reflect the general historical experience of Ireland in both linguistic and cultural terms. For further and more detailed information see the following works:- Brian Ó Cuív, *A View of the Irish Language* (Dublin, 1969); Rudolf Thurneysen, *A Grammar of Old Irish* (Dublin, 1961); Thomas F O'Rahilly, *Irish Dialects Past and Present* (Dublin, 1932); and *Gramadach na Gaeilge, an Caighdeán Oifigiúil* (Government Publications: Dublin, 1958). Regarding Dictionaries, see in particular *Contributions to a Dictionary of the Irish Language* (Royal Irish Academy: Dublin, 1913-1975); Niall Ó Dónaill / Tomás de Bhaldraithe, *Foclóir Gaeilge-Béarla* (Dublin, 1977).

The English language was first introduced to Ireland, with Anglo-French, by the Norman Invasion in the late 12th century. It did not gain a wide foothold in the country until the 17th century, with the introduction of southern English dialects into Leinster and elsewhere, and English and Scots dialects into Ulster. Due to its being the language of government, authority, and commerce, English has spread rapidly, bringing Irish near to the point of extinction. For detailed information on the history and nature of hiberno-English, see Jeremiah J Hogan, *The English Language in Ireland* (Dublin, 1927); Alan Bliss, *English Spoken in Ireland* (Dublin, 1979).

The guide to pronunciation here is arranged in three columns. The first gives the standard Classical Irish spelling of the name or word which is an entry heading in this Encyclopaedia, except for names of recent historical characters which are given in the contemporary Reformed Spelling. The second column gives modern (M) pronunciation in the international phonetic alphabet - the early (E) forms are given only when especially significant. The third column gives an approximate guide to pronunciation using English orthography. Full dialectal variants are not listed. The name with most variation is appropriately, though coincidentally, that of the character with the greatest range in both time and space, Fionn. His name is pronounced f′iN in the north, f′on in the west, and both f′u:n and f′aun in the south. The variation in his case results from the affect of 'nn' in final position. Where the early and modern pronunciations differ, the guide in English orthography approximates rather to the modern version, that being the most easily recognised in Ireland. Regarding characters who belong to the Modern Irish period, pronunciation of their names is generally given in the form current in their native areas. Regarding the letters used in the English orthography, it has been found necessary to add the letter 'h' to 'g' and 'k' in order to indicate that these should be pronounced as fricatives (for example, the non-palatal k-sound in Scottish 'loch', and the palatal k-sound in German 'ich').

ABÁN		aba:n	ob-aun
ADHAMHNÁN	(E)	aδavna:n	
	(M)	u:na:n	oo-naun
AILBHE		al′v′e	al-veh
AILILL ÓLOM		al′iL′ o:lom	al-il oe-lum
ÁINE		a:n′e	au-neh
AITHIRNE		ah′ər′n′e	a-hir-neh
AMHAIRGHIN	(E)	avar′γ′en glu:nγ′el	
GLÚNGHEAL	(M)	ourg′in glu:nγ′al	our-gin gloon-ghal
AMHAIRGHIN MAC ÉIGIT			
SALAIGH		ourg′in mak e:g′it′ sali	our-gin mok ai-git solly
ANÉRA MAC CONGLINNE		ane:rə mak kon g′l′iN′e	an-aira mok kun glinn-eh
ANIMAL TALES			
ANIMALS AND FOWL, DOMESTICATED			
ANIMALS AND OTHER CREATURES OF THE WILD			
AODH ALLÁN	(E)	e:δ aLa:n	
	(M)	e: ala:n	ai oll-aun
AODH EANGACH		e: angax	ai an-gokh
AODH SLÁINE		e: sla:n′e	ai slau-neh
AOIBHEALL		i:v′əl	ee-vul
AONGHUS	(E)	e:nγus	
	(M)	e:ni:s	ai-nees
ART		art	ort
BAILE MAC BUAIN		bal′e mak buən′	boll-eh mok boo-en
BALAR		balər	boll-ur
BANSHEE ('bean si')		b′an s′i:	ban-shee
BARRA		barə	borr-uh
BEAG MAC DÉ		b′eg mak d′e:	bay-ug mok dai
BEARACH		b′arəx	barr-ukh
BEARCHÁN		b′arəxa:n	barr-ukh-aun
BÓINN		bo:N′	boe-in
BÓRAIMHE		bo:rəv′e	boe-riv-eh
BRAN MAC FEABHAIL		bran mak f′evəl′	bron mok fev-il
BRANDUBH		bran duv	bron duv
BRÉANAINN		b′r′e:nəN′	bray-nin
BREAS		b′ras	brass
BREASAL BÓ-DHÍOBHADH		br′asəl bo: γ′i:və	brass-ul boe-yee-vuh

BRIAN BORU		b'r'i∂n boru:	bree-an bur-oo
BRICRIU		b'rik'ru:	brik-roo
BRIGHID (goddess)		b'r'i'y'id'	bri-yid
BRIGHID (saint)	(E)	b'r'i'y'id'	bri-yid
	(M)	b'r'i:d'	breed
BUTLER, THEOBALD			
BUTLER, MARGARET			
CAILLEACH BHÉARRA		kaL'∂x v'e:r∂	koll-yukh vai-ruh
CAILLÍN		kaL'i:n'	koll-yeen
CAINNEACH		kaN'∂x	kan-yukh
CAIRBRE CATCHEANN		kar'b'r'e katx'eN	karb-reh kot-kh-yun
CAIRBRE LIFEACHAIR		kar'b'r'e l'if'∂x∂r'	karb-reh liff-okh-ir
CAIRBRE MAC ÉADAOINE		kar'b'r'e mak e:di:n'e	karb-reh mok ai-ud-een-eh
CANO MAC GARTNÁIN		kano mak gartna:n'	kon-o mok gort-nau-in
CAOILTE		ki:l't'e	kweel-teh
CAOIMHGHIN	(E)	ki:v'γ'en'	
	(M)	ki:v'i:n'	kweev-een
CAOINCHOMHRAC		ki:n'xo:r∂k	kween-khoe-ruk
CATHAL MAC FIONGHUINE	(E)	kaθal mak f'inγin'e	
	(M)	kah∂l mak f'ini:n'e	koh-ul mok f-yun-een-eh
CATHAOIR MÓR	(E)	kaθi:r' mo:r	
	(M)	kahi:r' mo:r	ko-heer more
CATHBHADH	(E)	kaθvaδ	
	(M)	kaf∂	koff-uh
CÉADACH		k'e:d∂x	kai-dukh
CEALLACH		k'aL∂x	kal-ukh
CEALTCHAIR		k'altxir'	kalt-khwir
CEAT MAC MÁGHACH		k'at mak ma:x	kat mok maukh
CEITHEARN MAC FIONNTAIN		k'eh'∂rn mak f'iNt∂n'	kai-hurn mok f-yun-tin
CEITHEARNACH CAOILRIABHACH		k'eh'∂rn∂x ki:l'ri∂v∂x	kai-hurn-ukh kweel-reev-ukh
CÉITINN, SEATHRÚN		s'ahru:n k'e:t'in'	sha-hroon kai-tin
CESSAIR		k'esir'	kess-ir
CHRIST ('Críost')		k'r'i:st	kreest
CIAN MAC MAOLMHUAIDHE		k'i∂n mak me:lvui:	kee-un mok mwail-voo-ey
CIARÁN (of Cluain)		k'i∂ra:n	kee-ur-aun
CIARÁN (of Saighir)		k'i∂ra:n	kee-ur-aun
CLÍONA		kl'i:n∂	klee-nuh
COBHTHACH CAOL		kof∂x ke:l	kuff-ukh kwai-ul
COLLA		koL∂	kull-uh
COLM CILLE		kol∂m k'iL'e	kull-um kill-eh
COMHDHÁN	(E)	kovδa:n	
	(M)	ko:γa:n	koe-ghaun
COMHGHALL	(E)	kovγaL	
	(M)	ku:l	koo-ul
CONAIRE		kon∂r'e	kun-er-eh
CONAIRE MAC MOGHA LÁMHA		kon∂r'e mak mou la:v∂	kun-er-eh mok mou lau-vuh
CONALL CEARNACH		kon∂L k'a:rn∂x	kun-ul kaar-nukh
CONALL CLOGACH		kon∂L klog∂x	kun-ul klug-ukh
CONALL CORC		kon∂L kork	kun-ul kurk
CONALL GULBAN		kon∂L gol∂b∂n	kun-ul gull-u-bun

CONÁN MAOL		kona:n me:l	kun-aun mwai-ul
CONCHOBHAR MAC NEASA	(E)	konxovar mak n'esa	
	(M)	konəxu:r mak n'asə	kunna-khoor mok nassa
		krohu:r mak n'asə	kru-hoor mok nassa
CONGHAL CLÁIRINGNEACH		koni:l kla:r'iŋ'n'əx	kun-ee-ul klaur-ing-nukh
CONLAÍ		konli:	kun-lwee
CONN CÉADCHATHACH	(E)	kond k'e:dxaθax	
	(M)	koN k'e:dxahəx (also, koun)	kun kaid-kho-hukh (also, koun)
CORC DUIBHNE		kork div'n'e	kurk dwiv-neh (later variant, dwee-neh)
CORMAC MAC AIRT		kormak mak a'rt'	kurmok mok art
CORMAC CONN LOINGEAS		kormak koN lin'g'əs	kurmok kun lwin-gus
CRIDHINBHÉAL		kri:in'v'e:l	kree-in-vail
CRIOMHTHANN NIA NÁIR		k'r'ifən n'iə na:r'	kriffen neea nau-ir
CROM		krom / kroum	krum / kroum
CROMWELL, OLIVER			
CÚ CHULAINN		ku: xuləN'	koo khul-inn
CÚ ROÍ		ku: ri:	koo ree
CUMAINE FADA		kumən'e fadə	kum-in-eh fodda
CÚSCRAIDH MEANN MACHA		ku:skri m'eN maxə	koos-kri m-yun mokha
DAGHDHA	(E)	daγθa	
	(M)	daiə	daye
DÁIRE		da:r'e	dau-ir-eh
DÁITHÍ		da:h'i	dau-hee
DALLÁN FORGAILL		daLa:n forgiL'	doll-aun fur-gwill
DAMER, JOSEPH			
DANU		danu	don-u
DÉAGLÁN		d'e:gla:n	dai-ug-laun
DEARG		d'arəg	darr-ug
DEIRDRE		d'e:r'd'ir'e	dair-dir-eh
DIAN CÉACHT		d'iən k'e:xt	dee-un kai-ukht
DIARMAID MAC AODHA SLÁINE		d'iərmid' mak e: sla:n'e	dee-ur-mwid mok ai slau-in-eh
DIARMAID MAC CEARRBHEOIL		d'iərmid' mak k'arv'o:l'	dee-ur-mwid mok karv-yoe-il
DIARMAID UA DUIBHNE		d'iərmid' uə divn'e	dee-ur-mwid oo dwiv-neh
DOMHNALL MAC AODHA	(E)	dovnaL mak e:δa	
	(M)	do:nəl mak e:	doe-nul mok ai
DONN		doN / doun	dun / doun
DRUIDS			
DUBHTHACH DAOL ULADH		dufəx de:l olə	duff-ukh dai-ul ulla
DWYER, MICHAEL			
ÉADAOIN		e:di:n'	ai-ud-een
ÉIBHEAR		e:v'ər	ai-vur
ÉINNE		e:N'e	ain-yeh
ÉIREAMHÓIN		e:r'əvo:n'	air-uv-oen
EITHNE	(E)	eθ'n'e	
	(M)	eh'in'e	eh-in-eh
ELIZABETH I			
ENVIRONMENT			

EOCHAIDH	(E)	exiδ'	
	(M)	oxi	ukh-i
EOCHAIDH AIREAMH		oxi ar∂v	ukh-i arr-uv
EOCHAIDH FEIDHLEACH	(E)	oxiδ' f'eδ'l'ax	
	(M)	oxi f'eil'∂x	ukh-i fie-lukh
EOCHAIDH MAC LUCHTA		oxi mak luxt∂	ukh-i mok lukh-tuh
EOCHAIDH MAC MAIREADHA	(E)	oxiδ' mak mar'aδa	
	(M)	oxi mak mari:	ukh-i mok mar-ee
EOGHAN BÉAL	(E)	oγan b'e:l	
	(M)	o:n b'e:l	oe-un bai-ul
EOGHAN MÓR		eoγan / o:n mo:r	oe-un more
ÉRAINN		e:r∂N'	ai-rin
FAIRIES			
FEAR DIADH	(E)	f'er d'iaδ	
	(M)	f'ar d'i∂	farr-deea
FEARDHOMHAIN		f'arγoun'	farr-ghou-in
FEARGHAL MAC MAOLDÚIN	(E)	ferγal mak me:ldu:n'	
	(M)	f'ari:l mak me:ldu:n'	farr-eel mok mwail-doo-in
FEARGHUS MAC LÉIDE	(E)	f'erγus mak l'e:d'e	
	(M)	f'ari:s mak l'e:d'e	farr-ees mok lai-deh
FEARGHUS MAC RÓICH		f'ari:s mak ro:x'	farr-ees mok roe-ikh
FÉICHÍN		f'e:x'i:n'	fai-kheen
FEIDHLIMIDH MAC CRIOMHTHAINN		f'e:l'im'i mak k'r'if∂N'	fai-lim-eh mok kriffen
FEIRCHEIRDNE		f'er'x'e:r'd'n'e	ferr-khaird-neh
FEIRITÉAR, PIARAS		p'i∂r∂s f'er'it'e:r	pee-ur-us ferr-it-air
FIACHNA MAC BAODÁIN		f'i∂xn∂ mak be:da:n'	fee-ukh-nuh mok bwai-dau-in
FIACHU FEAR MARA	(E)	f'iaxu f'er mara	
	(M)	f'i∂xi f'ar mara	fee-ukh-ee farr morr-uh
FIACHU MUILLEATHAN		f'i∂xi miL'ah∂n	fee-ukh-ee mwill-ahun
FIANNA CYCLE			
FIND		f'ind	f-yund
FIND FILE		f'ind f'il'e	f-yund fill-i
FINN EAMHNA		f'iN' avn∂	finn av-nuh
FIONÁN CAM		f'ina:n kaM	fin-aun koum
FIONN MAC CUMHAILL	(E)	f'ind mak kuvaL'	
	(M)	f'iN mak ku:l'	f-yun mok koo-il
FIONNACHTA		f'iN∂xt∂	f-yun-ukh-tuh
FIONNCHÚ		f'iNxu:	f-yun-khoo
FIONNTAN		f'iNt∂n	f-yun-tun
FINNBHEARA		f'in'v'ar∂	finn-varr-uh
FÍOTHAL		f'i:h∂l	fee-hul
FIR BOLG		f'ir' bol∂g	fir bull-ug
FITZGERALD, GEARÓID IARLA		g'aro:d' i∂rl∂	gir-oed ee-ur-luh
FLANN MAC LÓNÁIN		flaN mak lo:na:n'	flon mok loe-nau-in
FLANNÁN		flaNa:n	flon-aun
FLIODHAIS	(E)	f'l'iδis'	
	(M)	f'l'ihis'	fli-hish
FOMHÓIRE		fovo:r'e	fuv-oe-reh

FOTHADH CANAINNE		fohə kanəNe′	fuh-uh kon-in-yeh
FRAOCH		fre:x	frai-ukh
FURSA			
GEIS		g′es′	gesh
GHOSTS			
GLAS GOIBHNEANN		glas giv′n′əN / glas goin′ən	gloss gwivnun / gloss gaye-nun
GOBÁN SAOR		goba:n s:er	gub-aun sai-ur
GODDESSES			
GODS			
GOIBHNIU		giv′n′u	gwiv-new
GOLL MAC MORNA		goL mak mo:rnə	gull mok moer-nuh
GUAIRE		guər′e	goo-er-eh
HORSES			
HUMAN LIFE			
HUMOROUS TALES			
ÍDE		i:d′e	ee-deh
JAMES II			
KILDARE, EARL OF			
KINGSHIP			
LABHRAIDH	(E)	lavriδ′	
	(M)	louri	lour-ee
LAOGHAIRE	(E)	le:γar′e	
	(M)	le:r′e	lai-ur-eh
LAOGHAIRE BUADHACH		le:r′e buəx	lai-ur-eh boo-ukh
LAOGHAIRE MAC CRIOMHTHAINN		le:r′e mak k′r′ifəN′	lai-ur-eh mok kriffen
LEPRECHAUN			
LÍ BAN		l′i: ban	lee bon
LIADHAIN	(E)	l′iaδin′	
	(M)	l′iən′	lee-en
LIR		l′ir′	lir
LUGH	(E)	luγ	
	(M)	lu:	loo
LUGHAIDH LÁGHA	(E)	luγiδ′ la:γa	
	(M)	lu:i la:	loo-i lau
LUGHAIDH LÁMHDHEARG		lu:i la:vγ′arəg	loo-i lauv-yarrug
LUGHAIDH MAC CON		lu:i mak kon	loo-i mok kun
LUGHAIDH RIABHDHEARG		lu:i riəvγ′arəg	loo-i ree-uv-yarrug
MAC DOMHNAILL, ALASDAIR MAC COLLA		aləstər′ mak kolə mak do:nəL′	oll-oster mok kull-uh mok doe-nil
MAC GIOLLA GHUNNA, CATHAL BUÍ		ka:l bi: mak g′iLə γonə	kaul bwee mok gill-uh ghun-uh
MAC LUGHACH		mak luəx	mok loo-ukh
MAC NA MÍCHOMHAIRLE		mak nə m′i:xo:rl′e	mok nuh mee-khoer-leh
MAC SUIBHNE, MAOLMHUIRE		mi:l′r′e mak siv′n′e	mweel-reh mok swiv-neh
MACHA		maxə	mokk-uh
MAINE		man′e	monn-eh
MANANNÁN		manəNa:n	monn-un-aun
MAODHÓG		me:o:g	mwai-oge
MAOL DÚIN		me:l du:n′	mwai-ul doo-in
MAOL FHOTHARTAIGH		me:l ohərti	mwai-ul uh-urt-ey
MAOLODHRÁN		me:l oura:n	mwai-ul our-aun

MARTIN, St			
MEADHBH	(E)	m′eδv	
	(M)	m′e:v	mwai-uv
MIDHIR	(E)	m′iγ′ir	
	(M)	m′i:r′	mee-er
MÍL		m′i:l′	meel
MIS		m′is′	mish
MOCHAOI		mo xi:	mu-khwee
MOCHUDA		mo xod∂	mu-khud-uh
MOLING		mo l′iη′	mu-ling
MOLUA		mo lu∂	mu-loo-a
MONGÁN		monga:n	mun-gaun
MONINNE		moniN′e	mu-nin-yeh
MOORE			
MÓR MUMHAN	(E)	mo:r muvan	
	(M)	mo:r mu:n	more moon
MORANN		mor∂N	murr-un
MÓR-RÍOGHAIN	(E)	mo:ri:γin′	
	(M)	mo:ri:n	moer-ee-en
MUIRCHEARTACH MAC EARCA		mir′x′art∂x mak ark∂	mwir-khart-ukh mok ar-kuh
MURCHADH MAC BRIAIN		mur∂x∂ mak b′r′i∂n′	murr-u-khuh mok bree-en
MYTHOLOGICAL CYCLE			
NEARA MAC NIADHAIN		n′ar∂ mak n′i∂n′	narra mok nee-yen
NÉIDHE MAC ADHNA	(E)	n′e:δ′e mak aδna	
	(M)	n′e: mak ain′∂	nai mok ay-nuh
NEIMHEADH	(E)	n′ev′eδ	
	(M)	n′ev′e	nev-eh
NÍ MHÁILLE, GRÁINNE MHAOL		gra:N′e wi:l n′i: wa:L′e	graun-yeh wee-ul nee waul-yeh
NÍ MHATHÚNA, MÁIRE RUA		ma:r′e ru∂ n′i: vahu:n∂	mau-ir-eh roo-a nee voh-oo-nuh
NIALL FRASACH		n′i∂L fras∂x	nee-ul fross-ukh
NIALL NAOI-GHIALLACH		n′i∂L ni: γ′i∂L∂x	nee-ul nwee ghee-ul-ukh
NOÍNE		ni:n′e	nwee-neh
NORSEMEN			
NUADHU	(E)	nuaδu	
	(M)	nu∂	noo-a
Ó CAOIMH, DÓNALL NA CÁSCA		do:n∂l n∂ ka:sk∂ o: ki:v′	doe-nul nuh kaus-huh o kweev
Ó CONCHUBHAIR, CATHAL CROBHDHEARG		kah∂l krovγ′ar∂g o: krohu:r′	koh-ul kruv-yarrug o kru-hoo-ir
Ó DÁLAIGH, CEARBHALL		k′aru:l o: da:l∂	kar-ool o dau-luh
Ó DOMHNAILL, AODH BALLDEARG		i: baLd′z′ar∂g o: do:n∂L′	ee boll-jarrug o doe-nil
Ó DOMHNAILL, MÁNAS		ma:n∂s o: do:n∂L′	mau-nus o doe-nil
Ó DONNCHÚ, DÓNALL NA nGEIMHLEACH		do:n∂l n∂ η′i:l′∂x o: don∂xu:	doe-nul nung-eel-lukh o dun-u-khoo
Ó FÁILBHE, CLUASACH		klu∂s∂x o: fa:l′v′e	kloo-us-ukh o faul-veh
Ó hANLUAIN, REAMONN		re:m∂N o: hanlu∂n′	rai-mun o hon-loo-in
Ó NÉILL, EOGHAN RUA		o:n ru∂ o: n′e:L′	oan roo-a o nail
Ó RATHAILLE, AOGÁN		e:ga:n o: rah∂l′e	ai-ug-aun o roh-il-eh
Ó RIAIN, ÉAMONN AN CHNOIC		e∂m∂n ∂ xnik′ o: ri∂n′	yo-mun u khn-wik o ree-en

Ó SÚILLEABHÁIN BÉARRA, DÓNALL CAM		do:nǝl kaum o: su:l'ǝva:n' b'eǝrǝ	doe-nul koum o soo-lev-au-in bai-ruh
Ó SÚILLEABHÁIN, EOGHAN RUA		o:n ruǝ o: su:l'ǝva:n'	oan roo-a o soo-lev-au-in
O'CONNELL, DANIEL			
OGHAM	(E)	oγam	
	(M)	o:m	oam
OGHMA	(E)	oγma	
	(M)	o:mǝ	oam-uh
OISÍN		os'i:n'	ush-een
OLLAMH FÓDLA		olǝv fo:lǝ	ull-uv foe-luh
OSCAR		oskǝr	us-kur
PARTHALÁN		parhǝla:n	por-hu-laun
PATRICK ('Pádraig')		pa:drig' / pa:rik'	pau-drig / pau-rik
PICTS			
PLACE-LORE			
POETS			
RAGHALLACH		raiǝLǝx	ray-ul-ukh
RELIGIOUS TALES			
ROMANTIC TALES			
RUADH RÓ-FHEASA	(E)	ruaδ ro:esa	
	(M)	ruǝ ro:asǝ	roo-a roe-ass-uh
RUADHÁN		rua:n	roo-aun
RÚMANN MAC COLMÁIN		ru:mǝN mak kolǝma:n'	roo-mun mok kullum-au-in
SAINTS			
SARSFIELD, PATRICK			
SEANÁN		s'ena:n	shen-aun
SEANCHÁN		s'anǝxa:n	shana:khaun
SEVEN BISHOPS			
SPECIAL POWERS			
SPORTS AND PASTIMES			
SUIBHNE		siv'n'e	swiv-neh
SUIBHNE MEANN		siv'n'e m'eN	swiv-neh m-yun
SWIFT, JONATHAN			
TADHG MAC CÉIN		taig mak k'e:n'	toy-ug mok kain
TARA			
TIGHEARNMHAS		t'iǝrnvǝs	tee-urn-vus
TIME			
TOMÁS MÓR		toma:s mu:r	tum-aus moor
TUÁN MAC CAIRILL		tua:n mak kar'iL'	too-aun mok kar-ill
TUATHA DÉ DANANN		tuǝhǝ d'e: danǝN	too-a-huh dai don-un
TUATHAL TEACHTMHAR		tuǝhǝl t'axtvǝr	too-a-hul tokht-vur
TURGESIUS			
UGHAINE	(E)	uγin'e	
	(M)	u:n'e	oo-in-eh
ULSTER CYCLE			
URARD MAC COISE		urard mak kos'e	ur-ord mok kush-eh
WEATHER LORE			
WILLIAM OF ORANGE			
WONDER TALES			

A

1. ABÁN *Model in gold of a prehistoric Irish boat.*

ABÁN Leinster saint of the early 6th century AD. A biography of him was compiled towards the end of the 8th century in the monastery of Magh Arnaidhe (Moyarney, near New Ross in Co Wexford), which monastery claimed him as its founder. Somewhat later recensions of this biography in Latin and Irish survive.

The Leinstermen ascribed their conversion to this Abán. His name (earlier, Abbán) is titular, meaning 'little abbot', and he was of the sept known as Dál Corbmaic. Thus he was known as 'Abban mocu Corbmaic', but his biography takes 'mocu' in the sense of son rather than of descendant. We accordingly read that he was son of a Leinster king called Cormac and that his mother Milla was sister to a bishop called Iubhar. In his youth he expressed a desire for the monastic life rather than for kingship, and as a result he was chained and held in captivity by his parents. The chains miraculously fell away, however, and he was then allowed to pursue the religious life.

When still a mere boy, Abán showed his miraculous power by restoring to life and wholeness a calf which had been devoured by a wolf. When he was twelve years old, he wished to accompany his uncle Iubhar on a journey to Rome, but Iubhar slipped away to the ship while Abán was sleeping. The youngster followed, and as the ship left port he walked on the waves to join its crew. In Italy, he again showed his power by lighting a lamp with his breath, by restoring to life a queen who had just died, and by overcoming ravenous monsters. On his return to Ireland, he banished demons from the sea by confronting them while riding his staff on the water, and angels told him that God had given him power over the sea.

Abán was reputed to have founded several churches outside of Leinster also, particularly in Munster, where the biography claims he performed several miracles. Other lore centred on his manner of establishing and defending monasteries - by his orders, the wolves acted as shepherds to protect his flocks, and ravaging armies found themselves transfixed until they abandoned their destructive intent. His feastday is March 16.

J F Kenney (1929), 318-9; Charles Plummer (1910) *1*, 3-33 and (1922) *1*, 3-10; John O'Hanlon (1875) *3*, 394-5; IFC 189:81-3, 203:11-2, 406:13-5.

ADHAMHNÁN (627-704 AD): Biographer of **Colm Cille** and abbot of the community founded by that saint on the island of Iona, off the west coast of Scotland. His father was of the same stock as Colm, and Adhamhnán himself was apparently born and reared in the region of Co Donegal. His name (originally Adamnán), was a diminutive of Adam but is anglicised as Eunan.

He went to Iona sometime around the year 670, became abbot in 679, and wrote the biography of Colm Cille some years later, using traditions of the saint which had survived both orally and in writings during the few generations since his death. One of his sources was an old monk who had known Colm Cille himself.

Among other works written by Adhamhnán was a description in Latin of the holy places of Palestine, based on what he heard from a Gallic bishop called Arculf who was shipwrecked and took refuge on Iona. In the year 697 a law drafted by him was enacted at a council in Biorra (Birr, Co Offaly). This law, entitled *Cáin Adamnáin*, was applicable to both Ireland and Scotland, and it specified that women, children, and clerics should be protected from attack both in times of war and of peace. It was claimed that he drafted the law to fulfil a promise he once made to his mother when she was upset at seeing a woman injuring another in battle.

2. ADHAMHNÁN *Engraving of an early Irish bishop riding a horse.*

Adhamhnán is featured in several mediaeval texts. He was especially associated with the high-king **Fionnachta**, his somewhat older contemporary. We read that when Fionnachta was riding along a road once, the young Adhamhnán ran out of the way but tripped on a stone and broke the milk-vessel which he had been carrying on his back. Realising that the youth was a clerical student, Fionnachta paid for the vessel and brought Adhamhnán with him to a banquet. Their friendship continued for a long time, until Fionnachta was tricked by St **Moling** concerning the **bóraimhe** tribute, whereupon Adhamhnán reproached the high-king bitterly for his foolishness. This is very dubious history, but the political situation described in it would have been current after the year 666 and we know that Adhamhnán had left Ireland to join the Iona community by the year 674. It seems quite unlikely that, before he had the prestige of the abbacy of Iona, he would have been involved in negotiations between Fionnachta and the Leinster king Bran Múit. This, as well as the several more localised accounts of Adhamhnán making legal and political arrangements, is doubtlessly an echo from the social importance of the *Cáin Adamnáin* tract.

Another role attributed to him does, however, have a historical origin. Two years after a fierce Saxon attack on Bréagha (the plain of Co Meath) in 684, he went to visit the king of Northumbria and secured the release of sixty captives who had been taken in the raid. The account given in the mediaeval literature is quite dramatised, claiming that, when he arrived with his monks on the shore of the Saxons' territory, the current was so rapid that his boats could not land. By a miracle, however, Adhamhnán made a great wall of the sea and therefore landed safely on dry land. Filled through this with dread of the saint, the Saxons submitted to him, surrendered their booty, and promised not to plunder Ireland again. One very pleasant little story describes how he once shut himself into his cell on Iona for three days, and how the monks grew anxious for him and went to investigate. Through the keyhole they saw the child Jesus, surrounded by a beautiful light, sitting in Adhamhnán's lap.

An additional text attributed to the authorship of Adhamhnán, but actually composed as late as the 10th century, is his 'vision' entitled *Fís Adamnáin*. It purports to describe a vision which he had when at Birr for the convention, in the course of which his soul went from his body and visited heaven and hell. This belongs to a genre which was popular in the literature of early mediaeval Ireland (see **Fursa** and **Bréanainn**).

The feastday of Adhamhnán is September 23.

[Biographical] A O Anderson / M O Anderson (1961), 92-8; R I Best in *Anecdota from Irish Manuscripts 2*, 10-20; John O'Donovan (1860), 72-85; S H O'Grady (1892) *1*, 404-6; Whitley Stokes (1905), 210-1, 244-5 and in *Revue Celtique 13*, 98-117; Kuno Meyer in *Zeitschrift für celtische Philologie 5*, 495-6.

[*Cáin Adamnáin*] Meyer in *Anecdota Oxoniensia 12*.

[*Fís Adamnáin*] Joseph Vendryes in *Revue Celtique 30*, 349-83. See also C S Boswell (1908); Myles Dillon (1948), 132-9.

[General] J F Kenney (1929), 245-6, 283-7, 429-33, 443-5, 799; John O'Hanlon (1875) *9*, 476-533.

AILBHE Saint who reputedly died in 527 AD, founder of a monastery at Imleach Iubhair (Emly, Co Tipperary).

The literature regards Ailbhe as having been a contemporary of **Patrick**, and portrays his mission as in progress in Munster before that saint. There are indeed some indications that his image took on aspects of pre-Christian tradition. Imleach Iubhair meant 'the lakeside at a yew-tree' and might originally have been a pre-Christian sanctuary, while the name Ailbhe itself - meaning 'rock' - may have been given to him as a reflex from ancient lore. An important place in central Leinster was anciently known as 'the plain of Ailbhe', and on that plain stood the monument known as the 'lia' (i.e. slab) of Ailbhe. The biographical accounts of the saint are, however, so late that it is difficult to claim that they contain vestiges of the earlier tradition.

The descriptions of his birth and youth show that at least the meaning of his name had not been forgotten. These state that his parents lived in Éile Uí Fhógartaigh (in north Tipperary), and his father's name is given as Ollchú ('great hound'), while we read that his mother was a servant of the local king, Crónán. That king was very hostile to Ollchú, and he ordered that the baby be exposed to wild beasts. The little boy was therefore placed under a large rock in a lonely place, but a wolf-bitch carried him away to her den and suckled him with her own pups. He was eventually found by some Briton slaves and reared by them.

When Ailbhe came of age he went to the Continent and was educated there by a bishop called Hilarius. Returning to Ireland, he was spreading the Christian faith in Munster when Patrick reputedly arrived there. He recognised Patrick as his superior and was given Emly as his see. In this role, Ailbhe was said to have been the mentor of several other Munster saints, and of **Éinne**, for whom it was claimed he got possession of Inishmore. According to one tradition, as he grew older Ailbhe wished to retire to some place where he could live in solitude, and chose the island of Thule near the Arctic Ocean. The king of Munster, Aonghus mac Nadfraoich, who did not wish to see so pious a saint leave his territory, placed guards at the sea-ports and so prevented him from doing so.

It is obvious that the Romulus-motif of suckling by a wolf was borrowed from heroic lore (see **Cormac mac Airt**). It was suggested by an epical story which concerned a wild hound called Ailbhe, from whom it was claimed the plain of Ailbhe had been named (see **Conall Cearnach**). This story of the saint's rescue by a wolf was imposed onto an earlier tradition that he was given directly to a group of Britons who were in bondage in the area, and that he had been looked after by them. The idea that he was reared by Britons might have some basis in fact, as it would explain how he could have been a Christian before the new religion became widespread in the south. The mention of Hilarius, if it refers to the 5th-century bishop of Arles, is almost contemporary with the dating of Ailbhe, but this connection is hardly more than speculation by a mediaeval writer.

Local tradition at Emly holds that Ailbhe was buried in the grounds of the monastery there. It was believed down to recent times that he protected the crops, and water from his well was sprinkled on the fields to prevent the sparrows from eating the corn. A legend in existence since the Middle Ages - and still current - claims that, when he was a boy and in service with a farmer, he miraculously confined these birds in a roofless barn (see **Saints**). His feastday is September 12.

J F Kenney (1929), 313-5; W W Heist (1965), 118-31; Charles Plummer (1910) *1*, 46-64; 'Fáinne Fionn' in *The Irish Rosary 16*, passim; Joseph O'Neill in *Ériu 3*, 92-115; Joseph Szövérffy in *Éigse 8*, 128-9; John O'Hanlon (1875) *9*, 278-97; IFC 556:141-2.

AILILL ÓLOM Mythical king of Munster, son of **Eoghan Mór**. His sobriquet (originally, Aulom) meant 'bare-eared', and he was sometimes called by the name Moshaulom ('beloved Aulom'). It is possible that the element Ailill, which was a common enough name, was added by the genealogists to give him a more normal designation.

Several details of him are found in 8th and 9th-century texts. We read that his dwelling was on the hill called Cláire (in the parish of Galbally, Co Limerick), and that he lived for ninety years - thirty years for each of three periods. The first period was before his reign, the second was as king, and the third after he was deposed by

Lughaidh mac Con. He was sometimes claimed to have been father of Eoghan Mór, rather than his son as the synchronisers had it. Possibly Ólom was in origin a mere nickname for Eoghan, for he was regarded - like Eoghan - as the ancestor and archetypal king of the Eoghanacht sept who ruled the province of Munster in the early Middle Ages. He was claimed by the Eoghanacht sept to have been the mate of the land-goddess **Áine**, and a dramatic but somewhat hostile description in one text has him raping her at her hill of Knockainey in Co Limerick. She tore his ears off in the struggle, and thus the appellation Ólom was explained. An elaboration of this episode states that, in anger at being maimed, he drove his spear through her. The mediaeval literature represents Ailill as having for wife Sadhbh, daughter of **Conn Céadchathach** and sister of **Art**. This, of course, is a synchroniser's trick, in order to portray as at friendship the great rival dynasties of the Connachta at **Tara** and the Eoghanacht in Munster.

Ailill Ólom, with his seven sons and his army, were said to have defeated the **Érainn** forces of Lughaidh mac Con (q.v.) at the battle of Ceann Abhradh (the Ballyhoura hills on the Limerick-Cork border). This was probably an echo of how the Eoghanacht first took the kingship of Munster. Some accounts state that Ailill acted treacherously towards Lughaidh, who was his foster-son, but all agree in having Lughaidh retire to Scotland and return from there at the head of a large army. At the battle of Magh Mucramha (near Athenry in Co Galway) the exile defeated the combined forces of Ailill and Art. Ailill's seven sons were slain, and he himself deposed from the kingship of Munster. Lughaidh took the high-kingship at Tara, but later handed it over to the renowned **Cormac mac Airt** and went south in order to restore his friendship with Ailill. It was said that Ailill had a barbed spear and that there was a prohibition (**'geis'**) on him against straightening it. It happened that he once put it under his tooth to straighten it, and the poison passed from it into the tooth. It corrupted his breath and blackened the tooth, causing great pain and anguish to him. When Lughaidh came, however, Ailill turned this ailment to advantage, for he infected his foe with it under pretence of kissing him.

A curious aspect of these accounts of Ailill is that their attitude is rather hostile to him. This can be explained by the hypothesis that elements of them derive from ancient rivals of the Eoghanacht in Munster, and that they have been further effected by propaganda of the Connachta - Uí Néill, who regarded the Eoghanacht as their principal competitors in the early mediaeval period.

Máirín O'Daly (1975), 38-65, 74-93; Kuno Meyer (1910), 6-13; Whitley Stokes in *Irische Texte 3*, 304-7; Myles Dillon (1946), 16-23; Mícheál Ó Dúnlainge in *Irisleabhar na Gaedhilge 18*, 75-81.

ÁINE Otherworld lady in Irish literature and folklore.

The name originally meant 'brightness', which was a typical attribute of Irish **goddesses**. In archaic times, it is apparent that this designation Áine was used for male as well as female deities, and it occurs in placenames in different parts of Ireland. The mediaeval literature has several mentions of an otherworld lady called Áine. She was, for instance, claimed to have been a daughter of **Manannán**, and one story told of how a warrior called Étar (later, Éadar) fell in love with her but died of a broken heart when she rejected him. He was reputedly buried at the place which since bears his name, Beann Éadair (Howth, Co Dublin). The major emphasis, however, was on a lady called Áine who was associated with Munster and particularly with the Eoghanacht sept (see **Eoghan Mór**). Her residence was an otherworld palace at Cnoc Áine (the hill of Knockainey in Co Limerick), which is situated in the centre of the pasture-lands of the rich Munster plain. She was therefore a version of the land-goddess, and as such became the patroness of sovereignty for the Eoghanacht.

This Eoghanacht connection is clearly expressed in an 8th-century text which has **Ailill Ólom**, son of Eoghan Mór, going at Samhain (the November feast) to attend his horses at Knockainey and lying down there to sleep for the night. The hill was stripped of its grass during the night, and he was puzzled as to who did that. He travelled to Leinster to a seer-poet called Fearcheas mac Comáin, who advised that they go together to investigate on the following Samhain. Ailill fell asleep on the hillside while listening to the cattle grazing, and the king of the 'sídh' (otherworld dwelling), called Eoghabhal, appeared accompanied by his daughter Áine. She was playing music on a bronze instrument. Fearcheas slew Eoghabhal and Ailill raped Áine, for which treatment she cursed the assailants. This text is hostile towards Ailill, but it is obviously based on a tradition that he was the mate of Áine. She was thus ancestress of the Eoghanacht, which was a way of further stressing the right of that sept to the kingship of Munster. It seems, indeed, that the name of the father who was invented for her, Eoghabhal, is a simple derivation from the sept's own name.

The mediaeval scholars considered it necessary to give an account of the 'prehistory' of Áine. They therefore claimed that, in the time of the **Tuatha Dé Danann**, Eoghabhal and his family sought territory from Nechtan (i.e. **Nuadhu**), and were advised to go and take the hill called Drom Collchoille. The tribes who were then in possession of the hill gave battle to Eoghabhal and his men, and the latter were being repulsed. Then Áine promised to gain the victory for Eoghabhal, on condition that her name be on the hill forever afterwards. This was agreed, and she scattered the foe by the force of magic and put them to flight. The hill was accordingly known as Cnoc Áine, and it was divided in four parts - Uainidhe's portion to the north, that of Fear Fí to the south, Eoghabhal's portion to the west, and Áine's to the east. This, of course, is a mere rationalisation and dramatisation of Áine's connection with the hill. Áine's real history was as a goddess appropriated by the Eoghanacht, probably as early as the 4th century AD, and made into a compound symbol of agricultural prosperity and septal sovereignty.

The claim of Áine's patronage and ancestry was stressed again in a striking manner by the great Norman lords of the area at the end of the Middle Ages. These were the Geraldines who, in the 14th century, called their first Earl of Desmond, Maurice, 'the king of Áine'. Maurice's son, Gearóid Iarla **FitzGerald**, they referred to as the 'son of the cavalier of bright Áine'. This Geraldine propaganda is reflected in folklore, which portrays Gearóid Iarla as her actual offspring. Maurice the first Earl, we are told, one day saw her bathing in Lough Gur, a short distance from Knockainey. He took her cloak, an action which magically put her in his power, and then lay with her, thereby causing Gearóid Iarla to be conceived. This story is the result of a fusion between the Eoghanacht myth of Ailill Ólom and a mediaeval continental legend concerning a swan-maiden. As a result of this fusion, Áine was supposed in folklore to be sometimes seen bathing in that lake in the form of a mermaid.

Independent of the Geraldine lore, Áine survived in folk tradition as a latter-day figure of the land-goddess. She is called Áine Chliar, the sobriquet being explained as 'cliar' (i.e. a wisp), but in reality it derives from Clíu or Cliach, the ancient name of the territory. The extended name of Knockainey in Irish is in fact Cnoc Áine Cliach. In the 19th century it was customary for local inhabitants to hold Midsummer festivities (see **Time**) on the hill. Bunches of straw ('cliara') were lit and carried to the summit of the hill and then scattered in the cultivated fields and among the cattle to bring prosperity. Áine was reputed to be sometimes seen on the hill on that night. She was said to be 'the best-hearted woman who ever lived', and a legend still current in the area tells of how she appeared in the form of a beggarwoman to a local poor family. The family was kind to the old woman, and when she had left they found a new sheep in their field. All their affairs prospered while they kept the sheep, but when they sold it the initial poverty returned. Áine was also given an aetiological role, and various large rocks in the locality of the hill were said to have been placed there by her.

The particular strength of the Áine tradition in east Limerick is due to the early appropriation of her by the Eoghanacht. That 'Áine' survived as a general designation for a goddess is clear, however, from the folklore associated with the name in widely scattered areas. At Dún Áine (Dunany in Co Louth), the weekend immediately after the Lughnasadh festival (see **Time**) was regarded as sacred to her, and people refrained from going on the sea for its duration. In Co Derry, the parish of Lissan (i.e. Lios Áine) has many associations with the same name, and it contains another hill called Cnoc Áine. Here she was also said to take an interest in local affairs. Once, when a cowherd was asleep, she awakened him and informed him that the cattle had strayed into an oat-field. She touched his head, leaving five grey finger-marks on his fair hair. She was supposed to have once been an ordinary woman, but was abducted into the hill, and the local family Corr were reputedly her descendants. She was their **banshee**, and her wailing was heard as a presage of the death of members of that family. Another hill called Cnoc Áine is in the parish of Teelin, Co Donegal, and here Áine is said to have been an ordinary girl who, tired of harsh orders from her father, went into the hill long ago. She lives there in a beautiful palace, and passes her time 'spinning the sunbeams and making gold cloth of the thread'.

[Literature] T F O'Rahilly (1946), 286-90; Edward Gwynn (1913), 114-5; Whitley Stokes in *Revue Celti-*

que 15, 330-1 and *Irische Texte 3*, 83 and (1900), 104-5; R I Best in *Ériu 3*, 162-3; Máirín O'Daly (1975), 38-9; S H O'Grady (1892) 2, 575-6; Láimhbheartach Mac Cionnaith (1938), 205.

[Folklore] David Fitzgerald in *Revue Celtique 4*, 186-90, 195; IFC 1799:8, 117-9; Máire MacNeill (1962), 30, 181, 307, 567, 591-2, 680; Énrí Ó Muirgheasa (1934), 403-4; Pádraig Mac Seáin in *Béaloideas 31*, 72-3; Seán Ó hEochaidh / Máire MacNeill / Séamas Ó Catháin (1977), 36-41, 375.

AITHIRNE Mythical poet and satirist in the **Ulster Cycle**. He had the various sobriquets Áilgheasach ('importunate'), Amhnach ('savage'), and Díbheach ('miserly'), and is said to have been son of the poet **Feircheirdne**.

Several mediaeval texts tell of the adventures of Aithirne. The magical power of his verse was said to have been demonstrated even before his birth. His mother, when pregnant, went into a house where a feast was being prepared, and the baby leaped in her womb when it got the whiff of ale. The aleman refused her a drink, however, and the unborn baby was heard to speak a stanza which caused the barrels to burst asunder. The ale spilled all over the house, and Aithirne's mother managed to drink three draughts of it from her palm. Another account has Aithirne, when a grown poet, satirising a river which yielded no fish to him. This, the river Mourne (in Cos Tyrone and Donegal) rose up in a flood of anger and swept people, animals, and property with it to the sea. The alarmed Aithirne then recited a verse of praise to 'clean away' the insult, and the river restored all and subsided. He is portrayed as ferociously demanding and so greedy that he would never share his food with anybody else. We are told that he used to always eat his meals in private for fear anybody would observe him and wish to join him. One day he went into a wood to cook a pig, but a stranger approached, much to his discomfiture. Aithirne demanded to know the stranger's name so that he could compose a satire on him, but the stranger gave a jumble of words which could not be rhymed. The stinginess of Aithirne is expressed metaphorically in an account which has him going to the otherworld dwelling of Brí Léith (near Ardagh in Co Longford) to acquire there the three 'herons of refusal and inhospitality' for his own house. One of these would tell a visitor not to enter, another would tell him to depart, and the third would tell him to keep away from the house.

Aithirne's acquisitive nature is illustrated in a long text of the 11th century called *Tallaind Étair* (the Battle of Howth). It describes how he went to **Eochaidh mac Luchta**, the one-eyed king of Connacht who was a most generous man. Eochaidh offered him any gift which he desired, and Aithirne demanded his only eye. The king plucked the eye out and gave it into the palm of the poet. On taking his leave, Aithirne remarked that this was proper vengeance for a raid which Eochaidh had made on the Ulster court at Eamhain Mhacha. Continuing on his journey to Munster, Aithirne visited the king of that province and insisted on sleeping with the queen, even though she had given birth on the same night. The people of south Leinster assembled before him offering all kinds of gifts in order to avoid his satire, but he refused all in the hope that they would kill him and thus draw on themselves the wrath of his native Ulster. He was finally appeased with a precious brooch which a horse accidentally kicked up from a grave-mound. On reaching the court of the Leinster king, Meas Geaghra, he demanded to sleep with the queen. Fearing satire and resultant dishonour, Meas Geaghra acquiesced. Aithirne remained a year there, and then took his leave, bringing with him thrice fifty wives of Leinster nobles. The Leinstermen escorted him courteously out of their territory as far as the borderland at Tealchuma (just north of Dublin), and he left them there, without giving any thanks. As soon as he had passed from their territory, the furious Leinstermen gave chase, but were intercepted by an Ulster force led by king **Conchobhar mac Neasa** himself and a fierce battle ensued. The Ulstermen retreated as far as Éadar (Howth in Co Dublin), where they ensconced themselves. For eight days they were besieged there, with no food or drink except clay and sea-water. Aithirne had seven hundred cows in the fortress, but he refused a drop of milk even to dying men. Meas Deadh, a pupil of **Cú Chulainn**, performed great feats in defending the fortress but was slain just as Ulster reinforcements landed by sea. Enraged by this, Cú Chulainn led a sortie from the fort and the Leinstermen were put to flight, but many warriors were slain on both sides. **Conall Cearnach** followed the Leinstermen and slew their king Meas Geaghra in single combat.

Aithirne was, however, once outwitted by his host. This was the poet **Amhairghin mac Éigit Salaigh**, himself a former pupil of the infamous satirist. Having stayed a night, Aithirne was about

3. AMHAIRGHIN GLÚNGHEAL *Standing stones near Kenmare, claimed to mark the grave of Amhairghin's wife Scéine.*

to leave but was persuaded by Amhairghin's rhetoric to remain for the duration of autumn. Again he was persuaded to remain for the winter and the spring, until summer came and Amhairghin made a poetic speech allowing him to depart. The pupils of Amhairghin wished to hear some of Aithirne's poetry, so Amhairghin called for a bull, a calf, and a sheep to be brought in and killed in his honour. Aithirne recited verses forbidding the killing of each, but finally was satisfied with a pig. Amhairghin had saved his house from satire by the high standard of his own poetry. The death of Aithirne came about when he overstepped himself with a demand. We are told that Conchobhar sought a new woman after the death of **Deirdre**, and a suitable maiden was found - Luaine, daughter of a chieftain of the Tuatha Dé Danann (see **Mythological Cycle**). When he heard of this, Aithirne and his two sons demanded that she become their lover. She refused, and Aithirne with a satire caused three blisters of shame to rise on her face. She died as a result, and Aithirne fled with his sons to a dwelling which he had at the river Boyne. The druid **Cathbhadh** warned the enraged Ulstermen that Aithirne could send 'destructive monsters against you - satire and ridicule and reddening, barking and burning poison and bitter words'. Cú Chulainn, however, advised them to kill Aithirne, and the satirist's dwelling was accordingly set ablaze by the Ulstermen. The bitter poet perished within.

It is apparent that Aithirne was originally a character who represented the magical power of the **poets**, but that his image was debased by anti-poet propaganda in mediaeval times. The stories which we have concerning him all belong to the period between the 9th and the 11th centuries, and no accounts of him survived in post-mediaeval folklore.

Rudolf Thurneysen in *Zeitschrift für celtische Philologie 12*, 398-9; E J Gwynn in ibid 17, 152-6 and in *Ériu 13*, 13-28, 57; Whitley Stokes in *Revue Celtique 8*, 47-64 and 24, 270-87; M E Dobbs in *Études Celtiques 5*, 154-61; R I Best in *Irish Texts 1*, 32-3; Kuno Meyer in *Ériu 7*, 1-9; Liam Breatnach in *Celtica 13*, 1-31; P L Henry (1978), 55-65, 240.

AMHAIRGHIN GLÚNGHEAL Mythical or fictional poet in early Irish literature. His name (earlier, Amorgein) probably meant 'song-conception' and would have originally been a kenning for the art of poetry itself. The epithet 'glúngheal' means 'bright-kneed', but its import is obscure.

He is featured in the pseudo-history, where he appears as one of the sons of **Míl** who lead the Gaelic people in their invasion of Ireland. The role assigned to him makes him the most important of the invaders, for he is the first of them to touch the soil of Ireland and he becomes the counsellor of his brothers and the chief negotiator with the incumbent race, the **Tuatha Dé Danann**. A dramatic detail is included to the effect that his wife Scéine was drowned off the shore where they landed, which harbour is thus claimed to have been called after her - Inbhear Scéine (Kenmare Bay in Co Kerry). That placename itself is of pseudo-learned derivation, being based on a corrupted reference in an early Latin geography. As Amhairghin first lands, he recites a great mystical rhetoric in which he exults in being a poet, claiming to be at one with the whole environment. He is wind, sea, bull, hawk, dewdrop, flower, boar, salmon, lake, and hill, and he further claims to be the point of a warrior's weapon and 'a god who fashions inspiration in the head'. This composition is really an argument by the professional poets of mediaeval Ireland for social primacy, but there is also an echo of ancient ritual concerning the metamorphic power of seer-poets (see **Find**).

He and his brothers having successfully effected the conquest of Ireland, we read that Amhairghin arbitrated on their various claims, and then himself settled at Inbhear Mór (Arklow, Co Wicklow), where he built a causeway. Contention broke out between the sons of Míl, however, and Amhairghin was slain by Éireamhóin in a battle at Bile Teineadh (Billywood, near Moynalty in Co Meath).

C-J Guyonvarc'h in *Ogam 12*, 448-9; R A S Macalister (1956), 30-47, 106-7, 110-21, 156-9; Liam Breatnach in *Ériu 32*, 45-93; P S Dinneen (1908) *2*, 80-107 and *3*, 30-3.

[Placename Inbhear Scéine] T F O'Rahilly (1946), 198.

AMHAIRGHIN MAC ÉIGIT SALAIGH Mythical character in the **Ulster Cycle**, professional poet to king **Conchobhar mac Neasa**. He is sometimes given the epithet 'iarghiunnach' ('shaven behind'), which is probably a reference to a tonsure employed by the **druids**.

This character was another development from the imagery associated with the name **Amhairghin**. The earliest reference to him is in a recension from the end of the 8th century of the birth-story of **Cú Chulainn**. There he is presented as Cú Chulainn's tutor, the drama of that young hero being heightened by the acquisition in this way of mythic wisdom. This indeed seems to have been the context in which a character called Amhairghin was first introduced into the Ulster Cycle. The mention of him in this text is at a secondary stage, however, for an already developed background is clear from a reference in it to how Amhairghin and his wife Fionnchaomh reared Cú Chulainn in their fortress of Dún Imbrith in Muirtheimhne (north Co Louth). It is further stated that **Conall Cearnach** was the foster-brother of Cú Chulainn, the former being son of Amhairghin and Fionnchaomh. It thus appears that Amhairghin was introduced into the cycle as Cú Chulainn's tutor in the early part of the 8th century and that he was soon put in the role of Conall's father in the rapidly developing lore. In this text, Amhairghin stakes his claim to be a suitable tutor for the child hero, and his words are the basis for his portrayal in the succeeding literature: 'I am praised for every quality, for my courage, for my wisdom, for my fortune, for my maturity, for my eloquence, for the nobility and bravery of my offspring. Whoever is a prince, I am a poet, I deserve the status of a king. I slay each warrior. I give allegiance to nobody but Conchobhar.'

The echoes in phraseology from the poetry and portrayal of his namesake **Amhairghin Glúngheal** show that that other poet is not far in the background. There are other passages in the literature which equally show the exalted status of Conchobhar's poet. A 9th-century text, for instance, refers to a three-headed monster which came out of the cave of Cruachain (Rathcroghan, Co Roscommon) and laid Ireland waste until 'Amhairghin father of Conall Cearnach slew it in single combat in the presence of all the Ulstermen'. This monster is called 'ellén', which can be related to the fiery Ailléan which was slain by the famous warrior-seer **Fionn mac Cumhaill**. Another 9th-century text tells of Amhairghin's childhood. Until he was seven years old he was an ugly backward child. His father Éigeat Salach was a blacksmith, and one day the poet **Aithirne** sent his servant to the forge to redden his axe. The child spoke a rhetoric to the servant, who raced back to Aithirne and told him what he had heard. Fearing that he would be upstaged, Aithirne went to kill the child. Éigeat, however, made a clay-statue of his son and Aithirne, in the dim light of the forge, struck that with his axe in mistake for the child. Hotly pursued, Aithirne then fled to his own fortress, where he was besieged by the enraged Ulstermen. Eventually peace was arranged, according to which Aithirne agreed to take the boy Amhairghin as his pupil and to teach him the skills of poetry. Thus, when Aithirne grew old, Amhairghin succeeded him as chief-poet of the province. This is a typical story concerning the youth of mythic heroes, and it can also be related to ancient Irish seer-lore (see **Poets**). Another mediaeval story tells of how, when Amhairghin was a qualified poet, Aithirne (q.v.) came to visit him and sought a pretext to satirise him, but Amhairghin was so good a host that he could find no pretext.

The general portrayal of Amhairghin is that of a faithful supporter of Conchobhar, who is nevertheless socially on a par with that king. Thus his wife Fionnchaomh is Conchobhar's sister, and he is portrayed as a mediator between Conchobhar and **Fearghus mac Róich** in their disputes. Invariably he is a stout fighter. An interpolation in *Táin Bó Cuailnge* (see **Ulster Cycle**) tells of how he had a portentous vision at Tailtiu (Teltown, Co Meath) and immediately afterwards went to confront **Cú Roí**, who was advancing against Ulster. He and Cú Roí began pelting each other and the stones met in the air. They then agreed to a truce between them, according to which Amhairghin would allow no armies to pass and Cú Roí would retire from the campaign, but when Cú Roí resumed his march Amhairghin began casting again. Conall Cearnach supplied him with stones and javelins, and the number of men he killed in this way was uncountable. In addition, Amhairghin is mentioned in several musters of Conchobhar's army, and he fought side by side with **Cormac Conn Loingeas** when the latter was slain by the Connachtmen in the house of Da Choga.

A G Van Hamel (1933), 6-8, 12, 30; Maud Joynt in *Ériu 10*, 133-4; Máirín O'Daly (1975), 48-9; Kuno Meyer (1912), 57; R I Best in *Irish Texts 1*, 32-3; Cecile O'Rahilly (1976), 103-6, 111-8; Whitley Stokes in *Irische Texte 3*, 390-5; Cormac Ó Cadhlaigh (1956), 465 ('Aimhirghean' and Aimhirghean mac Egetsalaigh').

ANÉRA MAC CONGLINNE The principal character in a satiric text composed in the 12th century and entitled *Aislinge meic Conglinne* (the Vision of mac Conglinne). The patronymic must have been applied to him rather spontaneously, as it means 'hound/warrior of the valley' and has no particular significance in the story. Perhaps it was the name or nickname of some person known to the author. There are two surviving recensions of the story, both going back to the same original. One of these seems to have been deliberately abbreviated, whereas the other is an expansive tour de force of humour and wit. It states that the name Anéra meant 'non-refusal', for he was refused nothing on account of his ability to praise and satirise.

We read that the Munster king **Cathal mac Fionghuine** (+742 AD) fell in love with Líogach, sister of his rival, the high-king **Fearghal mac Maoldúin**. Cathal had never seen the lady, but their mutual love grew through report of each other. Líogach used to send apples and sweets to Cathal, but her brother had a scholar put spells on these dainties and, as a result, when Cathal ate them parasites formed in his stomach and one of these grew into a 'lon craois' (i.e. demon of gluttony). Cathal thereby had a voracious appetite, and for a year and a half he impoverished the men of Munster as they tried to satisfy him.

At that time, the scholar Anéra mac Conglinne was studying at Ros Comáin (Roscommon), and he decided to go on his poetic circuit to the Munster king, since he had heard that there was plenty of good food wherever Cathal was. He arrived at the monastery of Corcaigh (Cork), the abbot of which was Mainchín (literally 'little monk'), but got no welcome there. The guesthouse - a mere hut - was open to wind, rain, and snow, the bed-clothes were full of fleas and lice, and the bathwater was putrid. There was nobody to attend to him, so he took out his book and began to sing the psalms. Hearing his voice, the abbot sent niggardly rations to him, but Anéra recited satiric quatrains on the monastery, and the servant reported these to Mainchín. The abbot, fearful that the quatrains would become known, ordered that the visitor be viciously flogged and drenched in the river Lee. This was done, and Anéra was flung naked and bleeding into the hut and locked therein till morning. On the next day he was brought before the assembly of monks, and Mainchín ordered that, since he had insulted the Church, he should be crucified.

Mac Conglinne was taken to the green of Cork to be executed, but he asked for one boon before dying. This was to be allowed to eat some food from his satchel, as viaticum for the journey ahead of him. The request was granted, and he took a tenth of the little food that he had and offered it as tithes to the poor. As a group of paupers gathered around him, he told them of the savage way in which he had been treated, and further delayed his execution by drinking water from a well using the point of his brooch as a vessel. Finally, he was forced to cut his own passion-tree, carry it on his back, and set it in the ground. All the while he reviled the monks, calling them curs and robbers until, stung in conscience by his remarks, they entreated Mainchín to give him a day's respite. After much persuasion, Mainchín agreed to this, and mac Conglinne was left overnight tied naked to a pillar-stone.

During the night, an angel came to him and recited a vision, and mac Conglinne put this vision into poetic form. When the monks came next day to crucify him, he recited the poem, which traced the descent of Mainchín back to Adam through a rich genealogy of food-names. On hearing this, the abbot was speechless with surprise and rage, and mac Conglinne continued to recite. His vision was of a journey through a sumptuous sea of milk and honey to a magnificent dwelling entirely comprised of delicious food and drink. Now it so happened that Mainchín had dreamt that only through such a vision could Cathal mac Fionghuine be cured of his affliction, and so he ordered mac Conglinne to go at once to the king. The scholar demanded that Mainchín's cloak be given to him if he succeeded, and the abbot reluctantly agreed to this.

Mac Conglinne then went to where Cathal was due to be that night, at the fortress of a noble called Piochán at Dún Cobha (somewhere in west Cork). Arriving there, he entertained the company with juggling and buffoonery. He offered to protect Piochán from the king's gluttony, and was promised as reward a golden ring, a British steed, and a sheep from every herd between there and Cork. When Cathal arrived, he inveigled thirteen apples, one after another, from the king, this being the first time that Cathal gave food away since the demon entered him. In anger, Cathal finally flung all the apples to him, and then mac Conglinne sought a boon and was promised it. He claimed that he had been cursed by the monks of Cork, and so he desired the king to sleep one night with him in order to have the curse removed. Cathal was infuriated when he heard this, but had no choice but to fulfil his royal promise.

Having prevailed on Cathal to fast with him, mac Conglinne had the king tied to the wall of the fortress and had delicious food of all kinds prepared. He began to cook most succulent meat and to eat it, as Cathal desperately tried to break his bonds and get to it. Mac Conglinne then began to recite a much inflated version of his food-vision, which made the king delirious with desire and rage. The demon came as far as his mouth, ravenous for the food, and mac Conglinne began to put pieces in front of it. Finally, the demon could restrain itself no longer, but sprang forth and seized a piece of meat in its claws and raced to the hearth with it. Mac Conglinne covered his own mouth and that of the king with his hands, and ordered that all leave the house. The doors were locked and the house set on fire, but the demon escaped onto a nearby rooftop. Mac Conglinne then addressed it, and it admitted that it could not have been overcome but by one as holy as himself. It was then banished into the air by mac Conglinne. Cathal was so grateful to the scholar for his cure that he ordered that a mighty reward be given to him. This encompassed the things already promised, with the addition of a cow from every yard in Munster and a cloak from every church.

This story combines two plots from ordinary folk narrative - a reptile enticed from its victim's stomach (see **Animal Tales**, Type 285B), and the liar who tells of a land of wondrous food (see **Humorous Tales**, Type 1930). The original text seems to have been written as a satire on the monastery of Cork in particular, whereas in its expanded form it is directed at monastic life in general. It may have been meant for public recitation by mediaeval gleemen, being very stylised and rich in descriptions. The style was, however, so complicated that no variant of the text passed into oral tradition.

Kuno Meyer (1892); Breandán Ó Buachalla in *Galvia 7*, 43-9.

ANIMAL TALES Of the three hundred types of international folktales concerning animals listed in the Aarne-Thompson catalogue, versions of over a third have been collected from Irish oral lore, and it is clear that such narratives have been equally popular in different parts of the country down to recent times. Being folktales, these stories are told for entertainment purposes, and the animals in them have roles which make the narrative attractive and interesting, but always fanciful. As such, they are easily distinguished from ordinary zoological lore and superstition (for which see the entries on **Animals**).

These folktales are almost all short and pithy, and the most frequent actor in them is the clever fox. For example, a story which has been collected in many different parts of the world, and which is listed in the catalogue as Type 1, was and remains very popular in Ireland. It tells of a fox which sees a man bringing a load of fish in a horse-cart. The wily animal lies down on the road at a place where the cart will pass and pretends to be dead. The man notices him and, thinking of the value of the fur, throws him into the cart and travels on. Once the fox gets the man's back turned he throws the fish one by one onto the road behind, and finally jumps quietly off the cart and collects the fish from the road. Type 2 tells of a trick which the fox plays on the wolf in icy weather when it is difficult to get anything to eat. He advises the wolf to make a hole in a frozen lake, put his tail through the hole, and fish will bite at it. He should then swish the tail quickly upwards, and so catch the fish. The wolf does as he is told but soon his tail becomes stuck in the ice. Men come on the scene to kill the wolf, and the unfortunate animal can only escape by leaving his tail behind. This story is usually told abroad concerning a bear rather than a wolf, and in these cases serves to explain why bears have short tails. There have been no bears in Ireland in historical times, but wolves survived until the 18th century. The latter animal was therefore a natural substitute.

Other stories which have the fox outwitting the wolf include Type 9B, which has both farming together, with the fox demanding the top of the corn and the bottom of the potatoes; and Type 32, which has both trapped in a well, the fox climbing onto the other's back in order to escape. A story which was very popular in Ireland, as abroad, concerns how the two enter a cellar at night and begin to gorge themselves with food (Type 41). The fox eases off at the eating after some time, and walks in and out through the narrow entrance, while the wolf jeers him for his apparently eccentric behaviour. The wolf eats so much that his body greatly expands, and therefore he cannot make his getaway when humans come. His more clever companion had kept a careful eye to his waistline and thus got cleanly away.

Other stories tell of the fox's attempts to catch animals to eat. One of these has the fox studying the character of a cock in order to entrap him. When they meet one day, the clever beast praises the beautiful singing voice of the cock and gives a friendly hint on how to make the voice even more musical. Even the best of singers, he states, improve on their voice when their eyes are closed, and the foolish cock does accordingly, only to be jumped on and gobbled up. A very simple, but widespread, little story tells of how the fox rids himself of fleas (Type 63). He does this by plucking a hair from his fur and holding it in his mouth while sitting in the river. Slowly but surely he submerges himself in the water, allowing just enough time for the fleas to travel upwards to avoid being drowned. He finally submerges his nose, leaving only the hair above, and then drops that into the water. One story, though found in different parts of Ireland, has not been widely collected abroad. This (a variant of Type 67) tells of how he steals into a butcher's shop but is trapped by the butcher who bars the door. The resourceful animal begins to throw everything on which he can lay paws into the fire. Eventually, when the whole shop is in danger of becoming a conflagration, the butcher leaves the door to quench the flames, and the fox slips out and away.

The clever fellow is not always so successful when he encounters domestic animals, however. Thus, a cat and a fox debate the matter of agility (Type 105). The fox boasts that he knows and can perform many tricks and challenges the cat to match him in this. The cat knows but one trick, and therefore has to concede the superiority of his opponent. Just then a savage dog comes on the scene, and the cat climbs up a tree with incredible speed, while the fox is unable to do so and is devoured. Climbing was the cat's one trick. A very interesting story found throughout most of Europe since mediaeval times and popular throughout Ireland concerns the death of the king of the cats (Type 113A). We are told that a man once met a huge cat, which attacked him and which he with difficulty managed to slay. Before it died, the fierce animal told him that it was the king of the cats. On his return home, the man told his wife that the king of the cats was dead and, hearing this, the old domestic cat which was sleeping by the fireside jumped up and left the house. Some versions have a more macabre ending, with the domestic cat leaping at the man's throat and killing him as the bearer of bad tidings.

Several of these folktales deal with the relationships between animals and humans. Irish versions of a worldwide story (Type 130) have an assorted group of animals joining forces to rout robbers from a house which is used as a hideout. Another story (Type 155) must be a comparatively recent borrowing from abroad, for a serpent is a main actor in it although no such creatures are found in Ireland. A man sees the serpent trapped under a tree and releases it, whereupon the ungrateful creature announces its intention of devouring its rescuer. The man remonstrates, and they agree to call on a passing fox to adjudicate. The fox states that he must see the situation re-enacted in order to help him to make up his mind and, once the tree is placed on top of the serpent again, he declares that it is most just to allow matters to remain as they were in the first instance.

The narratives can entail something of an aetiological sense. For instance, one story, which has been but sparsely collected abroad but which remains popular in Ireland, tells of an argument long ago between a cat and a dog regarding which of them should live inside the house. To settle the question they decided to have a race, and the one which reached the house first should have that privilege. The dog was winning the race, but stopped to attack a poor beggarman whom he did not recognise, and so the cat reached the house first. A more widespread story (Type 217) describes how a cat is destined to always behave according to its nature. A certain man has his cat so well trained that it holds a candle for him while he reads. However, a visitor (in Irish versions usually a poor travelling scholar) bets that he can make the cat drop the candle, and accordingly releases a mouse from his pocket. The mouse races across the table, with the eyes of the cat rivetted on it. When a second mouse is released, the cat can no longer control its nature, but flings the candle aside and gives chase.

Stories about birds also feature. The fanciful idea that these once held a parliament to decide on the functions and habitats of each of them is found widely (Type 220), as is the related story of how the wren became king of the birds (Type 221). It was decided that whichever of them could fly the highest would be given that exalted office, and in the contest the eagle flew away above every other bird. The wren hid in the eagle's tail, however, and when the great bird tired and could get no higher the wily little fellow jumped out and went higher still. According to another story (Type 222), a dispute between the wren and the mouse caused a great battle between the bird and animal kingdoms. The winged creatures sided with the wren, and the quadrupeds with the mouse, and as the two armies faced each other the fox offered to be umpire for them. He was to stand on a hill and indicate the trend of the battle by his tail. If the quadrupeds were winning he would raise it, and if the birds were winning he would lower it. The animals were soon overcoming their foes, and the fox accordingly raised his tail. However, the bee, who had not decided which side to take, threw in his lot with the birds and went and stung the fox's posterior. With a howl of pain, the fox lowered his tail to protect himself, and seeing this the birds were encouraged and they routed the animals off the field. Ever since, the birds have jurisdiction both in the air and on the ground, whereas the quadrupeds are confined to the earth. This is often told in Ireland as an introduction to another folktale (see **Wonder Tales**, Type 313).

One rare international folktale (Type 232C) is well evidenced in Ireland. We are told that a wren was once a farmer, and he had twelve sons which looked exactly like himself. A harsh winter came and he ran out of food and had to borrow some grain. When the following harvest came, the wren had a fine crop, but made no effort to repay the debt. The creditor went to collect his due, but was confronted with the thirteen identical birds and did not know to whom he should address his demand. The old wren was very pleased to in this way avoid paying, and he and his sons continued nonchalantly to thresh the grain as the bewildered creditor looked on. At last, the creditor thought of a plan. He shouted out enthusiastically that the old wren was a far better worker than any of his sons, and at that one of the wrens jumped up and beat his breast with pride. It was the old wren, pleased that at last his paternal chiding of the sons had been justified, but the creditor then knew to whom he should address his demand.

Regarding fish, the only folktale which has become widespread in Ireland is an explanation of why the flounder has a crooked mouth (Type 250A). We are told that it acquired this deformity because it once mocked a hungry saint who desired a fish, and a detail is often added to the effect that the salmon acquired its agile leap because it generously jumped into the breast of the holy man on the same occasion. A variant of Type 285B has been known in Ireland since mediaeval times. This international folktale tells of how a snake enters a person's stomach and is enticed out again by being made thirsty, and in the Irish adaptations a lizard is substituted for the snake. Two occurrences of the plot in mediaeval Irish literature (see **Anéra mac Conglinne** and **Fursa**) turn the offending creature into a demon of gluttony.

Antti Aarne / Stith Thompson (1961), 21-87; Seán Ó Súilleabháin / R Th Christiansen (1967), 33-57; Ó Súilleabháin (1942), 558-9, 650-3 and (1973), 14-6.

ANIMALS AND FOWL, DOMESTICATED A great deal of lore was concerned with the creatures with whom humans were in regular daily contact and on whom people's livelihood largely depended. Of these, the cow and the horse were the most important, but since horses figured in several other aspects of life besides agriculture a separate entry in this volume deals with them.

Cattle have been of paramount social importance in Ireland for a very long time, and this is reflected in the mediaeval literature concerning wars and raiding (see **Bóraimhe** and **Ulster Cycle**). The necessity of milk for sustenance and nourishment caused a quasi-mystical power to be often associated with it (see **Brighid, Corc Duibhne, Fliodhais, Glas Ghoibhneann**), and this was further stressed by perennial ideas which make cows stand at a kind of functional juncture between this life and the otherworld realms. The image of a divine white cow seems to have been early established in Irish myth (see **Bóinn**), but the literature repeatedly refers to white red-eared cows as being especially valuable and obtainable from otherworld sources. It has been plausibly suggested that this type of dual colouring derives its imagery from a breed which still survives in Britain, having been introduced there during the Roman occupation. Fairy cows are sometimes in later folklore claimed to have these colours, and it is believed that the fairies are more likely to take a white cow from a farmer's herd than any other colour. By extension of this, a white cow is said to be very unlucky on a farm. The type of cow most sought after by the old farmers was a 'droimfhionn', which signifies a dark-coloured animal with a streak of white on its back. These were believed to be great milkers, as also were cows with crooked horns.

An Irish proverb states that 'the cow is one of the pleasant trees of Paradise', and another states that she is leather and meat, milk and butter. Since cows were of central importance to the farmers' livelihood, and since they could be quite prone to illness, interference with them by otherworld beings was much feared. The **fairies** were believed to take a special interest in livestock, and so to placate them the first measure of milk taken from a cow would be thrown into the air for them. Notwithstanding this, it was thought that the fairies would not hesitate to take away a fine cow if they were in need of one in their realm. Cracks in a cow's hide were interpreted to result from fairy darts being shot at her, these darts being a preliminary to abduction. In order to prevent this, various methods were employed which were believed to be effective against the fairies, such as tying a red ribbon to the cow's tail, rubbing dung to her udder, or causing her to inhale some puffs of smoke. Since St **Brighid** was the special patron of cattle, crosses dedicated to that saint were hung in the cow-byre and were believed to give very good protection; while on St John's Eve (see **Time**), the cows might be driven through bonfires, or have their udders singed with a blessed candle at Easter. The same methods of protection were believed to be effective against the other chief source of danger to cattle, envious and avaricious neighbours. Certain people, who were reputed to have the evil eye (see **Human Life**), were much feared by farmers, and would at all costs be kept away from a herd. Similarly, if a neighbour used a whitethorn stick to drive one's cattle, the worst was suspected of him. Some neighbours were also suspected of attempting to take milk by magical means, especially on May Eve (see **Time**).

On the positive side, it was considered lucky to keep a goat or a virgin-cow with the herd, and in some places the cows were made to swim in a river or even the sea to bring them good fortune. Regarding the actual milking itself, it was believed that music caused a cow to increase her yield, and so milkers would often sing or whistle as they worked. It was customary in many places, at the beginning of summer, to bring the herd to new pasture until the end of autumn. The summer pasture would usually be unused land on a hillside or mountainside, and was known as 'buaile', hence the frequency of this element (anglicised 'booley') in Irish placenames. Temporary dwellings were erected on the chosen locations, and often the young people who tended the cattle would live in these for weeks on end. The practice of transhumance was current in other countries also, but in Ireland - a country with little sunny weather apart from these months - it had a special aesthetic attraction. It afforded the young people the opportunity of prolonged absence from the authority of their elders, and they availed of it to congregate, dance, and make merry. From the word 'buaile' comes the hiberno-English term 'hooley', which refers to an enjoyable get-together accompanied by singing and dancing.

A practice which was very common in mediaeval times, but which has died out in recent centuries, was to bleed cattle for food. A vein in the animal's shoulder was opened, and the blood caught in a vessel and when congealed heated into edible balls. This would provide much needed nutrition in times of scarcity. One of the valued staples of the traditional Irish diet was pork or bacon, and this is underlined in the literature by the importance attributed to pigs. Accounts of swine-herding and boar-hunts were very popular in the mediaeval stories, and pigs were often given otherworld associations (see, for example, **Fionn mac Cumhaill**). Pigs were kept by a large number of farmers in olden times, their sty often being an actual extension of the dwelling-house. In some places, it was customary to drive a pig into the house on May morning, so as to ensure luck for the summer season, and among the speculative capabilities of the animal was the ability to see the wind and thus forecast the weather. Pigs were naturally regarded as crude and dirty animals, and the likening of a person to one was the ultimate insult. Thus, in the literature, when otherworld beings appeared in the form of a pig, their hostile aspect was being stressed. A folk legend told of how a rich woman had once been unkind to a poor woman who came to seek alms, likening her and her children to a sow with a litter of bonhams. When the rich woman herself gave birth soon after, her child had a pig's head. Ominous **spirits** were often said to appear in the form of a black pig, and a late legend in north Leinster and adjoining areas tells of how an ill-tempered schoolmaster was turned into such a creature by one of his pupils who got possession of a book with magical spells. The raging teacher carved out a large trench through the countryside, and this was popularly given as the origin of the 'Black Pig's Dyke', a series of earthworks which stretch approximately along the southern border of Ulster and which were probably constructed in early centuries to prevent cattle-raiding.

Sheep also figure in the literature, but are not given a high profile, and folklore has little to say of them apart from their commercial value in terms of mutton and wool, although a ram is featured in an allegorical role in one widespread story of the **Fianna**. Like pigs, goats are said to be able to see the wind, and the most intriguing tradition associated with them was the custom in a few particular places of exhibiting a decorated billy-goat at goat markets, called puck-fairs. The most celebrated of such fairs is held at Killorglin, Co Kerry, in August, but another survived into the late 19th century at Mullinavat, in Co Kilkenny. Similar displays of 'king' animals included a decorated ram at a sheep-fair in Greencastle, Co Down, and a white stallion at a horse-fair in Cappawhite, Co Limerick. The custom probably originated with the fairs held by the Normans in late mediaeval Ireland, the animal being enthroned as a proclamation that the market was in progress. The popular explanation usually given for the origin of the Killorglin fair is that English soldiers were plundering the area long ago, but a billy-goat collected all the farm animals and led them up a mountain to safety. Another explanation, however, is that when the Killorglin fair was first set up, no animals were brought there except for a solitary billy-goat led by an old man. The townspeople were so grateful that they made the goat the symbol of the fair, and the spectacle of its enthronement attracted many sellers and buyers of animals. The billy-goat, decked out with ribbons and a crown, is placed on a high stage for the three-days duration of the fair, which has become a large tourist attraction.

Although continually associated with the country in tourist brochures, the donkey was a late introduction into Ireland and did not become common until the 19th century. Because of the international folk legend which claims that it got the cross on its back as a reward for carrying **Christ**, it was said to be a blessed animal which should always be treated with kindness. It was widely believed that a child suffering from chin-cough could be cured by being made to pass under a donkey's belly. A more ambiguous attitude was taken to the cat, it being on the one hand much valued for its service in keeping mice and rats at bay, but on the other hand suspected of having a deep and sinister side to its nature. The mediaeval literature has some fierce cats as opponents of heroes (see **Cú Chulainn**, **Fionn mac Cumhaill**, and **Seanchán**), yet domestic cats are portrayed as gentle companions of saints, as in one text which has a little pet cat supplying fish for three hungry monks on an island. In a humorous vein, folklore claimed that the cat had long ago bought three gifts for itself - these were equal light by night and day, the forgetfulness of the housewife, and the ability to keep its feet from getting wet. Dogs or hounds are also given two opposing roles in the literature. In stories of Fionn and the Fianna, for instance, some of them are faithful friends whereas others are fierce fighters in the armies of the foe. The hounds said to have hunted and fought for Fionn were undoubtedly examples of the huge and handsome breed known as Irish wolfhounds, which were in high demand abroad and were exported in great numbers in mediaeval times. A popular folktale tells of a prophecy that a prince will be killed by a black eight-legged hound, but he is saved by dogs which he meets. They kill the fierce hound, and then insist that the prince cut their heads off with an axe. By so doing he disenchants them, and finds that they are in reality a fellow prince and his two sisters. Dogs were appreciated, not just as good workers on the farm, but also as protectors of the house from both physical and spiritual marauders - it being believed that a dog could see ghosts and warn of them. It was said in Ulster that when St **Colm Cille** once saw a spaniel defeat an Irish hound in a fight, he prophesied that the Spaniards would one day control Ireland.

Regarding fowl, geese and ducks were widely kept, but most lore centres on hens and cocks. It was popularly believed that hens had been brought to Ireland by the **Norsemen**, and that they frantically prepared every night to fly back to Scandinavia on the morrow. However, when they fell asleep they forgot their plans and rambled about the farmyard the next day as before. They continue to harbour hostile feelings towards the Irish people, however, and their scraping on the floor of the kitchen is a vain attempt to set the house on fire. Much folk custom centred on their eggs. These were marked with a cross for good luck when the hen began to hatch, and at Easter baskets of fresh eggs were given as presents. Contrariwise, malicious individuals were reputed to put rotten eggs in the haystacks of neighbours in order to send bad luck to them. A crowing hen was believed to be unlucky in a farmyard and was not left alive for long. However, when the cock crew he was claimed to be saying 'Mac na hÓighe slán!' ('the Son of the Virgin is safe!') in memory of how he once bore testimony to the Resurrection of **Christ**. The crowing of a cock was believed to be efficacious against spirits, particularly that of a 'coileach Mhárta' (March cock). This was described as a cock, all black in colour, which had been hatched out in March ('Márta'), and in some cases specifically on a Tuesday ('Máirt). A legend, found in several coastal areas, tells of how a sea-captain once saw such a cock at a farmhouse near the shore. A thunderbolt was headed for the house, but the cock crew and thereby deflected disaster away. Realising the worth of the animal, the captain offered a substantial amount of money for it to the housewife, who foolishly accepted the bargain. As soon as the captain had taken the cock away, fire broke out and consumed the house.

Bees were more generally kept in former than in recent times. They were believed to be blessed creatures, to be possessed of special wisdom, and to take an acute interest in the affairs of their owners. If a bee entered the house it was regarded as a good omen, and the bees in their hive would be told in advance of projects which the family intended to undertake, in the belief that they might effect a beneficial influence. When a member of the family died, it was customary to place a black piece of cloth on the hive so that the bees could join in the mourning.

T P Cross (1952), 51-83; Seán Ó Súilleabháin (1942), 31-46 and (1967), 21-5; Séamus Ó Duilearga (1948), 371, 449; E Estyn Evans (1942), 47-55 and (1957), 27-38, 167-9; Máire MacNeill (1962), 289-302, 674-80; Kevin Danaher (1966), 93-100 and (1984), 12-6; Séamas Ó Catháin (1982), 45-53 and (1980), 75-80; Fionnuala Williams in *Emania 3*, 12-9; Geraldine Lynch (1976).

ANIMALS AND OTHER CREATURES OF THE WILD Tradition shows that the Irish people regarded the fauna with a good deal of intelligent curiosity, but also with a degree of fanciful imagination. In the literature there are mentions of some fantastic animals, especially great dragon-like creatures which inhabit watery realms and which have their origin in the biographies of **saints**. Some other fanciful creatures, such as griffins, massive cats, and fire-breathing hounds, are mere devices to heighten the drama in texts, and their rare occurrences in folktales are for the same purpose. There is a richer and more varied lore, however, concerning the ordinary creatures which are met with in the environment.

The various skills and characteristics of the fauna have long provided inspiration to poets and storytellers. In ancient times (see **Find**) seers were believed to be able to go about in the form of animals and thereby gain knowledge from other than human perspectives. From this grew the literary traditions which had such characters as **Fionntan** and **Tuán mac Cairill** living for long periods in the form of different creatures and becoming great repositories of ancient history. It also gave a narrative base to archaic ideas concerning how the deities could exist in non-human form, and by implication that certain individual animals, birds, and fish could have lived from time immemorial. The result of all this is a story in post-mediaeval folklore which with a degree of humour compares various long-living creatures. It tells of a man who, amazed at the coldness of a particular night, wonders if there was ever so cold a night before. He sets out to discover the answer to this, and first meets an otter which is lying in a deep hole on top of a rock. The otter tells him that it has been there for so long that the hole has been worn in the stone by its body, but it has never seen so cold a night as recently. Next the man meets a very old hawk, which is perched on an anvil and has been there for so long that the anvil is almost worn away from rubbing of its beak after eating. Neither has it seen so cold a night. Finally, the man encounters the one-eyed salmon of Eas Rua (the falls of Assaroe, at Ballyshannon in Co Donegal). This salmon tells him that it does indeed remember a colder night an extremely long time before. It had frozen so fast that night that, when the salmon jumped out of the water to catch a fly, the river was ice when it returned. The salmon had thus lain on the ice, and a bird came and plucked out one of its eyes. The blood from the eye melted the ice, and so the salmon had got back into the water. This story is a curious example of how a continuous tradition can remould its imagery, for in the early literature the one-eyed salmon was the form taken by the deity called the **Ruadh Ró-Fheasa** in the river Boyne, and by a confusion of this name it had become associated with the Donegal location.

The salmon was the favourite fish of the many generations of people, and thus has more lore attached to it than any other of its species. The famous 'salmon of knowledge', eaten by **Fionn mac Cumhaill**, must have been invented by the seer-poets, not only due to mystical ideas but also to the fine taste and nutrition of this type of fish. Because of its superb jumping ability, it was regarded as the epitome of good physical and mental condition, and so 'sláinte an bhradáin' (the salmon's health) was a standard term used in wishing a person well. It was so closely identified with human beings, indeed, that each person was said to have an internal 'salmon of life' in their body (see **Human Life**), and drowned people were sometimes said to appear after death in the form of large black salmon on a river.

Little narrative lore was current about other types of fish, but the eel was an exception. This creature, because of its unusual appearance and mode of travel overland, was an object of much speculation. Its tenacity gave rise to the idea that dead eels might sometimes come to life again, and that horse-hair left in water for a long time turned into an eel. There were some sinister echoes in the lore, such as a tradition that large eels could sometimes be seen going into graves to eat corpses. A story, common in Munster, told of how a man once caught a large eel and took it home. During the night, however, a voice was heard outside calling the eel. The captive eel spoke and said that its comrade was outside, and on investigation the man found that a similar large eel was outside the door. He therefore opened the door without delay and let the captive go.

Another agile water-creature which attracted attention was the otter, called in Irish 'dobharchú' or 'madra uisce', both of which terms mean 'water-dog'. In the biographies of the **saints**, otters are sometimes portrayed as assisting the holy men by providing fish for them. Folk belief held that otters slept with their eyes open, and a special and rare kind, called the 'king-otter', never slept at all. The king-otter, it was claimed, was an extraordinarily large male specimen, white in colour, but with the tips of his ears black and a black cross on his back. He was vulnerable only to a bullet made from silver, and the person who killed him would not live for more than twenty-four hours afterwards. The person who came into possession of a piece of his skin was, however, very fortunate indeed. That skin would guarantee safety at sea to any boat on which it was kept, safety from fire to any house in which it was, and safety from all accidents to any man who had a piece of it in his pocket.

Much speculation surrounded the seals also. They were sometimes said to have been the people who had been left outside the biblical Ark by Noah, and as a result they had been changed into that form. They could regain their human shape for short intervals, and stories were told of how benighted people sometimes saw the seals congregate on the sea-shore, cast aside their skins, and dance as humans. This notion probably sprang from contemplation of the human-like cry given by seals, and it was in time strengthened by the adaptation to the seal-context of the legend of a man who married a mermaid (see **Fairies**). Thus it is sometimes said that the strange bride in that legend was a seal-woman.

The fanciful belief that humans had been enchanted into animal-form is found also in the case of the creature known as a weasel ('easóg') in Ireland, but which is designated a stoat by the zoologists. It is said that these weasels hold

4. ANIMALS AND OTHER CREATURES OF THE WILD *Bull of the grey seal, the largest variety off the Irish coast.*

funerals for their dead, much as humans do, and that they show intelligence very like that of people. Its spit was believed to be poisonous, and a story was widely told of how it was prepared to use this as protection. A group of men were mowing a field where a weasel's nest was, and the weasel was worried that its young would be killed. It therefore went and spat into their tea-can, so that they would be poisoned before they reached the nest. One of the men, however, came upon the nest, and kindly put it to the side of the field where it would not be damaged. When the men went to drink their tea, the mother-weasel was seen to approach and knock the can over so that they would not be poisoned. Notwithstanding this, weasels were reputed to be vengeful against humans, and to see one early in the morning or when setting out on a journey was taken to be a bad portent. The folk fancy was that weasels had been the cats of the **Norsemen**, and that they had come to Ireland in this way.

The 'dogs' brought by the Norsemen, it was claimed, were foxes, but this animal was noted for its intelligence and wile long before the Middle Ages and in the legends of the saints he appears as a helpful but somewhat unreliable creature. The fox is famed in the international **Animal Tales**, versions of which were very popular in Ireland, and from ordinary observation many further accounts of him grew up in various localities. His tricks in order to evade the hunting-hounds were particularly the subject of interest, for example, how he would urinate in a circle and then jump outside the circle in order to put the hounds off his scent. He was also believed to be able to foresee events, including the weather, and his barking was taken as a sign that rain was approaching. In a few cases, most notably that of the Preston family of Gormanstown in Co Meath, a group of foxes was believed to assemble near the house and set up a continuous chorus of barking as a sign that a member of the household would soon die. Foxes, of course, were the subject of many songs - some humorous ones concerning their stealing of domestic fowl and others in praise of great hunts which they gave to the 'hard-riding country gentlemen'. Due to its colour the fox is the most conspicuous of land-animals and therefore it was regarded as unlucky to see one when going fishing. Fishermen conversing at sea would never refer to a fox by its name but would instead use a circumlocution such as 'bushy tail'.

The badger was also a clever animal, and among its accomplishments were the ability to save hay for farmers overnight, if it so chose, and a quite unusual way of making its getaway or otherwise travelling in a hurry. This was to put its snout into a special pocket under its tail, curl itself into a ball, and roll down hills or slopes. Rabbits were given a more spiritual significance, for the souls of dead people were sometimes said to return in this form. This belief was particularly applied to a white rabbit, no doubt because such an animal was unusual and eye-catching. Hedgehogs were understood to be animals of great perseverance in their difficult lives. One of them was said to have helped **Christ** after his forty days fast by rolling on the ground and collecting apples on its spikes for him. On the other hand, however, hedgehogs were believed to suck the milk from cows as they lay down on the field at night.

5. ANIMALS AND OTHER CREATURES OF THE WILD *The Irish hare with summer and winter pelage.*

Particularly notorious for this kind of milk-stealing was the hare, in which form it was said that malicious women could go abroad at night to take the dairy-profit of their neighbours. This idea is in Ireland for several centuries, and a common legend tells of how a farmer grew suspicious when the milk-yield of his cows diminished greatly. He stayed up at night to watch the cows, and saw a hare come to drink from them. His dog followed the hare, but could only manage to draw blood from its quarters as it fled. The farmer followed on and, coming to a house, asked an old woman who lived there had she seen a hare pass by. As she answered, he noticed that the woman was bleeding, and from this realised that the hare had in fact been her. Apart from such sinister human transformations, hares in their natural state could betoken bad fortune - for instance, if one crossed the path of a pregnant woman, the child could be born with a fissure in the upper lip. To avoid this 'hare-lip' in the child, it was advised that such a woman should tear the hem of her dress, thus transferring the destined fissure to another object.

Deer play a large part in much of the literature, especially in stories of the **Fianna**, where they are often portrayed as otherworld beings in disguise. They do not, however, figure much in folklore, which instead has a tendency to regard wild cats as being otherworldly. It is apparent that there have been no real wild cats in Ireland in historical times, and such cats in Irish folklore seem to be a combination in the popular mind of various things. These would include ordinary domestic cats either gone wild or engaged in nocturnal escapades, and reports from abroad of larger cats, such as the wild cats of Scotland or even lions. The latter would seem to account for the tradition that a wild cat ('fia-chat') has a claw at the tip of its tail. In some accounts, however, there are strong indications that what are meant by these 'wild cats' of Irish folklore are in fact pine-martens. When the wild cats congregate at night, they are said to discuss their private affairs and various stratagems which they will employ against humans. Irish versions of a very popular story (see **Wonder Tales**, Type 613) tell of how valuable secrets are discussed at these assemblies.

Rats were the principle pest-creatures in Irish life, since they stole and dirtied the grain, and they were therefore believed to be vile and vengeful creatures. A long-standing tradition, very strong throughout the whole Gaelic world, was that **poets** had the power to banish or control them with verse. Also feared were bats, whose appearance in or near a house was believed to betoken death. They were believed to stick in a person's hair and, if the hair were not cut immediately, that person would die. The mouse, however, had a more variable image. It was said that mice first came into existence due to a miracle of St **Martin**, who once placed some food under a tub and warned his companions to leave it there until the morrow. An inquisitive person lifted the tub during the night, and a plague of mice rushed forth. In order to control them, Martin threw his glove after them and it turned into a cat. This derives from an international legend, which has mice and rats created by the devil and sent into Noah's Ark.

Noticing them, however, Noah threw his glove at them and it became a cat. The legend, in its international form, is told in a 14th-century Irish text.

The heroic literature shows that in pre-Christian times birds were understood to be intermediaries between this world and the otherworld (see, for example, **Conaire** and **Cú Chulainn**). Deities could take on the form of birds, and in Christian lore this was adapted and transformed so that angels were portrayed as appearing in that form (see, for example, **Patrick**). There are several reports that the **druids** used the flight of birds as auguries, and they were believed to have been able to interpret the cry of the raven. A vestige of this survives in folklore, which claims that ravens and hooded crows are birds of ill omen, and that to hear them squawking near the house betokens the death of some relative. Similar ideas are still current regarding other types of birds. For instance, if, for the first time in the year, a person hears the cuckoo's cry in his left ear, that is a portent that the person will die before the year is out, and it is still widely believed that to harm a swan brings death or some other misfortune to a person. If a farmer harms a swallow, it is claimed that he will soon notice blood in the milk given by his cows, and it is regarded as a very unlucky thing to see a pigeon enter the dwelling-house. To see a single magpie betokens bad luck, but the effect of this can be removed if, on seeing it, a person immediately removes his hat.

Some curious ideas were current until recently concerning the nature of certain birds. For instance, the barnacle-goose ('gé ghiúrainn') was said to be hatched from barnacle-shells and thus was properly a fish. This meant that people would not break the Lenten fast by eating the barnacle-goose, a situation which in mediaeval times was accepted in Ireland and elsewhere by ecclesiastical authorities. The robin was said, in Ireland as abroad, to have got its red breast from its attempts to stanch the blood on the brow of **Christ** at the Crucifixion. It was also said to have assisted the Virgin Mary on the flight into Egypt. Mary was cut by brambles, but the little bird followed on and covered the trail of blood with leaves so that the pursuers would not find it. The robin was thus held in high regard as a blessed bird, and it should never be killed, nor should its nest be interfered with. Because of the assistance it rendered to Jesus, the robin was regarded as a bird anxious to console the sick and dying, and some people claimed that it was wont to alight on the window-sill of a house and sing to comfort a dying person within. In some Munster versions of folktales, the robin was described as a supporter and encourager of heroes in mortal combat, and these stories refer to the helpful bird as 'spideog mhuintir Shúilleabháin' ('the robin of the O'Sullivans'). Its particular association with that family is puzzling, but it may have arisen from the pseudo-tradition that the family's ancestor Súildubhán mac Maolughra gave away his eye through his generosity (see **Eochaidh mac Luchta**). In that case, the appearance of a helpful robin to stanch the blood from Súildubhán's face would have been a natural improvisation.

The wren's reputation was less respected. Although this litle fellow (called 'dreoilín' in Irish) was reputed to be king of all the birds in widespread narrative lore (see **Animal Tales**), it was regarded in Ireland as a treacherous bird. Various redactions of a legend told of how it had betrayed Irish soldiers by beating its wings on the shields or drums of a sleeping hostile army, whether of the **Norsemen** or the Cromwellians. It was even said to have betrayed St Stephen, the first Christian martyr, by flapping its wings to attract his pursuers when he was hiding. This is the popular explanation given for the custom of 'hunting the wren' on St Stephen's Day, when it is still customary in many parts of the country for groups of people in disguise and playing music to go from house to house collecting money to 'bury the wren'. In former times, they really brought with them, on a pole, the body of an unfortunate wren. The custom, known also in some other countries, seems to have been introduced into Ireland not more than a few centuries ago. It has been plausibly suggested, however, that antipathy towards the wren results from efforts by mediaeval ecclesiastics to abolish vestiges of druidic practices concerning the bird. A 9th-century glossary fancifully derives a term for the wren, 'dreán', from 'draoi-éan' ('druid-bird'), and similar echoes could be interpreted from a mediaeval text which gives a detailed list of prognostications from the wren's movements.

Less lore was current concerning other small animals. Frogs were in some narrative tales portrayed as enchanted people or fairies in disguise, but this idea was not strong in ordinary folk belief. Lizards were regarded as dangerous and quite sinister, and a voracious appetite was ascribed to them (see **Animal Tales**). A belief which probably derives from speculation regarding the chameleon is that the lizard, if cut into pieces, could join itself together again. If a person were brave enough to lick a lizard, it was said that he would have power to cure burns by applying his tongue to them. Snails were often used in divination, for example young people traced their track over a slate to decide whether a certain boy or girl would marry within the year. The spider was the most blessed of insects, having once used its web to hide the fugitive **Christ**, and therefore the spider was never killed and was regarded as a harbinger of good luck in the house. The spider's web was commonly used to stanch the blood from wounds. Contrariwise, the cockroach or black chafer was detested as the betrayer of Christ by giving information to his pursuers. It was said to have been the only insect to enter Christ's tomb, and its antipathy to Christians - according to popular fancy - is still shown by the habit of raising its tail to curse its beholder. The cricket was given both positive and negative significance - people believed that it was lucky to hear one in the house, but on the other hand it was said to betoken rain. If crickets left a house, this was taken to be an omen of an impending death in the family.

[Assaroe salmon] Seán Ó Súilleabháin / R Th Christiansen (1967), Type 1927.

T P Cross (1952), 48-83; Anne Ross (1974), 302-77, 417-46; Seán Ó Súilleabháin (1942), 289-303 and in *Béaloideas 10*, 132-40; W G Wood-Martin (1902) *1*, 116-51; Caoimhín Ó Danachair (1978), 25-6; J J O'Meara (1982), 37-52, 69-84, 128-33; Kevin Danaher (1972), 243-50; G E Evans / David Thomson (1974), 41-9, 156-77; Séamus Ó Duilearga (1948), 1-5, 371, 415-6; Kuno Meyer in *Irisleabhar na Gaedhilge 5*, 155 and (1912), 40; Liam Ó Dochartaigh in *Béaloideas 45-47*, 164-98 and 50, 90-125; RIA Dictionary s.v. 'dreán'; R I Best in *Ériu 8*, 120-3; Brian Ó Cuív in *Éigse 18*, 43-66.

AODH ALLÁN Son of **Fearghal mac Maoldúin**, and high-king of Ireland from 734 to 743 AD.

One annalistic source gives a dramatic account of his conception and birth. We read that his mother was the daughter of Conghal, who preceded Aodh's father Fearghal as high-king. She was a nun, but was the secret lover of Fearghal. Once, when he was told that she had a tryst with her lover, Conghal came in a rage to discover them, but his daughter hid Fearghal under the bed-clothes and sat on top of him. While in this position, a large cat came and ate chunks from his legs, but Fearghal seized the cat and quietly choked it. Believing his daughter to be innocent, Conghal drowned the man who had informed him of her affair and sought her forgiveness for his suspicion. Nevertheless, she conceived and gave birth, and secretly handed her baby boy to two women with instructions to drown him. Instead of doing so, they kept him, and four years later the nun-mother unwittingly admired the child and confessed that she was guilty of murdering a child born to herself. She was overjoyed to learn that this was in fact her son, and the boy was quietly delivered to Fearghal to be reared.

This story seems to be apocryphal, for elsewhere the name of Aodh's mother is given as Bríghe daughter of Orca mac Carrthain. One account states that, when he grew up, Aodh was boisterous and crude, in contradistinction to his younger brother **Niall Frasach**, who was well-mannered and kindly. It happened once that they simultaneously visited their father at the royal fortress of Aileach (Greenan Hill, in north-east Donegal). Fearghal had them put into separate quarters and, when he visited them in turn, he was very pleased with the gentle comportment of Niall but disgusted by the uproar and filth of Aodh's company. He therefore foretold that Aodh would be energetic and hard-willed, whereas Niall would be pious and prudent.

This reputation of Aodh was not general, however, and some of the literature regards him as a cultured man who was accustomed to compose verse. There is no doubting that he was an able, if ambitious ruler, and he succeeded in exerting his control over the regional kings by a combination of war and diplomacy. His most powerful opponent was the Munster king **Cathal mac Fionghuine**, but the two met at Tír Dhá Ghlas (Terryglass, Co Tipperary) in the year 737 and peace was arranged between them. Aodh fell six years later, fighting against his relative, Domhnall mac Murchadha, at Seireadh Magh (near Kells, Co Meath).

John O'Donovan (1848) 1, 326-41 and (1860), 22-31; R A S Macalister (1956), 390-3; P S Dinneen (1908) *3*, 146-9; Kuno Meyer in *Zeitschrift für celtische Philologie 13*, 143-4; F J Byrne (1973), 114-8, 147-8, 208-10.

AODH EANGACH A prophesied king in mediaeval Irish lore. The name 'Aodh' (earlier, 'Aedh') was a common one in both ancient and modern times, its original meaning being 'fire'. It is anglicised as Hugh. The epithet 'Eangach' has not been satisfactorily explained. Interpretations of it vary from 'brilliant' and 'pennoned' to 'vociferous' and 'bird-voiced'.

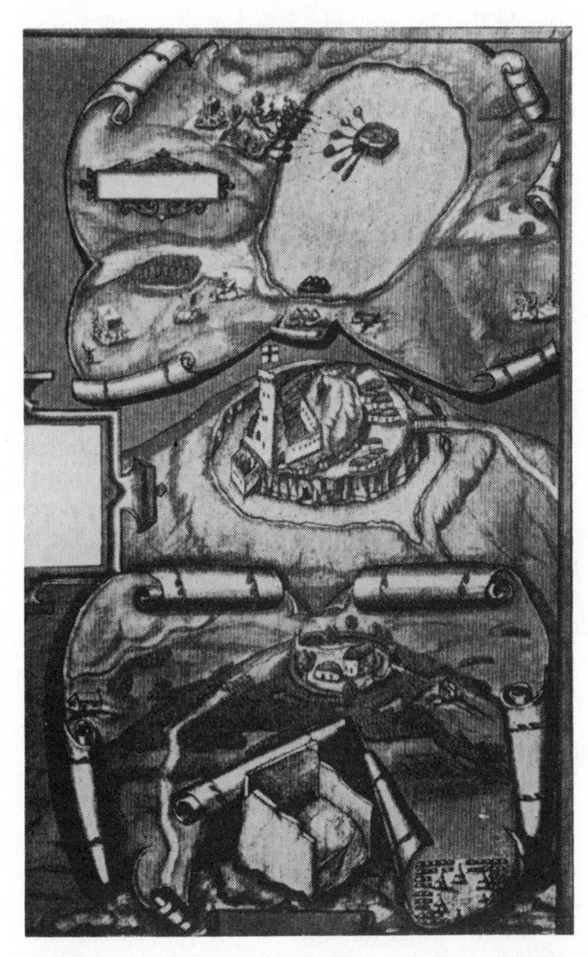

6. AODH EANGACH *Sketch from the year 1602 of the inauguration site of Uí Néill chieftains at Tullahogue near Dungannon.*

The idea that a great leader called Aodh Eangach would come was part of the propaganda of the royal Uí Néill sept in the latter centuries of their dynasty. It seems to have developed in or about the 9th century and was supposed to have been a prophecy made by the earlier saint **Bearchán**. The image may actually have sprung from the figure of Aodh Finnliath, the Uí Néill high-king from 862 to 879 AD who gained several victories over the Norse raiders. Especially when the sept's power began to decline from the beginning of the 11th century, poets were wont to flatter various Uí Néill leaders with the conceit that the lauded individual was the prophesied Aodh Eangach. A 13th-century poem claims that Bearchán had prophesied long before that 'a pillar would be erected by the side of Tara, and from it Aodh Eangach would emerge'. The imagery here suggests the fiery pillar of *Exodus* which led the Hebrews out of Egypt, and this is supported by one explanation of 'Aodh Eangach' as 'he who leaves a trail of fire'. Clearly both the name and the personality was left open to various interpretations, but the basic point is that he would lead from the royal centre **Tara**.

The prophecy attributed to Bearchán also states that the messianic figure would be a 'red-handed one' ('crobhdhearg'), that is his hand would be red from fighting and battles. Such an image was generally expressed by the term 'lámhdhearg' and was known to the earlier literature in the general sense of great warriors. For alliterative reasons it was applied especially to the warriors of Leinster. Once it became attached to the Uí Néill prophecy, however, it became domiciled in that context, and in post-mediaeval times the red hand was the family crest of the O'Neills and thus of the province of Ulster, where they predominated. Bearchán was reputed to have foretold that Aodh Eangach would defeat his rivals and win the battle at Liathdroim, which was a variant poetic name for Tara. Belief in such a prophecy lingered for a long time, and much reference was made to it during the rebellion of the great Aodh Ó Néill, Earl of Tyrone, against Elizabeth I at the end of the 16th century. Before the battle of the Yellow Ford in 1598, a professional poet told the Earl's assembled army that Bearchán had long ago prophesied a defeat of the English there. In this case the prediction was proved correct. An English report of the same time, in describing a push by the Earl towards Dublin, makes much of his arrival at Tara 'where the old doating prophecy was that if O'Neill could come and shoe his horse he should be king of all Ireland'.

Rudolf Thurneysen in *Zeitschrift für celtische Philologie 12*, 237-8; A O Anderson in *ibid 18*, 29-31; N J Williams (1980), 64, 280-1, 321; Pól Breathnach / Colm Ó Lochlainn *1* (1948), 178-9; Herbert Wood (1933), 173; James Carney in Myles Dillon ed (1968), 155-7; Dáithí Ó hÓgáin (1985), 124-7, 136, 333.

AODH SLÁINE High-king of Ireland, who reigned from 565 to 604 AD. He was son of **Diarmaid mac Cearrbheoil**. Sláine is the placename Slane in Co Meath, and its association with him suggests that he lived there at some stage.

A striking birth-tale is told of him in a 10th-century text. According to it, his father Diarmaid had two wives, Maireann and Mughain. The latter was jealous of Maireann and, knowing that her rival was bald, she determined to shame her at the festival of Tailtiu (Teltown, Co Meath). She therefore bribed a woman-satirist to knock from Maireann's head the royal diadem which hid her blemish. Immediately it fell, Maireann exclaimed: 'May God and Ciarán help me!' Through a miracle of St **Ciarán of Clonmacnoise**, beautiful golden hair grew on her head before anybody noticed that she was bald. Moreover, God caused Mughain to be barren for what she had done, and the king lost interest in her. In desperation, she sought the assistance of St Finnian of Magh Bhile (Moville, Co Down), and he blessed water and gave it to her to drink. As a result, she became pregnant and gave birth to a lamb. Again he blessed water for her, and she bore a silver fish. On the third occasion he blessed Mughain herself, and as a result of this she gave birth to Aodh Sláine.

This story was composed as propaganda for Aodh's descendants, and it was obviously intended to offset an earlier tradition which belittled them. Aodh, in fact, slew his cousin Suibhne mac Colmáin (see **Diarmaid mac Cearrbheoil**) and was in turn slain by Suibhne's son Conall. The 7th-century biography of **Colm Cille** has that saint warning the young Aodh Sláine against kinslaying, stating that, if he becomes guilty of it, his seed will have the kingship for a short time only. This would have been well remembered, for most of the high-kings from the 8th to the 10th century were direct descendants of Conall mac Suibhne.

S H O'Grady (1892) *1*, 74-5, 82-4 and 2, 469-72; Whitley Stokes in *Irische Texte 3*, 342-5, 417; R I Best / Osborn Bergin (1929), 133-6; A O Anderson / M O Anderson (1961), 236-7; R A S Macalister (1956), 372-5; F J Byrne (1973), 96-8, 281-2.

AOIBHEALL Otherworld lady and protectress of the Dál gCais sept in Co Clare. The name meant 'sparkling' or 'bright', and reflects a common attribute of **goddesses** in ancient Irish culture.

Aoibheall was associated particularly with the rock called Craig Liath (Craglea, near Killaloe), and all indications are that she was originally the patroness of the general area of east Clare and north-west Tipperary. The 12th-century tract on king **Brian Boru** states that, on the night before the battle of Clontarf, Aoibheall appeared to him and foretold that he would be killed in that contest and that the first of his sons whom he would see on that day would succeed him as king. The son was Donnchadh, and it is clear from the account that Aoibheall was acting in the capacity of goddess of sovereignty. Later adaptations of the theme have her appearing to either Donnchadh or his brother **Murchadh** and giving details of what would befall various members of the royal family. One account aptly names her as 'banfháidh Ó mBriain' (the prophetess of the O'Briens).

The post-mediaeval poets numbered Aoibheall as one of the principal otherworld women of Munster. The 18th-century Clareman Brian Merriman made her the chief actor in his celebrated Rabelesian poem *Cúirt an Mheán Oíche*. In this, she presides over the midnight court of frustrated women who complain of male impotency. Little folklore concerning Aoibheall exists, but in Co Cork she is made the sister of **Clíona** (q.v.) in a late oral legend.

T F O'Rahilly in *Ériu 14*, 1-6; J H Todd (1867), 200-1; W M Hennessy (1871) 1, 8-9; Láimhbheartach Mac Cionnaith (1938), 322-3; Eoin Mac Néill in *Irisleabhar na Gaedhilge 7*, 10; L P Ó Murchú (1982); T J Westropp in *Folk-Lore 21*, 186-7.

AONGHUS (earlier, Oengus) Mythical chieftain among the **Tuatha Dé Danann**. He resided at Brugh na Bóinne (the tumulus of Newgrange in Co Meath), and was thus often referred to as 'Aonghus an Bhrogha'. His father was the **Daghdha**, and his mother was **Bóinn**, the eponymous goddess of the Boyne river. The name Aonghus means 'true vigour' and must in origin have been a description of a divinity.

An alternative appellation for him was 'Mac ind Óc', which is a curious one, for 'óc' (modern, 'óg') is ungrammatical as a genitive if the appellation meant 'the son of the youth'. It is therefore accepted that the original form was either 'maccan óc' or 'in mac óc', both of these meaning 'the young boy'. 'Maccan' (later, Macán) corresponds to the Welsh mythical figure Mabon and to the British Celtic Maponos, who was identified in inscriptions with the Classical Apollo. It appears from this that Aonghus was the youthful expression

7. AONGHUS *Entrance to Newgrange tumulus, with inscribed slab.*

of some Celtic deity. To standardise the orthography, the alternative appellation of Aonghus is in this work cited as the Mac Óg.

A 9th-century text tells of the conception and birth of Aonghus. According to it, the Daghdha, who was king of Ireland, desired Bóinn, the wife of Ealcmhar (i.e. **Nuadhu**) who resided at the Brugh. In order to achieve his purpose, the Daghdha sent Ealcmhar away on a journey and then, by magic, made the night disappear and banished hunger and thirst from Ealcmhar so that the latter would not notice the passing of time. Nine months went by as one and in the meantime the Daghdha lay with Bóinn and she bore him a son. When Ealcmhar returned, he remained ignorant of what had happened. The child was called the Mac Óg, because his mother said that 'young is the son who was begotten at the beginning of a day and born between that and evening'. The Daghdha brought him to the rath of **Midhir**, where he was reared for nine years and became a champion hurler. One day he quarrelled with another player, however, and the opponent told him that Midhir was not his father. He demanded the truth of Midhir and learned who his real parents were. Accompanied by Midhir, he went to meet the Daghdha at Uisneach (Ushnagh, Co Westmeath), seeking land as his heritage. The Daghdha told him to go to Brugh na Bóinne at Samhain (the November feast), to threaten Ealcmhar there, and to demand possession of the Brugh for a day and a night. He did this, but when the day and night were over he refused to relinquish the Brugh to Ealcmhar. They went to the Daghdha to seek his judgement, and the Daghdha ruled that 'it is in days and nights that the world is spent', thus tricking Ealcmhar out of his dwelling. As compensation, Ealcmhar was given a nearby rath, and the Brugh became the property of Aonghus.

Other versions of how he came to possess the Brugh have him tricking the Daghdha himself rather than Ealcmhar. A 12th-century poem, which makes the Daghdha both the brother and lover of Ealcmhar's wife Bóinn, has Midhir directing Aonghus on how to trick his father out of the Brugh, with the same verbal ambiguity concerning day and night being used. This trick was part of ordinary folklore, and it was employed in this mythic context in order to dramatise the basic idea. That idea was that the blooming of youth denies the process of aging - at the youthful stage of life time passes slowly and vitality seems to be permanent. It was natural for the Irish to associate this feeling with a character from the divine realm, for one of the terms to describe the otherworld made it the timeless realm 'Tír na nÓg' (i.e. the Land of the Young People).

It is apparent that Ealcmhar was initially the victim of Aonghus' ambition rather than the Daghdha, for another early strand of tradition also had him being bested by a youth. This was the lore concerning how Ealcmhar, under his more usual name Nuadhu, was displaced by the young **Fionn mac Cumhaill**. The competition with Nuadhu was an early adaptation into the context of Fionn (q.v.), and so the suggestion is that a quite ancient myth told of how Nuadhu, symbolising aging adulthood, had been displaced by the Mac Óg, who personified the eternal appeal of youth. It might be inferred from the surviving evidence that there was a connection also between their British Celtic counterparts, Nodons and Maponos, in the north of England. If this were so, the myth of competition between these two deities would have come to Ireland with their names in ancient times.

In the text on the second battle of Moytirra (see **Mythological Cycle**), Aonghus is portrayed as a dutiful son to his father. When the Daghdha was in servitude to **Breas**, the satirist **Cridhinbhéal** was eating his food. Aonghus, called the Mac Óg, advised him on how to get rid of the satirist and also suggested what payment he should seek from Breas. This payment was one black heifer from among a great herd of the cattle of Ireland which Breas' **Fomhóire** people had taken as tribute. Breas thought the Daghdha's choice a stupid one, but later the whole herd followed the heifer back into the possession of the Tuatha Dé. The plot of the advisor and the ruse, occurring again in this case, must be a reflex from the old story which had Aonghus being advised to trick Nuadhu.

In line with the common triplication of deities in early Ireland, Aonghus was referred to in some sources as one of three sons of the Daghdha. His divine status is underlined by the prominent place among the Tuatha Dé which is accorded to him in several texts. Most dramatic of these is *Aislinge Oenguso* (the Vision of Aonghus). This story is one of the most 'otherworldly' of all narratives in the Mythological Cycle, and goes as follows:-

When Aonghus was asleep one night, he saw a beautiful maiden approach, but before he could touch her she disappeared. Such visits by her to him continued for a year, and he fell sick for love of her. His physician decided to call his mother Bóinn, and she searched Ireland for a year but failed to find the maiden. Then his father, the Daghdha, was sent for. The Daghdha enlisted the help of Bodhbh, the Tuatha Dé king of Munster who resided in Sídh ar Feimhin (the cairn on Slievenamon in Co Tipperary). Bodhbh discovered that the maiden was Caer Iobharmhéith, and that she was at Crotta Cliach (the Galtee Mountains in Co Tipperary), and he brought Aonghus to meet her. They found her at Loch Béal Dragan (Lough Muskry on the Galtees), accompanied by thrice fifty maidens linked together by a silver chain. Caer herself wore a silver necklace and her chain was of burnished gold. Bodhbh then explained that she was from Sídh Uamhain, an otherworld residence in the province of Connacht. When Aonghus returned to Brugh na Bóinne and told this to his father, the Daghdha went to Connacht and compelled Eathal Anbhuail, father of Caer, to reveal that his daughter went in the forms of a bird and of a girl on alternate years. At the following Samhain (November) she would be a bird at Loch Béal Dragan, and the Daghdha instructed Aonghus to go there and call her to him. He did so, and found her in the shape of a beautiful white swan, in the company of thrice fifty others. She went to him, and he too became a swan, and they embraced each other and flew three times around the lake. They then flew together to Brugh na Bóinne and put the dwellers of that place to sleep with their beautiful singing. Caer remained with Aonghus in the Brugh after that. The text confuses the narrative somewhat by having the Daghdha go to queen **Meadhbh** and her husband Ailill mac Máta to enlist their help against Eathal Anbhuail. These characters from the **Ulster Cycle** led an assault on Eathal's dwelling, and Ailill threatened to kill that king unless he gave information on his daughter. It is probable that the story was first written in the 8th century and that the material from the Ulster Cycle was introduced (on the pattern of the **Neara** narrative) in or about the 10th century.

Being the archetypal youth, several stories concerning love were told of Aonghus in mediaeval times. It was said that he loved a daughter of Ealcmhar, but that she went with Midhir instead, and Aonghus cast his food - 'the blood-red nuts of the wood' - onto the ground in anger. It was said also that he loved Dreibhriu, daughter of **Eochaidh Feidhleach**; and that **Clíona** was drowned while going to visit Aonghus after she had fallen in love with him. In the origin-legend of Loch nEachach (Lough Neagh in Ulster), Aonghus was described as assisting an eloping couple, **Eochaidh mac**

Maireadha and Eibhliu, wife of Eochaidh's father. Aonghus gave them the loan of his horse, which was so huge that it could carry them and all their chattels out of danger. When they stopped to rest, the horse urinated and thus gave rise to the great Lough Neagh. The exhuberance of youth is suggested in a mention of how Aonghus also had a wonderful multi-coloured mantle, which appeared to be of one colour only in the eyes of a man about to die. Another text makes **Manannán** the patron of Aonghus and the presenter to him of a wonderful dun cow, and further relates the story of **Eithne**, a beautiful maiden loved by him.

In late mediaeval and post-mediaeval literature Aonghus is introduced into some stories of the **Fianna Cycle** as a 'deus ex machina'. Most strikingly, he is made the patron and protector of the handsome young hero **Diarmaid ua Duibhne**. He intervenes to rescue the eloping Diarmaid and Gráinne when Fionn's men are close to capturing them and, after Diarmaid's death, he takes the corpse to his own residence at Brugh na Bóinne and lays it in burial under a great stone there. The reason why he became associated with Diarmaid was undoubtedly his fame in the context of youth and of love. One mediaeval text claims that Aonghus forged four kisses of his into 'four birds which charmed the young people of Ireland'. On the basis of his connection with Diarmaid, later stories have him intervening to assist the Fianna in a cattle-raid and rescuing them from dire straits in 'the land of the giants'. Despite his glamorous imagery, however, Aonghus is not featured in late folklore stories.

[Name] Jan de Vries (1961), 39; T F O'Rahilly (1946), 516-7; James Carney (1964), 112.

[Birth and gaining of Brugh] Osborn Bergin / R I Best in *Ériu 12*, 142-7; Lilian Duncan in *Ériu 11*, 188-92; Vernam Hull in *Zeitschrift für celtische Philologie 19*, 53-8; Lucius Gwynn in *Ériu 7*, 210-38; Edward Gwynn (1906), 18-21.

[Nodons and Maponos] Anne Ross (1974), 230-4, 463-6.

[Helping the Daghdha] E A Gray (1982), 30-1, 70-1.

[Three sons of Daghdha] R A S Macalister (1941), 156-7, 190-1; Edward Gwynn (1924), 92-3, 108-9.

[Dream of Aonghus] Francis Shaw (1934).

[Love-stories] Edward Gwynn (1913), 40-3, 386-9; Whitley Stokes (1892), 56-7.

[Mantle] Joseph Vendryes (1953), 13-4.

[Diarmaid] Nessa Ní Shéaghdha (1967), 22-3, 28-9, 38-9; Gerard Murphy (1933), 96-7.

[Helping the Fianna] Eoin Mac Néill (1908), 5-6; Murphy, *op cit*, 392-9; Stokes (1900), 13-4.

[Kisses] Stokes in *Revue Celtique 16*, 68-9; Eugene O'Curry (1873), 478-9.

[General] Gray, *op cit*, 127-8; Stokes, *CTS* (1905), 31.

ART Mythical king of Ireland, son of **Conn Céadchathach**. The name originally meant 'bear' - apparently a pseudonym for a warrior - and he had the sobriquet Aonfhear (earlier, Oenfer) which meant 'singular man' or 'champion'.

The literature, as was its wont, derives the sobriquet from a narrative episode. When his brother Connla departed in a boat for the otherworld realm, the disconsolate father Conn (q.v.) gazed upon Art and remarked that this remaining son was now 'the lone one' (i.e. 'oenfer'). He proved a dutiful son for, when Conn brought the polluted woman Bé Chuma to **Tara** and banished him for a year at her request, he accepted his father's wishes. He returned at the end of the year and found Conn unable to check the misfortune which had overtaken his reign. Bé Chuma challenged him to a game of 'ficheall' (the Irish form of chess). Art won the first game and demanded as his prize the warrior's wand which **Cú Roí** once had. Bé Chuma searched the otherworld dwellings of Ireland and found it for him. Then she won a game and imposed as a condition on him that he seek out and find a beautiful lady called Dealbhchaomh. Art set out abroad and eventually came to a wonderful island of women, where he was cordially received. They gave him directions to where Dealbhchaomh was, a place which could only be reached by overcoming several great obstacles. These included treacherous oceans and forests, fierce hags, and a nigh-invulnerable warrior. Art overcame all the obstacles and slew both of Dealbhchaomh's warrior parents in single combat. He and Dealbhchaomh became lovers, and he brought her back to Ireland with him. When he reached Tara, Dealbhchaomh advised him to expel his stepmother Bé Chuma from the country. This he did, thereby relieving Conn and the realm of the woman who had brought them such misfortune. This text dates from around the 13th century, and most of the episodes in it are taken from an international folktale which was very popular in Ireland (see **Wonder Tales**, Type 313) and in which a youth performs difficult tasks to gain a maiden and then elopes with her.

The theory of the mediaeval historians was that Conn was succeeded as king by his brother-in-law **Conaire mac Mogha Lámha**, and that Art in turn succeeded Conaire. In contradiction of the sagas, these historians also claimed that Art was the survivor of three sons of Conn - the other two, Connla and Crionna, having been slain by Conn's jealous brothers. Art's own reign is not much stressed in the literature. The historians claimed that his wife was called Meadhbh Leathdhearg, but this is merely an echo from the cult of the goddess of Tara kingship **Meadhbh**. Another woman associated with him was the wife of a certain Gnáthal mac Conruith, who is represented in a text of around the 9th century as having been king of Tara. This text is a rather confused one, and the king who is really meant seems to be Conaire mac Mogha Lámha. We read that the woman loved Art, and tricked her husband out of the kingship for his sake. This, however, was over-imaginative and conflicted with the generally held tradition that Art was king by right and by justice. As with his father Conn, he was portrayed as an ideal king. Although, living before the Christian period, he was a pagan, two angels hovered over him in battle on account of the 'truth of his rule'. It was also claimed that he won several battles against the Leinstermen and compelled them to yield the **bóraimhe** tribute to him.

An 8th-century text states that he had no male heir, but the night before the battle of Magh Mucramha (in east Galway) he slept with Achtan, the daughter of a druid, and in this way begot his famous son **Cormac**. He was slain in the battle next day, and his foe **Lughaidh mac Con** took the kingship of Tara. This situation is developed in a text from the 10th or 11th century, according to which Art was out hunting one day when he had a vision of angels and was inspired to foretell the coming of Christianity to Ireland. He also foresaw the battle of Magh Mucramha and how he would be defeated there.

Julius Pokorny in *Zeitschrift für celtische Philologie 17*, 204-5; Tomás Ó Máille, *ibid*, 138-9; Margaret Dobbs in *ibid 20*, 171-3; R I Best in *Ériu 3*, 149-73; Whitley Stokes in *Irische Texte 3*, 334-7, 360-1; John O'Donovan (1848) 1, 106-9; R A S Macalister (1956), 334-5; Lucius Gwynn in *Ériu 6*, 136; Máirín O'Daly (1975), 52-5, 64-9, 152; Best / Osborn Bergin (1929), xxxv, 296-9.

[Game-motif] Rosemary Power in *Scottish Studies 28*, 69-89.

B

BAILE MAC BUAIN Fictional youth of Ulster in a love-story written in or about the 11th century. He is given the epithet 'Binnbhéarlach', which means 'sweet-spoken'.

The story tells of how he arranged a love-tryst with a Leinster princess called Aillinn. They were to meet at a house in Ros na Ríogh (Rosnaree on the river Boyne), and Baile set off southwards towards that place. On the way, he and his companions stopped to rest their horses, and were approached by an ugly fleetfooted stranger who told them that Aillinn had been killed by the warriors of Leinster as she came to meet Baile. On hearing this, the young man fell dead with disappointment. His followers buried him there, and hence the place became known as Tráigh Bhaile ('the Strand of Baile', at Dundalk). The malicious stranger then went south to Suí Laighean (Mount Leinster) and, entering the bower of Aillinn, told her that her lover was dead. She also died from a broken heart, and was buried in that place. A yew-tree grew from the grave of Baile, with the likeness of his head in the upper branches, while an apple-tree grew from the grave of Aillinn, with her likeness on its top. Seven years later the Ulster poets made a writing-tablet from the yew-tree, while the Leinster poets made a writing-tablet from the apple-tree. At the feast of **Tara**, the high-king **Cormac mac Airt** was much taken with the beauty of the stories read by these two sets of poets, and wished to see their tablets. When he held them, the two tablets leaped together and became entwined in each other like woodbine on a branch. They could not be parted, and they were kept in the treasury of Tara for a long time until the citadel was burnt in a raid.

The character of Baile mac Buain was obviously invented due to speculation concerning the placename Tráigh Bhaile, while the story itself is a much ornamented version of an international narrative plot (see **Romantic Tales**, Type 970). The tragedy in the international plot is caused by feuding parents, but they have here been replaced by the malicious and spirit-like stranger, who seems to be an Irish development from mediaeval demon-lore.

Eugene O'Curry (1873), 472-5; Kuno Meyer in *Revue Celtique 13*, 220-5 and (1894), 84.

BALAR (also Balor, Bolur) Mythical tyrant, who was sometimes given the sobriquet Bailcbhéimneach ('strong-smiting').

His name seems to have originally meant 'the flashing one' and would have been 'Boleros' in ancient Celtic. Classical authors such as Ptolemy and Diodorus Siculus attest to a promontory in Cornwall being anciently known as Bolerion, and the inference is that a figure with such a name was associated with that place (probably Land's End). The Irish Balar is described in the early literature as grandson of an obscure personage called Nét and is said to have met his death at Carn Uí Néit ('the Cairn of Net's Grandson'). This is Mizen Head in Co Cork. Such associations with promontories in the extreme south-west of both Britain and Ireland strongly suggest the idea of the setting sun, and other imagery of Balar accords well with this. In one early text he is called Balar 'Birug-derc' (i.e. piercing-eyed), and he is represented in story as having a fearsome eye which destroyed hosts 'by its poison'.

Balar's role in Irish tradition is generally confined to the myth of **Lugh**, to whom his daughter gave birth against his wishes. In the mediaeval text on the second battle of Moytirra (see **Mythological Cycle**), he appears as a leader of the sea-pirate race called **Fomhóire** who oppress the divine race **Tuatha Dé Danann**. He is associated with the north and is said to have been king of the Hebridean Islands off the coast of Scotland. The general imagery of the Fomhóire has, however, been much influenced by that of the Norse raiders who harassed Ireland in the ninth and tenth centuries, and there is no reason to doubt the greater antiquity of his connection with the seas off the south-west coast.

The story of the second battle of Moytirra can be reduced to two basic levels of plot - the struggle between two supernatural races on the one hand, and the killing of a tyrant by his prophesied grandson on the other. This latter is the Lugh myth, and it is reasonable to assume that Balar properly belonged to that context. The fact that **Breas**, rather than him, is the over-all commander of the Fomhóire, and that Breas' role is much more fundamental to the plot of the battle, strengthens this assumption. The likelihood, then, is that when the harvest-myth of Lugh (q.v.) reached Ireland it appropriated to itself a leading personification of the scorching sun from the lore which was current at the time, and that Balar was thus made to fit the role of the tyrant-grandfather.

The clash of Balar with Lugh, as it has come down to us in both literature and folklore, shows the influence of the Biblical contest between David and Goliath. The weapon used by Lugh was the same as that used by David, a sling-stone, which we are told drove the eye back through Balar's head. Old Irish accounts of the slaying of an enemy by a hero in single combat usually have a great spear or javelin as the weapon of triumph, and this is likely to have been the case in the original version of this narrative also. Similarly, the portrayal of Balar has been tempered by the image of Goliath. He is of enormous size in our earliest text on the Moytirra battle, and when he falls dead 'thrice nine' of his own soldiers are crushed underneath him. Otherwise he is described with rather spontaneous dramatic touches. We read that the eye was never opened except on a battlefield - it had a polished ring in its lid, and it required four men to lift this lid. A rather ingenious, though superfluous, explanation is given of how the eye became poisonous - when the druids of his father had been brewing a magic concoction, Balar had come to observe the work and the fumes had settled on the eye, bringing with them their venomous power.

A variant description of Balar's death was current from at least the 12th century. According to it, he survived the loss of his eye in the battle and was pursued by Lugh all the way to Mizen Head. When cornered and certain of his doom, he tried to exact vengeance by telling Lugh that he could gain all the power of his grandfather by performing a certain act. This was to place the severed head of Balar on top of his own. Having decapitated the tyrant, Lugh instead laid the head on a large rock, which was immediately dashed to pieces. Variants of this episode have survived in folklore recensions of the Lugh myth down to our own time, though Mizen Head is no longer mentioned in them. In these tellings (see **Lugh**), Balar is said to have had his base on Tory Island off the Donegal coast, and he is said to have oppressed Ireland with cruel taxes. This is derived from the mediaeval literature, which situated the stronghold of the Fomhóire (q.v.) on that island and portrayed them as robbers and exactors of tribute. Various landmarks are pointed out on the island, such as the site of his fortress (Dún Bhalair), the nigh inaccessible peak on which he had a tower (Túr Bhalair) where his daughter was kept, and a deep cleft where he used to keep prisoners. The withering effects of his evil eye were pointed out in phenomena as varied as the black tips of the rushes and the barren slopes of the mountains Muckish and Errigal on the mainland.

In folk versions of the Balar myth, his grandson Lugh was assisted by a friendly smith called Goibhleann (see **Goibhniu**). This Goibhleann had a marvellous cow (the **Glas Ghoibhneann**), which Balar tried to steal from its owner. A variant account of these episodes was current in Co Monaghan, according to which Balar drove the cow and its calf down into Leinster, but when they reached the coast near Dublin the cow tried to turn back, and Balar raised the lid from his eye to see what was troubling her. Immediately the cow and her calf were turned into rocks, which are now the two Rockabill islands off Skerries. His eye was reputed to have had a similar effect in Co Mayo, the folk at Cong claiming that rocks in the locality were men who had been petrified by its glance. As might be expected, descriptions of how he employed his unique faculty are lavishly dramatised, for instance the following account from Mayo: 'He had a single eye in his forehead, a venomous fiery eye. There were always seven coverings over this eye. One by one Balar removed the coverings. With the first covering the bracken began to wither, with the second the grass became copper-coloured, with the third the woods and timber began to heat, with the fourth smoke came from the trees, with the fifth everything grew red, with the sixth it sparked. With the seventh they were all set on fire, and the whole countryside was ablaze!'

[Origin] T F O'Rahilly (1946), 58-60; E A Gray (1982), 133.

[Moytirra] Gray, *op cit*; Brian Ó Cuív (1945).

[His eye in literature] Gray, *op cit*, 60-1.

[Severed head] Ó Cuív, *op cit*, 6, 9; Eoin Mac Néill (1904), 35, 135.

[Landmarks in Donegal] Ordnance Survey Letters - Donegal (1835), 46-51, 81-97, 129-30, 229 and Westmeath (1837), 152; Séamus Ó Searcaigh in *An Claidheamh Soluis* 17/9/1910, 3; IFC 56:392.

[Monaghan lore] Henry Morris in *Béaloideas 7*, 244-6. Cf. also Éamonn Ó Tuathail in *Béaloideas 3*, 128-9.

[Mayo accounts of the eye] Ordnance Survey Letters - Mayo (1838), 110-2; Tomás Ó Cillín in *Béaloideas 4*, 88. Cf. also Máire MacNeill (1962), 598.

For versions of Balar's contest with Lugh, see references at **Lugh**.

BANSHEE (Irish, 'bean sí') Female spirit which, in folk belief, is heard to cry when the death of a member of an Irish family is imminent. The designation means 'otherworld woman', and the banshee is invariably a solitary being. Her cry is described as plaintive and very much like that of a keening woman of this world. It is usually heard in the vicinity of the family dwelling and therefore near in location to the person who is about to die. However, some accounts have her cry being heard at the family home although that person be far away, even in a foreign country.

The banshee tradition is peculiar to the Gaelic world, and it must originally have sprung from the idea that a **goddess** cares for the fortunes of specific noble families. In the early story of **Fraoch**, the impending death of that hero is announced by the cries of otherworld women, and in other texts we read of his own death being foretold to **Brian Boru** by the goddess **Aoibheall** and of the goddess **Mór** lamenting over the grave of **Cathal mac Fionghuine**. That there is continuity between this and the later folklore of the banshee is strongly suggested by the folk insistence that the banshee laments only those who have Ó or Mac in their surname, that is, families of noble Gaelic descent.

This notion provides a clue as to how the folk belief developed from the original idea that goddesses protected the rulers and inhabitants of their particular areas. Firstly, it is clear that the folklore is not totally in accord with the literary tradition, which uses the term 'bean sí' or 'sí-bhean' equally for an otherworld woman, but with somewhat different connotations. Such a woman in the literature is not solely associated with death, but is represented as appearing to inspire poets and through them to encourage the chieftains to success and prosperity. When she appears in order to lament a dead leader, it is usually after the death has occurred, and according to the age-old convention of **kingship**, her sorrow is magnified by the fact that the dead hero was her mystical spouse. In folklore, on the other hand, the banshee is concerned only with death, and with its announcement before it occurs. It is thus clear that the folk tradition has selected but one aspect of the original idea, and has placed it into the context of the general belief in omens presaging death. Such omens - for instance the appearance of certain birds or the hearing of certain noises - are expressions of the folk attitude to the enigma of death. So the banshee of popular belief, though originally a patron goddess, has become an enigmatic being, a strange voice crying from the portals of the unknown.

It is difficult to date precisely when this change occurred, but it seems obvious that stress on otherworld women as protectresses of distinctively Gaelic families has to do with the confiscations of land in Ireland by the English government. There are certain indications that the new profile of the banshee developed in the southern Leinster area, probably during the seizure of land there by the English in the 16th and 17th centuries. This area preserves a very special designation for the being. Thus the banshee is known in Carlow, Wexford, south Wicklow and south Kildare as the 'badhbh' (pronounced 'bow'); and in Kilkenny and south Laois as the 'badhbh chaointe' (meaning 'keening badhbh' and pronounced 'boheenta'). She is also known in Waterford as the 'badhb', a variant of the same word. The designation is in fact a survival of the name Badhbh which occurs frequently in the mediaeval literature as that of a goddess (see **Mór-Ríoghain**). The original meaning of the word, which it still preserves outside of this context, was 'scaldcrow', and it was a form which the corpse-hungry war-goddess was said to take. Its survival as the usual designation for the banshee in south Leinster is probably an echo of the fighting which was a necessary corollary to the claim on the land in that period.

Belief in the banshee has survived with surprising strength all over Ireland, and in urban as well as rural parts. Although it is claimed that she presages the death only of those with Ó or Mac in their surnames, in practice many names of non-Gaelic origin are included in the selection. She is much more often heard than seen, although some people claim to have caught a glimpse of her and in such accounts she is usually portrayed as old in appearance, and she combs her long white hair as she laments. A small number of narratives have become attached to her, and it is significant that these are particularly strong in Leinster. The most popular concerns how, after she has been heard to lament at night, a man finds her comb in the morning and takes it into his house. Next night a terrific wailing is heard outside his house, accompanied by knocks on the window. Realising that it is the banshee seeking her comb, the man puts it in his tongs and gives it out through the window. The comb is taken, and the tongs is twisted or broken, by which the man understands that that would have been the fate of his hand had he not used the tongs.

Patricia Lysaght (1986); Dáithí Ó hÓgáin in *Cóilín Owens* ed (1987), 63-5, 119.

BARRA (earlier, Bairre) Patron-saint of Cork city, which owes its origin to a monastery established by him at the end of the 6th century AD. His full name was Barrfhind or Findbhairre (later Fionnbharra, meaning 'fair-haired'). It is anglicised as Barry or Finbar.

His biographies, in Latin and Irish, are all late mediaeval and are very fanciful. They tell of an extraordinary incident preceding his birth. A certain Amhairghin was chief smith to Tighearnach, king of the Múscraighe sept (in west Co Cork). Against the king's commands, Amhairghin cohabited with a beautiful female slave and, when she became pregnant, the king ordered that the couple be burned alive. The fire could not be lit due to a rain-storm, however, and the unborn child spoke from its mother's womb, warning the king to abandon his intention. Amhairghin took the mother and child to his house at Achadh Durbchon (somewhere in the region of Macroom), and he was baptised there and given the name Loan. When he was seven years old, three clerics got permission to take him with them to study in Leinster. A doe gave her milk to feed him at Ros Coille (probably Muckalee in north Kilkenny) and the clerics tonsured him there, giving him the new name Fionnbharra ('fair crest').

We read that the saint's first foundation was at Achadh Bó (Aghaboe, Co Laois), but that he soon left this to **Cainneach** and moved on to Clíu (an area in east Limerick), where he raised from the dead the recently-deceased wife of a local king. He then established a school for clerics at the lake in west Cork which became known as Gúgán Barra. The founding of many other churches, and the counselling of many other clerics, were attributed to him, until eventually he was guided by an angel to the marsh at the mouth of the river Lee called Corcaigh. There he was given a site for a hermitage, which in time grew into the celebrated monastery. We read also that Barra went to Rome to obtain episcopal orders, and that a flame from heaven came onto the hand of Pope Gregory as he consecrated him. Later, when Barra asked St Eolang to be his confessor, the latter placed Barra's hand in that of God Himself. God was taking Barra to heaven, until beseeched by Eolang to allow him to remain on earth in order to continue with his good work. Nobody could ever after look on Barra's hand because of its radiance, but he used to cover it with a glove. When Barra died he was buried at Cork and the sun stood still in the heavens and shone brilliantly for twelve days while his obsequies were being performed.

Some foundations in other parts of Ireland and even in Scotland were attributed to him. A possible explanation for this is that various monasteries were founded under the direct or indirect influence of Cork, but it is more likely that the name was derived from myth and applied to various sea-saints. 'Barrfhind' is a term used to describe the sea-waves in the early texts concerning the mythic **Manannán**, and it is significant that some descriptions of St Barra resemble Manannán in that he rides on horseback across the sea and effortlessly picks a salmon from that watery 'plain'. The memory of Barra survived strongly in the lore of the south-west of Ireland. One folk legend claims that he banished a monster from the lake of Gúgán Barra, and that the monster fled up through the river Lee before departing through Cork harbour. His feastday is September 25.

J F Kenney (1929), 401-2; Charles Plummer (1910) *1*, 65-74 and (1922) 1, 11-22; Whitley Stokes (1905), 40-1; John O'Hanlon (1875) 9, 547-85; Liam Ó Buachalla in *Journal of the Cork Historical and Archaeological Society 68*, 104-6; Pádraig Ó Riain in *ibid 82*, 63-82; *The Irish Independent* 12/5/1932, 6; IFC 327:289-96, 437:396, 452:275-8, 939:304-5, 1014:262-4.

BEAG MAC DÉ A prophet, whose death is recorded at the year 553 AD. Beag (earlier, Becc) means 'small', and the earlier form of his patronymic was Ded or Deadh, a septal designation. In the mediaeval literature, this element of his name was changed to 'Dé' (genitive of 'dia' i.e. 'god') and was explained as referring to his having got the gift of prophecy from God. Due to this rather incongruous interpretation, he came to be regarded as a Christian saint, even though it is not certain that he was a Christian at all.

Several anecdotes are told of him in 10th-century literature, and these are clearly taken from oral tradition of the time. As with **poets**, it was claimed that he showed his ability from childhood. After he was born, people were talking about him, and they remarked that he was very small. The baby spoke and said that he knew as much as any big child concerning the end of the world, and then gave a series of pessimistic prophecies. Another account has him as a grown man in the house of Mac Arda, king of the Ciarraighe Luachra (a sept in Co Kerry) on the night that St **Bréanainn** was born. The king asked Beag what did he see, and Beag answered that he saw that a child had been born between them and the sea who would be king over Mac Arda forever. Similarly, Beag was said to have prophesied the beneficient rule of St **Ciarán** at Clonmacnoise, and the success of the monastery of **Colm Cille** at Ceanannas (Kells, Co Meath).

He spent the most notable part of his career in the employ of the high-king **Diarmaid mac Cearrbheoil**. We read that once, as he left the royal stronghold of **Tara**, he encountered three men, each of whom asked him a question. The questions related to how long would the fortresss be occupied, what was the depth of the nearby river, and how thick was the bacon-fat that year. Beag answered all three questions together with the four words 'pas go tóin amárach'. This phrase responds backwards to the questions - 'pas' being a three-finger measure, 'go tóin' meaning as far as one's backside, and 'amárach' being 'tomorrow'. We also read that Beag once spoke to nine people at once, and with a single discourse replied to all the different talk of the nine. Cryptic and accurate speech of this kind was an attribute of the most skilled poets according to Irish folk tradition.

The spontaneous knowledge of Beag was usually put to more practical uses. When Mughain, wife of the high-king Diarmaid, was pregnant, she and her husband went onto the green of Tara for fresh air, and they saw a troop of riders approach, led by Diarmaid's nephew Suibhne mac Colmáin Mhóir. Immediately Mughain cried out, and her husband suspected that she did this for love of Suibhne. Beag, however, explained that the cry was an indication that her unborn child would kill Suibhne. This was later proved correct, for the baby was **Aodh Sláine**, who slew Suibhne and was in turn slain by Suibhne's son. On another occasion, Diarmaid was being praised by his poets, but Beag remarked that he saw 'the fierce hound which shall destroy the mansion'. Diarmaid asked what he meant, and Beag replied that the high-king's foster-child would bring about his death. The foster-child was Aodh Dubh, son of king Suibhne of the Dál Riada whom Diarmaid himself had slain. Beag prophesied in detail how Diarmaid (q.v.) would die, and in order to avoid this the high-king had Aodh Dubh banished to Scotland.

Notwithstanding this precaution, Diarmaid was worried from that time onwards. One night he dreamed that two men came to him - one in clerical garb and the other a military man. They took his diadem from him and divided it among them. When he awoke and told of his dream, Beag explained it to mean that his reign was doomed, that his kingdom would be divided between the clergy and the laity, and that ill would come of that arrangement. On yet another occasion, Beag gave a long list of prophecies to the high-king concerning the future of Ireland, these being again of a very pessimistic nature. Diarmaid doubted the prophecies regarding his own death and questioned his **druids** on the matter, but they confirmed what Beag had said. Incensed at Diarmaid's distrust of him, Beag decided to leave Tara, but he had not gone far when he met Colm Cille. It had been foretold that Beag would give three false prophecies before his death and so, when the two met, Colm asked when would Beag himself die. Beag replied that he had seven years of life remaining, and on being further pressed reduced it to seven months. Colm expressed doubts, and he then admitted that he had a mere seven hours to live. All these prophecies were false, for death was nearer still, and the saint then said that he had come to prepare Beag for it. He administered the last Sacraments to him, and so the prophet died.

R I Best in *Ériu 4*, 162; Whitley Stokes (1890), 23, 28, 100, 118, 350 and (1905), 132-3; Charles Plummer (1912) *1*, 98 and (1922) *1*, 45; S H O'Grady

(1892) *1*, 74-5, 78-80 and *2*, 470; Kuno Meyer in *Zeitschrift für celtische Philologie 9*, 169-71; John O'Donovan (1848) *1*, 150-1, 196-7, 438-9; W M Hennessy / Bartholomew McCarthy (1887) *1*, 52-3, 154-6; Cormac Ó Cadhlaigh (1950), 77-87.

BEARACH (earlier, Berach) Saint of the 6th century AD. Two biographies of late date survive, one in Irish and the other in Latin.

We read that the coming of Bearach was prophesied by St **Patrick**, and that he was born at Gort na Luachra (Gortnalougher, Co Leitrim). He was fostered by a monk called Daigh mac Cairill at Magh Muirtheimhne (the plain of north Louth). Once, when a woman and boy refused to allow him to grind some wheat in a hurry, the boy fell into the mill and the woman died, but Bearach restored both to life. The boy's father, who was a nobleman, in gratitude gave him the site for a monastery in that place, Raon Bhearaigh (near Inishkeen). Bearach then went to the royal centre of **Tara**, but was refused a drink there and after he left all the beer disappeared from the vats. The king sent for him, and when he blessed the vats all was restored, whereupon he was given a site for another monastery. This was Díseart Bhearaigh (either Dysart in Co Westmeath or Kilbarrack in Co Dublin). Proceeding to the monastery of **Caoimhghin** at Glendalough, he was given control of the refectory there and worked many miracles to provide food for the monks when it was lacking. He also banished many demons from the place by ringing his bell and singing psalms.

We read that, after seven years, he left Glendalough, with his books being drawn in a chariot by a stag. The stag lay down at Cill Bhearaigh (Kilbarry, in Termonbarry, Co Roscommon), and it was there that he founded his most celebrated monastery. There also he performed many miracles, including the raising to life of warriors slain in battle. The site on which he built the monastery had earlier been given to a poet named Diarmaid, who refused to relinquish his claim to it. Bearach and Diarmaid searched Ireland for somebody willing to adjudicate between them, but nobody would do so for fear of the saint's curse and the poet's satire. In their search they finally visited the Scottish king Aodán mac Gabhráin. Finding two great mounds of snow at the entrance to the royal fortress, Bearach told Diarmaid to blow at these. Immediately he did so they blazed into fire. When Aodán was told what had happened he prostrated himself before Bearach, and he directed them to go to the kings of Teathbha and Breifne in Ulster.

Bearach performed several miracles in the presence of these kings, and they ruled in his favour. Diarmaid attempted to satirise them for this, but Bearach placed his palm over the poet's mouth and declared that he would never compose again. He also foretold that Diarmaid would die in a year from that day. At the end of the year, the poet shut himself into a church, but he was slain by a strong spear-cast made by a hunter at a passing stag. Diarmaid's son Cú Allaidh then undertook to curse Bearach's territory, but he was slain by Concheanann, a companion of the saint. Bearach was displeased at this act and imposed penance on Concheanann.

Other miracles attributed to Bearach included protecting the people against famine and sickness, and he was reputed to have changed a bog into a lake near Kilbarry in order to swallow up an aggressive army which was raiding the septs under his protection. His feastday is February 15.

J F Kenney (1929), 402-3; Whitley Stokes (1905), 74-5; Charles Plummer (1910) *1*, 75-86 and (1922) *1*, 23-43; John O'Hanlon (1875) *2*, 534-52; Donncha Ó Corráin / Fidelma Maguire (1981), 31.

BEARCHÁN Saint of the 6th century AD, founder of a monastery at Cluain Sosta (Clonsast, Co Offaly).

He reputedly was of the Dál Riada (a sept of Co Antrim), and had the nickname 'Fear Dá Leithe' (literally, 'man of two halves'), which is explained by his having spent half of his career in Scotland and the other half in Ireland. There is no surviving biography of Bearchán, but he must have had great prestige, as he was represented as the foreteller of many major happenings. The principal work attributed to him was a long verse-text which referred to events of the period from the 6th to the 12th century in Ireland and Scotland. It is difficult to decide on a date for the genesis of this text, but it is clear that it was supplemented and re-arranged from time to time. Further prophetic verses were attributed to him after the Middle Ages, and during the Elizabethan Wars much use was made of prophecies by which he was claimed to have foretold Irish victories over the English. He was reputed to have been one of the four great saint-seers of Ireland, the other three being **Colm Cille**, **Moling**, and **Bréanainn**.

No doubt on account of his fame as a prophet,

a curious anecdote concerning him has been collected from the folklore of west Cork. This anecdote - of obscure derivation - describes how he had a vision, in which it was revealed to him that his death would come when three kings came uninvited to his house. Three such guests did indeed come and, when he told them of his vision they promised to protect him. Placing him under an overturned vat, they stood on guard around it, but soon a cowherd arrived and lulled them to sleep with music. When they awoke in the morning, they found nothing left of Bearchán but his bones underneath the vat.

There was some confusion between himself and his namesake Bearchán of Glasnevin (in Dublin), who was better known as Mobhí. This particular saint was reputed to have been one of the mentors of Colm Cille, and his obit was given as 545 AD. The feastday of St Bearchán of Clonsast is December 4.

Whitley Stokes (1905), 76-7, 256-7; John O'Donovan (1864), 326-7; Donnchadh Ó Corráin / Fidelma Maguire (1981), 31-2; A O Anderson in *Zeitschrift für celtische Philologie 18*, 1-56; J H Todd (1867), 204-5, 225, 307; Eugene O'Curry (1873), 412-8, 421, 627-8, 670; Paul Walsh / Colm Ó Lochlainn *1* (1948), 178-9; Douglas Hyde (1899), 210-1 and (1915), 63-5; A Kelleher / G Schoepperle in *Revue Celtique 32*, 53-8.

BÓINN Eponymous goddess of the river Boyne. The name (earlier, Bóind or Bóand) is derived from a primitive Irish form 'bóu-vinda'.

The name of the river is one of the earliest cited Irish toponyms, occurring in Ptolemy's geography in the form 'Buvinda'. This dates from the 2nd century AD, but may be based on sources somewhat earlier still. The original compound would have referred to a goddess in bovine shape, and would have meant literally 'illuminated cow'. The Celtic word 'vind' covered a semantic range from the colour white to brightness and wisdom. In this latter sense it was personified as a great seer, known in old Irish as **Find**, and there is little reason to doubt that the name of the river was based on the cult of this personage. Thus Bóinn would originally have been the wisdom-giving cow associated with the archetypal seer. Her imagery is parallelled from another early Indo-European source, Sanskrit literature, which symbolises sacred rivers as milk flowing from a mystical cow. In early Irish literature, it is said that if a person drinks water from the river Boyne in June he will become a seer-poet.

Bóinn is described as the wife of Nechtan, which was a pseudonym for **Nuadhu**, and thus we can see that at some early stage of Irish tradition the cult of Find (q.v.) had that of Nuadhu superimposed on it. The reason for this seems to have been the rich aquatic imagery associated with Nuadhu, and hence it was claimed that the source of the river was a well called the Sídh ('otherworld dwelling') of Nechtan. The mediaeval **place-lore** states that only Nechtan himself and his cup-bearers could approach this well, and the eyes of anybody else who looked at its water would burst. One day, however, Bóinn boldly approached the well to examine it, and three gushes came from it, injuring her foot and hand, and blinding one of her eyes. She raced away from there, but the water rose after her and followed her all the way to the sea, thereby giving rise to the Boyne river. This account, though not in itself ancient tradition, incorporates at least one archaic idea concerning the craft of seers and **poets** i.e. the light of inspiration which blinds.

A 9th-century story tells of the **Daghdha** becoming the lover of Bóinn by a trick. He sent her husband away on business for nine months, although it appeared to be only a day, and in the meantime he lay with her and she gave birth to **Aonghus of Newgrange**, the archetypal youth. This story belongs to the Nuadhu context, and seems to be based on an original myth which had him being displaced by a young deity. Elements from the more archaic association of Bóinn with Find survived in the rich lore concerning the wisdom of the latter's heroic avatar **Fionn mac Cumhaill**.

Royal Irish Academy Dictionary (s.v. 'boand'); Alfred Holder (1896) *1*, 646-7; T F O'Rahilly (1946), 3; Eleanor Knott (1936), 6; Edward Gwynn (1913), 26-39, 286; Whitley Stokes in *Revue Celtique 15*, 315-6 and *CTS* (1905), 18-9; Osborn Bergin / R I Best in *Ériu 12*, 142-7; P K Ford in G J Larson (1974), 67-74; Dáithí Ó hÓgáin (1988), 17-8, 325.

BÓRAIMHE A tribute which the mediaeval historians claimed was due to the royal Uí Néill sept from the Leinstermen. The word (also spelt 'bóramha') meant 'cattle-computation', and the idea of this specific tribute was invented in or about the 8th century AD to explain and justify the record of warring by the Uí Néill against Leinster, which had been pursued sporadically for several hundred years.

A text written in the 11th century purports to give the history of this tribute. It describes how a Leinster king called Eochaidh mac Eachach married the daughter of **Tuathal Teachtmhar**, and then married a second daughter while pretending that the first was dead. When they discovered the truth, the ladies died from shame, and Tuathal as revenge defeated Eochaidh in battle, slew him, and ravaged his province. To secure peace, the Leinstermen agreed to pay a massive tribute. It consisted of thrice fifty hundreds each of cows, pigs, wethers, mantles, silver-chains, and copper cauldrons, as well as a special huge cauldron and thirty red-eared cows and calves with bronze halters and spancels and bosses of gold.

We read that Tuathal's successors continued to collect this 'bóraimhe', once in each reign, until the time of **Cairbre Lifeachair**. When this king tried to collect it he was faced by a Leinster army headed by Breasal Béalach and supported by **Fionn mac Cumhaill**. Cairbre was defeated, and the tribute was not again levied until thirty royal maidens were slain in **Tara** by the forces of the Leinster king Dúnlaing. The Leinstermen, however, continually rebelled against it, and were often successful, defeating even **Niall Naoi-ghiallach** himself in twelve battles. Niall's son **Laoghaire** next tried to impose the tribute, but he was captured on the first attempt and was slain on the second. Ailill Molt, son of **Dáithí**, also tried to take the 'bóraimhe', but the Leinstermen defeated him several times, as they did also his successors down to Aodh mac Ainmhireach, who suffered a momentous defeat and was slain by the Leinster king **Brandubh**.

A few of Aodh's successors managed to collect the tribute, but several others failed, until **Fionnachta** became high-king and took it twice. He tried to take it a third time, but the Leinster king Bran Múit enlisted the support of St **Moling**. This saint went to confer with Fionnachta, and by a verbal trick secured final remission of the onerous tribute. He persuaded the high-king to give the Leinstermen respite 'go Luan', which Fionnachta understood to mean 'till Monday' but which Moling interpreted as 'till the Last Day'.

Kuno Meyer in *Ériu 4*, 72; Whitley Stokes in *Revue Celtique 13*, 32-124; S H O'Grady (1892) *2*, 495-7.

BRAN MAC FEABHAIL Fictional character in a text which was written in the early 8th century. The name Bran (literally, 'raven') belonged to ancient Celtic lore, and was applied also to a mythic king in Welsh literature.

The text is the earliest example of the genre of 'imram' (later 'iomramh', and meaning 'rowing'). It describes how an otherworld woman with a silver branch came to the palace of Bran. The branch emitted beautiful music, and she revealed that it was from an apple-tree in the realm of Eamhain (for which otherworld realm, see **Manannán**). She further disclosed that this was a faraway island, and she described its wonders and invited Bran and his men to row there. She then disappeared from sight, and Bran set out on the sea with thrice nine for a crew. When they were two days on their journey they encountered Manannán, who described the sea as his estate and gave them instructions on how to reach the island of Eamhain before sundown. Coming to that island, Bran rowed around it and saw a crowd of people staring and laughing at his crew. One of his men went ashore, and immediately he began to stare and laugh like the rest. They next encountered the Island of Women, the inhabitants of which invited them ashore. They remained there in great delight and joy for what they thought was a year, though it was in fact many years.

Then one of the crew, called Neachtan, grew lonely for Ireland and decided to return home, and Bran agreed to accompany him. Bran's paramour advised him not to go, and if he did go not to set foot on the land. Reaching Ireland at Sruibh Bhrain (Stroove Point in north Donegal), they spoke from the boat to the people, who said that they had heard old lore of 'Bran's rowing'. Neachtan jumped from the boat, but as soon as he touched the soil of Ireland he withered away as if he had been buried for hundreds of years. Bran told of their adventures and wrote his account in **ogham**. Then he departed, and no more was heard of him.

This is a curious text, much of it in verse, and is undoubtedly based in part on pre-Christian ideas of the otherworld. The writer was, however, a Christian, and various references in the work suggest that he was an Ulsterman. He probably intended the voyage of Bran as a poetic tour de force rather than a serious philosophical work. The motif of a man who ages on his return from the timeless otherworld was an international one (see **Wonder Tales**, Type 470).

Séamus Mac Mathúna (1985); Kuno Meyer /Alfred Nutt (1895-7); A G Van Hamel (1941), 1-19.

See also Myles Dillon (1948), 101-31; H P A Oskamp (1970), 40-3.

BRANDUBH Leinster king who died c 605 AD. His father's name was Eochu, and the name Brandubh itself means 'black raven'. He was one of the characters who figure most prominently in stories of the kings.

A text from around the 11th century states that Eochu was for a while exiled in Scotland. His wife Feidhilm gave birth to twin boys; and on the same night and in the same house Ingheanach, wife of a king called Gabhrán, gave birth to twin girls. Feidhilm gave one of her sons in exchange for one of the baby girls, but she inserted a grain of gold into his shoulder so that he might be identified later. Eochu returned to Ireland with his family, and his son Brandubh became king of Leinster. The other boy grew up to be Aodán mac Gabhráin, a celebrated leader of the Dál Riada sept and king of Scotland. Aodán came to wage war on Leinster, but his real mother Feidhilm went to meet him and proved his identity to him through the grain of gold, as a result of which he made peace with Brandubh. This imaginative story has no basis in history, but derives from popular lore concerning confusion of new-born babies. Mediaeval romance also brought Brandubh into association with the adventures of **Mongán**, whose father was an ally of Aodán mac Gabhráin.

Brandubh was reputed to have delivered 'seven blows against Bréagha', but by far his greatest victory over the Uí Néill of Bréagha was in the year 598 at the battle of Dún Bolg (Dunboyke, near Hollywood in Co Wicklow). Here the high-king Aodh mac Ainmhireach, who was attempting to collect the **bóraimhe** tribute, was slain and his army scattered. By the 11th century a whole series of narratives had become associated with this battle, with quite dramatic representations of the participants. We read that the high-king Aodh had a son called Cumascach, who went about the country demanding the privilege of sleeping with the wife of each local king. When he came into Leinster, Brandubh spread the rumour that he was gone abroad and disguised himself and his men as servants. As a feast was being prepared for Cumascach, his satirist Glasdámh recognised by the great bounty that the cook was Brandubh in disguise, and accordingly put Cumascach on his guard. However, Brandubh had the doors of the house locked from the outside and set fire to it. Glasdámh begged to be allowed out, as he had been given food and was thus a true guest. Brandubh gave him permission to depart, but instead of himself doing so Glasdámh allowed Cumascach to escape in his clothes. However, Cumascach was slain by one of Brandubh's men as he left the territory.

The high-king Aodh, to avenge the death of his son, brought his army south, and encamped at Dún Bolg. Brandubh sent bishop Aodán of Glendalough to arrange a truce, but the high-king insulted him by insisting that the bishop touch his private parts. Aodán cursed him, saying that the king's own sexual organs would be taken by a she-wolf. Returning to Brandubh, Aodán advised him to bring his men into the enemy camp in baskets strapped to oxen, under the pretext of delivering food as tribute. He also recommended that a troop of unbroken horses be brought with rocks attached to their tails. Brandubh managed to make a truce with the Ulstermen in Aodh's force, and then challenged the high-king's champion to combat and slew him. He sent a spy, called Rón Cearr, disguised as a leper into Aodh's camp, in order to arrange the treacherous food delivery, but the high-king recognised 'a warrior's eyes in the leper's head' and continued his preparations for battle. Nevertheless, he was put off his guard when the Leinstermen arrived with a huge amount of food. The hidden soldiers sprang from the baskets and the wild horses were released, causing pandemonium in the camp. A wall of spears and shields was put around the high-king by his followers, and he retreated. Rón Cearr, however, attacked him, slew his bodyguard, and dragged him from his horse and beheaded him. He put the head of Aodh into his food-wallet and brought it to Brandubh. Variant accounts have both Cumascach and Aodh slain by Brandubh himself, thus further underlining the martial capacity of the Leinster king.

The death of Brandubh himself is dramatised in the hagiographical literature, which has St **Maodhóg** as his spiritual adviser and supporter. We read that a man called Saran 'the squinter' slew Brandubh and, when Maodhóg realised that the king had died without being shriven, he prayed and fasted for a long time and by this means had the king restored to life. Brandubh, however, was unwilling to return to the sinful world, and having received the last Sacraments desired to go to heaven and therefore died again immediately. He was buried at Maodhóg's monastery at Fearna (Ferns, Co Wexford). Saran repented of his deed

8. BRÉANAINN *Mount Brandon in Co. Kerry.*

and was forgiven, but as punishment his arm fell off.

Kuno Meyer in *Zeitschrift für celtische Philologie 2*, 134-7; R I Best in *Studies for G S Loomis* (1927), 381-90; Whitley Stokes in *Revue Celtique 13*, 54-95 and *17*, 160-1; Charles Plummer (1910) *2*, 149 and (1922) *1*, 185-6, 188, 215-7, 230-2 and 2, 383; W W Heist (1965), 238-44, 417; P S Dinneen (1908) *2*, 408-11 and *3*, 114-5; F J Byrne (1973), 142-9; Myles Dillon (1946), 41, 49, 106-11.

BRÉANAINN Saint of the 6th century, the date of whose death is variously given as 571, 575, and 581 AD. His name was rendered in Latin as Brendanus and thus in English as Brendan. He was a great founder of monasteries - the best known of these being at Clonfert and Annaghdown in Co Galway, Inishadroum in Co Clare, and Ardfert in Co Kerry. Reputedly also a great traveller, he was said to have visited Scotland, Wales, and Brittany, in which places his cult was strong in mediaeval times. Biographical accounts of him in Irish and Latin had their genesis in the 8th century, and his fame owed much to a fantastic text *Navigatio Brendani* which was written a hundred years or so later.

Bréanainn belonged to the Ciarraighe Luachra, a sept which inhabited the area around Tralee Bay in Co Kerry. Many placenames in that area reflect his cult, most notably the towering Cnoc Bhréanainn (Mount Brandon) in the Dingle Peninsula. The Ciarraighe were a maritime people, and no doubt their sea-travels helped to spread the cult of their saint and also to give him the image of a mariner par excellence. All of the surviving accounts of his life are conflations of the original biography and the *Navigatio*. From an analysis of these and some other material, the following emerges as a general outline:-

Bréanainn was born the son of one Findlugh of the Ciarraighe Luachra. Before she gave birth, Findlugh's wife dreamed that her bosom was full of pure gold and that her breasts shone like snow. A bishop called Earc explained to her the meaning of this, and the prophet **Beag mac Dé** also foretold the wondrous birth. This event was accompanied by several marvellous happenings, including a fair drop ('braen-fhind') which fell from heaven onto him, thus giving his name. The latter motif is transparently fanciful, for the name Bréanainn was apparently quite common in early Ireland, being a borrowing of the Welsh word for a king, 'brenhin'.

We further read that the child was fostered for five years by the nun, St **Íde**, and then was sent to be educated by Bishop Earc. Later he went to Connacht, and having studied there for some time returned to be consecrated by Earc. The love of God so increased in him, however, that he was given a vision of a secret island in the ocean to which he might withdraw from the world. This was Tír Tairngire ('the Land of Promise'). When he reached that island, he was told to return and teach the true way of living to the Irish people. This he did, and many more adventures are related of him. It was claimed that he cursed fifty rivers because fishermen on them were stingy with him, so that these rivers never after had fish; and that he blessed fifty more, with the opposite effect. He turned a man into an otter beacuse that man had stolen his cows, and on account of his short temper **Íde** instructed him to leave Ireland and go on missionary work to Britain. He rowed thither, and among his fantastic miracles there were the taming of savage lions and the banishing of sea-monsters. Notably, many of the miracles attributed to him are connected with water, such as the changing of fifty seals into horses to ransom a prisoner from the high-king **Diarmaid mac Cearrbheoil**. The horses proved unmanageable to the king's riders and raced to the river Boyne, where they reassumed their original form. Bréanainn died at the home of his sister at Eanach Dúin (Annaghdown) and, according to his instructions, his body was conveyed to his monastery at Cluain Fhearta (Clonfert) in a small chariot accompanied by one monk only.

Bréanainn's sea-voyage to Tír Tairngire is a Christian adaptation of the Celtic otherworld situated in an overseas island (see **Manannán**). Such a voyage to the otherworld was a striking and dramatic theme, and its occurrence in the legend of Bréanainn prompted a mediaeval scholar to compose the *Navigatio*. This scholar used some other material also from pre-existing Irish literature, particularly the account of the voyage of **Maol Dúin**. His text begins by having a monk called Barrfhind come to Bréanainn at Clonfert and tell of the marvellous Land of Promise. Bréanann, with fourteen of his monks, built a light wooden boat covered with ox-hides and set sail westwards, entrusting their fate to God. After forty days they reached land, where one of their company died, and then set sail again and reached the Island of Sheep. Later they began to cook their food on another island, which turned out to be in reality a great fish, and then they encountered a flock of birds, one of which spoke and gave them directions for their journey. They next reached an island where they were welcomed by a community of monks who had a beautiful church, and continuing on their journey they came to a marvellously smooth sea. Having revisited these places, they headed for the open ocean. They encountered huge sea-beasts, and spent some time on various other islands, one of which had three choirs of anchorites and another was luscious with grapes. A gryphon attacked them at sea, but the bird which had already advised them appeared and slew the gryphon, and they then came upon marvels such as a crystal clear sea and a pillar in the ocean which stretched to the sky and which contained a chalice for Bréanainn to celebrate Mass. They reached the Island of Smiths, the inhabitants of which threw burning lumps of clay at them as they sailed by. Bréanainn said that this was hell, and they also had to cope with a great fiery mountain from which demons came to take one of their number. Sailing south, they met with Judas seated on a lonely rock in the ocean enduring punishment for having betrayed Christ. On a small island they met a hermit called Paul, who was very old and clothed only in his long white beard. Paul explained that he had been educated by St Patrick, who had directed him to seek that lonely abode, and he had been fed for thirty years there by an otter which caught fish for him. For another sixty years he had been sustained by a marvellous well, and he now gave Bréanainn directions to the Land of Promise. Finally they came to that island, which was surrounded by mist and lit up by a mighty light. They met a youth there, who explained that God had kept them journeying for seven years so that they would see 'His varied secrets in the great ocean'. Bréanainn and his surviving companions returned home to a warm welcome by his own community.

Due to the several dedications to him, the memory of Bréanainn survived in many parts of the country. His feastday, May 16, is celebrated in west Kerry by the climbing of Mount Brandon.

J F Kenney (1929), 406-20; Charles Plummer (1910) *1*, 98-151 and (1922) *1*, xvi-xxii, 44-95; Whitley Stokes (1890), 99-115, 349-54 and (1905), 112-3, 404; James O'Meara (1978); H P A Oskamp (1970), 20-38; T C Croker (1829), 75-80; Máire MacNeill (1962), 682; Ordnance Survey Letters - Mayo (1838), 202-5; IFC 25:376-7, 124:138-40, 336:253-4,

492:67-119, 628:428, 945:passim, 947:passim.

BREAS A mythical king of the otherworld race, **Tuatha Dé Danann**. Breas (earlier, Bres) means 'beautiful' and, according to the text on the second battle of Moytirra (see **Mythological Cycle**), it was a sobriquet, the character's real name being Eochu Bres.

That text gives a detailed account of Breas' life. We read that a maiden of the Tuatha Dé called Ériu (i.e. Éire, the name of the country) was by the sea-shore when a stunningly handsome young man came to land in a silver vessel. He wished to make love to her, and she consented. Before departing he gave her a ring and told her to give it to nobody but the person whose finger it would fit. He also told her that he was Ealatha, king of the **Fomhóire**, and that she would bear him a son. Thus was Breas conceived. He grew up and, when **Nuadhu** was removed from the kingship because of his blemish, Breas was installed in his place on condition that if he became oppressive he would resign. He soon began to connive with the Fomhóire, however, in their levying of tribute on Ireland. He made virtual slaves of **Oghma** and the **Daghdha**, and further outraged the Tuatha Dé by refusing to entertain them as a king should do for his subjects.

Finally, a poet of the Tuatha Dé, **Cairbre mac Éadaoine**, satirised him for his stinginess, and 'from that hour there was nothing but blight on Breas'. The Tuatha Dé demanded his resignation, but agreed to his request to remain in office till the end of seven years. Intending to use this respite to assemble the Fomhóire, he went to his mother and enquired about his paternity. She gave him the ring which Ealatha had left with her, and it fitted his middle finger perfectly. He and she then set out for the domain of the Fomhóire, where they were welcomed and their dogs and horses outran those of the Fomhóire in friendly racing contests. Breas' father Ealatha recognised him from the ring, but refused him assistance to regain Ireland since he had not ruled justly. He did, however, direct Breas to **Balar** and to Inneach mac Dé Domhnann, two other Fomhóire kings. These assembled a mighty host and came with Breas to Ireland, but they were defeated by the Tuatha Dé in the great battle of Moytirra. Captured after the battle, in order to be given quarter by **Lugh** he offered to ensure that the cows would always be in milk and that there would be four harvests every year in Ireland. These conditions were refused by the Tuatha Dé, and then he offered agricultural advice to Lugh, viz that ploughing, sowing, and reaping should all be done on a Tuesday. On account of this advice Breas was released. The end of the text has him back with his father Ealatha in the latter's fortress in the realm of the Fomhóire.

It would be difficult to claim any great antiquity for the character of Breas, as distinct from the theme of the Fomhóire. His name seems to be a mere echo from the divine personage **Eochaidh**, borrowed into the Fomhóire context by some early mediaeval writer and made to suit that context. His birth-story follows a pattern which had some popularity with early mediaeval storytellers. This pattern is found also in the birth-story of **Mongán**, whose father was said to be the sea-deity **Manannán**. On the Continent it was the birth-story of the founder of the Merovingian dynasty. Common to these stories is the paternity by a sea-spirit and, just as the element 'maris' or 'mer' was the reason why the plot was applied to the Merovingians, so also the element 'muir' (i.e. sea) - as popularly applied to the Fomhóire - attracted the plot to Breas. Another motif borrowed from folklore is that of a father recognising his son through a ring-token left with the child's mother. It is noticeable that the motif does not suit the narrative context in the case of Breas, for there is no need of a recognition scene, but the author was anxious to dramatise his text with whatever material he had to hand. A further borrowing from folklore is the nature of Breas' advice regarding agriculture, for a common superstition held that it was unlucky to begin a new undertaking on Monday (see **Time**).

None of the other accounts given of Breas differ substantially from that in the Moytirra text, although there was some confusion regarding his ultimate fate. The first redaction of the pseudo-historical *Lebor Gabála* states that he was slain in the battle of Moytirra. An alternate tradition is found in other redactions i.e. that he met his death at the hands of Lugh at Carn Uí Néit (Mizen Head, Co Cork). This is a reflection from the lore concerning Balar (q.v.), but in his case Breas was said to have died through treachery. Lugh magically made bog-water appear as milk in his eyes, and he was poisoned from drinking it. In the post-mediaeval text on the Moytirra battle, he is said to have been beheaded by Lugh in single combat in the course of the fighting. Yet another account - given in the text on the 'first' battle of Moytirra - states that Breas died after taking a drink while hunting on Sliabh Gamh (the Ox

Mountains in Co Sligo). No accounts of him survived in post-mediaeval folklore.

E A Gray (1982), 26-39, 50-1, 66-71, 133-4; R A S Macalister (1941), 118-9, 148-9, 176-7, 228-9; Edward Gwynn (1913), 216-23; Joseph Frazer in *Ériu 8*, 58-9; Brian Ó Cuív (1945), 49-50, 73.

[Folkloric materials] Godefroid Kurth (1893), 137, 150-6, 501; Antti Aarne /Stith Thompson (1961), Type 873; Seán Ó Súilleabháin (1942), 356.

BREASAL BÓ-DHÍOBHADH Fictional high-king of Ireland in prehistory. He is described as having been son of the mythical Rudhraighe (see **Ulster Cycle**).

We read that he ruled for eleven years, and that during his reign a great pestilence came on the cattle of Ireland, so that one bull and one heifer alone survived. His epithet 'bó-dhíobhadh' means 'lacking in cattle', and on account of its alliteration seems to have been originally associated with a king called Breasal Beoil who had a prominent place in the early Leinster genealogies. The loss of cattle was not an unusual occurrence in early Irish warfare, and one story in fact told of how this Leinster Breasal resisted payment of the cattle-tribute called **bóraimhe** to the high-king **Cairbre Lifeachair**. The name is found in association with the seeking and taking of cattle in another mediaeval text also, for we read of one Breasal, son of the 6th-century high-king **Diarmaid mac Cearrbheoil**, forcibly taking a cow from a nun.

The attribution of a name such as Breasal Bó-dhíobhadh to a fanciful high-king of Ulster stock probably arose from the fame of the great cattle-raid in the Ulster Cycle, Táin Bó Cuailnge, and the meaning of the epithet was in turn re-interpreted by the writers of pseudo-history.

John O'Donovan (1848) *1*, 84-7; Myles Dillon in *Ériu 11*, 43-4; Kuno Meyer (1914) *2*, 15; R A S Macalister (1956), 294-5; P S Dinneen (1908) *2*, 180-1; T F O'Rahilly (1946), 268; F J Byrne (1973), 137-9, 320.

BRIAN BORU (926-1014 AD) Leader of the Dál gCais sept of Co Clare and high-king of Ireland from 1002 until his death. The name Brian had apparently come into general use in his time, being an adaptation of the earlier Briún, probably under the influence of the Breton name Brien. His epithet is usually written 'Bórumha' or 'Bóirmhe' in Irish. These are variants of the word **bóraimhe**, which meant a cattle-tribute, but in the case of Brian this meaning is but indirect. In a contemporary poem he is referred to as 'Brian from Bórumha', by which place was meant Béal Bóramha, on the right bank of the Shannon just north of Killaloe. The placename means 'the port of the cattle-tribute', and it is apparent that Brian was either born or reared there. Since Brian himself became in time a great collector of tribute, the term 'bóraimhe' was soon regarded as applying directly to his own activities.

Brian was the son of the Dál gCais chieftain Cinnéide, and he and his elder brother Mathghamhain waged a persistent war against rival septs, and particularly against the Norse settlers, until Mathghamhain was installed king of Munster in the year 968. Eight years later, however, Mathghamhain was treacherously slain, and Brian became the leader of the sept. He went from strength to strength until he compelled the reigning Uí Néill high-king, Maoilsheachlainn mac Domhnaill, to abdicate in his favour in the year 1002. Brian had his headquarters at Ceann Cora (Kincora, on the Shannon near Killaloe), and his power was unchallenged until a crisis which developed in 1014 and which led to the great battle of Cluain Tairbh (Clontarf, Co Dublin), in which he won a decisive victory over the Norsemen and their Leinster allies, but he was himself slain in the course of the battle. After his death there was over a century of contention between various powerful families for the high-kingship, and it was during this time that his Uí Bhriain (O'Brien) descendants had a text compiled to assert their leading claim. This text was entitled *Cogadh Gaedheal re Gallaibh* ('the War of the Irish with the Foreigners'), and it described in heroic terms the career of the great Brian.

The text states that, at an early stage, Mathghamhain was daunted by the power of the Norse in Munster and came to terms with them. Brian, however, continued a guerrilla campaign with a small band of men, and eventually persuaded his brother to resume the fight. Their victorious campaign against the Norse is described, culminating in a total victory at Sulchóid (Solohead, Co Tipperary) in 968, after which they took Limerick itself. Having described the subsequent events, and how Brian avenged the death of his brother, the text goes on to portray his reign as high-king as a period of unparallelled peace and prosperity in Ireland. We read that, during the reign, a lone woman travelled from Tory in the north of Ireland to Glandore in the south 'carrying a gold ring on a horse-rod, and she was neither robbed nor molested'. The text further claims that Brian appointed learned men as educators and funded the purchase of books from abroad, and had bridges, causeways, and roads constructed. He is also described as a great patron of religion, a reflection of the historical fact that Brian made a celebrated visit to Armagh soon after he gained the high-kingship, proclaiming that bishopric supreme in the Irish church and assigning to himself the title 'Emperor of the Irish'.

9. BRIAN BORU *Opening of **Codagh Gaedheal re Gallaibh** from a 12th-century manuscript.*

Brian's victory at Clontarf on Good Friday of the year 1014 is one of the great moments of history in the Irish mind. It marked the final overthrow of Viking power in Ireland, and the conventional account of the battle is based entirely on the *Cogadh* text. There we are told that, on the night before the battle, the otherworld lady **Aoibheall** appeared to Brian and told him that he would be killed next day. This proved true. As the tide of battle turned against the Norsemen, a fleeing Danish warrior called Brodir saw Brian praying in his tent and thought at first that he was a priest. Discovering who he in fact was, however, Brodir attacked him, and the elderly Brian defended himself stoutly. With a sword-stroke he severed Brodir's left leg at the knee and right leg at the foot, but the dying Dane smashed Brian's head to pieces with his axe. This may be inaccurate, and a varying account is given by a Norse writer. It tells of Brodir deliberately seeking out the king's tent during the battle, bursting through the bodyguards, and slaying Brian before being himself captured and put to death. The fact that the author of this Norse text was himself a Christian and very favourable to Brian adds some weight to his testimony.

10. BRIAN BORU *Harp, reputedly that of Brian Boru, but actually dating from the 15th or 16th century.*

All the later Irish literary accounts make use of the material in the *Cogadh* text, and it is not surprising that most of the stories concerning Brian in folklore are in one way or another derived from that text also. In these stories the courage and decisiveness of Brian is extolled, and one story common in Munster lore gives a scenario which is obviously derived from the capture of Limerick. We are told that he went secretly to examine the structure of a great Norse fortress, and decided that it could only be taken if the gates were opened to him. Riding by a hut, he saw a woman lamenting there and was told by her that she was married to a Dane and that, since no food was available, her husband had ordered her to cook their baby for a meal. Brian took pity on her and gave food to her, and in the conversation he discovered what the password to the fortress was. On the following night, Brian and a band of men gained access to the fortress by using this pass, and they fell upon the sleeping Vikings and slew them.

A more widespread story tells of how the Norsemen were so oppressive that they quartered a soldier in every house in Ireland - a detail sprung from the *Cogadh* text - but Brian sent word around secretly that every household was to kill their unwelcome guest on a certain night. At the appointed time this plan was put into operation, each household lighting a sheaf of straw as a signal to their neighbours that the deed was done and encouraging them to do likewise. Hearing of what had befallen their kinsmen in Ireland, the Norsemen abroad gathered a great force and invaded Ireland, thus leading to the battle of Clontarf. This is a curious tradition, and it must be an echo of the slaughter of the Danes in England at St Brice's feast by King Ethelred in the year 1002. This episode was described in various Saxon and Norman chronicles, and probably entered Irish lore from some such source. The *Cogadh* text itself is hardly more accurate in the reason which it cites for the great battle. According to this, the Leinster king Maolmhórdha, brother of Brian's wife Gormlaith, was a guest at Kincora and was observing a game of chess between Brian's son **Murchadh** and a relative. Maolmhórdha's prompting caused Murchadh to lose the game, and the latter taunted Maolmhórdha with having earlier been an adviser to the Norsemen when they lost against Brian. In high dudgeon, Maolmhórdha said that he would go to advise them again, and thus the renewed Norse activity which led to the battle. A Galway folk legend has Brian rather undecided as to whether he should wage total way on the Norsemen, but he is advised by a saint to go to a certain well on an island off the west coast. He does this, and notices the water of the well turn red, which he takes as a sign that he will triumph.

Late literary tradition makes much of Brian's reputed poet and adviser, the miniature Muircheartach mac Liag. There probably was a poet known as Mac Liag, but the verses on Brian and his court attributed to him are of much later date than the 10th-11th century. A story in one late text has Mac Liag returning to Kincora after a poetic trip around Munster. He tells Brian of how he has been very well received and loaded with presents by **Cian mac Maolmhuaidhe** and how another chieftain, Domhnall mac Dubhdhábhoireann, has given him but a belt and a piece of flint. Much to Brian's surprise, the poet values Domhnall's generosity the more, and Mac Liag explains that this was because Domhnall was the poorer of the two. Late folklore describes how Brian's affairs at Kincora were looked after for him in his absence by a dwarf counsellor, who probably is an echo of the personage Mac Liag.

Folklore contains some stray traditions about Brian which are nevertheless significant when taken in their broad context. A Cork account, for instance, claims that when a cow lies down in a field she sighs for the good life in the time of Brian, a notion which directly parallels northern lore of **Cormac mac Airt**. A Kildare source claims that plover were first introduced into Ireland by Brian beause of the wariness of these birds, and that the great king trained them to give the alarm if any enemy approached his camp. A Limerick tradition was that Brian had placed a massive chain across the river Shannon from Cratloe to Carrig so that the Vikings could not bring a fleet into the country at that point.

[Name] Kuno Meyer in *Ériu 4*, 68-73.

[Cogadh text] J H Todd (1867).

[Later texts] R I Best in *Ériu 1*, 74-112; Eoin Mac Néill in *Irisleabhar na Gaedhilge 7*, 8-11, 41-4, 55-7; A J Goedheer (1938).

[Folklore] Dáithí Ó hÓgáin (1985), 69-77, 328-9.

[Mac Liag] Colm Ó Lochlainn in *Éigse 4*, 34-43; Best, *op cit*, 94-102.

BRICRIU (later, Bricne) Mythical character in the **Ulster Cycle**, a trouble-maker who is described as 'poisonous' and 'evil-tongued'. He is stated to have been son of a certain Carbad (literally, chariot), which indicates that his characterisation was somewhat improvised.

Although little verse is attributed to him, it seems clear that Bricriu, like **Aithirne**, was understood to be a satiric poet. This would account for why his speech is always taken seriously and why his provocation never brings retaliation on him. The name apparently contains the adjective 'breac' (i.e. speckled) which in early Irish sources denotes a type of poetic satire which involved a clever mixture of praise and vituperation (see **Poets**). He was portrayed as a courtier of king **Conchobhar mac Neasa** - towards whom, as others, he combined friendship with malice. We are told that he could not refrain from encouraging strife, for 'if he made a secret of anything which was in his mind a purple boil would grow on his forehead as large as a man's fist, and he used to say to Conchobhar, It will burst from the boil tonight, o Conchobhar!'

He was particularly effective at causing dissension at drinking-feasts when the warriors were drunk and thus open to flattery and prone to competition. In the text on the dispute between the poets **Feircheirdne** and **Néidhe mac Adhna**, the blame for the dispute is placed on Bricriu. He encouraged the young Néidhe to sit in the chair of the chief-poet by falsely stating that Feircheirdne was dead, and then went to Feircheirdne to inform him of Néidhe's ambition. Similarly, at the feast given by Mac Da Thó (see **Conall Cearnach**), Bricriu did his best to promote strife between the warriors of Ulster and of Connacht who were ominously seated together. He proposed that the pig be divided by combat, adding 'you have all flattened each other's noses before!'. The principal story concerning his mischief-making is *Fled Bricrend* (the Feast of Bricriu) which was composed around the 8th century and survives in an 11th-century inflation. It describes how he had a special mansion built for a great feast, to which he invited Conchobhar and the Ulster nobles. They were reluctant to go, knowing that he would incite them against each other, but Bricriu threatened a worse fate if they refused. He said that he would cause them all to kill each other, would set son against father, and would even set the two breasts of every Ulsterwoman beating against each other until they were destroyed. The Ulstermen therefore agreed to go to the feast. Bricriu, meanwhile, spoke privately to three great warriors - **Laoghaire Buadhach, Conall Cearnach**, and **Cú Chulainn** - and promised each separately that he would give him the champion's portion of the food and drink at the feast.

Accordingly, when the guests arrived these three warriors began to argue and came to blows. They were separated at the request of Seancha, Conchobhar's peace-maker, who directed that the champion's portion be divided among them until it be decided which of them was the greatest. Bricriu had in the meantime sought to make matters worse by talking to the wives of the three warriors and saying to each of these that they should be first to enter the mansion. Hungry for precedence, the women raced each other and arrived outside the mansion with a great tumult. The doors were closed, but Cú Chulainn by his strength lifted a side of the mansion so that his wife Eimhear could enter. Next day, Conchobhar advised them to go to **Cú Roí** and that he would decide between them. On the way they met a giant, who overcame both Laoghaire and Conall but was overcome by Cú Chulainn. They returned to the Ulster court at Eamhain Mhacha, but once there the other two claimed that tricks had been played on them. They then set out for the court of queen **Meadhbh** in Connacht, where they faced an ordeal with three savage cats from the cave of Cruachain, and again Cú Chulainn alone triumphed. He further proved best at armed combat and horse-racing. Meadhbh privately gave a present to each of the three - a goblet of bronze to Laoghaire, a goblet of white gold to Conall, and a goblet of red gold to Cú Chulainn. On their return to Ulster, however, the other two claimed that Cú Chulainn had bribed Meadhbh, so they were again sent to Cú Roí in Munster. There a phantom overcame Laoghaire and Conall when they were put on night-watch at Cú Roí's fortress, but Cú Chulainn again prevailed. Cú Roí, who apparently was himself the phantom, awarded the honours to Cú Chulainn, but the verdict was once more disputed on their return home, and Cú Chulainn decided to forego his claim in the interests of peace.

Soon after, a monstrously ugly churl dressed in a grey cloak arrived at Eamhain Mhacha. The churl said that he had searched many foreign parts for a warrior the match of himself, but had so far failed. The test he proposed was that a warrior be allowed to decapitate him and that he be allowed to decapitate that warrior on the following night. Muinreamhar ('Fat Neck') was the first to accept the challenge. He cut the churl's head off, and the churl picked it up and went out. Next night, however, Muinreamhar absented himself, thus avoiding his side of the bargain. Similarly, Laoghaire and Conall decapitated the churl, but did not come to fulfil the second condition. Only Cú Chulainn was willing to lay his own neck on the block. The churl raised his axe but brought down its back rather than its blade. He then told Cú Chulainn to arise, for the champion's portion was undoubtedly due to him only. The churl was Cú Roí, who had come in disguise to ensure that his judgement was upheld.

Curiously, Bricriu does not figure at all in the second part of ths story, and it has been suggested that two separate narratives were combined. It is more likely, however, that the inventor of the story took a rather liberal attitude to his material, starting from a typically mischievous situation engineered by Bricriu and going on to adapt the beheading-game from floating mediaeval lore. It is significant that the order of events contradicts that in *Táin Bó Cuailnge* (see **Ulster Cycle**), where Meadhbh sees Cú Chulainn for the first time during the campaign and Bricriu is killed at the end of the campaign. Within his loose terms of reference, the writer of *Fled Bricrend* did nevertheless achieve some unity of plot, and the way in which Bricriu's mischief actually works to the benefit of Cú Chulainn is not discordant with tradition. In the accounts of the birth of Cú Chulainn (q.v.), he is one of the Ulstermen who first discover the otherworld house in which that hero's mother resides, and thus could be regarded as in some sense a patron of the hero. In the *Táin* and other stories, he stings Cú Chulainn into greater efforts in battle when such are required. Cú Chulainn accordingly improves his performance, though he resents such comments. In one 11th-century text, the hero is trying to slip into a feast when Bricriu announces his entry and calls for him to be attacked and killed. Cú Chulainn angrily threatens: 'I will give you a strong blow, o stupid Bricriu of the bitter words, which will quickly afflict you if you do not control your bad tongue!' In a later mediaeval text, the quest for the sons of Daol Dearmaid, incitement by Bricriu at another of his feasts is the cause of great trouble for Cú Chulainn (q.v.), culminating in a very difficult task which he must perform overseas.

Bricriu's more usual custom is to provoke trouble by suggestions and remarks made at the most sensitive times. 'I give my word,' he is quoted as saying, 'that a whisper is more valuable to me than a roar to another person!' Thus, in an account of why **Fearghus mac Róich** left Ulster, it was Bricriu who destroyed the truce between Conchobhar and Fearghus by reminding the latter of how he had been wronged. Then he advised Fearghus to go to the court of Meadhbh, and himself went to Connacht to fuel Meadhbh's ambitions. However, he could not refrain from sarcastically foretelling failure for Meadhbh's son **Maine** when that prince went to Ulster to court the maiden Feirbh. While at Meadhbh's court, he schemed to bring about Fearghus' raid on the king of the Gamhanra as told in the story of the lady **Fliodhais**. Fearghus, however, was so stung by one of Bricriu's insults at Cruachain that he once flung a chess-piece at him and fractured his skull, as a result of which the satirist spent a long time convalescing. When the two bulls were fighting fiercely at the end of the *Táin*, Bricriu came with the rest of Meadhbh's forces to watch them. In their violent struggle the bulls trampled on Bricriu and killed him. The satirist's name is perpetuated in the toponymic Loch Bricreann (Loughbrickland in Co Down).

[His boil] Whitley Stokes in *Ériu 4*, 32-3.

[Bricriu and Feircheirdne] Stokes in *Revue Celtique 26*, 12-3.

[*Fled Bricrend*] George Henderson (1899); Stith Thompson (1955-1958), Motif P632.2.

[Bricriu and Cú Chulainn] Cecile O'Rahilly (1976), 61; J C Watson (1941), 13-4, 39-40; Stokes in *Revue Celtique 14*, 424-7; Ernst Windisch in *Irische Texte 2 (2)*, 173-4.

[His whisper] Watson, *op cit*, 12-3, 39.

[Bricriu and Fearghus] Donald MacKinnon in *Celtic Review 1-4*, passim; Windisch in *Irische Texte 2 (2)*, 211, 214; Kuno Meyer in *Revue Celtique 10*, 227; O'Rahilly, *op cit*, 124.

[Maine's courtship] Windisch in *Irische Texte 3*, 445-556.

[Death] O'Rahilly, *op cit*, 124.

[General] Cormac Ó Cadhlaigh (1956), 467; M A O'Brien in Myles Dillon ed (1968), 67-78.
See also **Conghal Cláiringneach**.

BRIGHID (earlier, Brigit) Mythical lady of the **Tuatha Dé Danann**, originally a Celtic goddess. Her name meant literally 'the exalted one'.

This goddess is attested also for the British Celts, who called her Brigantī, and it is apparently from her that the tribe called Brigantes got their name. Branches of this tribe are also evidenced by placenames on the Continent, and it is therefore likely that the same goddess was worshipped there. She must indeed have been the Gaulish goddess whom Caesar equated with the Roman patroness of arts and crafts, Minerva. A 9th-century Irish glossary describes Brighid as a poetess and daughter of the **Daghdha**. She was 'a goddess whom the poets adored, because her protection was very great and very famous'. She had, the glossarian states, two sisters, both also called Brighid - a factor which exemplifies the Celtic tendencies to triplicate deities.

There are several indications that Brighid had agricultural fertility as her function besides the inspiring of poetry. The *Lebor Gabála*, in listing Brighid among the Tuatha Dé Danann (q.v.), calls her 'Brighid the poetess, daughter of the Daghdha', and states that she had two oxen. One of these was called Fea and the other Feimhean, and from them were named Magh Fea (the plain of the Barrow in Co Carlow) and Magh Feimhin (the plain in south-east Co Tipperary). Along with these oxen was 'Triath, king of the swine, from whom is named Treithirne'. Treithirne was the name of a plain in west Co Tipperary, and the mythical boar in question was more usually called the Torc Triath. It is further stated in the *Lebor Gabála* that these three animals used to cry out after rapine had been committed in Ireland, and all of this suggests that Brighid was a sort of guardian-goddess of domestic animals. The suggestion is strengthened by the cult of St **Brighid**, who is in folk culture the patroness of farm animals and whose feast-day is the first day of spring. It was once known as 'Oímelg' or 'Imbolg', which meant parturition, a direct reference to the birth of young animals in the spring. The festival may have been originally connected with the goddess, much of whose imagery was subsumed in that of the saint.

The mediaeval writers, in trying to normalise the connections between various characters of the Tuatha Dé, made Brighid (in the form of 'Brig') the wife of **Breas** and gave her a son called Ruadhán. In the statement that she was mother of the 'three gods of Danu', these writers may, however, have been reflecting early tradition. **Danu** was otherwise claimed as the mother of these three, and the suggestion is that Danu and Brighid were both aspects of a mother-goddess. The image is repeated in an account which claims that Brig was the first to lament the dead with weeping and shrieking. She did this when her son Ruadhán was slain in a treacherous attempt on the life of **Goibhniu**. It is apparent that a goddess with whatever name could in archaic times be called 'brigit', this being an epithet for 'exalted' **goddesses**. The 9th-century glossarian confirms her multiple personality by the statement that 'among all the Irish a goddess used to be called Brigit'. It is noteworthy, in view of this divine status, that some rivers in Munster bear her name.

Alfred Holder (1896) *1*, 533-43; D A Binchy (1970), 12-4; Anne Ross (1974), 452-6, 514; Proinsias Mac Cana (1970), 34-5; Émile Thevenot (1968), 180-4; Kuno Meyer (1912), 15; R A S Macalister (1941), 132-3, 158-9, 196-7; E A Gray (1982), 56-7, 119; Whitley Stokes in *Revue Celtique 16*, 150-3; Edmund Hogan (1910), 128.

BRIGHID (earlier, Brigit) Leinster saint who died c524 AD, foundress of a celebrated convent at Cill Dara (Kildare). Her name in modern Irish orthography is spelt Bríd, and in anglicised form appears as Bridget and Bride.

The earliest surviving reference to her dates from around the year 600. It occurs in an origin story of the Fotharta sept, and in it she is stated to have been of that sept and is called 'truly pious Brig-eoit' and described as 'another Mary'. All sources agree that she was of the Fotharta, and to this day a favourite designation for her is 'the Mary of the Irish'. The early development of her cult was closely connected with the rise to power in Leinster of a new sept, the Uí Dhúnlainge. The sept's leader, Faolán mac Colmáin, seized the kingship of the province around the year 633. He was married to a woman of the Fotharta, his brother was bishop of Kildare, and it would thus have been of great benefit to this new king to stress the importance of Brighid. At the request of the Kildare church, a Latin biography of the saint, *Vita Brigitae*, was compiled in or about the year 650 by a cleric known as Cogitosus. A striking feature of this work is the lack of real information on the historical Brighid, who had lived in the previous century. Is is basically a compendium of miracles, and the most valuable part of it is the description of Kildare as an ecclesiastical centre. It can be inferred from this that very little personal memories survived of the holy woman of the Fotharta who had founded the convent.

11. BRIGHID *Engraving of the Celtic goddess in Britain called Brigantia.*

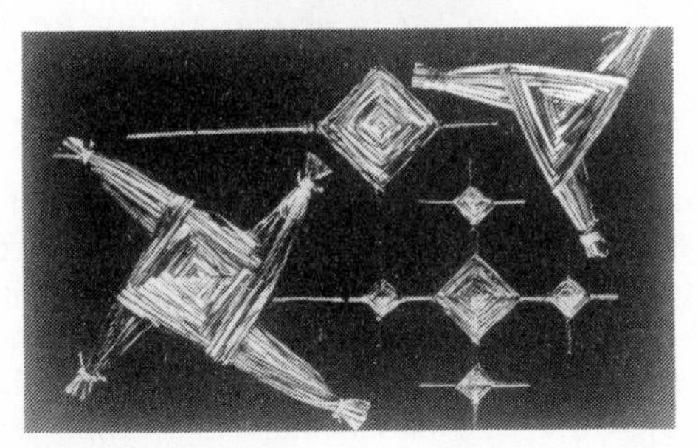

12. BRIGHID, SAINT *A selection of straw crosses dedicated to St Brighid.*

Cill Dara means 'the church of the oak-tree', and the presence of such a tree (see **Druids**) at the site suggests that it might have been regarded as a sacred place in pre-Christian times. The feastday of the saint, February 1, is the beginning of Spring and was anciently known as 'Oímelg' or 'Imbolg' (literally, 'parturition'). Cogitosus stated that it was the date of the saint's death, but it is safe to assume that this was a mere rationalisation of the cultic date. In Irish Christian tradition, St Brighid has always been regarded as the special patroness of farm-animals and of crops, and these are precisely the functions which one would expect of a pre-Christian divinity of spring. It is significant that the saint shares her name with the Celtic goddess **Brighid**, who in Ireland was honoured for her 'protecting care'. It is therefore probable that a pagan sanctuary at Kildare was Christianised by a holy woman of the Fotharta. This would have meant that the cult of that sanctuary became attached to her, including the goddess-name Brighid which probably was a title borne by the chief druidess there.

The synthesis of paganism and Christianity under the name of Brighid was, at any rate, easily achieved, and Cogitosus' own text betrays this in the nature of some of the miracles. The saint is portrayed as having the power to multiply such things as butter, bacon, and milk, to bestow sheep and cattle, and to control the weather. Celtic **goddesses** were frequently associated with fire, light, and thermal waters, and it is noteworthy that such images are also instanced by Cogitosus. The Christian ethos of the text should not, however, be under-estimated, for the basic theme running through it is Brighid's great charity due to her faith in God, and her sympathy for all His creatures. Moreover, the style in several places echoes phrases from the Bible and other early Christian literature. For instance, she changes water into ale, gives sight to a blind man, and renders fierce animals tame.

Some of the legends are localised variants of widespread motifs, such as the account of a maiden who has a silver brooch given into her charge by a cunning lustful man, who secretly steals it and casts it into the sea. He then demands either the brooch or that she become his sexual slave, but she sought the advice of the saint. As they were speaking, a man came with a fish for Brighid, and on opening the fish the brooch was discovered inside. The motif of a ring or coin miraculously recovered from a fish's stomach occurs in several early Christian sources, but the over-all plot here is an Irish development. Variants of it are found in the story of **Fraoch** and in the British biography of St Kentigern.

Another legend given by Cogitosus is of a pattern familiar in Irish hagiography i.e. a miraculous trick played by the saint on an overbearing king. In Brighid's case, we read that the king (presumably a Leinster monarch of an earlier dynasty than the Uí Dhúnlainge) had a pet fox which performed many kinds of tricks, and an unfortunate man killed it, thinking it to be wild. The man was seized and sentenced to death, and the angry king told him that this would be his fate unless he could produce a fox of equal intelligence and skill. A wild fox came to Brighid, sheltering under her cloak, and she produced it at the royal court, where it equalled the skill of the dead fox in every regard. The man was accordingly released, and soon after the fox escaped from the court and returned to its wild state. A direct borrowing of a motif from apocryphal lore of the child Christ in Continental literature is instanced by Brighid hanging her clothes on a sunbeam. Cogitosus states that she was dazzled by light and mistook it for a tree, and that the clothes stood there.

The theme of light and fire is especially stressed in 9th-century biographies of Brighid in Irish and Latin, texts which are based on sources somewhat older than themselves. Here we are told that the house in which she slept seemed to onlookers to be on fire, a detail which coincides with a 12th-century claim that a perpetual fire had been kept burning in the convent of Kildare. Although these motifs are borrowed from Continental sources, their application to Brighid is probably a reflection of older native tradition of the goddess. Cogitosus had stated that Brighid's father was called Dubhthach and her mother Broicseach, and that she had spent her youth at agricultural labour for them, such as churning butter, tending the harvest, and shepherding the flocks for them. The 9th-century biographies show the same awareness of her agricultural functions, but they differ from Cogitosus in stating that Brighid's mother Broicseach was the slave of Dubhthach and that he sold her to a druid. The druid therefore had care of Brighid as a child, but later he sent her back to her father. Such a lowly background of the saint could well reflect the original tradition, and an acquaintance with druidry would have been important to a person who undertook the task of Christianising a pagan sanctuary. These biographies also reflect imagery in keeping with druidic practice, such as the mystical production of milk and the feeding of the child Brighid on the milk of a special white red-eared cow (see **Corc Duibhne**). But much of this is rationalised in the context of Christian morality, Brighid being described as continually giving butter and even cows to the poor and the needy. In one touching scene, she does the servile work in place of her poor mother who has an eye disease, and she works so eagerly and well that the druid decides to set Broicseach free and himself accepts baptism.

Additional healings of the sick and injured are included in these biographies, but the most striking departure from Cogitosus is the bringing of Brighid into contact with saints of other paruchiae, such as Mel and **Bréanainn**, and especially with **Patrick** himself. The latter case reflects the success of the Kildare church in gaining recognition as the principal see of Leinster from the church of Armagh. We read that she met Patrick at Tailtiu (Teltown, Co Meath) and solved for him a problem which was affecting his retinue. A woman claimed that Patrick's assistant Bron was the father of her child, but Brighid caused the tongue of the woman to swell when she repeated the lie. Those present wished to burn the woman for her perjury, but Brighid did not allow them to do that and instead told the woman to do penance. A variant telling has the child itself speaking in Latin to Brighid and telling who the real father was. This story makes Patrick somewhat dependent on Brighid, and the circumstance is repeated when Brighid persuades a pagan man to accept baptism from Bron. Patrick's pre-eminence, however, is accepted when he instructs Brighid to bring a priest about with her always as her charioteer - this is so that converts can be baptised without delay.

The later mediaeval biographies increase her itinerary to cover areas of the country far from Leinster, and in this they doubtlessly reflect the spreading influence of her cult. They also add some material to the original portrayals, some of it cultural elements surfacing in the literature for the first time. For instance, an account in Irish from around the 8th century gives the druid's name as Maithghean and states that he knew from the noise of a chariot in which Broicseach was being conveyed that she had a marvellous child in her womb. The account also gives the striking detail that Brighid was born as her mother brought milk into the druid's house at sunrise - the mother had one foot outside the threshold and the other foot 'neither without nor within'. The mystery and paradox involved here, and the redolence of ancient beliefs concerning sacred **kingship** and sacred **poets**, seems to be another vestige of druidic lore.

Narratives of Brighid were developed through mediaeval times by further additions from Continental hagiography. A 9th-century text describes how a man comes to woo the young, and as yet unprofessed, Brighid. Her stepbrothers try to compel her to accept the marriage, but she knocks out one of her eyes so as not to be attractive to the suitor. When the family allow her to remain a virgin, she miraculously restores sight to herself. The story is repeated in later sources, and it survived in the recent folklore of north Leinster and south Ulster. The name of the suitor, Dubhthach mac Lughair, is borrowed from the early Patrician texts, and it is obvious that the story cannot be older than the 8th century. It was, in fact, taken from the lore of the Continental saint Lucy and was suggested by the symbolism of light associated with both of these holy virgins. It is apparent that the cult of Lucy influenced that of Brighid in other ways also in mediaeval times. Lucy's feastday, December 13, coincided with the winter solstice in the old calendar and was thus seen to usher in the lengthening of daylight. In Irish, the saying which refers to Brighid's feastday, February 1, is that 'from Brighid's feastday onwards the day gets longer and the night shorter', although in fact that change occurs from the winter solstice, and the presumption must be that this saying was in origin a rather inaccurate borrowing from the Lucy lore. It could well be, also, that some of the paraphernalia associated with the feast of Brighid in Irish folk life - such as processions of young girls with the leader dressed up as the saint - shows the influence of the Lucy cult, which was very popular in western European countries in the Middle Ages.

A very curious little folk legend, which was known throughout Ireland, illustrates the close connection made between Brighid, 'the Mary of the Irish', and the Virgin Mary. This, a quite anachronistic tradition, seems to have been invented for the purpose which it itself expressly states - to explain why Brighid's feastday comes immediately before that of Mary, Candlemas or February 2. We are told that, when Mary and the **Christ** child were fleeing into Egypt, they found the road blocked by a party of soldiers, and Mary did not know what to do. Just then Brighid came on the scene and offered to deflect the attention of the soldiers from the fugitives. She did this by donning a garish head-dress with lighted candles attached to her hair, and the soldiers were so intrigued by this that they did not notice Mary and Jesus slip by. In thanks for this assistance, Mary told Brighid that henceforth the feast of the Irish saint would come one day before her own.

Another folk legend found throughout Ireland was more recent in origin and even more anachronistic. According to this, the mythical Leinster king **Labhraidh**, who had horse's ears, came to Brighid to seek her assistance. He sorrowfully placed his head in her lap, begging pity for his hideous blemish, and she blessed him and rubbed his head. 'I see no blemish,' she said, and he immediately stood up and found that the horse's ears had disappeared and that he had the natural ears of a man. The genesis of this folk legend is obvious, for the literary biographies of Brighid described how she once miraculously gave eyes to a flat-faced man. Based on this, and because of the mutual associations of Brighid and the horse-eared Labhraidh with Leinster, some imaginative person devised the new narrative.

The best-known of all the folk legends of Brighid purports to explain how she obtained the land for her convent at Kildare. We are told that the local chieftain refused to give her any more ground than the amount which her cloak would cover. At that, she took off her cloak and laid it on the ground, and it began to miraculously spread. It spread so much and encompassed such a wide area that the dumbfounded chieftain begged her to stop it before he had lost all his territory. She did so, and the area covered by the cloak, we are told, became the site for her foundation. Some variants of the legend have an aetiological dimension, explaining that the ground was levelled by the cloak and thus includes the great flat plain known as the Curragh of Kildare. This folk legend dates to the late Middle Ages and is, in fact, an Irish version of a well-known folktale. This (see **Humorous Tales**, Type 2400) has a trickster gaining as much land as an ox-hide can enclose by cutting the hide into thin strips and encircling a large area with these strips. It may well be that the Irish version concerning Brighid was devised by a mediaeval clergyman who knew the version of the folktale concerning Dido of Carthage in Virgil's *Aeneid*. In his or in other hands, the rather unethical act of the international folktale was transformed and given the moral force of a miracle.

It is clear that the Fotharta sept, branches of whom were scattered throughout Leinster, played a large part in the dissemination of the Brighid lore in early times and, apart from Kildare, her cult is strongly localised at Faughart in Co Louth, which place derives its name from the sept. It was, however, undoubtedly ecclesiastical sources which in the Middle Ages caused the spread of the lore of St Brighid throughout Ireland and even to Wales and Scotland. This is still evidenced by the widespread occurrence of her name in toponymics, but - at least in the post-mediaeval era - lore of her has depended less on local dedications than on the high profile of her feastday in the traditional year-cycle (see **Time**). Until recent generations, this day, February 1, was marked by a great variety of folk custom and belief, particularly in association with agricultural matters.

Foremost among the customs was that of the 'Cros Bhríde' (Brighid's Cross), a small cross woven from rushes or straw and placed under the rafters of the dwelling-house so as to ensure health and good fortune for the ensuing year. Sometimes such a cross was put in the cow-byre also to protect the farm-stock. The most common kind of cross throughout the country was lozenge-shaped, with the rushes or straw wound around sticks, and sometimes five such cross-lozenges would be formed into the shape of a larger cross. Also common were crosses with unaligned arms and ones with interwoven patterns. A cross within a circle was a variant found only in Munster, and in Ulster a simple three-legged type was sometimes used for cow-biers. Equally prevalent was the custom of leaving a piece of cloth outdoors from sunset to sunrise on the eve of the feast in the belief that the saint would touch it overnight and thus confer on it protective and curative properties. This was known as the 'brat Bhríde' (Brighid's mantle) and was kept in the house for the following year. It was believed to be efficacious in healing sick animals, and if placed on the head of a calf or foal would ensure that the young animal's mother would suckle it. In Co Galway a belt, decorated with little crosses, was woven from hay or straw ropes, and both people and cattle were passed through it in order to secure the protection of the saint. A more general practise was to include the residue from the making of Brighid's Crosses in new spancels for the cows, so as to protect them during the ensuing year. In most of the country it was customary on the eve of the feastday for groups of people, particularly young girls, to go in disguise from house to house, singing and dancing, and to collect either eggs or money from the householders. The leader of the group was usually a girl dressed as the saint and carrying a home-made doll, called a 'brídeog' ('little Brighid') or in English a 'biddy'.

[Earliest reference] M A O'Brien (1962), 80-1; Donncha Ó hAodha (1978), 42.

[Faolán mac Colmáin] F J Byrne (1973), 131-56.

[Cogitosus] Johannes Bollandus / Godefridus Henschenius (1863), February, *1*, 135-41; Seán Connolly in *Journal of the Royal Society of Antiquaries of Ireland 117*, 5-27.

[Brooch and fish] Antti Aarne / Stith Thompson (1961), Type 736A (see **Wonder Tales**).

[Cloak on sunbeam] see Robert Wildhaber in *Festschrift Nikolaus Grass*, 228-37.

[Other biographies] Ó hAodha (1978); Bollandus / Henschenius, *op cit*, 118-34, 141-55; Paul Grosjean in *Irish Texts 1*, 2-21; Whitley Stokes (1890), 34-53, 318-36; W W Heist (1965), 1-37.

[Other early material] Stokes / John Strachan (1903) *2*, 327-49; Rudolf Thurneysen in *Irische Texte 3*, 71; Kuno Meyer, *HB* (1912).

[Folk Customs] Kevin Danaher (1972), 13-37; S C Ó Súilleabháin (1977) and in Alan Gailey / Dáithí Ó hÓgáin (1982), 242-53.

[Folklore] Ó hÓgáin (1985), 16-26, 323-4; Máirtín Ó Briain in *Béaloideas 53*, 52-7; IFC, much material.

[General] J F Kenney (1929), 356-64, 801; E G Bowen in *Studia Celtica 8-9*, 33-47; John O'Hanlon (1875) *2*, 1-224.

BUTLER, MARGARET (c1466-c1539) Wife of Piaras Rua Butler, 8th Earl of Ormond, and a celebrated woman of her time. She was daughter of Gearóid Mór FitzGerald, the great Earl of Kildare and hence was popularly known as Máiréad Ní Ghearóid. Her marriage to Piaras in 1585 was an attempt to form a bond between the two great rival Norman families, the Geraldines and Butlers, but this did not have the desired result and Margaret witnessed the destruction of her nearest relatives by the English authorities, aided by her husband.

Before he became Earl of Ormond, Piaras Rua had to contend with a cousin, but he was staunchly supported by the Kildare Geraldines. For some years he led a very difficult life and, according to near-contemporary accounts, 'was forced to hover and lurk in woods and forests'. He was accompanied by Margaret in these miserable circumstances, and we read that in the wilderness once when she was heavily pregnant she begged her husband to bring her some wine to drink. This spurred her husband on to greater efforts, and he slew his rival and gained the Earldom. It is clear that Margaret had a reputation for a great appetite in her own time. Writing in 1571, Edmund Campion describes her as 'a rare woman, and able for wisdom to rule a realm, had not her stomach overruled herself'. Richard Stanihurst, who wrote six years later, was quite hostile to her, because of the manner in which she sided with her husband in his scheming against her Kildare kindred. Nevertheless, he admitted that there was some ambiguity in her nature. 'She was a sure friend, a bitter enemy, hardly disliking where she fancied, not easily fancying where she disliked', he writes, and goes on to describe her as 'man-like, tall of stature, very rich and bountiful'. Several writers refer to her as religiously devout and charitable, and one source credits her with being 'the very best woman of her time for hospitality and munificence'.

It is likely that the faction of the Butlers which had been defeated by Piaras would have been even more hostile to her than to her husband, for it was through her that Piaras got the assistance to defeat them. Secondly, the Geraldine family themselves would have felt quite hostile to her on account of her connivance with the ungrateful plotting of Piaras against them. At any rate, her portrayal in folklore is that of a powerful, but greedy and vindictive, woman. Legends concerning her were current until recent times in Co Kilkenny, where she was known as Máiréad Ní Ghearóid and also as 'the great Countess'. A 19th-century source relates that 'she emulated, if not excelled, her lord in feats of arms' and goes on to describe her as 'having always a numerous train of armed followers, well-trained and accoutred, at her command, by whose aid she levied blackmail on her less powerful neighbours'. Folklore, however, tends to focus on more immediate and personal details, and so the folk legends tell of tricks and ruses by which the Countess tried to inveigle possessions from various individuals.

We are told that, when she resided in Grannagh Castle, in the south of Co Kilkenny, she often visited the head of the Mandeville family, who had a fine estate at Ballydine, near Carrick-on-Suir. While there she noticed a contrivance by which a bell rang in the mansion every time a salmon was caught in a net placed by Mandeville's servants in the river Suir. Overcome with envy, she exclaimed aloud that Ballydine would yet be hers, but Mandeville indignantly rebuffed her. Not to be outdone, the Countess bestowed 'the praise of the envious' on Mandeville's sixteen fine sons, as a result of which all of the boys soon died. This story combines two different elements - the motif of a bell attached to a salmon-net (see **Cano mac Gartnáin** and **Comhdhán**), and the folk belief that an 'evil tongue' can be physically destructive. It is probably on account of the association of this belief with Margaret that she was sometimes referred to as 'an Chuntaois mhallaithe' ('the cursed Countess').

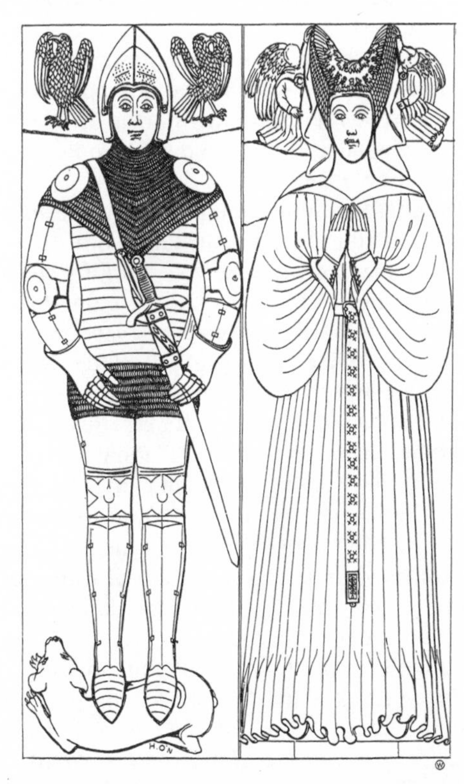

13. BUTLER, MARGARET *Figures of Margaret Butler and her husband from a tomb in St. Canice's Cathedral, Kilkenny.*

Another legend has the Countess visiting the head of the Walsh family, called 'an tOidhre Breathnach', who lived at Inchacarran Castle. He was a very generous host, and on one occasion he asked the Countess to name any dish in the world and he would have it prepared for her. She said that she desired more than anything else a plateful of special morsels of meat, and she specified that the type of morsel which she had in mind can only be found in a tiny part of the thigh of an ox. Walsh realised how he had been fooled, but he had given his word and he had no choice in honour but to order the slaughter of as much of his cattle as necessary for the purpose. Thus seven whole herds were sacrificed in order to appease the craving appetite of the Countess of Ormond. We are further told that she wished to take his lands from Walsh and, with this in mind, again chose an unguarded moment while being merrily entertained in his house. She begged as a small request of him that she could have the use of as much fertile ground as one bottle of flax-seed might be sown in. He instantly granted the request, but soon realised that he had again been tricked and that she intended to spread the seed far and wide. On this occasion he was prepared, however, so when she came with her servant and the bottle of seed he directed her to start the sowing in the thick brush of Coolanass, where the seed would soon be used up to no avail.

Another tradition claims that she kidnapped the son of the Walsh chieftain, and that this episode gave rise to extreme hostility between them. So great did their hatred grow that the Countess and Walsh hanged messengers sent from each to the other. The tree on which Margaret hanged her unfortunate victim was long known as 'Sceach na Cuntaoise' (the Countess' Bush), a large white-thorn in the parish of Tullahought. In north Kilkenny, the Countess was said to have hanged people from a jutting stone in front of her stone 'seat' on the top of Ballyragget Castle. Though the tradition must preserve some grain of truth, such a reputation for cruelty was hardly deserved. That reputation seems rather to have been a relic of the violent tenor of her time and the anomalous situation in which she lived. The fact that she was a Geraldine living among Butlers is echoed in a legend of her sept (see **FitzGerald, Gearóid Iarla**) which in Kilkenny was attached specifically to her. Thus we are told that when she was in the great castle at Carrick-on-Suir once, she looked through the window and saw Butler of Kilcash driving in his carriage. By use of magic she caused his horses to sink into the pavement, but he in return caused a pair of horns to grow on her head so that she was stuck in the window, much to the amusement of the spectators.

See also **Seven Bishops**.

Edmund Campion (1809), 161; Donough Bryan (1933), 92-5, 214-5; S H O'Grady (1929), 167; Lord Dunboyne in *Old Kilkenny Review 18*, 45; William Carrigan (1905) *3*, 53; Brian FitzGerald (1951), 129-30; IFC 2104:486-507.

BUTLER, THEOBALD (+1206) Ancestor of the Butler family, Earls of Ormond. His real name was Theobald Walter, and he was brother to the Archbishop of Canterbury and was a favourite courtier of King John 11. He came to Ireland with that king, and was granted large tracts of land in north Tipperary and south Wicklow. Equally important, he was given the lucrative control of the wine-patent for Ireland, from which derives the family name de Bouteillier ('bottle-bearer' - gaelicised as 'de Buitléir'). The family held this patent, which entitled them to a payment on all imported wine, until 1811, when they sold it to the Crown for a huge sum.

The very powerful Earls of Ormond felt it appropriate to give a heroic profile to their ancestor. Thus, in a genealogical text written in the 16th century, we are told that Theobald first landed in Ireland at 'an tInbhear Mór' (the bay of Arklow) and, when he came ashore, he drew his sword and put its point into the earth beneath him. He then announced: 'I pledge my word that I will not return this sword to its sheath or its protective scabbard until I attain to the farthest part of Ireland, unless my demise come!' The text goes on to state that he made good his words, never stopping until he reached Inis Umhaill (Innishowle in west Mayo). Then he returned to Arklow, put up his sword, and declared that the surrounding coastal area was so fine that he wished to live his life there and be buried there.

This account is highly fanciful, changing the status of Theobald to that of a great conqueror and attributing to him several different episodes in the history of the family. Quite skillfully, the author converts the wine-patent into a much more resounding commission, namely 'the first patent from the English king to make conquest in Ireland'. King John did indeed confer Arklow on him, but he was not buried there, although his direct successors were. The writer of the text was borrowing imagery from the lore of **Amhairghin Glúngheal**, reputedly the first of the Gaelic people to set foot on the soil of Ireland in prehistoric times and also the reputed builder of the causeway at Arklow. The Butlers did acquire land by conquest in Co Mayo, but not until Theobald was long dead, and the district in question was suggested to the author by the fact that it officially became Ormond property in the 16th century. In the meantime the Butlers had come to control most of Cos Tipperary and Kilkenny, where their fine castles can still be seen.

Edmund Curtis (1923), 100-2, 170, 430; William Carrigan (1905) *3*, 51-2; S H O'Grady (1929), 162-77; Lord Dunboyne in *Old Kilkenny Review 18*, 37-52.

C

CAILLEACH BHÉARRA (literally, 'hag of Beare') Mythical old woman in Irish literature and folklore, associated with the Beare peninsula in west Cork. The early sources state that her name was Boí, and also refer to her as the 'sentainne' ('old woman') of Beare.

In origin, she was undoubtedly one of the **goddesses**, or a special manifestation of the land-goddess. The southwest of Ireland was anciently associated with the otherworld, especially that of the dead (see **Balar** and **Donn**), and the idea of a hag of great age domiciled there seems to have been a combination of such sombre imagery with the negative aspect of the land-goddess. Her name Boí was synonymous with the word for a cow, and ancient Irish lore seems to have contained the notion that an old cow-goddess lived on an island off the western coast (see **Corc Duibhne**). At the tip of the Beare peninsula is an island called 'Inis Boí' (later 'Oileán Baoi') which was regarded as the residence of this celebrated hag. The Corca Loighdhe, a leading sept of west Munster whose territory encompassed the Beare peninsula, claimed this Boí as their ancestress; and a neighbouring sept, the Corca Dhuibhne, claimed that she had been the foster-mother of their ancestor, Corc Duibhne.

She is featured in a poem written around the year 900 AD, which portrays her as a miserable old yellow-skinned woman lamenting her youth. She says that in the past she has been beautiful and has drunk mead and wine with kings, an image which shows that she represented the goddess of sovereignty (see **kingship**). All of this has been reset by the poem in a moral context, however, and she speaks as one who, after a pleasurable life in youth, is taking the veil of a nun in her old age. The word 'cailleach' (from the Latin word for a veil, 'pallium') originally signified a nun, but had come to mean an old woman, and this was probably what suggested to the author that Boí had become a nun. That **Cumaine Fada** is claimed to have been the saint who invested her suggests that the poem is of Munster derivation.

The hag of Beare is not traditionally portrayed as a nun, but rather as a wise and somewhat sinister old woman. In early stories, however, she could also have the aspect of youth. One such, now lost, but current in the 10th century, told of a love-affair which she had with the warrior **Fothadh Canainne**. Another mediaeval description centres on her more prominent image. We read that 'she had fifty foster-children in Beare' and that 'she passed into seven periods of youth, so that every husband used to pass to death from her of old age, so that her grandchildren and great-grandchildren were peoples and races'. It is this portrayal of her as an old woman surviving from the distant generations of the past which is found in folklore. In fact, it was commonly said of a person of very advanced years that he or she was 'as old as the Cailleach Bhéarra!'

Aetiological lore concerning her was, as one might expect, strongest in west Munster. Again as an echo of her origin as a goddess, she is triplicated by the claim that she had two sister-hags, who lived respectively on the Kerry peninsulas of Dingle and Iveragh. One folk legend tells of how she fell on hard times, and the Dingle hag decided to render her some assistance by presenting her with an extra island. The Dingle hag put a straw rope around the island and began to drag it south, but it split in two and the straw broke off the Iveragh peninsula, and so the islands of Scariff and Deenish remain in that place. Another legend tells of the extremely sharp eyesight which the hag of Beare had. It happened that the Iveragh hag was one day working in her house at Bólas, when she heard a shout outside. It was the hag of Beare warning her that her cow had gone into the corn-field outside the house. The hag of Beare had seen this happening at a distance of almost twenty miles across the sea. Another legend has her being asked how she has lived for so long. Her answer is that the top of her head had never seen the air, the sole of her foot had never touched the ground, she had never ate except when she was hungry, and she had never stayed in bed after awakening.

In this context she personifies ideas of

healthy living, and a Connacht variant adds to these some principles of hygiene. The hag of Beare, we are told, never carried mud on her feet from one place to another, and she never threw out dirty water until she had first brought in clean water. The lore of west Galway tells of how, when at sea one night with her sons, they complained of the severe cold. She told them to scoop water into the boat and fill it, and then to scoop the water out again, and in this way they kept themselves warm with the exercise until morning. We are also told that she had a great bull called the Tarbh Conraidh, and every cow who heard his bellow calved within a year. The bull once swam after a cow across a creek, and the hag jumped after him, struck him with her rod, and turned him into a rock in the sea. This simple account is obviously of late derivation, but the general tradition which connects her with the landscape in different parts of the country is older. Standing-stones are often said to have been people and animals transformed by her, and she is said to have described how various aspects of the landscape came about, such as lakes drying up and mountains taking their place. All of this must reflect the spread of her fame from Munster in mediaeval times, when she had not yet lost the imagery of a land-goddess. In fact, lore surviving from land-goddess cults in various parts of the country were preserved by the application of her name to them. This is especially clear in the folklore of Scotland, where the Cailleach Bhéarra has undergone radical transformation, being represented as a female spirit of the wilderness and protectress of wild animals.

In the folklore of Connacht and the north midlands, the hag of Beare was closely associated with corn and harvesting. There was a widespread belief in a spirit of the harvest, which was said to race from the scythes in the form of a small animal, especially that of a hare. The cutting of the last sheaf in a field was therefore alluded to 'as driving out the hare', and - probably from its resemblance to a hooded old woman - this sheaf was known as the 'cailleach'. A lay concerning the great athlete **Caoilte**, composed in the 13th century, has the Fianna warriors reaping a corn-field at Bréagha (Co Meath), in order to expel a little deer from it, and this can be taken as evidence of the existence of such a folk fancy already at that time. It is curious to note that neither lore of the harvest-animal or of the Cailleach as a great reaper was known in Munster. The strong likelihood, therefore, is that - at some time since the Middle Ages and in the northern half of the country - the imagery of this harvest 'cailleach' got confused with lore of the Cailleach Bhéarra, thereby causing the latter to become a kind of embodiment of the harvest-spirit.

There are good reasons to believe that the little deer in the Fianna-lay was deliberately forged by the writer from a hare ('giorrfhia', literally 'short deer'). A man who could work as fast as a racing hare would, of course, be a phenomenally fast reaper, and so the idea could develope of a contest between a reaper and the hag of Beare. Thus we are told that the Cailleach Bhéarra once had a huge corn-field and that she issued a challenge to all and sundry to engage in a reaping contest with her. Every man who took up the challenge was defeated by her in the reaping-race, and had his legs cut from under him by a stroke of her sickle or scythe. Eventually a wily man discovered that she had a black beetle hidden in the handle of her implement and, realising that this was a magical device to give her great speed, he killed the beetle and then defeated the hag in the contest. She then revealed to him her great age and told him some details from her life, which vary from version to version but usually contain some accounts of her love affairs when young.

A common tradition tells of how she used to sow in late winter and harvest the green corn before the autumn gales came. This corn was known as 'coirce na bhFaoillí' ('the oats of February'), and it was contrasted in a proverb with the mixed oats and straw of a crop sown in March and the wisps and bags of chaff which resulted from April-sowing. We are also told that the hag revealed to people a better method of threshing than that which had hitherto been current. She did this with a verse, recommending that the flail should be made with a holly-stick as handle and a hazel-stick as striker, and sheaves should be threshed one at a time on a clean floor. Such items of lore were obviously mnemonic devices for farmers which became attributed to the hag of Beare so as to underline conventional wisdom.

Gerard Murphy (1962), 74-83, 206-8 and in *Proceedings of the Royal Irish Academy 55:C*, 83-5; Kuno Meyer (1892), 6-7, 131-4; Proinsias Mac Cana (1980), 48, 58; M C Dobbs in *Revue Celtique 49*, 440; F J Byrne (1973), 166-8, 211; Gearóid Ó Crualaoich in *Béaloideas 56*, 153-78; Séamus Ó Duilearga (1948), 255-7, 428-9; Seán Ó Súilleabháin (1942), 493; Máire MacNeill (1962), 160-1, 573; S P

Moore in *Éigse 8*, 78.

[Harvest-hare] G E Evans / David Thomson (1974), 127-41; E E Evans (1957), 162-3; Eoin Mac Néill (1908), 55-7.

CAILLÍN Saint of the 5th or 6th century, who founded a monastery at Fiodhnacha (Fenagh, near Ballinamore, Co Leitrim). The name means 'little cowl', and he was of the Conmhaicne sept of west Connacht.

A long account of him in Irish survives, devoted to his founding of the monastery and citing many poems concerning him. This, 'the book of Fenagh', was compiled in the year 1516, but incorporates the contents of an earlier text which probably was written in the 12th century. The account given of Caillín is a quite fanciful one, with much added by the later author. We read that Caillín was fostered and educated by the longevous **Fionntan** and sent by him to Rome to be educated as a Christian. Twelve years after the arrival of St **Patrick**, he returned to Ireland as a bishop and was given much honour and authority by Patrick and the other early saints. When founding his monastery at Fenagh, he was at first opposed by the local king Feargna and his druids. Through the saint's prayers, however, Feargna was swallowed up by the ground, and the druids were turned into stones. Feargna's son, called Aodh Dubh, was an extremely ugly fellow, but he was helpful to the saint and was therefore rendered handsome and had the kingdom conferred on him by Caillín.

We read that God sent an angel to Caillín to give him great knowledge, and this allowed for Caillín to be portrayed as a great sage and harbinger of social and political events. The 14th and 15th century chieftains of the northwest of the country, and their poets, found this portrayal suitable as background to events of the time, and so the book of Fenagh has much material - couched in prophetic terms - relating to the triumphs and ambitions of the Uí Dhomhnaill, Uí Néill, and Uí Ruairc. The latter sept (rulers of the Cavan-Leitrim area) had Caillín as their special patron. The saint, whose feastday was November 13, was portrayed fancifully in another late mediaeval text also, where he is claimed to have been a step-brother of the 7th-century poet **Seanchán**.

The folk memory of Caillín in Leitrim is derived from the book of Fenagh, and in the area especially associated with the Conmhaicne sept, Conamara in west Galway, he is said to have built a church at Bannon and to have had a bell with a tremendously loud sound.

J F Kenney (1929), 400-1; W M Hennessy / D H Kelly (1875); R A S Macalister (1939); Seán Mac Giollarnáth (1941), 11-3, 259; IFC 62:264, 75:158-9, 158:64-6, 559:200-1, 655:187-99.

CAINNEACH (c521-c599 AD) Saint who founded the monastery of Achadh Bó (Aghaboe, Co Laois). His name (which meant 'pleasant person') is anglicised as Canice, Kenneth, and Kenny.

Cainneach was for a while a member of the community of **Colm Cille** on the island of Iona. Three Latin texts on his life survive, and these are based on an original biography compiled perhaps as early as the 8th century. We read that he was born in Gleann Ghaimhin (Glengiven, Co Derry), and that his father Laidheach was an accomplished poet. In his youth Cainneach was employed as a cowherd, but he soon opted for ecclesiastical education. He went to Wales, where he was ordained a priest by St Cadoc, and on his return home to Glengiven he converted to Christianity the chieftain of his own sept, the Corca Dálann. We read also that, while with Colm Cille in Scotland, Cainneach founded several churches in that country. Returning to Ireland, he clashed with the king of Meath, called Colmán Beag, who had carried off a nun from her convent and held her captive on an island. The king, seeing Cainneach approach in a fiery chariot, was terrified and repented of his action. Soon after Colmán died, and Cainneach prayed over his grave and had his soul released from torment into heaven.

Cainneach became a close friend of the king of Osraighe (south Co Laois and Co Kilkenny) and, when that king was besieged by enemies and his fortress set on fire, the saint miraculously passed through the flames and brought him to safety. On another occasion, Cainneach came upon a gruesome sight when a group of Leinstermen were sacrificing a boy by flinging him into the air so that he would fall on the points of their spears. By the saint's prayer, the boy was not injured by his fall, but he was so terrified by the ordeal that his eyes were crooked to the end of his days. This boy, called Dalua, later became himself noted for sanctity, and founded the monastery of Cill Dalua (Killaloe, Co Clare). The literature describes Cainneach as in appearance a low-sized bald-headed man. He was celebrated for his beautiful handwriting in copying sacred texts, and also for his eloquence in speech, and it was said that he had been taught these special skills by Christ himself, who came to him once when he was in solitude at Inis Locha Cré (Holy Island, near Roscrea in Co Tipperary).

14. CAINNEACH *Mediaeval sketch of a monk illuminating a manuscript.*

Although it is not mentioned in the surviving literature, it is apparent that he founded a church at Kilkenny, thus giving that place its name (Cill Chainnigh). The folklore of the Aghaboe area claims that, after his death, the people of Laois and the people of Kilkenny argued over which of them should have his body for burial. They fell to blows, ignoring his coffin, and when they looked again there were two coffins, thus allowing both parties to be pacified. This story is in fact a borrowing from the lore concerning the burial of the national saint, **Patrick**. The feast-day of Cainneach is October 11.

J F Kenney (1929), 394-5; A O Anderson / M O Anderson (1961), 220-1, 352-7, 500-1; W W Heist (1962), 182-98; Charles Plummer (1910) *1*, 152-69 and *2*, 18; IFC 946:124-31/134/217-9.

CAIRBRE CATCHEANN Fictional character who, it was claimed, had led a revolt of the 'aitheach-thuatha' (subject-peoples) against the nobility in ancient Ireland. His epithet means 'cat-headed', and he was said to have been of the Luaighne sept, who lived near **Tara**.

The story of him was an invention by the pseudo-historians as part of the propaganda of the royal Uí Néill sept, who fancifully applied the term 'aitheach-thuatha' to the septs collectively known as **Érainn**. We read of how Cairbre, with two other leaders called Monach and Buan, spent three years preparing a feast for the nobles at Magh Cró (apparently in Co Leitrim). When the guests were drunk, Cairbre and his men slew them all. The plan was not, however, a complete success, for a great famine came on Ireland on account of the unjust **kingship** of the usurpers. Accordingly, when Cairbre died, messages were sent to the three young heirs to the kingship, who had been in their mothers' wombs when the revolt had occurred and who had since been refugees in Scotland. These three - Fearadhach Fionn, Corp Ólom, and Tiobraide Tíreach - were invited to return to Ireland, and the subject-peoples offered them their loyalty forever. Fearadhach became king of Tara.

Another tradition had a character called 'Cairbre Catutchenn' as an ancient king of the Érainn of Munster. In this case, the epithet meant 'hard-headed', and it is obvious that the pseudo-historians shortened it to mean 'cat-head', which image was seen by them as suitable to a usurper.

Toirdhealbhach Ó Raithbheartaigh (1932), 60, 107-14, 122-6, 210; T F O'Rahilly in Eóin Ua Riain (1940), 101-10.

CAIRBRE LIFEACHAIR Fictional high-king of Ireland, son of the celebrated **Cormac mac Airt**.

His name (earlier, Coirpre Lifechar) was based on a vestige of myth concerning the **Tara** kingship. This, of Leinster provenance, had the element 'Corb' in names of archetypal kings at that centre, and from it also the name of Cormac mac Airt himself (q.v.) may have come. One emanation of this name is Cairbre Cluithechair, also associated with the ancient Leinster control of Tara. His sobriquet probably meant 'lover of games', and it is apparent that Cairbre Lifeachair was an analagous name. The sobriquet in this case meant 'lover of the Liffey', this latter being now the name of a river but in former times the designation of the plain of Kildare through which the river ran. The character as delineated by the mediaeval pseudo-historians was a son of the high-king Cormac, but his Leinster connections were kept alive by the sobriquet, and we find it variously stated that his mother was a daughter of the great Leinster king **Cathaoir Mór** and that he was fostered by the Leinstermen.

The writers did not, however, hesitate to depict Cairbre Lifeachair as a staunch scion of the Connachta sept which had taken Tara from the Leinstermen. He is several times mentioned as a prince at the court of his father, not only in stories of the celebrated Cormac, but also in stories of the great Leinster hero **Fionn mac Cumhaill**. The annalistic record claims that he was killed in battle against the Fotharta, branches of which sept inhabited various parts of Leinster, in a battle at Gabhra (Gowra, Co Meath) in the year 284 AD. This, of course, is pseudo-history, but it attests to such a tradition having been known to the mediaeval storytellers. This battle was reinterpreted, in or around the 11th century, to have been fought by Cairbre against the **Fianna** troop of Fionn, and this latter idea became the accepted one. We read that, seated on a white horse in that battle, Cairbre cast his spear at the great Fianna warrior **Oscar**, mortally wounding him, but that he was himself slain by the dying Oscar.

Whitley Stokes in *Irische Texte 3*, 336-7 and in *Revue Celtique 13*, 50; Kuno Meyer in *Zeitschrift für celtische Philologie 11*, 110; T F O'Rahilly (1946), 139-40, 268-9; John O'Donovan (1848) *1*, 120-1; Ernst Windisch in *Irische Texte 1*, 158; Myles Dillon in *Ériu 11*, 44; Gerard Murphy (1933), 32-57; Neil Ross (1939), 148-51; Pádraig Ó Siochfhradha (1941), 200-12.

CAIRBRE MAC ÉADAOINE (earlier, Corpre mac Étaíne) Mythical poet of the **Tuatha Dé Danann**, his mother being a poetess called Éadaoin.

He was reputed to have composed the first satire in Ireland. It so happened that when he visited **Breas**, then king over the Tuatha Dé, he met with the inhospitality which was typical of that king. He had to spend the night in a dark and bare little hut with nothing to eat but stale cakes. Next morning he made a quatrain deriding the stinginess of his host and declared that 'the prosperity of Breas is no more!' As a result, the good fortune of that king began to fade. Before the second battle of Moytirra (see **Mythological Cycle**), Cairbre again assumed the role of the archetypal **poet** by promising to use his magical power as a weapon, satirising the foe so that 'through the spell of my poem they will not be able to contend with warriors'.

There are a few other incidental references to Cairbre. We are told, for instance, that he composed a praise-poem on the great shield of **Manannán**, and as a result was given the shield, but he passed it on to the **Daghdha**. The mediaeval tradition was that he died of sun-stroke, and that his mother died from sorrow for him.

E A Gray (1982), 34-5, 52-3, 119-20; Kuno Meyer (1912), 25, 98; H A de Jubainville (1903), 96; Eoin Mac Néill (1904), 35, R A S Macalister (1941), 226-7; Vernam Hull in *Zeitschrift für celtische Philologie 18*, 63-9.

CANO MAC GARTNÁIN Warrior who died in 688 AD and is the subject of a mediaeval romance entitled *Scéla Cano Meic Gartnáin*.

The essence of the romance was composed in the 9th century, but the full surviving text dates from over a century later. The events described in it are unhistorical, for Cano died a generation or two later than the kings and chieftains who are made to figure in the action. The story describes how one Gartnán mac Aodha and his uncle Aodán mac Gabhráin contended fiercely for the kingdom of Scotland. Gartnán lived in Inis Moccu Chéin (an island near Skye) in a fine palace surrounded by wealth and prosperity. He had fifty fishing-nets attached to ropes, with a bell at the end of each rope so that whenever a fish was caught a bell would ring. A son was born to him, and the child was called Cano and put into fosterage. Gartnán had a vat full of gold and silver concealed in the sand at low-tide, and had the four men who hid it killed, so that only he, his wife, and his son knew of it. Some time later his foe Aodán mac Gabhráin sacked and ravaged the island and slew Gartnán himself. Cano escaped to Ireland with some followers. The joint-kings of Ireland, **Diarmaid mac Aodha Slaíne** and his brother Bláthmhac, welcomed them.

Meanwhile, Aodán searched for the hidden vat of treasure and found it, reputedly with the help of the devil. With this treasure, he sent servants to bribe the joint-kings of Ireland to murder Cano, but the daughter of Diarmaid overheard the plotting and warned the intended victim. Cano went with twelve swordsmen and broke in on the discussions between Aodán's men and the two joint-kings. Diarmaid and Bláthmhac gave assurances that they would not betray him and advised him to follow the bribers and take the treasure from them. This he did, but he allowed these men to go free in return for promises of loyalty.

Cano went hunting with his followers and was amazed when, for the first time, he failed to shoot swans and ducks. Arriving in the province of Connacht, however, he met and fell in love with Créidh, daughter of king **Guaire** and wife of the warrior Marcán. She put all to sleep with a magic spell at a feast, but Cano refused to lie with her or to elope with her. Before he departed, however, he left a stone as a token with Créidh, promising to return for her when he secured the kingship of Scotland. This was a stone received by his mother from two otherworld women who came to her when she was in child-bed, and its preservation was linked to the preservation of Cano's own life. On leaving Connacht, he went south to Dún mBaíthe (Dunboy in west Cork), where he was received with great hospitality by a chieftain of the Corca Loighdhe sept called Iollann mac Scanláin. Soon, messengers arrived from Scotland to announce that the kingship had been awarded to him, and he departed for his native land, loaded with presents from Iollann. As he left the shore, a dark red wave splashed into his boat, and he interpreted this as a presage of death for Iollann. A year later, Iollann was indeed slain by two Munster rivals, and Cano brought an army of Saxons, Britons, and Scots to avenge him. He established the son of Iollann as over-king of the Corca Loighdhe sept.

Cano tried on several occasions to meet Créidh, but was always prevented from doing so by armed bands under the control of Colcu, son of Marcán. On one occasion as he crossed the sea to meet her, he was intercepted by three ships under the command of Colcu and he was cut down. When Créidh saw the pallor of death on his face, she dashed her head against a rock and Cano's life-stone was shattered underneath her. Cano died in Scotland nine days later.

The writer of this text used a variety of elements in his plot. He seems to have been under the influence of the story concerning the above-mentioned Diarmaid mac Aodha Sláine (q.v.) and his wife Beagfhola; but he also forged some of the narrative from the three-cornered plot which was popular in early mediaeval times i.e. the old husband opposed by the lover of his young wife (see **Deirdre**). Several folklore elements are also utilised, such as the idea of hidden treasure, the motif of an external soul (see **Wonder Tales**, Type 302), and the bloody wave as a presage of death.

D A Binchy (1963). Cf. James Carney (1955), 189-242; Seán Ó Coileáin in *Ériu 32*, 115-36.

CAOILTE A great athlete and faithful comrade of **Fionn mac Cumhaill** in the **Fianna Cycle**. His full name is Caoilte mac Rónáin, and he figures prominently in stories of Fionn in both literature and folklore.

In a Leinster genealogy from the 6th or 7th century, Fionn, Tulcha, and Caoilte are referred to as three descendants of Baoiscne. Tulcha was represented in mediaeval lore as a brother of Fionn and Caoilte as Fionn's nephew, but this early reference groups the three together as if they constituted a unit. It may be that such a unit echoed the triplication of Fionn (see **Find**). The earlier form of Caoilte was Caílte, and it seems to have been a contrived compound of 'cael' (meaning slender or exact) and 'te' (meaning hot or fierce), so Caoilte may have been envisaged as a dexterous and keen warrior. Already in texts from the 8th-9th centuries, he is said to have had special athletic skills, and texts of comparable date describe him as Caoilte 'cos-luath' ('fleet-footed'). He was so celebrated for such accomplishments that a 12th-century Welsh author borrowed him under the guise of 'Sgilti ysgawndroet' ('Sgilti light-foot'). The Welsh text utilises a common folklore plot concerning a number of characters with extraordinary abilities (see **Wonder Tales**, Type 513), and there are many indications that this plot had already influenced the lore of Caoilte in Ireland in the 10th or early 11th century. Thus we find an old friend and helper of Fionn, Fiacail Fí, being described as so fast a runner that he wears balls of lead around his neck to check his speed. This motif parallels one in the folklore plot, which has a fast runner tying one leg under his belt to slacken his speed. Nowhere else is Fiacail claimed to have been a great runner, so it is reasonable to assume that in the case of Fiacail Fí the motif has been borrowed from the folklore plot through the medium of Caoilte.

It may well be that it was a text concerning **Mongán**, written at the end of the 8th century, which cast Caoilte in the definite image of a great runner. Here he comes from the realm of the dead in the south-west of Ireland in order to settle a dispute concerning the site of a warrior's burial between Mongán and his poet in east Ulster. This portrayal of him running across the whole sweep of Ireland is repeated in later sources, such as the 12th-century text *Agallamh na Seanórach* which has him speeding from Tonn Chlíodhna (Dingle Bay) to Tráigh Rudhraighe (Dundrum Bay) in a single day. The title of this text means 'the Colloquy of the Old Men', and it focusses strongly on Caoilte who, along with **Oisín**, is described in it as a survivor of the ancient Fianna troop who lives on to meet **Patrick** and to relay much of the ancient lore to that saint. The occurrence of Caoilte in such a role is probably due to the 8th-century text above, which has him as one coming from the past to convey antiquarian lore.

The Colloquy gives other insights, too, into the development of the character Caoilte. His speed is compared to that of the wind, and it has him running two tense races. In one case, an ugly hag comes to the Fianna at Cruachain (Rathcroghan, Co Roscommon) and demands that they race against her. When the contest begins, Caoilte runs ahead of her, and then turns around and cuts her head off with a sword. In another case, the challenger is a beautiful young lady from the otherworld dwelling at Beann Éadair (Howth, Co Dublin), who is defeated in a long race by Caoilte. The motif of racing against a woman comes from the folklore plot (Type 513 referred to above), but the contrasting images of Caoilte's two competitors here - ugly hag and beautiful maiden - are those of the **goddess** of sovereignty. This suggests a connection between Caoilte and the struggle of Fionn with Cormac, a struggle of which the character Gráinne is an echo (see **Diarmaid ua Duibhne**). The connection is seemingly confirmed by a story written towards the end of the 10th century, which tells of how Fionn wooed Gráinne at Tara, but she demanded as a gift from him the male and female of each wild animal in Ireland to be brought in one drove to her. Caoilte undertook this seemingly impossible task, and succeeded in bringing that great straggling drove to Tara.

Other recensions of this story, though written somewhat later, preserve echoes of the original struggle between Fionn and Cormac. We read that Fionn attempted to seize power at Tara, but his plan was thwarted by Cormac and he was taken prisoner. In order to secure his release, Caoilte engaged in a campaign of attrition against the high-king, and so swift was he that he could not be captured. Eventually, he went in disguise to Cormac and demanded to know what ransom the king would accept for Fionn's release. The ransom was the straggling drove, and Caoilte accordingly succeeded in bringing it to Tara and thus had Fionn set free. This story of the 'straggling drove' is in fact drawn from two different sources - folklore concerning a man who can herd rabbits by blowing his magic pipe (see **Wonder Tales**, Type 570), and the account of Noah's Ark in the Bible.

It was a good and dramatic story, and soon became very popular in folklore, where Caoilte was said to have brought a herd of hares to Tara and to have placed them in a house with nine open doors there. By his speed and continuous racing around that house, he kept all the hares within until morning. Other suitable motifs were joined by the folk to the image of Caoilte the mighty runner. A late folk story from Co Galway illustrates this well by its deft selection of materials from various Fianna stories and from ordinary lore. We are told that the king of Ireland wished to have a fistful of sand brought to him every morning from each of the four shores of Ireland, for he would know by smelling them whether the foot of a foe had landed during the night. Three men offered to do this for him each day. The first man said that he would have the sands collected as quickly as a leaf falls from a tree, but this did not satisfy the king. The second man said he would do so as fast as a cat slinking between two houses, but again the king was not satisfied. The third man was Caoilte, and he said that he would do it as fast as a woman changes her mind. The king was impressed and asked him to go and collect the sands. 'I have just returned with them!' said Caoilte.

Kuno Meyer (1895), 45-8 and (1910), xxiii and in *Revue Celtique 5*, 198, 200 and in *Zeitschrift für celtische Philologie 1*, 458-61; Whitley Stokes (1900), 1-3, 103, 115, 136, 182, 189, 205; Eoin Mac Néill (1908), 6, 19-21; Gerard Murphy (1933), 124-40; Nessa Ní Shéaghdha (1945), 67-83; Neil Ross (1939), 40-59; Dáithí Ó hÓgáin (1988), 177-85, 296-8, 337, 344, 357 and in Bo Almqvist / Séamas Ó Catháin / Pádraig Ó Héalaí eds (1987), 241-2; IFC 1010:85-6 etc.

[Sgilti] J G Evans (1907), 232.

CAOIMHGHIN Saint who died c618 AD, founder of the monastic settlement at Gleann Dá Loch (Glendalough, Co Wicklow). His name (earlier, Coemgen) is anglicised as Kevin.

The surviving biographies of him, in Latin

15. CAOIMHGHIN
The valley of Glendalough.

and Irish, date from several centuries after his time,being compiled principally to add to the prestige of the famous monastery of Glendalough. We read that his coming was foretold by both St **Patrick** and the epical hero **Fionn mac Cumhaill**. His father's name is given as Caomhlugh, of the Dál Messin Corb sept of Leinster, and his mother was reputedly called Caomhall. Both names, containing the adjective 'caomh' (i.e. gentle) seem to have been invented by the biographers. The texts state that he was borne without any pain to his mother, and such an easy pregnancy may have been the reason why the child was given the name Coemgen (literally, 'gentle conception'), although the texts themselves explain the name as 'beauteous birth'. He read that twelve angels with golden lamps attended his baptism by St Crónán, and that the fort in which he was reared was never subject to frost or snow. A mysterious white cow used to come to give its milk for the child's sustenance.

When Caoimhghin grew up. he was told by an angel to study for the priesthood and, when he received holy orders, the same angel instructed him to go to the lonely place called Gleann Dá Loch (literally, 'the valley of the two lakes'). There he wore only the skins of wild animals and would lie by night on bare stones doing penance. He banished a great monster from the lesser of the two lakes into the larger one, and as a result sickness of men and of beasts was healed by a visit to the lesser lake. The monster in the other lake takes the illnesses and is thereby left too weak to inflict harm on anybody. When, however, the monster turns on its side, the water rises as high as the peaks of the surrounding mountains, and a person who sees that is destined to die within a week.

Caoimhghin performed great self-mortification. For seven years he ate only nettles and sorrel and was accustomed to stand up to his waist in the water while reciting the vespers. His psalter once fell into the lake, but an otter came and saved it from being wetted. The saint went to live all alone in a cave, and was on the point of death from fasting and penance when he was discovered. It happened that the cow of a certain farmer of the locality had a marvellous milk-yield. The herdsman grew curious and, following the cow, found that she got her marvellous milk through licking the feet of the saint. When the farmer heard of this, he arranged that the saint be brought in a litter to his house, and the dense trees of the wood bent of their own accord to allow the litter to be carried through them. The rescuers looked after the saint and helped him to build a church and the residence which was the basis of the great monastery. In the valley he was at peace with all nature, and we read that, when he prayed, the little birds would often perch on his hands and shoulders. One fanciful little anecdote told of how, while fasting during Lent, a blackbird landed on one of his outstretched palms and made its nest there. Noticing this, the saint kept his hand in the same position until the blackbird's young were hatched.

Soon he was joined by others seeking the monastic life. It was claimed that, in order to gain recognition for the foundation, he travelled to Rome and was granted the boon that seven pilgrimages to Glendalough were equal in spiritual value to one pilgrimage to that great city. Among the miracles attributed to him were the restoring to life of recently deceased people, the provision of food for his community of monks when such was not available, and making a wolf substitute itself for a doe in providing milk for a foster-child of his. The helpful otter used to bring a salmon from the lake for the monks every day, but one member of the community decided to kill the otter in order to make a glove from its skin. Understanding this, the animal disappeared, and the angry Caoimhghin ordered that monk to leave the community. It was also said that, during a time of scarcity, the saint sought food for his monks from some women who were carrying cheese in their baskets. The women pretended that the baskets contained nothing but thread, whereupon Caoimhghin turned the cheese into stones.

Most of the legends related of him in the mediaeval literature survived in local folklore, though often altered and embellished. One striking instance is that concerning a maiden who fell in love with him, and who according to the literature was driven away with nettles by the celibate saint and afterwards became a nun. Later folk versions of this legend have Caoimhghin causing the persistent lady to fall from a precipice into the larger lake at Glendalough. A folk legend which is post-mediaeval and has no counterpart in the literature purports to tell of how he gained the site for his monastery. A chieftain of the local noble family Ó Tuathail, we are told, ridiculed the saint's entreaties for a site. Observing a goose with a broken wing, Ó Tuathail mockingly promised as much land as that goose would encircle in its flight, whereupon the injured bird rose into the air and encircled all of the valley. It is hardly necessary to point out that this legend is apocryphal, and it is also anachronistic, for the family of Ó Tuathail (anglicised O'Toole) did not settle in the area until the 12th century. Another popular tradition has it that no larks ever sing at Glendalough, the saint having so ordained because he was aggrieved at larks who caused the builders of his cathedral to rise too early in the morning and thus feel tired and listless at their work.

Glendalough was one of the greatest centres of monasticism and of learning in early mediaeval Ireland, and the remains of the foundation are particularly striking in their beautiful surroundings. Caoimhghin's feast-day is June 3.

J F Kenney (1929), 403-4; Charles Plummer (1912) *1*, 234-57 and (1922) *1*, 125-67; W W Heist (1965), 361-5; P Ó Nuanáin (1936); IFC 143:1771, 485:269-70, 946:128-34, 1140:275-7, S917:245-7/327/337/370/414-4, S918:139-40/207.

CAOINCHOMHRAC A bishop of the monastery of Clonmacnoise, with whom a mystical adventure is associated in the mediaeval literature.

We read that he was wont to retire with his monks to Inis Aondaimh (Devenish Island in Lough Ree on the river Shannon) in order to pray there. One day they were cooking a little pig which had been given to them by hunters, when they saw a stranger come from the lake towards them. The stranger said that the dead pig was a monk who had been transformed along with other young members of his community, for disobedience. The stranger was the monk's father, and on hearing his account Caoinchomhrac had the pig buried honourably. At the stranger's invitation, Caoinchomhrac then dived into the lake and accompanied him to the underwater monastery. He repeated his visits often to that place. One Easter Thursday he noticed that his own monks had cooked pork for their meal and, angered at this breach of Lenten abstinence, he left them and was never seen again. It was not known whether he had gone to the underwater monastery or had been brought to heaven by angels.

S H O'Grady (1892) *1*, 87-9.

CATHAL MAC FIONGHUINE (+742 AD) King of Munster, whose reign began in the year 721.

He was of the Eoghanacht, the royal Munster sept, and belonged to the branch which inhabited the area of Gleanndamhain (north-east Cork). His father Fionghuine had been king of the province for a short period, as had his uncle and his cousin. After acceding to the kingship, Cathal undertook a campaign against the Uí Néill high-king **Fearghal**

mac Maoldúin. For a while he was allied to the Leinster king Murchadh mac Brain, but was not involved in the decisive battle of Allen in 722 when Fearghal was defeated and slain by the Leinstermen. The account of that battle has the severed head of Fearghal being brought to the court of Cathal at Gleanndamhain and being accorded high respect there. In the following years Cathal was in continuous conflict with both the Uí Néill and the Leinstermen, barely escaping with his life from the latter at the battle of Bealach Éile (near Borrisoleigh in Co Tipperary) in 735. Two years after this he had a conference with the new high-king **Aodh Allán** at Tír Dhá Ghlas (Terryglass, Co Tipperary), at which the two magnates appear to have reached some sort of agreement, and Cathal was involved in no other serious conflict. He was buried at the famous monastery which had been founded by St **Ailbhe** at Emly in Co Tipperary. In a text concerning a lady called Mór, he was confused with his great-grandfather Cathal mac Aodha, and as a result the goddess **Mór Mumhan** was claimed to have uttered a verse of lamentation over his grave.

Mediaeval Munster writers represented Cathal as having been in effect the king of all Ireland. They claimed that he was a great patron of poets and an extraordinarily generous host. This was the main reason why he was featured in the goliardic text concerning **Anéra mac Conglinne** and a vision of abundant food. There we read that Cathal had a demon of gluttony within him as a result of dainties which he ate and which had been tampered with by the magician of the high-king Fearghal.

F J Byrne (1973), 205-11; Séan Mac Airt (1951), 104-9; John O'Donovan (1848) *1*, 314-9, 328-9, 334-5; Pádraig Ó Riain (1978); R I Best / M A O'Brien (1957), 627-8; Tadhg Ó Donnchadha (1940), 147.

CATHAOIR MÓR (earlier, Catháir Már) Ancient Leinster king, possibly historical. The name Cathaoir apparently meant 'battle-lord', and his epithet meant 'the great', especially in the sense of a famous progenitor. The early mediaeval writers regarded him as the ancestor of the foremost septs of the Laighin (Leinstermen), and claimed that he had ruled in **Tara**.

There was no small amount of confusion concerning his floruit. The annals and sagas regard his reign as having belonged to the 2rd century AD, but this contradicts the more reliable genealogical sources, whose evidence would place him two hundred years later. His ambit at least is historical, for it is clear that the Leinstermen held Tara for some time before the rise of the Connachta (the race of **Conn Céadchathach**) in the 4th-5th century. He is referred to in literature dating from the late 6th or early 7th century as a kindly, generous and noble leader. The genealogists claimed that he ruled Tara for thirty years, and that he had the same number of sons, but only ten of these were given prominence. A fictional document, styled 'the Testimony of Cathaoir Mór', seems to have been in existence by the 8th century. It describes the grants of wealth and privilege bequeathed by Cathaoir to the various Leinster septs. Listed are his sons from whom the leading septs traced their descent, and the major royal sites of the Leinstermen are enumerated, significantly including Tara. A mediaeval prose commentary on the Testimony states that 'Cathaoir Mór was for three years in the kingship of Ireland' and that he was defeated and slain at the battle of Magh Agha (near Teltown in Co Meath) by Conn Céadchathach.

It may well be that a title 'Cathaoir' was borne by the last Leinster king of Tara, although the battle between himself and Conn was an invention and did not become well established in tradition. One late version portrays Conn as a child and has his people already in possession of the citadel. We read that Conn was playing hurley at Cruachain (Rathcroghan, Co Roscommon) when a **druid** told him that Tara was being sacked by Cathaoir. The youngster gathered together a band of soldiers and set out to defeat the Leinstermen. No full account of these matters survives from the Leinster viewpoint, but there is an echo of such in the mentions of how Cathaoir fell in the battle of Magh Agha at the hands of the Luaighne. This sept, mercenaries to the Connachta, were portrayed as bitter enemies of the Leinstermen in the early accounts of the hero **Fionn mac Cumhaill**.

The mediaeval Dinnsheanchas (**Place-lore**) has several mentions of Cathaoir. One story describes him celebrating the feast of Tara, and when the assembled host was inebriated a warrior called Garman stole the queen's golden coronet. He was pursued from Tara by Cathaoir's men and, after a long chase, seized at the mouth of the river Slaney and drowned there - hence, we are quite speculatively told, that place was known as Loch Garman (i.e. Wexford). Another story tells of how Cathaoir dreamed that a beautiful lady appeared to him. She was pregnant for a long time and then gave birth to a son. Cathaoir next dreamed that he saw nearby a fragrant tree which gave all kinds of fruit and from which most pleasant music came. On awakening, Cathaoir's druid, Brí mac Baircheadha, interpreted the dream for him. The lady was the Sláine (river Slaney), her son was the harbour of Loch Garman, and the great tree was Cathaoir himself. Its music was his 'noble eloquence when appeasing a multitude' and the wind which shook down its fruit was his great generosity. Yet another story has the place being named from the death there of Cathaoir's swineherd, while Cathaoir himself and his ten sons were said to have been buried at Tulach Eoghain (near Morett in Co Laois). Though these references are quite contrived, they illustrate how, in the mediaeval mind, Cathaoir was regarded as synonymous with the ancient culture of Leinster.

T F O'Rahilly (1946), 268, 549; M A O'Brien (1962), 121, 535; Kuno Meyer (1914), 14-6; Myles Dillon (1962), 148-78; R A S Macalister (1956), 330-1; Whitley Stokes in *Irische Texte 3*, 370-1; Edward Gwynn (1913), 168-83, 508-10 and (1924), 172-5, 282-7, 450-1; Denis Murphy (1896), 57-8; L P Ó Caithnia (1984), 97-8.

CATHBHADH Mythical warrior-druid in the **Ulster Cycle**. His name would have meant 'battle-slayer' originally.

According to one version of the birth of king **Conchobhar mac Neasa**, Cathbhadh slew the twelve tutors of the girl Neas. She then went armed in search of the killer, whose identity was unknown to her, and was surprised by Cathbhadh while bathing. He forced her to become his wife and brought her with him to his rath in the district of Ros (in south Co Armagh), where Conchobhar was born. Other accounts do not mention his warrior-prowess, but instead concentrate on his magical and prophetic powers. He is said to have taught his magical skills to the noble youths in Conchobhar's warrior-academy at Eamhain Mhacha, and to have thus given instruction to **Cú Chulainn**. He announced what was the most auspicious day to first take arms, which knowledge was quickly put to effect by Cú Chulainn; and he also specified to Conchobhar's son, **Cormac Conn Loingeas**, which magical injunctions (see **'geis'**) that prince should abide by in his life. Cathbhadh's status was high in the royal court. For instance, there was a prohibition on the Ulstermen to speak before the king spoke at an assembly, but the king himself was prohibited from speaking until Cathbhadh had his say.

His function of advisor to Conchobhar is evidenced in the story of **Deirdre**, for when that lady was born he foretold that she would bring disaster to the Ulstermen. He is referred to as the maternal grandfather of Deirdre's lover Naoise and his two brothers, but was tricked into supporting Conchobhar in the king's treachery against them. When they were fighting invincibly against Conchobhar's men who attacked them in violation of guarantees, the king asked Cathbhadh to restrain them, saying that he feared they would destroy Ulster. He gave a solemn promise that if they were restrained he would not harm them. Cathbhadh accordingly used his magic to bring a great surge of sea under their feet on the plain, and so they were seized and done to death on Conchobhar's orders. One account states that Cathbhadh cursed Conchobhar after that treachery, declaring that none of his progeny would rule at Eamhain Mhacha; but the Cycle in general has him remaining loyal to Conchobhar. His advice is always mentioned as being farsighted and wise. For instance, when the cattle-raid of Cooley was over and the king thirsted for revenge against Connacht, he was advised against further warring by the druid. Cathbhadh also tried to restrain Cú Chulainn (q.v.) from going to his death when a trap had been set for him by hostile magicians.

C J Guyonvarc'h in *Ogam 12*, 197, 449-50; Kuno Meyer in *Revue Celtique 6*, 173-82; Whitley Stokes in *Ériu 4*, 22-3; Cecile O'Rahilly (1976), 19-20, 105; J C Watson (1941), 4-16; Vernam Hull (1949), 43-6; Whitley Stokes in *Irische Texte 2*, 122, 143, 146-52; Edmund Hogan (1892), 2-13; Cormac Ó Cadhlaigh (1956), 467.

CÉADACH Fictional character in the **Fianna Cycle**.

The late mediaeval literature has several mentions of a warrior called Céadach, variously claimed to have been a son of the Scandinavian king, the Saracen king, and the king of Thule. There does not seem to have been any specific narrative of him in existence at that time, and the mentions were simply a way of stressing how the fame of the Fianna was so great that foreign princes came to join it. However, it is virtually certain that a romance-story concerning him was composed in the 16th or 17th century, although no manuscript of that text survives. Versions of the story have been collected from folklore all over Ireland and western Scotland in the last two centuries, which suggests that manuscripts of it were once quite common. The story tells of how Céadach was the son of a foreign king and that he joined the Fianna and became a close confidant of the troop's leader, **Fionn mac Cumhaill**. He and another young man, usually called Lon Dubh, were in love with the same girl. She chose Céadach, and Lon Dubh sought as recompence the right to strike one undefended blow on his rival. Soon afterwards, Fionn was embarking on an overseas adventure, and he took the two young warriors with him. Céadach showed great valour on the expedition, but on their return home Lon Dubh struck the promised blow and in the ensuing struggle both young men were killed. Fionn had arranged with Céadach's sweetheart that he would raise a black sail if her lover were dead, but he raised a white sail instead. When she saw the dead body she was disconsolate, but, noticing two birds magically revive a third, she copied their actions and brought Céadach to life again.

The composer of this story clearly had a good imagination, and it is difficult to trace any possible sources used by him, apart from some version of the mediaeval romance of Tristan and Isolde, which is clearly echoed by the sails motif.

Alan Bruford (1969), 123-33, 258-9; Dáithí Ó hÓgáin (1988), 257-8, 341.

CEALLACH Cleric of the mid-6th century, bishop of Cill Alaidh (Killala, Co Mayo).

Memory of his career seems to have survived orally until mediaeval times in his native area of Uí Fiachrach Muaidhe (in east Mayo). He was the son of the Connacht king **Eoghan Béal**, who died in the year 543 and was succeeded by his brother Ailill Ionbhanna. It is apparent that this Ailill contended with Ceallach for the kingship and deprived him of it, but there is no direct evidence regarding this. A biography of Ceallach written in the 12th century purports to give details of these events, but it creates a great distortion by substituting for Ailill the celebrated Connacht king **Guaire**, who in fact lived a century later.

The text of this story, entitled *Caithréim Cellaig*, describes how before he died Eoghan Béal instructed his followers to instal Ceallach as king in his place, as his other son Muireadhach was too young. Ceallach was a monk at the monastery of St **Ciarán at Clonmacnoise**, and the men of Uí Fiachrach Muaidhe persuaded him to leave that monastery and to become king of Connacht. Ciarán was displeased at this, and cursed Ceallach for abandoning his vocation. The king of the southern Uí Fiachrach - here called Guaire - plotted to depose Ceallach and eventually drove him in flight from his territory. Ceallach returned to Ciarán's monastery and resumed the clerical life there, sending what remained of his followers to join his young brother Muireadhach.

The fame of Ceallach's holiness spread, and he was appointed bishop of Killala. He was extremely popular, a great host and patron of the arts. Once, when he approached near to a fortress of Guaire, he did not go to meet the king. Guaire sent an invitation to him, and Ceallach promised to come as soon as his Sunday observances were completed. Guaire's messenger, however, misrepresented his reply as a refusal and, as a result, Guaire grew angry and ordered the bishop to leave his territory. Ceallach went to an island on Loch Claon (a pseudonym for Lough Conn in Co Mayo) and spent Lent there, accompanied by four young clerics. Meanwhile, Guaire became aware the the youth Muireadhach was frequently visiting Ceallach there and grew frightened that Ceallach would advise his young brother to make a bid for the kingship. Guaire's own advisers fed his fear, and on their instructions he bribed Ceallach's four clerical companions to murder him. This they did, by driving their spear-points into him and rending him with their swords. His body was left to the carrion-crows and wild beasts, but all of these which consumed his flesh and blood died as a result.

When Muireadhach came to the island and found his brother missing he set out in search of him. A fierce wolf came from the woods and slew nine of Muireadhach's men, whereupon Muireadhach attacked and slew the wolf. Thus he got the nickname Cú Choingeilt ('consuming hound') from his companions. Finding Ceallach's body, he realised what had happened and swore vengeance. He cursed a graveyard where burial was refused to the body, for fear of Guaire, and it was struck by lightning and destroyed. Two wild stags came drawing a hearse and, when the corpse was put into the hearse, they brought it to a cemetery in the Eisreacha (an area near Killala in Co Mayo). After the burial, the stags used to plough for the local people by day and come to lick the grave of holy Ceallach in the evening.

Cú Choingeilt collected a force of men and made several alliances, including that of the high-king at Tara. On his return to Connacht, he met a swineherd guarding pigs which belonged to the four murderers of Ceallach. The swineherd welcomed him, and brought him disguised as a servant to the fortress of the four. Noticing that all were becoming drunk inside, he sent the swineherd to call his men. They came and seized the four murderers - the ex-clerics Maol Chróin, Maol Dalua, Maol Seanaigh, and Maol Deoraidh. Cú Choingeilt had the four taken out next morning, and had them impaled, dismembered, and gibbetted. Following this savage revenge, conflict broke out between Cú Choingeilt and Guaire, the latter being forced to sue for terms. Guaire gave his daughter Geilghéis in marriage to Cú Choingeilt, but he also plotted treachery. Using the unwitting St Ciarán as a mediator, he invited his young rival to his fortress, promising to cede the kingship of Connacht to him. When he got Cú Choingeilt in his power, however, he wasted no time in having him slain.

Kathleen Mulchrone (1933); J F Kenney (1929), 456-7; Tomás Ó Concheanainn in *Éigse 11*, 35-8.

CEALTCHAIR Fictional warrior of Ulster. The name, meaning 'mantel' or 'concealment', was a metaphorical term for a spear.

He is said to have been son of an otherwise unknown character called Uitheachar, and to have resided at Dún Leathghlaise (Downpatrick, Co Down). Huge and ugly in appearance, he had large nose and ears and rough grey hair. Rugged also in manners, he fought alongside **Conchobhar mac Neasa** in all that king's major engagements and is mentioned as present in several dramatic scenes of the **Ulster Cycle**. Usually a background figure, one text from the 11th century focuses attention on him. We are told that his wife Brígh Bhreathach once went to the house of a very rich man of Ulster called Blái Briugha. There was an injunction (**'geis'**) on this Blái that he must sleep with a woman who came alone to his house, and so he slept with Brígh. Cealtchair heard of this, and he drove his spear through Blái as the latter was playing chess with Conchobhar. The spear stuck in the wall behind Blái, and a drop of blood from it fell on the chess-board near the enraged king. Fleeing Conchobhar's anger, Cealtchair went to the territory of the Déise (Decies, in east Munster), but a settlement was reached and he was allowed to return home. Conchobhar imposed on him as compensation for Blái's death that he must relieve the Ulstermen of the three worst misfortunes that should befall them.

Soon after, a Munster warrior called Conganchneas came to ravage Ulster as vengeance for the death of his brother **Cú Roí**. This Conganchneas (i.e. 'horny-skin') got his name from the fact that javelins and swords did not wound him but merely glanced off his skin. Cealtchair was sent by Conchobhar to rid the province of him. Encountering Conganchneas, Cealtchair beguiled him by offering his daughter Niamh to him as well as a massive dinner every evening. Niamh soon inveigled from Conganchneas the secret of how he might be killed. 'Red-hot iron-spits must be driven into my soles and through my shins,' he said. She told her father, and when Conganchneas was asleep Cealtchair drove the irons into him and then beheaded him. Cealtchair had the fallen warrior buried at the place of his démise and a cairn erected over him. The second misfortune which Cealtchair had to tackle was a vicious hound called 'the Brown Mouse', which every night devastated some dwelling in Ulster. It used to return to a cave in a certain valley and sleep there during the day. One morning, it found Cealtchair at the cave waiting for it. He thrust a hardened alder stick into the hound's mouth, and when its teeth locked on the stick he shoved his hand down its throat and tore its heart out. Exactly a year after that, three whelps were found at the cairn of Conganchneas. One of these became the hound of Mac Da Thó (see **Conall Cearnach**), a second was the hound of Culann the smith which **Cú Chulainn** killed, and the third was raised by Cealtchair. He called it Daolchú ('chafer-hound') because it was jet-black. This hound was ferocious to everyone except Cealtchair himself, and when he was away from home one day it escaped and began to devastate the province. This was therefore the third misfortune from which Cealtchair had to deliver Ulster. He went to the valley where the hound was and called it. It came and licked his feet, but he speared it through the heart. When he withdrew the spear and raised it, a drop of the hound's blood ran along it and fell on Cealtchair himself. It went right through him and killed him.

The source for this story is clearly the tradition regarding the death of Cú Roí (q.v.). Conganchneas is described as brother to that hero, and the narrative employs a folktale plot (see **Wonder**

Tales, Type 302) already used in the context of Cú Roí. From that folktale we have the motif of the secret betrayed by a giant's wife, and that of the external soul of the giant - here complicated by the extension of his personality onto hounds. These animals were no doubt suggested by the name of Cú Roí, and the influence of the slaying of a great hound by Cú Chulainn is also clear. The name Conganchneas is borrowed from the text of *Táin Bó Cuailgne* (see **Fear Diadh**), while the venomous drop of blood from a slain opponent is probably taken from accounts of the death of the tyrant **Balar**.

Cealtchair's spear, called the 'luin', was famous. We are told that, when it expected to be used, it had to be bathed in a cauldron of blood, for otherwise its shaft would burst into flame and it would go through its bearer. It was discovered by Cealtchair on the field of the great second battle of Moytirra (see **Mythological Cycle**), and after his death it passed into the possession of **Dubhthach Daol Uladh**. Dubhthach was himself slain by it, as was **Cúscraidh Meann Macha** later. It is apparent that the character of Cealtchair was originally invented around the motif of a fantastic spear. His weapon was called the 'luin Cheltchair', but this probably was originally the 'luin cheltchair' (meaning, 'flashing of spear'). An offshoot of the association of Cealtchair with spears is a reference to a great javelin-cast made at him by **Ceat mac Mághach**. This javelin entered his thigh and passed through his testicles, so that from that day forward he had no progeny.

Cecile O'Rahilly (1976), 107, 113, 301; Kuno Meyer (1906), 24-31, 43-5; Eleanor Knott (1936), 37-8; J C Watson (1941), 33; Rudolph Thurneysen (1935), 12-3; Cormac Ó Cadhlaigh (1956), 467.

CEAT MAC MÁGHACH Mythical Connacht champion who figures in several stories of the **Ulster Cycle**.

The name (earlier, Cet) is apparenly identical with the Gaulish name Cettos, both indicating endurance, which was probably an attribute of some antique Celtic deity. Both it and the patronymic (earlier, Magu) may have belonged to the native population of the western province before the Connachta sept took over (see **Ulster Cycle**). In view of Ceat's leading profile as a Connacht warrior, it is significant that the part he plays in the cattle-raid of Cooley is minimal, and this further suggests that his origins do not lie in the ambit of Ulster lore. The strong likelihood is that he was a figure of such celebrity in the early folklore of the western province as to be naturally included in an Ulster-Connacht conflict once that conflict became an accepted context for writers to situate their stories. In these stories, Ceat always plays the role of a hostile outsider, the greatest single warrior with whom the Ulstermen must contend.

According to one source, the mother of **Conall Cearnach** was a sister of Ceat, and when Ceat came to visit and saw the baby he knew that it would be a great slaughterer of Connachtmen. So he put his foot on the baby's neck, intending to kill it, but was prevented by the mother. Conall's neck was twisted ever after. Similarly, Ceat left his mark on several other leading Ulster warriors In his continual attacks and combats, he left Lámh Ghábhaidh with only one arm, knocked an eye out of the head of Eoghan mac Durthachta, cut the heel off Sál Cholgan, made the same warrior's son Meann dumb, wounded Muinreamhar mac Gheirginn so that his neck was continually swollen, wounded **Cúscraidh** in the throat so that he spoke ever after with a stammer, and rendered **Cealtchair** infertile with a cast of his javelin. He had thus a victory to boast of over the various great warriors of Ulster who were present at Mac Da Thó's feast, when he demanded the right as leading warrior to carve the pig. When Conall Cearnach (q.v.) entered, however, Ceat relinquished that privilege to him.

The literature represents Ceat as having been for a time at the court of the high-king **Eochaidh Feidhleach** and as having shared with Conall Cearnach the leadership of Eochaidh's army (see **Finn Eamhna**). When the conflict between Ulster and Connacht gathered momentum, however, his main function was raiding and plundering the northern province. He is described as 'a slaughterous hound' and 'a perpetually foraying enemy against the Ulstermen for as long as he lived'. In one of his daring raids he took the brain-ball of Meas Geaghra which was held as a trophy in Eamhain Mhacha; and it was with this that he delivered his most devastating blow of all. He waited the opportunity to shoot it from a sling at king **Conchobhar mac Neasa**, and it was as a result of this deadly shot that Conchobhar eventually died. Ceat followed up this triumph by slaying Conchobhar's son and successor, **Cormac Conn Loingeas**, and soon after made another deadly raid into Ulster. When he departed with the heads of thrice nine men, Conall Cearnach was sent after him. Snow had fallen, and Conall followed his track as far as Breifne (in the Cavan-Leitrim area), where he saw his chariot-horses outside a house. Reluctant to engage so fierce a warrior, Conall contented himself with placing as a token a wisp from one of the horse's manes on the front of Ceat's chariot. When Ceat found this he recognised Conall's work and went to seek him out. They met at Áth Cheit (i.e. 'Ceat's Ford' on the river Shannon) and fought so furiously that both fell. Conall rose again, badly wounded, but Ceat was dead.

Notwithstanding the indications that his origins lay in the oral lore of western septs in ancient times, the character of Ceat figures only in Ulster Cycle literature and is not known to the folklore of recent centuries.

T F O'Rahilly in *Ériu 13*, 166-7; Whitley Stokes in *Irische Texte 3*, 392-5, 404-7; Rudolf Thurneysen (1935); M E Dobbs in *Revue Celtique 43*, 284-7, 304-31; Kuno Meyer (1906), 2-21, 36-41, 45; P S Dinneen (1908) *2*, 200-9; Cormac Ó Cadhlaigh (1956), 468.

CEITHEARNACH CAOILRIABHACH (literally, 'Narrow-Striped Kern') Designation of the principal character in a humorous text composed around the year 1514.

We read that the chieftain Aodh Dubh Ó Domhnaill was feasting with his retainers in his dwelling at Béal Átha Seanaigh (Ballyshannon, Co Donegal) when a stranger appeared among them. His costume had narrow stripes on it, his boots let in the water, his mantle was old and tatty with a naked sword protruding from it behind, and in one hand he carried three javelins of charred hazel. Aodh Dubh asked who he was and received the answer: 'My use and wont is to be in Islay one day, another in Cantyre, a day in Man, a day in Rathlin, and yet another on Slievecarn - for I am a ranting rambling roving fellow!' He had passed by the doorman unnoticed, and he boasted that he could not be prevented from leaving whenever he wished. Furthermore, he insulted the musicians of Aodh Dubh, saying that their playing sounded worse than the devils wielding sledge-hammers in hell. He then himself took a harp and played, and so sweet and enchanting was the music that it would heal the sick and the wounded, and Aodh Dubh recognised that it was of the otherworld. However, the stranger continued with his saucy answers. 'One day I am sweet, another I am bitter!' he declared, and refused a fine suit of clothes proffered to him. Aodh Dubh had twenty footsoldiers within and twenty horsemen without to ensure that he could not depart, but the stranger passed out between them while they struck each other thinking that they were striking him. He gave an herb to the gatekeeper, telling him that if rubbed to the gums of the men killed in the tussle it would revive them. He instructed the gatekeeper to demand land and twenty cows from Aodh Dubh as payment for this service.

Just at that very time, Seán Mac Gearailt (i.e. Fitzgerald), son of the Earl of Desmond, was holding an assembly in his dwelling at Cnoc Áine (Knockainey, Co Limerick), and the kern dressed in striped clothes approached, announcing that he had come from Ó Domhnaill in the north. He was given a drink and fell asleep until the following morning, and when he arose Seán asked him to play music and show his learning, but the stranger failed dismally at both tasks. Being ridiculed, he took the book and harp and performed magnificently. Seán remarked that he was a man of truly sweet art, and received the reply: 'I am sweet one day, and sour another day!' In the afternoon, Seán took him walking around the hill, and the stranger described how he had seen long ago there great hunts by **Fionn mac Cumhaill** and his men. Engrossed in this account, Seán turned to look at him, but found that the visitor had disappeared in the twinkling of an eye.

In Leinster, the head of the bardic Mac Eochaidh family, was laid up with a broken leg for a long time, and all the best twelve physicians of his province had failed to cure him. To him the narrow-striped kern next appeared, claiming to be a medical student and saying that if Mac Eochaidh abandoned his stinginess and churlishness he would be healed. The poet promised this, and his visitor then applied an herb to his leg. Immediately, Mac Eochaidh leaped up and began to run so swiftly that his twelve physicians could neither restrain or catch him. Then the kern warned the poet to remain generous, or else he would come to him and break the two legs so badly that they could never again be healed. In a flush of gratitude, Mac Eochaidh offered the kern three hundred each of horses, cows, sheep, and pigs, as well as his daughter in marriage. A great feast was prepared for the kern, but he raced away from them faster than a hare.

He ran so swiftly that he reached Sligo in an instant. The chieftain of that area, Ó Conchubhair, was preparing to go on a campaign against Munster on account of a dispute between two hags over the ownership of a basket. One of the hags, from Munster, had taken the basket from the Connacht one, and Ó Conchubhair was determined to avenge this insult to his province. The kern enlisted in his force, and the Connachtmen took great prey in Munster - including two cows and a hornless bull from the southern hag as compensation for her Connacht rival. The kern took his bow and arrow, and alternately repelled the Munster pursuers and drove the prey, ensuring that the raiders crossed the river Shannon safely. On their return home, Ó Conchubhair drank a draught without offering one to the kern, and the latter took his leave of him. The chieftain tried to persuade him to stay and offered him his choice of reward, but in an instant the kern had disappeared.

He next visited Tadhg Ó Ceallaigh, and offered to perform tricks for the company at the residence of that chieftain. His first trick was to lay three rushes on his palm and to blow away the middle one only, which he did by holding the other two with his finger-tips. One of Tadhg's men protested that he could also do this, but when he tried his fingers got magically caught in the palm. The kern, having won the bet, cured him with an herb, and then said that he had another trick - he could wag one ear while the other stood still. He did this by wagging one ear with his hand. When the same retainer of Tadhg tried to do it with his own ear, it came clean away from his head, and he again had to be cured by the kern. Then the latter took a thread of silk from his bag and threw one end of it into the air. It stuck in a cloud; and he further took from his luggage a hare, a beagle, a servant-boy and a pretty girl, who all climbed up the thread into that cloud. Commotion was heard from the cloud above, and the kern remarked that harm was being done. He pulled in the thread, and it transpired that the beagle had killed the hare and the boy had gone 'between the two legs of the lady'. The kern cut the boy's head off with a sword-stroke, but Tadhg protested at this, and he resuscitated the boy, putting the head on backwards. Again Tadhg protested, and he turned the head around to its proper position, but then immediately disappeared.

The kern next appeared at the house of Mac Murchadha Caomhánach, styled 'king of Leinster', where he announced himself as the 'giolla deacair' ('difficult servant'). He criticised the harpers of that chieftain, and they seized their swords to kill him. All of their blows fell on their own heads, however, and on seeing this slaughter the nobles ordered that the kern be seized and hanged. He was accordingly taken to the gallows and despatched, but on the executioners' return to the house they found him waiting for them there alive. They realised to their consternation that they had hanged the closest confidant of Mac Murchadha Caomhánach, but the kern restored to life him and the harpists who had been killed in the earlier melée. The chieftain turned to check if all were alive, and when he looked back again the kern had gone. He went to Cill Scíre (Kilskeer, Co Meath) to the house of Seán Ó Domhnalláin, where he was given a meal of thick milk and wild apples. He departed unexpectedly from there also, and no tidings of him were ever found after.

16. CEITHEARNACH CAOILRIABHACH
Knave in 16th-century playing-cards, portrayed as a foot-soldier.

Some later manuscripts state that the kern was **Manannán** in disguise 'because he used to be thus visiting everybody as a trickster', but this is merely a rationalisation of the story based on such appearances of Manannán in other accounts. The author seems to have been an Ulsterman, for he has Mac Eochaidh praise the people of that province and say that the kern came from there. It is clear that he made a compilation of trickster material based on lore of travelling **poets** and gleemen. The Ceithearnach Caoilriabhach has the attributes of such men, including the characteristic saucy and antithetical answers. It is very likely that the author himself was one of them. The noblemen mentioned, being his contemporaries, must have been among his hosts when he went on tour. The specific imagery of the kern would have been suggested to the author by card-playing, which was extremely popular in 16th-century Ireland. The knave in a suit of cards was represented as both a trickster and a soldier (i.e. kern), and was portrayed with striped trousers. It therefore appears that the noblemen who occur in the text enjoyed playing at cards, and that the author was teasing them on this account.

The text was very popular in manuscripts, and no doubt it passed into popular lore. In recent generations good oral versions of it have only been collected in Scotland, but some of the episodes have been collected in connection with other characters from the folklore of Ulster.

S H O'Grady (1898) *1*, xii-xiii, 276-89; Alan Bruford (1969), 153-4, 253; IFC 169:387-8

CEITHEARN MAC FIONNTAIN Fictional character in mediaeval Irish literature.

He first appears in the **Ulster Cycle** as one of twelve leading champions of that province. His name Ceithearn (earlier, Cethern) meant 'soldier' or 'kern', and he was apparently invented as a character-type to add to the drama of the great cattle-raid of Cooley. In that text he comes alone to attack the army of queen **Meadhbh**, taking the place of the hero **Cú Chulainn** who is worn out by wounds and fatigue. He himself suffers a grievous wound, but resumes the fight and is slaughtered in the midst of the foe. His father Fionntan then comes to avenge him.

Because the name given to his father corresponded to that of the famous seer **Fionntan**, Ceithearn appears in a slightly later text as the tutor of another great hero **Fionn mac Cumhaill**. We read that, after the young Fionn got the gift of wisdom from tasting the salmon of the Boyne, he went to Ceithearn to receive instruction from him in the craft of poetry. Here Ceithearn is described as a sage, and his role is no doubt due to the associations of his patronymic.

Ernst Windisch in *Irische Texte 2.1*, 174; Cecile O'Rahilly (1976), 96-101; Kuno Meyer in *Revue Celtique 5*, 202.

CÉITINN, SEATHRÚN (c1580-1650) Priest, poet, theologian and historian, his name in anglicised form is Geoffrey Keating. Born in Burgess, near Cahir in Co Tipperary, he was educated at Bordeaux and Salamanca and returned to Ireland as a priest in or about the year 1610.

It is said that he delivered a sermon critical of the life being led by a certain powerful lady, and that she complained him to the English President of Munster, Sir James Perrot, after which he was proclaimed an outlaw. Betaking himself to the Glen of Aherlow, he set about collecting manuscript material for his most celebrated work, a history of Ireland. Folklore claims that he travelled much of the country in pursuance of this task, which he finished in 1634. The history was entitled *Foras Feasa ar Éirinn*. It circulated widely in manuscript form and in the succeeding centuries was a basic source of information for poets, scholars, and antiquarians.

He was parish priest of Cappoquin, Co Waterford, in 1634, and it is reported that he died at a castle belonging to the Butler family at Reahill, near to his birthplace. One tradition, however, had it that Céitinn was murdered by a Cromwellian soldier in Clonmel. A Kerry folk account is in general accord with this, claiming that he was saying Mass in a lonely place when his congregation noticed soldiers approaching. When they told this to the priest, he instructed everybody to stay where they were, for if they ran they might be shot. He continued with the Mass then, but when the soldiers came they could see neither priest nor congregation there. Three days later, however, Seathrun Ceitinn was caught and decapitated. This legend is of a type usually told of fugitive priests in 17th and 18th-century Ireland, according to which the priest is saying Mass at a rock in the wilderness for fear of arrest. A group of soldiers come to the spot but cannot see him. However, it is often said that one of the soldiers, who was baptised a Roman Catholic, has the power to see the priest, who is accordingly arrested and put to death.

Eoin Mac Giolla Eáin (1900), 3-7; Brian Ó Cuív in *Éigse 9*, 263-9; Robin Flower in *Béaloideas 2*, 204; Dáithí Ó hÓgáin (1985), 206-8.

[*Foras Feasa ar Éirinn*] David Comyn (1902) - Vol 1 and P S Dinneen (1908-1914) - Vols 2-4.

CESSAIR Fictional lady, leader of the imagined first ever settlement in Ireland.

The mediaeval writers of pseudo-history claimed that she was a grand-daughter of the Biblical Noah and that she came to Ireland to escape the Deluge. 'She thought it probable that a place where people had never come before, and where no evil or sin had been committed, and which was free from the world's reptiles and monsters, that place would be free from the flood.' She arrived forty days before the Deluge, but two of her three ships were wrecked and only one came ashore at Corca Dhuibhne (the Dingle Peninsula in Co Kerry). The total crew of that ship was fifty women and three men. Cessair's father, Bith son of Noah, was one of these, as well as Ladra the pilot, and the celebrated **Fionntan**. They divided the women among them, with Cessair being part of Fionntan's share. The other two men soon died and, being left alone with all the women, Fionntan felt inadequate and fled from them. Cessair died from a broken heart on account of his absence, and the other women did not long survive her. Fionntan (q.v.) alone remained.

A variant account states that Noah had refused entry into his Ark to these three men because he considered them robbers, and that Cessair had offered to bring them to safety if they accepted her leadership. She consulted an idol, which directed them to travel to Ireland. Cessair was also given an agricultural role, it being claimed that she brought into Ireland the first sheep ever to be in the country. The mediaeval historians had a further tradition that, whereas Cessair and her group were the first settlers in Ireland, three fishermen from Spain had earlier discovered the country, having been blown hither by a gale. They returned to Spain to collect their wives, but the Deluge overtook them and drowned them at Tuagh Inbhir (the estuary of the river Bann) before they could land.

R A S Macalister (1939), 166-252; H A de Jubainville (1903), 36-42; Alwyn Rees / Brinley Rees (1961), 113-5.

CHRIST, JESUS (Irish, Íosa Críost) In addition to the canonical texts of the New Testament, many accounts of Jesus and of his companions were current throughout Europe in apocryphal works in Latin and Greek. These works were very popular in mediaeval Irish Christianity, and many of them were translated into Irish. The Church in Ireland, indeed, was more tolerant of the apocryphal literature than it was in other countries, and as a result the Irish sources are very important to a study of this whole phenomenon of unapproved accounts of Christ. Particularly important in early Irish devotional literature were versions of the works known as 'the Gospel according to the Hebrews', 'the Book of James' and 'the Gospel of Thomas' which gave fanciful descriptions of Jesus' youth, and 'the Gospel of Nicodemus' which told of Jesus' passion, death, and harrowing of hell.

17. CHRIST, JESUS *The arrest of Jesus, from the Book of Kells.*

It was, of course, considered in Ireland that Jesus had been born in mid-winter, with all the attendant harshness of climate at that time of year. Thus we read of several marvels which occurred at his birth, such as grapes ripening, palm-trees flowering, wheat sprouting, lights appearing in temples, and babies speaking in their mothers' wombs. The sun shone in Bethlehem at midnight, and all those who were sick or afflicted were healed immediately in that hour. More obviously derived from Continental apocrypha are accounts of a great fragrance which filled the cave in which the Christ-child was born, and how he conversed with the three wise men who came with beautiful presents for him. He soon showed his great wisdom and miraculous power. As a little boy, he shaped some clay into the form of birds and, when an over-pious man upbraided him for doing this on the Sabbath, he clapped his hands and the clay-images became alive and flew away to heaven. When sent to school, he showed that he knew more than the master, and other boys who tormented him were miraculously struck down but were revived by himself. The cross on which Christ was crucified, we read, was made from four different timbers - cedar, cypress, pine, and beech.

The Gospel of Nicodemus, written in Greek in the 4th century AD, describes how, after the crucifixion, the traitor Judas was going to hang himself, fearful of the prophecy that the dead Christ would rise again. Judas' wife, who was roasting a cock at the time, tried to reassure him by stating that this would no more happen than the dead cock would crow. Whereupon the cock flapped its wings and crowed three times. Versions of this in mediaeval Irish literature have the woman as Judas' mother or sister rather than his wife, and have Judas himself boasting that the cock will not crow. The motif became very popular in post-mediaeval Irish iconography, the cook and cooking-pot being on many tombstones and at the foot of little wooden crosses carried by penitents. Oral versions of the legend were current throughout Ireland. According to these, the soldiers who had crucified Jesus were cooking a cock when one of them remarked that it was rumoured that the executed man would come back to life again. Another soldier denied this by reference to the cock, whereupon the dead bird arose from the cauldron, flapped its wings and cried out 'mac na hóighe slán' ('the son of the virgin is safe'). Ever since, it is claimed, cocks say this when they crow. These Irish folk versions have assimilated the situation to the canonical account of the cock crowing to signal Peter's denial of Christ, an account on which the original apocryphal story was itself probably based.

Folklore tends to reflect philosophical ideas in its own physical way. Thus the Christian theory of history, which has the birth of Jesus ushering in a new era, gives rise in European folklore generally to the notion that the physical and cultural environment was reshaped in many ways during the life of the Saviour. This is very much the case in Ireland also. We are told that Christ was once a fugitive and that the spider covered him with its web so that his enemies could not see him. This insect is thus regarded as blessed. The chafer beetle, however, is cursed, because it betrayed Christ. Some men were at work sowing corn when Christ passed by, and he told them that if questioned by his pursuers they should not lie. The corn grew up overnight, and therefore when the search-party arrived next day the sowers told them that the fugitive had passed by when they were sowing. The soldiers were about to abandon their pursuit, but a chafer treacherously cried out 'yesterday!' It is also said that a pig rooted clay over Christ to conceal him, but a hen scraped it away, and that as a result hens lay eggs painfully while sows bear their young with ease. The elder-tree once refused to shelter Christ, but the ivy did so, hence the elder is the last tree to bear leaves while the ivy is evergreen. In a similar vein, the donkey got the cross on its back because it carried Christ on his triumphant entry to Jerusalem, and the robin got its red breast when it tried to remove a thorn or wipe the blood from the brow of the dying Saviour.

18. CHRIST, JESUS *Holy well at Kildare, one of many such sites where people congregated to pray.*

In human terms also, it is regarded as the time of beginnings. For instance, the Virgin Mary once remarked to her little son Jesus that he was her 'seven loves', and the child replied that she had left a sad inheritance to mothers, for ever after they would love their children so much as to cause heartbreak to themselves. A legend which has been international since mediaeval times tells of how, when Mary was pregnant, she asked her husband Joseph to fetch some fruit from a nearby tree. Joseph replied peevishly that she should ask the father of her child to do that for her, whereupon the tree bent down of its own accord so that she could get the fruit. Ever since, pregnant women long for fruit while old men get jealous of their young wives. There is an element of humour in such lore, which does not however preclude piety. Another international story current in Ireland tells of how Jesus and Mary once met a blind man, and Mary privately asked Jesus to give him his sight. Jesus remarked that that might not be a good idea, because the man's wife was misbehaving with another man. Mary then asked that the wife be given an excuse also. So, when the cure was effected and the man saw what was happening, his wife remarked: 'If I was not fooling you, these people would not have taken pity on you and would not have given your sight to you!' Ever since, we are told, women have an excuse on the tip of their tongues.

An international story which was very popular in Ireland told of how Christ pointed out a mistake made by his leading apostle, St Peter (see **Religious Tales**, Type 774K). Less popular in oral tradition, though quite influential in the literature, was a story of how Christ miraculously caused a coin to be retrieved from the belly of a fish (see **Wonder Tales**, Type 736A). This motif, popular throughout the Christian world, occurs in fact in the Gospel of Matthew (17:26). One of the best-known religious legends in Irish folklore has an even older source. This tells of how the child Jesus and his mother once sought lodgings at a house where a kind man was married to a high-handed woman. The wife curtly refused to allow them in, but the man told them that they could sleep in an outhouse. During the night, the man was severely smitten with a pain in his side, and his wife in desperation went to Jesus and Mary for help. Jesus told his mother to place her palm on the afflicted part, and to recite the following prayer: 'A gentle man had a rude wife who put Jesus Christ sleeping in the straw, Mary's palm to the wound, in the name of the Father and the Son and the Holy Ghost!' The man was healed immediately, and so this prayer, called 'ortha an ghreama' ('the charm-prayer for the stitch') was commonly recited to heal such an ailment. Similar stories were current in Hungary and Italy, and there can be little doubt but that these are survivals of a tradition once common in Europe. The ultimate source, in fact, seems to be a pre-Christian Egyptian story of how a rich woman refused shelter to the goddess Isis. When the woman's young son was stung by a serpent, Isis took pity on him and healed him with an incantation.

Popular piety in traditional Ireland was of such an immediate nature that there were folk prayers for almost all situations and to counteract many common ailments. The greatest devotion, however, centred on the passion and crucifixion of Jesus and on the sorrow of his mother. Many variants of a heartrending song described a conversation between the dying Christ and his mother as she stood at the foot of the Cross.

[Irish versions of apocryphal works] Edmund Hogan (1895), 38-85; James Carney (1964); Brian Ó Cuív in *Éigse 15*, 93-102; Robert Atkinson (1887); Gearóid Mac Niocaill in *Éigse 8*, 76-7; Cainneach Ó Maonaigh (1944); Áine Ní Chróinín (1952); Maoghnas Ó Domhnaill (1940); Martin McNamara (1975), 37-125.

[Folklore] Seán Ó Súilleabháin (1942), 548-51 and (1951), 3-31, 304-7; Anne O'Connor in *Sinsear 2*, 34-42; Pádraig Ó Héalaí in *Léachtaí Cholm Cille 14*, 151-72 and in *An Sagart* 1-2/1979.

[Prayers] Pádraig Ó Siochfhradha (1932), 360-404; Diarmuid Ó Laoghaire (1975).

[Origin of stitch-legend] Tekla Domotor in *Arv 28*, 21-35.

[Virgin Mary] Angela Partridge (1983); Peter O'Dwyer (1988).

CIAN MAC MAOLMHUAIDHE (c960 - 1015) Son of the king of Munster. His father Maolmhuaidh was slain in battle against **Brian Boru** in the year 977 AD, but he himself made peace with Brian and married his daughter Sadhbh. He fought on Brian's side at the battle of Clontarf, but was afterwards slain in the struggle for the kingship of Munster which followed on Brian's death.

He is the subject of a romance composed in the 15th century, entitled *Leigheas Coise Chéin* (the Healing of Cian's Leg). According to this, the stewards of Brian Boru went to collect rent in west Munster, and when they came to the house of Ó Cronagáin of Coireall (an unidentified place), that man was not at home. The wife of Ó Cronagáin, however, refused the rent to them. Hearing this, Brian in anger despoiled the land of Ó Cronagáin, but he encountered the culprit's wife, and she insisted that their overlord was Cian and that he had never sought rent from them. Impressed by her speech, Brian returned her greyhound and sheep to her, and promised to make restitution to her husband for the damage which had been done to him if he reported to the royal fortress of Ceann Cora (Kincora, Co Clare). Soon after, Ó Cronagáin set out for Brian's court, and on the way he caught a greyhound which was half-white and half-green. Brian welcomed him, and Ó Cronagáin asked for a set of beagles which the high-king had received as a gift from the king of France. This was granted to him and, foregoing the promised compensation, he went off towards home on the following day. At Sliabh Luachra (east of Killarney), his hounds coursed a hare, and the hare jumped into his bosom and became a beautiful young woman. She brought Ó Cronagáin to an otherworld dwelling and, at his request, slept with him that night. In the morning she went with him to his home at Coireall, and when they arrived there they found that his wife had gone away.

For three years the otherworld woman stayed with Ó Cronagáin, and at the end of that time she persuaded him to entertain Brian Boru there. Cian also was invited and, when he saw the woman, he fell completely in love with her. She rejected his advances, whereupon Cian knocked her down, but she was immediately changed into a mare and raced from the house. Cian tried to restrain her, but she kicked him, breaking his leg. Next day, Cian was brought to his own home, but his physicians failed to heal the leg. On the exact same day at the end of a year, he was alone in bed while his household was at Mass. A stranger came to him, announcing that he was his nephew and that he had heard Mass at Réamas na Ríogh (Rheims in France) that very day. He further said that he had once had a sweetheart in an otherworld dwelling at Cnoc Rafann (Knockgraffon in south Tipperary). He had slighted her, however, and she had laid conditions (**'geis'**) on him to leave Ireland. In France he had procured a foreign princess as wife for the French king and had himself married a daughter of the German Emperor. She bore him three sons, but was taken from him by a warrior who overcame him and left him bound for a year. After his release, he had accidentally wounded himself with his own spear. A young princess of Orkney had healed him with a special poultice, and he now applied that same poultice to Cian's leg and cured it immediately.

The nephew called himself Macaomh an Fhágáin ('the Vagrant Youth'). Cian wished to know more of his adventures, and the Macaomh explained that he had had affairs with other women besides his wife, and by the Orkney princess he had a son who called himself Macaomh an Uaignis ('the Solitary Youth'). He met with this son on the search for his wife, and eventually they found her. His other three sons had refused to accept the pre-eminence of the Solitary Youth, and thus the Vagrant had to depart without delay in order to settle matters between them. Thus ended the account given to Cian by his adventurous visitor.

This story is found in a mere two manuscripts. It is a loose and ill-contructed text, but better manuscripts of it must have existed, and the story became popular in folklore, especially in Gaelic Scotland. Oral versions give an explanation for the disappearance of Ó Cronagáin's otherworld wife which seems to have been a vital part of the narrative in the lost manuscripts. She had, we are told, threatened to leave him if he ever reminded her of how she had been a hare at the mercy of his dogs. This motif is reminiscent of the folk legend of the O'Briens of Inchiquin (see **Fairies**), from which it was probably borrowed. The influence of literary stories of **Cú Roí** is evident from the motif of binding a vanquished rival in love, from the designation 'man of the grey cloak' for one of the Vagrant's associates, and also from his speedy travel abroad. However, the specific reference to mystical travel between Rheims and Ireland seems to be derived from the lore of bilocation of saints.

J H Todd (1867), cxl, cxcii-cxciv, 212-5; S H O'Grady (1898) *1*, 296-305; Alan Bruford (1969), 134-6, 144, 262.

CIARÁN of Cluain Saint who died c550 AD, founder of the great monastery of Cluain Mhac Nóis (Clonmacnoise, Co Offaly). This monastery, in the 7th and 8th centuries, claimed ecclesiastical precedence over most of Connacht and Munster, as

19. CIARÁN OF CLUAIN *Remains of monastery at Clonmacnoise.*

well as a large part of Leinster. The name, as in the case of his older namesake **Ciarán of Saighir**, is anglicised as Kieran.

His biography was written at Clonmacnoise in or about the 9th century, and versions of it survive in both Latin and Irish. We read that he was son of a carpenter called Beoán of the Dál nAraidhe sept (in Antrim and Down) and of Darerca, a woman of the Ciarraighe sept (in Co Kerry), and that even before his birth there were signs of his future greatness. His coming was, it was claimed, prophesied by the three major saints of Ireland, **Patrick**, **Brighid**, and **Colm Cille**. When Darerca was pregnant with him, the high-king's druid announced that the chariot in which she travelled resounded as it did under one destined for **kingship**. His youth is also much dramatised. The first miracle performed by him was the restoration to life of a dead horse belonging to the son of the high-king and, to give him the profile of a young hero par excellence, he was described as slaying a savage hound which attacked him, as **Cú Chulainn** had done. He was sent by his parents to herd cattle, and while engaged at this work a fox befriended him and carried about his psalter for him. The fox, however, began to eat the book and, while doing so, was set upon by hounds. He had no choice but to race for safety into Ciarán's cowl, and thus both book and fox were saved.

One day, he insisted on joining his mother in dyeing cloth, and did his task so well that the cloth turned all it touched into its own colour. Having performed several other miracles, he went to the monastery of St Finnian at Cluain Ard (Clonard, Co Meath). His mother refused him permission to take a cow from the herd with him, but he blessed a brown cow and it followed him. This was the celebrated 'odhar Chiaráin' ('dun one of Ciarán') which used to give enough milk for all the monastery's needs. While studying at Clonard, a stag used to come and hold his book on its antlers while he read. Once, when a girl fell in love with him, Ciarán persuaded her to become a nun by saying that if she offered her maidenhood to God she would be united with himself in a true sense. Ciarán became very famous as a sympathetic saint, ransoming slaves and befriending the poor with special fervour. He also had a marked agricultural function, and several of his miracles are concerned with reaping and milling, ensuring copious harvests and plenty of food.

We read that he decided to found his monastery at Clonmacnoise on account of the beauty of the place. He was assisted in the building by

Diarmaid mac Cearrbheoil, and as a reward he promised Diarmaid that he would be high-king of Ireland. When this came to pass, the two maintained their friendship, and Ciarán became the confessor of the high-king. This situation allowed for lore to develope of Ciarán playing a leading part on a very public stage. We read that once, when Diarmaid held the fair of Tailtiu (Teltown, Co Meath), a woman accused her husband of being unfaithful to her. The husband denied this, but his wife insisted that he swear on the matter 'under Ciarán's hand'. He accordingly swore with the saint's hand laid upon his neck, but he was swearing falsely and as a result a tumour came upon him and his head fell off. All wondered at this, and Ciarán took him to the monastery of Clonmacnoise, where the headless man remained for seven years, being reconciled to his wife before his death. The saint was also said to have miraculously come to the rescue of Maireann, one of Diarmaid's wives, who was being shamed by a rival wife at the fair of Tailtiu (see **Aodh Sláine**). Maireann had no hair, but when her diadem was knocked off at the instigation of the rival, Ciarán caused beautiful tresses to grow on her head. On yet another occasion, Ciarán was asked by the high-king's assembly at Uisneach (Ushnagh, Co Westmeath) for assistance in a period of drought, and he consented and caused a downpour of much-needed rain on the land.

One story connects Ciarán with his namesake who, to distinguish the two, was known as 'old Ciarán of Saighir'. It happened that Crichid, the farmer of Clonmacnoise, went to Saighir and impiously quenched the perpetual fire which burned there. On his way home, Crichid was devoured by wolves, whereupon Ciarán of Clonmacnoise went forth, obtained fire from heaven in place of the quenched fire, and restored Crichid to life. While the two saints feasted together at Saighir, Ciarán of Clonmacnoise prayed that that monastery be wealthy, whereas the older Ciarán prayed that wisdom be always in Clonmacnoise. When he felt his death approaching, Ciarán of Clonmacnoise had the monks bring him out into the sunlight. He looked at the sky and said 'hard is that road, but necessary'. We read that he was thirty-three years of age at the time of his death. This latter detail is obviously based on the life of Christ who, like Ciarán, was 'the son of a carpenter'. Another tradition had it that Ciarán died young because the saints of Ireland grew jealous of him and prayed for his death.

Several relics of him survived until mediaeval times. The hide of his dun cow was kept at Clonmacnoise, and it was believed that the soul of a person who was placed on it when dying would gain heaven. The stone which had always served as a pillow for him was also preserved; as was a robe which allegedly was given by him to St **Seanán**, who sent it floating down the river Shannon to the latter's monastery. We further read that, at his death, he presented his bell to **Caoimhghin** - this bell was called the 'bobán' and was long preserved at the monastery of Glendalough.

Several of the stories passed from the written texts into popular lore, and some other details were added. In the folklore of west Offaly, for instance, a sudden gust of wind was known as 'Ciarán's wind', and this was explained by a legend. Ciarán and St Manchán, we are told, decided to arrange the boundary between their paruchiae by rising early one morning and walking towards each other. The dividing line would then be drawn from where they would meet each other. Manchán accordingly left his monastery (at Leamonaghan, Co Offaly) with the first light of day and began to walk towards Clonmacnoise. Ciarán was a heavy sleeper, and was only woken by the voice of Manchán insisting that the boundary must be at Clonmacnoise itself. Ciarán, however, prevailed on his rival to allow him as far as he would throw his cap. He uttered a prayer, and a sudden squall blew the cap far away into the air. The two saints ran after it, and it came down at Bloomhill, which henceforth was the boundary between them. In the folklore of Co Meath, a humorous account was given of how Ciarán was said to have had a difference of opinion with **Colm Cille**. The two saints had churches at Castlekieran and Kells respectively, and we are told that Ciarán took a cross from Kells and Colm went to Castlekieran in high dudgeon and took it back. Ciarán followed on and caught up with him as he crossed the river Blackwater, whereupon the two holy men struggled with each other in the water and the cross fell and was broken.

Several legends of the saint were current in the folklore of the Clonmacnoise area. It was said that a local chieftain once refused him food though he was starving, and Ciarán threatened that the chieftain would die of thirst. This happened so, for each time the chieftain put a goblet to his mouth the drink disappeared through it. It was also said that Ciarán was once mocked by a local man who said that he was 'no more a saint than the robin on yonder bush'. No sooner had he said these words than Ciarán changed into a robin and flew to a hawthorn bush which grew nearby. The man fell on his knees and begged pardon, and the saint returned to his usual shape.

The feastday of Ciarán of Cluain is September 9.

J F Kenney (1929), 376-82; Ludwig Bieler (1979), 146-7; Whitley Stokes (1905), 202-5 and (1890), 117-34; Charles Plummer (1910) *1*, 200-16; W W Heist (1965), 78-81; R A S Macalister (1921); S H O'Grady (1898) *1*, 72-4, 82-3, 416; John O'Hanlon (1875) *9*, 199-237; Ordnance Survey Letters - Meath (1836), 18-22; IFC 157:505-6, 179:141-3, 946:157-60/256, 947:222-4, 1103:421-4, 1910:148-9.

CIARÁN of Saighir Saint of the 5th and early 6th centuries, founder of the monastery of Saighir (Seirkieran, near Birr in Co Offaly). He was reputed to have been 'the first-born of the saints of Ireland'. His name implies that he was dark-haired, and is anglicised as Kieran.

It is apparent that a biography of him was composed by a monk of the Seirkieran community around the 8th century, but the surviving accounts have added much to that original. Though they differ considerably among themselves, the general outline is clear. His father Lughna was from the territory of the Osraighe (south Laois and Kilkenny), and he settled in Corca Loighdhe (west Cork) and married a woman called Liadhain there. Before the saint's birth she had a vision of a star coming from heaven and entering her mouth. The young Ciarán was fostered in Cléire (Clear Island) and, having spent thirty years there, he set out for Rome.

In Italy he met St **Patrick**, who gave him a bell and told him to return to Ireland and to found a monastery at the place where the bell would ring of its own accord. He did this and, when the bell rang at Saighir, he commenced the building of his monastery there. He was helped in his task by a wild boar, a wolf, a badger, and a fox, which animals became his first monks. An anecdote tells of how the fox once stole the saint's shoes to eat them in his den, but Ciarán sent the badger to bring him forcibly and ordered him to do penance for the misdeed. Soon a large number of men and women arrived to become his monks and nuns. A series of miracle stories are related of him, including raising people from the dead, providing food where none previously existed, and healing the sick and afflicted.

When Patrick reputedly arrived in Munster, Ciarán went to join him on his missionary work. One anecdote tells of how a man was seized by the king of Munster because he had stolen Patrick's horse, and of how Ciarán ransomed the man for his weight in gold. After the king had received the gold, however, it melted away and vanished. A similar story tells of cattle paid by Ciarán to ransom his namesake **Ciarán of Clonmacnoise** from a local king - these cattle also melted away and vanished when their purpose was fulfilled. The idea that Ciarán preceded the mission of Patrick must be old, for in some striking instances he is made to parallel John the Baptist, the precursor of Christ. We read of him as a pioneer of monasticism in the wilderness, wearing nothing but skins of wild animals and refusing ordinary food, all of which sounds like residue from an ancient portrayal. Another striking motif is his reputed custom of keeping a fire perpetually lighting in his monastery - this has all the marks of a borrowing from Irish pre-Christian ritual (see entry on St **Brighid**).

His association with Cape Clear on the southwest coast seems to be historically accurate. The surviving literary accounts have him spending his youth there, and they make the association again in a different context, stating that he used to go to pray with his foster-mother on a lonely rock off the southern coast of Munster. He would return miraculously to Seirkieran on the same day. Ciarán is still remembered in the folklore of Clear Island, and his feastday is March 5.

J F Kenney (1929), 316-8; Charles Plummer (1910) *1*, 217-33 and (1922) *1*, 103-24; S H O'Grady (1892) *1*, 1-16; W W Heist (1965), 346-52; Paul Grosjean in *Analecta Bollandiana 59*, 217-71; John O'Hanlon (1875) *3*, 115-48; IFC 40:96-8, 88:198-201.

CLÍONA (earlier, Clidna, Clíodhna) Otherworld lady in literary and oral tradition. Her name was sometimes accompanied by the epithet Ceannfhionn ('fair-haired').

A mediaeval story tells of how she fell in love with **Aonghus** and went from her dwelling in Magh Meall ('the Pleasant Plain') in a bronze boat to meet him. She was accompanied by a man called Iuchna, who acted treacherously towards her. He played magic music so that she fell asleep, and a great flood came and drowned her at Cuan Dor (the bay of Glandore, Co Cork). An alternative account makes her one of the **Tuatha Dé Danann**, and states that she eloped from Tír Tairngire ('the Land of Promise') with a handsome young warrior called Ciabhán. They landed at Trá Théite (the strand at Glandore), and Ciabhán left her in his boat while he went to hunt. The wave then came and drowned her. These accounts seem to have arisen from an actual designation of the tide at that place as the Wave ('Tonn') of Clíona. This was one of the great waves of Ireland, according to the ancient topographical system, and her association with it was an expression of the idea that the deities resided in water.

In post-mediaeval tradition, Clíona was regarded as one of the principal otherworld women of the province of Munster. She was said to reside in a palace under Carraig Chlíona, a conspicuous large rock surrounded by smaller ones in a lonely part of the parish of Kilshannig, south of Mallow in Co Cork. To the poets she was an inspirer of their art, but she also had the reputation of being a seducer, as evidenced by a poem composed as a colloquy in west Munster in the 18th century and which became very popular in the folklore of that area. In this text she comes to the celebrated poet Cearbhall **Ó Dálaigh**, inflicts a terrible thirst on him, and then promises to relieve him of it if he will lie with her. Cearbhall realises that to go with her means death, and so refuses to comply.

A folk legend, told in Co Cork, concerned Clíona and her reputed sister **Aoibheall**, who were claimed to have been daughters of a druid who lived in the rath of Castlecor, near Kanturk. Both of the ladies were in love with a young chieftain of the Ó Caoimh (O'Keeffe) family, but Aoibheall was his favourite and he was engaged to be married to her. Clíona enlisted the help of an old nurse skilled in magic, and so caused Aoibheall to pine to the point of death. She then told Aoibheall that she would have her cured if she renounced her love for Ó Caoimh, but Aoibheall refused and Clíona struck her with a magic wand, turning her into a white cat. The unsuspecting chieftain later married Clíona, and they lived happily for a long time until the old nurse took ill and on her deathbed was struck by remorse. She sent for the chieftain and told him what had happened. The wand was by that time lost and the beautiful white cat could not be restored to its former shape, but Ó Caoimh in his fury ordered Clíona from his dwelling. She went to live at Carraig Chlíona and remains there ever since. She had given birth to a son of Ó Caoimh, and was thus regarded as the otherworld ancestress of that sept.

With the same general theme, another curious legend of her was told throughout Munster in recent centuries. According to this, a young man called Seán mac Séamais Mac Gearailt (John fitz-James Fitzgerald) was betrothed to a lady and a great dance was held to celebrate the engagement. Seán, who was a very handsome fellow, was dancing magnificently when he suddenly dropped dead, and it was believed that he had been 'carried away' by the **fairies**, and specifically by Clíona. A young girl, Caitlin Óg Chéitinn, daughter of a 'wise woman' (i.e. folk-healer), went to Carraig Chlíona and demanded that he be returned. She spoke in verse outside the rock and Clíona answered in the same metre from within. A long contest in poetry ensued, with Clíona insisting on holding on to the handsome young man, but when Caitlín Óg demanded a massive dowry for Seán she released him back into the world. This legend is connected with an actual event which occurred in August 1737, when John Fitzgerald, the young Knight of Glin, suddenly fell ill at a ball in Youghal to celebrate his engagement to Isabel Butler. He died next day in Cork and was buried there. This John had seven years earlier formally renounced the Catholic religion and had conformed to the official Protestant Church. He was a Gaelic poet, and was a close friend of several of the leading Munster poets of his time. His change of faith was motivated by a desire to avoid confiscation of his property, and was generally believed to have been contrived. As such it would have been the subject of humorous repartée between himself and other versifiers, and it is apparent that some such versifier alluded to the change as if it were an abduction of him by the fairies. This was a type of poetry often remembered in oral tradition, and his tragic death would in time be confused with it, thus giving rise to the legend.

According to local lore in north Cork, Clíona was many times seen leading the fairies in a nocturnal dance at her conspicuous rock, and it was also claimed that she sometimes gambolled about in the form of a large white rabbit. The stone circle of Carraig Chlíona was regarded as an eerie place, and nobody would venture there at night for fear of being abducted by her and her fairy host.

[Legend of wave] Whitley Stokes (1892), 12-3 and *Revue Celtique 15*, 437-8 and (1900), 108-9; Edward Gwynn (1913), 206-15.

[Clíona and Cearbhall Ó Dálaigh] Dáithí Ó

hÓgáin (1982), 215-23.

[Legend of Clíona and Aoibheall] Patrick Kennedy (1870), 133-5; J G White in *Journal of the Cork Historical and Archaeological Society 17*, part 2, 45-50, 74-82; IFC 42: 130-3, 98:268-86.

[Seán mac Séamais] Brian Ó Cuív in *Béaloideas 22*, 102-11; IFC Catalogue (numerous versions).

[John Fitzgerald, Knight of Glin] J A Gaughan (1978), 66-9, 148-50; Risteárd Ó Foghludha (1937), 5-10 and (1946), 14, 84-6; Royal Irish Academy Ms 12 F 6:21-5.

COBHTHACH CAOL Fictional king of Ireland, whose reign was put down to the 4th century BC. Sometimes his name has the appendix Bréagha (earlier, Breg) i.e. pertaining to the area around **Tara**.

Son of **Ughaine**, he was said to have reigned for fifty years, but he figures narratively only in the Leinster myth of **Labhraidh**. He treacherously killed his brother Laoghaire Lorc, Labhraidh's grandfather, and seized the kingship. He also killed Ailill, Labhraidh's father, but was in turn slain by Labhraidh in the conflagration at Dinn Rígh. The name Cobhthach means 'victorious', while Caol (earlier, Coel) is 'meagre' or 'thin'. The sobriquet is explained by reference to the great envy which he bore towards his brother Laoghaire, which caused him to waste away. The name of Cobhthach occurs in the genealogies as an ancestor of **Conn Céadchathach**, and thus of the Connachta and Uí Néill, and it was apparently on that account that the Leinstermen selected him as the hostile tyrant in the Labhraidh myth.

R A S Macalister (1956), 268-79; T F O'Rahilly (1946), 102-16. See further the references under **Labhraidh**.

COLLA (earlier, Conlae) Three mythical brothers of the name - Colla Uais, Colla Meann, and Colla Fochra - who, according to the mediaeval pseudo-historians, made singificant conquests in the south of Ulster in the 4th century AD. The actual conquests referred to were the work of **Niall Naoighiallach** and his sons a century later.

The tradition of the three Collas was already established by the 8th century. It was claimed that they were nephews of the high-king Fiachu Sraibhthine, who was himself son of **Cairbre Lifeachair**. Fiachu had a wonderful son called Muireadhach Tíreach, who was his champion in battle. Once, when Muireadhach was away in Munster leading his father's army, the three Collas made an attempt at seizing the throne. Fiachu's **druid** told him that he had a choice, victory and no more kings among his descendants, or to be slain and his descendants to be kings. Fiachu decided on the latter, and he thus was defeated and slain by the Collas in the battle of Dubhchumar (where the Boyne and Blackwater meet at Navan). Alarmed at the approach of Muireadhach's army, however, the Collas fled to Scotland, where they spent three years. Finally, they returned to **Tara** all alone and were received and forgiven by Muireadhach for having slain his father. They remained loyal to the high-king, and after some time he advised them to go north and make 'sword-land' of Ulster. Enlisting allies from the province of Connacht, the Collas advanced north and won six great battles against the Ulstermen. The seventh battle lasted a whole day and night, until blood reached the girdles of the warriors. The Ulstermen were completely routed, and the Collas pursued them all the way east to Gleann Righe (the Newry valley). Thereafter the conquering brothers carved out a kingdom for themselves in the district known as Airghialla (Oriel, comprising Cos Armagh and Monaghan, and parts of Louth and Tyrone). This story of the conquests by the three Collas was one of the several literary traditions which grew out of the northward expansion of the Connachta - Uí Néill (see **Conn Céadchathach**) and the overthrow of the Ulster royal centre at Eamhain Mhacha (see **Ulster Cycle**).

M A O'Brien in *Ulster Journal of Archaeology* (Series 3) *2*, 170-7; Kuno Meyer in *Zeitschrift für celtische Philologie 8*, 317-20; Gearóid Mac Eoin in *ibid 36*, 63-82; Edward Gwynn (1913), 200-5, 512; S H O'Grady (1892) *2*, 461-2, 505-7; P S Dinneen (1908) *2*, 356-65; T F O'Rahilly (1946), 224-32; F J Byrne (1973), 72-4.

COLM CILLE Saint and missionary, born at Gartan (Co Donegal) around 521 AD of the royal Uí Néill sept, his father Feidhlimidh being a grandson of **Conall Gulban**. In the year 546 he founded a monastery at a place which became known as his 'oakwood', Doire Cholm Cille (i.e. Derry), and later several other monasteries, including ones at Dairmhaigh (Durrow, Co Laois), and Ceanannas

(Kells, Co Meath). In 563 he left Ireland with twelve companions and settled on Oileán Í (Iona, an island off the south-west coast of Scotland). From there he began a mission to the **Picts** and to the Irish settlers of Scotland. He died on Iona in the year 597. He was originally called Criomhthann, 'Colm Cille' being a nickname meaning 'dove of the church'. The word 'colm' is derived from Latin - which form, Columba, is often used as the saint's name.

A large number of poems and prophecies has been ascribed to Colm down through the centuries, but only one of these is likely to have been his actual composition. This is the *Altus Prosator*, an acrostic hymn which lists the various aspects of the Christian view of the world. It is apparent that a short biography of him was written by Cuimíne Ailbhe, seventh abbot of Iona, in the middle of the 7th century, but the earliest full work on him was the celebrated *Vita Columbae*, written in or about the year 685 by the ninth abbot **Adhamhnán** who, like Cuimíne, was a relative of Colm. This is in three sections or 'books'.

The first section gives accounts of Colm's feats of clairvoyance and of his prophecies relating to immediate events and to people whom he knew and met. The second section describes miracles performed by him - such as producing food, healing illnesses, controlling the weather at sea - and the deaths of several tyrants who were hostile to the Iona community. The third section is probably a reproduction of the work of Cuimíne Ailbhe and is more directly biographical. We read that, before the birth of Colm, an angel appeared to his mother to announce that he would be a great saint; and further that when the baby was born light radiated from the room where he slept. He was educated by a bishop called Finnian, who observed an angel continually accompanying him. Reference is made to how, after he became a monk, he was 'excommunicated by a certain synod for some trivial and quite pardonable offences' and how the charges against him were proved to be incorrect. In this controversy **Bréanainn** took his part, announcing that he had seen a bright pillar precede him as a sign that he was ordained by God to lead souls to heaven. Accounts are given of various visions, in which Colm saw angels and demons, as well as the souls of the blessed departing to their reward. The most dramatic account concerns how he, when on Iona, realised that a monk had fallen from the round tower of his monastery at Durrow, and sent an angel to rescue him. Before the monk reached the ground the angel caught him, with the result that he suffered no injury. During his visions Colm was surrounded by light, and on these occasions he 'saw openly manifested many secrets hidden since the beginning of the world'. He foresaw his own death and announced this to his monks on Iona. As the final hour approached, weary with age, he went to sit in the monastery's granary, and a white horse which used to carry the milk-pails galloped up to him. The horse laid its head upon the saint's breast and began to whinny, to shed tears, and to foam at the mouth in sadness. A monk tried to drive the horse away, but he was restrained by Colm, who said: 'Let him be, for he loves me!' Returning indoors, he appointed his colleague Baíthéne as his successor, and died before the altar in the monastery chapel, blessing his community. It was night-time, and a great light in the shape of a pillar was seen in the heavens over a wide area as his soul departed. For the three days of his obsequies a great tempest blew, but it subsided immediately he was buried.

In the second section of *Vita Columbae* is related the most engrossing of all the stories concerning the saint. This concerns the renowned monster of Lough Ness in Scotland. We read that when Colm came to the bank of the river Ness, he met there a group of people preparing to bury a man who had been seized and bitten by a water-monster ('aquatilis bestia') as he swam there. The body had been recovered by some boatmen using hooks. Colm told one of his men, called Lugne moccu Min, to swim across and collect a boat from the other bank, but as Lugne was in midstream the monster roared and rushed on him with open maw. Colm made the Sign of the Cross in the air with his hand and commanded the monster to retreat, whereupon it fled terrified back into the water. This is the earliest recorded instance of the common Irish motif which has water-monsters being banished by **saints**. The motif sprang from the influence of the Apocalypse of John on the folk imagination, and in the case of Colm a direct link can be traced between his use of the Apocalypse in preaching and the Lough Ness account. In the poem *Altus Prosator*, Colm had referred to the 'great horrible frightening dragon' of the Apocalypse ('draco magnus deterrimus terribilis') which dwells in the depths of land and sea. It thus appears that the relayer of the image was made into the actor in the legend which sprang from it.

It is probable that several other hymns were composed by Colm, and down through the centuries a vast number of poems has been fancifully attributed to him. These vary in subject from prayer and celebration of the beauties of nature to occasional stanzas and prophecies of all kinds. He thus came to be regarded as the saint with a special partiality to those who made verse, and it was claimed that he had himself been trained in the schools of the poets. The nucleus of this tradition may have existed in his own lifetime, for Adhamhnán refers to poems composed in Irish in praise of the saint and claims that one of these protected its composer from enemy attack. The text of a long verse eulogy on Colm survives. It is called the *Amhra* ('Marvel') of Colm Cille, dates to around the year 600 AD, and is attributed to the chief-poet of Ireland at the time, **Dallán Forgaill**. The text is in extremely obscure language, of a type known as 'bélra na filed' ('rhetoric of the poets'), and various glosses were written on it by mediaeval scribes. According to these glosses, Dallán Forgaill began the eulogy in gratitude for the saint's intervention on behalf of the poets when they were in difficulty. Adhamhnán recounted how Colm was present at a convention in Drom Ceat (Daisy Hill, near Limavady in Co Derry), at which the high-king Aodh mac Ainmhireach made an agreement with the king of the Dál Riada of Antrim and western Scotland, Aodán mac Gabhráin. The glossarians claimed that one of the issues discussed at that convention was the situation of the poets, who had been guilty of extortionate behaviour and had become a major problem to the nobles, and that Colm had saved them from banishment by suggesting that their numbers and privileges be reduced. When Dallán began to compose his eulogy in thanks for this, the saint directed him to postpone composition of it until after his death. By the time that Colm died, Dallán had lost his eyesight, but it was miraculously restored to facilitate him in carrying out his task.

The mediaeval biographies, in both Latin and Irish, are based on Adhamhnán's text, but they add some striking traditions. One of these concerns how he came to be called Colm Cille - when he was a child, the other children noticed how often he visited the church to recite the psalms and they used to enquire 'has the little dove come to the church today?' Another such tradition concerns how his teacher, the monk Cruithneachán, taught him the alphabet - for each letter the child learned Cruithneachán gave him a bite of sweet-tasting bread, and so he soon knew all the letters.

A very dramatic innovation was introduced into lore of him in or about the 12th century. This has no historical foundation, but has become one of the best-known stories of Colm. According to it, he got a loan of a book of the Gospels from St Finnian of Maigh Bhile (Moville, Co Down) and secretly copied it. Finnian, on realising what had been done, demanded the return of the book and the copy as well. Colm objected, saying that the copy was his, and the matter was referred to the high-king **Diarmaid mac Cearrbheoil** for judgement. Diarmaid ruled 'to every cow her calf and to every book its copy'. Colm angrily retorted that it was a bad judgement and would be avenged. Another quarrel added to the tension, for Colm gave sanctuary to a prince who had killed a man in violation of the high-king's protection. Ignoring Colm's sanctuary, Diarmaid put the prince to death. Nurturing these two grievances against the high-king - who was of the southern branch of the Uí Néill - Colm encouraged the northern Uí Néill to make war on him. As a result, Diarmaid was defeated by the northerners with great bloodshed at the battle of Cúl Dreimhne (Cooldrevny, at the foot of Benbulben in Co Sligo). Colm later repented of having caused so much slaughter, and vowed that as penance he would never again set foot on the soil of Ireland, never again set eye on the Irish people, and never again partake of the country's food or drink. So he departed in sorrow for Iona. Years later, when he attended the convention of Drom Ceat, he avoided breaking his vow by having a sod of Scottish clay under his feet, having his eyes shrouded in cloth, and using only food and drink brought from Scotland.

The battle of Cúl Dreimhne was fought in the year 561, and in it Diarmaid mac Cearrbheoil was indeed heavily defeated by an alliance of the northern Uí Néill and the Connachtmen. Colm's sympathies would naturally have been with his own close relatives in that battle, but apart from this there are several indications that he was generally on good terms with the high-king. None of the early sources make reference to the copying of a book as the cause of Colm's exile, and indeed Adhamhnán mentions two return visits which Colm made from Iona to Ireland. It appears that some mediaeval scholar invented the idea of 'the battle of the book' on foot of the rather quaint way in which Adhamhnán dated the departure of Colm to Iona. 'Two years had passed after the battle of Cule Drebene,' he wrote, 'as it has been told to us, when the blessed man first sailed away from Ireland.' It is not possible to say if the 'trivial and very pardonable offences' mentioned by Adhamhnán were at all related to manuscript-copying or to partiality towards the northern Uí Néill, but the very reference to accusations would have helped to develope the legend. The plot of how Colm circumvented his vow was borrowed from popular storytelling of mediaeval times (see **Humorous Tales**, Type 1590).

All of this lore is featured again in the celebrated biography *Beatha Colaim Chille* compiled by Mánas **Ó Domhnaill** in the year 1532. This makes use, not only of many of the earlier texts, but also of oral tradition concerning the saint which was current in the Donegal area at the time. Much of this oral tradition survives to the present day. We are told that, before Colm was born, an angel directed that a particular flagstone which was floating on a lake be brought to his mother, and that it was on this stone that she gave birth. His mother bled, staining the earth, and therefore the red clay of that place, Gartan, is said to have curative and protective powers - especially against rats. Concerning his public life, the most dramatic of the many legends in Donegal folklore concerns how he converted the inhabitants of Tory Island to Christianity. We are told that the ruler of the island was at first hostile to the saint, but agreed to give him as much land as his cloak would cover. When Colm spread his cloak it covered the whole island, whereupon the ruler grew angry and set a savage hound on him. Colm made the Sign of the Cross and the hound fell down dead, and following this the ruler submitted to the saint. Colm left as a blessing that the clay of the island would always be effective in banishing rats, wherever it was brought. The cloak-spreading motif is an obvious derivation from the lore of St **Brighid**; whereas the idea of the efficacious clay - not mentioned by Mánas Ó Domhnaill - seems to have been supplied by some partisan of Tory who was acquainted with Adhamhnán's text. There it is stated that Colm blessed Iona, so that 'the poison of vipers shall in no way have power to harm either men or cattle within the boundaries of this island'.

There was indeed a Columban monastery on Tory Island in early mediaeval times, and a kindred legend based on a monastic foundation concerns Glencolmcille in the south of Co Donegal. There it is said that the saint banished a horde of demons from the glen and ordained that ever after the area was to be a sanctuary for the weak and for all those in need. Probably on account of the legend of 'the battle of the book', Colm was popularly regarded as having been a short-tempered saint. Thus it was said that, though very charitable, he was impatient and quite haughty with beggars who came to seek alms outside of the time of day set aside by the saint for this purpose. He was cured of this high-handedness, however, when Christ appeared one day disguised as a beggar seeking alms. On being impatiently handed a lump of dough, the beggarman threw it into the fire and immediately ears of corn sprouted from the fireplace. Recognising who his visitor was, Colm begged forgiveness, and ever after gave generously to the poor at any hour of day or night.

There was a persistent tradition that, after his death on Iona, the body of Colm was miraculously transferred home to Ireland. Norse raiders of Iona in the year 825 sought out the shrine in which his body had been placed in order to plunder it, and the tradition grew up afterwards that these raiders - finding no treasures there - cast the coffin out to sea and it floated over to Ireland. When his body was discovered by monks on the north-eastern coast, they brought it to Downpatrick and interred it there alongside **Patrick and Brighid**. The belief that these three great saints of Ireland are buried together is unhistorical, but it proved very attractive to the popular mind. One folk account has it that, when Colm's coffin came ashore, a cow licked it and her milk-yield increased greatly as a result. The local people went to investigate what had caused the cow to give so much milk, and they discovered the coffin and the body of the saint inside. When they brought the corpse to Downpatrick, the graves of Patrick and Brighid moved apart so as to allow room for Colm to be buried between them.

The Ó Domhnaill sept of Donegal claimed the special protection of Colm Cille, and down to Elizabethan times they always brought into battle a special relic, which was believed to guarantee them victory. This relic was a copy of the Psalms and was known as the 'Cathach' ('battler') of Colm Cille. The manuscript, which was said to have been written by the hand of the saint himself, still survives, as does the casket in which it was carried. An anthology of prophetic poems traditionally ascribed to the saint was published in the year 1856 and several times subsequently. This anthology has had a great influence on popular lore in

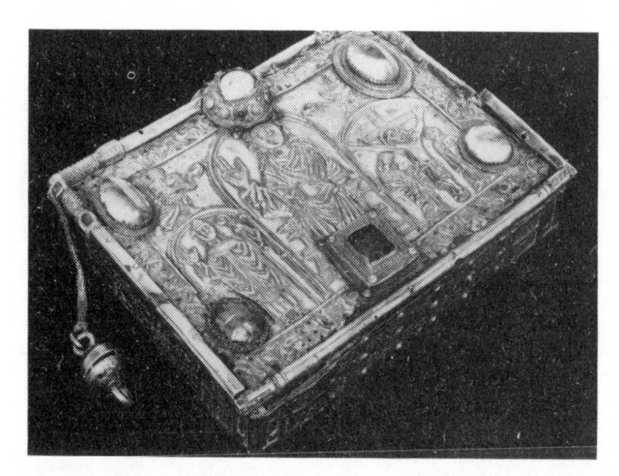

20. COLM CILLE *Shrine of the 'Cathach' of Colm Cille.*

Ireland, as these 'prophecies of Colm Cille' are taken to refer to many of the developments of the 20th-century world. The feastday of the saint is June 9.

[*Altus Prosator*] J H Bernard / Robert Atkinson (1898) *1*, 62-89.

[*Amhra*] Whitley Stokes in *Revue Celtique 20*, 30-55, 132-83, 248-9, 400-37 and *21*, 133-6. See also P L Henry (1978), 191-212.

[Adhamhnań's text] A O Anderson / M O Anderson (1961).

[Mediaeval biographies] Stokes (1890), 20-33; W W Heist (1965).

[Ó Domhnaill text] Andrew O'Kelleher / Gertrude Schoepperle (1918).

[Folklore] Dáithí Ó hÓgáin (1985), 26-35, 51-2, 324-5; Seán Ó hEochaidh in *Irisleabhar Muighe Nuadhat* 1963, 33-50; Joseph Szövérffy in *Éigse 8*, 108-32; IFC, numerous items.

[Cathach] J F Kenney (1929), 629-30.

['Prophecies of Colm Cille'] Nicholas O'Kearney (1856).

[General] Kenney, *op cit*, 263-5, 422-42, 802-3; Fergus Kelly in *Ériu 24*, 1-34 and *26*, 66-98; P S Dinneen (1908) *3*, 48-113; Séamus Ó Searcaigh (1967); John O'Hanlon (1875) *6*, 255-593; Szövérffy (1988).

COMHDHÁN (earlier, Comgan) A celebrated jester of Munster who reputedly lived in the 7th century AD, said to be stepbrother to the saint **Cumaine Fada**.

Several stories are told of Comhdhán in the mediaeval literature, and in these he is equally well-known by the nickname Mac Dá Chearda. This nickname ('Son of Two Skills') is explained by his possessing wisdom and madness in equal measure; and it is significant that the secondary form of his name itself, 'Comhdhán', could be taken to mean 'equal arts'. He was the archetypal wise fool, and one source refers to him as 'the chief poet of Ireland and the leading fool of Ireland'. He is described as son of Maolochtraigh, king of the Déise sept (of Co Waterford), and of Mughain, mother of Cumaine. He and Cumaine are credited with having jointly composed a learned poem on the place-lore of Magh Feimhin (the plain of south Tipperary), and anecdotes concerning them are related in a text from in or about the 12th century. According to this text, Comhdhán was the chief fool of Ireland, yet when he was in his senses he would deliver judgements the wisdom of which nobody could contradict. When the foolishness predominated, he could walk dryshod on water, and he could sleep underwater and the aquatic creatures were friendly towards him, nestling in his palms. Likewise, he slept on dry land when there was inclement weather and the birds would come and shelter him. How he became a fool is explained by an affair which he had with the wife of his father's **druid**. The druid sang an incantation on a wisp and cast it in his face, confusing his senses. He became a perpetual wanderer, but Cumaine loved him and delighted in his conversation. Cumaine used to ask him all types of questions concerning morality, and received in return the most profound answers.

It happened that a Munsterman called Mac Teléne, who was a formentor of strife, was once at the court of king **Guaire** of Connacht. He boasted that Munster excelled Connacht, citing Cumaine for sportsmanship, bishop Moronóc for foolishness, and Comhdhán for poetry. Guaire thought such attributes rather incongruous for these three characters, and he detained Mac Teléne until the boast could be investigated. A year later, the three characters came to the Connacht court, and Guaire hid an egg under the cover of Cumaine's chair, but the saint sat on it without breaking it, thus proving his agility. He also showed superb ability at chess. Moronóc took fifty hurley-sticks from a group of youths and closed the door on the sticks so that it knocked the curved heads off them all. He then lay in the king's bed with his boots full of mud, and tied his laces to the bed so that when he arose he knocked both Guaire and Cumaine to the floor. Meanwhile, Comhdhán recited an extempore stanza which proved his ability at poetry, so Guaire had to admit the truth of Mac Teléne's assertion and accordingly had to release the boaster.

Several of the details from these anecdotes are retold in a long text written a few centuries later. This text gives a humorous biography of Comhdhán, and is entitled *Imtheachta na nÓinmhididhe* (the Adventures of the Fools). It describes how, after the death of his wife Mughain, the Déise king Maolochtraigh remarried, and the new queen fell in love with Comhdhán. This love was not returned, and so his stepmother grew to hate Comhdhán and to plot his destruction. Once, when he won a horse-race, the king's druid was praising him, but the queen told the druid that Comhdhán was courting his wife. The druid grew jealous and, as Comhdhán was washing his horse in a river, he struck him with a magic wand, as a result of which Comhdhán was sick for a year. His hair fell out, and he became a complete idiot. A young man called Odhrán pitied him, and he developed a special affection for Odhrán and gave him all his possessions. One day, Comhdhán followed the women to the forest to collect fruit, and he remained there overnight. He was attacked by wolves, and next day went towards his father's house, stopping at an oratory on the way.

Meanwhile, his half-brother Cumaine had come to seek tidings of him. By promises of all kinds of food, he was prevailed on to follow Cumaine to his hermitage. Comhdhán did not wish it to be known that he was following on, and covered his head with a lump of moss, foolishly thinking that this concealed him. Soon after, Cumaine and Comhdhán came upon a group of men erecting a wall from felled trees and the men explained that they were building a barricade between them and the property of a monastery. On the saint's advice they desisted, however, and they brought Comhdhán and Cumaine with them to their master, Fínghein king of Munster. The two guests were royally received there, but Comhdhán misunderstood a joke made by Fínghein's queen to the effect that he must marry her as yet unborn daughter, and he fled from that place. He ran all the way until he came to the court of king Guaire in Connacht. On being told that a 'huge red-haired churl' was outside trying to fell a tree, Guaire went to welcome him. Comhdhán recited enigmatic poems, which Guaire understood to refer to his condition and his recent adventures. Guaire instructed the local children to put their hands around the tree, and this ruse succeeded in preventing Comhdhán from trying to cut it with his axe. The king then brought the fool into his fortress.

Soon after, Guaire's horses were stolen and Comhdhán followed the robbers, being under the impression that they were preparing the horses for racing with the king's consent. He met with the robbers, who found it feasible to go along with his delusion but, on his amicable return to Guaire, the king was furious with him for befriending them and plotted treachery against him. He sent him to collect heron's eggs in a lonely place, and then sent cut-throats after to kill him. Comhdhán unwittingly led the pursuers to where the horse-thieves were, and the latter took this to be a warning from him and fled. Guaire and his party came upon Comhdhán sitting alone in the robbers' hut and, angry at their chiding, the fool left them and returned to Munster. He next visited the court of the Leinster king Conaing, and there met again with St Cumaine, after which he returned to Connacht.

The exasperated Guaire sent messengers to collect the high-king's jester **Conall Clogach**, in the hope that the latter might be able to teach some sense to the fool. Conall, however, was an equally great fool and, in order to entice him to come with them, Guaire's men had to pretend that there was much better food in Connacht than at the Ulster fortress of the high-king **Domhnall mac Aodha**. They left lumps of rich food along their track all the way to Guaire's court, and Conall followed along at a distance. When the two fools met they kissed each other, eyed each other, and engaged in conversation about each other's physical appearance. They were given massive cauldrons of meat and porridge from which to eat. Noticing a fly alight on Conall's nose, Comhdhán plastered him with roasting porridge in an attempt to kill it. Conall thanked Comhdhán for defending him, and the latter was very pleased with his new reputation for heroism. Then Guaire decided to have a bath and requested their assistance. They went to a wood to get timber for the fire, and Guaire arranged to have a golden ring mounted on a stick in their path. When they saw this they made little of it, saying that they had come to seek timber rather than gold. Conall found a suitable piece of timber, and the disappointed Comhdhán begged him to exchange it for the ring. Returning to the palace, Conall cast the ring aside with indifference.

One of Guaire's retainers suggested that the fools should make a circuit of Connacht, and so they set out next day and reached Ros Comáin (Roscommon). They were well received there, but complained of the quality of the butter and Conall flung it onto the fire. It blazed up, and in an attempt to quench it Comhdhán threw flax onto the fire, and Conall threw straw after it. The house caught fire, and soon the whole town was in a state of conflagration. The fools fled, and as it was a dark night they thought that the saint of that place had deprived them of their sight for what they had done. Reassured by the sunrise next day, they stopped at a house on their way but, being badly received there, they walked withershins around the house and cursed it. Eventually they met with Cumaine, who treated them very well, and then they set out on a circuit to many different parts of the country. They soon began to bicker and to insult each other, however. When they came to the dwelling of the Munster king Fínghein, Conall stole some meat from the steward and Comhdhán disapproved of this. They then decided to part company, Conall returning to Ulster and Comhdhán going to visit Cumaine. The latter gave a hermitage to Comhdhán at a place called Inis Glinne, and Comhdhán made a fish-weir for himself there. He arranged a bell on the weir in such a way that it rang whenever a fish was caught. He spent the rest of his life in prayer and devotion and died in the arms of his saintly stepbrother.

The author of this text was well read in the mediaeval literature, and was quite selective in his treatment of the materials. He altered the story of the druid's wife so as to avoid accusing Comhdhán of adultery, introducing the well-known motif of a lustful and treacherous stepmother - probably on the pattern of the story of the Leinster hero **Maol Fhothartaigh**, whose name resembles that of Maolochtraigh (see also **Romantic Tales**, Type 870C). The companionship of the two fools may have been suggested by a similar setting in the story of **Suibhne**, while the bell announcing the catching of a fish is borrowed from the story of **Cano mac Gartnáin**. The emphasis on tricks associated with food may have been suggested by the story of **Anéra mac Conglinne**, in which Comhdhán had a mention. The author also had a good sense of humour, and did not hesitate to borrow from oral lore current in his time. Such adaptations by him included popular tales concerning fools frightened, dealings with robbers, and fatal results from swotting an insect (see **Humorous Tales**, Types, 1321, 1527, and 1586A). He also seems to have known the **Animal Tale**, Type 130, which concerns robbers and the burning of a house; and the text recounts concerning Conall Clogach (q.v.) other far-flung **Humorous Tales** (Types 1313 and 1600).

Comhdhán occurs also in the love-story of **Liadhain**, in which he brings a secret message in verse to that lady from her lover Cuirithir. Despite his entertaining character, however, he is not featured in the later folklore, under either name Comhdhán or Mac Dá Chearda.

J G O'Keeffe in *Ériu 5*, 18-44; Edward Gwynn (1913), 200-5, 512; Kuno Meyer (1892), 6-7 and (1902), 12-7; Cormac Ó Cadhlaigh (1939), 113-56, 217-22; Gearóid Mac Eoin in *Zeitschrift für celtische Philologie 36*, 74-82; George Calder (1917), 372; Seán Ó Coileáin in *Ériu 25*, 103-13.

COMHGHALL (c515-602 AD) Saint who founded the monastery of Beannchair (Bangor, Co Down). His name is anglicised as Congall.

He was of the sept called Dál nAraidhe (in south Antrim and north Down). A friend of **Colm Cille**, Comhghall spent some time with that saint on the mission to Scotland. He was also the teacher of the renowned missionary Columbanus (c543-615), who carried the message of Christianity to many parts of continental Europe and founded the famous monastery of Bobbio in Italy. Although the prestige of Comhghall himself was great, the two versions of his biography which survive seem to date from as late as the 12th century. These texts are in Latin, but they make use of much earlier material which was probably in Irish.

We read that the priest who baptised him was blind, but got his sight from a well which miraculously sprang up to give water - a detail borrowed from the lore of **Patrick**. When Comhgall grew up, he had to substitute for his father in a local war, because the father was too old to fight, but was allowed to go home when snow fell on the army camp and miraculously left him untouched. On opting for the religious life, he went to the monastery of Cluain Eidhneach (Clonenagh, Co

Laois), the abbot of which was St Fionntan, and then visited **Ciarán** at Clonmacnoise. Returning to Ulster, he took holy orders and established the monastery of Bangor. Several miracles of healing and even of raising the dead are attributed to him, and we read that due to his holiness his cell was brilliantly illuminated when he retired there. Once, when grain was scarce, a rich man refused to give of his copious store to the monks, and Comhghall told him that mice would eat all his corn. This accordingly happened, and other anecdotes tell of how the saint overcame various tyrants and robbers.

Comhghall crossed over to the community of Colm Cille on the island of Iona, and we read that, together with Colm and **Cainneach**, he set out to convert the king of the **Picts**, Brude. Coming to Brude's fortress, Comhghall caused the gate to open, Colm opened the doors, and Cainneach caused the king's hand to wither when it brandished a sword against them. On accepting the faith, Brude's hand was restored to him. We further read that, after Comhghall returned to Bangor, a foreign monk visited that monastery to contend with him in austerities. Comhghall brought the visitor to a river at midnight, with an invitation to join him in singing the psalms there. As they stood in the river, the water alternated between great heat and great cold, and the stranger had to admit defeat. On another occasion, Comhghall restored to health Caointighearn, wife of the Dál nAraidhe king **Fiachna mac Baodáin**, after she had been given poison by one of her handmaids. The handmaid repented, and was forgiven and saved from punishment by the saint.

Several churches in both Ireland and Scotland were dedicated to Comhghall, and his feastday is May 10.

J F Kenney (1929), 395-7; A O Anderson / M O Anderson (1961), 314-9, 490-3, 500-1; Whitley Stokes (1905), 410; Charles Plummer (1910) *2*, 3-21; W W Heist (1962), 332-4, 420; Kuno Meyer in *Irisleabhar na Gaedhilge 4*, 229 and in *Anecdota from Irish Manuscripts 3*, 9-10; John O'Hanlon (1875) *5*, 152-84.

CONAIRE Mythical king of **Tara**. His name is a compound of 'cú' (hound, figuratively warrior), and probably meant 'warrior-lord'. He is sometimes given the epithet Mór ('great'), or Caomh ('handsome').

The principal text concerning Conaire is *Togail Bruidne Da Derga* (the Destruction of Da Dearga's Hostel). This was compiled in the 11th century from two distinct texts of earlier date. The story was already in writing in the 8th century, containing material which seems to be an echo of how the Leinstermen displaced an earlier **Érainn** group. Conaire, who represents such a group, is a somewhat enigmatic figure, but it is clear that the motifs associated with him derive from a cult of sacral **kingship**. We read that his father, a king called Eterscéle, had no issue until he married a young girl, Meas Buachalla, who had been abandoned by her parents. The girl had been impregnated by an otherworld man who came to her in a bird-skin. This spectre had told her that she would give birth to a son 'and that boy may not kill birds, and Conaire shall be his name'.

The young Conaire was sent into fosterage in Magh Life (the Curragh of Kildare) and, when he grew to early manhood, Eterscéle died. Conaire was summoned to attend a 'bull-feast' at Tara, which involved a seer sleeping on a bull-hide in expectation of a vision which would reveal who should be the new king. He set out in his chariot, and on his way he saw some huge birds and pursued them as far as the sea near Áth Cliath (Dublin). There the birds took off their skins, taking human form, and one of them told him that he was forbidden to cast at birds. He further instructed Conaire to go naked to Tara, where he would be installed as king. Meanwhile, the seer at the bull-feast had a vision of 'a naked man coming along the road to Tara at dawn, bearing a stone in his sling'. Conaire came thus, and his fosterers met him on the road and clothed him with royal garments. The motto he adopted as king was 'to enquire of wise men so that I myself may be wise'.

Conaire's reign ushered in a period of great happiness and good fortune in Ireland. His three foster-brothers, however, began to reave and plunder. Conaire, out of love for them, refused to put them to death, but instead banished them to Scotland. Meanwhile, he unwittingly broke several prohibitions (see **'geis'**) which the bird-men had imposed on him when they told him that he was to be king. Finally, when benighted on the road called Slíghe Chualann, he decided to visit the hostel of his friend Da Dearga (probably at Bohernabreena in south Co Dublin). He perceived three red men riding along in front of him and remembered that one of his prohibitions was against following three such men into Da Dearga's house. Failing to dissuade the three strangers from preceding him, he resigned himself to his fate. He entered the hostel, and the three red men sat down with him. A horrid-visaged woman came to the door and foretold that 'neither skin nor flesh of you will escape from the house you have entered, except what the birds will take in their claws'. His three foster-brothers had, in the meantime, landed at Trácht Mhuirbhthean (Merrion Strand in Dublin) with an army of marauding Britons, and they were marching towards the hostel. They made a surprise attack, but Conaire killed hundreds of the foe before he could reach his weapons and hundreds more when he grabbed the weapons. The raiders set fire to the hostel three times, but each time the conflagration was quenched by the defenders. Then **druids** who were with the raiders put a magic thirst on Conaire and, since all the liquid in the hostel had been expended in quenching the flames, he grew weak and was slain by two of the foe. His severed head spoke a verse in praise of his champion, Mac Cécht, who had fought tremendously by his side.

Other fragmentary sources shed light on aspects of this story. We read, for instance, that the foster-brothers of Conaire were also known as 'the three red-heads of the Leinstermen', and it is obvious that the three mysterious strangers who rode ahead of him to the hostel were originally the same trio as these. It is also striking that the name of his host Da Dearga, also called simply Dearg, signifies redness; and the original story must have had that character in the role of foe rather than of friend. **Dearg**, indeed, was a common personification of death in early Irish literature. In the basic stratum, therefore, Dearg as death would have been one of the aspects of the fated life of the sacred king. Memories of Leinster aggression were superimposed on, and confused with, such rituals of kingship.

A different account of Conaire's accession to the kingship states that his mother, Meas Buachalla, was of otherworld origin and was herding for king Eterscéle when she was made pregnant by him. She kept the child's paternity secret until Eterscéle died, and then she told Conaire to go to Tara, for he was the son of the dead king. She collected an otherworld army for him, and when they reached Tara the steeds stood still when he entered the ritual chariot, the royal cloak fitted him, and the flag-stones magically moved to let him pass. The upright stone, the Lia Fáil, cried out against the axle of his chariot as it always did for the true king. This account also refers to variant traditions concerning Conaire's birth, including the ideas that Meas Buachalla was the daughter of her lover Eterscéle and that she had sojourned for a while in the otherworld dwelling called Sídh Bréagha Léith near Tara. It is clear that the sacral kingship was the central and basic subject of the Conaire legend, and that this was underlined by the use of a variety of motifs relating to the otherworld.

Several of the non-dominant septs regarded Conaire as their ancestor, thus giving them a claim on the kingship and indirectly preserving the memory that the Érainn once controlled Tara. The dominant Uí Néill dynasty also used his name for their own benefit, and one tradition had it that Conaire took compensation from the Leinstermen for the death of his father at their hands. He is thus, rather anachronistically, claimed to have originated the **bóraimhe**, a tribute imposed by the Uí Néill on Leinster. The mediaeval literature also exhibits a duplication of this mythical king by the annalists - for which see **Conaire mac Mogha Lámha**. There are no late literary accounts of Conaire, and he was unknown in the folklore of recent centuries.

Eleanor Knott (1936); Lucius Gwynn in *Ériu 6*, 130-41; R A S Macalister (1956), 300-1; Edward Gwynn (1913), 116-9; M A O'Brien (1962), 120; P S Dinneen (1908) *2*, 230-3; T F O'Rahilly (1946), 82, 117-30, 202; F J Byrne (1973), 59-63, 323; Myles Dillon (1948), 25-31.

CONAIRE MAC MOGHA LÁMHA Fictional king of Ireland, son-in-law and successor of **Conn Céadchathach**.

This character is clearly a double of **Conaire Mór**, and was invented by the historians in order to facilitate chronology. Like his prototype, the epithet 'caomh' (handsome) is added to his name, and the mediaeval writers themselves were sometimes confused as to which Conaire they had in mind. This Conaire mac Mogha Lámha was one of the three joint-kings of Munster, and was favoured by Conn after **Eoghan Mór** took the whole province of Munster to himself. Conaire married Sárait, daughter of Conn, and Conn designated him his heir. He reigned for eight years, and was slain by one Neimheadh mac Sraibhghind (see **Neimheadh**), who then married the bereaved queen. However, the three sons of Conaire went to their uncle **Art** for assistance. These three were each called Cairbre, and they travelled to Munster and gave battle to

Neimheadh, who had as ally Lughaidh mac Con. This was claimed to have been the battle of Ceann Abhradh (the Ballyhoura hills on the Limerick-Cork border), other and differing accounts of which exist (see **Lughaidh mac Con**). At any rate, Neimheadh was defeated, and he fled to the protection of his new wife at Ard Neimhidh (the Great Island in Cork harbour), but one of the three brothers slew him in her arms. Sárait remarked that the deed was a great disgrace ('aisc') - hence the slayer became known as Cairbre Músc, the epithet being explained as a derivative of 'mó a áisc' (i.e. 'greatest was his disgrace'). A variant tradition had it that the disgrace of Cairbre Músc resulted from his lying with his own sister (see **Corc Duibhne**).

T F O'Rahilly (1946), 201-3; Lucius Gwynn in *Ériu 4*, 144-53; Kenneth Jackson (1938), 1-14, 31-4, 74-5; Whitley Stokes in *Irische Texte 3*, 312-7; P S Dinneen (1908) *2*, 276-81.

CONALL CEARNACH Mythical warrior in the **Ulster Cycle**. The name Conall derives from a Celtic 'Cuno-valos', meaning 'strong like a wolf', and in origin this character seems to have been an ancestor-hero of the Conailli sept which inhabited parts of Cos Armagh, Down, and Louth. His sobriquet meant 'triumphant', an appropriate one for such a hero.

Conall Cearnach was probably adopted into the nascent Ulster Cycle in the 7th or early 8th century, perhaps following the rise to prominence of the Conailli at this time. He was soon given a major role. The literature makes him son of the poet **Amhairghin mac Éigit Salaigh**, his mother being identified as Fionnchaomh daughter of the druid **Cathbhadh** and sister of king **Conchobhar mac Neasa**. Fionnchaomh was for a long time childless, but on a druid's advice she went and washed at a certain fountain. She took a drink of water there, and a chafer was in the drink. As a result, she gave birth to a baby boy. The chafer was stuck in the baby's hand, and she had to cut it out. This story parallels the birth-narrative of Conchobhar and is obviously borrowed from that source.

Another account deviates from the genealogy ordinarily given to Fionnchaomh, and claims that she was of the Connacht people and sister to the warrior **Ceat mac Mághach**. According to this, Ceat heard it foretold that Fionnchaomh would give birth to a child who would 'never be a night without a Connachtman's head hanging on his belt'. Ceat therefore placed the baby under his heel to crush its neck, but before the marrow of the neck was destroyed Fionnchaomh intervened and had the baby returned to her. As a result of this, Conall ever after had a slanted neck. This account gives a false etymology for his name, stating that Fionnchaomh condemned Ceat's act as 'wolfish treachery' (i.e. 'con-fheall'). Several artificial attempts were also made to explain the sobriquet Cearnach - such as relating it to the protuberance ('cern') cut from his hand to release the chafer, or a protuberance from the side of his head after a blow struck on him in battle. One imaginative interpretation was that the epithet derived from the Latin root 'cern', meaning 'perceive', and it was said that Conall could see as well by night as by day so sharp was his eye.

Conall Cearnach was much used as a character in the filling-out of the Ulster Cycle in the early mediaeval period, and in this regard his occurrence in the text *Táin Bó Fraích* is of special significance. The original of this text seems to have been written towards the end of the 8th century. It features, with Conall, the hero **Fraoch**, and these two characters may have been suggested to the author by their rather incidental appearances in early versions of *Táin Bó Cuailnge*. That author tells of how Fraoch, when setting out to search for his wife, his sons, and his stolen cattle, met Conall at Beanna Bairche (the Mourne Mountains in Co Down). They went together to the Alps, where they found the cattle being guarded at a fortress by a savage serpent. Conall, 'the finest hero of the Ulstermen', attacked the fortress and destroyed it. The serpent went harmlessly into his belt, and having released it again he and Fraoch brought the kidnapped people and cattle back to Ireland. The most plausible explanation of the serpent's strange behaviour is that the episode was suggested to the author by a similar episode in the 7th-century Life of St Samson of Dol in Brittany. That the author of *Táin Bó Fraích* was a cleric is indicated by the occurrence of the Lombards as hostile people. The Lombard kingdom was overthrown by the Franks, who had Papal backing, in the year 775 AD, and this probably was the event which prompted the author to include them.

The literature represents Conall Cearnach as having been for a while in the employ of the high-king **Eochaidh Feidhleach**, for whom he and Ceat were army commanders during the rebellion of Eochaidh's three sons, the **Finn Eamhna**. This may be an echo of an alternate tradition to the more general one that he was among the leading warriors in the Ulster court of Conchobhar. A certain instability in the role initially assigned to him in the literature is evidenced by the fact that he is erroneously mentioned among Meadhbh's soldiers in *Táin Bó Cuailnge*, while later in the same text he is one of Conchobhar's foremost fighters. One unsupported source has Féibh, daughter of Conchobhar, as his wife, and therefore he is made father of Fiacha mac Fir Féibhe, one of the Ulster exiles in Connacht (see **Cormac Conn Loingeas**).

A text written about the year 800 made Conall Cearnach the foremost warrior of Ulster. This was *Scéla Mucce Meic Dathó* (the Story of the Pig of Mac Da Thó). It told of how Mac Da Thó, a Leinster king, had a great hound called Ailbhe, which was sought after by both Conchobhar and queen **Meadhbh of Connacht**. The hound's owner cleverly promised it to both sides and, when both Ulstermen and Connachtmen arrived to collect the animal, he invited them to a feast in his huge house. A massive pig was cooked for the feast, and the two companies sat ominously opposite each other. The satirist **Bricriu**, as was his wont, started mischief by suggesting that the only way to divide the pig was by feats of arms. A boasting contest began, and Ceat mac Mághach went to the pig, knife in hand, and challenged any Ulsterman to equal his feats. He described how he had humiliated in battle their leading champions, and it seemed that the apportioning of the pig must be left to him. Then Conall Cearnach entered the house, exchanged greetings with Ceat, and told him to leave the pig. Ceat questioned his accomplishments and Conall answered: 'I swear as my people swear that, ever since I took a javelin in my hand, I was slaying a Connachtman every day, and destroying them by fire every night, and I have never slept without a Connachtman's head under my knee!' Hearing this, Ceat backed down, but he remarked that if another Connacht warrior, by name Anluan, were present that warrior would have been able to contend with Conall. 'But he is,' said Conall, drawing Anluan's head from his belt and flinging it at Ceat's chest so that a spurt of blood came through his lips. Conall then apportioned the pig. He allowed but a fourth part of it to the Connachtmen, however, and fierce fighting broke out between the two sides. Mac Da Thó released the hound to see which side it would take, and it chose the Ulstermen. The Connachtmen were routed, and the hound pursued the chariot of Meadhbh and her husband as far as the Plain of Ailbhe in central Leinster. It was slain there by the charioteer Fear Logha. This type of contest at a feast was a very ancient aspect of Irish culture. Writing of the Continental Celts, Diodorus Siculus and other authors mentioned how leading warriors among these were honoured with the finest pieces of meat and how disputes and challenges to duels were common at their feasts. Athenaeus referred to how the Celts allowed the thigh-bone of the cooked animal to the bravest warrior, 'and if anyone challenged this the two arose and fought a duel to the death'. These Classical writers also described how the heads of slain enemies were brought about by the Celts as trophies.

The cult of heads is reflected also in a text of the 10th-11th century. This tells that Conall's two brothers were slain by the men of Leinster in the battle at Howth which was brought about by the satirist **Aithirne**. The Leinster king, called Meas Geaghra, later had his hand cut off by a servant in a quarrell. Conall, thirsting to avenge his brothers, caught up with Meas Geaghra at the ford of Casán Claonta (Clane in Co Kildare). Meas Geaghra protested that it was ignoble to fight a one-handed man, so Conall tied one of his own hands to his side. The river was reddened by the fierce combat which ensued between the two, but Conall proved superior. Meas Geaghra, before being slain, suggested that Conall place his head on top of his own. Having decapitated him, however, Conall placed it on a rock, and a drop came from it and cut through the rock to the ground. When he then placed the head over his own, it straightened his neck so that the twist which had caused him to be called 'Conall Claon' was removed. Conall left that place in his own chariot, putting his charioteer into that of Meas Geaghra. On his way he met the dead king's wife Buan, showed her the head, and took her into his chariot. The head reddened and whitened alternately, and Buan explained that her dead husband was smarting from having once declared in an argument with Aithirne that no Ulsterman would take her. She then began to lament her husband, and herself fell dead from the trauma. Conall told his servant to cut the brains from Meas Geaghra's head and to mix them with lime into a ball. This was done, the head itself being left with the body of Buan, and Conall took the brain-ball with him and deposited it in Eamhain Mhacha, the Ulster capital. It was later snatched away by Ceat mac Mághach and used as a projectile to inflict a mortal wound on

Conchobhar mac Neasa (q.v.). This adventure of Conall again shows signs of being a literary compilation, its purpose being to explain the origin of the brain-ball which killed Conchobhar. The episode of the destructive drop from Meas Geaghra's head parallels a motif in the account of the death of **Cealtchair**, both based in all probability on a similar motif in the mythological lore of **Lugh** and **Balar**. It is also apparent that the situating of Meas Geaghra's death at Casán Claonta (literally, 'the twisted pathway') was due to a play on Conall's reputed nickname Claon (earlier 'claen', referring to the twist in his neck).

Conall Cearnach was accorded a special role in the youth-biography of **Cú Chulainn**, who was given as a child into the care of Conall's mother Fionnchaomh. Thus the two heroes were reared together, Conall being somewhat older in years. On the day that Cú Chulainn took arms, Conall was guarding a frontier post, and the younger hero asked him to leave the duty to himself. Conall refused, and Cú Chulainn insisted on going further south to find combat. Conall followed on in his chariot to give protection, but the youngster flung a stone and broke the harness of the chariot, which caused Conall to return to his post in a fit of pique. Later on, Conall was bested by Cú Chulainn in the tests for the leading warrior which resulted from the feast of **Bricriu**, but no real hostility between the two is ever portrayed. When Cú Chulainn was treacherously slain Conall wreaked vengeance on those responsible. This is described in the text *Deargruathar Chonaill Chearnaigh*, the earliest version of which dates from the 11th century. According to this, Cú Chulainn and Conall had arranged that if one of them were killed the other would avenge him. After Cú Chulainn's slaying, therefore, his wife Eimhear sent for his foster-brother, who was then at Inbhear Mór (Arklow in Co Wicklow). Conall set out, and on his way his charioteer, in anticipation of the 'deargruathar' (i.e. crimson-raid), was overcome by fear and died. Conall released one horse from his chariot and continued on horseback. He met the great steed of Cú Chulainn, the Grey of Macha, which led him to where its master lay dead. Astride his own fierce mount, called the Dearg Drúchtach, Conall tracked the retreating killers of his friend, and met with Lughaidh mac Con Roí at a ford. He agreed to allow Lughaidh to return to his native Munster, on condition that he face him in single combat later. Conall next met and slew **Maine**, son of Meadhbh, and put the head of the dead man on a withe. Continuing his offensive, he slew among others the family of Cailitín who had by magic brought about Cú Chulainn's death, and then headed south to keep his appointment with Lughaidh. The latter had lost one hand at the killing of Cú Chulainn, and to equalise the combat Conall tied his own hand to his side. Having cut Lughaidh's head off, Conall left it on a stone and it split the stone. He then went to Ulster and presented the heads of the dead enemies to Eimhear. It is clear that the description of the combat with Lughaidh is based on the somewhat earlier description of that with Meas Geaghra.

It is noticeable that the story-writers were anxious to give cohesion to the major stories of the Ulster Cycle, and Conall Cearnach was seen as a suitable personage to employ in that context. So, after the death of **Cormac Conn Loingeas**, we are told that the Ulster nobles appointed Conall as administrator of the kingdom and then offered the throne to him. He, however, declined this since he considered himself too old to lead them into battle, and instead he recommended that his pupil **Cúscraidh Meann Macha** be made king and he gave a series of wise counsels to Cúscraidh on how to govern. When Cúscraidh was duly installed, he divided his territory among the nobles, allotting the land between Drogheda and Iveagh to Conall. We are further told that that area was as a result known as Caoille Chonaill ('Conall's Division'), but this designation is merely a reflection of the fact that it was the ancient territory of the Conailli, the people who had Conall Cearnach as ancestor-hero.

The versatility of Conall is clearly shown in the story of one of his greatest feats, the slaying of the ferocious Ceat mac Mághach (q.v.). Indeed, the ongoing contest between these two 'slaughter-hounds' ('árchoin') is a background theme running through most of the Ulster Cycle. After one of Ceat's most devastating raids on Ulster, Conall followed him through the snow to Breifne (an area in Cavan-Leitrim) and slew him in single combat at a ford on the river Shannon. Conall himself was nearly dead after the furious contest. A hostile warrior, Béalchú of Breifne, found him lying on the ground and took him to his house with the intention of allowing him to recover and then slaying him in combat. As Conall's condition improved, however, Béalchú grew fearful and plotted treachery. He accordingly told his three sons that he would leave the doors of his house open and directed them to go at night and kill Conall in his bed. Suspecting this, Conall forced Béalchú to lie in the bed. Béalchú first closed the doors, but when he had fallen asleep Conall reopened them and thus Béalchú was slain in mistake by his own sons. Conall then attacked the sons and slew them also. This account, found in an 11th-century text, is an adaptation of the plot of a folk story which has a giant being thus outwitted by a smart man (see **Humorous Tales**, Type 1119). The plot was considered appropriate to Conall's dexterity.

All of this presupposes a long martial career continuing for Conall after the main events of the Ulster Cycle were over, but a variant account has him repairing to the court of queen **Meadhbh** in Cruachain after the deaths of Conchobhar and Cú Chulainn. 'Great sorrow and misery and leprosy befell him, so that there was no strength in his feet to go about.' Meadhbh and her husband Ailill mac Máta had him fed for a long time, even though he ate mighty meals. He used to entertain the men of Connacht rather riskily every day by describing how he had slain their sons and brothers and fathers. Finally, when Meadhbh became jealous of her husband's affair with another woman, she prevailed on Conall to kill him. Conall was in turn slain by the enraged Connachtmen. His head was kept in the western province, but the Ulstermen had a prophecy that if they drank milk out of the skull they would become strong again.

Conall Cearnach was so celebrated a character in mediaeval culture that several septs claimed descent from him. He remained well-known to the literati, and some of the texts in which he played leading roles continued to circulate in manuscript down to recent centuries. His name was thus well known to those oral storytellers who were influenced by written sources. In Ulster folklore, it was said that he joined the Roman army and was present at the Crucifixion of **Christ**. On his return to Ireland, when asked why he was so dejected, he remarked that anybody who had seen what he saw could never again be merry. This legend is a simple development of the tradition that Conchobhar mac Neasa (q.v.) was informed of the Crucifixion. Local onomastic lore at Ballyconnell in Co Cavan insisted that Conall had been slain there by some of Meadhbh's soldiers who followed him from Connacht, and the same claim was made on behalf of Rathconnell in Co Westmeath, but both these are late identifications of the hero with some other men called Conall referred to in placenames.

[Name and origin] Julius Pokorny (1959), 1112; Kuno Meyer (1912), 25; F J Byrne (1973), 89-90, 118, 323; Whitley Stokes in *Irische Texte 3*, 390-5.

[Conall and Fraoch] Wolfgang Meid (1974), 13-6, 44; James Carney (1955), 26-7, 57-60.

[Conall and Eochaidh Feidhleach] M E Dobbs in *Revue Celtique 43*, 284-7, 304-27.

[Conall in the *Táin*] Cecile O'Rahilly (1976), 5, 105, 120, 122.

[Fiacha mac Fir Féibhe] Stokes, *op cit*, 406-7.

[Contest over heads] Rudolf Thurneysen (1935); Kenneth Jackson (1964), 35-7; N K Chadwick in *Scottish Gaelic Studies 4*, 120-6; Michael Tierney in Joseph Raftery ed (1964), 31-2.

[Meas Geaghra] Stokes in *Revue Celtique 8*, 47-64.

[Conall and Cú Chulainn] Cecile O'Rahilly, *op cit*, 17, 21; R I Best / M A O'Brien (1956), 451-3; A G Van Hamel (1933), 115-33.

[Conall and Cúscraidh] Best in *Ériu 8*, 170-90.

[Deaths of Ceat and Béalchú] Meyer (1906), 36-42, 45.

[Death of Conall] Meyer in *Zeitschrift für celtische Philologie 1*, 102-11.

[Genealogies] T F O'Rahilly (1946) 349-50; O'Brien (1962), 555.

[Folklore] Seán Ó Súilleabháin in *Béaloideas 21*, 25-6, Seamus MacManus (1951), 159-61; Ordnance Survey Letters - Cavan (1836), 96 and Westmeath (1837) *1*, 215-7; IFC 89:152, 1126:2-3/283; 1141:117-51; S964:173; S966:135, 354; S967:329.

CONALL CLOGACH Foolish man who figures in Irish literature, reputed to have been a step-brother of the 6th-century high-king **Domhnall mac Aodha**.

In the celebrated biography written by **Adhamhnán**, St **Colm Cille** is said to have blessed the boy Domhnall at the Convention of Drom Ceat (Daisy Hill, near Limavady in Co Derry) in the year 575 and to have foretold that he would excel his brothers. This was developed by mediaeval writers with the suggestion that

Domhnall's mother was pleased, but the legal queen of Aodh mac Ainmhireach was angry that her own son had been superseded by this. She bitterly referred to the saint as 'a crane-like cleric' and, on hearing this, Colm Cille remarked that she and her maid-servant - who assisted her in plotting against him - might themselves be cranes until doomsday. They accordingly were turned into two cranes and remained in a nearby river ever after.

One of Domhnall's step-brothers, called Conall, had a distinguished career and died in 604 AD, but this did not deter the writers from giving a quite bizarre account of him. We read that Conall incited the rabble to throw stones at Colm Cille and his monks at Drom Ceat, and that in retaliation the saint cursed him and deprived him of the kingship. Colm assembled his monks and had them ring their bells against the transgressor, on account of which he came to be known as Conall 'Clogach (i.e. 'of the bells'). He was deprived of his reason by the saint's curse, and thus became the royal jester at his brother's court at Dún Chinn Craoibhe (somewhere to the south of Ballyshannon, Co Donegal).

One late mediaeval text gives details of his folly, stating that he used to spend each day guarding the frontier against Tír Chonaill (i.e. the Donegal area), and would strike three blows with his cudgel on the ground there to keep the boundary from moving overnight when he returned to his brother's royal fortress. As he went home one night he met with the high-king's men, who had just hanged the mother of a gang of robbers and were burying her in a bog-hole. Noticing that Conall had seen them, they secretly replaced the body with that of a dead goat. The foolish Conall later pointed out to the robbers where he thought their mother was, but they found the goat there instead. 'Had your mother a beard and horns?' he asked. Later, his royal brother Domhnall played a trick on him by having some Connacht visitors pretend to be messengers with tidings that Conall Clogach had been eaten by wolves at his frontier-post. Conall wept at the news of his own death, but one warrior seized him and declared that he had rescued the fool and brought him safely there. This text goes on to tell of how Conall Clogach went to Connacht and met the Munster fool **Comhdhán** there, and of their numerous escapades together. This account incorporates several plots from folklore (see **Humorous Tales**, Types 1600 and 1313 and other Types referred to under **Comhdhán**).

A O Anderson / M O Anderson (1961), 230-1; Brian Ó Cuív in *Éigse 11*, 183-7, 290; Whitley Stokes in *Revue Celtique 20*, 426-8; Kuno Meyer in *Zeitschrift für celtische Philologie 10*, 48-9; Andrew O'Kelleher / Gertrude Schoepperle (1918), 346-51, 376-7; P S Dinneen (1908) *3*, 88-91; Cormac Ó Cadhlaigh (1939), 136-56.

CONALL CORC King of Munster in the 5th century AD. Little can be deduced regarding his history from the legends which are told of him in literature of the 8th and succeeding centuries.

He is described as son of a certain Luightheach and fourth in line of descent from **Ailill Ólom**. His mother was called Boilce, a female satirist of the Britons, who put a binding request on Luightheach to lie with her. In this way Conall was conceived, and he was fostered by a sorceress called Feidhilm, who was nicknamed Láir Dhearg ('Red Mare'). Hence he was also known as 'Corc mac Láire'. A group of sorceresses once gathered at Feidhilm's house, and she concealed the boy under the hearth. One of the visitors remarked: 'I destroy only what is under the cauldron', and immediately the fire darted at the child and burned his ear. Thus he got the nickname Corc, which meant 'red'. Next day, a diviner examined the boy's palm and told him that, if he freed captives whenever he could, his name would be famous.

The boy was later adopted by his cousin, the Munster king Criomhthann mac Fiodhaigh. When he grew up, Criomhthann sent Conall to Leinster to collect tribute, and while there he ransomed three captives - one of whom, Gruibne, went to Scotland. However, Criomhthann's wife tried to seduce him and then, in spite, lyingly told her husband that Conall had asked her to lie with him. This is an early Irish example of a farflung storytelling motif (see **Romantic Tales**, Type 870C). Criomhthann sent Conall to the king of the **Picts** in Scotland, with a coded message in **ogham** on his shield. Arriving in that country, Conall was caught in a snowdrift and was rescued by Gruibne, who was herding swine there. Gruibne understood that the message on his shield was a signal to the Pictish king Fearadhach to kill the bearer, so he changed it to mean that Fearadhach's daughter should be given to Conall. Fearadhach hesitated, but Conall and his daughter came together and she became pregnant by him. She gave birth to a son, and after some wrangling Fearadhach accepted Conall as his son-in-law.

21. CONALL CORC *The Rock of Cashel, with mediaeval ecclesiastical buildings.*

Conall had two more sons by his Pictish wife and, on Criomhthann's death, he returned to Munster, bringing her and the children with him. As they arrived snow fell, and they lost their way in the storm. On the very same day a swineherd had seen a vision of a yew-tree on top of the great rock of Caiseal (Cashel, Co Tipperary) and angels descending to an oratory in front of it. The swineherd told this to his master Aodh, king of the Múscraighe sept, and Aodh's **druid** explained that this meant that the kingship of Munster would be centred there and that the first person to light a fire under the yew-tree would be king of the province. Aodh wished to go at once, but the druid advised him to wait till morning. Thus it happened that Conall arrived at the rock before him and, quite unaware of the prophecy, lit a fire there. When Aodh arrived and submitted to him, Conall understood all, and within a week had established himself as king of Munster. The place was accordingly known as Caiseal Coirc ('the castellum of Corc').

This legend of Corc, with its early folkloric material, was obviously put together at the behest of the royal Eoghanacht sept of Munster, of whom Conall Corc was one of the most famous ancestors. The placename Caiseal is a borrowing from Latin and it seems that all the tradition of that place had Christian sources - as in this legend. For that reason, the lore cannot be much older than the texts; but the stress on pagan elements is so marked, and the lore so clearly illustrates the transition of the Eoghanacht from paganism to Christianity, that its origin probably belonged to the 6th or 7th century.

Conall Corc is little referred to in the later tradition, but a 17th-century source gives a slightly varying account of how he got his name. According to this, his mother was called Bolgbháin, and the hero's father was legally married to another woman. Two idiots deliberately injured the child Conall. He was hidden from them under the cauldron, but they lifted the cauldron and burned his ears.

Kuno Meyer in *Anecdota from Irish Manuscripts 3*, 57-63; Vernam Hull in *Publications of the Modern Language Association 56*, 937-50 and in *Zeitschrift für celtische Philologie 18*, 420-1; Whitley Stokes in *Irische Texte 3*, 311-2; P S Dinneen (1908) 2, 368-87; Myles Dillon (1946), 34-7; F J Byrne (1973), 183-9; David Sproule in *Ériu 36*, 11-28.

CONALL GULBAN Son of **Niall Naoi-ghiallach**, who in the mid-5th century carved out a kingdom for himself in west Ulster.

In the push northwards from **Tara**, he was accompanied by his brothers Eoghan, Cairbre, and Éanna. Conall's new territory came to be known from him as Tír Chonaill (most of Co Donegal), and his descendants were called Cinéal Chonaill. Similarly, Eoghan's name was given to Inis Eoghain (the northern Donegal peninsula) and Tír Eoghain (Tyrone), and his descendants were called Cinéal Eoghain (the northern branch of the Uí Néill). Conall got his epithet from the conspicuous mountain Beann Ghulban (Benbulben) in the south of his territory. His fame was promoted in succeeding centuries by his descendants, the Cinéal Chonaill, whose leading family from mediaeval times onwards took the surname Ó Domhnaill. Later genealogists claimed that Conall had been the favourite son of his father Niall, but in reality Niall was succeeded as high-king by **Laoghaire**, who probably was the eldest son. In the province of Connacht, Niall's brothers Fiachra and Brian (earlier, Brión) had formed their own kingdoms, their descendants being known as Uí Fiachrach and Uí Bhriúin. Fiachra was an outstanding warrior, as also was his son **Dáithí**.

The mediaeval Cinéal Chonaill writers weaved old memories of politicking between all these powerful relatives into a comprehensive narrative which heroised Conall. According to it, when Conall was a boy his uncle Fiachra was so impressed by the lustre in his face that he took him as a fosterson from Niall. The boy was sent by Fiachra to be educated by Muireadhach Meann, king of the Calraighe sept (in Co Sligo). Part of his training was to run each day from a pillarstone towards Beann Ghulban, and the place where he halted to draw his breath was marked by Muireadhach. Next day he would have to run further, until eventually he could reach the peak without pausing at all. When people remarked that 'Conall runs bravely on Gulba', the druid of Muireadhach called him 'Conall of Gulba', hence his full name. Once, when Conall's uncle Brian visited Muireadhach's dwelling, a leading soldier among the visitors boasted that he could do the same feat, but he dropped dead in the effort. Soon a war broke out between Ulster and Connacht, and the Ulstermen burned the fortress of Muireadhach and slew that king. Conall went to Tara for assistance, and his brothers joined him. Their father Niall counselled that compensation should be accepted from the Ulstermen, but Fiachra urged Conall against this. In a fierce battle at Áth Cró ('the ford of blood' i.e. Ballyshannon, Co Donegal) Conall and his brothers, assisted by Fiachra and Dáithí, defeated the Ulstermen. Conall himself beheaded

22. CONALL GULBAN *Benbulben, the great razor-shaped mountain.*

the Ulster king Cana. Laoghaire then returned to Tara, taking Cana's wife with him, and Fiachra and Dáithí returned to their fortress at Cruachain (Rathcroghan, Co Roscommon). Conall, supported by Eoghan, Cairbre, and Éanna, continued his campaign against the Ulstermen. Finally, in a battle at Cruachan Droma Lighean (near Lifford, Co Donegal) the other three were facing defeat, but the wounded Conall rose from his sick-bed, slew the enemy leader and inspired his army to rout the foe. The four brothers then divided their conquered territories between them, Conall's portion being from Loch Súilighe (Lough Swilly) to Drobhaois (river Drowes). Following this, war broke out in Connacht between Fiachra and Brian, and Dáithí came to Conall seeking help. Conall gathered his forces, defeated Brian and cut a trail of destruction southwards, defeating even the Munster king Lughaidh Meann. However, Brian captured Fiachra and sent him to Niall at Tara as a prisoner. Conall again defeated the reassembled forces of Brian at Damhchluain (near Tuam in Co Galway), after which Brian was slain. The combined armies of Conall and Dáithí subdued all Connacht, after which Dáithí was installed as king of the province. The two leaders then went to Tara, where they were reconciled to Niall, and Fiachra was released.

A later mediaeval text retells much of this, and further increases Conall's status by claiming that he was chosen as high-king of Ireland as successor to Niall, but that Laoghaire coaxed the kingship from him. A long list of battles gained by Conall in many parts of the country is given, and we read that 'the valour of Niall of noble deeds was in no son of his except in Conall'. This text describes the hero as meeting his death at Dún Chonaing (near Fenagh in Co Leitrim), while chasing a group of raiders of the Masraighe sept (of Co Leitrim), who had stolen horses from Tara. Conall was slain while unarmed and accompanied by but a few of his men, and he was buried at Dún Bhaile (now Fenagh).

The Cinéal Chonaill had long been interested in gaining ecclesiastical prestige for themselves. Thus we read in a 7th-century biography of **Patrick** that Conall was the most receptive of all Niall's sons to the message of the great saint. He welcomed Patrick, accepted baptism, and gave him land for a church at Domhnach Phádraig (Donaghpatrick, Co Meath). There may well be some truth in this, but it is much developed in the 9th-century biography of the saint, which has Patrick telling Conall that 'your brothers' seed will submit to your seed forever'. A later mediaeval source claims that, on that occasion, Patrick drew the sign of a red cross on Conall's shield, thus giving to the hero's Ó Domhnaill descendants their family crest.

The fame of Conall Gulban was so great that when, in the 16th century, an anonymous Donegal writer decided to compose a romantic story, he made this celebrated ancestral figure the hero of it. This text, entitled *Eachtra Chonaill Gulban*, departs almost completely from the genuine tradition, situating most of its action overseas in the general manner of post-mediaeval romances. It opens by describing how Conall was trained by Muireadhach Meann by making him run up Beann Ghulban, and then we read of how - quite anachronistically - the German Emperor sought help from Niall after Italy was over-run by the Turks. Niall is here described as having three sons - Laoghaire, Eoghan, and Conall - and the first two insist on joining their father on the expedition. Only Conall is willing to remain at home and protect Ireland. After Niall's fleet has departed from Beann Éadair (Howth, Co Dublin), Conall decides to visit the beautiful Eithne, daughter of the Leinster king. She is strongly guarded at Nás (Naas, Co Kildare), but Conall vaults into her apartment and departs carrying her on his shoulder. She complains that he is carrying her away in flight, and so he waits for her guard and slays an entire company of them. On reaching Beann Éadair, he falls asleep with his head on her lap, and a stranger called the Macaomh Mór ('Large Warrior') arrives in search of the Leinster king's daughter. Eithne pretends that she is not her, but the Macaomh is so enamoured of the lady who addresses him that he takes Eithne anyway and departs with her over the sea.

When Conall awakens he finds out from a local shepherd what has happened. The shepherd also tells him that a ship is always at Beann Éadair when an Irishman needs it, and so Conall sets sail in search of his loved one. He lands in Scandinavia, where he defeats a whole team of young hurlers and then goes to 'Teach na nAmhas' ('the House of Mercenaries') where he is attacked. Seizing one man by the ankles, he uses him as a club to ward off the rest. When Conall falls asleep, the Scandinavian king sends a hundred warriors to attack him, but Conall dreams of fierce lions and awakes and slays them all. The king's daughter Doireann falls in love with him and sends her druid Dúnadhach to cure him of his wounds. The druid then places him in the princess' bed, but Conall puts a sword between them and she grows angry. She engages a great warrior called Amhas Órarmach ('Golden-Armed Mercenary') to kill him, but in a fierce and protracted combat Conall overcomes and binds the Amhas. He then puts the king's whole army to flight and binds the king himself, but Dúnadhach intervenes and makes peace between them.

A great feast is held, and a strange warrior called Ridire an Ghaiscigh ('the Knight of the Feat') arrives, seizes the king, and throws him to the floor. Conall fights the newcomer, defeats him, and then demands to know if he was ever in a more difficult position than now. The Ridire tells of how he met the Macaomh with Eithne, and how he had fought for Eithne but had been overcome by the Macaomh and thrown over a sea-cliff. He had landed in a griffin's nest and eventually managed to kill the griffin. Next he had fallen in with man-eating giants but had again escaped, and then had proceeded to Scandinavia. Hearing from him that Eithne had won a promise from the Macaomh not to be made his wife for a year, Conall enthusiastically sets out again on his quest, accompanied by Dúnadhach, the Amhas, and the Ridire. In Crete, Conall defeats in single combat the prince **Iollann Armdhearg**, and enlists him also as a supporter.

They arrive in Syria and, coming to the Macaomh's fortress at a place called Pampilana, they kill hordes of the foe. Then Conall fights the Macaomh, and after four days of combat defeats him but spares his life on promise of tribute. In order to compensate the Macaomh for the loss of Eithne, Conall and his men go to Caledonia to win a fine princess for him. They encounter great opposition there, finding that five hundred men they kill each day come alive again overnight. Conall lies among the dead, and thus discovers that a hag comes with a bottle of balsam to revive them. He slays the hag, and some days later strangles three poisonous hounds with his bare hands. In a general battle, the army of the Caledonian king is defeated, and the princess is won for the Macaomh. News arrives, however, that Eithne has been kidnapped by the Greek king to be his son's wife. In a great battle Conall and his followers defeat the Greeks and sack Athens.

Learning that the Turks have won many battles against the German Emperor and have advanced into Europe, Conall and his helpers set out to the rescue with a mere hundred knights. Slipping into the Turkish camp, Conall slays the enemy emperor, but he and his five companions have to retreat in the face of great odds. In the darkness and confusion Conall's brother Laoghaire unwittingly fights the Amhas, and similarly with Eoghan and the Macaomh. Conall, however, recognises in each case an Irish groan from his brothers, and calls off their opponents. Next day Conall and his men join the army of the German Emperor, and in a massive battle the Turks are completely overthrown. Conall returns to Ireland with his father and brothers, and his later career is summarised in keeping with the earlier sources.

As well as using a version of the earlier biography of Conall, the author of this text borrowed some plots from current folklore (see **Romantic Tales**, Type 953 and **Humorous Tales**, Type 1137). The motif of a hag magically reviving slain warriors is found also in the 13th-century Norman-French romance *Perceval*, and this may have drawn on the same lost Irish source from which the author of *Eachtra Chonaill Gulban* got it. This romance of Conall Gulban, with its colourful imagery, became very popular in manuscripts, and from being read out it was picked up by oral storytellers in the 18th and 19th centuries. Several versions have been collected from folklore - all shortened and tending to omit the details which are not necessary to the basic plot. That plot, as preserved by the oral tellers, centres on the abduction of Eithne, Conall's adventures in Scandinavia, his defeat of the Macaomh, and his final routing of the Turks.

[Biographies] Pól Breathnach in *Irisleabhar Muighe Nuadhat* (1932), 43-52 and (1933), 34-41; Gustav Lehmacher in *Zeitschrift für celtische Philologie 14*, 212-69; W M Hennessy / D H Kelly (1875), 138-55, 312-31.

[St Patrick] Ludwig Bieler (1979), 132-3 and (1971), 149-50; Kathleen Mulchrone (1939), 46; Whitley Stokes (1887), 70-3, 148-51, 464-7, 478-81; Bernard Burke (1884), 747; Andrew O'Kelleher / Gertrude Schoepperle (1918), 12-3.

[Romance and oral versions] IFC 1121 (edition by Riobard Ó Scannláin). Discussions and lists of versions in Alan Bruford (1969), 15-7, 72-9 253-4, 279 and in *Béaloideas 31*, 1-50.

CONÁN MAOL Mischievous character in the **Fianna Cycle**, brother of the great warrior **Goll mac Morna**. The name Conán is a diminutive of 'cú' (literally 'hound' but figuratively 'warrior'), and the epithet means 'bald'.

His mischief-making is probably a survival from the early hostile portrayal of Goll and thus of the whole Morna clan. There is an early reference to a certain Maol mac Morna, and such a character may have been envisaged as having a druidic tonsure, an image also found in relation to the great Fianna leader, **Fionn mac Cumhaill**. It is of interest that Conán Maol shares his first name with another character who was hostile to Fionn, namely Conán son of the Liath Luachra. We read that this latter character waged a long campaign against the Fianna, killing many of them. His father's designation ('the Grey of Logher') shows him to have belonged to west Munster, hostile territory for Fionn (q.v.), and it was in that area that he eventually crept up on and captured Fionn himself. He told Fionn that he wished to enlist in the Fianna, and the latter had no choice but to agree. However, Fionn never forgave him and eventually encompassed his death by sending him to woo the daughter of a man who had vowed to kill any such wooer.

Accounts of Conán Maol mac Morna begin in the 12th-century literature, and it is noticeable that the author of the most developed Fianna text of that period confuses the son of Liath Luachra with Goll's brother. It may therefore be that Conán Maol was in origin a composite figure drawn from a certain Maol mac Morna and this other Conán. Already in the 12th-century sources he has a comprehensive personality as an impulsive and quite malicious man. A very sinister side to his character is illustrated by one episode, in which, during the great war between Fionn and Goll, he and two of his supporters seize three young women who are under Fionn's protection. When they are brought to Goll's camp, that warrior wishes to return them as a means of making peace with Fionn, but Conán Maol insists on killing them. This is probably an echo of the cruel nature of Fionn's archetypal foe who originally gave rise to the more noble Goll (q.v.). It represents an extreme in the portrayal of Conán, whose mischief is usually of a more mundane type.

We read that 'he never sought justice from anyone, and he gave his curse to whomsoever did justice to him', and he was notorious for jibes and incitement. A 15th-century lay goes so far as to call him 'the destructive man of the Fiann-troop' ('fear millte na Féinne'). This word for destruction has a special meaning in the term for a magically destructive eye, 'súil mhillte', so it is not surprising that folklore attributes to Conán the power of killing his enemies by looking at them through his fingers. He had requested that power, we are told, from an otherworld lady in an allegorical house which Fionn (q.v.) and some of the Fianna once visited, and the lady had granted it to him. However, on Fionn's advice she did not let him know that his request had been granted, for if he knew it he might kill the Fianna themselves if a fit of pique took him.

Conán Maol was portrayed as a troublesome buffoon in the post-mediaeval literature of the Fianna Cycle (q.v.). and his actions afford comic relief in some texts. A favourite situation is to have him tussling with hideous hags, resisting their amorous advances or fighting viciously with them. According to one such text, when many of the Fianna were released after being stuck to the floor in a magical dwelling, there was not enough liquid to release Conán, so he had to be forcibly torn free, leaving the skin of his back behind him. Folk narrative added some details in its retellings of the popular text, claiming that the other Fianna warriors attached a sheepskin to his back in place of his own skin, and that he was sheared each year and thus provided socks for all the Fianna! He is further ridiculed in a verse-text composed in south Ulster in the late 18th-century. According to this, he is invited to an otherworld dwelling by a little man called Cab an Dosáin ('Tufty Mouth'). During the night there, he tries to go to the bed of a beautiful young woman, but imagines that he is being sucked into a bog and that savage cats are attacking him. His shouts awaken the other dwellers, and they find him sitting on a candlestick, with a kitten licking his mouth. When all had again retired, he succeeded in reaching the woman's bed, but she made him reverse sexual roles, and then he imagined that he was going to give birth and called for a midwife. Fionn, however, managed to have Conán freed from his weird surroundings 'because he had some magic himself'. This story is a combination of a somewhat earlier text on a character called **Mac na Míchomhairle** and of an international narrative plot (see **Humorous Tales**, Type 1739).

Whitley Stokes (1880), clxxii and (1900), 52, 113, 186, 203-5; Nessa Ní Shéaghdha (1967), 24; Eoin

23. CONCHOBHAR MAC NEASA *Eamhain Mhacha from the air.*

Mac Néill (1908), 57; Gerard Murphy (1933), 258; Dáithí Ó hÓgáin (1988), 165-6, 272-3, 295-6, 336, 342, 344, 357.

[Conán son of the Liath Luachra] Stokes (1900), 101-2; Eoin Mac Néill (1908), 1-3; Edward Gwynn (1924), 362-6; L-C Stern in *Revue Celtique 13*, 7-10; Ní Shéaghdha (1967), 56-64. See also **Feardhomhain**.

CONCHOBHAR MAC NEASA Mythical king in the **Ulster Cycle.**

The name Conchobhar is a compound of 'cú' (i.e. hound, figuratively 'warrior') and 'cobhar' (i.e. desirous). Its original meaning would then appear to be 'one who is desirous of warriors', a typical designation for the king in heroic society. As holder of the office of sacral kingship, the figure of Conchobhar must have been of importance in the legends of the ancient Ulaidh people, from whom the province of Ulster got its name. Echoing lore of him which circulated in antiquity, we have several embellished accounts of Conchobhar from early in the literature, and by mediaeval times the corpus of the Ulster Cycle functioned as a kind of general biography of him.

It is curious that he is designated from the name of his mother Neas (earlier, Nes). This might be a vestige of some matriarchal system, but it more likely derives from the convention of personifying sovereignty as a woman (see **Goddesses**). In accordance with this, descriptions of his birth were invented which, in underlying his royal status, gave pride of place to his mother. Neas, it is claimed, was daughter of a fictional earlier king of the province called Eochu Sálbhuidhe. She had twelve foster-fathers, who were all slain by the druid-warrior **Cathbhadh** as they drank together one night. The identity of their killer was not known, and Neas was so enraged that she took to reaving the countryside in blind fury. One day, while she was unarmed and bathing in a lake, she was seized by Cathbhadh who made her swear to become his wife. One account states that Conchobhar was their offspring; but another has a high-king of Ireland, Fachtna Fáthach, as his father. Yet another source states that Neas was fertilised by a drink of water which she had brought to Cathbhadh and some drops of which she herself consumed. The water was from the Conchubhar, which was the name of a stream (apparently in the vicinity of Lough Ross in Co

Armagh). Thus, it is said, the child got its name. This explanation is based on the false identification of two different words, the stream's name being a compound of 'con' (i.e. cumulative) and 'cubhar' (foam). An additional motif used in order to connect him with this river seems to have been borrowed from lore of **Fionn mac Cumhaill**. According to it, Conchobhar was born holding a worm in each hand, and immediately fell into the river, from which Cathbhadh rescued him.

The tradition which gained currency was that Fachtna Fáthach was the real father and that Cathbhadh acted as guardian to the child; and this allowed for a story to develop which rationalised Conchobhar's accession to the throne of Ulster. The reigning king, **Fearghus mac Róich**, wished to have Neas as wife, and she agreed on condition that he allow her son to hold the kingship for one year. The province prospered during that year, and Neas advised Conchobhar to win the support of the nobles by favouritism and bribery. This strategem worked so well that, at the end of the year, the nobles decided to retain Conchobhar as king. He then ordered that Fearghus be banished, and a civil war followed between the two. Peace was eventually made between them, the basic conditions of it being that Conchobhar should remain king and that Fearghus should become seneschal of the province. The king of **Tara**, **Eochaidh Feidhleach**, who had supported Fearghus in the war, now gave his daughter in marriage to Conchobhar. That daughter was **Meadhbh**, but she soon left her bridegroom through vanity and returned to her father at Tara.

Conchobhar is portrayed as a good and able administrator of his kingdom. During his reign in Ulster, the crops grew lusciously, cattle were easily fattened, and the rivers and lakes gave plenty of fish. Peace and prosperity radiated from his court at Eamhain Mhacha (Navan Fort in Co Armagh), where he had fine buildings erected. As an ideal king, he is imagined as having been in step with the logic of the cosmos. His household, for instance, consisted of 'the number of men which is the number of days in the year'. He held a great assembly each year at Samhain (November), the feast with greatest emphasis in the old Irish calendar, and all the Ulstermen were duty-bound to attend this assembly. Any man who failed to do so lost his reason and died. He was also a model of systematic planning, establishing depots and armouries and instituting an academy at Eamhain Mhacha where boys were trained in feats of arms. Regarding his duties as king, he spent each morning in solving the administrative problems of the province, and then divided the day into three parts. The first part he spent observing the boys perform athletic feats, the second part playing chessboard games, and the final part feasting with music and entertainment. Echoes of more primitive features survive through the model patterns, however, features which accord with the fertility symbolism of the Ulster kingship evidenced by the character of Fearghus mac Róich (q.v.). Thus we read that Conchobhar slept with the bride of each of his subjects on the first night after a wedding, and slept on one night also with the wife of any householder whom he visited on his royal circuit. His sister Deichtine was the mother of the great **Cú Chulainn**, but one tradition had it that Conchobhar was in fact the father of that hero through an incestuous union with Deichtine. He certainly was quite amorous, for we read that, after Meadhbh, he married three of her sisters - Clothra, Eithne, and Mughain.

As a warrior, Conchobhar is represented as brave and resourceful, as in *Táin Bó Cuailnge* (see **Ulster Cycle**) when he shows his valour after he and his men are released from the magical debility previously imposed on them by the lady **Macha**. When the *Táin* campaign was over, he languished in Eamhain Mhacha impatiently planning vengeance on Meadhbh and the rest of Ireland for the damage they had inflicted on his province. Gathering his forces by land and sea, he made such preparations for terrible war that the three great waves of Ireland shook portentously. The various kings who had opposed him now offered huge compensation in gold, but Conchobhar refused and moved his army south to Ros na Ríogh (Rosnaree on the river Boyne). He was confronted there by the forces of Cairbre Nia Fear, king of Tara. During the fighting, Conchobhar's shield, the Óchaoin, shrieked out and was answered by all the other shields of the Ulstermen. When Cú Chulainn slew Cairbre the enemy took to flight, and he entered Tara in triumph. Cairbre had been married to Conchobhar's sister Feidhilm, and the victor now gave the prestigous kingship of Tara to the son of that couple, called Earc. This story first appears in a 12th-century manuscript, and is obviously a late addition to the *Táin* story, but it is interesting to note that there is no attempt - even at that late stage - to have Conchobhar installed at Tara as high-king of all Ireland.

The unsavoury manner in which he ousted

Fearghus from the Ulster throne was not seen to reflect overmuch on Conchobhar's character. It was based on a vestige of ancient ritual which had Fearghus (q.v.) as a divine patron entrusting that kingship to the reigning sovereign - the story itself being no more than a rationalisation of this vestige. The early mediaeval writer, who thus rationalised the material, found it necessary to dramatise it in personal terms, and for this purpose he attributed a shrewd opportunism to Conchobhar. This trait of opportunism was not perpetuated by other writers, but one notable exception was a story which developed early in the 9th century - the tragedy of **Deirdre**. This story in fact goes further than its precedent, allotting to Conchobhar a cynically cruel and treacherous role, but in general the older type of portrayal held firm and Conchobhar was envisaged in a remarkably consistent light through the centuries.

True to the original meaning of his name, he is invariably described as a figure of authority surrounded by his great martial champions, and significantly his death occurs when for once the sacred person of the king is exposed unprotected to the foe. This, his death-tale, is found in several versions and seems to have originated in the 11th century. According to it, the Leinster king Meas Geaghra was slain by **Conall Cearnach** and his brain, mixed with lime, was preserved as a trophy in Eamhain Mhacha. **Ceat mac Mághach**, the Connacht warrior who continuously ravaged Ulster, stole the trophy away. Mindful of a prophecy that Meas Geaghra would avenge himself after death, Ceat kept the brain-ball by him as a missile, with which he intended to do maximum harm to the Ulstermen when the opportunity should arise. Eventually, during a skirmish between the two provinces, he got his chance. He persuaded a group of Connacht women to beg Conchobhar to go apart from the Ulster army and show his kingly person to them, and then lost no time in shooting the brain-ball from a sling at his quarry. The missile lodged in Conchobhar's head and, thus seriously wounded, the king was rescued and taken away by the Ulster warriors. On examining the wound, the surgeon Finghein decided that Conchobhar's life would be endangered if the ball were removed, but that he would live if he avoided all exertion. For seven years Conchobhar remained seated, but then one day he noticed the earth trembling and the sun darkening and, on enquiring of the druid Cathbhadh what was the meaning of this, was told that a good man called **Christ** had been crucified in the east. Outraged by this news, Conchobhar rose up in great anger, and the ball fell from his forehead. The blood which sprang from his head baptised him before he died, and so he was the first Irishman to become a Christian. Variants of this story have, as bearer of the sad tidings to Conchobhar, not Cathbhadh but a Leinster poet called Bachrach, or even a Roman tribute-collector called Altus. One version of the story has the king rising from his throne and racing furiously to a nearby wood, where he slashes at the trees, in his delirium imagining them to be the crucifiers of Christ.

This story became popular in the folklore of Ulster, but the idea of baptism by blood was too enigmatic, and that detail dropped out and was replaced by a whole new extension to the account. His body only had died, it was said, and God had preserved his soul and deposited it in the hollow of his skull. Much later, when St **Patrick** was preaching the Faith in Ireland, he heard a voice speaking to him from a clump of rushes. This was the voice of Conchobhar's soul, and Patrick soon discovered the skull in the rushes. The voice explained how the brain-ball had been lodged there, and Patrick said that in order to reach heaven the body must be revived and baptised. Conchobhar's soul then cried out pathetically that it feared to endure death a second time, whereupon Patrick was so overcome with pity that tears flowed from his eyes down onto the skull and Conchobhar was thus baptised. His soul ascended to heaven in the form of a dove. This legend is derived from a mediaeval Latin tradition which claimed that St Gregory the Great had baptised the dead Emperor Trajan, Patrick and Conchobhar being seen as good substitutes for these two worthies in the Irish context.

Conchobhar does not figure prominently in recent folk tradition, apart from this latter legend and occurrences in oral versions of stories like that of Deirdre and Macha, as well of course as the fragmentary oral survivals of the Cú Chulainn stories.

[Name] Calvert Watkins in *Ériu 19*, 114-6.

[Birth and accession] Kuno Meyer in *Revue Celtique 6*, 173-82; Whitley Stokes in *Ériu 4*, 18-38.

[Reign] Stokes, *op cit*; A G Van Hamel (1933), 20-1, 64-5. Also references under **Ulster Cycle**.

[Battle of Ros na Ríogh] Edmund **Hogan** (1892).

[Death] Kuno Meyer (1906), 2-21; P S Dinneen (1908) *2*, 198-205; Joseph Szövérffy in *Zeitschrift für celtische Philologie 25*, 183-210; Alan Bruford (1969), 99; Dáithí Ó hÓgáin (1985), 11-2.

[General accounts] Cormac Ó Cadhlaigh (1956), 38-44, 135-61, 371-82, 427-9, 469.

CONGHAL CLÁIRINGNEACH Fictional king of Ireland, situated in prehistory. The name means 'warrior-valour' and the sobriquet 'flat-nailed'. There apparently were several stories in mediaeval literature concerning him, but no good early account survives. There is, however, a long text, dating from around the 15th century, which retells episodes known to the literature for several centuries anterior to it. These episodes have synchronised Conghal with the **Ulster Cycle**, thus bringing forward his reign to the end of the 1st century BC.

The text, which was written in east Ulster, tells of how Lughaidh Luaighne, king of Ireland, divided the province of Ulster into two parts, placing Conghal Cláiringneach over one part and **Fearghus mac Léide** over the other. The nobles demanded that their province be united under one king, and the poet Fachtna Fionn brought the two rulers to **Tara** to request this of Lughaidh Luaighne. In Tara, Lughaidh's daughter Fionnabhair fell in love with Fearghus and prevailed upon her father to give the Ulster kingdom to him. Tracts of land in each province were offered in compensation to Conghal, but he rejected this and left Tara in anger. He went to the king of Meath, Cairbre Crom, who encouraged him to avenge the insult, and several banished princes joined him there. As he returned to Ulster, he met Criomhthann Caomh, son of Lughaidh Luaighne, at the Boyne and killed him. When Lughaidh was given news of this, he was in great sorrow. He gave Fionnabhair in marriage to Fearghus mac Léide, who then undertook to go home to Ulster and banish Conghal. Fearghus held a great feast at the Ulster capital, Eamhain Mhacha, at which his namesake Fearghus mac Rosa (i.e. **Fearghus mac Róich**) was present. Contention arose between the followers of the two, and when mac Rosa grew doubtful that a military tribute due to him from mac Léide would be honoured he withdrew his forces from Eamhain and joined Conghal's army. Conghal sent the poets Fachtna Fionn and Bricne (i.e. **Bricriu**) to Eamhain to ask his friends and kinsmen to join him, but Bricne began to make threats against these and they refused to come over. On the advice of his tutor, Conghal turned away from fighting his fellow-Ulstermen, but he allowed Fearghus mac Rosa to attack and destroy the fortress of Niall Niamhghlonnach at Dún Dá Bheann (Mount Sandel near Coleraine) in revenge for the insults he had received at the feast. In retaliation, Niall attacked the army of Conghal and mac Rosa at Aonach Inbhir Thuaighe (at the mouth of the river Bann). In a fierce battle, Niall was slain and his forces scattered. The poet Fachtna Fionn then advised Conghal to go overseas with his followers, and they did accordingly. After several adventures in Scotland and elsewhere, they returned to Ulster and were rejoined by Fearghus mac Rosa and headed for the hostel of Boirche (in south-east Co Down) where Fearghus mac Léide was then sojourning. Mac Léide and his men came out to face the foe but they were routed, and Conghal then decided to advance on Tara. He sent Fachtna to challenge Lughaidh Luaighne, who asked for a night's respite in order to gather his forces. He was given that, but in the battle next day he came face to face with a rampant Conghal and was beheaded. His Luaighne sept were decimated, and Conghal then took the kingship of Ireland. Fearghus mac Léide came to Tara to surrender, and Conghal did not banish him but gave the throne of Ulster to a warrior called Ros Ruadh.

The portion of the text which describes Conghal's adventures abroad is obviously a late mediaeval invention, and indeed may have been composed by the writer of the text himself. It tells of how Conghal was betrothed to Taise Thaoibhgheal, daughter of king **Donn** of the otherworld, who is here said to have lived on Rathlin Island. The king of Uardha ('cold country'), called Nabgodon, desired Taise. When Conghal and his men were feasting with Donn at the latter's hostel, this Nabgodon attacked them with a great force, and in a vicious struggle Conghal beheaded Nabgodon and all the attackers were slain. Conghal and his men were a long time recuperating from their wounds, and meanwhile emissaries were sent to Fearghus mac Léide, who bestowed a tract of land on Taise and even offered the Ulster kingship to Conghal. The latter, however, decided to go to Scandinavia, and he and his men were royally entertained by the king of that country, called Amhlaoibh. Bricne mischievously went to the king's beautiful daughter Beiuda and told her that Conghal was in love with her. She said that he must bring her three wonderful birds, a certain great chariot-yoke, and a certain great helmet. These things were on a faraway sea-fortress which was controlled by the amazon Muirn with a great force, but after many fighting feats Conghal and his men procured them. On his return to Scandinavia he refused to marry Beiuda, since she had sent him into such danger. Then he went to Scotland and took several islands, and received the homage of the kings of the Britons and Saxons before deciding to return to Ireland.

The death of Conghal was made to follow logically on his great campaign for the kingship. It was said that he went to Munster to take hostages on account of the help that Lughaidh Luaighne had received from that province. The Munstermen refused the hostages, and in the ensuing battle they were defeated and Lughaidh's son Cairbre was wounded and remained lame ever after. This Cairbre had two sons, Duach (alternately, Duí) and Deadhadh. These contended with each other, and Duach had his brother blinded. He was therefore known as Duach Dallta Deadhaidh ('Duach who blinded Deadhadh'). Conghal died at the hands of this Duach, who then assumed his grandfather's throne, but no details of this episode survive.

R A S Macalister (1956), 296-7: P M MacSweeney (1904); P S Dinneen (1908) *2*, 180-3.

CONLAÍ (later, Conlaoch) Son of **Cú Chulainn** in the **Ulster Cycle**, tragically slain by his father in single combat.

The story of Conlaí first appears in a text of the late 9th century, *Aided Oenfir Aífe* (the Death of Aoife's Only Son), and is a version of an international hero-tale plot (see **Romantic Tales**, Type 873). When Cú Chulainn was learning arms in Scotland, we are told, he overcame in combat the female warrior Aoife, and she consented to lie with him. He gave her a ring and requested her, if she gave birth to a baby-boy, to send the child to Ireland as soon as he could wear that ring. He further said that the boy should be instructed to tell his name to no single warrior. Seven years later, the Ulstermen were assembled on the shore of Trácht Éise (at the Newry estuary) when they saw a youth coming over the waves in a boat. The youth refused to tell his name to various warriors who went one by one to meet him, and he overcame them all. Eimhear, the wife of Cú Chulainn, suspected the youth's identity, and she tried to restrain her husband from going to face him; but Cú Chulainn ignored her entreaties and demanded his name of the youth. The latter begged that two men be sent against him so that he might tell it, but to no avail, and a terrible combat commenced between the two. They went fighting into the water, and Cú Chulainn shot his javelin, the 'ga bolga', at his opponent through the water. The youth's entrails were torn out and he died. Cú Chulainn took the body in his arms and laid him before the Ulstermen. 'Here is my son for you, men of Ulster!' he said.

It is clear that the starting-point for this narrative was the older account of the wooing of Eimhear by Cú Chulainn (q.v.), which described how that hero learned arms in Scotland and fought Aoife. The spirit of the international hero-tale was not properly integrated into the context, as the author - mindful of the short life of Cú Chulainn - had to make Conlaí an accomplished fighting warrior at the tender age of seven. Two other versions, which do not long post-date that text, exhibit a desire to make the story more logical. One of these, a verse redaction, makes Conlaí nine years old when he comes to Ireland. The other, in prose, mentions no age, but changes the background to his conception in order to render it less complicated. Thus, whereas both Aoife and another lady, Uathach daughter of Scáthach, were lovers of Cú Chulainn in Scotland according to the story of the wooing of Eimhear, here Aoife herself is made Scáthach's daughter.

The manuscript copyists of the Middle Ages intruded an account of Conlaí's conception into their text of the Wooing of Eimhear, thus gaining respect and acceptance for the new narrative. In later literary tradition, the two stories were usually paired together, and inflated versions of both were written in the 16th century and recopied in several manuscripts for the following two hundred years. So it is not surprising to find that in folklore the story of Conlaoch, son of Cú Chulainn, is invariably told as a sequel to the latter's sojourn in Scotland. Several versions of this combination have been collected from the recent oral lore of Cos Donegal and Galway, and in them Aoife is always fused with the daughter of Scáthach. Not surprisingly, the story of Conlaoch was popular also in the west of Scotland, where a special lay concerning his tragic biography was composed and passed on orally. The celebrated Irish writer W B Yeats knew the story in translation from the old literature, and he made it the subject of his play 'On Baile's Strand'.

[Oldest version] A G Van Hamel (1933), 9-15.

[Other recensions] Edward Gwynn (1924), 132-5. J G O'Keeffe in *Ériu 1*, 123-7.

[Later version] Seán Ua Ceallaigh (1935), 25-38.

[Folklore] Seán Ó Súilleabháin (1942), 598; Alan Bruford (1969), 94, 256-7; J F Campbell (1872), 9-15.

CONN CÉADCHATHACH (earlier, Cond Cétchathach) Mythical king of Ireland. His name means 'head', and the sobriquet 'of the hundred battles'. The imagery in these names is that of a great conquering leader.

'Conn' is the Irish version of an old Celtic word for sense or intelligence, and its Gaulish equivalent 'Condos' was also in use as a personal name. It was natural that a sept emerging to power and predominance in Ireland should regard such an ideal name as being that of their ancestor. The sept which seized control of the Boyne valley and triumphed over all their rivals in the 4th and 5th centuries accordingly called themselves Connachta ('descendants of Conn'), and to them is due the origin of this mythical king. By the time that Irish saga-lore was committed to literature the political and military interests of the Connachta sept had caused many traditions of him to develop. Much of this can be instanced from the surviving mediaeval texts.

The earliest stratum of tradition is echoed in a text which dates from around the 9th century, but which undoubtedly reflects much earlier material. This tells of how a certain Fínghein mac Luchta was visited each November-feast (see **Time**) by an otherworld woman called Rothniamh. She used to relay to him information concerning all the affairs of Ireland. One year, when she came she told him that many wonders were to occur on that night. A son would be born to a king called Feidhlimidh, and that son would unite the five provinces and be the progenitor of fifty-three kings of Ireland. On the same night a stream would break from the earth which would be the river Boyne. Also, an ancient tree called Mughain which had been sown by **Fionntan mac Bóchna** would be uncovered, and Fionntan himself would awake from a long slumber and would relay ancient lore. Furthermore, lost treasures would be discovered by the **Tuatha Dé Danann** in their otherworld dwellings, the five great roads of Ireland would be discovered; and among other wonders great lakes and rivers would appear and nine bright birds would sing beautiful music over the rampart of **Tara**. Later, when Conn became king of Ireland, he was told by his druid that Fínghein was the only man in the country who did not give fealty to him. He sought out Fínghein, who then served him for fifty years until falling in battle. Conn himself, it was claimed, reigned for no less than fifty-three years, and his floruit was put down to the 2nd century AD. It was claimed that he immediately succeeded the great Leinster king, **Cathaoir Mór**, as ruler of Tara, and some sources state that he in fact defeated and slew Cathaoir in a battle at Magh Ágha (the plain around Teltown in Co Meath). No reign ever was better than his. There was no robbery, no sickness, no bad weather; and the trees were well foliated, the crops were copious, and the rivers were full of fish. No sharp weapons were carried, one ploughing in spring yielded three crops, and the cuckoo's cry was heard on the cows' horns. 'A hundred clusters grew on each stem, a hundred nuts in each cluster.'

It is clear from this text that when the Connachta took over the Boyne valley they expropriated the cultic lore of that area (see **Find**) and connected it to their mythical ancestor. Their anxiety to make Conn the culture-hero of the Boyne valley was, as the text shows, equalled by their anxiety to make him the perfect king of Tara. The Connachta were successful in their ambitious policies, but they did have to contend with long and sustained opposition from other septs. Memories of this are embodied in the tradition of a great conflict between Conn and the Munster hero **Eoghan Mór** (also known as Mugh Nuadhat). Eoghan, it was said, made himself king of the southern province by ousting the three incumbents. One of these three, called Aonghus, sought help from Conn and received six battalions. He was, however, defeated and slain by Eoghan, who thereby came into direct conflict with Conn. Eoghan defeated the high-king in ten successive battles, forcing him to divide Ireland in halves between them. Conn had the northern half, and Eoghan took the southern half. Hence the names 'Leath Choinn' and 'Leath Mhogha' for the two halves of the country. The dividing line ran from Áth Cliath Meadhraidhe (i.e. Maaree, south-east of Galway) to Áth Cliath Duibhlinne (i.e. Dublin). It consists of a number of low mounds across the centre of the country which could be imagined as a series, and was known as Eisgir Riada ('the Careering Ridge').

24. CONN CÉADCHATHACH *Stone figures of prehistoric kings or druids, from Co. Fermanagh.*

A developed and inflated telling of the conflict between Conn and Eoghan is given in a 13th-century text, *Cath Maighe Léna* (the Battle of Moylena). Here Eoghan's father is described as displacing two rivals for the Munster kingship and as gaining that office for Eoghan. The two displaced men were called Macnia mac Luighdheach and **Conaire mac Mogha Lámha**, and they went to Conn for help. They were well received at Tara and Conn gave them his daughters in marriage as well as a third daughter to Iomchadh Airmdhearg, a prince who had been banished from Ulster. Relations between Conn and Eoghan deteriorated as a result, and Conn gathered his forces and advanced into Munster. After several skirmishes, he encountered the Munster forces at Carn Buidhe (near Kenmare in Co Kerry). A fierce battle ensued, with Eoghan on the losing side. He escaped in a boat and departed the country for Spain. Some time later he returned to Carn Buidhe with a strong Spanish force and demanded of Conn that Ireland be divided in two halves between them. Left with no choice Conn agreed, and the division lasted for a long time. When Eoghan went on a circuit of his territories later, he noticed that many ships belonging to Conn were in Dublin Bay, and he demanded that the bay should also be divided equally. Conn refused, and a new war began between them. Eoghan brought his forces to Moylena (just north of Tullamore in Co Offaly), and Conn made an unexpected attack on him there. In a prolonged struggle, Eoghan's armies were wiped out and he himself slain. Conn was then the unchallenged king of Ireland, and he re-established Macnia and Conaire as joint-kings of Munster.

Another tradition told of a special clash with the Leinstermen, whose king Eochaidh mac Earca once refused to pay the **bóraimhe** tribute. At Maistiu (Mullaghmast in Co Kildare) Conn was routed by the Leinster forces. As he fled he was overtaken by two Leinster warriors and wounded by them. He slew the two, but Tara was taken and remained in the possession of Eochaidh for seven years. However, Conn's fortunes revived and he regained the royal citadel and compelled Eochaidh to once more yield the tribute. Such traditions of Conn's struggles against provincial kings echo the emerging power of his sept, the Connachta, although in the form in which they have come down to us the stories anachronistically portray Conn like a mediaeval king claiming sovereignty over the whole country.

Accounts vary concerning the length of his reign, ranging from twenty to fifty-three years, but there is general agreement that he was succeeded - according to his own wishes - by his son-in-law Conaire mac Mogha Lámha. Conaire was succeeded by Conn's son Art, father of the most celebrated personage in the whole lore of the sept, **Cormac mac Airt**. Since Conn was therefore the great progenitor of the Connachta, a sept from which sprung the Uí Néill and other leading families (see **Niall Naoi-ghiallach**), it was important to emphasise his role as ideal king and founder of a dynasty. One early text is entitled *Buile Chuind Chétchathaigh* (the Vision of Conn of the Hundred Battles), and it gives a long list of kings who succeeded him. Another text, put together in the 11th century, turns this into the form of a story. One day, we are told, Conn went for a walk on the rampart of Tara, accompanied by his druids and his poet Cessarn. He trod on a stone, which screamed under his foot. Cessarn explained that the number of cries which the stone made signified the number of his descendants who would rule Ireland. Then a great mist descended, and they found themselves in a beautiful plain. Entering a magnificent house they found there a girl with a crown of gold and a golden cup, and a phantom sitting on the throne. The phantom was **Lugh**, and the girl was the sovereignty of Ireland. She gave a giant ox-rib and hog-rib to Conn, as well as a cup of red ale (see **Kingship**), and the phantom named the future kings. Cessarn wrote them down in **'ogham'** script on staves of yew, and then the vision disappeared.

Such vision stories had some vogue in the mediaeval literature concerning Conn. We read that he was on the hill of Uisneach (Ushnagh, Co Westmeath) one day, accompanied by his son Connla, when a beautiful lady from the otherworld approached. Only Connla saw the lady, and she called on him to go to Magh Meall ('the Pleasant Plain'). Conn's druid sang a spell against her so that she departed, but as she did so she threw an apple to Connla. For a whole month, Connla would partake of no food but that apple. Then, when they were at the sea-shore one day, the otherworld lady returned. She had a boat of glass, and Connla entered that vessel and went away with her.

Conn's other son **Art** also features in a late mediaeval narrative involving the otherworld. According to this, when his beloved queen Eithne died, Conn was very depressed and went alone one day to Beann Éadair (Howth, Co Dublin). There he met a young woman of the **Tuatha Dé Danann**, called Bé Chuma, who had been expelled by her own people for an indiscretion which she had committed with a son of **Manannán**. She went with Conn to Tara and lived with him for a year. She demanded that he banish Art, and he did so, but as a result there was neither corn nor milk for the whole year in Ireland. The **druids** were consulted, and they blamed the misfortune on the presence of the woman and further revealed that deliverance could only come through the sacrifice of the son of a sinless couple. Conn undertook to seek out such a youth. He went to Beann Éadair, where he found a boat which brought him to a beautiful island called Tír na nIongnadh ('the Land of Wonders'). He found there a prince called Séaghdha Saorlabhraidh, whose parents had never come together except at his conception. Conn told Séaghdha that if he bathed in the waters of Ireland, the country would be delivered from its misfortunes, and Séaghdha agreed to go with him. On reaching Tara, preparations were made to slay the boy, but Conn and his men relented. Realising the situation, the boy called on them to slay him, but just then a strange woman approached with a cow and told them to kill the cow instead. This they did, and two birds emerged from the carcase. One bird had twelve legs and the other but one leg. They fought, and the one-legged bird conquered the other. The woman then explained that Séaghdha was as the one-legged bird, with justice on his side, while the druids were as the other. She was the boy's mother, and she declared that the druids should be hanged and advised Conn to put his concubine Bé Chuma from him. Conn could not get himself to do this, and Bé Chuma remained at Tara for some time until Art (q.v.) defeated her at chess, outdid her in questing, and banished her from the country. The theme of the innocent boy who is to be sacrificed on the advice of druids is borrowed from Nennius' account of the boy Ambrosius in *Historia Brittonum*, but it has been reshaped here in a rather awkward attempt to insert Christian symbolism into Celtic otherworld lore.

The death of Conn, as befitted a great hero, could only come about through treachery. He had, we are told, a brother called Eochaidh 'Yellow-Mouth' who continually upset his reign. This Eochaidh went into Ulster, and Conn sent five envoys after him to ensure that he was well-behaved. These envoys met Eochaidh on Sliabh Bréagha (a range of hills north-west of Slane in Co Meath) and slew him there. The Ulstermen were displeased at this, but peace was made between them and Conn. However, an Ulster king called Tiobraide set out for Tara with a group of his men. They were all disguised as women. Conn was standing on an eminence, preparing for the Festival of Tara, and he considered that they were a group of visiting Ulsterwomen. Seizing the opportunity, they fell upon him and slew him. One account states that the otherworld woman Rothniamh reappeared just before this episode to foretell disaster, and that on the death of the great high-king war broke out again between the provinces, rivers overflowed, great trees fell, the salmon in the Boyne river screamed, and the four great waves of Ireland (see **Environment**) lamented him. It is significant that Conn was born at Samhain (the November vigil) and died also at Samhain, for this was reputedly the date of the Festival of Tara (q.v.), the major cultic centre of kingship. The antiquity of this lore of Conn is evidenced by the occurrence of the episode of Eochaidh 'Yellow-Mouth' in a saga which has been dated to the 7th or 8th century. Here Eochaidh is described as Conn's uncle who was his rival for the kingship and who, after doing much harm to Conn, sought and was granted protection in Ulster. Eochaidh is slain by Conn's son Asal, accompanied by five other men, and Conn has to give heavy compensation to the Ulster king **Fearghus mac Léide** as a result. The compensation included a noblewoman of his own sept and a parcel of land known as Níth, just north of the Boyne. The episode is briefly mentioned in a poem of even earlier date, perhaps as early as the 6th century. Here Conn is described as 'cétchorach' (i.e. 'of the hundred treaties'), which may be either an alternative or an older form of his epithet.

[Birth] Joseph Vendryes (1953); Edward Gwynn (1913), 238-9.

[Magh Ágha battle] Myles Dillon (1962), 168-9.

[Conn versus Eoghan] Vernam Hull in *Zeitschrift für celtische Philologie 19*, 59-61; Kenneth Jackson (1938).

[Vision] Rudolf Thurneysen (1912), 48-52; Kuno Meyer in *Zeitschrift für celtische Philologie 12*, 232-8 and 13, 370-82.

[Connla story] Julius Pokorny in *ibid 17*, 193-205.

[Bé Chuma] R I Best in *Ériu 3*, 149-73. Ambrosius story in A G Van Hamel (1932), 52-61.

[Death] Osborn Bergin in *Zeitschrift für celtische Philologie 8*, 274-7; Margaret Dobbs in *ibid 20*, 161-72; D A Binchy in *Ériu 16*, 33-48.

[General] R A S Macalister (1956), 332-5; P S Dinneen (1908) *2*, 260-9; Edward Gwynn (1935), 156; M A O'Brien (1962), 563; T F O'Rahilly (1946), 184-92, 281-5; Myles Dillon (1946), 11-4; L P O Caithnia (1984), 94-8.

CORC DUIBHNE Fictional ancestor of the sept called Corca Dhuibhne in west Munster.

His name was a fanciful personification of the septal designation - the word 'corca' in fact meant 'a race of people' and Duibhne was a goddess whose name appears in the earlier form Dovinia on several west Munster **'ogham'** stones. The legend of the character Corc Duibhne first appears in a text of the 10th or 11th century. We read that his parents were Cairbre Músc and the sister of that warrior, Duibhind. They were the children of **Conaire mac Mogha Lámha**, king of Munster, and twin boys were born of their incest. The first of the twins to emerge had a ruddy colour, and thus was called Corc (literally 'red'). The men of Munster wished the child to be burned and so avoid the shame on their province, but a druid offered to take Corc out of Ireland. He brought the baby to an island off the west coast, called Inis Boí after his wife Boí, who was better known as the **Cailleach Bhéarra**. There Corc was reared by the druid and Boí, being bathed in the sea each morning on the back of the white red-eared cow which his fosterers owned. Eventually the boy, through magic, changed the cow into a rock in the sea, and the druid brought him back to the mainland. The young Corc joined with the Déise sept who, according to the story, were soon after banished from **Tara** by **Cormac mac Airt**. They went to Munster and settled there, and Corc Duibhne chose as his habitation the peninsulas in the west of that province.

There is no mention of the character Corc Duibhne in the earlier, 8th-century, account of the expulsion of the Déise from Tara, and it is clear that this story was invented by the Corca Dhuibhne in the interval. The principal source used by them was the legend of **Conall Corc**, reputed founder of the royal Munster dynasty of the Eoghanacht sept.

Vernam Hull in *Zeitschrift für celtische Philologie 27*, 28-37; F J Byrne (1973), 166-7.

CORMAC CONN LOINGEAS Mythical warrior, son of Ulster king **Conchobhar mac Neasa**.

Cormac's mothar was Clothra, daughter of **Eochaidh Feidhleach** and sister of **Meadhbh**. The scattered fragments of biography devoted to him in the mediaeval literature bring him into the ambit of his famous aunt. We are told that he was one of the guarantors for **Deirdre** and, when his father treacherously reneged on that agreement, he joined with **Fearghus mac Róich** in rebellion. Together they went to Cruachain and joined the forces of Meadhbh there. This group of Ulster defectors to Connacht was called the 'dubhloingeas' (meaning, numerous exile band), and thus was explained Cormac's sobriquets Conn Loingeas ('head of exile bands'). He was in Meadhbh's great muster for the cattle-raid of Cooley but, like Fearghus, could not disguise his sympathy for his fellow-Ulstermen and his reluctance to oppose them. He praised **Cú Chulainn** to his Connacht listeners, grew violently angry when Meadhbh denigrated Conchobhar's military skills, restrained an enraged Fearghus from slaughtering myriads of Ulstermen in the last great battle, and vehemently urged on the brown Ulster bull in its combat with its Connacht rival. All of this is literary fiction, post-dating the Deirdre story which was seen as a rationalisation of Cormac's sobriquets.

The original import of his name, however, would have had the element 'Conn' going with the first word rather than with the third. Thus 'Cormac Conn' (meaning, the Leader Cormac) would have been the character's proper designation, both of these elements having mythic dimensions in early Irish tradition and being interchangeable in that context as names for a hero. In fact, the names Cormac and Conn were used for heroes of great importance in early Irish lore (see **Cormac mac Airt** and **Conn Céadchathach**), and a significant part of the biographies of these heroes was a period of displacement or exile ('loingeas'). It is therefore obvious that the designation Cormac Conn Loingeas had roots far anterior to the story of Deirdre and even to the idea that some Ulstermen defected to the court of Meadhbh.

An indication of what those roots were is provided by the only full story concerning the character, the text *Togail Bruidne Da Choca* which was fashioned in or about the 9th century and tells of how he died. According to this, after the death of his father Conchobhar, the Ulstermen sent **Amhairghin mac Éigit Salaigh** and other emissaries to Cruachain offering Cormac the kingship of his native province. He set out with three hundred men, but on the way he broke several prohibitions (see **'geis'**) which the druid **Cathbhadh** had put on him at his birth. These prohibitions forbade hunting at particular places, repairing his chariot with a yoke of ash, and swimming in a particular lake. Another broken prohibition involved listening to the music of the harper Craiftine who came to play for him. Craiftine did this out of malice because Cormac was the lover of his wife Sceanbh. Reaching the river Shannon at Athlone Cormac saw a woman there before him. She was the Badhbh (see **Mór-Ríoghain**), and she was washing a bloody garment. When she raised her hand, all the water rose up with it, and so Cormac crossed over without wetting his feet. Such a crossing was, however, also one of the things prohibited to him by Cathbhadh. Soon after he and his men encountered and routed a Connacht army which was returning from raiding Ulster. One of his men, Loiniach, was angered by this change in alignments and returned to inform the Connacht court while, weakened from the fighting, Cormac's force decided to rest at the hostel of Da Coga (near Drumraney in Co Westmeath) - again in violation of a prohibition on him. Amhairghin tried to dissuade them from doing so, saying that Da Coga was a subject of Meadhbh, but he was over-ruled, and when reinforcements from Ulster arrived all settled down at the hostel for the night. Amhairghin had a dream of doom, and they were soon surrounded and attacked by a large force of Meadhbh's soldiers. The hostel was set on fire by the attackers, and in a ferocious conflict almost all of Cormac's men were slain. He himself fell in hand to hand fighting with a certain Corb Gaillne and the formidable **Ceat mac Mághach**. Only three survived, Amhairghin, **Dubhthach Daol Uladh**, and Fiacha mac Fir Féibhe, and they were met by a desolate Fearghus mac Róich, who had rushed from Cruachain in an attempt to prevent the slaughter.

This story is a close parallel to the death of **Conaire** at the hostel of Da Dearga, and is obviously derived from that source. The reason seems to have been an old tradition that a character called Cormac Conn Loingeas was also slain in a besieged hostel, and it may even be that Cormac was originally a double of this mythical **Tara king**, Conaire. Sources outside of the **Ulster Cycle** refer to a Cormac Conn Loingeas who was apparently regarded as a Tara king. Such a mythic figure, sharing imagery with such as Conn, Cormac, and Conaire, and sharing with them the theme of exile, would be the source from which was formed the character of Cormac son of Conchobhar mac Neasa.

Kuno Meyer in *Anecdota from Irish Manuscripts 5*, 18; Joseph O'Neill in *Ériu 2*, 176-7; Vernam Hull (1949), 47-8; Cecile O'Rahilly (1976), 1, 52; Whitley Stokes in *Irische Texte 3*, 402-5 and in *Revue Celtique 21*, 149-65, 312-27, 388-402; T F O'Rahilly (1946), 130-40, 284, 485-6.

CORMAC MAC AIRT Mythical high-king of Ireland. The most celebrated of all kings in Irish tradition, the mediaeval historians put down his reign to the period from 227 to 266 AD. Being son of **Art**, he was also known as Cormac ua Cuinn (i.e. 'grandson of Conn'). He was sometimes given the epithet Ulfhada (earlier, Ulfhota), which meant 'longbearded'.

It may be that there was a spectacular local king of **Tara** called Cormac in the 3rd century, but he could not have been ruler of all Ireland at that time. The name is an abbreviation of 'Corbmac' which, with the components reversed, would be the same as 'Mac-corb'. The noun 'mac' (literally, a son) was sometimes in Old Irish sources used in warriors' names, but the element 'corb' has not been satisfactorily explained. It occurs in ancient septal designations of sections of the Laighin (Leinstermen), and indeed a certain Cú Chorb was regarded as the ancestor of all the kings of the Leinstermen. This Cú Chorb was reputed to have had four sons - Nia Corb, Cormac Lusc, Cairbre (earlier Coirpre) Cluitheachair, and Meas Corb. The latter was claimed as their progenitor by the Uí Gharrchon, the sept to which the earliest definitely historical kings of Leinster - in the 5th century AD - belonged. This sept, like others of the Cú Chorb line, fell into relative obscurity in succeeding centuries. The strong likelihood, therefore, is that the appellation Corb was associated with a section of the Leinstermen who had controlled Tara in the 3rd or 4th century. 'Cormac Lusc' is the most suggestive of the names, but another striking echo of the nomenclature is a certain Cairbre Nia Fear. The first element in this character's name is a diminutive of 'Corb', the word Nia meant 'champion', and Fear (literally, 'man') was sometimes used as a synonym for Mac ('son'). This character was cited by the synchronisers of history as having been king of Tara, but not a high-king of Ireland - a position which would suit the political reality of late prehistoric Ireland.

It therefore appears that a figure known as Cormac was the fanciful ancestor of, or the actual leader of, a Leinster group which for a while controlled Tara, and that he therefore came to be seen as an archetype of the sacral kingship associated with that place (q.v.). When the ascendant Connachta sept (see **Conn Céadchathach**) gained control of Tara they expropriated the cult of kingship and adopted Cormac into their own genealogy. They made him out to have been a son of Art, son of their own eponymous ancestor Conn, and in their own propaganda interests portrayed this 'Cormac mac Airt' as the man to whom Tara owed all its splendour and as an ideal king whose power brought good fortune and prosperity to the whole country. That legendary royal names could be borrowed from the genealogy of one dynasty into that of another is evidenced also by the way in which the Leinstermen - impressed by the prestige attaching to the mythical Ulster king **Conchobhar mac Neasa** - claimed that one of their great ancient kings had been called Conchubhar Abhradhrua. In turn, the Ulstermen borrowed the name Cormac from the Connachta, hence their character **Cormac Conn Loingeas**. Perhaps this latter borrowing accounts also for the rather inconsequential epithet which describes Cormac as longbearded, for 'Ulfhota' may be a deliberate corruption of 'Uladhta' ('pertaining to Ulster') and thus an attempt in the Connachta interest to negative the Ulster borrowing.

25. CORMAC MAC AIRT *Early Irish stone carving of a king.*

The Connachta propaganda developed from the 5th to the 7th century, and from it derives the image of Cormac which is found in all the mediaeval literature. In his reign, we read, the rivers of Ireland were overflowing with fish, forests were difficult to travel due to the amount of fruit on the trees, and the plains were difficult to travel because of all the honey. Peace reigned supreme, crops grew copiously, and cows had a massive milk-yield. An echo of the taking of Tara survived in a tradition that 'Cormac grandson of Conn' was defeated by the Leinstermen and banished to Caladh Truim (Galtrim, Co Meath). We read that the Leinstermen were led by Meadhbh Leathdhearg, demonstrably the goddess of sovereignty (see **Meadhbh**), and that she herself held the kingship for fourteen months and lay with Criomhthann Cas, son of the celebrated Leinster king **Cathaoir Mór**, before Cormac managed to regain power. Other sources state that Meadhbh had been the wife of Art, and that she would not allow Cormac - Art's son by another woman - to come to Tara. These are stray echoes from earlier Connachta propaganda concerning Cormac, but it is clear that the Connachta - Uí Néill historians soon decided that it was better to delete all claims of the Leinstermen to the Tara kingship. Accordingly, an epical biography of Cormac mac Airt was composed, the surviving text of which dates from the 8th century. It can be synopsised as follows:-

On the night before the battle of Magh Mucramha (in east Galway), Art slept with the daughter of a druid. Her name was Achtan and, before he left, Art gave her as tokens his sword and a golden ring. He was slain in the battle next day, and his foe **Lughaidh mac Con** took the kingship. Achtan gave birth to her baby, Cormac, and the **druid** signalled five protective circles about him - against wounding, drowning, fire, sorcery, and wolves. Then one day, when Achtan was asleep on a green, a wolf-bitch came and took the child away. This wolf suckled him until he was discovered by a trapper called Luighne and returned to his mother. Fearing the hostility of Lughaidh mac Con, Achtan took the child to the north of Ireland to seek the protection of Art's foster-father Fiachna Casán. While crossing a mountain at night-time, the wolves of Ireland gathered to take back Cormac, but a herd of wild horses protected the mother and son. They reached the dwelling of Fiachna, and Cormac grew up there. On reaching the age of thirty, his druid-grandfather told him that a certain day was auspicious to begin an attempt at gaining the kingship. Taking the sword and ring of his father Art, he set out for Tara all alone. As he approached the citadel, he met with a woman who was crying because the king had declared her sheep forfeit for grazing in the queen's field of woad. 'One shearing for another would have been more just!' said Cormac. When word of this was brought to Lughaidh, the usurper recognised the truth of the judgement. He suspected that this was a son of Art and realised that his own false reign was at an end. Therefore, when Cormac came, Lughaidh received him and handed over the kingship to him.

The elements of Connachta tradition which went to invent this biography are obvious. Lughaidh's moral acceptance of Connachta supremacy is an obvious case in point. Less obvious, though also significant, is the role played by the character Fiachna (or Fiachra) Casán, otherwise associated with the Airghialla sept to the north of the Connachta, and who would therefore reflect a diplomatic function. He was also featured as a helper of Cormac's fancied ancestor **Tuathal Teachtmhar**. Furthermore, there is the helpful role played by a character called Luighne or Luaighne - this was the name of a sept in the vicinity of Tara who were permanently loyal to the Connachta.

An alternate version of Cormac's birth-story also echoes Connachta propaganda of early centuries. In these Cormac's mother is said to have been a legal wife of Art, called Éachtach, and we read that when she became pregnant she had a vision of her head being taken from her body and a great tree growing from her neck. Her husband explained this to mean that she would give birth to a great king who would rule all Ireland. Art was slain at the battle of Magh Mucramha, as he had foretold, and Éachtach went in a chariot to Connacht, seeking the protection of her brother-in-law Lughna (an obvious corruption of Luighne). On the way, she gave birth to the baby Cormac within the chariot. This is based on a false etymology for the name viz. 'carb-mhac' ('chariot-son'). Éachtach told her handmaid to make a bed of leaves for them on the roadside and to watch over them as they slept, but the handmaid herself fell asleep also and a wolf-bitch came and brought the baby away to its den. When Lughna heard of this, he offered a rich reward to anybody who would recover the child, and soon after a man noticed a little boy crawling among wolf-cubs. Thus he was recovered by Lughna, and he grew up to be extremely handsome, strong, and kindly. One day, he and Lughna's sons were playing and he struck one of them. The other boy teased him with having no father, whereupon Cormac went to Lughna and demanded to know the truth. Having told him that he was the son of Art, Lughna brought him to Tara and put him into service there minding sheep for a widow. These were the sheep which Lughaidh mac Con declared forfeit later for grazing the field, and when Cormac corrected the judgement Lughaidh realised who he was. He charged at the boy, who raced from him three times around Tara before jumping the rampart and making his getaway. The men of Ireland, however, having experienced the ill-fortune of the usurper's reign, were pleased that Cormac had come. Lughaidh remained for another year in the kingship - during which time no grass or foliage or corn grew - and then was driven out of Tara and Cormac was installed in his place. One curious description dramatises the ritual contrast between 'true' and 'false' kingship (q.v.) - when Lughaidh gives the wrong verdict on the sheep one side of his palace collapses, but it stays and falls no further when Cormac gives the correct verdict. Thus Cormac is made the founder of true kingship, and this is underlined by the claim that he restored Tara 'as it had never been before' and built the great 'Fortress of the Kings' and other edifices there.

Some ideas used in the development of the myth are quite clear. Cormac is portrayed as the Solomon of the Irish, several accounts referring to his wise decisions and counsels; like Romulus he is suckled by a wolf-bitch; and like Jesus he had a threatened youth and began his public life at the age of thirty. The founding of the Connachta - Uí Néill dynasty, therefore, was patterned along the lines of three other great foundations i.e those of the Jerusalem Temple, of the city of Rome, and of the Christian faith. These ideas cannot have been earlier than the Christianised Ireland of the 6th-7th centuries, but some more ancient ideas can also be traced. Since Lughaidh mac Con (q.v.) belonged to the **Érainn** people, his contest with Cormac could well reflect the taking of Tara by the Leinstermen from the **Érainn** in or about the 3rd century (see **Conaire**). Because of the appellation 'mac Con' (literally, 'son of hound/wolf') the image of suckling by such an animal was very probably first associated with him in particular, and in the perspective of the Leinstermen his reign could be symbolised as a wolf herding sheep - thus introducing the idea of sheep into the embryonic myth. The wolf-imagery would naturally have transferred to Cormac due to the Classical account of Romulus.

In the mediaeval literature, elaborate descriptions are given of the splendour of Cormac's great banqueting hall at Tara, called the Teach Miodhchuarta, and of his methods of administration. Neither was the dramatic potential of his personal life ignored. A 10th-century text tells of a beautiful girl called Eithne, daughter of the Leinster king **Cathaoir Mór**, who was in fosterage with the exceptionally generous hospitaller Buichead. The brothers of Eithne so played upon Buichead's generosity that he became impoverished, his seven herds of cattle reduced to a mere seven cows and one bull. He left Leinster and went to live at Ceanannas (Kells, Co Meath), bringing only his small herd, his wife, and his foster-child. Eithne worked hard for her foster-patents, and one day Cormac met her as he rode through the countryside on his horse. He admired the diligence with which she worked and, on learning who she was, proposed marriage to her. Buichead, however, hesitated with his permission saying that he could not give her as he was not her father, whereupon Cormac had her carried off at night and she conceived by him. Later the marriage was arranged, and Cormac gave a massive bride-price to Buichead - all the animals that he could see from the rampart of Ceanannas for a whole week. Thus Buichead returned to the Leinstermen, with an even bigger herd than before. Other texts tell of how Cormac fell in love with a beautiful woman called Cearnait, daughter of the king of the **Picts**, whom an Ulster raiding-party had brought as a captive from Scotland. Cormac asked for her, and she became his mistress, but Eithne through jealousy made her a slave whose work was to grind a large amount of grain with a quern-stone every day. Cormac contrived to meet with her again, and she became pregnant by him. He pitied her when he saw how hard she had to work, and so sent abroad for a tradesman to construct a mill - the first ever in Ireland. Thus Cearnait was freed from her gruelling labour.

Another story concerning Cormac's family life occurs in a 14th-century text, which seems to be based on earlier materials. According to this, he was alone in Tara on a May morning (see **Time**) when he saw a young beautifully-dressed stranger approach. The stranger had a branch with three golden apples on it, which when he shook gave forth exquisite music capable of healing all illnesses. Cormac asked him for the branch, and was given it in exchange for three requests. He then departed, but returned exactly a year later and asked for Cormac's daughter Ailbhe to go with him. The king reluctantly agreed. Exactly a year later he returned again and in similar manner took Cormac's son, **Cairbre Lifeachair**, with him. Finally, on the third May Day he took Eithne herself. Cormac was disconsolate, and he followed the stranger. He came to an unknown land, where he saw several strange sights. There the stranger revealed that he was **Manannán** and that his country was Tír Tairngire (the Land of Promise). Manannán had brought him there to show to him the nature of true wisdom (see **Poets**). Cormac had his family returned to him, and was given a present of a beautiful goblet, which broke into three pieces when a lie was spoken in its presence and became whole again when the truth was told. He was entertained with a banquet, at which he fell asleep, and next morning awoke on the green of Tara with all his family and the goblet.

The famous high-king had another treasure, a wondrous sword which shone in the darkness like a candle and was so sharp that it could cut a hair on water. It had belonged to a young man called Socht, but one of Cormac's administrators, Duibhdhriu, took it from Socht while he was drunk and had his own name inscribed on the inside of the hilt. Afterwards, Duibhdhriu claimed the sword as his, offering the inscription as proof. Socht replied that the sword was found driven through his grandfather and that this proved that Duibhdhriu was the murderer. Hearing this, Cormac ordered Duibhdhriu to pay wergild for Socht's grandfather. Duibhdhriu confessed the trick he had played, and was given an additional fine by Cormac for that. Cormac then revealed that the sword had once belonged to **Cú Chulainn**, and that it had been used by the Ulstermen to slay his own grandfather Conn (q.v.). The judge Fíothal agreed with Cormac that he should have the sword as wergild; and it, with the branch and the goblet, constituted the three special treasures of Cormac. This story is in fact a variant of a folk plot which was quite popular in mediaeval Europe (see **Romantic Tales**, Type 978).

A striking aspect of the Cormac lore is how he was on several occasions forced to go into exile ('loingeas') from Tara. This theme must have originated in the context of the struggles of the Connachta to gain and hold that sacral centre of kingship from contending peoples such as the Érainn, the Leinstermen, and the Ulstermen. It had special emphasis in the myth of the eponymous ancestor of the Connachta, Conn (q.v.), and its antiquity in the lore of both Conn and Cormac is evidenced by the appellation Cormac Conn Loingeas (q.v.), which was borrowed as the name of an exile prince into the **Ulster Cycle**. In the specific case of Cormac mac Airt, at least three exiles are described by the mediaeval literature. The Ulstermen are given the chief role as his enemies, and one source rationalises this by having them depose him for a year on two separate occasions. This must ultimately reflect the 4th-5th century conflicts as the Connachta attempted to extend their sway north of the river Boyne. A text entitled *Cath Crinna* was composed, probably in the 9th century, describing such a conflict, and an expanded version of it dates from the later Middle Ages.

According to this text, Cormac brought the Ulstermen to a feast in the north of Bréagha (the plain of Meath), but hostilities were scarcely disguised and the servant of the Ulster king scorched Cormac's hair with a candle. To avenge the insult and re-establish his power, Cormac went to his maternal cousin, **Tadhg mac Céin**, and sought his help, promising him as much land of Bréagha as his chariot would encircle after the battle until sunset. Tadhg told Cormac how to come unawares upon the great warrior **Lughaidh Lágha**, as the latter was taking a bath. Cormac stood over Lughaidh with naked sword and demanded wergild for his father Art. Lughaidh, who had slain Art, promised the head of Fearghus 'Black-tooth', king of Ulster. The battle against the Ulstermen was fought at Crionna (on the river Boyne near Mellifont), and Cormac stayed apart, accompanied by a servant dressed exactly like himself. Lughaidh Lágha brought a head to the servant, thinking it that of the Ulster king and that the servant was Cormac. He made the same mistake with a second head and, when he came the third time with the real head of the Ulster king, he slew the servant in a fit of pique. Tadhg fought magnificently, and when the battle was won he demanded fulfilment of the promise of land. Swooning from the effects of the fighting, he set off in his chariot, intending to encompass Tara itself on his route, but the charioteer - a partisan of Cormac - headed away from Tara every time he swooned. Finally, the unfortunate Tadhg found himself at the river Liffey and knew that he had been tricked. Returning to

Tara, he sought medical attention for his wounds. Cormac arranged that both he and Lughaidh Lágha should be treated by physicians whom he bribed to insert beetles into their wounds. When Lughaidh was near to death, Cormac came and asked him how his father Art had comported himself when slain. Lughaidh was livid at the question, and answered bitterly: 'He bleated like a he-goat, he bellowed like a bull, he screeched like a woman!' His anger was indeed so great that his wounds burst open, the beetles fell out, and he was healed. Tadhg got a message to the Munster king **Ailill Ólom**, who sent good physicians to him. They feigned to pierce his stomach with a red-hot iron and, through his terror, he thrust the beetles and other vermin from himself and was also healed. In order to avoid war with him, Cormac gave the fee of the land which his chariot had encircled. The attribution of treachery to Cormac is untypical, and this story was obviously written in the interests of Munster - to which province Ailill Ólom, Lughaidh Lágha, and Tadhg mac Céin belonged.

The second push against Cormac occurred when Eochu Gunnat succeeded Fearghus as Ulster king. One night Cormac saw in a dream this Eochu coming and taking the captives' pillar from Tara and placing it in Cruachain (Rathcroghan, Co Roscommon). He also saw his wife Eithne lying with Eochu for a year and then returning to himself. His druids explained this to mean that the Ulstermen would drive him from Tara and that Eochu would take and hold his kingship for a year. This proved true, for the kings of the other provinces joined with Eochu and defeated Cormac's army. They slew his stepbrother and close ally, Nia son of Lughna, and drove Cormac's own mother Éachtach out of her dwelling. The disconsolate Cormac fled west to Cruachain, where he gathered his supporters about him. Returning to Tara, he defeated the Ulster army, Lughna's other son Lughaidh slaying Eochu Gunnat, and thus Cormac regained his power.

Towards the end of the 9th century, a genealogical text was compiled which claimed that Cormac was expelled for a time from Tara by Fiachu Araidhe, ancestor of the Dál nAraidhe sept of north-east Ulster. He had to go to Rafainn (Knockgraffon in south Tipperary) and submit to the Munster king **Fiachu Muilleathan** in order to get his support. With the help of a strong southern force, therefore, Cormac gave battle to Fiachu Araidhe and defeated him at the battle of Fochaird (Faughart, Co Louth). Cormac regained Tara, and it is clear that this text was written in the Munster interest. A notable aspect of it is the role of counsellor in the battle assigned to the **druid** Mogh Ruith, who resided at Dairbhre (Valentia Island, off the Kerry coast). For his services, this druid was awarded territory in Magh Féinne (near Fermoy, Co Cork). The same selection of Munster characters is found in the text *Forbhais Droma Damhghaire* (the Siege of Drom Damhghaire, now Knocklong in Co Limerick). In its present form, this text dates from as late as the 14th century, but the basis of it must be several hundred years older. Again, it is a Munster story, and this time the southerners teach a lesson to Cormac rather than lend him assistance. It describes how the high-king once ran short of beef to feed his numerous household. One of his administrators reminded him that he collected only one tribute from Munster, even though that province was divided into two parts. However, the Munster king Fiachu Muilleathan refused to pay double tribute, and so Cormac brought his army south and besieged Fiachu at Drom Damhghaire. Fiachu was in a desperate position, but the druid Mogh Ruith came from Dairbhre and magically supplied the besieged Munstermen with water. Cormac's own druid Ciothruadh advised him to have his men cut down trees and set fire to them. If the wind blew south towards the besieged army, they should attack, and if it blew north they should go home. Mogh Ruith advised the Munstermen to do likewise, and then blew a magic breath which became a black cloud and floated towards Cormac's men. The cloud fell among them as a sinister shower of blood. Mogh Ruith also caused the Munster fire to explode into a conflagration, and the smoke from it blew north. The men of Munster then charged after it, sweeping Cormac's army before them, and to stave off utter ruin Cormac had to pay compensation and give hostages to Fiachu at the fortress of Rafainn. Another Munster tradition described how this Fiachu Muilleathan (q.v.) was treacherously slain at the instigation of Cormac.

A particularly interesting development was the association of Cormac with the hero **Fionn mac Cumhaill**, who came to be portrayed as the leader of troops serving the high-king as a semi-independent army (see **Fianna Cycle**). This arose from a conflation of the Connachta - Uí Néill lore of Cormac and the Leinster lore of Fionn. It must have been effected by writers of the 8th century and, as a vestige of the ancient hostility between the Connachta and the Leinstermen, it continued to evidence within it a certain amount of tension between the two characters (see entries on Fionn and **Caoilte**). The writers developed the idea that Cormac's daughter, Ailbhe, had been Fionn's wife, and the celebrated Gráinne of Fianna romance (see **Diarmaid ua Duibhne**) was another reputed daughter of the high-king. Moreover, the eventual overthrow of the Fianna in battle was attributed to Cormac's son, Cairbre Lifeachair (q.v.).

The way in which Cormac's reign was used to punctuate ancient events is well exemplified in a story which was invented in or about the 9th century. This was an attempt to explain the origin of the Déise people of south-east Munster, based on the fact that a similar name, Déis, was borne by an ancient people who resided near Tara. The main actor in this story, and the reputed leader of the Déise, was one Aonghus (earlier, Oengus) Gaíbhuaibhtheach, who was a vestige of Érainn myth, otherwise known as Oengus Bolg. This Aonghus had a terrible spear, from which his epithet derives, and to which three heavy chains were attached. The story tells of how a son of Cormac, called Ceallach, abducted a girl from Aonghus' territory and, chided by a woman from whom he once sought food, Aonghus determined to avenge the act. He went to Cormac's palace at Tara and ran Ceallach through with his spear. As he withdrew it, a link from one of its huge chains struck Cormac and blinded him in one eye. As a result, seven great battles were fought between the armies of Aonghus and Cormac, with the result that Aonghus and his Déise were banished from their territory and had to retire to Munster. Since a blemish disqualified one from holding the kingship (q.v.), Cormac had to abdicate, and his son Cairbre Lifeachair became high-king in his place. Cormac left Tara for the last time and went to live at the rath of Cleiteach (near Slane in Co Meath).

This story provided a rationale for accounts of Cormac's final days. A text of the late 9th or early 10th century quotes a long list of advices given by him to his son Cairbre concerning how a king should rule. This is one of several Old Irish texts which are based on the type of Latin gnomic writings known as 'speculum principis'. Not long after this, an account developed of how the great high-king died, imputing Christian sanctity to him. It was claimed that his goodness, and his insistence that not things themselves but the creator of things should be adored, meant that he was in effect a Christian even though he lived before the coming of **Patrick** to Ireland. We therefore read of how he ordered that, after his death, he not be buried in Brugh na Bóinne (Newgrange, on the river Boyne) because the pagan kings had been buried there. Instead, he wished to be buried at Ros na Ríogh (Rosnaree), a short distance down the river on the opposite bank, with his face eastwards towards the rising sun. He went to a feast at the rath of a noble called Spealán, and a piece of bread which was given to him at the feast contained a fish-bone. As he was eating, a dispute broke out between two kerns. Cormac was startled by the commotion, and the fish-bone caught in his neck and he choked from it. Accounts differ as to the reason why the fish-bone was in the bread - the original explanation being that it was inadvertantly kneaded into it, but later versions suggest that the druids were responsible as they disapproved of his Christian leanings. After his death, these druids determined that he be buried in Brugh na Bóinne despite his orders, but a flood rose on the river as they attempted to cross it. His bier was swept down to Ros na Ríogh, and on the following morning the body was found lying there. So he was interred at that place in accordance with his wishes.

His fame lived on in the folklore of the northern half of the country. A quatrain known in oral tradition throughout Ulster, Connacht, and north Leinster stated that 'in the time of Cormac mac Airt / life was pleasant and enjoyable / there were nine clusters on each branch / and nine branches on each stem'. It was also said that when a cow lies down on the grass, the great sigh which she heaves is for the happy days of his reign long ago. In the same broad region, versions of his coming to Tara as a youth to claim the kingship from Lughaidh mac Con (q.v.) continued to be told by word of mouth. Furthermore, it was said that he was posthumously baptised by Patrick when the saint one day came across a clump of rushes from which a voice spoke. The voice explained that it was Cormac's soul, which had been confined there because it could not enter heaven. Patrick shed tears of sympathy, which baptised his soul, and it rose to heaven in the form of a white dove. This legend was borrowed from the lore of **Conchobhar mac Neasa**, but in recent centuries the Cormac-versions have become more numerous than those concerning Conchobhar.

A late recension of the story of Cormac's quest to the land of Manannán was current in manuscripts of recent centuries, and it gave rise to a new narrative in Donegal folklore. This told of how Cormac had to go to a strange country to recover 'the sword of light' and how he succeeded in this task with the help of a shaggy-looking but very fleet pony. It was told as a loose version of an international folktale which was quite popular in Ireland (see **Wonder Tales**, Types 313 and 550).

[Corb in septal names] M A O'Brien (1962), 9, 23-8, 94-5, 565; A P Smyth (1982), 15-20, 186.

['Ulfhada'] Whitley Stokes in *Irische Texte 3*, 336-7; T F O'Rahilly (1946), 486.

[Salutory reign] S H O'Grady (1892) *1*, 89-90.

[Meadhbh and Leinstermen] Maura Power in *Zeitschrift für celtische Philologie 11*, 42-3, 52-3 Nessa Ní Shéaghdha (1945), 174.

[Biographies] Tomás Ó Cathasaigh (1977), 107-33; Vernam Hull in *Ériu 16*, 79-85; Máirín O'Daly (1975), 52-3, 56-9, 64-73; O'Grady (1892) 1, 89-90, 253-6; Margaret Dobbs in *Zeitschrift für celtische Philologie 20*, 173-82.

[Administration] O'Grady (1892) *1*, 90; Stokes, *op cit*, 198-9; Edward Gwynn (1903), 20-37.

[Eithne] Stokes in *Revue Celtique 25*, 18-39, 225-7; David Greene (1955), 27-44; Proinsias Mac Cana in *Études Celtiques 8*, 86-7.

[Cearnait] Kuno Meyer in *Hibernica Minora 2*, 75-6; Gwynn, *op cit*, 20-3.

[Manannán] Stokes in *Irische Texte 3*, 193-8.

[Sword] Stokes, *ibid*, 199-202. See Dag Strömbäck in Arthur Brown / Peter Foote eds (1963), 178-90.

[Exiles and battles] Rudolf Thurneysen in *Zeitschrift für celtische Philologie 20*, 222-3.

[Crionna] O'Grady (1892) *2*, 491-3 and *1*, 319-26.

[Eochu Gunnat] James Carney in *Éigse 2*, 187-97.

[Fiachu Araidhe] Meyer in *Zeitschrift für celtische Philologie 8*, 313-4.

[Drom Damhghaire] M-L Sjoestedt-Jonval in *Revue Celtique 43*, 1-123 and *44*, 157-86.

[Déise] Meyer in *Ériu 3*, 135-42; Hull in *Zeitschrift für celtische Philologie 27*, 14-63.

[Advices to Cairbre] Meyer (1909).

[Salter of Tara] Stokes in *Irische Texte 3*, 199; John O'Donovan *1* (1848), 116-7.

[Religion and death] R I Best / Osborn Bergin (1929), 127; R M Smith in *Irish Texts 4*, 16-7; Hull in *Ériu 16*, 85; Power, *op cit*, 43; Ní Shéaghdha *op cit*, 175-6; O'Donovan, *op cit*, 114-7.

[Folk quatrain] Seosamh Laoide (1905), 111 and (1913), 61; G Nic Gréagóir in *An Claidheamh Soluis* 20/6/1908, 6; Éamonn Ó Tuathail in *Béaloideas 3*, 123, 131; IFC (several versions).

[Cow] IFC 706:535.

[Folk biographies] Ó Tuathail (1933), 123-4 and (1934), 13. For other versions and discussion, see the entry on **Lughaidh mac Con**.

[Baptism] Ó Tuathail (1934), 13-4; Seán Ó Súilleabháin in *Béaloideas 21*, 178; IFC (several versions).

['Sword of light'] IFC 56:321-44, 104:263-81.

[General] O'Donovan, *op cit*, 110-21; P S Dinneen (1908) *2*, 282-353; Ó Cathasaigh, *op cit*; Cormac Ó Cadhlaigh (1927).

CRIDHINBHÉAL (earlier, Cridenbél) Mythical satirist, one of the **Tuatha Dé Danann**.

When king **Breas** oppressed the Tuatha Dé, the **Daghdha** was made to construct an earthwork around the king's fortress. Cridhinbhéal, described as 'an idle blind man', asked the Daghdha for the three best bits of his food each night. The requests of satirists were not normally refused, so the Daghdha complied and as a result was miserable and hungry. He was, however, advised by his son, the Mac Óg (i.e. **Aonghus**), to put three gold coins into the food for Cridhinbhéal. He did this, and the gold stuck in the satirist's stomach and killed him. When the Daghdha was accused of murder by Breas, he protested that he had but given gold to Cridhinbhéal. The satirist's stomach was cut open, and when the gold was found there the

Daghdha was released. It is not expressly stated in the text, but what the Daghdha was implying was that Cridhinbhéal had consumed the coins out of greed. In folklore, behaviour of this type was often humorously ascribed to misers (see **Humorous Tales**, Type 1305C).

Otherwise Cridhinbhéal is described as one of the Tuatha Dé host in battles. Various attempts were made to explain his name. One such was 'heart in mouth' ('cridhe ina bhéal'), meaning that he could not keep a secret. Alternately it was said that he was so ugly that his mouth was in his breast. Another explanation for his name was 'mouth of sparks' ('crithir-bhéal') from the fierceness of his poems; and yet another claimed that he was the first lampooner ever to quench a torch with the power of his words. The real meaning of the name - alternately given as Crichinbél, Crithinbél, and Crichinphél - is unclear, but the most likely interpretation is 'heart in mouth' in the sense that **poets** were believed to speak directly from their emotions without thinking.

E A Gray (1982), 28-31, 120; Whitley Stokes in *Irische Texte 3*, 384-5, 422; R A S Macalister (1938), 154-5, 184-5.

CRIOMHTHANN NIA NÁIR Fictional king of Ireland situated in prehistory. His sobriquets were originally Nia Nár and meant simply 'noble warrior'.

He was said to have been begotten by **Lughaidh Riabhdhearg** on Lughaidh's own mother Clothra. One mediaeval text tells of how he went on an adventure to Éadar (Howth, Co Dublin) with an otherworld woman called Nár, thus deriving his appellation Nia ('warrior') of Nár. He spent a month and a fortnight in the otherworld rath there and brought many treasures from it, but died soon after. The treasures included a golden chariot, a great chess-board, and a mysterious 'mantle of Criomhthann'. A variant account speculates that Nár refers to the shame ('náir') which he felt on account of his incestuous birth. It states that his reign lasted for sixteen years in all, and that he died after falling from his horse.

R A S Macalister (1956), 302-5; P S Dinneen (1908) *2*, 234-5.

CROM Archetypal pagan in folk tradition, represented as an opponent of **Patrick** in that saint's mission.

In an 11th-century text he is called Crom Cruach and described as an idol of the pagan Irish. The personage intended is synonymous with an idol called Cenn Cruaich which is referred to in a biography of Patrick from the 9th century. Cenn Cruaich has twelve sub-gods, and his statue in Magh Sléacht (the plain of Tullyhaw, Co Cavan) is demolished by the saint and it sinks into the ground. Crom Dubh, like Cenn Cruaich, originally derives from the image of the Antichrist in Christian thought. In folklore he is usually called Crom Dubh. The name has been taken to mean 'black stoop', but it may have actually signified 'dark croucher', an image of the devil.

A late mediaeval legend evidences a change in the characterisation of Crom Dubh, portraying him as a great sinner who after his death was being carried away by demons, but Patrick intervened and saved him. The saint's reason for doing this was that Crom had each year given a bullock to the poor for their sustenance. It is obvious that the Antichrist image of Crom had been forgotten and that he was now seen as a mere mortal. Another and connected development was the substitution of Crom for **Dáire** in the legend of how the latter gave a cauldron as a gift to Patrick. Thus in folk versions of that legend, it is always Crom Dubh who presents Patrick with either a cauldron or a bullock, and the saint shows that his thanks written on a piece of paper outweighs the gift on a scales. Convinced by this, Crom is converted. Other and more ancient imagery is reflected in the assigning of the encounter between Crom and the saint to the festival of Lughnasa (see **Time**). This festival has long been celebrated on the Sunday nearest to the 1st of August, which was therefore known in most of the country as 'Crom Dubh's Sunday'. Since Lughnasa is a harvest festival anciently dedicated to **Lugh**, it is likely that the myth once represented Lugh's contest with **Balar** and that Patrick and Crom have taken the place of these.

Edward Gwynn (1924), 18-23; Kathleen Mulchrone (1939), 55-6; Máire MacNeill (1962), 26-32, 452-74, 598-600, 681; Dáithí Ó hÓgáin (1985), 6-8, 323.

CROMWELL, OLIVER (1599-1658) English parliamentary leader and Lord Protector of the British Commonwealth. The merciless nature of his nine-month campaign in Ireland in the year 1649 left a deep imprint on Irish feeling, and 'the curse of Cromwell' ('scrios Chromail') is regarded as an imprecation of the worst kind.

26. CROMWELL, OLIVER *Commonwealth coin showing Cromwell.*

With his large and seasoned army, Cromwell cut a pathway of slaughter through the country, but folklore strikingly concentrates on some personal accounts of him which have little or nothing to do with his actual campaign. In fact, the corpus of oral narrative concerning him in Ireland clearly reflects propaganda against him by the Royalists in England in his own time. No doubt the Irish, from their own experience of him, felt that they had little reason to doubt what his English enemies said about him. The Royalist party in England claimed that a tapestry of the devil hung in the room where he was born, and this is developed in Irish folklore into the claim that, when Cromwell drilled his soldiers in a field, he had a picture of the devil hanging on the gate at the entrance, and every time he himself passed through the gate the devil bowed to him. Royalist cartoons of his own time in England usually represented him in the company of the devil, and an echo of this in Irish folklore is the story of how a friar once encountered Cromwell, who was mounted on a fine horse. The terrified friar saluted the 'two gentlemen' and, when Cromwell queried who the other gentleman was, he found that the devil could be seen riding behind him.

It was noticed in England that Cromwell's death on the 3rd of September 1658 came exactly seven years to the day after his last great victory, at the battle of Worcester in 1651. The story thus grew up that he had sold his soul to the devil before that battle in return for seven years of success. This idea too became very popular in Ireland, where it was believed that Cromwell had got his great military power from that infernal source. The correspondence was even closer than this, for a great storm was raging in the south of England as Cromwell lay dying, and the Royalists interpreted this as the devil coming for the soul of his agent. Memory of this storm and of its supposed significance survived in Irish folklore, and accounts collected in this century describe how, at the time of his death, a hellish vessel was seen on the sea, being dragged along by black dogs and its sinister captain announcing that he was coming for Cromwell. A satiric poem written at the time of Cromwell's death and published in broadsheet described the deceased tyrant being brought over the river Styx to Hades, and one Kerry folk account echoes actual lines from that poem.

27. CROMWELL, OLIVER *Royalist cartoon of Cromwell seated on the left-hand side of the devil.*

In a play performed in Cork city in the year 1685, Cromwell was represented 'with a gilded nose tweaked by Beelzebub as he carried him off'. The emphasis on his large nose was derived from contemporary propaganda in England, which nicknamed him 'Copper Nose', 'Ruby Nose, and 'Nose Almighty'. Irish folklore preserves this also, it being claimed that Cromwell had a nose of either copper or brass. Some aspects of his image in Irish lore seem, however, to be independent developments. An example is a story which claims that he once came to Ireland in disguise in order to discover what kind of people the Irish were and how he could overcome them. He arrived at a house where a man was being waked, and after a while he offered money to the widow if she would cut a slice from the corpse. She indignantly refused, but relented when he increased his offer. He further bribed a man at the wake to trip up a drunken friend and knock him into the fire. Very satisfied when he noticed this weakness of character, Cromwell remarked 'Ireland is mine' and said that the Irish would sell and roast one another for money. This story is no doubt a rationalisation of an unfortunate tendency in the Irish experience, but it may echo some vestiges of the propaganda against the Irish which was current in England in Cromwell's own time. This propaganda painted the Irish as barbaric and cannibalistic monsters, and to its influence was largely due the ruthlessness of Cromwell's actions in Ireland.

One particular story was widely told in both Munster and Connacht. This purports to tell of dealings which Cromwell had with a prophet called Maoilsheachlainn Mac Amhlaoibh, chieftain of Duhallow in Co Cork (the surname is anglicised as MacAuliffe). There really was a chieftain of that name living at the time, and he did compose some verses of prophecy concerning the general state of Ireland, but accounts of his involvement with Cromwell must have been a special narrative growth unconnected with the historical Maoilsheachlainn. We are told that his mother was taken away into a fairy-rath, where she became the lover of an otherworld man, and that when she was pregnant she was left back into the ordinary world. Her husband, the chieftain, was unaware that he was not the father of the child she was bearing, and so that child grew up and in time succeeded the old chieftain. This was Maoilsheachlainn and, because of his otherworld origin, he had the power of prophecy. One night he dreamed of a cobbler in England who would rise to great power and would one day control all Ireland. This cobbler's name was Cromwell. Maoilsheachlainn lost no time in setting out for England and, after a long search, located that cobbler. The latter turned out to be a genial fellow who was amused at what he regarded as the mad fantasies of the Irishman, so he agreed to sign a covenant in his blood that he would never evict Maoilsheachlainn from his property. Time passed, and when Cromwell rose to power and was ravaging Ireland, he came to Duhallow to seize land there. However, when shown his signature on the covenant, he honoured his word and did not evict Maoilsheachlainn.

Being quite curious as to his future, Cromwell queried the prophet on it, and was given apparently reassuring answers. Some tellings claim that Maoilsheachlainn prophesied that he would never again be in danger if he survived that day. Cromwell, however, went to a forge to have his horse shod and, being impatient, he stuck a gun-barrel into the furnace to convert it into a shoe and was shot by a bullet which had been left in the discarded gun. Other versions state that the prophecy was that Cromwell would live as long as he liked, but that he cut his own throat in a fit of anger as he shaved. Yet others have it predicted that his power would last in Ireland as long as he was in the country, and he accordingly left instructions for his body to be buried here. The soil of Ireland, however, rejected his corpse and cast it out into the sea between the two countries, the resultant tussle between English and Irish waters causing that sea to be rough ever since.

The story of Cromwell's dealings with this prophet is basically borrowed from the biography of Merlin, whose reputed prophecies were taken very seriously in the political life of 17th-century England. Merlin, according to the account of him given by Geoffrey of Monmouth, was the son of a demon-spirit and gave ambiguous prophecies to the tyrant ruler Vortigern. Some conceit which placed Cromwell in the role of Vortigern must have been current in Royalist circles, and when this was borrowed to Ireland an Irish prophet associated with that period would have been substituted. Maoilsheachlainn was the one chosen for this role, for that name is pronounced in Munster as 'mlokhlin' and Merlin not dissimilarly.

Seán Ó Súilleabháin in Linda Dégh / Henry Glassie / F J Oinas eds (1976), 473-83; Dáithí Ó hÓgáin (1985), 281-6, 345-6 and in *Sinsear 2*, 73-83.

[Royalist pamphlets] Rolv Laache in *Edda 2*, 175-227 (compare especially verse on p. 218 to IFC 667:206-8).

[Mac Amhlaoibh] T F O'Rahilly (1925), 20; Tadhg Ó Donnchadha (1940), 214.

CÚ CHULAINN Mythical champion who predominates in the **Ulster Cycle**.

His name is traditionally interpreted to mean 'the hound of Culann'. 'Cú' (i.e. hound) was a common designation for a warrior in early Irish literature, and whatever the original import of the second part of his name it is clear that he had his source in a cult of martial prowess. The literature tells that, prior to his first great exploit, he was called Sétanta, which corresponds to the name of a Celtic tribe in Britain, the Setantii. His javelin is called the 'ga bolga', reminiscent of the Belgae, a prominent Celtic people of western Europe; while the name given to his father-in-law, 'Forgall Manach', preserves that of the Menapii of Gaul. The literature describes Cú Chulainn as a native of Muirtheimhne (in present-day Co Louth), and the indications therefore are that his cult originated among some group of British or Gaulish Celts which had settled in that area.

The oldest surviving stratum of lore concerning Cú Chulainn is that found in the epic *Táin Bó Cuailnge*. There he single-handedly defends the province of Ulster against the great army of queen **Meadhbh** of Connacht. The text has several curious descriptions of him. His body becomes transformed by the 'riastradh', which is a kind of battle-frenzy. He shakes from head to foot and revolves within his skin, his features turn red, one eye becomes monstrously large while the other becomes tiny, his mouth grows huge and emits sparks, his heart booms in his chest, his hair becomes spiked and glowing, and the 'warrior-light' rises from his brow. This description is obviously an echo of ideas concerning inspiration of warriors in ancient culture. At the height of the battle-campaign, Cú Chulainn risks his life to 'show himself to the women and the poets', and this can be viewed as a survival in narrative of some ancient warriors' ritual. Relevant also is the fact that his character covers a wider range than feats of arms alone, and that there is a mystical significance in some of his actions. In order to delay the enemy army, for instance, he twists an oak-sapling into a hoop and writes a message on it while using but one arm, one leg, and one eye. This was apparently a ritual of war employed by magical **poets** and parallels the pose adopted by **Lugh** during battle. In fact, Lugh is introduced into the *Táin* as the otherworld patron of Cú Chulainn, who comes to relieve him when he is fatigued from fighting, thereby allowing him to sleep for three whole days.

The introduction of Cú Chulainn himself into the narrative of the *Táin* is probably to be dated to the seventh century (see **Ulster Cycle**). An early 8th-century text tells the story of his conception and birth, giving him a close blood-relationship to the Ulster king **Conchobhar mac Neasa**. We are told that a flock of birds landed on the plain of Eamhain Mhacha, where the royal court was, and devoured the grass there. Some of the Ulster warriors pursued the birds in their chariots, with Conchobhar's sister Deichtine acting as his driver. Night overtook them at Brugh na Bóinne (Newgrange in Co Meath), and a great snow fell. The Ulstermen were given shelter by a couple who lived in a solitary house there. The man told them that his wife was in birth-pangs, and Deichtine went to her assistance. A baby boy was born, and at the very same time a mare dropped two foals at the door of the house. The Ulstermen brought the foals to the baby, and Deichtine nursed him. When morning came they found themselves alone at the Brugh, except for the baby and the foals. They returned to Eamhain Mhacha, but the baby grew ill and died on them. When the heartbroken Deichtine took a drink, a tiny creature slipped into her mouth. She dreamed that night that Lugh came to her and said that he was the father of the baby and that it would be born again through her. She became pregnant, and it was suspected that her brother the king was responsible, so Conchobhar gave her in marriage to one of his warriors called Sualdamh. She miscarried and grew pregnant again - this time by her husband - and gave birth to a son, whom she called Sétanta.

The patronage of Lugh for Cú Chulainn, as shown in these texts, indicates that there was some connection between the two personages. One explanation would be that the personage of Cú Chulainn was developed from Lugh before his introduction into the Co Louth area in the early centuries AD. Another explanation would be that his image was influenced by the Lugh cult in the Louth-Meath area some time after his introduction. The latter seems the more likely, as the intensive, and seemingly basic, warrior focus of Cú Chulainn is quite distinctive as opposed to the polytechnic imagery of Lugh.

The text on Sétanta's birth further states that the child was given to a smith called Culann, who was to be his tutor. When at play, Sétanta killed Culann's hound, and then said to the smith: 'I will be your hound'. Hence his acquired name 'Cú Chulainn'. This episode is a secondary invention, for the name originally meant 'warrior of Culann', whoever or whatever Culann may originally have been. It is clear that from at least the 7th century onwards it was being felt necessary to give some description of the hero's youth, and those accounts which were given differed considerably. The text, for instance, betrays some confusion as to who Sétanta's real father was and the reader suspects that Lugh and Conchobhar were also seen in that role. One account, from the 9th century has his mother called Deichtire rather than Deichtine. She is here also the sister of Conchobhar, but her husband is apparently of the otherworld. She and her maidens were the fifty birds who allured the Ulstermen to the strange house, where **Bricriu** met her and her husband. Mischievous as usual, Bricriu returned to Conchobhar and spoke of the lady's great beauty, without mentioning who she was, and when the king heard of the lady he desired that she be brought to him. On her way hither, however, she revealed that she was in travail, and so she was excused from sleeping with the king. The night passed thus, and when the Ulstermen awoke next morning they found the baby Sétanta in Conchobhar's lap. This version, with its extra attempts at dramatisation, confuses the tradition still further, and it is significant that general indecision also relates to the question of the hero's rearing. One version of the birth-story states that he was given by Conchobhar to another sister, Fionnchaomh, and was reared by her and her husband, the seer **Amhairghin mac Éigit Salaigh**, in their dwelling on the plain of Muirtheimhne. This also states that the seneschal **Fearghus Mac Róich** wished to be the child's tutor, and elsewhere Fearghus is indeed given this function.

The compiler of the first recension of the *Táin* attempted to reconcile the differing strands by having Fearghus relate a youth-biography of the hero. According to this, the boy Sétanta persuaded his mother (who is here said to have lived with her husband in the plain of Muirtheimhne) to allow him to go to Eamhain Mhacha and play with the youths there. He set off, continually casting his javelin ahead of him and catching it before it touched the ground, until he reached his destination. Seeing the youths hurling there, he joined the game without their permission. The enraged boys flung all their sticks, their playing-balls, and their shields at him, but he rained off all the blows and the battle-frenzy came upon him with the usual bodily transformation. He laid low fifty of the youths, and the rest fled before him. Conchobhar and Fearghus had their chess-game upset by the rout, and Conchobhar seized the boy. On learning that he was Sétanta, the king made peace between him and the other boys, and those who had been injured were restored to health by their guardians. Sétanta, however, refused to sleep in Eamhain Mhacha until his head and feet were propped up with stones so that they were equidistant from the floor. He insisted on not being disturbed in his sleep thus, and once broke the forehead of a man who tried to awaken him. Once, when the boy was sleeping, the Ulstermen were defeated by their enemies in a great battle. Awakening, Sétanta went to the battlefield with his hurley-stick, rescued Conchobhar and his son **Cormac Conn Loingeas**, and brought them home safe. When Eamhain Mhacha was attacked on another occasion, and the Ulstermen laid low with the curse of debilitation which was on them (see **Macha**), the boy repelled the marauders with stones and with his hurley. We are told that, when he rescued Conchobhar and Cormac, Sétanta was egged on by the war-goddess Badhbh who spoke to him from among the corpses on the battlefield. This goddess (see **Mór-Ríoghain**) is repeatedly associated with him, appearing in various forms when he is locked in battle. She again underlines the intensive imagery of war in his portrayal.

Regarding the idea that the boy Sétanta killed a hound, the youth-biography which is inserted into the *Táin* rationalises this through use of a monster-slaying motif. The account is put into the mouth of the warrior **Conall Cearnach**, supplementing what has been said by Fearghus. Since Sétanta excelled all his fellows at games and athletic feats, the account goes, the king was intensely proud of him. Once, when Conchobhar was invited to a feast, he asked the boy to accompany him and his nobles, but Sétanta was busy playing games and said he would follow on. The feast was being hosted by the smith Culann, who kept a monstrous hound to guard his fortress by night. Conchobhar forgot that the boy was coming, and the hound was released. Soon Sétanta came, playing his tricks with his hurley and ball, and the hound attacked him. The boy seized the ferocious beast by the throat and back, and dashed its head against a pillar-stone. Conchobhar's men rushed out of the fortress, and to their amazement and relief found the boy safe and the hound dead. Culann, however, felt the loss of his great hound, and Sétanta offered to guard his property for him until another dog could be found. Thus he came to be known as 'Cú Chulainn'. Some mediaeval sources in fact give him a secondary or alternative designation viz. 'Cú na Ceirde' (the Hound of the Craftsman/Smith).

The inserted passage in the *Táin* then has another warrior, Fiacha mac Fir Féibhe, tell of how Cú Chulainn gained official recognition as a warrior when he was a mere seven years old. One day the druid **Cathbhadh** prophesied that whoever took up arms on that day would forever be remembered in story and, overhearing this, the boy went to Conchobhar seeking weapons. He broke the first fifteen sets of spear and shield, and then was given the king's own set. When Cathbhadh said that his life would be short, Cú Chulainn answered that he would be content with this if he achieved fame. Similarly, when Cathbhadh prophesied that the name of whoever mounted his first chariot on that day would live forever in Ireland, Cú Chulainn broke twelve chariots and was given the chariot of Conchobhar. He set out and slew the three sons of Nechtan Scéine, who had killed as many Ulstermen as were then living. He also captured live a fine stag and twenty swans, roped them to the chariot, and returned thus to Eamhain Mhacha with the heads of the three conquered warriors. In his frenzy he threatened to slaughter all, but Conchobhar ordered the women of Eamhain to go out naked to him. Seeing the women thus, Cú Chulainn covered his face, and the Ulster warriors seized him and plunged him consecutively into three vats of cold water. The first vat burst asunder, the second boiled up with huge bubbles, and the third was lukewarm. Then he went and sat on the king's knee, which henceforth was his public seat.

It is clear from this that various ideas from antiquity, particularly those associated with initiation rites of warriors, are embedded in the tradition of Cú Chulainn. The *Táin* portrays him as the complete warrior, excelling in all the tricks of the trade, and parts of the text look like echoes from lore which had the function of a training manual. His accomplishments include athletic skills, deft use of a sling, controlled and accurate wielding of

28. CÚ CHULAINN *Detail of a chariot from a stone cross at Clonmacnoise, Co. Offaly.*

a sword, methods of throwing a javelin and warding it off with a shield, and howling to upset a foe. The descriptions given of his skills greatly exaggerate human potential - he could, for instance, cut the sod from under his opponent or shave him with sword-strokes, leap onto the opponent's shield and leap over a flying javelin - but this may be as much the result of oral preservation of the tradition as of deliberate dramatic inflation. The names given to many of his martial tricks are quite obscure and seem equally to be the débris of ancient skills. Of special interest is his mode of fighting with his great Carbad Searrdha ('Scythed Chariot'), which had cutting instruments attached to its axle on either side. Latin writers describe how the Continental Celts used similar devices, and this constitutes yet another distinctive parallel between Cú Chulainn and Celtic culture outside of Ireland. Perhaps it is in this very imagery that the origin of his name lies, for an archaic word 'cul' was used in Irish for a chariot. A compound of this word, or a corrupted genitive form, might have been the basis for the element 'culann', and if so 'Cú Chulainn' would have originated in a designation meaning something like 'chariot-warrior'. Probable support for this interpretation comes from the fact that the personal 'Culann' of the early literature is described as a smith, a type of tradesman who would play the leading role in the manufacture of war-chariots. The most plausible theory for the hero's origin would therefore be that he symbolised a particular war-cult introduced by a group of Celts who in Roman times crossed from Britain to the area of Muirtheimhne, which bordered on the territory of the Ulstermen. It is noteworthy that in the accounts of his birth and youth the roles of paternity and fosterage played by figures such as Lugh and Culann have been duplicated by the inclusion in these roles of figures who are central to the Ulster Cycle - characters such as Conchobhar mac Neasa and Fearghus mac Róich. This confusion suggests that, at the time of Cú Chulainn's first occurrences in the literature, his lore had only quite recently been Ulsterised. A synopsis of the *Táin* narrative from the early 7th century does not in fact mention him at all, but instead features a young warrior called Fiacc as the leading fighter for the Ulster forces. The warrior-imagery of Cú Chulainn of Muirtheimhne was so impressive as to cause him to be sustituted for the Ulster Fiacc, and in the developed *Táin* narrative a series of heroic exploits are attributed to him (see **Ulster Cycle**) which are the most striking epical descriptions in all Irish literature.

Another text is worthy of study with regard to the development of the biography of the new hero. This is *Tochmarc Emire* ('the Wooing of Eimhear'), the original of which was written in the late eighth century but which underwent much reworking and expansion during the following two hundred years. It tells of how Cú Chulainn outdid all the Ulster warriors at walking on ropes and 'the apple-feat and the feats of the javelin and the sword-edge', and how the Ulstermen grew jealous of their women's admiration of him and decided that a wife must be found for him. Conchobhar had all Ireland searched for a suitable girl, but nowhere could such be found. Then Cú Chulainn himself went to woo one Eimhear (earlier, Emer), daughter of Forgall Manach in the Lughlocht of Lugh (south of the river Boyne in Co Meath). They spoke in riddles to each other, and she set conditions on her love. She said that he must first slay hundreds of men, do 'the feat of the salmon-leap', deliver a sword-stroke which slew several but spared men selectively, and go sleepless from November to August. Cú Chulainn promised to perform the feats and left her. When Eimhear's father heard of their encounter he went in disguise to Eamhain Mhacha and advised that Cú Chulainn should go to Scotland to study the warrior's art with a female tutor called Scáthach. He thereby hoped to have the young hero killed. Cú Chulainn set out for Scotland and learned tricks from a warrior called Domhnall there - how to walk over fire and to perform on the point of a spear. Going to meet Scáthach he came to a bouncing bridge which knocked off it all but the most accomplished warriors. His battle-frenzy came upon him and he crossed the obstacle by performing the salmon-leap. He then became the lover of Scáthach's daughter Uathach, and forced Scáthach herself to give him further martial training. War broke out between Scáthach and another warrioress called Aoife, and Cú Chulainn overcame Aoife in single combat and she lay with him. He learned many tricks from her, relating to such things as juggling, leaping, running, casting, fighting, and chariot-driving. Returning to Ireland, he found Eimhear's home so well guarded that he could not take it for a whole year. Then he charged the defenders with the scythe-wheeled chariot and slew three hundred and nine of them. Giving the salmon-leap over the rampart, he thrice over slew nine men, sparing one man in the middle of them each time. Having thus performed all the tasks required of him by Eimhear, he took her away to Eamhain Mhacha. The mischievous **Bricriu** stated that Eimhear must sleep the first night with king Conchobhar as was the usual custom. To allay the hero's rage at this and deflect his attention, Conchobhar ordered him to gather a herd of swine and deer and birds and to bring them to Eamhain. The nobles saw to it that further trouble was avoided by having Fearghus and Cathbhadh sleep in the same bed with Conchobhar and Eimhear and thus assure that the honour of Cú Chulainn was not compromised.

A story which was composed soon after the Wooing of Eimhear also survives in a somewhat later recension than its original. This is *Serglige Con Culainn* ('the Wasting-Sickness of Cú Chulainn'), and it tells of how the hero fell in love with an otherworld lady called Fann (earlier, Fand). On the feast of Samhain (November) some wonderful birds settled on a lake in the plain of Muirtheimhne and each of the women longed to have a pair of them. Cú Chulainn got the birds for them with his sling, but there were none left for his wife (identified in the text variously as Eimhear and Eithne Inghubhai), and he promised to find some for her. He failed to catch two magic birds soon after, however, and then fell asleep. Two women came and beat him, and as a result he was sick in Eamhain Mhacha for a whole year. At the next feast of Samhain a man appeared beside his bed and told him that an otherworld woman called Fann awaited him. He returned to where he was a year before and was told by a lady called Lí Ban there that if he fought for her husband for the duration of one day in the otherworld he would have the love of Fann. He did this, and spent a month with Fann in the otherworld. When he bade her farewell, they arranged a tryst at Iubhar Cinn Tráchta (Newry in Co Down). His wife, however, came to that place to attack Fann, and the latter returned to the otherworld, leaving Cú Chulainn to her.

Other adventures related of the hero in the mediaeval literature include the awarding of the champion's portion to him after the feast of **Bricriu**; his contest with **Cú Roí** for the lady Bláthnaid; and the tragic single combat he fought against his own son **Conlaí**. There is rich personal colouring in the various accounts, and much of this can be related to the heroic milieu. For instance, he is described as having three faults, being 'too handsome, too brave, and too young'. He has two marvellous chariot-horses, the Grey of Macha and the Black of Saingliu. These are presumably the same as the two foals mentioned in the birth-story, but they had to be recovered by him as described in a recension of the text on the feast of Bricriu. There we are told that the Grey came out of a lake (see **Horses**) and was mounted by Cú Chulainn and ridden rough throughout Ireland before he brought it tame to Eamhain at nightfall. The Black was acquired in similar circumstances. He had great weapons, too, especially the 'ga bolga', which is described as a barbed javelin which hacked at its victim causing multiple wounds. He also had a great spear called Duaibhseach (literally 'grim'), a massive shield and helmet around which demons of the air shrieked, and a visor which he got as a present from the deity **Manannán**. Much extravaganza is employed in describing his appearance. His hair was of three different colours, and he had four colourful dimples in each cheek, seven pupils in each eye, seven fingers on each hand and seven toes on each foot. He had some distinctly magical powers, such as when he wrote a message in **'ogham'** script compelling the enemy to cease their advance in the *Táin*. Also in that text, when mocked by the women on account of his youth, he 'took a handful of grass and chanted a spell over it, and they all thought that he had a beard'. The more practical side of his adventures is also stressed - his charioteer Laogh accompanies him on most of his great exploits, performing the service of chiding him into greater efforts when such are required.

As champion of the Ulster Cycle, Cú Chulainn is described in many accounts as saving king Conchobhar and his men when they are in dire straits. Thus, in the 9th-century text *Mesca Ulad* ('the Intoxication of the Ulstermen') he and another warrior called Fionntan argued over which of them should host the king and his company at an ale-feast. It was decided that the night should be divided into two halves, with Fionntan having the first. But the disgruntled Cú Chulainn, when his turn came, brought the company on a drunken tour all over Ireland, ending up in the fortress of Cú Roí (q.v.) at Teamhair Luachra (in Co Kerry). Here Meadhbh and her husband Ailill were already visiting, and the Ulstermen received a feigned welcome and were then locked into an iron-walled house. The house was made red-hot, but Cú Chulainn broke a way out with his sword. He broke down the door of a second house in which they were confined, and led the Ulstermen in an all-out attack on their tormentors. The fortress was destroyed, and Cú Chulainn later entertained Conchobhar and the other warriors in his own fortress of Dún Dealgan (Dundalk, Co Louth).

An account of the death of Cú Chulainn was already in circulation by the tenth century. Cú Chulainn, we are told, had killed a warrior called Cailitín during the war with Meadhbh, and Cailitín's wife gave birth posthumously to sextuplets - three sons and three daughters. Meadhbh sent these children abroad to study sorcery, and on their return she incited them against Cú Chulainn. Then she herself invaded Cuailnge (the area of Cooley in Co Louth), thereby drawing Conchobhar and his Ulster warriors into battle again. Conchobhar, having got a report that treachery was planned against Cú Chulainn, called him to Eamhain and ordered him to remain there until the war was over. The hero was kept there in the company of Eimhear and the women and druids of Ulster. The children of Cailitín came, however, and by magic made it appear that Eamhain was being attacked. For three days this continued, with Cú Chulainn being restrained by his guardians. Then Conchobhar sent word that the hero be brought to the Valley of the Deaf, where he could no longer hear the din of battle. He was followed there by the children of Cailitín, and one of them put herself into the shape of Niamh, a young lady for whom Cú Chulainn had a particular attachment. She went to where he was and told him that he was needed in the battle. He set forth, and on his way met the three daughters of Cailitín who were roasting the meat of a dog. They invited him to eat with them. There was a prohibitive **'geis'** on him against refusing an invitation to a meal, but equally he was prohibited from eating dog-meat on account of his name. He tried to extricate himself by taking the meat in his hand and hiding it, but much of his strength left him nevertheless. When he joined the battle the sons of Cailitín had prepared three special javelins, and three sons of men whom Cú Chulainn had slain were ready to throw these javelins. The first cast killed the charioteer Laogh, the second lodged in the side of the great Grey, and that horse raced into the lake from which it had come. The third javelin struck Cú Chulainn. It was flung by Lughaidh, son of Cú Roí, and it caused the hero's intestines to fall out. He staggered to the nearby lake to take a drink, and a raven which was drinking his blood tripped over the intestines. Amused at this, the hero gave a last great laugh. He tied himself to an upright stone so that he would face his enemies standing, and then died. For three days the foe did not dare approach him, until one of Cailitín's daughters put herself in the shape of a crow and landed on the stone. Realising that he was dead, the warriors approached, but they could not remove the sword from his hand. Lughaidh cut the veins of the hand, and the sword fell, severing Lughaidh's own hand as it did so.

The fame of so great a warrior caused one 11th-century writer to make a connection between him and St **Patrick**. This writer described how, when the saint was trying to convince the high-king **Laoghaire** of the truth of Christianity, Cú Chulainn appeared as a phantom driving his great chariot and told Laoghaire to believe in the new religion. He described some of his own great feats in arms and outlined the values which he had held in life. These were to protect his people, and to be 'a boy among boys, a man among men, triumphant at a ford, strong in face of satire, stronger still in face of praise'. As a result, we are told that Laoghaire was converted to Christianity and Cú Chulainn was released from hell into heaven. It is clear from this that the lore of Cú Chulainn was being made more adaptable to the mentality of mediaeval culture, and that the writers were growing more fanciful. One text, for instance, has Cú Chulainn meeting on the Boyne river an otherworld man called Seanbheag ('old dwarf'), who travels in a small boat of bronze. Seanbheag presents the hero with clothes which protect their wearer against burning and drowning, as well as a shield and spear which guarantee victory in combat. A text in the same manuscript tells of how Eimhear eloped with a Norse prince called Tuir Gleasta, but Cú Chulainn followed them to Norway, slew his rival, and recovered his wife.

A 12th-century text evidences an effort to set Cú Chulainn in the context of mediaeval romance without losing the flavour of the indigenous lore. This tells of a feast held in Cooley by Conall mac Gleo Ghlais, who invited Conchobhar and the nobles of Ulster. The king however, neglected to bring Cú Chulainn with him, and the hero set off in a huff to find adventures for himself. He told his charioteer Laogh that there was a **'geis'** on him to kill a man on every journey he made from Eamhain Mhacha. At the sea-shore he met a huge warrior, Goll mac Carbada from north Germany, who was coming to put Ireland under tribute. In a fierce contest Cú Chulainn, encouraged by Laogh, beheaded the intruder with his short-sword, called the 'Cruaidín Cadadcheann'. Returning then to Eamhain, he found the court empty of its nobles, who had all gone to the feast, and in a pique he decided to burn the place. He was restrained, however, by the verse of Suanan Sailcheann, the king's poet. He then set out for Cooley and on the way met a ferocious character called Garbh who lived in Gleann Ríghe (the Newry Valley in Co Down) and refused to allow any warrior to pass through his territory. This Garbh had just killed fifty of Conchobhar's men as they travelled to the feast. Cú Chulainn slew Garbh with his short-sword, and also slew a horrific hound which Conall mac Gleo Ghlais had released at night to protect his fortress. Refused entry to the feast, he tore a great standing-stone from the ground and slew thrice fifty of the servants with it. Bricriu urged the warriors to combine and kill Cú Chulainn, but Fearghus mac Róich and Conall Cearnach took his part. The tumult continued until Conchobhar's diplomat, Seancha mac Ailealla, waved his 'branch of peace'. Then Cú Chulainn told of his adventures and he was reconciled to the others. He intended to leave Ulster for a year on account of the insult he had received, but Conchobhar offered him whatever compensation he sought. Cú Chulainn was satisfied to leave the amount to be decided by the judges and poets, and even then took only a third of what he was awarded.

In the story of the feast of Bricriu (q.v.) Cú Chulainn got public recognition as the champion of Ulster, but he had to undergo many ordeals to prove his pre-eminence. The situation in that text would naturally have appeal to later writers, and so - in the 13th century - another story was composed which made use of it, again having the hero undertake adventures as a result of Bricriu's machinations. This story told of how Bricriu held another feast and, when all were assembled, said that no warrior should partake until he had first performed a great martial deed. Cú Chulainn accordingly set out for Connacht, and took away from there a girl who loved him. She was called Fionnchaomh and was the daughter of Eochaidh Ronn, king of the Uí Mhaine sept. When Cú Chulainn spent the night at Meadhbh's court, Eochaidh came in most aggressive mood, but Cú Chulainn drove a spear through the neck of his horse and seized him with his hands. Meadhbh made peace between them, but Eochaidh enjoined on Cú Chulainn to discover what caused the exile of three sons of a warrior called Daol Dearmaid. The hero returned to Eamhain Mhacha, but could not rest there on account of what had been enjoined on him. He felt as if the clothes on his body and all surrounding him were ablaze, so he set out to find the answer. At Dundalk he saw a boat, and in his anger slew all its crew except a prince who was on board. This prince told him that the boat was a magical one and would itself direct him on his quest. It accordingly brought him to a strange island where, in answer to his question about the sons of Daol Dearmaid, he was directed to another island where their sister Achtland lived. She slipped away from her husband with Cú Chulainn and brought him to the land in which the sons of Daol Dearmaid were. There Cú Chulainn fought a tremendous duel with a fierce warrior called Eochaidh Glas. The answer to the question is not clarified in the text, but apparently this Eochaidh Glas was holding the three young men in subjection. Cú Chulainn, using astounding acrobatic skills in the duel, slew his opponent with the 'ga bolga'. He then returned to Eamhain Mhacha in Ulster and told of his adventures.

This story, although using the traditional background, is strongly influenced by a new genre which was being adopted from other languages into Irish storytelling at the time. This genre, the 'romain d'aventure', featured quests which led to curious adventures in strange and faraway countries. Although the theme of great heroes making conquests abroad was found in the Ulster Cycle and other Irish heroic literature from an earlier date, plots dependent on fantastic places and loosely-strung episodes were a novelty. The romain d'aventure was of a quite different character to the indigenous lore of Cú Chulainn, and it had comparatively little vogue in his case. However, in the 17th century a group of anonymous writers from the Armagh-Louth area composed a half-dozen prose-texts which were inspired by the story of the quest for Daol's sons. The earliest and best of these was the Pursuit of Gruadh Ghriansholais, a beautiful lady who came to Ireland fleeing from a hideous giant and seeking the help of Cú Chulainn. She was daughter of the king of Antioch. Protection was given, but the giant snatched her from Cú Chulainn, and the hero set out overseas to recover her. After many ferocious encounters with giants and formidable warriors he rescued the lady and re-united three love-crossed couples before returning in triumph to Ireland.

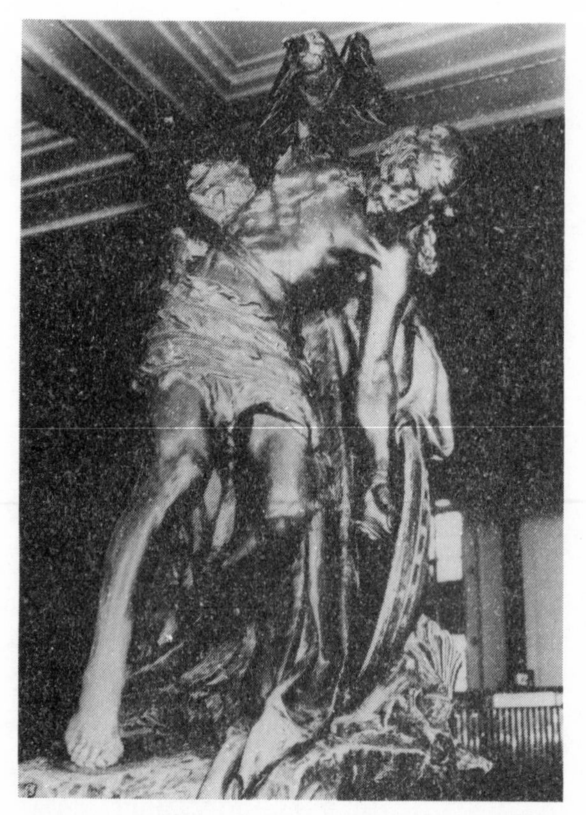

29. CÚ CHULAINN *Modern statue of Cú Chulainn in the General Post Office, Dublin.*

The author of this text took great liberties with pre-existing material of the Ulster Cycle, for example turning Conchobhar's physician Finghein Fáithliaigh into a fairy who comes in a cloud to cure the hero's wounds. Much play is also made of Cú Chulainn's great war-chariot, the Carbad Searrdha, which is claimed to have exuded poison in battle. Similar motifs occur in the other texts of this group, with Cú Chulainn and comrades like **Conall Cearnach**, **Fear Diadh**, and Ailill Fionn (see **Fliodhais**) contending with giants and dragons, overcoming sorcery, rescuing ladies, and always returning in blood-stained victory.

Some garbled versions of these late prose-texts have been collected from the folklore of the north of Ireland, arising no doubt from readings of manuscripts. Popular also, particularly in Connacht, was a lay concerning Cú Chulainn, which had been composed in the 16th or 17th century after the pattern of many such lays in the **Fianna Cycle**. This has a Scandinavian champion called Garbh mac Stairn coming to Ireland to demand tribute. At **Tara,** rather inappropriately for the Ulster Cycle, he met Conchobhar mac Neasa and the Ulster warriors, and all agreed to render the tribute except Cú Chulainn. Bricriu chided Garbh with this, and as a result those two warriors fought a combat non-stop for seven days and nights. On the eighth morning, Garbh was beheaded by Cú Chulainn with a mighty sword-stroke. No original manuscript of this lay has been found, but such must have been in the background. The fact that so dramatic a character as Cú Chulainn has not been accorded a higher profile in folklore mirrors the fortunes of the Ulster Cycle generally, for that cycle seems to have been almost exclusively a learned tradition for the past five hundred years or more. General folk biographies of him have indeed been collected from the oral lore of Connacht and Ulster, as well as from western Scotland, and these derive most if not all of their material from literary accounts compiled in modernised language from the 14th to the 17th centuries - accounts which continued to be copied by scribes down to recent generations. Accordingly, some details from his birth-story have been current in Donegal folklore, while in Galway a confusion of the sources has led to him being identified with one of the children born to **Macha** after her race against the horses of Conchobhar. His slaying of Culann's hound is general, as is an abbreviation of his training with the female warriors and the tragic story of how he slew his son Conlaí. Some of his feats in the *Táin*, as well as episodes from his death-story, were well-known in the lore of Co Louth, due no doubt to their local associations.

There is also a burlesque narrative which has no literary parallel but which was known over most of the Gaelic world. In it a humorous plot from the common stock of folklore has been adapted to the context of Cú Chulainn (See **Humorous Tales**, Type 1376A). According to this narrative, Cú Chulainn agrees to tell a smith about an adventure of his, provided that no woman is listening. He describes how he had come upon a giant who had stolen a cow and was roasting it. Cú Chulainn tried to interfere, but all his martial efforts were in vain and he ended up by being flung by the giant into the cow's horn! The smith's wife was listening to this account of the hero' humiliation, and she shouted out that he should properly be called, not 'Cú na gCleas' (the hound of the skills), but 'Cú na hAdhairce' (the hound of the horn). When Cú

Chulainn heard this he was humiliated and angry, and he killed the eavesdropper in a fit of pique, thus leaving the remainder of the engrossing story untold. This narrative, with its deflation of heroism and its joking at the learned respect given to the Ulster Cycle, exhibits the typical playful humour often found in oral narrative. The distancing of Cú Chulainn from the ordinary stock of oral tales did not generally result in ridicule, however, for the learned respect for him which persisted among literary men guaranteed his status. To antiquarian speculation of recent times is due the practice of explaining placenames in different parts of Ireland by reference to the literary stories of Cú Chulainn. The Ulster Cycle, and in particular the heroic personality of Cú Chulainn, have exerted a strong influence on the literature and on the popular imagination in the past hundred years, through the work of writers such as Standish James O'Grady, Lady Augusta Gregory, W B Yeats, P H Pearse, Austin Clarke, and Thomas Kinsella.

[Origins] Kenneth Jackson (1964); M-L Sjoestedt (1982), 75-98; Jan de Vries (1963), 72-86; C-J Guyonvarc'h in *Ogam 13*, 592-8 and *19*, 266.

[Ritualistic descriptions] Cecile O'Rahilly (1976), 14-5, 24-5, 68-72; A G Van Hamel (1933), 102-4; R I Best in *Ériu 5*, 72; William Sayers in *ibid 32*, 163-7.

[Birth] Van Hamel (1933), 1-8; Ernst Windisch in *Irische Texte 1*, 134-45.

['Cú na Ceirde'] Edward Gwynn (1913), 256-9; O'Rahilly (1976), 13; Kuno Meyer (1906), 44; Whitley Stokes in *Irische Texte 3*, 398-9; Myles Dillon (1953), 13.

[Boyhood deeds] O'Rahilly (1976), 13-26.

[Wooing of Eimhear] Van Hamel, 16-68.

[Wasting sickness] Dillon (1953).

[His horses] Van Hamel, 4, 92, 107-17; George Henderson (1899), 38-40; R I Best / M A O'Brien (1956), 448-53.

[Personal descriptions] Cormac Ó Cadhlaigh (1956), 103-5.

[Intoxication of Ulstermen] J C Watson (1941).

[Death] Best / O'Brien (1956), 442-53; Van Hamel, 69-118.

[St Patrick] R I Best / Osborn Bergin (1929), xxxiv-xxxv, 278-87.

[Seanbheag and Eimhear stories] Kuno Meyer in *Revue Celtique 6*, 182-5.

[Goll mac Carbada and Garbh] Stokes in *Revue Celtique 14*, 396-449.

[Daol Dearmaid] Windisch in *Irische Texte 2(1)*, 164-217.

[Late romances] Cecile O'Rahilly (1924); Meadhbh Ní Chléirigh (1941) and (1942); Máire Ní Mhuirgheasa / Séamus Ó Ceithearnaigh (1952).

[Garbh mac Stairn] R T Christiansen (1931), 86-9; Áine Bhreathnach in *An Stoc* 6/1919, 2; IFC 793:406-10, 1012:421-3, 1236:60-6.

[Late manuscript versions of mediaeval stories] Séan Ua Ceallaigh (1935); Stokes in *Revue Celtique 29*, 109-52, 312-4; O'Rahilly (1961), xlvii-lix.

[Folklore] Seán Ó Súilleabháin (1942), 597-9; Alan Bruford (1969), 93-9, 104-5, 237-8; Douglas Hyde (1901), 330-8; Conor Maguire in *New Ireland Review 25*, 181-9; E C Quiggin (1906), 236-41; Seán Mac Giollarnáth (1936), 37-46; Liam Mac Coisdealbha in *Béaloideas 9*, 55-8; Ordnance Survey Letters - Louth (1836), 94-7, 103-4, 155; IFC Catalogue.

CÚ ROÍ Mythical Munster king who figures in the **Ulster Cycle**.

'Cú' (hound) was a frequent appellation for a warrior in ancient Ireland, but the meaning of the second part of the character's name is unclear. It was sometimes written 'Ruí', and an earlier form would have been 'Raui', which seems to be a genitive of a Celtic word meaning 'roarer' or the like. The lack of clarity in the name has led to several different suggestions concerning its origin, one theory going so far as to claim that Cú Roí was an echo of the historical character whose name was Latinised as Carausius and who seized the reins of government in Britain in the year 286 AD. This Carausius held out against the might of Rome for seven years, until he was killed by treachery. Obviously the career of such a great leader would make a deep impression on the surviving Celtic peoples, but the theory that the character Cú Roí represents a confused memory of him is impossible to prove. It is at any rate certain that several mythical elements are involved in Cú Roí. In mediaeval Irish literature he was usually said to be 'son of Dáire'. This **Dáire** was claimed as ancestor by the Érainn, which was the designation given to septs other than the predominant Connachta and Eoghanacht. Among the leading septs of the Érainn were several Ulster groups and in the south the Corcu Loighdhe (in present-day Co Cork). The Corca Loighdhe claimed descent from Lughaidh son of Dáire. This is significant, for a mythical character who figured prominently in early Munster tradition was **Lughaidh mac Con**. The Ulster Cycle has a son of Cú Roí, called Lughaidh mac Con Roí, as slayer of **Cú Chulainn**, and there is little doubt but that originally all of these three Lughaidhs were one and the same character. A corollary of this is that Cú Roí and Dáire were also one character, or at least that they had been identified with each other. If Cú Roí was derived from some historical person, that person may have already borne the title 'son of Dáire'. Otherwise, the title is due to the fancy of genealogists who were acquainted with the identification of the characters Cú Roí and Dáire and wanted to rationalise it.

A 7th-century Latin text represents Dáire (q.v.) as the possessor and bestower of a cauldron, which sets him in the role and function of the Celtic god of plenty. This imagery is parallelled in a 9th-century poem, which states that Cú Roí had a cauldron into which thirty oxen would fit, as well as a huge vat and a dish wrought from silver and gold. Another reference in the poem gives an indication of the source from which the composers of the Ulster Cycle borrowed Cú Roí. He is described as 'the high-king of the mounds of Tara'. This gets indirect support by the text on the Intoxication of the Ulstermen (see **Cú Chulainn**), where Cú Roí is said to reside at a place called Teamhair Luachra in Munster. There was in fact no such place, and scholars believe that the whole story told in this text was originally concerned with the real Teamhair (**Tara** in Co Meath). A petrified toponymic 'Temhair Érann' survived in the ancient literature, and its original meaning must have referred to Tara having been in the possession of the Érainn people before the Laighin (Leinstermen) and Connachta - Uí Néill in turn gained control of that citadel.

This situation is also reflected in the tradition of another Érainn king, **Conaire**, who is cast in the role of ritual king to whom many fateful prohibitions (see **'geis'**) attach. Among the conditions are that Conaire should not stay away from Tara for nine nights in succession, that he should not stay in a house from which firelight could be seen after sunset, and that a single woman or man should not enter his house after sunset. These seem to echo ancient ideas concerning a cosmic function of the king as guarantor of the life-giving enregy of the sun. One very old text states that the king was prohibited from being in bed in Tara at sunrise and from travelling over the plain of Cuileann (in Co Louth) after sunset. An idea which corresponds to all of this occurs regarding Cú Roí, though much ornamented and enhanced by a style-conscious mediaeval writer: 'Cú Roí never reddened his sword in Ireland from when he took arms until he died, and the food of Ireland did not pass his lips since when he had reached the age of seven for as long as he lived, because Ireland could not contain his pride or his fame or his supremacy or his valour or his strength or his courage... In whatever part of the world Cú Roí should happen to be, he chanted over his fortress every night, so that it revolved as quickly as a millstone, and the entrance was never to be found after sunset.'

Other references to him are in a similarly striking vein. He wages campaigns in foreign parts, conquers countries in the eastern and southern world, and is even called by the title 'king of the world'. Such references accord with the theory that Cú Roí was Carausius, who was a great admiral, but the general drift of the ideas suggest a more ancient origin. Cú Roí 'traverses the briny stream', he 'holds helm on the southern sea', and his appearance is that of 'a blazing lion'. Notwithstanding their mediaeval flavour, these references all have solar symbolism, and it is not accidental that Conaire is haunted by the colour red and is consumed in a great fire, while the figure of Dáire was often associated with fire, with redness, and even with one-eyed figures (see **Goll mac Morna**). It is unlikely that Cú Roí and his corresponding figures were sun-deities. Rather does the evidence suggest that they represent the function of the sacred king as mediator who guarantees good fortune, particularly in the context of weather.

The Ulster Cycle, in which he occurs, preserves no direct accounts of Cú Roí's ritual role, but instead associates him with the west Munster area.

This is to be expected, for the Érainn people were strongest in that area in the early literary period. His fortress is designated as Cathair Chon Roí (Caherconree on the Slemish mountain west of Tralee), and it is from this base that he operates in the general corpus of the Cycle. In the text on the feast of **Bricriu**, for instance, the three leading Ulster warriors went to Caherconree to have him decide which of them was the greatest. Cú Roí was not present when they arrived, but the huge phantom who tested them on their night-watch was apparently him in disguise. He finally settled the matter between them by going to the Ulster court at Eamhain Mhacha in the shape of a massive and very ugly churl wearing a great dark-grey cloak. He proposed to each of the three warriors that they decapitate him and that he do the same to them in return. Of the three, only **Cú Chulainn** was willing to fulfil his side of the bargain, and so Cú Roí named him as the champion. In the story of the Intoxication of the Ulstermen, however, Cú Roí is represented as their foe and as foe even of Cú Chulainn. He is a close ally of **Meadhbh** and her husband Ailill mac Máta and the fosterer of their son. Again, in *Táin Bó Cuailnge*, his forces (the Clann Deadhadh) are among Meadhbh's combined armies, although their part is a minor one. Cú Roí himself was a reluctant participant in that campaign. His only spectacular act during it was to engage in a great stone-throwing contest with the Ulster warrior Muinreamhar. Like **Conall Cearnach**, his role in tradition depended on other lore of the Ulster Cycle besides the *Táin*.

The best-known story of Cú Roí concerned his death, of which there were several mediaeval renderings. The story seems to have developed, or at least to have been put into the context of the Ulster Cycle, in the late 9th century. The earliest surviving version tells of how Cú Roí, disguised in a grey cloak, assisted the Ulstermen in a raid on a sept called Fir Fálgha. In the raid several treasures were taken, including 'the three cows of Iuchna', a fine cauldron, and Bláthnaid daughter of the Fir Fálgha king. When he was refused a share of the spoils, the enraged Cú Roí took these three best treasures - cattle, cauldron, and woman - for himself. Cú Chulainn tried to prevent him, but was overcome by Cú Roí and had his hair shorn and daubed with cow-dung. The great Cú Chulainn had to hide himself with shame for a year until his hair grew again. Bláthnaid, however, loved Cú Chulainn, and she schemed with him to come to Caherconree and destroy Cú Roí. The earlier recension of the story states that she betrayed to Cú Chulainn the fact that Cú Roí's soul resided in a salmon in a certain pool, and that when Cú Chulainn killed that salmon with his rival's sword Cú Roí's strength drained away. The somewhat later recensions have Bláthnaid asking Cú Roí to have a fine dwelling built for her. She arranged that when all his warriors were thus engaged collecting and erecting stones she would give the signal to Cú Chulainn that her captor was undefended. This she did by letting some milk from the cows flow downstream to where Cú Chulainn was waiting with his forces. She secretly tied Cú Roí's hair to the bedpost after bathing him, and thus discommoded he was slain by Cú Chulainn and most of his men slaughtered. Bláthnaid paid for her treachery, however, for Cú Roí's poet **Feircheirdne** watched her closely until he found her standing on a cliff at Ceann Bheara (probably on the Antrim coast). He threw himself at her, and both he and she were dashed against the rocks below. An obscure praise-poem on Cú Roí is also attributed to Feircheirdne, but it contains no references to further narratives.

The 'Fir Fálgha' were in reality the mid-Leinster sept known as the Uí Fáilghe, and this story has incorporated an independent legend which told of a herd of cows owned by an ancient king of that people called Iuchna Eachbhéal. According to that legend, the cows loved Iuchna so much that they broke their horns in lamentation at his death. One speculative genealogical text has the same Iuchna as maternal uncle of Cú Roí, and this may have suggested the idea that Cú Roí would attempt to take the celebrated cows.The pre-existing theme of Cú Roí's cauldron provided another valuable item for the story, while his reputation as a great warrior betrayed would attract the motif of a treacherous wife. It is obvious that two sources have been used in connection with this latter motif - one being the Biblical account of Samson and Delilah, and the other a plot from the common stock of folklore (see **Wonder Tales**, Type 302). Cú Roí's appearance to the Ulstermen in disguise, and wearing a grey cloak, was borrowed from the story of Bricriu's feast.

The death-tale of Cú Roí was popular with manuscript writers of the 11th to the 13th century. These writers did not understand who the Fir Fálgha of the story were, with the result that they situated the great raid by Cú Roí and the Ulstermen at Cantyre in Scotland, or alternately on the Isle of Man. This latter was the place mentioned in the retelling by the historian Seathrún **Céitinn** in the 17th century. A few tellings of the story have been collected from folklore, deriving directly from Céitinn's work, and otherwise no accounts of Cú Roí survived in later oral tradition.

[Origins] T F O'Rahilly (1946), 5-6, 77-80, 321-2; John Rhys in *Journal of the Royal Society of Antiquaries of Ireland 21*, 651-7.

[Poems on him] Whitley Stokes in *Ériu 2*, 1-14; Kuno Meyer in *Zeitschrift für celtische Philologie 3*, 37-46; Rhys, *op cit*, 652-3.

[Bricriu's feast] George Henderson (1899).

[Intoxication of Ulstermen] J C Watson (1941).

[Death] R I Best in *Ériu 2*, 18-35; Meyer in *Revue Celtique 6*, 187-8; Rudolf Thurneysen in *Zeitschrift für celtische Philologie 9*, 189-234; Joseph Baudiš in *Ériu 7*, 200-9.

[Folklore] Alan Bruford (1969), 95-7, 251.

CUMAINE FADA (c589-c661 AD) Munster saint of whom several accounts are given in the mediaeval literature. His epithet (earlier, Fota), means 'long' or 'tall'.

A short biography in Irish dates from the 9th or 10th century. According to this, he was son of Fiachna, king of the western section of the royal Eoghanacht sept of Munster. Fiachna, when intoxicated, begot the child on his own daughter and then ordered that it be thrown to the wild beasts. However, the baby was put in a milk-pail and left on the arm of a cross outside a monastery and the abbot discovered him there and fostered him, giving him the name Cumaine ('little pail'). When Cumaine learned of his origin, he went away to be educated by St **Barra** at Cork, and spent twelve years studying there. An inspired fellow-student told him that he would die in Corcach, so Cumaine hastily left that place. He went to visit his father's royal court - situated in the text at Cashel - and gave wise counsel to the king, who did not realise who the young cleric was. Everybody remarked on how closely the two resembled each other, and Cumaine spoke a verse to his father suggesting their relationship. When Fiachna understood, he promised Cumaine authority over all the monasteries in his territory, and in return Cumaine promised heaven to his father. Cumaine spent the rest of his life preaching throughout Ireland, and eventually came to a monastery at Corcach Bheag in the territory of the Uí Fidhgheinte (a sept in east Limerick). He had been avoiding a place called Corcach all his life, and realised too late what name this location bore. The text is damaged at this point, but the account must have ended with his death. A praise-poem, reputedly composed at his death and apparently of very early date, is found in the manuscripts.

Variant recensions of the story have Cumaine's mother as queen of the Déise sept (in Co Waterford), and have him as a baby being saved from the river Suir by the fisherman of St **Déaglán** and being reared by St **Íde**. As he grew up, he left her convent and wandered about idly until one day he took shelter in the hollow of a tree. A continuous dripping of rain filled that hollow, and meanwhile he noticed a man nearby building a house patiently with lathe upon lathe. Realising that learning could only be acquired in similar manner through patience, he returned to Íde's convent and resumed his studies. A long tradition of verse and story makes Cumaine the half-brother of a famous Munster jester, **Comhdhán**, and both are involved in the early mediaeval story of **Liadhain**.

One source states that Cumaine was 'the vessel of wisdom in his time', and his feastday was November 12.

J F Kenney (1929), 241, 266, 420-1; Gearóid Mac Eoin in *Béaloideas 39-41*, 192-205 and in *Ériu 28*, 17-31; F J Byrne in *Ériu 31*, 111-22; J H Bernard / Robert Atkinson (1898) *1*, 16-21 and *2*, 108; John O'Donovan (1864), 304-5; Kuno Meyer (1902), 16-23; Cormac Ó Cadhlaigh (1939), 188-9; Seán Ó Coileáin in *Ériu 25*, 92-113.

CÚSCRAIDH MEANN MACHA Fictional Ulster warrior and king, son of **Conchobhar mac Neasa**.

The name Cúscraidh lacks a clear meaning, but was probably fabricated by an early mediaeval writer from 'coscradh' (i.e. overthrowing or destroying). The sobriquets mean 'the stammerer of Macha', and it may be that this appellation is a vestige of cultic lore, **Macha** being the goddess of Ulster sovereignty. The literature explains Cúscraidh's stammering as a commonplace feature. We are told that he met and contended with the fierce Connacht fighter **Ceat mac Mághach** in a lonely place. Ceat wounded him in the neck with a jevelin, and his vocal cords were thus damaged. Another source states that Ceat wounded him in the mouth, cutting away the tip of his tongue, and that the women of Ulster used to woo him afterwards by themselves affecting a stammer. He is said to have had a magnificent spear, with ferrules of silver which of their own accord whirled around bands of gold on the spear when conflict was imminent. Cúscraidh was the pupil of **Conall Cearnach** and, after the death of Conchobhar, Conall tried hard to secure the kingship for him. He refused that office, however, in order to avoid civil war among the Ulstermen. After the death of his brother **Cormac Conn Loingeas**, he accepted the kingship and was given a series of wise counsels by Conall concerning how a king should behave. He ruled well, but after three years a dispute broke out again with Connacht over a patch of territory, and this led to war. The two armies met in a fierce battle at Airteach (Frenchpark in Co Roscommon), and the Connachtmen were defeated, but Cúscraidh himself was slain by a warrior called Mac Éacht wielding a famous spear which once belonged to **Cealtchair**.

Rudolf Thurneysen (1935), 13-4; Whitley Stokes in *Irische Texte 3*, 404-5 and in *Revue Celtique 21*, 150-1; R I Best in *Ériu 8*, 170-90; Cecile O'Rahilly (1976), 110, 302 and (197O), 120, 346; Cormac Ó Cadhlaigh (1956), 471.

D

DAGHDHA (earlier, Dagdae) A leading mythic character in Irish literature, one of the **Tuatha Dé Danann**, who was demonstrably a principal deity in ancient times.

The name meant 'good god', though good not specifically in the moral sense but in the sense of technical precision. This explanation is given in the important text on the second battle of Moytirra (see **Mythological Cycle**), when the Tuatha Dé were making their military preparations. The surviving portrayals cause him to be identified with the 'Dis Pater' whom Caesar claimed was regarded by the Gauls as their ancestral deity. Mediaeval texts in fact state that the Daghdha had the alternative name Eochaidh Ollathair (see **Eochaidh**), the sobriquet here meaning 'father of many'. He was also known by the appellation '**Ruadh Ró-Fheasa**' (i.e. the All-Knowing Noble). This makes him a god of wisdom, and references to him under that name effectively portray him as a wise ancestral figure (see **Find File**).

Some basic attributes of the Daghdha are described in the account of the second battle of Moytirra. These attributes are hugeness, generosity, and a voracious appetite. He possesses a mighty cauldron from which 'no company ever went away unsatisfied', and the narrative again and again stresses the massive and momentous nature of his imagery. He is represented as willingly building a fortress for king **Breas**, and then being forced to build a great rampart around that fortress. During this work, he was deprived of food due to the demands of the satirist **Cridhinbhéal** and his life was miserable. However, through the advice of his son, the Mac Óg (i.e. **Aonghus**) he outwitted both Cridhinbhéal and Breas, and chose as payment for his work a single black heifer from Breas' herd. This heifer he later used to entice back all the cattle which the **Fomhóire** oppressors had taken from the Tuatha Dé.

The images of progenitor and gourmand also surface in the text. Before the battle, we are told, he went to a tryst with the **Mór-Ríoghain**, goddess of land and of war, on the bank of the river Unshin in Connacht. She had one foot on either side of the river when the Daghdha mated with her there. Then he went to a parley at the Fomhóire camp, and they - knowing that he loved porridge - filled a great cauldron with it for him and added vast quantities of milk and meat. They poured all this mixture into a hole in the ground and forced him to eat it. He took his ladle, which was big enough for a man and a woman to lie together in it, and ate the whole meal, scraping up even the gravel in the process. His belly was greatly distended as a result, and he fell asleep. On wakening he left the camp, dragging his mighty club after him. The club was so massive that eight men would be required to carry it. He had it mounted on wheels, and as he dragged it along the wheels made a track as deep as a dyke between provinces. He soon met a beautiful young woman of the Fomhóire and sought intercourse with her, but his huge belly made this impossible. The woman mocked him and flung him to the ground, and after he had disgorged himself he mated with her. She then promised magical assistance to the Tuatha Dé in the forthcoming battle, as the Mór-Ríoghain had also promised. When the battle was joined, the Daghdha wrought havoc on the foe with his mighty club.

30. DAGHDHA *Bronze cauldron from the 7th century BC.*

These passages are full of crude humour, but in them the writer is burlesquing what were in reality ancient mythical ideas of copiousness and fertility in association with the deity. At the end of the text, a more exalted capability is attributed to the Daghdha when he expertly plays the three kinds of magical music on a harp. In the text on the first battle of Moytirra, he is claimed to have been a god of druidry, and is described as using the great club with deadly effect in the fight. His magical power is stressed in direct association with the club in a passage in an 8th-century text. Here we are told that the club had a rough end and a smooth one. When he put the rough end on the heads of nine men together it slew them immediately, and when he put the smooth end on them they were revived. The emphasis on his club and cauldron recall the Gaulish deity Sucellos (literally 'good striker') who was portrayed on monuments as having a mallet and a jar. Sucellos was often represented in the company of the river-goddess Nantosuelta, so it is reasonable to assume that both the Gaulish 'Sucellos' and the Irish 'Daghdha' were pseudonyms for the same ancient Celtic deity.

Although by all indications an ancestral and therefore original figure, the mediaeval writers were very keen to attribute a genealogy to the Daghdha. In pseudo-history he is claimed to have been, like **Breas**, a son of Ealatha, which would give him Fomhóire paternity. This might well be a reflection of his association with fecundity, which would coincide with the agricultural imagery of the Fomhóire. In the account of the second battle of Moytirra he is said to have had two brothers, **Nuadhu** and **Oghma**, but this is no more than a late instance of the tendency to triplicate deities. Elsewhere there is no scarcity of references to his immediate family. One mediaeval account, obviously echoing earlier lore, makes him the husband of the Mór-Ríoghain, and he is also stated to have been lover or husband of the eponymous river-goddess **Bóinn**. By the latter he was father of Aonghus (q.v.), for whom he gained possession of Brugh na Bóinne (the Newgrange tumulus in Co Meath). That landmark, we are told, was built by the Daghdha himself, and another great edifice attributed to his labours was the Grianán of Aileach (in Co Donegal, a few miles from Derry city).

Several Tuatha Dé worthies were said to have been children of the Daghdha, including Aodh Caomh, Cearmaid, and **Brighid**, and one source even goes so far as to make **Dian Céacht** his son. An account of a daughter called Ainge states that the Daghdha made a tub for her which would drip while the sea was in flood and became stable when the sea subsided. His hugeness is emphasised in one text by the casual, though serious, remark, that his countenance was 'broader than half a plain'. Another text has him clearing twelve plains in one night, and cutting the path of twelve rivers in another night, and describes him as controlling the weather and the crops for the Tuatha Dé. This aetiological and environmental sense in the lore of the Daghdha underlines his divinity. The story of how his son Cearmaid was slain by Lugh (q.v.), after he sought to seduce the latter's wife, reflects some ancient lore of sexual jealousy connected with the Daghdha, for similar themes occur in accounts of two other sons of his. These were Aodh Caomh, who was slain by the jealous husband after he had seduced the wife of Corrchend; and Conán who was killed while trying to win a maiden called Cealg from her father.

The literary writers did not hesitate to invent new stories of the Daghdha. A 10th-century source has him using his club to expel a sea-monster and making the sea itself recede, thereby causing to surface the plain of Muirtheimhne (in north Co Louth). Continuing fascination with the great club is evidenced by a text from around the 12th century which purports to tell its origin. In this, after Cearmaid was slain by Lugh, the Daghdha put the dead body of his son on his back and set out for the eastern world in search of a resuscitating cure. He met three men who were carrying treasures along the road, and one of these treasures was the club. He inveigled it from them to examine it, and then touched the three with its killing-end. He touched Cearmaid with the revivifying end, and his son was restored to life and health. He then revivified the three strangers, and they allowed him to keep the club on permanent loan.

The Daghdha's own death was claimed by the pseudo-historians to have taken place as the result of a wound inflicted by a woman. This was Ceithleann, wife of Balar, with whom - according to some versions of the second battle of Moytirra - he engaged in single combat. She stabbed him with a javelin and, though he survived the wound, it continued to trouble him. He succeeded Lugh as king and ruled over the Tuatha Dé for eighty years, but eventually the wound took its toll and he died from it. This reworking of the tradition, with its strained chronology, is due to the pseudo-historians. A text of around the 9th century, with its timelessness, is nearer to the mythic perspective. Here the Daghdha is represented as still living when the Tuatha Dé were overcome by their successors, the sons of **Míl**. As part of the struggle, the Tuatha Dé destroyed the corn and milk of the newcomers, but when the sons of Míl made peace with the Daghdha he returned these products to them.

Post-mediaeval mentions of the Daghdha make him the father of other Tuatha Dé personages such as Bodhbh Dearg and **Midhir**, but these are mere spontaneous identifications, and he figures little in the later lore.

[Names] E A Gray (1982), 44-5; T F O'Rahilly (1946), 466-7; Kuno Meyer (1912), 98; Whitley Stokes in *Irische Texte 3*, 354-7; R A S Macalister (1941), 120-1.

[Cauldron, club] Gray, *op cit*, 24-5; J C Watson (1941), 27-9.

[Moytirra] Gray, *op cit*, 28-31, 42-51; 54-5, 70-1; Joseph Frazer in *Ériu 8*, 16-7, 30-3, 38-9, 44-5.

[Sucellos] Émile Thevenot (1968), 133-42; M-L Sjoestedt (1982), 52-7.

[Mór-Ríoghain] Gray, *op cit*, 44-5; Edward Gwynn (1906), 18-9 and (1924), 196-201.

[Bóinn] Gwynn (1906), 10-1, 18-21.

[Edifices] Gwynn (1906), 18-9 and (1924), 92-121.

[His children] Macalister, *op cit*, 120-1, 158-9; Gwynn (1924), 92-121, 292-3, 350-3, 362-7; Osborn Bergin in *Mediaeval Studies for G S Loomis* (1927), 400-2. For Cearmaid cf. also **Lugh**.

[Environment] Stokes (1892), 8-9; Gwynn (1924), 108-9; Osborn Bergin / R I Best in *Ériu 12*, 142-51.

[Muirtheimhne] A G Van Hamel (1933), 35-6; Gwynn (1924), 294, 454.

[Acquisition of club] Bergin, *op cit*, 402-6.

[Death of Daghdha] Brian Ó Cuív (1945), 7, 48; Macalister, *op cit*, 184-5.

[War with sons of Míl] Vernam Hull in *Zeitschrift für celtische Philologie 19*, 55-7.

[General] Gray, *op cit*, 121.

DÁIRE Name of a mythic personage in ancient Irish lore. Literally it meant 'the fruitful one', and there are several indications that it was an alternative designation for the **Daghdha**.

The Daghdha was regarded as a great ancestor, and Dáire fulfils the same function through his frequent occurrences in the early portions of genealogies. In these, he is given various guises - such as Dáire Doimhtheach, Dáire Barrach, Dáire mac Sídhe Bhoilg, Dáire mac Deadha - in order to render the different pedigrees credible. In a 7th-century biography of St **Patrick**, he parallels the Daghdha more immediately by being represented as the possessor of a fine cauldron. The cauldron motif occurs again in the context of the mythical **Cú Roí**, who is represented as son of Dáire. Like Cú Roí also, a character called Dáire Sírchréachtach was fancifully claimed to have made many conquests abroad, and it is thus apparent that the images of Cú Roí and Dáire were synonymous at some stage of tradition. Elsewhere we find the name Dáire being given to the owner of the great bull, the **Donn Cuailnge**, and appellations of characters such as Dáire Donn and Dáire Dearg indicate that the name was originally on a functional par with others such as **Donn** and **Dearg**.

In the early literature, the name Dáire occurs in alignment with **Goll** to designate a figure hostile to **Fionn mac Cumhaill**, and this can be explained by the early influence of the **Lugh** myth on the image of Fionn (q.v.).

T F O'Rahilly (1946), 7, 48-9, 210, 275-6, 454-5, 551; John O'Donovan (1849), 4-5; Cecile O'Rahilly (1952), 1, 39; Kuno Meyer in *Revue Celtique 5*, 197; Gerard Murphy (1933), 66-73; Dáithí Ó hÓgáin (1988), 14-5, 357.

DÁITHÍ (also, Nath Í) Historical king, who died c 445 AD. The mediaeval historians held that he had been king of Ireland, but in reality his realm was confined to either the north midlands or Connacht.

The name Nath Í originally meant 'nephew of Eo' ('eo' being a tree, figuratively a champion), but already by the early Middle Ages it was considered as an eclipsed form of 'daithe' (meaning 'swiftness', hence 'the swift one'). The fanciful interpretation thus given was that Dáithí never delayed to take up arms. There was a tradition that his real name was the relatively common one Fearadhach, but Nath Í was also current as a name in early Ireland. His father is said to have been Fiachra, brother of the celebrated **Niall Naoi-ghiallach**, and accordingly he was distinguished from other characters with the same name by the designation Nath Í (or Dáithí) mac Fiachrach.

He had the reputation of being, from the beginning, a fierce warrior. We read that, after Niall was installed as high-king at **Tara**, the province of Connacht was assigned to Fiachra and his brother Brian. The two contended with each other, however, and war broke out between them. Brian defeated Fiachra's army at Damhchluain (near Tuam in Co Galway), and Fiachra was taken prisoner and sent as a captive to Niall at Tara. Dáithí managed to escape, and he re-assembled his father's army and, with a surprise attack, defeated Brian in a second battle at Damhchluain. Brian fled, but was pursued and slain, after which Niall released the captive Fiachra and installed him as king of the province of Connacht. Fiachra was later slain as he campaigned against Munster, fifty Munster hostages being buried alive with his corpse at Forrach (Farrow, near Mullingar in Co Westmeath). Dáithí became king in his place.

Something of the actual savagery of these wars comes across, even in the late mediaeval texts. The predatory activities engaged in by Dáithí outside of Ireland probably consisted of no more than brief raids on the west coast of Britain, but one long list of his battles included some fought abroad. Referred to are engagements in Scotland, such as at Strathclyde ('Sraith Chluaidhe') and Kincardine ('Magh Circinn'), and also mentioned is an expedition across the English Channel ('muir nIocht') to the Alps ('Elpa'). The latter location probably resulted from a misinterpretation of Alba (meaning Scotland, or in the earlier literature all of Britain). A mediaeval text describes how the king of Thrace, called Formenus, who was on a Christian pilgrimage, had a great tower built in the Alps. Dáithí and his men knocked down this tower, and as a result Formenus prayed to God against him. When Dáithí was inspecting the area a thunderbolt from heaven struck and killed him. On their way back to Ireland with the corpse, his followers fought and won nine further battles. He was buried at the royal Connacht centre, Cruachain (Rathcroghan, Co Roscommon), where a red pillar-stone is still pointed out as marking his grave. It is clear that his encounter in the Alps with Formenus was invented by some mediaeval writer who had come across a reference to the 5th-century Frankish king Faramund.

A text written as late as the 17th century gives an extended account of Dáithí's great campaign overseas. According to this, his druid Doghra prophesied for him at the feast of Samhain (November - see **Time**) the he would conquer Scotland, and he accordingly set sail for that country at the head of a great army. In a bloody battle at Magh an Chairche (an obvious derivation from the Magh Circinn of earlier tradition) he defeated the Scottish king, called Fearadhach Fionn; and then proceeded through Britain and France, receiving submission from all and sundry, until his sudden démise in the Alps.

T F O'Rahilly (1946), 211-5; RIA Dictionary ('Dathi'); S H O'Grady (1892) *1*, 333-4; Vlad Bănăteanu in *Zeitschrift für celtische Philologie 18*, 160-88; Whitley Stokes in *Irische Texte 3*, 352-3, 418; Edward Gwynn (1906), 40-1; Julius Vendryes in *Mélanges à Ferdinand Lot* (1925), 743-67; John O'Donovan (1844), 17-27; P S Dinneen (1908) *2*, 412-3; Eugene O'Curry (1873), 284-8. See also **Conall Gulban**.

DALLÁN FORGAILL Poet who lived at the end of the 6th century AD, composer of a celebrated hymn in honour of St **Colm Cille** entitled the *Amhra* (literally, 'marvel'). 'Dallán Forgaill' meant 'the blind man of eloquence' and was really a nickname.

According to the mediaeval literature, Dallán was the chief-poet of Ireland and was indebted to Colm Cille for this position. It was claimed that the saint had successfully pleaded the case of the **poets** at the Convention of Drom Ceat in the year 575. Dallán had been banned from composing and the poets in general were in danger of being banished from the country until Colm reconciled them to the high-king Aodh mac Ainmhireach and to the nobles. As part of the solution Colm insisted that Dallán, on account of his surpassing knowledge and skill, be made the chief-poet ('ard-ollamh'). Dallán began soon after to compose the *Amhra* for Colm, but the latter out of humility forbade him to go beyond the prologue. The saint did, however, give him permission to compose the full eulogy when he had died, and told him that his sight would be restored for the purpose. Dallán asked how he would know if and when Colm had died, and the saint told him that a man on a speckled horse would bring the news and that the first words which that man would speak to him should be used to begin the poem. Dallán did accordingly, and so the *Amhra* began with the words 'ní dísceoil d'uíbh Néill' ('it is no paltry news for the descendants of Niall'). Colm was the great saint of this royal sept, the descendants of **Niall Naoighiallach.**

31. DALLÁN FORGAILL *Bronze figures of layman and ecclesiastic from the 7th or 8th century.*

The mediaeval writers knew quite little about **Dallán** himself, but the general tradition was that he belonged to the Masraighe sept and that he was a native of Maighin (Moynehall, just south of Cavan town). His real name is given as Eochaidh son of Colla, and some writers identified him with **Eochaidh Éigeas**. This seems to be a confusion due to a shared name, however, and one mediaeval quatrain mentions as three leading and distinct poets **Seanchán**, **Eochaidh Éigeas**, and **Dallán Forgaill**. There are some indications that Eochaidh Éigeas was the eldest of these three, and that Dallán inherited his position as leading poet, while Seanchán (q.v.) was definitely the youngest. Early sources refer to Dallán as 'mac Forgaill' ('son of Forgall') or even as 'ua Forgaill' (indicating a grandson). Neither of these appellations intend Forgall as the name of a progenitor, but rather that the poet Dallán was the 'essence' of wise declaration. In two early stories, a poet called Forgall is described as being present at the palace of **Mongán** at Moylinny in Co Antrim. It is possible that this is a genuine tradition, for the cycle of stories concerning Mongán apparently derives from eulogies composed for him by poets. Forgall is here described as proud and rapacious, a factor which leads to suspicion that the lore of the Drom Ceat convention is in the background. The strong likelihood is that by this Forgall was meant Dallán himself, albeit portrayed in a manner which is not necessarily true to character. Mongán died a reasonably young man in the year 624, and the dating would thus accord with the idea that he and Dallán were acquaintances.

The mediaeval literature claims that Seanchán succeeded Dallán as chief-poet, and there is no compelling reason to doubt this. However, an account grew up of the circumstances which is definitely romance rather than history. We read that he was inveigled by Aodh Fionn king of Breifne (the Cavan area) to go and seek a fine shield from a rival Aodh mac Duach, king of Airghialla (the general area of south Ulster). Dallán accordingly went and recited a poem in praise of the Airghialla king and then demanded the shield as payment. The king offered gold and silver and herds of cattle, but refused to part with his shield, and then Dallán threatened to satirise him. Aodh mac Duach protested that such extortion had been forbidden by Colm Cille and the other saints at Drom Ceat, but Dallán recited a demeaning poem and then departed. Because he had abused his art, he lived but three days thereafter. On his deathbed he proclaimed that Seanchán was the most worthy to succeed him, and that poet came and recited an eulogy over his corpse, describing him as the greatest poet of Ireland and comparing his intellect to 'a great flooding of the sea-tide'.

His association with Colm Cille, and the pious

nature of his celebrated poem in praise of that saint, caused Dallán himself to be regarded as an especially holy person by ecclesiastical historians. Already by the 8th century, he was being described as a saint and had a feastday, January 19, allotted to him. Furthermore, due to the fame of the *Amhra* for Colm Cille, a tendency grew for similar associations to be made between him and other saints. Thus, in or about the 9th century, a short *Amhra* for **Seanán** was attributed to him, undoubtedly at the instigation of that saint's community in Scattery Island on the Shannon. In later mediaeval times, Dallán was claimed to have composed a praise-poem for St Conall Caol of Inishkeel in Co Donegal, and this type of pious portrayal of him continued in stark contradiction to the secular lore. We read that he was once visiting the monastery of Conall Caol when sea-pirates attacked and beheaded him. They flung his head into the sea, but it was swept ashore, and when one of Conall's monks placed it on his body it stuck thereto as before, so that he was buried whole at Inishkeel. This story, though unhistorical, is the only account of Dallán which has survived in folklore.

The real place of Dallán's burial is unknown, but he can hardly have lived long into the 7th century.

Whitley Stokes in *Revue Celtique 20*, 31-55, 132-83, 248-89, 400-37 and *ibid 21*, 133-6 and in *Zeitschrift für celtische Philologie 3*, 220-5 and (1905), 54-5, 414; John O'Donovan (1864), 30-1; Owen Connellan (1860), 258-62; James Travis in *Speculum 19*, 89-103; Kuno Meyer (1895) *1*, 45-56; Maud Joynt (1941), 1-9; Andrew O'Kelleher / Gertrude Schoepperle (1918), 486; John O'Hanlon (1875) *1*, 496-503; Seán Ó Coileáin in *Ériu 28*, 33-7; Séamas Ó Searcaigh (1967), 23-5, 42-3; IFC 948:45.

DAMER, JOSEPH (1630-1720) An English entrepreneur who moved to Ireland in 1662 and bought up large estates from Cromwellian settlers in Co Tipperary. He filled these lands with sheep, and set up a very successful business in the export of wool. He also set up a banking business in Dublin and became so rich that the English government itself was heavily in debt to him.

Damer had the reputation of being a miser. Dean **Swift**, who disliked him, wrote that 'he walked the streets and wore a threadbare cloak, he dined and supped at charge of other folk'. He never married, and at his death he left his great wealth to two nephews - the property at Roscrea to his namesake Joseph and his own house and surrounding estate at Shronell to John. The total will amounted to nearly half a million pounds, a stupendous sum for the time, and it is doubtlessly from this that the common Irish proverb 'as rich as Damer' derives. Amazement and speculation gave rise to much folklore concerning how he first became rich. Joseph Damer had begun his career as a civil servant in Cromwell's administration, and so it was said that he had stumbled onto the treasures of one of the monasteries which were confiscated in Ireland. The treasure had been hidden by the monks in barrels covered with tallow, and it was fancied that Damer had been a chandler who bought these 'tallow-barrels' and found to his surprise and delight what they contained.

After his death, the mantle of archetypal magnate fell on his nephew John, who married in 1726. It was, however, an unsuccessful alliance. Folklore claims that his wife eloped with an army officer, and this Damer also was childless. Around the year 1740 he commenced the building of a huge mansion at Shronell. This mansion, of which only a portion of the wall now remains, was said to have had a window for every day of the year. Folk accounts of John have a large element of farce. It is said that he went about in rags, while he had his servants magnificently accoutred for the sake of pomp, and that he used even to come in disguise to the servants and beg money from them. There was reputedly a secret room in his mansion, with its doors heavily padlocked, and in this room he had stored an incredible treasure of golden sovereigns. He loved to spend long periods alone in this vault, gazing at the glittering sovereigns and delightedly letting them run through his fingers. A story grew up about him, which is in reality a variant of one of Aesop's fables (see **Humorous Tales**, Type 1305A). According to this, a travelling tailor came to him one day and offered to make a proper suit of clothes for him. He immediately asked how much would that cost, and the tailor said that all he required as payment was one look at Damer's gold. The magnate thought that the tailor was a foolish fellow and that this was a good bargain, so he agreed. When the fine suit was finished, he brought the tailor to his secret room and showed him the gold. The tailor looked at it for a little while and Damer, growing curious, enquired what could he gain from this. 'It does me the same good to be looking at it,' said the tailor, 'as it does yourself!'

When John died in 1768, the enormous wealth

passed to his nephew, again called Joseph, and the son of this Joseph was an inveterate spendthrift who frittered away his vast inheritance on gambling, drinking, and expensive clothes. The theme of futility was thus complete, and folklore continually added to its accounts of the gold of 'great Damer' - who was, in reality, a composite character drawn from the various eccentric members of that family. Many kinds of motifs involving acquisitiveness became attached to the name in Munster tradition. A popular international folktale told of a trickster who made a contract for as many sovereigns as would fill his hat, and so it was said that Damer struck such a bargain with the devil in return for his soul. The shrewd Damer tricked the evil one by putting a hole in his hat and placing it over a hole in the floor of his mansion. There was a huge room underneath, into which the sovereigns continued to shower, and in exasperation the devil withdrew from the deal, forfeiting the huge amount of sovereigns to Damer. Another story had it that Damer was originally a poor rat-catcher and that he was employed by a rich lady to clear her house of the pests. He stole a huge amount of gold sovereigns from her by secreting them in the bellies of the dead rats as he disposed of them.

The final loss of Damer's great wealth was also the subject of speculation. It was said that jackdaws found their way into his vault and, coin by coin, took away all the bright metal objects in their beaks. Some tree-cutters in the area were reported to have become wealthy later through the unexpected windfall from the birds' nests. There is some evidence that the charge of callous greed laid against Damer was not justified in the cases of any of the bearers of the name. However, the vast wealth contrasted strongly with the general living conditions of the time, and was in itself a very dramatic phenomenon. It therefore was ideal material for folklore, which has a strong tendency to personalise memories and to put ideas into physical form.

A M Fraser in *Dublin Historical Record 3*, 41-53; J M Hone in *Studies 39*, 419-26; D J O'Sullivan in *Journal of the Irish Folk Song Society 25*, 37-9; Áine Bhreathnach (1972); Dáithí Ó hÓgáin in William Nolan / T G MacGrath (1985), 139-47, 446-8.

[Folklore plots] Antti Aarne / Stith Thompson (1961), Types 1130, 1305A; Thompson (1955-1958), Motifs B756, M210-211, N527, Q272.

DANU Goddess who is referred to in the **Mythological Cycle** and in some ancient toponymics. The name occurs only in the genitive 'Danann' (earlier, Danand'), most significantly in the description of the otherworld beings **Tuatha Dé Danann**.

It is probable that this goddess was worshipped from antiquity by the Celts, for several river-names in Europe - most notably the Danube - are based on a Celtic word Danŭv. This is cognate with Dānu, the name of a river-goddess in Sanskrit literature. In mediaeval Welsh literature, a lady called Dôn is described as the mother of a family of mythical wizards, a factor which strongly suggests her identity with the Irish goddess.

The name Danu was identified by mediaeval Irish writers with 'Anu'. This latter (alternately, Ana) is connected with an Old Irish word 'anai', which meant 'wealth', and Anu is described as the goddess to whom the province of Munster owed its special prosperity. Two mountain-tops near Killarney in Co Kerry were called Dá Chích nAnann (literally 'the Two Paps of Anu'), and a 9th-century glossary states that 'good was the food which she gave'. The form Anu may thus have developed through the role of food-provider being applied to Danu. The status of mother-goddess is strongly suggested by the glossary, which declares that Anu was 'the mother of the Irish gods' - a near enough equivalent to the Welsh Dôn. It is clear that the Irish goddess was associated with the land rather than with rivers, but this change in function could have taken place in antiquity. Another early text calls Ireland 'iath nAnann' ('the land of Anu'). This usage, like the toponymic Dá Chích nAnann, would have rendered the final element identical in sound with 'nDanann', and it may indeed have been such usages which caused Danu to be referred to as Anu. As a land-goddess, she was identified by the writers with the **Mór-Ríoghain**. It seems likely, indeed, that Danu was originally the proper name which lies behind designations like the Mór-Ríoghain, **Brighid**, and other titular names of Irish **goddesses**.

Little narrative concerning Danu is found in the literature. She is said to have been the mother of the three brothers who killed the father of **Lugh**. Their father was Tuireall, and Danu's association with them is due to the designation of Tuatha Dé Danann (q.v.) as Trí Dé Danann, which left the impression that she had three sons. Tuireall was claimed to have been an alternative name for Dealbhaoth, described as Danu's own father - but

32. DANU *The 'Paps of Danu' near Killarney.*

this piece of incestuous scandal is nothing more than a product of the imagination of some mediaeval writer. Danu was in fact given varying paternities, leading to the situation in which several mythical ladies were said to have had the same name. Ultimately, as mother-goddess, Danu was not in need of parentage.

Alwyn Rees / Brinley Rees (1973), 50-3, 364; Alfred Holder (1891) *1*, 1224-38; Gerard Murphy (1953), 208-10; Kuno Meyer (1912), 3; Whitley Stokes in *Irische Texte 3*, 288-9; E J Gwynn in *Ériu 13*, 40, 63; R A S Macalister (1941), 128-9, 156-7, 192-3; E A Gray (1982), 122-3.

DÉAGLÁN Saint who founded the monastery of Ard Mhór (Ardmore, Co Waterford). He was reputedly one of the missionaries who predated **Patrick** in the south of Ireland, but it is difficult to confirm this and his floruit may in fact have been in the late 5th and early 6th century AD. His name (earlier, Déclán) is anglicised as Declan.

His biography, surviving in Latin and Irish, dates from the 12th century but incorporates some older material. We read that his father was called Earc mac Tréin and was of the Leinstermen, and that he was borne by his mother Déithín without pain. At his birth, his head struck against a stone, and this caused the stone to have a cavity. Rain from this 'carraig Dhéagláin' ('Declan's rock') afterwards used to heal all types of sickness. Until he was seven, he was fostered by his maternal uncle Dobhrán who lived in the Déise territory (Co Waterford), and then was educated by a bishop Colmán and a holy hermit called Diomna. When he came of age, seven men who had seen a ball of fire in the sky at his birth came to him and became his followers. They set out to Rome with him, and met St **Ailbhe** who was sojourning there. Déaglán was appointed as a bishop by the Pope, and while in Italy he also met Patrick, who had not yet undertaken his mission to Ireland. We read that, while Déaglán was saying Mass one day, a little black bell came from heaven to him. He entrusted this bell for safe keeping to one Rúnán, son of the king of Rome, who wished to accompany him on his return to Ireland.

They set out on the homeward journey, but could not find a ship to bring them over 'muir nIocht' (the English Channel). Then an empty

33. DÉAGLÁN
Images in stone at the monastery of Ardmore.

ship miraculously appeared and took them from the mainland to England, and after spending some time there they embarked for Ireland. Rúnán, however, left the little black bell on a rock on the shore and did not remember it until they were well out to sea. Discovering this, Déaglán prayed to God and that rock began to float on the sea. The saint directed that the boat follow the floating rock, and in this way they landed at Inis Aird na gCaorach (High Sheep Island), whereupon the king of the Déise gave this island to him. Déaglán struck the water with his crozier, and immediately the sea drained and the island was joined to the mainland. This was the site on which he began to build his great monastery of Ardmore.

The biography attributes several other miracles to Déaglán. He banished a plague from the people of Caiseal (Cashel, Co Tipperary) and restored to life seven noble hostages who had died from that plague while in the custody of Aonghus, king of Munster there. As a result of this, tribute from the Munster kings was ever after due to his monastery. It is also claimed that he welcomed and assisted Patrick when that great saint reputedly arrived in Munster, for they had formed a mutual bond of friendship when they met on a highway in Italy.

A series of more personal legends are also cited in the biography. Once, a certain wealthy man named Dearcán invited him to dinner and served up the meat of a dog under pretence that it was mutton. Déaglán, however, noticed the dog's claw in the meat and upbraided his host, whereupon Dearcán repented and was converted. On another occasion Déaglán was on a journey and his horse went lame. He harnessed a stag to the chariot in its place and, when the journey was finished, released the stag back into the wilderness. We also read of how the palace of the Déise king

Cionaodh took fire and how Déaglán cast his crozier into the conflagration, thereby quenching it immediately. Furthermore, when an enemy fleet approached with the intent of plundering and destroying Ardmore, he sent the holiest member of his community, Ultán, to confront them. Ultán raised his left hand against the ships, and they all sank immediately. The sailors were turned into stone, and they are the rocks in the sea off Ardmore. The latter story has been borrowed into this context, for elsewhere Ultán is described as banishing a massive invasion fleet at the request of the high-king **Diarmaid mac Cearrbheoil**. We read that he was busy caring for the children of women who had died in a great plague, and only his left hand was free when the messengers from Diarmaid arrived. He therefore raised that hand, remarking that if his right hand were free he would have raised it and as a result 'no foreigner would ever invade Ireland'.

Much of the material of the literary lives survived also in the folklore of Co Waterford. A boulder which lies on the shore at Ardmore is identified as the rock which floated over the sea carrying his bell. It rests on two other rocks, thus leaving a little passage underneath, through which people crawl on all fours to relieve themselves of ailments. The legend of the dog-meat is a derivative of a folktale plot concerning the divining power of a wise man (see **Wonder Tales**, Type 655). In oral lore of Déaglán, however, it is much developed by having the saint make the Sign of the Cross over his plate, and the dog jumps up, restored to life, and races barking from the house. This oral form results from the addition to the literary account of a story of a holy man who miraculously brings a dead animal back to life after eating its meat (see **Religious Tales**, Type 750B).

An early tradition had it that Déaglán first brought rye into Ireland, the full of his shoe of it, as St **Fionán Cam** first brought wheat. The feastday of Déaglán is July 24.

J F Kenney (1929), 310-3; Charles Plummer (1910) *2*, 32-59; Patrick Power (1914), xvi-xxvi, 1-73, 150-77; Whitley Stokes (1905), 112-3; John O'Hanlon (1875) *7*, 307-54; Ordnance Survey Letters - Waterford (1841), 159-66; IFC 22:70/413, 84:8-10, 87:86, 251:329-31, 259:54-68, 492:331, 614:162-5, 947:307.

[Ultán and Diarmaid mac Cearrbheoil] Stokes, *op cit*, 198-201.

[Restoration of eaten animal] Plummer (1910) *1*, cxliii.

DEARG (earlier, Derg) Name of a mythic personage in ancient Irish lore. Literally it means 'red', and Dearg had rather sinister associations with slaughter and death.

In the surviving sources, he does not have a uniform identity, and it is apparent that the name and personality had by the literary period become a dramatic device to build tension in texts. The character Da Dearga, in whose hostel **Conaire** was slain, is a case in point. Da Dearga is also directly referred to as 'Derg' in the text, and indeed the element 'da' seems to be a shortening of 'dia', meaning 'god'. His divinity is further suggested by the occurrence of three horsemen called 'Derg' who presage death for Conaire and who ride 'the horses of Donn', as it is by the parallelism between 'the house of Derg' and 'the house of Donn' in the text itself. The conclusion must be that Dearg is in some way equivalent with the better known death-god **Donn**. Perhaps Dearg was an appellation for Donn in the context of violent death or, given the history of the Conaire myth, it might well be that it was the name by which Donn was generally known to the early Leinstermen.

In the tradition of the Leinster hero **Fionn mac Cumhaill**, Dearg appears as a hostile otherworld figure, and this seems to have originated in a fanciful dialectic between Donn and Fionn's prototype **Find**. 'Dearg', like 'Donn', occurs in several texts as an epithet with the name **Dáire**, who in turn also appears to have been a double of the **Daghdha**. The whole complex of ancestral figures would have been borrowed, some centuries before Irish literature began, into the context of Find (q.v.). One offshoot of this is a very curious story found in an 8th-century text, which describes how Fionn mac Cumhaill had a servant called Derg Corra. A paramour of Fionn made advances to this servant, who rejected her, and she in revenge claimed that he had tried to rape her. Believing the false charge, Fionn banished the servant from his presence, but later while hunting came across him again in the forest. Derg Corra was eating a meal along with a blackbird, a trout, and a stag. His identity was hidden by 'a cloak of concealment', but he was recognised through the magical knowledge of Fionn. The plot of this story has been borrowed from an extraneous source (see **Romantic Tales**, Type 870C), but the imagery onto which it has been superimposed is quite distinctive.

That imagery corresponds to Celtic engravings in several parts of western Europe, which have a human figure, accompanied by a stag and other animals. One of the engravings preserves the name Cernunnos, which meant 'the horned (or peaked) one', an interpretation which can also be put on the name Dearg Corra ('the red peaked one'). This suggests that surviving vestiges of ancient Celtic belief became attached to the divine appellation Dearg. Such imagery of sacred deer, of course, proved attractive to the developing lore of Fionn mac Cumhaill, which had deer-hunting as one of its favourite themes. The connection of Dearg with wild deer continued within that context, and mediaeval storytelling had his daughter coming in the shape of a doe to Fionn (see **Oisín**).

T F O'Rahilly (1946), 125-9, 276; Eleanor Knott (1936); Kuno Meyer in *Revue Celtique 25*, 344-9; Dáithí Ó hÓgáin (1988), 15, 46-9, 324, 328.

DEIRDRE Mythical or fictional lady of great beauty in the **Ulster Cycle**.

The story of Deirdre is a version of the three-cornered tragic plot concerning competition between an old man and a young man for the hand of a lady. Other versions include the romance of Tristan and Isolt and the elopement of **Diarmaid ua Duibhne** with **Gráinne**. It is apparent that the plot circulated in the folklore of antiquity and became popular among the Celts of northern Britain and of Ireland. The first surviving text of the Deirdre story dates from the 9th century and is entitled *Loinges Mac n-Uislenn* (the Exile of the Sons of Uisliu). It tells of how king **Conchobhar mac Neasa** and the Ulstermen were drinking at the house of the storyteller Feidhlimidh when an unborn baby cried out in the womb of Feidhlimidh's wife. The lady gave birth to a girl. The druid **Cathbhadh** foretold that the child would cause great slaughter, and the warriors called for her to be put to death. Conchobhar, however, said that he would take the child, who was called Deirdre, and he had her fostered in a place apart in the care of the nurse Leabharcham. She grew up to be the most beautiful woman in Ireland. One day, as she watched her foster-father flaying a calf in the snow, a raven came and drank the blood; and she remarked that the man of her desires must have hair dark like the raven, cheeks red like the blood, and body as white as the snow. Leabharcham told her that there was such a man, and his name was Naoise (earlier, Naise), one of the three sons of Uisliu. Deirdre soon after contrived to meet Naoise. 'A fine heifer is passing by,' said Naoise. 'The heifers are always fine,' she answered, 'where there are no bulls.' 'You have the bull of the province, the king of Ulster,' said he. 'Between the two of you, I would choose a young bull like you!' answered Deirdre. Remembering Cathbhadh's prophecy, Naoise rejected her; but she seized him by the ears and threatened him with shame and derision if he refused to take her away (see **'geis'**).

Naoise then collected his two brothers, Aindle and Ardán, and took her away with him. Unable to avoid Conchobhar's vengeance in Ireland, they crossed to Scotland, but Deirdre's beauty soon attracted the jealousy of the king of that country to Naoise, and they had to repair to a lonely island in the sea. The Ulstermen pitied their plight and prevailed upon Conchobhar to allow them to return. Three celebrated warriors, **Fearghus mac Róich**, **Dubhthach Daol Uladh**, and **Cormac Conn Loingeas** went to Scotland and escorted them home on Conchobhar's surety. On their arrival at the royal court of Eamhain Mhacha, however, the king had the three sons of Uisliu treacherously slain by his mercenaries. Fearghus and his fellow-guarantors were livid at this, and they ravaged the province in vengeance and departed to the hostile court of queen **Meadhbh** in Connacht. Conchobhar forced the grieving Deirdre to live with him for a year. At the end of the year, he asked her whom of all men she hated most, and she answered Eoghan mac Durthacht, for it was Eoghan who had killed Naoise. 'Well, you will live with Eoghan!' said the king. Next day she was made to travel in a chariot, with Conchobhar and Eoghan on either side of her. The king mockingly remarked that her eye was like that of a sheep between two rams. Deirdre, unable to bear any more, dashed her head to pieces against a rock.

This story did not long predate its first occurrence in literature. It was introduced into the Ulster Cycle as an explanation for the desertion of Fearghus mac Róich (q.v.), a happening which had previously been explained in other ways. Also, the portrayal of Conchobhar is conspicuously more ruthless than in other stories. Elsewhere he is ambitious but not cruel, and the aging vindictiveness shown by him here is a direct result of the role of the old suitor in the borrowed three-cornered plot.

An expanded version of the romance was written in the 14th century, and became quite popular in manuscripts; and again the 17th-century historian

Céitinn gave a short retelling in his influential work. There is also an 18th-century redaction, written in Ulster, which gives more detailed descriptions of some of the episodes; while in Scotland a lay was composed which tells the story in a more conversational form. It is therefore not surprising that the romance of Deirdre has survived strongly in folk tradition, many tellings having been recorded in both Ireland and Scotland in recent generations. These oral versions have been current for a long time, for they include the beginning of the story (not found in the 14th-century text) and the motif of the unborn child's cry (missing in all but the earliest text). They also have two important innovations. Conchobhar has a house built with a leaden roof for Naoise and his brothers and, when they are inside the house, the doors are locked on them and the house set on fire. The intention is to leave them to a horrid death, but in most versions they break out and die fighting. This motif is borrowed from the firing of an iron house in the mediaeval literary tale called the Intoxication of the Ulstermen (see **Cú Chulainn**). Secondly, when Deirdre dies she is buried in the same graveyard as Naoise, and a tree grows out of each grave. Branches of the two trees intertwine. This is an adaptation of an international motif which has been current in Ireland for many centuries (see **Romantic Folktales**, Type 970).

The Deirdre story in distorted form is the subject of James Macpherson's once celebrated poem 'Darthula'. In somewhat more recent times the story has featured in the work of such writers as Lady Gregory, W B Yeats, J M Synge, James Stephens, and George Russell.

[Earliest text] Vernam Hull (1949).

[Other literary versions] Whitley Stokes in *Irische Texte 2 (2)*, 109-84; Donald MacKinnon in *Celtic Review 1*, 12-7, 104-31; P S Dinneen (1908) *2*, 190-7; Sean Ua Ceallaigh (1927), 65-88; Breandán Ó Buachalla in *Zeitschrift für celtische Philologie 29*, 114-54.

[Scottish lay] J F Campbell (1872), 19-29.

[Folklore] Alan Bruford (1969), 99-105, 264-5; Seán Ó Súilleabháin (1942), 599 and (1974), 23-9.

DIAN CÉACHT Mythical physician in early Irish literature. The original meaning of the name seems to have been 'he who swiftly travels', and it may in fact have been a pseudonym for a god of healing.

Dian Céacht is mentioned very early in the literature. Reference in 7th and 8th-century texts have him as a physician and as an arbitrator on matters concerning leeches. An incantation against ailments refers to 'the salve which Dian Céacht left with his family so that whatever it is laid on is healed'. A 9th-century glossary directly calls him 'the healing sage of Ireland' and a later writer repeats this description and calls him a 'god of health'. Caesar refers to such a god among the Gauls, but does not give his name and calls him 'Apollo'. It is likely that Dian Céacht, the one who travels swiftly when required to heal his devotees, is the Irish version of this deity. In a 10th-century text, Dian Céacht is indeed described as 'going roads of great healing'. The mediaeval writers in general made him the physician of the **Tuatha Dé Danann**, an adept at magical cures, and in that role he occurs in several texts. In the **Mythological Cycle**, he and his three brothers are mentioned as physicians in the first battle of Moytirra. In the second battle, however, two sons and a daughter are the trio who feature with him. They make a well, into which the wounded of the Tuatha Dé are cast to be healed while Dian Céacht and his family sing incantations by it. Before the same battle, he makes a promise which typicalises his image: 'Any man who is wounded, unless his head be cut off, or the membrane of his brain or his spinal cord be severed, will be fully healed by me.'

It was appropriate, then, that it was he who healed the blemish of the Tuatha Dé king **Nuadhu**. That king having lost his hand in the first battle of Moytirra, Dian Céacht put a silver arm on him which had 'the vigour of every hand in it'. The great physician's son Miach, however, interfered and himself set about healing the king. In nine days skin grew on the hand, it became manageable, and it became so deft as to catch wisps of burnt bulrushes. Dian Céacht was displeased at being upstaged by his son and struck him three times on the head with a sword, but Miach cured himself of each wound. Then Dian Céacht struck him a fourth blow, which cut his brain and killed him. Three hundred and sixty-five herbs grew out of Miach's grave, one for each of his joints and sinews. The young man's sister Airmeith collected the herbs, and Dian Céacht mixed them so that nobody would ever again know their full healing qualities. We are also told that Dian Céacht put every type of herb that grew in Ireland into a well between Moytirra and Lough Arrow. This well was known as Tiopra Sláine and was reputed to have been his great healing well. All of this lore can be viewed as débris of the ancient mystique and rituals associated with the art of healing.

Some mediaeval sources invent further details of relatives and associates, but very few adventures are related of him. We are told that he cured Tuirill (see **Lugh**) by making an emetic draught for him, and that he destroyed serpent-like creatures which infested the heart of a son of the **Mór-Ríoghain**. In a more heroic vein, he is described as slaying a great serpent which threatened to devastate the countryside surrounding the river Barrow in south Leinster. This is clearly an echo of the mediaeval imagery which equated plagues with dragons and the like (see **Saints**). It is also stated that he restored the eye which **Midhir** had lost in an accident, and a late variation on this particular theme is given some humorous colouring. According to this, Miach, the son of Dian Céacht, replaced the eye of **Nuadhu's** doorkeeper with that of a cat. Skilled though this operation was, it left the doorkeeper at a disadvantage, for the eye remained open at night watching mice and birds, whereas by day it slept while its bearer should be at work. The same late text burlesques the motif of the replacement of Nuadhu's arm by stating that Miach performed the operation in a bizarre manner. First he removed a beetle which had nested in the king's other arm, and then he replaced the lost limb with that of the king's swineherd. This is an echo from a folk plot (see **Wonder Tales**, Type 660).

T F O'Rahilly (1946), 472-3; Daniel Binchy in *Ériu 20*, 1-3, 22-3; Whitley Stokes / John Strachan (1903), *2*, 249; Kuno Meyer (1912), 36; Stokes in *Irische Texte 3*, 356-9; Joseph Frazer in *Ériu 8*, 34-5, 44-5; E A Gray (1982), 24-5, 32-3, 40-3, 50-1, 54-7, 122-3; Edward Gwynn (1906), 62-3 and (1924), 182-5; R A S Macalister (1941), 112-5, 122-3, 216-7, 228-9; R J O'Duffy (1888), 1-3.

DIARMAID MAC AODHA SLÁINE High-king of Ireland, who reigned jointly with his brother Bláthmhac from 642 to his death in 664 AD. Both he and Bláthmhac died of the plague called the 'Buidhe Chonaill' (literally, Yellow of Conall).

Diarmaid was said to have been reared by a woman called Sineach Cró, and a saga entitled *Cath Chairn Chonaill* was compiled in the 10th century concerning her influence on him. We read that the men of Connacht were taking her cattle and that she chided Diarmaid with doing nothing to stop this. She said that he had the nickname Ruanaidh ('scarlet') because he was a coward and, smarting under this, Diarmaid gathered an army in order to invade the western province. Eventually the Connacht king **Guaire** opposed him at Carn Chonaill (Ballyconnell, near Gort in Co Galway). Guaire was defeated, and had to submit to the high-king, but so generous was he that Diarmaid knelt before him in respect, and the two kings were reconciled.

From the same period comes another story of Diarmaid, which tells of how he left the citadel of **Tara** one day with his fosterson Criomhthann and travelled to Áth Truim (Trim, Co Meath). A beautiful woman approached them in a chariot there, and she agreed to return to Tara with Diarmaid and be his wife. He gave her as token a little brooch, and hence she became known as Beagfhola (earlier, Becfola, meaning 'little wealth'). She, however, tried to seduce Criomhthann, and he agreed to a tryst with her. She set out for the appointed place on a Sunday morning, accompanied by a handmaid, but wolves attacked them at Dubhthor (the northern boundary of Meath) and killed the handmaid. Beagfhola fled into a tree to avoid them. From the tree she saw a fire in the forest and, going there, she met a handsome young man magnificently accoutred. He paid no heed to her, but she followed him into his boat on a nearby lake. They crossed over to an island, where she shared his meal and got into his bed, but still he paid her no attention. Three warriors exactly like him came in the morning, and he joined them. The group fought four other warriors who arrived on the scene, until all were bloody. The young man then returned to her and revealed that his name was Flann, grandson of Feadhach. His three companions were his brothers, and the other group were relatives. The island had belonged to Feadhach, and the two groups were fighting for it. It was a marvellous island, with sufficient food always available for its inhabitants. Beagfhola wished to remain with him, but he told her to return to Diarmaid and said that if he gained possession of the island he would come for her. She found her handmaid alive and well - for the wolves had merely been calves from the island - and they returned to Tara. There she found Diarmaid rising from his bed as if no time had passed since she left him.

Exactly a year later, she and Diarmaid saw a wounded man passing the door of their dwelling. The man was Flann, and Beagfhola went away with him. Soon after, four clerical students arrived and announced that St Molaise of Damh-Inis (Devenish on Lough Erne) had sent them, for a farmer on the island had that morning seen two groups of four warriors fighting there. All had fallen but for one wounded man. The saint had buried the other seven, and Diarmaid directed that the gold and silver of their accoutrements be used to ornament Molaise's shrine and satchel and crozier. Beagfhola was never seen again.

This story provides a unique blend of pre-Christian and Christian tradition, with Devenish being portrayed as an island sanctuary for both worldviews. It is clear that the author, who initially presented Beagfhola as an immoral being, could not resist portraying the otherworld of pre-Christian belief in an attractive light.

Diarmaid also figures in the mediaeval literature concerning **Cano mac Gartnáin** and **Seanchán**, and of several of the saints, including **Féichín** and **Mochuda**.

R A S Macalister (1956), 378-81; Whitley Stokes in *Zeitschrift für celtische Philologie 3*, 203-19 and in *Irische Texte 3*, 344-7; Kuno Meyer (1912), 98; D A Binchy (1963), 5; S H O'Grady (1898) *1*, 85-7; Máire Bhreathnach in *Ériu 35*, 59-91.

34. DIARMAID MAC CEARRBHEOIL
An upright decorated stone at the monastery of Clonmacnoise.

DIARMAID MAC CEARRBHEOIL High-king of Ireland who reigned between the years 544 and 565 AD. His father was Fearghus 'Cearrbheoil', this epithet (earlier, Cerrbeoil), meaning 'crooked-mouthed', and Diarmaid's patronymic therefore comes from his father's nickname. In later texts his name is written as Diarmaid mac Cearbhaill.

After the death of **Muircheartach mac Earca**, the two claimants to the throne were Diarmaid and his distant cousin Tuathal Maolgharbh. The latter won the contest, and he forced Diarmaid to go into hiding. One text describes an incident which reputedly occurred during this period. Being at Snámh Dá Éan (now Farnagh, Co Westmeath), Diarmaid saw the smoke of a fire in the distance and, going to investigate, found St **Ciarán** building the foundations of his monastery at Clonmacnoise. One of Diarmaid's druids remarked that it was an inopportune time for beginning a building, but Diarmaid disregarded this and assisted the saint in driving a stake into the ground. Ciarán prophesied to him that, as a result of this, he would be high-king on the next day.

Hearing this, one of Diarmaid's followers, Maol Mór, volunteered to go and assassinate Tuathal Maolgharbh. His plan was to bring a pup's heart on the point of his spear and to tell Tuathal that this was the heart of Diarmaid, and then to stab the unsuspecting high-king with the same spear. Diarmaid agreed to the plan, and lent his own horse to Maol for the venture. This was a black horse, and it was very fleetfooted. Maol accordingly went and slew Tuathal, but he failed in his effort to escape and was himself slain. Diarmaid then advanced on **Tara** and, encountering no opposition, assumed the office of high-king for himself. This tradition is a curious one, and it is difficult to determine what basis it had. The account of the assassination may preserve some historical data, for we read that an expression grew up from it, viz. 'éacht Mhaoil Mhóir' ('the feat of Maol Mór'), to denote a pyrrhic victory. We read that, in appreciation of his prophecy, Diarmaid offered to Ciarán all of the plain around Clonmacnoise. That place had been until then occupied by one Flann Fionn, an enemy of the king. Diarmaid attacked the house of Flann and set fire to it. Flann was wounded and jumped into a bath-tub to escape the heat, but notwithstanding this he perished in his own house. Ciarán grew angry at the manner in which the land was acquired for him, and he declared that Diarmaid himself would suffer a similar triple death by wounding, drowning, and burning.

Diarmaid, as was customary, began his reign by celebrating the feast of Tara. The nobles of Ireland demanded that the arrangements regarding precedence at this feast should strictly accord with ancient ordinances, and Diarmaid brought the various wise men of Ireland to detail what these ordinances had been. None could do this satisfactorily, however, until the ante-diluvian seer **Fionntan** came on the scene and gave a full description of the ancient history and lore of Ireland. This account, by selecting Diarmaid's installation as the occasion for Fionntan's mythical announcements, shows how important his reign was regarded by the mediaeval writers. One reason for this was the fact that Diarmaid stood chronologically between two worlds, the ancient pagan one and the new Christian one. Diarmaid himself may have still been a pagan. He was at least a half-pagan, for he is represented as having **druids** in the forefront of his retinue and as mixing their counsels with those of Christian **saints**. There is much ambiguity. We read that when his son Breasal stole a cow from a nun, she complained to Diarmaid and he brought Breasal to a river and drowned him there. Then he regretted having done this, and went to **Colm Cille** to implore the assistance of that saint. Colm brought him to the ascetic Beagán who, when he saw Diarmaid, spoke crossly to him. 'Into the ground with you, o kin-slayer!' he said, and the high-king sank to his knees in the earth. Nevertheless, Colm prevailed upon Beagán to help, and the ascetic raised his hand and began to pray. He brought fifty men called Breasal from hell, and eventually brought the desired Breasal and restored him to life.

In the 7th-century biography of Colm Cille, Diarmaid is referred to as 'ruler of all Ireland', ordained by God's will, yet his relations with Colm himself were - if tradition is to be credited - far from good. Mediaeval writers state that the saint gave his protection to Curnán, a Connacht prince who had killed a man in a hurling-match at Tara, and that - notwithstanding this - Curnán was put to death by the high-king. A further development in the saga of their relations was the legend of how Colm secretly copied a book and how Diarmaid adjudged that the copy must be surrendered to the owner of the original. These disagreements were cited as the incidents which brought about the battle of Cúil Dreimhne (Cooldrevny, between Drumcliff and Sligo) in the year 561, a battle which Diarmaid and his southern Uí Néill forces lost to a combined army of Connachtmen and northern Uí Néill. The actual role of the saint in this battle was probably no more than as a supporter of his northern kindred, and the theme of bitter personal hostility between himself and Diarmaid seems to have originated from no more than an attempt to synchronise their respective careers.

Individuals gifted with prophecy, whether saints or druids, were given significant roles in the lore of Diarmaid. This emphasises the ritual nature of the kingship which he embodies, but its special focus is the question of his death. One account gives the leading part to the celebrated prophet **Beag mac Dé**, who was among the high-king's retinue. Beag, we are told, had suggested that Diarmaid's fosterchild Aodh Dubh, a prince of the Dál nAraidhe sept of east Ulster, would cause his death. Aodh would give him a poisoned drink while Diarmaid would be wearing a shirt woven from a single seed of flax and a cloak of wool from a single sheep, moreover his ale would be brewed from a single grain, his bacon would be a pig that was never farrowed, and the ridge-pole of the house would fall on his head. Hearing this, Diarmaid was alarmed and had Aodh Dubh banished from Ireland. To test Beag's prophecy, he consulted his druids on the matter, and to his dismay found that their prognostications were similar. There was obviously much duplication in the tradition of prophecies concerning Diarmaid's death - these being variously attributed to Ciarán, Beag, and the druids.

To further complicate the matter another saint, **Ruadhán** of Lorrha, was portrayed as a portender of doom for the king. We read that Diarmaid's reign was generally a good one, and that he was wise and kindly. However, one of his administrators, called Aodh Baclámh, was an evil fellow who swaggered about the countryside collecting the taxes. His custom was to carry the high-king's spear crosswise in his arms and to demand that the entrance to each nobleman's fortress be made wide enough to allow him to thus pass through it. A Connacht noble, Aodh Guaire by name, was enraged at his fortress being knocked down to suit this whim, so he slew Aodh Baclámh and then fled to Ruadhán for sanctuary. For fear of Diarmaid, Ruadhán sent him to Britain, but soon he had to leave there also through Diarmaid's threats.

Aodh Guaire returned to Ruadhán, and the saint hid him in an underground chamber called Poll Ruadháin in one of his monasteries (Pollrone, in south Kilkenny). Diarmaid went there, demanding to know where the fugitive was and, unwilling to tell a lie, the saint said that he did not know 'unless he be under where you are standing!' The high-king departed in frustration but, knowing that Ruadhán would not lie, he soon realised where Aodh Guaire was. He therefore returned and seized the fugitive in violation of the saint's sanctuary. Aodh Guaire was brought to Tara to be put to death, but Ruadhán followed on, accompanied by St **Bréanainn**, demanding that the prisoner be released. Diarmaid refused, insisting that as king he had the necessary legal authority, and the saints chanted curses and rang their bells against him. Then they fasted against him, and one night he dreamed that a great tree was cut down by foreigners. Realising that the foreigners signified clerics, he called Ruadhán and began to upbraid him. They exchanged maledictions, Diarmaid insisting that Ruadhán's monasteries would be deserted and that his body would be blemished. Ruadhán laid his curse on Tara, and then pointed out the ridge-pole which would fall on the high-king. Finally Diarmaid agreed to release Aodh Guaire, and they were reconciled.

The multiple prophecies must, however, be fulfilled; and so it happened that, When the high-king was on his royal circuit, he was approached by a strange warrior who invited him to visit the fortress called Ráth Bheag (near Donegore in Co Antrim). The warrior had a beautiful daughter, and he invited Diarmaid to sleep with her. She gave him a shirt and cloak, and her father gave him bacon and ale - all of the unusual types which had been foretold. Then he noticed that the house had new rafters, and was told by his host that they were made from a ridge-pole which had been found floating on the sea. Realising that his doom was at hand, Diarmaid tried to rush from the house, but his former foster-child Aodh Dubh was at the door and ran him through with a spear. The house was set on fire, and he climbed into a vat of ale to avoid the flames. The beam of the house fell on his head, and he thus died a triple death from wounding, fire, and drowning.

That Diarmaid was slain by Aodh Dubh is a historical fact. **Adhamhnán**, in his biography of Colm Cille written in the 7th century, describes how this Aodh Dubh later sought to be ordained a priest in Scotland but was cursed by Colm for killing Diarmaid. The curse was that he would be 'pierced with a spear' on the prow of a ship and would fall into the water and 'die by drowning' - which indeed was the way in which he died. There is little reason to doubt the statement that Colm rejected Aodh Dubh, but the claim that his death was caused by the saint's curse seems to be a narrative accretion. Aodh probably did perish in a sea-fight, but the description of the death as being multiple must have been borrowed from folklore (see **Romantic Tales**, Type 934A). It is evident that the legend of Diarmaid's death was based on this story of Colm Cille. There was a notable similarity between Aodh's murder of Diarmaid and Diarmaid's own murder of his enemy Flann Fionn. So, by making Ciarán's curse on Diarmaid result from that incident, the text reveals that the curse on Aodh Dubh was being developed and extended into the description of the death of Diarmaid himself.

A similar story was told in the mediaeval literature concerning the death of Muircheartach mac Earca (q.v.). Although Muircheartach preceded Diarmaid in the high-kingship by some years, there can be little doubt but that the motif of the triple death was initially connected with Diarmaid. The kernel of his saga seems to be the opposition between druidic and Christian advices - in other words the struggle of the two religions for influence over him. His actual violent death would have been a suitable event to which a striking moral could be attached. The claim that a saint had warned him of it beforehand would illustrate the ultimate powerlessness of an earthly king and also demonstrate the divine accuracy of Christian prophecy. That there were remnants in existence of sacrificial imagery in connection with the deaths of kings is evidenced by the myth of **Conaire**, and three-fold enigmatic circumstances would highlight such drama. The basic idea that Diarmaid was unable to compete with the Christian religion and with its saints is echoed also by an episode in his saga which has St Ruadhán outsmart him regarding **horses**. We read that, after he had released Aodh Guaire, Ruadhán sent thirty dark-grey sea-horses to him as a gift. Not realising the unusual origin of these fine steeds, Diarmaid put them racing, but they would accept neither bridle or whip and returned to the sea.

A O Anderson / M O Anderson (1961), 71-5, 84-9, 278-83; R A S Macalister (1956), 384-7; S H O'Grady (1892) *1*, 66-84; Kuno Meyer in *Zeitschrift für celtische Philologie* 7, 305-7; R I Best / H J Lawlor (1931), 102-7; Paul Walsh in *Irisleabhar Muighe Nuadhat* 1926, 3-11.

[Theme of three-fold death] Kenneth Jackson in Eoin Ua Riain ed (1940), 535-550.

[General] Cormac Ó Cadhlaigh (1950); Proinsias Mac Cana (1970), 29-31; F J Byrne (1973), 87-105. See also **Maolodhrán**.

DIARMAID UA DUIBHNE Handsome young hero in **Fianna** romance. The name Diarmaid was derived from 'dí-fhormaid', meaning 'unenvious', and was common in early Ireland. The second part of his name signifies 'descendant of Duibhne', which connects him with the Corca Dhuibhne sept of west Kerry.

In the mediaeval literature, he is also referred to as Diarmaid Donn, Diarmaid mac Duinn uí Dhuibhne, and Diarmaid mac Duinn meic Donnchadha. All of these appellations connect him with the Kerry area - containing echoes not only of Corca Dhuibhne but also of the deity **Donn**, and the branch of the western Eoghanacht known as the Uí Dhonnchadha. The indications are, therefore, that the original appearance of the character in lore of **Fionn mac Cumhaill** was connected with that part of the country. Some stories of Fionn (q.v.) from the 8th century onwards have him opposed to the western Eoghanacht and abducting women from them, and it would have been natural to have a character with such appellations portrayed as an opponent of his in these matters. Simultaneously, in the midlands, Fionn was being portrayed as an opponent of the high-king **Cormac mac Airt**, as part of the conflicting claims of the Connachta sept and the Leinstermen on the Boyne valley and the cult-centre of **Tara**. Sovereignty was envisaged alternately as a beautiful lady and as a miserable hag, thus the contest between Cormac and Fionn (q.v.) could be viewed as a struggle concerning a beautiful lady called Gráinne, a name which in fact meant 'ugly one'.

There are several references which show that an account of how Diarmaid eloped with Fionn's woman Gráinne was part of the repertoire of storytellers from the 9th century onwards. This indicates that a fusion had taken place between Fionn's hostility towards Cormac and his hostility towards the western Eoghanacht. The narrative structure which was used to rationalise this fusion was a quite popular one in early mediaeval Irish storytelling i.e. the three-cornered plot of old man, young man, and young woman such as is found in the case of **Deirdre**. Although it was well-known, we have no full version of this romance of Diarmaid and Gráinne from mediaeval times, the earliest surviving recension dating from the 15th century. This recension contains some late accretions, but no doubt it preserves faithfully the original structure. It can be summarised as follows:-

After the death of his wife Maighnis, Fionn was a widower for a year and, having been told that Cormac had a beautiful daughter called Gráinne, he sent a message to the high-king concerning her. Gráinne consented to marry Fionn and a great betrothal feast was held at Tara. At the feast, however, Gráinne saw the young warrior Diarmaid among Fionn's company and fell in love with him. She gave a sleeping-draught to all those present at the feast except Diarmaid, and then tried to persuade him to carry her away. He was reluctant to do so, out of loyalty to Fionn, but she threatened him with magical destruction (see **'geis'**) if he refused. They departed from Tara and went west, crossing the river Shannon and encamped in a wood called Doire Dá Bhaoth. Next day Fionn set out in pursuit, and his trackers found their trail. **Oisín** sent Fionn's great hound Bran to warn the fugitives and also got a man with a massive voice to shout a warning, but Diarmaid ignored both messages, and instead gave three kisses to Gráinne in the full sight of the enraged Fionn. The spiritual **Aonghus**, who had been the fosterer of Diarmaid, came to support the elopers, and he took Gráinne away from that place under a cloak of concealment, while the athletic Diarmaid vaulted over Fionn's men and escaped.

The fugitives next went to the south-west. Diarmaid caught a fish in the river Laune and they spent the night there. A young warrior called Muadhán came to them and became their servant. Going further west over the Caragh and Beigh rivers, they met with three mercenaries from the Channel Islands who had come to Ireland at Fionn's request with a thousand men and three poisonous hounds to hunt Diarmaid. Not recognising Diarmaid, they took up his challenge to athletic contests of riding a barrel downhill, jumping onto a pointed spear, and walking on a sword-edge, and in this way lost many of their men. Finally they realised who Diarmaid was and set their hounds on him, but Diarmaid, with the help of Muadhán, slew both hounds and themselves. Soon after, Muadhán left them, and Diarmaid and Gráinne travelled northwards again. As they crossed a stream, a spurt of water struck Gráinne's leg and she remarked that it was bolder than Diarmaid. It was then that they became lovers, for hitherto Diarmaid had left a fishbone between them as they slept as a proof to the pursuing Fionn that they had not been unfaithful to him.

Coming to a forest, they got permission from an ogre called the Searbhán to settle there, providing they did not interfere with the fruit on his tree. However, Gráinne became pregnant and craved for some of these berries, and Diarmaid had to slay the ogre in a horrific combat. Fionn with his trackers reached that place and surrounded the tree, in the branches of which the lovers had taken refuge. Again Aonghus came to their assistance, and they escaped in similar manner as before. Aonghus then went to Fionn and to the high-king Cormac and agreed terms with them regarding Diarmaid. The fugitive couple were allowed to return to his native territory of west Kerry, and he and Gráinne got further land from Fionn and Cormac in Leinster and Connacht. They lived happily for a long time and had several children. However, Fionn still secretly planned revenge against Diarmaid.

While residing in north Connacht, the couple were awakened one night by hounds baying and the sounds of a boar-hunt. Fionn had organised this hunt, because it had been prophesied of Diarmaid, when he was a child, that he would meet his death through hunting the great boar of Beann Ghulban (Benbulben, Co Sligo). Suspecting treachery, Gráinne tried to restrain her husband from going to face the boar, but next day when Diarmaid heard that the Fianna warriors were being slaughtered by the boar he went to face it. When the fierce beast charged him, Diarmaid leapt onto its back, and after a tremendous struggle was thrown off and his stomach ripped open. Then with the stump of his sword he stabbed the boar through the navel, killing it. Diarmaid was in the pangs of death, and Fionn refused twice to bring him a drink of water, even though water from Fionn's palms contained a cure. On the third occasion, Oisín threatened his father that he would kill him if he did not comply with Diarmaid's request. Fionn therefore brought the drink, but before he reached him Diarmaid was dead. Aonghus then came and brought the body of Diarmaid to his otherworld dwelling on the river Boyne.

There are several points of similarity between the portrayal of Diarmaid and that of Adonis in Classical myth. As with Adonis, the literature often refers to the beauty of Diarmaid's person and to the lustre of his countenance, and his death fighting a fierce boar is a direct parallel. This can best be explained by postulating that the early mediaeval composer of the Diarmaid and Gráinne story had read the account of Adonis given in Ovid's *Metamorphoses*. This would also explain why Diarmaid is associated with Benbulben, a place so far away from his native territory, for Ovid describes how the boar which killed Adonis had a savage and crooked snout. An Irish word for such a snout would be 'gulba', and thus it is likely that Diarmaid's boar had some such designation, which suggested Beann Ghulban as the locale of the fight. Regarding the involvement of Aonghus in the story, it seems that this was occasioned by the special concern of Aonghus (q.v.) for young lovers, and that it was patterned on the assistance rendered to the beleaguered **Cú Chulainn** by Lugh.

This story of Diarmaid and Gráinne has been current in the folklore of both Ireland and Scotland for several centuries, and the main events of it are situated in various localities by the oral tradition. Indeed, the dolmens (ancient burial portals) which consist of a flat stone raised on top of two others and which are so common in the Irish landscape, have long been known as 'beds of Diarmaid and Gráinne'. The folk fancy is that the lovers slept on top of these during their flight from Fionn, and it is believed that if a childless woman sleeps on one of them she - like Gráinne - will conceive. These folk versions have contained two special motifs since the end of the Middle Ages. One concerns the manner of Diarmaid's death. Instead of dying in combat with the boar, he is said to have slain it without sustaining any mortal injury to himself. The wily Fionn, however, realised that the boar had one poisonous bristle and therefore asked Diarmaid to measure the beast from snout to tail. To do so, Diarmaid stood on its back, but he slipped and the bristle pierced him, with fatal results. The other motif in oral versions is Diarmaid's celebrated love-spot. This was situated on his forehead or neck, and any woman who saw it would fall helplessly in love with him. Marks on the body, made from various concoctions, were part of love-magic in ancient and mediaeval tradition, and it must have come into

35. DIARMAID UA DUIBHNE *A dolmen in Co. Clare, of the type popularly known as 'Bed of Diarmaid and Gráinne'.*

this narrative from such a source. Diarmaid's love-spot ('ball seirce') became his great distinguishing mark in folklore, and he was known as 'Diarmaid of the women'.

In post-mediaeval oral versions of a visit made by Fionn (q.v.) to an allegorical house, Diarmaid is said to have got his love-spot as a gift from an otherworld lady representing youth there. It seems clear that the character of Diarmaid owes its origins to the story of his elopement with Gráinne, but in the subsequent literature he figured prominently in many stories. For accounts of other adventures involving him, see **Fianna Cycle**.

Proinsias Mac Cana (1980), 46, 57, 86; Nessa Ní Shéaghdha (1967); Neil Ross (1939), 70-6; Dáithí Ó hÓgáin (1988), 166-77, 336-7, 358-9 and in Bo Almqvist / Séamas Ó Catháin / Pádraig Ó Héalaí eds (1987), 216-8, 227-31; Alan Bruford (1969), 106-9, 283.

DOMHNALL MAC AODHA High-king of Ireland who reigned from 628 to 642 AD. He was son of another high-king, Aodh mac Ainmhireach (for whom see **Colm Cille** and **Brandubh**). In his biography of Colm Cille, **Adhamhnán** describes how that saint blessed the boy Domhnall, and foretold that he would outlive all his brothers, be a famous king, and die peacefully in his bed - all of which proved to be true.

Domhnall was a shrewd and able king. Initially he had as ally the Ulster king Conghal Caoch, but when the two quarrelled and clashed Conghal had to flee to Scotland. He enlisted the support there of Domhnall Breac, king of the Dál Riada sept who controlled western Scotland and some territory in Antrim. The result of this was a great battle fought at Magh Rátha (Moira, Co Down) in the year 637. In this battle, the high-king gained a complete victory over the forces of Domhnall Breac and Conghal Caoch. A text which dramatised these events was composed early in the 10th century, being based on surviving tradition at that time. According to it, Conghal Caoch was the fosterson of the high-king Domhnall and his epithet 'caoch' (i.e. one-eyed) was due to his having been stung in the eye by a bee in Domhnall's orchard. The Ulstermen demanded the eye of Domhnall's son as compensation, but the high-king decreed only that the swarm be destroyed so that the guilty bee should perish.

The text goes on to describe how, when Domhnall held the feast of **Tara**, Conghal sat on his left-hand side. A dozen eggs were brought to the high-king, and Conghal ate one of them secretly. When Domhnall began to divide the eggs he noticed that one was missing and accused Conghal of stealing it. Conghal refused to remain at the feast, despite Domhnall's attempt to resolve the quarrel by offering him a golden egg. He went to Scotland to the Dál Riada king and, returning with a strong force, began to ravage the territory of the high-king's mother. The saints of Ireland attempted to effect a reconciliation between himself and the high-king, but Conghal was determined to become ruler of Ireland. The armies met at Magh Rátha. Domhnall the high-king entrusted command of his forces to a warrior called Dúnchadh, while he himself played chess in his tent with his dwarf acting as a look-out. The battle lasted for three days. Dúnchadh killed Conghal's horse, but gave him his own in place of it. Similarly he destroyed Conghal's shield and sword, but replaced them with his own. Hearing that the high-king was at his tent praying, Conghal thought of going to make terms with him, but in the continuing fighting he slew the royal jester **Conall Clogach**. Then the high-king himself went into the fighting, calling on the name of God, and his forces overwhelmed the foe. Conghal was slain, as well as the Dál Riada king, but one strong man of the Scots escaped by swimming. The loyal Dúnchadh was also slain, and the high-king lamented him in verse. Domhnall also honoured the head of his slain opponent Conghal, reciting a poem of praise for him.

A more intricate narrative is given in a text from the 11th century entitled *Fled Dún na nGéd* (the Feast of Dún na nGé, a fortress near Dowth in Co Meath). According to this, the high-king Domhnall dreamed that his pet whelp went raging from him and gathered the Irish and Scottish packs, as well as those of the Saxons and Britons, against him. These hounds were only defeated by Domhnall and his men after seven battles. Alarmed by the dream, Domhnall leaped naked from his bed, but he was restrained by his wife who assured him that his forces were so strong that he had nothing to fear. Domhnall went to his hermit-brother Maol Cobha to have the dream interpreted, and Maol explained that the whelp was his fosterling, and that the fosterling would rebel and get the support of foreigners and only be defeated after seven battles. Domhnall had two princes in fosterage, Conghal Caoch and **Raghallach** of Connacht, and Maol recommended that these two be dismissed, but the high-king refused to do so out of honour and affection for them.

Domhnall prepared for the feast of Tara, sending out his stewards to collect as many goose-eggs as possible. These stewards forcibly took eggs from the maidservant of a saint who used to stand all day to his armpits in the river Boyne and then eat an egg each evening together with some cress from the river. When the saint discovered what they had done, he laid a curse on the feast which the high-king was preparing. Just before the feast was held, a hideously ugly couple arrived, bringing a tubfull of goose-eggs. Domhnall welcomed them and gave them food, but they could not be satisfied and departed saying that they were from hell and that they had come to be first at the feast and thus ensure that trouble would ensue.

When the kings of all the provinces had assembled Domhnall welcomed them but, before they sat to eat, Conghal took a bite from one of the eggs. Domhnall was told of the saint's curse, and he then realised that Conghal, who had been the first to partake of the eggs, would be the one to oppose him. The twelve leading saints of Ireland were brought to bless the feast and have the curse removed from it, and they did so, but the effect on Conghal could not be undone. At the feast, Conghal was not put sitting in his customary place beside the high-king, and furthermore he was served the egg of a hen rather than of a duck. Urged on by his outraged Ulstermen, Conghal was seized with rage and began to recite his grievances against Domhnall. Among the things he mentioned was the fact that he had gained the high-kingship for Domhnall by slaying his predecessor

Suibhne Meann. He had run Suibhne through with his spear as that high-king was playing chess, and the dying Suibhne had flung a chessman at him and completely destroyed his eye, which had earlier been stung by the bee. Then Conghal stormed out of the feast, despite all Domhnall's efforts to pacify him.

He gathered his forces in Ulster, and then crossed to Scotland to seek support from the king of that country, Eochaidh. The latter had promised never to oppose Domhnall mac Aodha, but he allowed his four sons to go with Conghal. Eochaidh's chief-druid Dubh Diadh, and the other **druids**, cautioned against the undertaking, but Conghal pushed ahead and went to seek the support of the king of the Britons. While he was at that court, a strange warrior arrived who demanded the marrow-bone given to the greatest warrior at a feast. He won this through combat, and then proved that he was Conán Rod, the long-lost son of the British king and queen. He wore a ring on his finger given him by his mother when he had left twenty years before to learn feats of arms, he had a grain of gold under his shoulder which the queen had long ago inserted there, and he gave conclusive proof by removing a stone which no liar could move and by riding two horses which no liar could ride. He also joined the force of Conghal.

Fortified by warriors of the Scots, Britons, and Saxons, Conghal crossed to Ireland, but in the massive slaughter at Magh Rátha he was defeated and slain. Conán Rod was slain by Ceallach, son of Maol Cobha, and of all the foreigners only one man escaped alive. This was the druid Dubh Diadh, who by magic flew through the air and reached Scotland with a dead warrior attached to each leg, for Conghal had tied his men together for the battle. The text relates also that it was in that battle that the Dál n-Araidhe king **Suibhne** went mad, and several echoes from the Suibhne story are found in the text. Other sources known to the writer obviously included an account of the sojourn of **Lughaidh mac Con** in Scotland and his triumph in the battle of Magh Mucramha; the story of the birth of the Leinster king **Brandubh** (motif of gold-grain in shoulder); and the tradition of the Connacht king **Guaire**, who also had a hermit-brother who was a prophet. Domhnall's brother Maol Cobha was not in actual fact a hermit, but had been high-king until defeated and slain by **Suibhne Meann**. His survival as a hermit in this instance is therefore an anachronism.

A O Anderson / M O Anderson (1961), 47-50, 230-1, 316-7, 474-7; Karl Marstrander in *Ériu 5*, 226-47; John O'Donovan (1842); Ruth Lehmann (1964); R A S Macalister (1956), 376-7.

DONN Mythical figure in Irish literature and folklore. The name simply represents the adjective 'donn', meaning 'brown'. This was sometimes written 'dond', which is incorrect, for the word in fact derives from a Celtic 'dhuosnos'.

In ancient times the adjective could also signify 'dark', and the character Donn is perennially associated with the shadowy realm of the dead. He is, however, also represented as an ancestor of those who die, and his name therefore seems to have been originally an epithet of the deity known as the **Daghdha**. Donn is referred to in several early texts. Particularly striking is a reference in the death-tale of **Conaire**, who is slain by three red-haired men, 'sons of Donn, king of the dead at the red tower of the dead'. These three are further quoted as saying, 'we ride the horses of Donn - although we are alive, we are dead!'

In treating of this shady personification of death, the writers of pseudo-history rationalised him into one of the leaders of the fanciful ancient migration to Ireland of the Gaelic people. These writers described how one Donn, son of **Míl**, was drowned at Inbhear Scéine (Kenmare Bay in Co Kerry). In this, they were echoing an earlier belief that in that area the deity inhabited the island known as Teach Duinn (literally 'Donn's House', and now called Bull Rock). One 9th-century source attributes a very significant line to this personage: 'To me, to my house, you shall all come after your deaths'. Other sources, from the 8th to the 10th centuries, refer to Teach Duinn as the place 'where the dead assemble', and describe deceased people as travelling to and from it. Repeated references in the literature show that Teach Duinn was regarded as the western extremity of Ireland, and it is tempting to connect the locating of Donn there with some accounts given by the 2nd-century Greek writer Plutarch. Referring to a deity who lives in a sleepy state on an island off the land to the west of Britain, Plutarch calls him by the name of a Greek god of the dead, Cronus; and again the same writer describes how fishermen in that land were wont to hear strange boats travelling at night to a distant destination where the names of those who disembarked were called out.

The word 'donn' could be viewed as the opposite of 'find', which meant 'illumination' or 'brightness', and that the Celtic otherworld included a dialectic between these two colours is clear from the early lore of the personage **Find**. Such a dialectic was, indeed, the background to the conflict in the **Ulster Cycle** between the two great bulls called the Finnbheannach and the **Donn Cuailnge**. Its genesis must be quite old, but originally the figure represented by Donn was not in any way dependent on Find (q.v.) and Donn survived in tradition as a great personage in his own right. Mediaeval literature tends to associate his name with each and every otherworld place, but since the name had come to be used in a generalised sense to mean 'otherworld lord' it is clear that most of these allusions are not to him specifically. Folk tradition testifies that two locations, in addition to Bull Rock, preserved definite vestiges of his cult. These were Cnoc Fírinne (Knockfierna, a very conspicuous hill in the middle of Co Limerick) and the 'Dumhcha' or great sand-dunes at Dunbeg on the west coast of Co Clare.

At Knockfierna he was known as Donn Fírinne, and the entrance to his palace was believed to be through a cavity near the summit of the hill. Folklore told of people being brought into the hill to be with Donn when they died, and this was not seen to conflict with Christian belief since it was rationalised by the opinion that such people were not really dead but had been kidnapped by him. He was said to often leave his residence at night, riding a white horse, and such folk accounts of him have been influenced by legends of other spiritual beings. For instance, he once took a man with him on a terrifying ride throughout Ireland (see **Ghosts**), and he was said to take away accomplished hurlers to join his team in hurling-matches against rival otherworld communities (see **Fairies**). Like the fairies also, he resented people interfering with his hill by ploughing on its slopes but, being quite genial, he preferred to appear and warn people to stop rather than to take immediate action against them.

One type of narrative illustrates how a cluster of motifs got attached to him. We are told that he visited a blacksmith one night and asked for his horse to be shod. He wrenched off one of the horse's legs and gave it to the blacksmith to have the shoe put on it. The terrified smith complied, and then Donn replaced the leg on the horse perfectly, saying that he was to lead his cavalry that night in a battle against a rival host. The unorthodox method of shoeing the horse is borrowed from a far-flung folklore plot (see **Religious Tales**, Type 753), but the general situation described is of special interest. That situation corresponds to a legend found in a mediaeval Norse text concerning the Norse god Odin, who similarly appeared to a blacksmith to have his steed Sleipnir shod before a great battle far away. It seems likely, therefore, that this account of Donn is indebted to a residue of lore from the Norse settlements of mediaeval Limerick.

Other items of lore concerning Donn can also be related to Odin. Like the Norse deity, he sometimes rode his horse through the sky, and he was regarded as a great personification of the weather. Thunder and lightning meant that he was travelling wildly in the sky, and if clouds were over the hill of Knockfierna that was taken to mean that he was gathering them together and would soon release them in the form of rain. The portrayal of Donn as a phantom rider led to a connection being drawn between him and another ghostly figure of Limerick lore, the Earl of Desmond (see Gearóid Iarla **FitzGerald**), and as a result of this the image of a wizard was borrowed from that Earl to Donn. Thus one folk narrative has a man being brought into a fine palace in Knockfierna and finding there Donn as an old man clothed in white and instructing a large number of young students in 'the mysteries of the creation since the stars began to shine'.

In Co Clare he was known as 'Donn na Duimhche' ('Donn of the Dune') and was also often encountered as a night-horseman, and one legend developes the motif of his fairy army. We are told that a hostile fairy host was driving away all the cattle from a local farmer when Donn and his army intercepted them and, in a bitter otherworld battle, rescued the herd. This Clare tradition of Donn stretches back for a considerable time. It was well-known to the poet Aindrias Mac Cruitín who, around the year 1740, alluded to Donn na Duimhche in one of his works. Complaining of his miserable circumstances and of the niggardly treatment he had received from the gentry of the area, the poet begged Donn to open his door to him and receive him into his palace 'under the waves'. The maritime aspect of this lore of Donn in west Clare is a close parallel of the tradition of Bull Rock ('Teach Duinn'). The mediaeval pseudo-historians described several people as being drowned at the sand-dunes ('dumhcha') at Teach Duinn, and the literature also referred to this great personage of the south-west Kerry coast as Donn

Dumhach or Donn Dumhaighe (i.e. 'of the dunes'). The shore off Doonbeg in Co Clare was very dangerous for boats, and it was therefore easy to make the mistake of identifying the Kerry dunes with the larger ones on the Clare coast. The identification was probably first made by some scholar in post-mediaeval times, and as a result the lore of Donn became associated with the latter area.

In his poem, Aindrias Mac Cruitín made an offer to Donn to 'groom the steeds of your phantom cavalry'. It is apparent from this that the poet knew of the fairy-horseman image, this having been borrowed into the Clare lore from that of Donn Fírinne at some time previous to the 18th century. The origin of this earlier Donn Fírinne of Limerick is more complicated. His epithet is a corruption of Frigrinn, which was an ancient name for the locality, the hill being originally called Cnoc Frigrinne. The likelihood is that this tradition grew out of some rhetoric or text which situated Donn at various hill-cairns regarded as otherworld dwellings. As a result of the corruption to 'Fírinne' (literally, 'truth'), and of Donn's associations with the elements, the people of Co Limerick claimed that the hill was so called because its aspect enabled 'truthful predictions to be made about the weather'. The connection with Odin and the variety of the fairy legends attached to Donn Fírinne would suggest that his lore was well established in Limerick by the late Middle Ages.

Julius Pokorny (1959) 1, 271; Käte Müller-Lisowski in *Béaloideas 18*, 142-99; T F O'Rahilly (1946), 481-4 and in *Hermathena 23*, 203-4 and in *The Irish Monthly 53*, 257-63; Liam Ó Luaighnigh (1935), 7-9; Ristéard Ó Foghludha (1952), 211-3; Dáithí Ó hÓgáin (1985), 152-4, 234-6, 337.

[Plutarch references] *Moralia*: 419, 941; A C L Brown (1943), 339-41.

[Odin material] Gudhni Jónsson (1957), 390-2; C-M Edsman (1949), 117-9.

DONN CUAILNGE Mythical bull, the chief object of the great cattle-raid (*Táin Bó Cuailnge*) in the **Ulster Cycle**.

When the compilers of the *Táin* narrative in the 6th or 7th century decided to feature cattle-raiding in the account of an epical war, they naturally sought material with bovine imagery which could be dramatised. The god of the dead was called **Donn**, and since death was a major theme in the context the compilers were inclined to give a leading role to a great bull called Donn. Cuailnge (Cooley in Co Louth) was an obvious area on which an Ulster versus Tara war would focus, and thus the bull was said to belong to that area. The mythical background to this Donn Cuailnge is clear from the fact that he is contrasted with another great bull called the Finnbheannach (earlier, Findbennach). The name of this latter bull is interpreted as 'the white horned one', but the first element in it suggests that it is an emanation from the ancient divine personage **Find**.

There are several indications that metamorphosis was an attribute of deities in ancient Irish tradition, and a 9th-century text underlines the mythic significance of these two bulls in accordance with this. They are described as the final manifestations of two opposing beings after a whole series of transformations. Originally, we are told, they belonged to the otherworld community, being two pig-keepers there called Friuch and Rucht. These two quarrelled and cast spells over each other's pigs, with the result that they were dismissed by their employers. Then they turned themselves into birds of prey and continued their contest, and later took on respectively the forms of fish, stags, warriors, phantoms, and dragons, fighting each other all the while. Eventually they became maggots. One of them went into a spring in Cooley and was consumed by a cow belonging to Dáire mac Fiachna. The other was consumed from a Connacht spring by a cow of queen **Meadhbh** and her husband. These two cows bore bull-calves, the former the Donn Cuailnge and the latter the Finnbheannach. The plot of this story is borrowed from folklore (see **Wonder Tales**, Type 325), but the basic idea can be accepted as reflecting divine transformations of Donn and Find which have been carried over into the new context of the *Táin* epic. The name of the Donn Cuailnge is taken to reflect a brown colour ('donn'), but the bull is also called the Dubh Cuailnge ('black of Cooley'). This colour variety in fact reflects the imagery of the deity Donn, who was also sometimes called Dubh. The designation of the bull's owner further reflects ancient lore of the deity, for the name **Dáire** was often used in association with Donn.

The same text on the pig-keepers' transformations describes the Donn Cuailnge as being fierce, strong, and so huge that thirty boys could ride on its back. In the *Táin*, we are told that it could bull fifty heifers in a single day, that the heifers which did not calve on the following day would burst, and that no demons would dare come into the canton where the great animal was. Its role is further dramatised in related texts. For instance, the **Mór-Ríoghain** once took a cow from Connacht to be bulled by the Donn Cuailnge, and the calf which resulted grew into a fine young bull which was slain in combat by the Finnbheannach. On seeing this, queen Meadhbh swore that she would not rest until she saw that calf's sire being confronted by the Finnbheannach. The great cattle-raid began when Meadhbh was refused a loan of the Donn Cuailgne by its owner. Later, when Meadhbh's army was in a position to capture the bull, the Mór-Ríoghain appeared to it in the form of a bird and warned it to go with its heifers to a safe place. Eventually Meadhbh succeeded in taking the bull, and she retained it on her retreat to Connacht after defeat at the hands of **Cú Chulainn** and the Ulstermen. On reaching Meadhbh's court at Cruachain, the final inevitable clash occurred when the Donn Cuailnge and the Finnbheannach encountered each other. The most dramatic account states that they fought all day and all night, travelling throughout Ireland and terrifying everybody who heard their rending and bellowing in the darkness. When morning came, the Donn Cuailnge was seen passing by Meadhbh's court at Cruachain with the carcase of its rival on its horns. It then headed towards home, dropping parts of the dead bull at various places and thus giving rise to several placenames. Reaching Cooley, it slaughtered many people in its rage, then put its back against a mound, and the heart burst in its breast.

Ulrike Roider (1979); Ernst Windisch in *Irische Texte 2(2)*, 239-56; Kuno Meyer in *Revue Celtique 10*, 212-28; Cecile O'Rahilly (1976), 30, 46-8, 124 and (1970), 35-6, 48-9, 133-6 and (1961), 44-5, 58-9, 157-62; M E Dobbs in *Zeitschrift für celtische Philologie 14*, 395-420.

DRUIDS Members of the learned caste or priestly profession in Celtic and early Irish culture. The word 'druid' is probably derived from a Celtic 'dru̯id-', which would have meant 'very knowledgeable'.

The Greek and Latin writers attest to the importance of the druids among the Gauls. They were at the centre of society, making decisions on matters of tradition, custom, and law, and also on general questions concerning nature and human life. Continental and Irish sources alike make it clear that the druids in their teaching placed great emphasis on the five elements - sky, earth, sea, sun, and moon - holding these to preside over human affairs. According to the Classical writers, they also taught the doctrine of transmigration of souls and practiced divination of the future from auguries, and several echoes of such beliefs and practices can be found also in Irish tradition (see **Find** and **Poets**).

We read that the terminology used to describe a practitioner of mystical knowledge among the Gauls was 'druid', 'vātis', and 'bardos', and the same terms were used in early Irish literature in the form of 'druí' (later, 'draoi'), 'fáith' (later, 'fáidh'), and 'bard'. In mediaeval Ireland, these terms were used respectively in the senses of 'magician', 'prophet', and 'versifier'. Whatever the nature of original druidic grades, these specific senses which came to be applied to the terms give a good insight into the general functions of the profession. The druid was believed to have mystical powers, to be a seer, and to utter sacred rhetoric. Irish tradition tends to use the word 'bard' in the context of minor poets, and the more prestigious term for a poet is 'file'. This word derives from a root meaning 'to see', and there are indications that it was used (in an original form 'velet-') in connection with the druids of the Continental Celts also. In Ireland, the 'file' was a leading figure in the social order and his verse was reputed to have magical power. It is in fact clear that vestiges of druidism survived in the imagery of Irish **poets** after the introduction of Christianity made more overt expressions of the older beliefs unfeasible.

Some early Irish sources describe rituals whereby the druids gained knowledge. We read of how, to decide on who should be king, they organised a bull-feast ('tarbhfheis') which consisted of killing a white bull, drinking its soup, and sleeping on its hide. The required information would be revealed through a dream in that situation. Similarly, their custom of lying on their 'wattles of knowledge' is described, and it is evident that the source of such inspiration was believed to be the spirits of dead ancestors (see **Find**). There can be little doubt but that much of the paraphernalia of the supernatural, as found in early Irish literature, emanated from teachings of the druids. These matters would include the idea of the otherworld realm whether on oversea islands or in burial-mounds, at least some aspects of the cult of kingship, and devices such as magical cloaks of concealment and magical fogs and winds.

In his account of the druids of Gaul, Julius Caesar describes the island of Britain as a kind of headquarters of the profession in his time, and he says that Gaulish druids resorted there to improve their education. Certain parallels to this are found in early Irish sources, which use the term Alba for the whole island of Britain. For instance, the druid-poetess Feidhilm, from whom queen **Meadhbh** of Connacht seeks a prophecy, is described as having come from Alba where she had learned 'filidheacht' (seer-craft). There are several mentions of druidesses in Continental sources also. The word used by the Gauls for a centre of druidic ritual was 'nemeton'. This appears in Irish in the form 'neimheadh', which had the meaning 'sacred place' and is in fact given as the name of a fictional druid of old. These places seem to have often been close to trees, hence the Irish term 'fiodhneimheadh', where 'fiodh' means a tree, and there are many indications that the cult of trees was very strong among druids. A somewhat fanciful derivation of the word 'druid' - first cited by Pliny and still held by some scholars - is 'oak-scientist' (Gaulish 'dru-', Irish 'dair', meaning oak). The favourite tree of the druids, however, was clearly the rowan, and it was on wattles of this tree that the Irish practitioners slept in order to have prophetic visions. The hazel-tree was also important, as evidenced by the druid's name Mac Cuill ('son of hazel') and also by the lore concerning nine hazel-trees at the source of the river Boyne, the nuts of which had a nucleus of wisdom (see **Bóinn**). Both Continental and Irish sources also stress the druidic custom of drawing auguries from the flight of birds, especially of the raven.

The narratives concerning druids in Irish literature all come from Christian sources, and in them these pagan priests are portrayed in a generally negative light. Aspects of their original status, however, come through in some texts. A good example is the druid **Cathbhadh** who is portrayed as on a par with the king of Ulster, and in some contexts even has precedence over him. Thus we read that nobody could speak before this druid in the assembly of the Ulstermen, and an incident is related to illustrate this. When trying to rouse the warriors from their debilitation, Sualdamh, father of **Cú Chulainn**, shouts a warning to them concerning the rampant armies of Meadhbh. He does not wait for Cathbhadh to speak first and so, when he mounts a horse, it rears under him and his shield turns against him and severs the head from his shoulders.

Not surprisingly, the druids were portrayed as opponents of the **saints** in mediaeval hagiography. Already in a 7th-century biography of **Patrick** a verse is attributed to two druids who sadly prophesy the end of their own power and the coming of new ways. These two are called Lochru and Lucet Mael, and we read of a great contention at **Tara** between Patrick and the latter. This is druidism through a hostile perspective, and Lucet is patterned on Biblical figures such as the Babylonian wizards of Nebuchadnezzar and Simon Magus, the magician who opposed St Peter. However, certain of his attributes may be authentic, such as his name Lucet which is meant to indicate a devotee of **Lugh**, and his epithet (later, Maol) which means bald and may refer to a druidic tonsure. The skills attributed to Lucet are probably a reflex of lore then current concerning druids - he causes snow to fall and brings a thick fog over the land. Other skills attributed to druids in the mediaeval literature are creation of illusions, interpretation of dreams, curing of illnesses, discovery of thieves, giving of shrewd military advice, and cursing of people and places hostile to them. A principal means of performing all these functions was through chanting spells or uttering rhetorics. This custom lies at the basis of the culture of the Irish poets (q.v.), and there is continuity between the ancient lore of druids and the traditional images of the latter.

Whereas the tradition could survive under the guise of versification, it was handled with varying degrees of tolerance. When the context being described was explicitly belonging to old pre-Christian times, druids and their craft could figure in the literature because of their antiquarian and dramatic value. This is so in cases of druids associated with the **Tuatha Dé Danann** and with pseudo-historical kings such as **Cormac mac Airt** and **Eoghan Mór**. In other contexts, prophecies supposedly made by druids and pagan seers could be used as an argument in favour of Christianity, as is evident from prophecies concerning Patrick and several other saints which were attributed to the celebrated **Fionn mac Cumhaill**. Finally, there are traditions which reflect the historical situation of the Christian mission confronted with druidism. A realistic echo of this is found in the accounts of the 6th-century high-king **Diarmaid mac Cearrbheoil**, who is represented as having both druids and saints as advisers at his court. His leading prophet, in fact, is an interesting example of how the mystical imagery from the two cultures could influence each other. This is **Beag mac Dé** whom the writers converted retrospectively into a saint.

Although the druid survived as a dramatic personage in ordinary narratives of ancient heroes (see **Conall Gulban**), the tendencies in the hagiographical literature were different. There the general picture is of druids as malicious wizards. Nowhere is this clearer than in the case of Mogh Ruith, a druid who in the secular literature performs heroic services for the Munstermen when they are beleaguered by the high-king Cormac mac Airt (q.v.). It is probable that his name was a survival of that of an ancestor figure of the Rothraighe sept in Munster, but it was early subjected to antiquarian speculation. It was therefore taken to mean 'servant of wheel', and Mogh Ruith was said to have possessed a 'roth rámhach' (literally 'oared wheel'). The idea of such a wheel seems to have been suggested by the survival of prehistoric solar symbols inscribed on stone. One such stone, at Cnámhchoill (Cleghile, near Tipperary town) was even said to have been a remnant of the great wheel of Mogh Ruith. Lore of this druid must have developed in the early mediaeval period, for in the ecclesiastical literature of the 11th century he has already been adapted into an apocryphal Christian setting. Here he plays a sinister role, it being claimed that he was trained by the biblical wizard Simon Magus and that he entered the service of King Herod. In that position, he was the man who beheaded John the Baptist. This belief led to panic in 1096 AD, which was the year of a great pestilence, and moreover it was a leap year and the feast of John fell on a Friday. It was therefore feared that the wrath of God would fall on the country because of Mogh Ruith's action, and it was necessary for the bishops to proscribe special prayers and fasting in order to allay popular alarm.

N K Chadwick (1966); Stuart Piggott (1968); P L Henry (1978), 40-8; F le Roux / C-J Guyonvarc'h (1986); Charles Plummer (1910) *1*, clviii-clxiii; Ludwig Bieler (1979), 74-7, 92-7.

[Mogh Ruith] A M Scarre in *Ériu 4*, 173-81; Käte Müller-Lisowski in *Zeitschrift für celtische Philologie 14*, 145-63; Martin McNamara (1975), 64-7; J F Kenney (1929), 749-53; T F O'Rahilly (1946), 519-22.

DUBHTHACH DAOL ULADH Fictional warrior in the **Ulster Cycle**.

Dubhthach (literally, 'the black-haired fellow') was one of the warriors who constituted the exile band of **Fearghus mac Róich** in Connacht. His sobriquets (earlier, Doel Ulad) mean 'chafer of the Ulstermen', and he is described as particularly ruthless, killing several women on his first foray when Fearghus rebelled against king **Conchobhar mac Neasa**. In retaliation all of his family were put to death, and he in turn continually wreaked vengeance for this on the Ulstermen. Sometimes he worked with company, but he was equally effective when raiding alone.

His portrayal is sinister, having rough jet-black hair, a bloody eye, and the head of a ravenous wolf on each shoulder of his armour. For a while he was the possessor of the great spear of **Cealtchair**, and he was accustomed to bathe its point in a vat of dark blood. Dubhthach is obviously a character invented to heighten the drama in the texts. One mediaeval source states that 'as everybody deems it a horror to see the insect called the chafer, so the Ulstermen deemed it a horror to see Dubhthach'. We are told that he also had the nickname Daolteangach ('chafer-tongued') because his speech was poisonous and bitter, as a result of which the tongue had grown black in his head. When his wife was among the women who admired the beauty of **Cú Chulainn** during the cattle-raid of Cooley, Dubhthach was overcome by jealousy and suggested that the young hero be attacked unawares and killed. Hearing this, Fearghus reprimanded him severely for his cruelty in killing women and youths. Despite his hatred for his native province, Dubhthach remained loyal to **Cormac Conn Loingeas** and fought alongside him in Cormac's last stand. He was one of the few survivors on that occasion, but was eventually slain by his frightful spear when it was in the hands of a certain Feidhlimidh.

J C Watson (1941), 32-3, 37, 40-2; Whitley Stokes in *Irische Texte 3*, 398-9; Vernam Hull (1949), 47-8; Cecile O'Rahilly (1976), 7-8, 72-4, 107; Eleanor Knott (1936), 37-8; W M Hennessy (1889), xiv-xvi, 37-9; Cormac Ó Cadhlaigh (1956), 472; Donald MacKinnon in Celtic Review 2, 112-21, 202-5.

DWYER, MICHAEL (1772-1825) Leader in the Rising of 1798 in Wicklow. He held out against the English authorities in the fastnesses of his native county for five years after the rebellion had failed, and eventually secured acceptable terms of surrender. Having been imprisoned in Dublin for two years, he agreed to go to Australia and spent the remainder of his life there.

36. DWYER, MICHAEL *Near-contemporary portrait of Michael Dwyer.*

As a guerrilla leader, Dwyer was daring, resourceful and effective, and he became a great popular hero. Many stories were told of his agility and cleverness in evading capture. He often used disguise, and he could mislead and confuse the soldiers in a variety of ways. Once, it is said, he put a troop to flight by placing hats on haystacks, thereby giving the impression that he was accompanied by a large body of men. When all else failed, he could use his great running and swimming ability to make his getaway. A whole new road, which allowed for the rapid deployment of troops, was constructed by the authorities in a futile attempt to capture him. This, known as the Military Road, runs southwards right across the Wicklow Mountains. No doubt many of the accounts of his breath-taking escapes were current in his own time, spreading among the community as soon as they were effected. Much of the folklore concerning him has an air of desperate humour. For instance, we are told that soldiers once surrounded the house in which he was staying in the Glen of Imaal, and Michael had no choice but to slip into the piggery, where he hid behind a big and rather fierce sow. The soldiers came to look in the sty, and the sow stood on her hind-legs and began to attack them. Michael prodded her into the fray, and the confused soldiers decided that nobody could stay there with such an illtempered animal, and departed.

Michael was an expert climber, and used the mountain-slopes to fatigue his enemies and to speed his own progress. Not only the terrain, but wild nature itself, was in sympathy with the popular hero, as is clear from an account of what befell him when he once spent the night sheltering in a cave on Lugnaquilla Mountain. When he woke up, it was a beautiful sunny morning, and he began to light his pipe and relax. A robin flew in to the cave and began to upset his blanket. He attempted to grab the bird, but it flew away. The bird soon returned with an aggressive air, as if it were going to attack him, and Michael thought this strange. He went to the cave-entrance and, when he looked out, he saw that the hillside was red with soldiers. He drew out his strong sea-whistle and blew a blast on it. When the soldiers heard this they thought that he was giving a signal to a large body of men to attack them, and they fled. Michael himself wasted no time in running down the opposite side of the mountain, thankful to the little bird for its timely warning.

Luke Cullen (1938); Charles Dickson (1944); Pádraig Ó Tuathail in *Béaloideas 5*, 174-8.

E

ÉADAOIN (earlier, Étaín) Mythical lady of the **Tuatha Dé Danann**. One source mentions a poetess of the Tuatha Dé with this name (see **Cairbre mac Éadaoine**), while another introduces her as an otherworld helper of the Munster king **Eoghan Mór** in his travails.

She is featured in a very colourful story written in the 10th century. According to this, after **Aonghus** had got possession of Brugh na Bóinne (the Newgrange tumulus in Co Meath), his foster-father **Midhir** went to visit him there. Midhir attempted to separate two fighting youths, and had one of his eyes knocked out by a holly-prick in the struggle. **Dian Céacht** came and healed him, but he nevertheless demanded compensation of Aonghus. What he sought was the most beautiful maiden in Ireland, Éadaoin Eachraidhe daughter of Ailill, king of Ulster. Aonghus went to Ailill, who demanded that twelve plains be cleared for him and twelve rivers be created. All of this was done by Aonghus's father, the **Daghdha**, and after Aonghus gave Éadaoin's weight in gold and silver he was allowed to bring her home with him. He gave her to Midhir, who tarried for a year thereafter in the Brugh. At the end of the year, Midhir and Éadaoin went to Midhir's own dwelling at Brí Léith (now Slieve Golry near Ardagh in Co Longford). Éadaoin was not long there, however, when Midhir's first wife Fuamnach, with a stroke of a magic wand, turned her into a pool of water. The water turned into a worm, and the worm into a beautiful fly which followed Midhir wherever he went. Midhir knew that it was Éadaoin, and he loved only her. However, Fuamnach caused a magic wind to blow the fly away from Brí Léith and out onto the sea-shore, where the transformed Éadaoin lived for seven years in misery. Then she managed to reach Brugh na Bóinne, where Aonghus protected her and kept her in a beautiful sun-bower. Fuamnach contrived to go to the Brugh when Aonghus was absent, and again she blew the fly away. It alit on a house in Ulster and fell into the drink of the wife of a warrior called Étar. The woman conceived, and in this way Éadaoin was born a second time.

When **Eochaidh Aireamh** became king of Ireland, his subjects refused him tribute until he got a queen. He sought out the most beautiful woman in the country, and found that she was Éadaoin daughter of Étar. He took her to **Tara** and married her. The king's brother Ailill Anghubha fell sick from love of her and, in order to save his life, she arranged a tryst with him on a hill near the court. However, the man who came in the shape of Ailill was none other than Midhir, who had kept Éadaoin under observation since her second birth. She refused to go with him, and returned to Eochaidh. Ailill Anghubha, whose love-sickness had been magically caused by Midhir, regained his health. Some time later, Midhir arrived at Tara and invited the king to play chess. Eochaidh won several games and exacted great prizes from him. These included horses, pigs, cattle, and sheep, as well as magical tasks such as the clearing of stones from a large plain, the placing of rushes over another plain, the construction of a forest over yet another, and the building of a causeway over a bog. Finally Midhir won a game and demanded as prize a kiss from Éadaoin. This was arranged for a month hence, but at the appointed time Eochaidh had his court at Tara surrounded with warriors inside and outside. Notwithstanding this, Midhir suddenly appeared among them and, taking Éadaoin in his arms, took her out through the skylight. In the form of swans they flew together to Sídh ar Feimhean (the cairn on Slievenamon in Co Tipperary).

In a vain search for them, Eochaidh and his men began to dig up the cairn on Slievenamon and, realising that the lovers were not there, they turned their attention to Midhir's own dwelling at Brí Léith. Midhir immediately appeared to them and offered to let Eochaidh have the lady back. Accordingly, fifty women arrived at Tara, all looking exactly like Éadaoin. She was the best woman in Ireland at serving drink, so Eochaidh asked the women to do that. He chose one lady, and the others departed. But he had chosen wrong, for the lady was his own daughter, with whom Éadaoin had been pregnant when she left him.

Before he realised his mistake, he lay with his daughter, and of that was born a baby girl. This child was cast out on Eochaidh's orders, but she grew up to be a fine maiden and became the wife of Eterscéle and thus mother of the great **Conaire**.

This story of Éadaoin has the background of myth, but the plot uses a variety of motifs borrowed from folklore (see **Wonder Tales**, Types 313, 325). These motifs include the transformations of Éadaoin, the magical flight of the lovers, and the attempt by Eochaidh to select her from among the identical women. The motif of incest at the end of the story was borrowed from mediaeval hero-lore and employed to make unique the ancestry of a famous character. An alternate tradition, represented in a text of the same period, refers to Éadaoin as the otherworld wife of **Eochaidh Feidhleach** rather than Eochaidh Aireamh, but has none of the great adventures of the above account.

Osborn Bergin / R I Best in *Ériu 12*, 137-96; Eleanor Knott (1936), 1-3. For folklore motifs see R Th Christiansen (1959), 148-50.

ÉIBHEAR Son of the fictional **Míl**, and one of the imagined leaders of the Gaelic people in their settlement of Ireland. His name (earlier, Éber) was forged by the pseudo-historians out of Ēberus, a hiberno-Latin form of Hibernus ('Irishman'). The epithet Fionn ('fair-haired') was sometimes added.

After their victory over the **Tuatha Dé Danann**, Éibhear ruled the south of Ireland for a year, while his brother **Éireamhóin** ruled the northern half. A border dispute, however, led to a battle between them, in which Éibhear was defeated and slain. The pseudo-historians claimed that all the septs of the southern province of Munster were descended from Éibhear.

R A S Macalister (1956), 10-175 (passim); T F O'Rahilly (1946), 195-9.

ÉINNE (earlier, Enda): Saint who died c530 AD, founder of a monastery on Inis Mór (Inishmore, the largest of the Aran Islands, Co Galway).

The surviving biography, in Latin, is a late conflation of several earlier accounts. We read that his father was called Conall Dearg and that his mother, Aoibhfhinn, was a grand-daughter of the king of Arda (Ards, Co Down). He had several sisters - one of whom, Fanchea, was celebrated as a saint in her own right. Initially he pursued a warrior's life, but Fanchea persistently tried to direct him towards the Church and eventually succeeded in this. He went to Britain and to the Continent for his education, and on returning to Ireland founded several churches near the river Boyne. Having, with the support of St **Ailbhe**, got permission from the Munster king to set up a monastery on Inishmore, he and his monks set out for that island but could find no boat to bring them there from the mainland. They stood on a large rock which was on the shore, and this rock miraculously floated on the water and conveyed them over. We read that he had ten monasteries in all built on Inishmore, assigning half of the island to himself, but contention arose concerning this division. An angel appeared to him with two gifts - a copy of the Gospels and a priest's chasuble - and on account of this heavenly intervention the dissenting monks accepted his decision.

Several dramatic miracles are attributed to him. Once his monks complained that a dangerous rock was troublesome to them at sea, and Éinne brought an angel to split the rock with a sword of lightning. The result was a chasm through the rock, allowing a safe passage to the port. Éinne was celebrated for the strictness of his rule, and one tradition has it that, to ensure that each of the monks had a clear conscience, he used to order them one by one to go on the sea in a little timber boat. If there was any sin on the monk's soul, the salt-water would penetrate the body of the boat. Only one man of the community continually passed this test - he was called Gigniat, and had entered the monastery as a boy. Many of the famous saints of Ireland were said to have visited Éinne on Inishmore, and to have been instructed by him. A late literary tradition has **Colm Cille** visiting him, but we read that the two saints quarrelled, and Colm left the island with their friendship rather strained after Éinne refused him permission to build a church there.

The literary sources are embellished by local folklore concerning Éinne and his community. It is said, for instance, that the inhabitants of Inishmore at first resented his coming to them, but that he miraculously drove the horses of the island's chieftain, Corbán, across the sea to the other islands and this convinced Corbán that he should submit to the saint. The contention between his monks concerning the division of the island is also remembered in folklore, as is his quarrel with Colm Cille. In the latter case, we are told that Éinne agreed to divide the island with

Colm and that they made an arrangement concerning the division. Éinne was to go to the eastern end of the island and Colm to the western end and, having both said Mass at sunrise, they would start to walk towards each other. The point at which they met would be the boundary between them. However, Colm cheated by starting to walk without saying Mass, and as a penance he was ordered to leave Inishmore and not to build a church within earshot of Éinne's bell, which had a very wide range. The feastday of Éinne is March 21.

J F Kenney (1929), 373-4; Charles Plummer (1910) *2*, 60-75; Andrew O'Kelleher /Gertrude Schoepperle (1918), 158-61; John O'Hanlon (1875) *1*, 1-11 and *3*, 911-21; IFC 77:26-9, 157:522-3, 158:121-8, 238:617-22, 303:112, 413:12-3, 461:72-85, 669:135-7.

ÉIREAMHÓIN Son of the fictional **Míl**, and imagined leader of the Gaelic people in their settlement of Ireland. The name (earlier, Éremon) was invented by the pseudo-historians on the basis of Ériu (later, Éire), the name of the country.

After the **Tuatha Dé Danann** delayed them by tricks and magic, Éireamhóin led his people into Ireland through the Boyne estuary (see **Míl**). Having defeated the Tuatha Dé at the battle of Tailtiu (Teltown, Co Meath), he and his brother **Éibhear** divided the kingdom of Ireland between them, he reigning in the northern half and Éibhear in the south. It was said that the two brothers cast lots concerning their men of art, and that Éireamhóin won the poets for the north, while Éibhear won the harpers for the south. Within a year, the brothers had a dispute concerning border territories and, in a battle between them at Brí Damh (near Geashill, Co Offaly), Éibhear was defeated and slain. Éireamhóin was then unchallenged king of Ireland, and he dug two royal forts - Ráth Oind in Cualu (north Wicklow), and Ráth Bheathaigh (Rathbeagh, in north Kilkenny). He fought several other battles, in one of which his opponent was his brother, the poet **Amhairghin Glúngheal**. Having reigned for seventeen years, Éireamhóin died at Airgeadros (Silverwood, by the river Nore), and was buried at Ráth Bheathaigh nearby.

The historians, in their attempts to derive all the Irish septs from the sons of Míl, imagined that Éireamhóin was the ancestor of the peoples of the north and east of the country.

R A S Macalister (1956), 10-175 (passim); T F O'Rahilly (1946), 195-9.

EITHNE Mythical or fictional lady of the **Tuatha Dé Danann**.

Her story is told in a text from about the 14th century. According to it, she was a daughter of the steward of **Aonghus** and was reared along with Curcóg, daughter of **Manannán**, in the fosterage of Aonghus at Brugh na Bóinne (the Newgrange tumulus in Co Meath). When Eithne grew up she was a beautiful girl, but was insulted by a remark passed by a visitor to the Brugh and as a result would touch neither food or drink. After seven days Aonghus offered her the milk of a dun cow, one of two marvellous cows which he and Manannán had brought from India. She herself milked the cow and drank its milk, which tasted like honey and wine. When Manannán in his dwelling at Eamhain Abhlach heard the news he summoned the maiden to him, for he knew the remedy for every ailment. When Eithne arrived she would only partake of the milk of the other marvellous cow from India, the speckled animal which Manannán had. Then Manannán understood that when she was insulted in Brugh na Bóinne her 'guardian demon' had left her and had been replaced by a guardian angel. She was thus no longer one of the Tuatha Dé, but had become a Christian and would accept nourishment only from the righteous land of India. For many ages she lived on the milk of the two cows, until St **Patrick** came to Ireland. After bathing in the river Boyne one day, the 'féth fiadha' (invisibility of the Tuatha Dé) left her and she met a cleric and went with him to his hermitage near the Brugh. Patrick himself soon arrived there, as did Aonghus and his people in search of her. The latter demanded her back, but Patrick refused and tried unsuccessfully to convert Aonghus, who departed with a cry of anguish. Eithne was baptised, died a fortnight later, and was buried with Christian honour.

Lilian Duncan in *Ériu 11*, 184-225.

ELIZABETH I (1533-1603) Queen of England from 1558 until her death.

Because of her oppressive policies towards Ireland, and the devastation caused by her armies, Elizabeth is remembered with hostility in the popular tradition of the country. The major charge laid against her is that of promiscuity. A poem from the mid-17th century refers to her as

37. ELIZABETH I *Contemporary woodcut of Elizabeth.*

'monstrous Elizabeth who did not marry but who refrained from no man' and adds that she was treacherous and made a wasteland of Ireland. A folk legend collected in Co Leitrim in the following century accords well with this. It tells of how Brian 'na Múrtha' Ó Ruairc, chieftain of the O'Rourkes of Breffny, was invited to London by her in order to pledge his fealty. When she saw that he was a handsome man she arranged that he be accommodated in a sumptuous apartment in her palace. He was visited in his bedroom on several nights by an unknown lady, and he noticed by the moonlight on one occasion that his visitor was wearing a fine ring. Next day he saw the same ring on the Queen's finger and hinted genially that he recognised her. On the following night an assassin was sent to despatch him. This story is apocryphal, for in reality Brian had been in rebellion against Elizabeth and had travelled from his homeland to Scotland to seek assistance. However, the Scottish king James (later James I of England) handed him over to the English and he was kept in the Tower of London until he was hanged in 1591. Brian was a very brave man, and some contemporary sources suggest that he had some correspondence with the Queen when he was imprisoned in London. On one occasion, he refused to bow to her Privy Council and, when asked did he bow to the images of saints, replied that there was a great deal of difference between the saints and them. Respect for Brian's courage seems to have been confused in Ireland with rumours of Elizabeth's amours, thus giving rise to the legend.

Later folklore accounts claim that Elizabeth slept with a different man each night, and in the morning had each of her lovers sent to the block. The motif of an anonymous nocturnal lover is found in the reverse form, under the influence of an international folktale which tells of how a princess tries to identify a rogue. Thus we are told that Elizabeth used to have a man brought to her boudoir each night and, since she could not see him properly in the dark, she would quietly cut a piece of his coat or a lock of his hair and thus be able to identify him on the morrow in order to have him executed. An Irishman outwitted her, however, by cutting the hair of all her soldiers while they slept. Next day, she failed to pick out the man, but she uttered a verse warning whoever had fooled her not to try it again.

The context which has people visiting her to advance their interests in Ireland puts Elizabeth in a somewhat better light. There were indeed some celebrated visits by Irish leaders to her court - such as that in 1562 of the proud Ulster chief Seán Ó Néill who spoke only Irish and kept his kerns by him as bodyguard, and 1593 the dramatic Gráinne Mhaol **Ní Mháille** whose wits were well equal to those of Elizabeth herself. Folklore has Elizabeth behaving with wisdom and humanity on such occasions. A legend from Cork tells of how she conferred one side of the river Bandon on a man called Fitzgerald in return for services rendered to her cause in Ireland. He remarked, however, that things were better in pairs, and then she told him to take the two sides. An account from Wicklow claims that one of her officers brought the head of the chieftain Feidhlim Ó Tuathail to her, in expectation of a grant of that chieftain's land. Elizabeth, however, conferred no more on the opportunist than a smile and the shawl that she was wearing on her neck.

We are told that Elizabeth was very superstitious, and that she kept a playing-card, the ace of hearts, under the seat of her throne, believing that as long as it was there she would not die.

One story claims that she had a servant-girl from Ireland, whom she relied on greatly. As she grew old she became quite demented, and one day she called the servant-girl to her as she lay prostrate in her bed of gold. In their conversation, the girl referred to all the Irish people whom the Queen had caused to be killed and remarked that death was now near and all her gold could not keep her alive. After her death, it is claimed that a terrible stench came from her coffin, this obviously being a hostile perspective on the fact that her corpse had been kept for five weeks before her royal funeral in London.

Cecile O'Rahilly (1952), 21; Dubhglas de hÍde (1933), 144; J C Walker (1786 -Appendix), 81-2; Donal O'Sullivan (1958) *2*, 121-2; James Hardiman (1831) *2*, 286-305; Lady Gregory (1926), 37-8; Dáithí Ó hÓgáin (1985), 162-3; IFC 259:457/648, 924:403-5, 1007:784, 1114:175-6, S507:142.

ENVIRONMENT People in Ireland, as everywhere else, have speculated on the nature of the physical world around them, giving rise to a rich imaginative lore.

The sky and its phenomena are an obvious subject of such lore. The **druids** are said to have been keen students of the heavenly bodies, and the early literature has several mentions of oaths being taken by reference to sun, moon, and stars. The sun figured most prominently in ancient tradition, and the myth of **Lugh** and **Balar** shows how it could be personified. There are other indications, such as in descriptions of the mythical **Brighid**, **Conaire** and in seasonal lore generally (see **Time**), of how the sun was understood to be the source of energy, both agricultural and mystical. In folk speech, the sun and moon are sometimes referred to as if they have influence on human affairs, and in Irish 'by the strength of the sun and moon' was a common exclamation. What appear to be echoes of ancient beliefs are the idea that if a woman slept in the sunlight she was more likely to become pregnant, and that the waxing of the moon was a propitious time to undertake new work, whereas its waning was the opposite. The light of the full moon was said to make **fairies** more active in their affairs, and it was also supposed to cause insanity in some people.

Fanciful explanations were offered, especially to children, of the obvious aspects of these bodies. The sun was said to be inhabited by a fox, and food melting due to its heat was said to be eaten by him, while the 'man in the moon' was said to have once been a boy who was transported there due to his laziness at sweeping with a brush or drawing water with a bucket. Thunder and lightning were similarly claimed to be the angels drilling and flashing their swords, and December snow was picturesquely explained as the geese being plucked in heaven for the Christmas feast. The young ones were also told that a crock of gold was hidden at the foot of the rainbow. On a more serious note, the latter phenomenon was said to be a token of God's promise to mankind that the world would never again be destroyed by flood, but it was not altogether auspicious, for its appearance over a house was taken to portend the death of some member of that family. Various stories told of how persons were born under a certain star and as a result had either good or bad fortune in their lives, while a meteor was taken to be a soul passing from purgatory to heaven. A sunburst through clouds, causing clear rays to descend to the earth, was interpreted as the track made by the souls of good people passing to heaven immediately after death.

Landscape and sea had many traditions attached to them. Lonely places and regions far out on the ocean were regarded as special haunts of **fairies** and kindred beings. In early Irish myth the otherworld was thought of as an overseas realm (see **Manannán**), and the survival of such a mythical idea in folk belief is instanced by the fancy that there was a mystical island called Uí Bhreasaíl somewhere off the west coast. The imprint made on the sea by the sunrays was sometimes pointed out as the image of this island. The early literature describes four great waves of Ireland which cried out on the death of a true king. These were the Wave of **Clíona** in Tralee Bay and the Wave of Tóim in Kenmare Bay on the southwest coast, and the Wave of Rughraidhe in Dundrum Bay and the Wave of Tuaidhe at Ballintoy on the northeast coast. Because of its danger and unpredictability, folklore tends to personalise the ocean. It was believed that 'the sea takes its own share', by which was meant that a person who saved another from drowning was himself in danger of meeting with such a tragic end.

It was fancifully said that various lakes came about when a woman forgot to replace the lid on a copious well, or when some supernatural person or animal urinated in that place. Almost all Irish rivers have feminine names, and the early literature associates several of them with variants of the land-goddess (see **Goddesses** and **Bóinn**). A common folk legend tells of how a voice is heard at a river every seven years declaring 'now is the time, where is the person?' by which is meant that it is destined that individuals will be drowned there periodically. Lakes were also much feared and speculated upon. Some of them were said to be so deep as to have no bottom, and traditions abounded of ancient cities having sunk beneath them. Boatmen could often at night see lights and hear the muffled sounds of bells coming from these underwater cities.

The veneration accorded to holy wells, each of them dedicated to a particular saint, seems to have had its origin in pre-Christian religion, but it became thoroughly christianised due to the importance of wells for baptism by early missionaries. Thus we are often told, in both literature and folklore, of a **saint** causing a well to miraculously spring up by striking the ground with his crozier. On the feastday of the particular patron-saint, people gathered at the local holy well to pray, and this 'pattern' (Irish 'patrún', from the actual word 'patron') were great occasions for, in addition to prayer, communal celebration such as music, dancing, and even drinking. Many cures were associated with these wells, and it was usually said that a supplicant saw a mystical fish in the water as a sign that a cure was to be obtained. Traditions told of how a holy well was desecrated by some individual, and as a result it became dry but reappeared at a new location nearby. A special tree grew beside most of these wells, and pilgrims attached a piece of cloth to it or inserted a coin into it as a token of their veneration.

Lonely parts of the countryside, especially at night, were reputed to be places of contact with the otherworld, and some quite disturbing traditions were associated with them. Most striking was the belief in the 'hungry grass', said to be a patch of grass - mostly on mountainsides - on which a person might unwittingly walk with the result that he or she became afflicted by a great hunger. This could cause death, and to avoid such an eventuality many wayfarers brought some bread with them in their pockets, for eating the bread could obviate the effects of the magical hunger. In lonely places, also, a 'magic fog' was believed to sometimes descend around a person, causing him or her to stray interminably until light of day brought release from the ordeal. This belief can be compared with accounts in the mediaeval literature of how heroes found themselves surrounded by a fog as an introduction to an otherworld adventure.

Of the flora, most attention was focussed on trees. The early literature describes several great trees of ancient Ireland, and these seem to have been landmarks for assemblies. Most celebrated of them was the Bile Tartain at Ardbraccan in Co Meath, said to have been an ash of gigantic size. Others were the yew of Mughain near Ballaghmoon in Co Kildare, the yew of Ros at Old Leighlin in Co Carlow, an ash called 'Dáithí's Branch' at Farbill in Co Westmeath and another ash called 'the Branch of Uisneach' at Ushnagh in the same county. The sites of many of the great trees were taken over by monastic communities, and there are several mentions of such in the lives of the **saints**. The belief long survived that a very old and notable tree, termed a 'bile', was in some way sacred, and accounts in both literature and folklore tell of misfortune befalling people who interfered with such a 'bile' or cut it down. Concerning magical properties, the early literature associates the hazel with seers (see **Bóinn** and **Druids**), but in ordinary folklore pride of place is very much accorded to the rowan. This, called in Irish 'caorthann' and also known as 'mountain-ash', was believed to be especially efficacious. A piece of rowan was put in the milk-pail and around the churn to prevent magical milk-stealing (see **Time**: Bealtaine), and it was kept in the house in the belief that it prevented fire.

T P Cross (1952), 20-32, 46-7; W G Wood-Martin (1902) *2*, 46-115, 152-9, 206-61; Seán Ó Súilleabháin (1942), 251-88; Kevin Danaher (1964), 67-78, 114-9; A T Lucas in *Journal of the Cork Archaeological and Historical Society 68*, 16-54; Caoimhín Ó Danachair (1978), 24-5.

EOCHAIDH (earlier, Eochu): A name which occurs as that of several characters in mediaeval literature, and the origin of which was demonstrably mythic. It seems to be a derivative of 'ech' (later, 'each') which means 'horse', for the name is often associated with equine imagery. The suggestion is that a deity could be envisaged as a great horseman, but in some contexts the name could indicate stallion-like reproductive ability (see **Fearghus mac Róich**).

The most striking instance of the name being attached to a divinity is that of the **Daghdha**, who had the alternative designation of Eochaidh Ollathair (i.e. 'Eochaidh the Father of Many'). In accordance with this, there was a tendency to give the particular name Eochaidh to antique characters in the genealogies of several septs. In the Eoghanacht pedigrees a character called Echdae was mentioned as husband of the goddess **Áine** - his name would have meant either 'horse-like' or 'horse-god'. Furthermore, a persistent theme in the mythology of Celtic **goddesses** was the race in which these ladies showed their speed, sometimes in contention with **horses**. There are some indications that the sacrifice of a horse was an archaic ritual connected with the inaugeration of kings in Ireland, and if so such a ritual would have had both social and mythic connotations.

Designations of deities were frequently used as names for mythical or, in some cases, historical kings (see the following entries).

T F O'Rahilly (1946), 34, 290-4, 467-9, 552-3; M A O'Brien (1962), 613-7; Myles Dillon / Nora Chadwick (1973), 126.

EOCHAIDH AIREAMH Fictional king of Ireland situated in prehistory. His sobriquet means 'ploughman'.

He is described as brother and successor of **Eochaidh Feidhleach**, and his reign as lasting fifteen years. In the original lore, he was probably in fact a double of Eochaidh Feidhleach, and since the names of both suggest agriculture they may be remnants of a divine patron of that skill. In the 9th-century text on the wooing of **Éadaoin**, Eochaidh Aireamh appears as a king of Tara and human husband of that metamorphosed lady of the otherworld. Various sources place his death at Freamhain (Frewin in Co Westmeath), where he was burned by one Siugmhall. Elsewhere this character, Siugmhall, appears as an otherworld being or deity who resided in Sídh Neanta (a rath near the north of Lough Ree on the river Shannon). His name may originally have meant 'powerful thunderbolt', and the tradition that he killed Eochaidh Aireamh could be a remnant of myth. A secondary account, in the Éadaoin story, develops the lore by making Siugmhall the grandson of Midhir, Eochaidh's rival for the lady. According to this, Eochaidh had a fortress in Frewin, and the burden of his sustenance fell on the sept called Fir Chúil who belonged to that district. Mórmhaol was king of the Fir Chúil, and his brother was Siugmhall. These two gathered their forces and attacked Eochaidh's fortress. They burned it and slew the king himself.

R A S Macalister (1956), 298-9; Osborn Bergin and R I Best in *Ériu 12*, 137-96; Edward Gwynn (1935), 161: P S Dinneen (1908) *2*, 228-9; T F O'Rahilly (1946), 52-3.

EOCHAIDH ÉIGEAS Poet of the 6th century AD who is mentioned as having been present at the Convention of Drom Ceat (Daisy Hill, near Limavady in Co Derry) in the year 575. His epithet means 'sage' or 'poet'.

Some mediaeval writers identified him, probably incorrectly, with **Dallán Forgaill**, whose real name is also given as Eochaidh. It seems likely that he was somewhat older than Dallán and was the leading poet in Ulster before the latter came to prominence. His prestige must have been considerable, for he was described in the mediaeval literature as the chief-poet of Ireland. Little detail is given concerning him, except that in one story he is claimed to have been employed as court poet by the king of Dál nAraidhe (in south Antrim and north Down), **Fiachna mac Baodáin**. In that capacity, we read, he was upstaged by Fiachna's brilliant young son **Mongán**.

Although they knew next to nothing of him or of his life, the writers of pseudo-history were so impressed by the fame of his name that they projected it backwards in their chronology onto a fictional king of ancient Ireland, **Ollamh Fódla** (literally, 'high-poet of Ireland') whose real name, they claimed, was Eochaidh Éigeas. Another compliment was paid to the dim memory of him in the post-mediaeval period, when the leading poetic family of Leinster, surnamed Mac Eochadha (anglicised Keogh and Kehoe) fancifully traced their descent to the celebrated 6th-century poet.

Whitley Stokes in *Revue Celtique 20*, 42; Maud Joynt (1941), 1; P S Dinneen (1908) *3*, 80-1, 94-5; Eleanor Knott in *Ériu 8*, 155-60; Seán Mac Airt (1944), 256.

EOCHAIDH FEIDHLEACH Fictional king of Ireland, who was claimed to have been contemporaneous with Julius Caesar. The sobriquet 'feidhleach' probably meant 'one who yokes', and a mediaeval text supposes that it was during his reign that the ox-yoke was first used in Ireland. An alternative explanation, 'righteous', is given for Eochaidh's sobriquet, but this seems to be incorrect, as he is said to have had a brother called **Eochaidh Aireamh** - the epithet here meaning 'ploughman'. This brother is probably a double of Eochaidh Feidhleach himself, and suggests that the name was in origin the appellation of the deity **Eochaidh** in the context of agricultural patronage.

The actual character of Eochaidh Feidhleach is not, however, regarded as in any way supernatural. He figures in the **Ulster Cycle**, where he is described as king of Ireland and the first descendant of **Cobhthach Caol** to gain that primary office. We are told that he took the kingship by defeating and slaying the Ulsterman **Fachtna Fáthach** at the battle of Leitir Ruibhe (in the area of Corran, Co Sligo). Fachtna was the father of **Conchobhar mac Neasa**, who as a result continually battled and schemed against Eochaidh. The latter, for his part, supported **Fearghus mac Róich** against Conchobhar and made several attempts to have the province of Ulster submit to him. He reigned for twelve years, and during that time, we are told, there was a golden age in Ireland. Peace, generosity, courtesy towards women, and love of the arts prevailed. Cows gave milk copiously, trees gave much fruit, and the waters were full of fish. 'No noise was heard from woods of howling wind or showers of rain, but the great plains were covered with dew until the middle of each bright fine day.' This was so, because in the third year of Eochaidh's reign Jesus **Christ** was born in the Holy Land.

Eochaidh, however, had some bitter disappointments. Two of his sons were killed in the victorious battle of Leitir Ruibhe. Then three other sons, called the **Finn Eamhna**, rebelled against him. It was said that he had an argument with his queen Cloithfhionn over a chess-game, and she as a result left **Tara** and went to live at the Ulster court in Eamhain Mhacha. She took her three sons, the Finn, with her, and at her instigation they declared war on their father. They ignored all his entreaties and were defeated and slain in the battle of Comar (near Navan in Co Meath). Eochaidh was disconsolate, and his heart burst in his breast with sorrow. He was buried with his three rebellious sons, as he had directed, in a great mound at Croghan. Eochaidh was said to have had several other children, including Conall Anghlonnach, who later became a leading warrior in Ulster, and the celebrated **Meadhbh**. He gave the kingdom of Connacht to one Tinne mac Connrach after Tinne and his men built a fossa around the rath of Croghan in one night. When Tinne later slew Meadhbh's suitor, Fiodhach mac Féig, however, Eochaidh turned against him, deposed him, and gave the Connacht throne to Meadhbh. On account of the episode concerning the three Finn, it was said that Eochaidh recommended that any future king have somebody other than a son to succeed him, for in that way sons would not be rivals of their fathers. According to the pseudo-historians, Eochaidh's brother became king after his death.

Whitley Stokes in *Irische Texte 3*, 330-1; M E Dobbs in *Revue Celtique 39*, 1-32 and *40*, 404-23, and *43*, 277-342; Kuno Meyer in *Anecdota from Irish Manuscripts 5*, 17-22; Joseph O'Neill in *Ériu 2*, 173-81; R A S Macalister (1956), 298-9; Edward Gwynn (1935), 161-2; P S Dinneen (1908) *2*, 182-7; Eleanor Knott (1936), 1-2.

EOCHAIDH MAC LUCHTA Fictional character in mediaeval literature, said alternately to have been king of south Connacht and of Munster.

We read that he was a very generous man and had but one eye. When **Aithirne** visited his court, Eochaidh offered that importunate poet the choice of his wealth as a gift. Aithirne demanded 'the only eye in your head to be given to me in my fist', and Eochaidh complied. He knocked the eye out with his own finger and presented it to the poet. He then asked his servant to direct him to water so that he might wash his face. The servant remarked that the socket ('dearc') was red ('dearg') from the blood and Eochaidh said that that water should ever after be called Deargdhearc (hence Lough Derg on the river Shannon). God was so impressed with the magnanimity of Eochaidh that He miraculously gave him two eyes as reward. A variant of this story has **Feircheirdne** as the importunate poet, rather than Aithirne. It is apparent that the motif is very old, it being an exemplary one to demonstrate how generous the true king should be to **poets**. It may have become attached to the deity **Eochaidh** on account of solar imagery associated with that personage. Elsewhere there is mention of a character called Eochaidh Aonshúile (i.e. 'of the One Eye'), and there can be little doubt that Eochaidh mac Luchta was a character invented from the débris of the cult of the deity.

The later mediaeval literature gives a further twist to the story. Here we read that a Munster king, Eochaidh mac Maolughra plucked out his eye to satisfy the extortionate demand of a Scottish druid called Labhán. St **Ruadhán**, who witnessed this, prayed to God that the druid's two eyes should pass into the head of the king, and so it happened. Thus the king acquired the nickname

'Súil Labháin', and from him was derived the Munster family surnamed Ó Súilleabháin. This version was quite anachronistic with regard to its characters, connecting the 6th-century Ruadhán with Súildubhán mac Maolughra who flourished in the late 9th century. The name Súildubhán in fact meant 'dark-eyed', and a false etymology 'súil amháin' ('one eye') led to the claim that his real name was Eochaidh and also to the invention of a character named Labhán.

Whitley Stokes in *Revue Celtique 8*, 48-9 and *15*, 461-3; Edward Gwynn (1913), 338-47; T F O'Rahilly (1946), 59, 175-9; Kenneth Jackson (1938), 182; Myles Dillon in *Proceedings of the British Academy 33*, 248; Charles Plummer (1922) 1, 329; Tadhg Ó Donnchadha (1940), 147-8; P S Dinneen (1908) *3*, 58-9.

EOCHAIDH MAC MAIREADHA Fictional character in a mediaeval story which may preserve echoes of ancient myth.

The story claims that Mairidh was a king of Munster, and that he had two sons, Eochaidh and Ríbh. Eochaidh fell in love with his father's wife, a young woman called Eibhliu who had been fostered by **Aonghus** of Newgrange. Eochaidh carried Eibhliu away, accompanied by many of his retainers. On their way, a stranger killed their horses, but Aonghus appeared and gave them a marvellous steed which carried all their baggage. Aonghus warned them not to allow the steed to rest and urinate, else it would cause their death. On reaching Ulster, however, the horse did urinate, causing a spring to rise. Eochaidh built a house by the spring and settled there, but one day a woman forgot to replace the cover on the well and it flooded the area, drowning Eochaidh and most of his family. Thus was formed Loch nEachach ('the Lake of Eochaidh' i.e. Lough Neagh).

One version duplicates the plot by having another otherworld lord **Midhir** first killing their horses and then offering them a marvellous steed. This animal urinated and thereby gave rise to Lough Ree on the Shannon. We read that, later, when their horses were killed again, Aonghus presented them with the second steed. All of the versions are somewhat disjointed, being retellings of an original account. It is likely that that account described how Eibhliu (see **Goddesses**) was abducted by Eochaidh. Midhir - perhaps the original name of Mairidh - tried to prevent the abduction by killing the horses, and Aonghus came to the rescue with the wondrous steed. This steed later gave rise to Lough Neagh by urinating there. This, the largest lake in Ireland, in fact got its name from the sept Uí Eachach, who inhabited the area and whose name signifies 'descendants of Eochaidh'. It is quite likely that the sept was so called from the cult of the deity **Eochaidh** and that the story is an elaboration of the equine imagery of that deity.

Edward Gwynn (1913), 450-9, 560-1 and (1924), 62-9, 388-91; Whitley Stokes in *Revue Celtique 16*, 151-3; S H O'Grady (1892) *1*, 233-6; T F O'Rahilly (1946), 291, 499; Kuno Meyer in *Zeitschrift für celtische Philologie 8*, 307-8.

38. EOGHAN BÉAL *Warrior from the Book of Kells.*

EOGHAN BÉAL King of Connacht who died in 543 AD. His epithet (earlier, Bél) means 'mouth' and is explained as meaning that he was 'the spokesman for all the people around him'.

A brief account of his career is given in the 12th-century text on his son **Ceallach**. This states that he raided all the other provinces of Ireland

and was continuously successful on his campaigns. Eventually he clashed with the sons of **Muirceartach mac Earca**, who brought a great force from Ulster to plunder Connacht. As they were returning north with massive booty, Eoghan attacked them at Sligo. The Ulstermen were put to flight, but Eoghan himself was mortally wounded. Before he died he told his people to instal Ceallach as king in his place. He also instructed them to bury him in the plain of Uí Fiachrach (now north Mayo and west Sligo) with his javelin in his hand. He was to be standing upright and facing north, and this would ensure that the Ulstermen would not triumph over Connacht. This was done, and the Uí Néill of the north were continually defeated by the Connachtmen until they came with a great force, took the body of Eoghan from its grave, and reburied him at Loch Gile (Lough Gill, Co Sligo) with his face downwards. This burial-motif is apparently a borrowing from the lore of **Laoghaire**.

Kathleen Mulchrone (1933), x, 1-3; Kuno Meyer in *Archiv für celtische Lexikographie 3*, 303-4.

EOGHAN MÓR Mythical ancestor of the dominant sept in early mediaeval Munster, the Eoghanacht. 'Eoghan' meant 'good conception', and the epithet 'mór' signified 'great', especially in the sense of a family ancestor.

He was also known as Mugh Nuadhat ('servant of Nuadhu'). **Nuadhu** was a divinity and ancestor figure held in high regard by the Leinstermen, and this designation of Eoghan seems to be the result of Leinster influence on the Eoghanacht in the 6th century. The Leinstermen had previous to that time been engaged in a long struggle against the growing dominance of the Connachta, and their anti-Connachta propaganda would have had appeal to the rulers of Munster. The whole lore of Eoghan, indeed, involves a bitter struggle against the mythical ancestor of the Connachta, the celebrated **Conn Céadchathach**.

The literature, as was its wont, gives a fabricated explanation of the designation Mugh Nuadhat. According to this, Eoghan was the foster-son of the Leinster king Dáire Barrach, who once undertook to fortify Dún Aillinne (Knockaulin in Co Kildare) and engaged a famous builder Nuadhu for the work. A servant was digging the trench and was unable to remove a huge stone which he came across. Eoghan was among a group of onlooking youths, and they refused to help, so he went into the trench and lifted the stone on his own. With one throw, he placed it in the southern angle of the fortress, where it remained ever after. 'You have a noble servant today, o Nuadhu,' remarked a druid, and thus Eoghan became known as 'Mugh Nuadhat'.

A series of epithets was connected to his name, such as Eoghan Taidhleach ('bright'), Eoghan Fial ('generous'), and Eoghan Fithiceach. This latter was interpreted in several ways. It was claimed that he invented wooden spades ('fidhfheaca') so that his men could dig out the site of a fortress; and alternately that he had three forts, each called 'Fighfhec', because they were made of trees 'woven and bent' into each other. The real explanation seems to have been in the word 'fithec' which meant a tunnel, for - as we shall see - Eoghan was said to have constructed cellars for storing provisions. Already by the 9th century, the Munster genealogists were promoting the fancy that Eoghan had come to Ireland from abroad, landing with his followers at Inbhear Colptha (the estuary of the Boyne). He was informed by his prophets that a great famine was coming in Ireland, and they advised that he store up a large amount of food. This he did, storing the provisions away in souterrains connected with his three fortresses, and when the famine came he shared this food with the men of Ireland in return for the kingship of the country. This is obviously contrived by some early mediaeval scholar to bolster the prestige of the Eoghanacht. The coming of Eoghan to Ireland is somewhat confused, for the surviving text at some points suggests that it was his sons who came rather than himself. It clearly echoes the *Lebor Gabála* account of the sons of **Míl**, while the famine-motif is borrowed directly from the Old Testament account of Joseph in Egypt.

A text compiled in the 13th century, *Cath Maighe Léna*, gives a full account of the deeds of Eoghan, incorporating details from several early sources. This again explains his nickname, it being claimed here that he helped the servant of a Munster rath-builder called Nuadhu Dearg. We read that Munster was at that time divided into three parts, one portion being ruled by Eoghan's father, who is called - apparently as a reflection of Eoghan's nickname - Mogh Néid. Eoghan's mother, Síoda, had a dream of seven emaciated black cows which gored and killed seven fine white cows, and a druid explained this as a presage of seven bounteous years followed by seven years of famine. Eoghan and his father had cellars constructed, in which they stored a great quantity of grain in the good years. With the onset of famine, the other Munster lords came to them in desperation seeking food, and Mogh Néid promised to assist them on condition that the whole kingdom of Munster be given to his son. This was agreed, but the other two regional kings, **Conaire mac Mogha Lámha** and Macnia mac Luighdheach, went to Conn Céadchathach for help. Conn gave them his daughters in marriage, and he divided Munster on their behalf.

The armies of Conn and Eoghan met at Carn Buidhe (near Kenmare in Co Kerry), and Eoghan was defeated. An otherworld lady called **Éadaoin** who resided in that area came to his assistance, making rocks appear as soldiers in the eyes of the foe, and under cover of this she spirited away Eoghan and what remained of his army. She placed them in seven ships in Kenmare harbour, and that night the unyielding Eoghan made three sorties ashore against the forces of Conn. They spent nine more nights having their wounds healed by Éadaoin, and then Eoghan sailed with his followers to Spain. Arriving there, he was given a bright ('taidhleach') cloak by the daughter of the Spanish king. She had made that cloak from the skin of a wondrous salmon which she had caught. Eoghan married this princess, and all went well for nine years, until he grew lonesome for home. The Spanish king gave him a fleet and an army, and thus he set out for Ireland, bringing his wife with him.

When he reached Carn Buidhe, both Conaire and Macnia submitted to him, and many other nobles of Ireland came into alliance with him, including the Ulster and Leinster kings. Conn had no choice but to compromise, and accordingly Ireland was divided into two equal portions between himself and Eoghan. The dividing line was from Áth Cliath Meadhraighe (Maaree, south-east of Galway) to Áth Cliath Duibhlinne (Dublin), and this arrangement lasted for a long time. When Eoghan demanded that Dublin Bay be divided equally between them, however, hostilities resumed. Conn made a surprise attack on Eoghan's forces at Magh Léana (Moylena, just north of Tullamore in Co Offaly) and, in a prolonged and vicious contest, Eoghan's army was routed. Eoghan stood alone, fighting fiercely against the foe. He and Conn wounded each other, and then several warriors transfixed the dying Eoghan with their spears.

Kuno Meyer in *Zeitschrift für celtische Philologie 8*, 312-3; Vernam Hull in *ibid 19*, 59-61; Kenneth Jackson (1938); Eugene O'Curry (1855); F J Byrne (1973), 199-201.

ÉRAINN (also, Érna) General name applied to several septs in early Ireland. It is derived from Ériu, the name of the country, and thus meant literally 'Irish people'.

In the early literature, the Érainn are postulated as being distinct from other groups, such as the Connachta, Eoghanacht, Laighin, and Cruithin. The distinction between them and the latter two groups has some warranty. The Laighin (from whom the province of Leinster got its name) were a special, and to all appearances a comparatively late, Celtic migration into Ireland (see **Labhraidh**). The Cruithin seem to have been either a non-Celtic or very early Celtic group (see **Picts**). The evidence suggests, however, that the distinction between the Érainn and the Connachta and Eoghanacht septs was a fabrication. The Connachta (see **Conn Céadchathach**) were, from the 4th or 5th century AD onwards, the leading sept in the country. They captured and held **Tara**, put many other septs under tribute to them, and claimed to be high-kings of Ireland. In the south, the Eoghanacht exercised comparable power from their royal seat at Cashel, making most of the Munster septs their tributaries. They seem to have established their sway over Munster at around the same time as the Connachta gained control of all the north Midlands, and the early mediaeval literature portrays the respective mythical ancestors of both septs, Conn Céadchathach and **Eoghan Mór**, as two ancient magnates who divided Ireland between them. This caused the idea to develop that these two leading septs were different from the rest of the people, whom they termed 'aitheachthuatha' ('vassal-tribes'). In line with this, the designation Érainn came to be restricted in meaning to these same tributary septs - that is, they were the ordinary Irish as opposed to the pre-eminent groups.

Prior to their coming to power, however, the Connachta and the Eoghanacht must have sprung from the same stock as the Érainn. Irish was the common language of both noble and tributary septs, as is clear from the provenance of **ogham** inscriptions, most of which belonged to 'Érainn' territories. The literature indicates that, in the period roughly from the 5th to the 7th centuries, the term Érainn was applied particularly to non-Eoghanacht septs in Munster, but it is clear that the ordinary septs of other areas were similarly regarded. The Ulaidh, who gave their name to the province of Ulster and who are the subject of the **Ulster Cycle**, were undoubtedly Érainn, as were all the prominent septs from the western province. In northern and western parts of the country, however, there was a tendency to use a term from the débris of Celtic tribal names i.e. **Fir Bolg**, for the less prominent Érainn groups. The Érainn of Tara were long remembered - that is, the old rulers of that area before the Laighin took it from them. When the Laighin were themselves displaced from Tara by the Connachta, this was seen not as a reversion to the stock who originally held it, but a passing of the sacred citadel into the hands of a 'new' class of nobility.

In time, however, the adoption of a novel term to refer to an Irish person weakened the force of most of the older designations. This was the Welsh word 'Gwyddel' (i.e. an Irishman) which was, in or about the 6th century, borrowed into Irish in the form 'Goidel', and soon became 'Gaedheal'. The Connachta and Eoghanacht may have originally tried to restrict this new borrowing to a description of themselves, but the genealogists and historians assured that it had the widest application. Thus the pseudo-historical tract called *Lebor Gabála* derives all the people of Ireland - including even Laighin and Cruithin - from the fictional Míl Easpáine, whose ancestor was the equally fictional Gaedheal Glas (see **Míl**). The Irish language also came to be known as Goidelg (becoming Gaeidhilg), due to the Welsh term for it, 'Gwyddeleg'. The genealogical and historical tracts continued to reflect the dominance of the Connachta and Eoghanacht, but there was an insistence that all were of common stock, and several septs had their heritage doubly secured through their lines being fancifully connected with those of the official nobility.

The term Érainn thus became obsolete, both in its original meaning and in its narrowed sense. Its original meaning, however, had something of a rebirth in post-mediaeval speech with the use of the word Éireannach (plural, Éireannaigh) to describe an inhabitant of Ireland. It retains this general meaning in contemporary speech, with the term Gael (the modern form of Gaedheal), being used of a person who belongs to, or identifies with, the Irish language (Gaeilge) and the native culture.

T F O'Rahilly in *Ériu 14*, 7-28; Liam Ó Buachalla in *Journal of the Cork Historical and Archaeological Society 49*, 25-9; Toirdhealbhach Ó Raithbheartaigh (1932), 53-92, 101-31.

F

39. FAIRIES *A typical Irish fairy-fort.*

FAIRIES (in Irish, sí) The otherworld community which, according to Irish folklore, inhabits the countryside side by side with, but usually invisible to, the human race.

The word 'sí' (earlier, 'sidh') originally meant a mound, and the early literature has several references to otherworld dwellers in the tumuli and cairns which dot the Irish countryside. One ultimate source of the Irish tradition of fairies, therefore, was the idea of the community of the dead living on in their burial chambers, and it is noticeable that lore of the dead (see **Ghosts**) still tends to become confused with that of the fairies in living oral narrative. In a more basic sense, there are some indications that the concept of the living dead was one of the fountain-heads of the ancient Celtic pantheon of mythic beings (see especially **Donn**). These mythic beings were, however, also understood to be a kind of spiritual community whose nature was on a different plane to that of the human race. As such, they were called by the literati the **Tuatha Dé Danann** and were described as living in a timeless realm, from which they could appear to people at will and provide glittering visions of their existence. The evidence indicates that, at some stage in antiquity, Irish versions of widespread beliefs about otherworld communities were assimilated to lore of the living dead, and that from this evolved the 'sí' people of general Irish tradition.

The Tuatha Dé were portrayed as patrons and bestowers of things involving social prestige, such as arts and skills, and even **kingship** itself. That the fairies of folklore are indebted to them is obvious from the special intensity with which this motif is found in Irish folk legend. Many such legendary accounts tell of how **poets** and other people with powers of magic got their skills as gifts from the fairies. The occasions and methods of communication with the fairies in such cases is also enlightening. Usually the person who is to receive the gift falls asleep at some location not ordinarily frequented by humans and therefore regarded as otherworldly. It may be a 'fairy rath' (an ancient tumulus or relic of an earthenwork fort), a riverside (water being anciently associated with Celtic deities), or a cairn on a hill-top. The fact that the sleep parallels shamanic rites, and that the locations are the same as those involved in ancient seer-craft (see **Find**), makes it clear that this aspect of fairy legend is a survival from native rituals.

The fairies are said to live in the air and in the sea as well as on land, and thus all folklore concerning communal otherworld beings can be classified under this general heading. Among the aspects of fairy lore to which a pre-mediaeval origin can be attributed are the numerous traditions concerning otherworld animals - especially cattle and horses - which come from raths or lakes or the sea and mingle with animals of this world. Similarly, the fairies sometimes take animals away into their world, a form of economic thieving which probably owes its orgin to ancient animal-sacrifice. The fairy-dwellings, when a human gains access to them, are beautiful places, decorated with precious metals and with sumptuous food and drink and melodious music, and therefore can be seen to preserve the standard traits of the realm inhabited by the Tuatha Dé.

The mediaeval literature concerning the seer-hero **Fionn mac Cumhaill** has many references to visits to Tuatha Dé strongholds which, like the dwellings of the fairies in the late folklore, are often situated within cairns and raths. As in folklore, Fionn is given gifts in these residences, for example a marvellous knife or goblet. Gift-items of a similar nature are also brought from the otherworld in texts which situate it in a marvellous land overseas (see **Bran mac Feabhail** and **Cormac mac Airt**), and it is therefore clear that we are dealing with one continuous tradition which derives ultimately from the divine realm of mythology. We read in one 12th-century text that every otherworld dwelling in Ireland was open at Samhain (the November feast - see **Time**), an idea that is reflected in folk beliefs that the fairies are especially to be encountered at May and November, as groups of them are wont to change their residence from one rath to another at these two basic junctures of the Irish year.

It is likely also that the folk belief that great battles are sometimes fought between different fairy communities is a reflection of ancient lore, for instance the mythic battle described in the literature between the Tuatha Dé and the Fomhóire (see **Mythological Cycle**). In line with this battle imagery, folk belief holds that the most dangerous type of encounter is with the 'slua sí' ('trooping fairies'), a kind of battalion of shock-troops which are sometimes abroad at night and which lay low anybody who gets in their way. There was a strong folk assumption that one should never refer to the fairies by their name (whether 'sí', or the diminutive and somewhat disparaging 'sióga', or the English 'fairies'), and so such circumlocutions as 'na daoine maithe' ('the good people') or 'na daoine uaisle' ('the noble people') were used. This also is redolent of early belief and there can be little doubt that similar caution was employed in connection with mythical and quasi-mythical beings in ancient Ireland.

The survival of early Irish myth in folklore is amply illustrated by the portrayal of several individual personages as functionaries in the landscape, for example **Áine**, **Clíona**, **Donn**, **Fionnbheara**, and it is noticeable that these are usually assimilated to the fairies in the living lore. There is an interesting duality in the folk attitude to these personages and to the fairies themselves. On the one hand they are exalted beings who can be good patrons; but on the other hand they are understood to be on a parallel with humans and even in competition with us, engaged in their own agricultural pursuits and wishing to keep their own sections of the landscape as their special property. This tendency to regard the otherworld community as a parallel to the human one could well be as old as Celtic myth itself, and it is evidenced at all stages of Irish literature. For instance, otherworld women could become the lovers or even wives of mortal men, an idea which is at least as ancient as the theme of the goddess of sovereignty, symbolising **kingship**, who is mate to the reigning king. Such alliances occur again and again in the literature - for examples, see the entries under Aonghus, Art, Bran mac Feabhail, Conaire, Cormac mac Airt, Criomhthann Nia Náir, Cú Chulainn, Diarmaid mac Aodha Sláine, Éadaoin, Fionn mac Cumhaill, Laoghaire mac Criomhthainn, Muircheartach mac Earca, Niall Naoi-ghiallach, Oisín).

The 9th-century account of **Macha** as an otherworld wife is found in a new form in later

Munster folklore. We are told that a certain Earl of Inchiquin (of the Uí Bhriain, the O'Brien family of Co Clare) was one day walking by the side of Lake Inchiquin when he met and fell in love with a beautiful maiden. She became his wife, but laid one condition on him - that he was never to bring any of his friends to the house to see her. They lived happily together, until one day he went to horse-racing, and brought a friend home with him to show him the beautiful wife. Heartbroken at how the Earl had disregarded the prohibition, the lady returned to the lake and was never afterwards seen. This legend parallels that of Mélusine in mediaeval French lore, but is so different in detail that it is obviously not borrowed directly from that source. There was a fashion for mediaeval families on the Continent to claim an otherworld ancestress, and it is likely that the O'Briens adopted it from some such heraldic source prior to the 15th century (see **Cian mac Maolmhuaidhe**). In doing this, they were probably following the fashion set in Ireland by the **FitzGeralds**, who borrowed for themselves the Continental legend of a swan-maiden). The Macha story, however, had been an earlier Irish prototype, and because of the identity of plot it exerted an influence on the imagery of the Inchiquin legend, such as the detail of horse-racing.

The Macha story seems to have been itself an early Irish adoption of the plot to the context of this Ulster horse-goddess, and it seems sensible to suggest that there was in circulation in ancient Ireland some account of a man marrying a spirit-woman and she leaving him when a ritual taboo was broken. The likelihood is that this was an offshoot of the idea that the sacred and much-tabooed office of **kingship** involved taking the land-goddess as mate. A legend found in the folklore of coastal areas of western Ireland sprang from a specific application of the account to the marine context in mediaeval times. We are told that a man once saw a beautiful maiden on a rock by the shore. She had laid aside her cloak, and when he seized this she was in his power. She therefore went home with him and married him. They had several children, and all the time the husband kept the cloak hidden from her. Then one day she discovered the cloak and returned to the sea. Certain families are said to be descendants of this mermaid, and as proof of their origin these families were said to have webbed feet. The legend, some versions of which describe the lady as a seal-maiden rather than a mermaid, spread to Scotland and to Iceland, probably in the late Middle Ages.

All of this raises the much-debated issue of Celtic influence on the romantic literature of mediaeval Europe, especially in so far as fairy lore is concerned. It seems likely, for instance, that the French legend of Mélusine was based on a Celtic, or even an Irish, source; and, whatever the reality behind the problem of the 'Breton lays' in mediaeval French, there was undoubtedly a great Celtic influence on the way in which the fairy realm was portrayed in the Arthurian cycle and its related lore. Continental romance in turn had a marked influence on Irish literature of the late Middle Ages, but little of that influence is mirrored in the folk tradition. The mediaeval Irish attitude to the otherworld did, however, undergo a profound change due to one external influence, that of Christianity. The monks who committed the ancient lore to writing had, from the beginning, been somewhat uncomfortable theologically when describing the otherworld of pre-Christian belief. At times, these writers regarded it as a simple realm of story, at other times they felt compelled to reduce its characters to the plane of ancient history, but when its mythical and spiritual nature became too awkward to handle they resorted to demonising it. Theologians on the Continent were less tolerant, tending to opt exclusively for the latter approach when faced with surviving otherworld beliefs, and they developed a rationale in Biblical terms for the spiritual communities which were popularly believed to live on beside the human one. So the fairies were claimed to have been remnants of the fallen angels who had been driven out of heaven by God after the revolt of Lucifer.

This idea spread to Ireland and was adopted into the lore of the Irish 'sí', probably towards the end of the Middle Ages. It is referred to in a text of the early 15th century, which identifies the fairies with the Tuatha Dé Danann. Describing them as dwellers in mounds and under water, the writer comments: 'Some say that they were demons of a different grade who came with the exiled band of Lucifer from heaven. They assume airy bodies for the purpose of destroying and tempting the descendants of Adam.' Irish folklore developed this portrayal, claiming that, as the fairies fell from heaven, God relented somewhat and said that 'where they are, may they stay there'. Thus the fairies came to inhabit air, land, and water. In order to fill the seats left in heaven by their expulsion, God created the human race with the distinctive trait of having red blood in their bodies, whereas that of the fairies is white. Any whitish coloured liquid seen on the ground in the early morning might accordingly be explained as blood spilt when two hostile groups of fairies clashed and fought a battle during the night.

Having lost their places in heaven, the fairies were believed to be anxious to regain them, and to underline the situation a special Irish folk legend was developed and became very popular. We are told that a priest, while travelling at night, was met by a group of fairies who asked him would they ever gain salvation, and when he answered in the negative they began to wail pitifully. A variant of this has the fairies asking a man to put the question to the priest as he consecrates the Host at Mass. The priest again gives the negative answer, and warns the man that when he goes to tell this to the fairies they will be very angry and he must dig a hole in the ground, enter it, and place a shovel and spade in the form of a cross over himself as protection. The notion that fairies are in contention with humans for places in heaven was further developed as a rationale for why the fairies sometimes abducted people. Thus we are told that they wished to assimilate and intermarry with humans so that their race would gain more red blood, the qualifying trait for the lost seats. Belief in abduction by otherworld beings must be quite ancient in Ireland. The mediaeval literature has several instances of young men and young women being enticed away by the Tuatha Dé (see, for examples, **Cormac mac Airt**, **Cú Chulainn**) and, apart from the context of courtship, such abduction would be a natural explanation for sudden death or unexplained deterioration in health. Fairy-lore, however, mostly concentrates on children and young mothers being taken away. The emphasis on children reflects the function of the fairies as a means of warning children to stay safely near their home, while the vulnerability of the health of young women who have just given birth would have given rise to the belief in their abduction. However, the need for explanation by way of narrative meant that the young mothers would be abducted due to the death of a fairy mother and the resultant need for a wetnurse. Narrative explanations for the abduction of young children were more involved. Boys were said to be especially vulnerable, not only because they were reputedly more able workers but also because of the traditional idea that the male gives more of its properties to offspring and thus more human blood to the fairy race.

Regarding the abduction of children, a legend which spread throughout western Europe became very popular in Ireland. This describes how parents leave their child, who is pining and causing them great worry, in the care of a baby-sitter, usually a tailor. Much to the astonishment of the baby-sitter, the child begins to act like an intelligent adult. He stands up in the cradle and begins to speak of events long ago, perhaps also asking for a drink of liquor or even playing fine music on a set of pipes. Realising what he is, the tailor reddens his pin or some other metal implement in the fire and approaches the child while wielding it. At that the child jumps from the cradle and races screaming out through the door. The baby-sitter warns the departing changeling to send the stolen child back, and soon afterwards the real child, for which the strange creature had been substituted, is returned. A popular formulation of the legend has the baby-sitter applying a special test to the changeling - he heats a drink for it in an egg-shell and, on seeing this, the child laughs and says it has never seen such a silly thing in its long life - thus betraying its real nature.

Another legend, also found throughout Ireland, describes an attempted abduction of a young woman by three strange old women who come on each of three nights to help her at her spinning. Growing suspicious, the young woman on the third night goes to the door and shouts out that the top of the nearby hill is on fire. Duped by this, the three old women race from the house and up the hill to save their otherworld residence from the supposed flames. This legend was inspired by two international folktales - one of which tells of how an impish little man tries to inveigle her child from a young woman by helping her at spinning, and the other telling of how three old women help a girl to spin an impossible amount in one night and thus become the bride of a prince. Particularly developed recensions of the legend state that the three fairy women lived on Slievenamon in Co Tipperary. The name of that eminence, Sliabh na mBan, means literally 'the mountain of the women', and it has a cairn on its top long associated with the otherworld. It may well be that this Irish folk legend originated in that area.

The 'slua sí' can sometimes be understood as a fairy cavalcade abroad at night seeking to take some human away with them for no apparent reason. This appears to be an indigenous Irish theme, in which they are synonymous with the otherworld of the dead, and there are even accounts given of 'fairy funerals' seen at the time of the death of some local person. A legend told in several parts of the country describes how a recently deceased young woman appears to her husband as he sleeps one night and asks him to be in a certain place on the following night, when she will be riding with the fairy host. When the cavalcade comes by, he must watch for the grey horse on which she will be mounted, and if he grabs her without delay she will be returned to him. He goes to the place as directed and sees the cavalcade passing. Among them he recognises several people of his acquaintance who have died. When he rushes to grab his wife, however, the grey horse shies and bolts, and the cavalcade immediately disappears, leaving him alone. The idea upon which this legend was constructed, that of a man recovering his wife from the otherworld, can be traced back in Irish tradition to the 10th century at least, as it occurs in the story of **Éadaoin**.

Common in different parts of Ireland also was a northwest European legend which tells of how a midwife was once called out to tend to a fairy woman who was giving birth. When the child was born, she was given some ointment to rub on it, and by accident rubbed her own eye with the ointment. She was then brought back to her own house safe and well. Some time later, however, she was at a market and recognised one of the men there who had been in the fairy dwelling. She spoke to him, and he realised that she could see him because of the ointment which she had rubbed to her eye. Angered at being thus visible to her, he put his finger in her eye and blinded it. The idea that the fairies are resentful of human intrusion into their world is common. For instance if a house is, either advertently or inadvertently, built over a pathway used by them, great tumult will be heard and items will get flung about. One of the fairies may appear and explain that the dwellers in that house will have no peace until the situation is corrected, either by demolishing the house completely or by removing whatever part of it is blocking the path.

The fairies can, however, be quite benevolent to people in some ways. They might confer gifts or skills on people, and they might even come to the rescue of an individual who badly needed help. Several individuals, especially those with **special powers** of healing, were said to be 'in the fairies' and to travel the countryside with them at night, gaining all types of information in the process. Another Continental legend was adopted to illustrate this notion of quick magical travel, and versions of it were common throughout the country. It concerns a man who meets the fairy host one night, and they invite him to come with them. They give him a special cap and tell him to mount a ragwort-weed as if it were a horse. When he does so he finds himself brought into the air and, travelling thus with the fairy host, comes to a wine-cellar in a foreign country. There he drinks his fill, but when morning comes he finds himself alone and is arrested for breaking into the cellar. He is sentenced to be hanged, and is placed on the gallows with a rope around his neck. He manages, however, to draw the fairy cap from his pocket, and when he puts it on his head he is raised into the air. Soon he finds himself back home, standing beside the ragwort in the very place that he met the fairies.

The Irish fairies were not imagined as being very different in form or appearance to the human race, except that they might be somewhat paler in hue and might be dressed in clothing of silk and satin. The idea that they were smaller in size than humans was not general in Ireland. Similarly, a wide range of activities paralleling those of the human community were attributed to them. They were believed to be ruled by kings and queens, inside their dwellings there were many chambers and great assembly halls, and they often held great feasts. It was usually said, however, that a human visitor who partook of their food could not return to the ordinary world. The fairies engaged in farming, went incognito to the the humans' markets to buy and sell stock, and could appear at will to seek the loan of some implement from a farmer or his wife. They often rewarded those who assisted them in some way. In sport and entertainment, too, their tastes resembled those of humans. Their music, often heard at night, was exceedingly beautiful, and they were much given to hunting and to playing hurley. A story told in many parts of the country concerns a great hurler who was taken away at night to play for a team of fairies in a match against another such team in a field beside a rath. The hurler scores, following which the vision of the match suddenly disappears and he finds himself at home in bed.

The hostile aspect of the fairies included their supposed propensity to shoot tiny darts at fine cattle or fine horses and thus cause them to pine away and belong to them. A ribbon or other piece of cloth of red colour was believed to be an effective protection against them, and various religious amulets were used for that purpose also. Another means of protection arose from the fact that the fairies themselves were very fastidious and disliked anything which was dirty. Therefore, it was believed to be a good thing to keep the foot-water in the house, and in some places it was customary to sprinkle a drop of urine on children before they left the house, so as to keep fairy abducters at bay. Their dwellings may be of many types, all relatively remote from human concourse and all with a certain aura of mystery. The oldest attributions must have been to tumuli and cairns, but in late mediaeval times the no longer understood earthenwork forts (popularly called 'raths', 'lisses' and 'moats') were added. Further variety of location was provided by stone circles, hills, and even invisible caverns in mountainsides, not to mention fanciful underwater palaces. If any person damaged a place believed to be a fairy-dwelling, misfortune or even death would befall him - a belief which was indeed instrumental in preserving many archaeological sites in the countryside. A solitary bush or tree was often regarded as belonging especially to the fairies, and if it were cut down they would similarly exact vengeance.

Although such beliefs in a parallel otherworld community may never have been unanimously held in Ireland, they were widely held at all stages of history, so strongly indeed that stories and superstitions have become intertwined in each other with many kinds of permutations. Rather spontaneous beliefs, too, could spring up. For instance, strange lights seen at night were believed to be the fairies trying to send a benighted traveller astray, and a heavy mist was believed to be caused by them with a similar intent. It was thought necessary to be diplomatic towards the fairies in ordinary human nourishment, for instance the first drops of milk from a cow, or of newly-distilled whiskey, should be thrown into the air for them. The belief that a whirlwind is caused by fairies as they pass by is of a kind likely to be quite ancient, but it must have been reinforced by the similarity in sound of its title 'sí gaoithe' (originally 'sidhe gaoithe' and literally meaning 'thrust of wind') with the word 'sí' (originally 'sidh') for the fairies themselves.

[Indices and discussions] T P Cross (1952), 243-73; Séan Ó Súilleabháin (1942), 450-79 and (1967), 82-6; Caoimhín Ó Danachair (1978), 32; W G Wood-Martin (1902) *2*, 1-25; W Y Evans Wentz (1911); Katharine Briggs (1977) and (1978).

[Dwellings open at November] Kuno Meyer in *Revue Celtique 5*, 202; Ó Súilleabháin (1967), 83.

[Inchiquin legend] Séamus Ó Duilearga (1948), 439; Cross, *op cit*, Motif F302.2; Briggs (1978), 145-50.

[Mermaid legend] Ó Duilearga, *op cit*, 314-6, 438; David Thomson (1965); Séamas Ó Catháin (1985), 28-30, 80-1; Bo Almqvist (1988), 61; IFC, many versions.

[Origin of fairies] R Th Christiansen in *Béaloideas 39-41*, 95-111.

[Tuatha Dé as fallen angels] Toirdhealbhach Ó Raithbheartaigh (1932), 197-201.

[Query re salvation legend] Ó Catháin (1985), 79; Michéal Briody (1977).

[Changeling legend] Séamas Mac Philib (1980).

[Spinning women legend] Ó Súilleabháin / Christiansen (1967), Types 500-501*; Almqvist, *op cit*, 49-53; John Dunne in James Maher ed (1954), 68-9.

[Abducted wife legend] Ó Duilearga, *op cit*, 291-3, 435; Cross, *op cit*, Motifs F322.2-5; B Hunt (1912), 155-8.

[Midwife legend] Christiansen in *Lochlann 6*, 104-17; Críostóir Mac Cárthaigh (1988).

[Fairy cap legend] Christiansen (1958), Type 6050; Briggs (1976), 148-50, 409-12; Ó Duilearga / Dáithí Ó hÓgáin (1981), 257-60; IFC, several versions.

[Anthologies] Ó Duilearga (1948), 291-323, 434-40; Dermot MacManus (1959); Séan Ó hEochaidh / Máire Ní Néill / Séamas Ó Catháin (1977).

FEAR DIADH Mythical or fictional warrior in the **Ulster Cycle**.

Several variants of his name are found in the mediaeval literature - including Fer Déa ('man of a goddess'), Fer Deoda ('divine man'), Fer Dedh ('man of fire'). One variant, Fer Deadh, preserves what is apparently the original meaning. An earlier form of this would have been Fer Dedad or in the plural Fir Dedad, which looks like a tribal name. In fact, the many **Érainn** were often called Clann Dedad, which is equivalent in meaning to

Fir Dedad. The identifying element 'Ded' for the Érainn tended to become confused with the different word 'déa' (goddess). This latter was in use as a name of several rivers, one of which was in northeast Leinster - the river Dee. It is apparent that, due to a confusion of the words, the territory through which this river flowed was fancifully regarded as having anciently belonged to the Fir Dedad. Accordingly, a ford ('áth') on that river was given its name from this people and known as Áth Fher Dedad.

Etymology, be it true or false, was regarded by the mediaeval writers as crucial to the acceptance and development of lore. In the Cycle the river Dee is called by an alternative name, Níth, which suggests that these writers did indeed regard the word Déa as an ancient population name pertaining to the surrounding territory. This people, the Fir Dedad, would have been quite obscure in the context, and so their designation could easily be reshaped into an imagined heroic personage of old. Moreover, the obscure name of that personage was given a new form and interpretation, Fer Diad (literally 'man of smoke'). To the compilers of the literature, and doubtlessly also to their oral sources, it presented no problem to identify the ford on the river Dee with this particular character, and so that ford became known as Áth Fhir Diadh (later anglicised as Ardee, in Co Louth). The proximity of this to the area of the cult of **Cú Chulainn** meant that a connection could be made between the two warriors. The first mention of the warrior Fear Diadh is in a text written in or about the 9th-century. He is there described as son of **Fearghus mac Róich** and slayer of **Ceithearn mac Fionntain**, and it is clear from this that he had already by that time become associated with the Ulster Cycle.

As that cycle developed and its characters became synchronised, Cú Chulainn and Fear Diadh were represented as having as youths been trained in arms together. Thus in a 10th-century text we are told that they were educated by the female warrior Scáthach in Scotland. One of the other students of Scáthach was one Lóch Mór, who is represented in the epical story *Táin Bó Cúailnge* (see **Ulster Cycle**) as a former companion who was slain in single combat by Cú Chulainn. There are several indications that it was on the pattern of this episode that a combat between Fear Diadh and Cú Chulainn was introduced into the text of the *Táin* in the 11th century. Lóch is described as having a horny skin ('conganchnes') which entails that he cannot be killed by ordinary means, and Cú Chulainn has to use his deadly javelin, the 'ga bolga', to achieve his purpose. Both details are repeated in the account of Fear Diadh's clash with the great hero. Again, the *Táin* describes how another young comrade of Cú Chulainn, called Fear Baoth, is weaned away from his friendship by queen **Meadhbh**, who offers her daughter Fionnabhair to him if he will fight Cú Chulainn. This is repeated also in the case of Fear Diadh. Furthermore, the *Táin* account shows signs of forced rearrangement in order to make Fear Diadh fit into the context. He had been, for some reason, described as the son of Damhán, and the writer who planned his introduction into the *Táin* used phonemic similarity to add a wider dimension to this patronymic. Thus he described Fear Diadh as coming from Iorras Domhnann (Erris in Co Mayo). The Domhnainn sept of that area were reputed to be one of the fiercest fighting groups in Meadhbh's army, and it was thus considered appropriate to identify Fear Diadh as one of them, even though such a western origin contradicted the ambit which he shared with Cú Chulainn.

The inserted episode in the *Táin* has Fear Diadh at first refusing to fight Cú Chulainn on account of their friendship. Meadhbh plied him with drink and offered her daughter to him, but he continued to refuse until she lyingly suggested that Cú Chulainn had boasted of superiority over him. So he went to face his former comrade in single combat, a combat which is made to accord with tradition by situating it at Áth Fhir Diadh. The confrontation at the ford of the two erstwhile friends is described with great drama. In the first recension of the *Táin*, Fear Diadh insults his opponent by calling him a squint-eyed fellow and the two then fight fiercely, using all their tricks learnt from Scáthach. Cú Chulainn, however, has his charioteer Laogh pass the 'ga bolga' downstream to him and, catching this between his toes, he casts it into the anus of Fear Diadh. The latter lowers his shield, and Cú Chulainn pierces him through the heart. Badly wounded himself from the combat, Cú Chulainn then laments his fallen friend. This account is amplified in the later recensions to include a preliminary conversation between the warriors in which each beseeches the other to withdraw from the ford and in which they dolorously recall their past friendship. They are described as fighting for four days before Fear Diadh is slain. Each evening after the first two days fighting they embrace each other and exchange food, drink, and healing herbs. On the third evening, however, they break off all contact, and after a fierce conflict Cú Chulainn slays him with the 'ga bolga'. Fear Diadh dies in the arms of his friend turned foe.

This is the only major episode in the whole tradition which features Fear Diadh. He is mentioned incidentally in other texts, and figures as a comrade in arms in some postmediaeval romances concerning Cú Chulainn (q.v.).

Kuno Meyer in *Zeitschrift für celtische Philologie 8*, 305; A G Van Hamel (1933), 49; Cecile O'Rahilly (1976), 78-95, 275 and (1970), 71-100 and (1961), 83-110; R I Best in *Zeitschrift für celtische Philologie 10*, 274-308; Max Nettlau in *Revue Celtique 10*, 330-46 and *11*, 23-32, 318-43. For an alternative understanding of the name, see E P Hamp in *Ériu 33*, 178.

FEARDHOMHAIN Mythical or fictional young warrior in the **Fianna Cycle**. The name seems to have been a common one, meaning 'minor' or 'young man'.

The mediaeval literature mentions him several times as one of the followers of **Fionn mac Cumhaill**. It varies as to his identity, but generally regards him as a Leinster scion. Texts from the 11th to the 13th century give varying recensions of a story concerning his tragic death. According to this story, he had a sister called Finnine and she was either illtreated or killed by her husband, Conán mac an Léith Luachra, as a result of which Feardhomhain engaged Conán in combat, and both were slain in the fierce duel. There is an indication that Fionn was in some way responsible for the tragedy. Another mediaeval source mentions how Feardhomhain slew a monster in Loch Lurgan (a lake west of the bog of Allen in Co Offaly), and there can be little doubt but that a substantial literary account of Feardhomhain once existed, though it is now lost.

An oral story, very popular in the folklore of Co Donegal, seems to be based on that lost text. A folk identification of Loch Fhinne (Lough Finn) in that county with Finnine was the probable reason for the survival of the story in this form. We are told that Fionn wished to bring about the death of Feardhomhain and, knowing him to be a brave youth, advised him to avoid a fierce pig which inhabited a certain glen. Feardhomhain, as expected by Fionn, went to the glen with his three dogs. Each dog was killed in turn by the pig, and then Feardhomhain and the fierce beast fell fighting each other. The young hero's sister, called Finngheal, went to assist him, but she was drowned in Lough Finn in her haste.

There are elements in this story concerning Feardhomhain which seem to have been unknown to the mediaeval writers, and the likelihood therefore is that the lost literary romance was written like other works of its kind in the 16th or 17th century. Its author would have read the mentions of Feardhomhain in the earlier texts, from which he took the character of Feardhomhain's sister and the theme of Fionn's treachery. He portrayed the water-monster slain by Feardhomhain as a fierce pig, for he knew of the situation whereby a brave youth acts on ambiguous advice concerning such an animal from the biography of Fionn (q.v.) himself, as well as from the story of **Diarmaid ua Duibhne**.

P L Henry in *Ériu 18*, 158-9; Whitley Stokes (1900), 78-9, 101-2, 113, 123-4, 355; M E Dobbs in *Ériu 14*, 166-9; Eoin Mac Néill (1908), 13, 12-3, 25; Myles Dillon in *Ériu 11*, 44; Edward Gwynn (1924), 362-7; Charles Plummer (1910) *2*, 250; Gerard Murphy (1953), 3-6, 181; Séamas Ó Catháin (1985), 69-70, 85-6; Dáithí Ó hÓgáin (1988), 255-7, 341, 358.

FEARGHAL MAC MAOLDÚIN High-king of Ireland from 710 to 722 AD. He died in that year in battle against Leinster, a battle which is the subject of the text *Cath Almaine*, composed in the 10th century and rewritten some time later.

The original author derived the character and general milieu from the historical annals and dramatised these in his narrative. According to the text, Fearghal and the Munster king **Cathal mac Fionghuine** were old adversaries, but peace was arranged between them. Fearghal planned to invade Leinster to collect the **bóraimhe** tribute, and he gathered a large army for this purpose. One of his recruits was a youth called Donn Bó, a widow's son, whose mother allowed him to go only on his safety being pledged. The invasion force went astray in the winter weather and Fearghal's men took from a leper his only cow and burned his house. The leper cursed them for this. At their camp, Fearghal called on Donn Bó to entertain the company, for he was the best in Ireland at storytelling and poetry and music. Donn Bó refused, however, and the jester told stories instead. At Almhain (Allen, Co Kildare), the Leinster army opposed them in a fierce battle, and both Fearghal and Donn Bó were slain.

That night the Leinstermen held a triumphant

feast, and when one of them went out to the battlefield he heard the voices of the dead singing for Fearghal and their musicians playing. The voice of Donn Bó was the sweetest of all, and so the Leinsterman brought that head into the feast. It was placed on a pillar and, when asked to sing for the men of Leinster it turned to the wall so as to be in darkness, and then sang. All the company wept, so sad was its voice. When brought back to the battlefield, the head asked to be replaced on its body and, when this was done, Donn Bó revived and so returned safe to his mother as pledged. Cathal mac Fionghuine, however, was angry at the slaying of Fearghal, with whom he had made peace. To placate him, his erstwhile Leinster allies brought the head of the high-king to a feast at Gleann Damhain (Glanworth, Co Cork) where Cathal was then residing. Cathal had the head washed and combed and dressed in satin, and then prepared a great feast. The head blushed in the presence of the Munstermen and thanked God for the reverence shown to it, after which the feast was distributed among the poor. Cathal then brought the head back to the Uí Néill, Fearghal's royal sept.

The most striking aspect of this story is the motif of the speaking heads of the dead. This was an ancient feature of warrior-lore (see **Conall Cearnach** and **Fionn mac Cumhaill**), to which the author of this narrative gave an aura of mystery and of pathos. Fearghal was the father of two other celebrated highkings, **Aodh Állan** and **Niall Frasach**.

Pádraig Ó Riain (1978); John O'Donovan (1860), 20-49; R A S Macalister (1956), 384-9.

FEARGHUS MAC LÉIDE (earlier, Fergus mac Léte) Mythical king of Ulster. He seems to have originally been a double of the better known mythical king of the province, **Fearghus mac Róich**, and as such would be another version in saga of the patron deity of ancient Ulster kingship.

The major account of him dates from the late 7th or early 8th century. According to this, he gave his protection to Eochaidh 'Yellow-Mouth', who had been exiled by **Conn Céadchathach**. When Eochaidh was slain by Conn's men, Fearghus demanded compensation. This was agreed, and it included the handing over of a parcel of land called Níth to Conn, as well as the handing over of the mother of one of the assassins. She was Dorn, a noblewoman of Conn's people, and she was treated by Fearghus as a menial servant. Soon after this, Fearghus went on a trip to the sea-coast with his charioteer, and fell asleep there. Sprites ('luchorpáin' - see **Leprechaun**) came to him and took away his sword. Then they carried him to the sea, and when his feet touched the water he awoke and seized three of the sprites. He demanded that they grant him three wishes, viz. the power of swimming under seas and pools and lakes. His desire was granted to him, with the stated exception of going under Loch Rudhraighe in his own territory (i.e. Dundrum Bay in Co Down). Time passed, and one day Fearghus decided to swim under Loch Rudhraighe. While in the lake he encountered a dreadful monster ('muirdris'), which alternately inflated and contracted itself like a bellows. At the sight of it his mouth was turned to the back of his head, and he fled to the land. He fell asleep there, and the charioteer went to the wise men of Ulster at the court of Eamhain Mhacha. Realising that a man with a blemish should not be king (see **Kingship**), but wishing to retain Fearghus in that office, the wise men decided to conceal the blemish. They arranged that only nobles would attend him in his palace, and this stratagem succeeded for seven full years. Fearghus remained unaware of his condition, but one day the enslaved Dorn was washing his head. Judging that she was working too slowly, Fearghus struck her with a whip, whereupon she was overcome by anger and taunted him with the blemish. He cut her in two with his sword, and then went straight to Loch Rudhraighe to contend with the monster. For a day and a night they fought in the water, and eventually Fearghus emerged showing the head of the slain monster to the Ulstermen. Overcome by his efforts, however, he fell down dead, and for a whole month the bay remained red from the struggle which had taken place there.

Some early myth obviously lies behind this account. We are told that the sprites put into his ears herbs which enabled him to be a prodigious swimmer, and a variant description has one of them giving him a cloak which, when wound around his head, gave him the power. It is noteworthy that his supposed double Fearghus mac Róich is portrayed as a great swimmer who is also killed while in water, and this suggests that some aquatic symbolism attached to the ritual of ancient Ulster kingship. Some further support for this is given by the classification of Tonn Rudhraighe (the tide in Dundrum Bay) among the great waves of Ireland which cried out upon the death of a king. It is likely that such aquatic symbolism combined with memories of a 4th-5th century conflict between the Ulstermen and the Connachta sept at **Tara** (see **Ulster Cycle**), and that the result was the legend of how Conn gave to Fearghus the land and woman as compensation. This much is indeed described in a poem predating the text which has been summarised here. The poem mentions Dorn's taunt to Fearghus and states that the latter was killed in Loch Rudhraighe. The monster is not mentioned, and both it and the sprites must be an addition to the legend. They are apparently derived from the influential writings of the early 7th-century scholar Isidore of Seville, who describes such fantastic sea-dwelling creatures.

Around the 13th-century some writer developed the story of Fearghus' death into a burlesque narrative, laying greatest stress on the sprites. According to this, on the very night that Fearghus hosted a great banquet at Eamhain Mhacha, the king of the land of the leprechauns hosted a feast for his own people. This king, called Iubhdán, boasted of the greatness of his warriors, but his poet Eisirt burst out laughing, saying that one of Fearghus' warriors could overcome all of Iubhdán's battalions. Eisirt was allowed to depart in order to prove his assertions, and he travelled to Ulster, where he was received with much amusement. He was so small that he could stand on the palm of Fearghus' dwarf-poet Aodh. After three days and three nights Eisirt, accompanied by Aodh, returned to his own country. Iubhdán and his court were terrified when they saw the 'giant' Aodh, and Iubhdán decided to go himself to see Ulster. He set out, with his queen Bébó, and arrived secretly at Eamhain Mhacha by night. Attempting to eat porridge there, he fell into the cauldron and was rescued next morning by the amused courtiers. Fearghus ordered that he be put with the rabble of the household, but relented when Iubhdán promised to remain with him. He was accordingly given excellent quarters, and he and his queen became celebrities in Eamhain Mhacha. Eventually the leprechaun people came with seven battalions to take him back. They bargained for his release, using both threats and offers of ransom. The only ransom which Fearghus would accept was Iubhdán's shoes, and so the leprechaun king was released. The reason why Fearghus desired the shoes was that he had, previously, while swimming in Loch Rudhraighe, encountered a monster ('sinach') there and had barely escaped with his life. The monster's breath had twisted his mouth towards the back of his head. The blemish was kept a secret from him until one day he and his queen quarrelled over precedence in the use of the bath stone. He struck her, breaking one of her teeth, and she in anger told him of his blemish. He therefore chose Iubhdán's shoes, for he believed that they could protect him when he went to encounter the monster again. Accordingly, he confronted it a second time, and in a ferocious fight slew it with his great sword (called the 'caladhcholg'). But the monsters vicious tooth tore his heart, and so he expired, mourned by his poet Aodh and the rest of the Ulster people.

It has been suggested that a manuscript version of this story was read in English to Jonathan **Swift**, and that he got from it the idea of contrasting a land of giants and a land of pygmies which is the basis of his famous work *Gulliver's Travels*. At the other end of the timescale, it is believed that the sword of Fearghus derives from ancient Celtic myth. The mediaeval literature lists Fearghus mac Léide among the several heroes who for a time had possession of the 'caladhcholg', and for his part Fearghus mac Róich was also the wielder of a great sword. Another mythical Ulster king, who seems ultimately to be identical with both of these, was known as Fearghus Foga (literally, 'Fearghus of the Spear'). He was said to have been the inventor of the spear, and it emerges from this that a typical weapon of great warriors was associated with the personification of Ulster kingship. It has been argued that such a great weapon, called 'bolgos' (meaning 'lightning') was an attribute of the original Celtic war-deity, and it is significant that in Irish the compound 'caladhbholg' (i.e. 'hard-spear') was used to designate a fearsome weapon of war. The word 'bolg' was easily confused with the ordinary word for a bag (see **Fir Bolg**), and since 'colg' means a sword it was natural that 'caladhcholg' should be substituted for the earlier form, so the typical weapon became a sword. In Welsh sources it is also a sword, though the original 'bolgos' survived there in its aspirated form, viz. 'caledvwlch' - hence Arthur's great 'Caliburnus' or 'Excalibur' in later romantic literature.

Apart from the saga of his death, Fearghus mac Léide is given an occasional background role in the developed **Ulster Cycle** in the Middle Ages. As if to echo their ultimate identity, he is there stated to have been 'the close colleague of Fearghus mac Róich'. He is given a major role in the post-mediaeval romance of **Conghal Cláiringneach**. Here it is said that the province of Ulster was divided between himself and Conghal, but relations broke down between them and Fearghus was defeated in battle by Conghal and deprived of his realm.

[Early texts on his death] D A Binchy in *Ériu 16*, 33-48.

[Isidore influence] James Carney (1955), 125.

[Burlesque text] Standish H O'Grady (1892) *1*, 238-52.

[Possible influence on Swift] Vivian Mercier (1962), 27-31, 187-8.

[Name of sword] T F O'Rahilly (1946), 43-74.

[Fearghus Foga] O'Rahilly (1946), 68, 226-8.

[General] D A Binchy in Myles Dillon ed (1968), 40-52.

FEARGHUS MAC RÓICH Mythical king and seneschal in the **Ulster Cycle**.

The name Fearghus (earlier, Fergus) meant 'virility'; and the original form of his patronymic, 'ró-ech', meant 'great stallion'. He is represented as possessing great sexual energy, having large genitals and requiring seven women to satisfy him. Several other figures in the regnal lists of the ancient Ulaidh people (from whom the province of Ulster got its name) were also called Fearghus, and since these lists were fabricated from myth it is apparent that the name had some ritual significance. He was sometimes referred to as Fearghus mac Rosa Ruaidh, which designation must be of secondary origin. According to this tradition, his mother had the unlikely name, for a woman, of 'Róch', and his father was Ros Ruadh son of Rudhraighe (for whom see **Ulster Cycle**). There can be little doubt, however, that this Ros Ruadh originated in an attempt by genealogists to connect the Ulaidh with the prestigious cult of the Boyne valley (see **Find** and **Ruadh Ró-fheasa**). Otherwise the character of Fearghus mac Róich springs from genuine ancient Ulster tradition. We are told in the literature that he was king of the province at first and that he later became seneschal. This is a strange arrangement biographically, and it suggests that he was anciently regarded as an original king of Ulster who was the patron of successors to that office. In all probability 'fergus' had once been a cultic attribute of kingship, entailing equine imagery (see **Eochaidh**), and had in time become a cult name for the monarchs of the Ulaidh people. When the fortunes of the Ulaidh waned in the 4th and 5th centuries AD, this attribute and its mythic personification would have been understood as in some way abandoning them.

40. FEARGHUS MAC RÓICH *The Lia Fáil at Tara, known locally as 'Bod Fhearghusa'.*

There is evidence that Fearghus mac Róich was a leading figure in the saga *Táin Bó Cuailnge* (see **Ulster Cycle**) from its inception. An obscure verse-text which dates from the early 7th century has him deserting his own people because of his attachment to queen **Meadhbh**, and further states that, having been proclaimed by the Ulster king

Conchobhar mac Neasa, he and his associates went south to **Tara**. A somewhat later text *Fochond Loingse Fergusa meic Róig*, describing the cause of his exile, has him resenting the lavish way in which Conchobhar entertains strangers compared to the lack of respect shown for himself, and has him dallying with Meadhbh unknown to her husband when he reaches her court. The motif that Fearghus had left Ulster and joined the foe was obviously open to several rationalisations. In the biography of Conchobhar we are told that he was tricked out of the throne. He was king of Ulster until falling in love with Neas, the mother of Conchobhar, and she agreed to become his wife on condition that he relinquish the kingship to her son for a year. When the year was ended, the nobles of the province were so pleased with Conchobhar that they decided to keep him permanently in the office, and Fearghus was displaced. Yet another account has Fearghus being banished by the ambitious Conchobhar and going to Tara where king Eochaidh Feidhleach gave him his daughter in marriage. From there he commenced a war against Conchobhar and, when peace was eventually restored between them, Fearghus was allowed to return to Ulster and was made seneschal. This, despite the confused rationalising, preserves an echo of an original role as patron of the monarchy.

The notion that Fearghus became seneschal neutralised the theme of desertion, but it did not obliterate it, and so a new explanation was felt necessary. This was done by having him desert the province a second time, and a plot was adopted from floating lore external to the Ulster Cycle, one which also had a woman as the cause of conflict between two men. Thus the tragic story concerning **Deirdre** came into existence. Memory of Fearghus' cult was weakening, and here he was confined to a secondary role in the action, being not the lover of Deirdre but her guarantor. We are told that he deserted Conchobhar after that king had treacherously violated his sureties for the beautiful young woman and her lover. Fearghus declared war on Conchobhar, burned the royal fortress of Eamhain Mhacha, ravaged the province, and departed with many Ulster warriors to the hostile court of Meadhbh in Connacht. Later he fell in love with **Fliodhais**, wife of the king of the Gamhanra sept (who lived in the Erris area of Mayo). She abandoned her husband, who was slain and his fortress plundered by Fearghus. Fliodhais then became Fearghus' wife, and she brought her great herd of cattle to him.

The literature also states that, in retaliation for his desertion, Conchobhar had all of Fearghus' kin who remained in Ulster slaughtered. Fearghus thirsted for revenge, and was thus in the forefront when Meadhbh launched her great attack on Ulster in *Táin Bó Cuailnge*. His loyalties were, however, divided as he had not lost his affection for Ulster and, since he had once been the tutor in arms of **Cú Chulainn**, he resorted to several ruses to protect his native province and in particular his beloved pupil. He was the owner of a great sword (see **Fearghus mac Léide**), which was stolen from him by **Ailill mac Máta**, when the latter had discovered him dallying with his wife Meadhbh (q.v.). Ailill restored this sword to him before the final great battle in the *Táin*, and with it he sheared the heads off three hills so as to quench his martial vigour and not wreak havoc on his fellow Ulstermen.

When the great campaign was over Fearghus grew homesick and returned to Ulster against Meadhbh's wishes. He settled in the south-east of the province and remained there until his wife Fliodhais died. Then, in yet another departure, he went back to Meadhbh's court at Cruachain (Rathcroghan, Co Roscommon). He went swimming once in a lake called Loch Finn, near Cruachain, and so great a swimmer was he that all of the gravel and stones from the bottom of the lake came to the surface. Meadhbh dived in after him and entwined herself about him, and he swam thus around the lake. Her husband Ailill, growing jealous, remarked to his brother, the blind **poet** Lughaidh, that 'the stag and the doe are acting splendidly in the lake' and encouraged the oracular Lughaidh to cast a javelin at them. This Lughaidh did, with unerring aim, and the javelin struck Fearghus in the breast. The great man managed to swim ashore before he died, and he was buried in that place. The motif of death in water is apparently part of the ancient lore concerning him (see **Fearghus mac Léide**), but otherwise this story is a creation of the 10th or 11th century. The original tradition - as evidenced by the 7th century text - was that Fearghus had met his death at Látharna (Larne, Co Antrim). The nearby town of Carraig Fhearghuis (Carrickfergus) seems to have taken its name from the original local tradition of the Ulaidh.

Although the sexual prowess of Fearghus, and his association with women like Neas, Meadhbh, and Fliodhais must represent old tradition, most of the narratives concerning him which are found in the literature were invented as linkages in the complex of lore which centred on *Táin Bó Cuailgne.* This function is brought out clearly in the idea (which first appears in 12th-century sources) that he was responsible for the preservation of the *Táin* epic itself. According to this, the story of the great cattle-raid had been lost and the poets of Ireland failed to recover more than a few fragments of it. The chief-poet **Seanchán** began a great quest for the story, and success was finally achieved by going to the grave of Fearghus beside Loch Finn and addressing an incantation to the dead warrior. Fearghus arose from the grave, surrounded by a mist, and revealed the story from beginning to end before returning to the clay.

Fearghus mac Róich does not figure prominently in the later literature. He is described in one 11th-century text as travelling to Spain to avenge a Munster chieftain who was beheaded by marauders, and he is given background roles in the post-mediaeval romance of **Conghal Cláiringneach** and in some rambling literary tales of the 17th century (for sources see **Cú Chulainn**). Little memory of him survives in folklore, apart from some examples of the story of Fliodhais (q.v.) collected in Co Mayo. When he was driving away the cattle-herd of Fliodhais from the Erris peninsula, it is said, a giant slew him with holly-darts shot from a bow. This giant, called 'the Fool of Barr Uisce', pretended to be a simpleton, whereas in reality he was a very clever fellow. This is obviously a distorted echo from the manuscript descriptions of how Fearghus was killed by the blind poet Lughaidh. The hero's grave was pointed out at Tammy, north-east of Bangor-Erris, but this was but one of several onomastic identifications - no doubt inspired by the tradition of how the poets sought out his grave. The most striking onomastic detail echoes his basic image of virility, for the upright stone at Tara (q.v.) was known to local Irish-speakers in the 19th century as 'bod Fhearghusa' (i.e. the phallus of Fearghus).

[Origins and sexuality] T F O'Rahilly (1946), 480-1; F J Byrne (1973), 51-2; Whitley Stokes in *Ériu 4*, 26; M E Dobbs in *Ériu 8*, 136.

[7th-century text] Kuno Meyer in *Zeitschrift für celtische Philologie 8*, 305-7; James Carney in *Ériu 22*, 73-80.

[Fochond text] Vernam Hull in *Zeitschrift für celtische Philologie 18*, 293-8; Donald MacKinnon in *Celtic Review 1*, 208-27.

[Other accounts] see **Conchobhar mac Neasa**, **Deirdre**, **Fliodhais**, **Cú Chulainn**.

[Dallying with Meadhbh and loss of sword]: Cecile O'Rahilly (1976), 76 and (1970), 68; MacKinnon, *op cit*, 228-9.

[Mediaeval account of death] Meyer (1906), 32-5.

[Spanish sojourn] Edward Gwynn (1924), 346-51.

[Bod Fhearghusa]: Byrne (1973), 51.

[General Accounts] Cormac Ó Cadhlaigh (1956), 38-42, 228-33, 267-83, 439-46, 473-4.

FÉICHÍN Saint who died in 665 AD, founder of a monastery at Fobhar (Fore, Co Westmeath) and at several other places. His name was a common one in early Ireland, and meant literally 'little raven'.

Concerning his life, one Latin text and two Irish ones survive. One of the Irish texts may be a translation from the original but lost Latin biography which was compiled in or about the 9th century in one of the monasteries founded by the saint. We read that his coming had been prophesied by **Colm Cille**, and that his father Caolcharna was of the royal Uí Néill sept of **Tara** and his mother Lasair was of the royal Eoghanacht sept of Munster. As a baby, he used to be put sleeping between his parents, but when morning came they would find him on the bare floor with his arms outstretched in the form of a cross. A flock of angels hovered over his head, and as he grew up he performed many miracles. Having been educated at the monastery of St Náithí at Achadh Chonaire (Achonry, Co Sligo), he was instructed by an angel to go and found a monastery at Iomaidh (Omey Island, off the Galway coast).

He reputedly had several dealings with the joint high-kings, the brothers **Diarmaid mac Aodha Sláine** and Bláthmhac. We read that he sought recognition for their claims from their predecessor as high-king, **Domhnall mac Aodha**. Domhnall at first refused Féichín's request, but the saint fasted against him and brought snowdrifts to his kingdom and a fiery sword between himself and his queen. Domhnall then relented, but the royal druid - who continued to oppose the saint, was swallowed up by the ground. Notwithstanding this account of his friendship towards them, Diarmaid and Bláthmhac are sometimes represented as in conflict with Féichín. Once, when Bláthmhac seized hostages from him, he caused that king's fortress to burst into flames and thereby gained his submission. On another occasion, Diarmaid had seized a friend of Féichín, called Aodán. Féichín went to the royal fortress, miraculously entered through the closed gates, and caused a man who opposed him there to drop dead. On restoring the man to life, he was allowed to take Aodán with him. This Aodán, who became one of Féichín's monks, was the strongest man of his time, with a huge stomach, and the saint was sore pressed to limit his appetite.

Having been instructed by an angel to go to Fore, Féichín set up his famous monastery there. We read that he never sought the help of kings or nobles, for fear of slipping into arrogance. He was, however, assisted by the generous Connacht king **Guaire** in time of famine. The queen of the high-king Diarmaid also assisted him in looking after a leper, whom Féichín carried on his back to her fortress. This leper was Christ himself in disguise, and he left a crozier as a gift for the saint. When on an urgent journey once to secure the release of a hostage, one of Féichín's chariot-horses dropped dead, and a water-horse from a nearby river-pool came and took its place. The hostage was beng held by the king of Leinster, Ailill mac Dúnlaing, at Dún Náis (Naas, Co Kildare), and when Ailill refused to release him an earthquake shook that place and the chains fell off all the hostages there. Ailill died, but was returned to life by Féichín in return for the release of the hostages and an end to the tribute paid by the saint to him for the site of Fore. Féichín returned the strange animal to its pool, instructing it to never again appear to man (see **horses**). The biography claims that, when Féichín died, a multi-coloured column was seen ascending from Fore to heaven, and for the following seven days the devil and his minions found it impossible to visit Ireland.

One mediaeval source gives a speculative little anecdote by way of explaining the saint's name. We read that, when he was a child, his mother noticed him one day gnawing a bone and remarked 'yonder is my little raven!' As well as Féichín, the saint was sometimes referred to by a hypocoristic form of his name, Mo-éca. His memory survives in the folklore of the Fore area, the monastery there being reputed to have 'seven wonders' associated with it. These are the situation of the edifice over a bog, the image of an anchorite in a stone, water in a well which will not boil, a mill without a mill-stream, a stream which flows uphill, a tree the timber of which will not burn, and a massive stone lintel raised by an angel over the church-entrance in response to Féichín's prayers. His feastday is January 20.

J F Kenney (1929), 458-9; Whitley Stokes (1905), 48-9, 421 and in *Revue Celtique 12*, 318-53; Charles Plummer (1910) *2*, 76-86; John O'Hanlon (1875) *1*, 356-82; Ordnance Survey Letters - Westmeath (1837), 1-28, 80-5 and Louth (1835-6), 41-3, 47-8; IFC 62:264, 75:64-6/158-9, 656:83-115, 946:201-2, 1133:50-5/69-70, 1160:551-3.

FEIDHLIMIDH MAC CRIOMHTHAINN (770-847 AD) king of Munster from 820, and also celebrated as an ecclesiastic.

He became a lay-member of the ascetic community of monks called 'céilí Dé' ('companions of God'), and also reputedly held the office of bishop of Cashel. A renowned warrior, he gained several victories in battle over Munster rivals, over the royal Uí Néill, and over the men of Connacht and of Leinster. As well as his military triumphs, he forced many monasteries to submit to his ecclesiastical authority. In the year 837 he met the high-king Niall Caille at the monastery of Clonfert (in Co Galway) and they arranged a pact of non-aggression between them. However, they clashed three years later at Carman (Wexford). Feidhlimidh was defeated in the battle and, in his flight, left his crozier behind him in the brambles.

Feidhlimidh had quite a reputation for composing extempore verse, and the mediaeval literature cites anecdotes concerning repartée between him and various characters. One such has him arguing in verse with a young cleric by the Samhaoir (Morning Star river in Co Limerick); and another has a cleric of the Uí Chormaic sept (of Co Clare), as he sang to the harp, poetically seeking Feidhlimidh's help against those who had laid waste his monastery. Yet another has the king expounding in verse a crude witticism concerning a senior of Clonmacnoise, after he had ravaged that Leinster monastery. We read that Feidhlimidh had previously been refused hospitality by the senior while travelling outside his own territory disguised as a pauper and accompanied by his wife, servant, and dog. Now he triumphantly ordered in verse how the foul reception accorded to him on that occasion be avenged. The wife, servant, and dog of the senior should be joined with the senior himself by the nose of each being put into the anus of another.

A longer text, written in the 11th century, describes Feidhlimidh going on his royal circuit to west Munster. It was snowing heavily and, since there was nowhere else to go, he decided to visit the house of the satirist Gulaidhe at Áth Lóiche (Dunloe, Co Kerry). This Gulaidhe had often benefited from the king's bounty, but he was himself a bitter and stingy old fellow. He had a young daughter who was just as sharp in her speech as himself and, on hearing the king's arrival trumpeted outside, he sent this girl to greet the visitors. She spoke to Feidhlimidh in rich rhetoric, protesting that everything was miserable and scanty about the house. So daunted was the king by her speech that he offered her a large tract of land, and she then took him by the hand and led him into the house. For three days he was entertained there with fine food.

A longer version of this story, in modernised form, is found in manuscripts from the 17th century onwards. In it the satirist is called Gul, and his daughter is called Sadhbh and is allotted a much developed series of stylised and slick replies. She routs the three leading poets of Feidhlimidh with her clever remarks when she comes upon them relieving themselves. 'The poets were bulled together,' she says, and they state that she should tie the newly-born calves, but she retorts that the cows should first be allowed to lick their calves! When, having been well entertained, Feidhlimidh is leaving the house, he promises her a gift the next time he meets her. She slips out through a backdoor and meets him outside, and he therefore is constrained to give her his suit and his horse. Feidhlimidh sends a scholar called Donnúir to seduce the girl, and after Donnúir succeeds he goes to Feidhlimidh's palace at Cashel seeking payment. At table, Donnúir insists on dividing the goose, which he rhetorically does and allots the major portion to himself.

Most of the jokes and anecdotes found in these texts seem to have been borrowed from folklore, and some are still to be found in oral tradition quite independent of Feidhlimidh (see **Poets**). The account of the smart girl outwitting the king has the appearance of a distorted version of a popular folklore plot (see **Romantic Tales**, Type 875) and the expanded version of that story has taken into its ambit another such plot (see **Humorous Tales**, Type 1533). This expanded version has, in its turn, had an influence on the folklore concerning poets, particularly in Munster, where manuscripts of it were quite popular.

In the Munster literature Feidhlimidh appears as 'a brave, saintly, and well-spoken king' who travelled around with a bishop at each shoulder and surrounded by clerics and wise advisers. In other words, he was seen as a sort of Irish Charlemagne, a role which possibly he himself tried to emulate. Like the Frankish Emperor, he was even regarded by some as a saint, and - doubtlessly under Munster influence - August 28 was allotted to him as a feastday. The infamy of his deeds was, however, remembered elsewhere, and the annals report that his death resulted from the destruction by him of the famous monastery of Clonmacnoise in the year 846. When he returned home to Munster after this escapade, he dreamed one night that he was visited by the patron-saint of the monastery, **Ciarán**, who prodded him in the stomach with his crozier. As a result of this, Feidhlimidh was overtaken by a 'flux of the belly', from which affliction he died in the following year.

[Biographical] Séan Mac Airt (1951), 114-5, 124-31; Denis Murphy (1896), 131-40; John O'Donovan (1848) *1*, 434-73; Kathleen Hughes (1966), 182-212; F J Byrne (1973), 211-29.

[Anecdotes and poetry] Kuno Meyer in *Zeitschrift für celtische Philologie 3*, 34 and *5*, 500 and *10*, 44-5; Tadhg Ó Donnchadha (1940), 95-103.

[Story of clever girl] Kuno Meyer (1894), 65-9; Tomás Ó Gallchobhair (1915), 93-114.

See also **Mis**.

FEIRCHEIRDNE (earlier, Ferchertne); A mythical poet, who occurs in a number of different contexts in the early literature. His name is a personification, meaning 'man of precise craft', the craft referred to being poetry. To the writers, such a name was suggestive of a **poet** par excellence, and thus it could serve as an archetype of the profession in whatever context.

One of the 7th-century biographers of St **Patrick** refers to onomastic information preserved by an ancient poet of that name and calls him 'one of the nine druid-prophets' who belonged to Bréagha (the Co Meath area). This formulaic description suggests that Feircheirdne was known only through verse attributed to him, and given the name such verse might have been composed by any expert of the poetic craft. This interpretation is borne out by the way in which Feircheirdne is accorded differing situations in the scheme of things. The earliest context in which he is set is the myth of the Leinster king **Labhraidh**, whose poet he is claimed to have been. He is there credited with the composition of the very archaic poem on the destruction by Labhraidh of the fortress of Dinn Rígh. In the developed story concerning this event, it is said that he, together with the harper Craiftine, accompanied Labhraidh when that king was banished from Ireland. His statements are represented as invariably containing the truth, and he is absolutely loyal to the Leinster culture-hero Labhraidh.

Feircheirdne is again the name of an archetypal poet in an 8th-century text which assigns his most dramatic role to him. This text is entitled *Immacallam in Dá Thuarad* (the Colloquy of the Two Sages), and in it he is represented as an elderly poet of the Ulstermen. When the chief-poet of the province, Adhna, died, his official robe was conferred on Feircheirdne. Adhna, however, had a young beardless son, called **Néidhe**, who was studying poetry in Scotland, and he got tidings of what was happening by interpreting the sound of a sea-wave. He immediately went to the Ulster capital, Eamhain Mhacha, to claim the robe for himself. Feircheirdne was absent when he arrived, and the mischievous **Bricriu** persuaded the youngster to don the robe. He fixed grass on his face and sang a charm over it to make it appear as a beard, and sat in the chief-poet's chair. Feircheirdne was indignant when he returned and discovered this, and a vehement contest in words ensued between him and Néidhe. They contended in rhetorics and riddles and metaphors in the obscure poetic speech. Eventually, Néidhe yielded precedence to the older man, who then made a series of prophecies about evil times to come in Ireland. Néidhe surrendered the prestigious robe to Feircheirdne, and was about to throw himself at his superior's feet when Feircheirdne graciously stayed him and bestowed lavish blessings on him. A later gloss on the text states that the earth was swallowing the young poet for his discourtesy until Feircheirdne prevented this by proclaiming 'stay!' Finally, Néidhe hailed Feircheirdne as 'comrar dána' (i.e. a casket of poetry), and accepted him as a second father.

That text was part of the **Ulster Cycle**, but it was quite unique there and was not really synchronised with the cycle's other stories. Feircheirdne is mentioned en passant in some of the other texts, but the cycle generally has other characters, such as **Aithirne** and **Amhairghin mac Éigit Salaigh**, as the chief-poets of the Ulster king. Though claimed as Aithirne's father, he really duplicates him. For example, the story of how an importunate poet demands to be given the one eye of a generous king, was properly told of Aithirne, but a late mediaeval text substitutes Feircheirdne for him. Another text of the same period borrows a description of Aithirne and relates it of Feircheirdne viz. 'the lakes and rivers drain before him when he satirises, and they rise up when he praises them'. The name Feircheirdne is also given to the poet of the warrior **Cú Roí** in that cycle. Here he avenges the death of Cú Roí by jumping to his death from a cliff-top bringing with him Bláthnaid, the false wife of the warrior. A long poem on Cú Roí, which praises his qualities and laments his tragic death, is attributed to this Feircheirdne.

Ludwig Bieler (1979), 84-5; Kuno Meyer (1914) *2*, 7-9 and in *Anecdota from Irish Manuscripts 3*, 43-4 and in *Zeitschrift für celtische Philologie 3*, 40-6; Whitley Stokes *CTS* (1905) and in *Irische Texte 3*, 364-5, 380-1; J C Watson (1941), 24-5; Cecile O'Rahilly (1961), 141. See **Cú Roí**, **Labhraidh**.

FEIRITÉAR, PIARAS (c1610-1653) Nobleman and poet from the Dingle Peninsula in Co Kerry. He fought for several years against the Cromwellian army. When returning home from peace-negotiations, he was seized in violation of a promise of safe conduct, and was hanged in Killarney.

Folklore concerning Piaras is very popular in the Dingle peninsula, most of the anecdotes centring on some verse or other said to have been composed by him or by somebody whom he encountered. His nobility is stressed by traditions which associate him with fine horsemanship. He was said to have had seven fine stallions, all of different colour and all possessed of great speed, stamina, agility, and courage. Apart from the delight which he took in horse-racing, it is said that he also loved gambling and that he was an expert at cards. The poetry composed by him and which survives in manuscript treats especially of love, and this aspect of his personality emerges as a basic theme in his folk portrayal. It is said that he once courted a rich lady and was preparing to marry her. While visiting her father's mansion, however, a blind but wise man who was sitting in the corner of the parlour spoke a quatrain to the effect that 'the white mare has foaled'. The import of this was unclear, but Piaras understood it to be that the lady was of easy virtue, and he took the warning and cancelled the wedding. It was alleged that, when he was captured later, this lady spared no effort to have him hanged.

The historical Piaras was in fact the leader of a group of several hundred men, and with this little army he managed to hold out longer against the Cromwellian forces than any other leader in the country. All of this is much personalised in the folk legends, which visualise him as outwitting and tricking the enemy with a mere handful of soldiers of his own. His castle was situated on a cliff overlooking the sea near Sybil Head, and it is said that a large body of English soldiers once came to attack it. The sea had made a cleft beside the castle, and Piaras told his men to increase the size of this cleft and to build a false bridge over it. When the enemy came in sight of him and his working party, he quietly gave a signal to his men and they raced towards the castle as a feint. The soldiers rushed after them directly, crowding onto the false bridge, which gave away under their weight, and large numbers of them dropped into the sea far below and were drowned.

There is even a tendency to envisage Piaras as a solitary fugitive, and we are told that a favourite hideout of his was a cave in a nigh inaccessible part of the Great Blasket island. We are told that several groups of soldiers were sent into west Kerry to apprehend him, and that he was captured once. The soldiers, however, were hungry and tired after their long search, and they decided to stop at a local house for a meal. Piaras gave a hint to the woman of the house to quietly pour water into the barrels of the soldiers' guns, which had been left aside as they ate. Then he himself jumped up and ran away. The soldiers tried to shoot him, but their guns would not fire. They followed him on foot as far as his cave, which could only be entered through a narrow gorge. Unknown to them, there was a hole in that entrance, and as they came in he flung them one by one through that hole and into the perilous sea below. He used this hideout for a long time, but it was a lonely life there, and he is said to have once composed a quatrain complaining to God that he had no company there but the darkness of the cave and the noise of the waves.

Piaras, who in one of his poems described the English policy towards the Irish as 'the games played by the brave little cat with the mouse', was taken treacherously by the enemy forces at Castlemaine. One folk legend states that the arresting officer noticed a sea-gull at some distance from them and that he promised Piaras his freedom if he could compose a stanza and twenty, every one ending with the word 'siar' ('west') before the gull rose from the ground. Piaras began to compose with absolute fluency, but the gull rose when he had sixteen stanzas made. He was brought to Killarney, where he was put to death on Cnocán na gCaorach (Fair Hill). Folklore states that a priest and a bishop were hanged along with him. The bishop handed a little stone to him, saying that while he held that in his mouth he could not be hanged. So it was, the rope failing to choke Piaras twice. On the third occasion, however, he spat the stone from his mouth, saying that none of his descendants would be called remnants of the gallows, and so he was hanged. The motif of the miraculous stone was part of general folk beliefs, but there is no evidence that Piaras was in the company of two clergymen when executed. The folk account may have developed from a well-known reference in a 17th-century poem by Seán Ó Conaill, a cleric of Kerry. This reference is to 'the wise and generous man, Piaras Feiritéar of fine traits, Conchubhar, Tadhg, and Bishop Baothlach, who were hanged on the gallows of Cnocán na gCaorach'. The two priests referred to, Conchubhar Mac Cárthaigh and Tadhg Ó Muircheartaigh, were hanged at the same place a year after Piaras, whereas Bishop Baothlach Mac Aogáin was hanged three years before. The folk accounts of Piaras' death seem therefore to have sprung from a misinterpretation of these lines.

Pádraig Ua Duinnín (1903); Kenneth Jackson *SB* (1938), 37-40; Cecile O'Rahilly (1952), 78, 156-7; Dáithí Ó hÓgáin (1985), 174-8, 219, 338.

FIACHNA MAC BAODÁIN (earlier, Fiachnae mac Baetáin) King of the sept called Dál nAraidhe (in south Antrim and north Down), who died in battle against his cousin and namesake Fiachna mac Deamháin of the Dál Fiatach (in Co Down) in the year 626 AD.

He was also known as Fiachna Lurgan, and was a celebrated warrior. A lost saga described an attack which he made on the Saxons of Dún Guaire (i.e. Bamborough in England), and elsewhere the mediaeval literature describes him as having been king in Ireland and Scotland. He may even have claimed the high-kingship for a while. One annalistic account borrows from the youth-biography of the epical hero **Cú Chulainn** in order to underline the greatness of Fiachna. His mother was of the rival Dál Fiatach sept, and we read that, on seeing a wolf attack sheep, she wished that she would conceive a son who would thus treat her husband's people. When the young Fiachna was born, his father disliked him because he resembled his mother too much, and so she brought him to a place apart to be reared. One day, however, the child seized some meat from his fellows and went to his father's court with the meat on a spit. Baodán set a fierce hound on him, but the young Fiachna stabbed the animal through the heart with the spit. At the same time he grabbed a hawk, which had swooped for the meat, in his other hand; and on seeing this his mother was so shocked that she could never conceive again.

We further read that Fiachna was given the epithet 'find' ('fair-haired') in order to distinguish him from his rival namesake, Fiachna mac Deamháin, who was accordingly given the epithet 'dubh' ('black-haired'). These two fought many battles, and Fiachna Find was always the victor because St **Comhghall**, who was of his sept, supported him with prayers. However, Fiachna Dubh went to Comhghall and insisted that the saint pray for him also, as Comhghall had been fostered by the Dál Fiatach. Both men were preparing for another battle, and the perplexed saint offered Fiachna Find the choice of victory and loss of heaven or defeat and eternal happiness. Fiachna Find chose the latter, and so was defeated and slain.

Fiachna mac Baodáin figures prominently in the stories which grew up around the name of his more famous son **Mongán**.

F J Byrne (1973), 111-2; S H O'Grady (1892) *1*, 390-3.

FIACHU FEAR MARA Fictional character situated in prehistory.

The mediaeval writers claimed that a king of Ireland called Aonghus Tuirmheach lay with his own daughter in drunkenness, and as a result the girl gave birth to Fiachu. The child was put by Aonghus into a little boat, dressed in the purple robe of a king's son, with a golden fringe on it. He was put out to sea at a fortress called Dún Aighneach (apparently on the Donegal coast), but was discovered on a nearby beach by fishermen, who took him ashore and reared him. Hence he was known as Fear Mara ('son of the sea'). Fiachu was said to have been father of Eterscéle and thus grandfather of **Conaire**. The account of his birth must have been prompted by the suggestion of incest in Eterscéle's fathering of Conaire, but the plot used is an international one, probably based in this instance on the pseudo-account of the birth of Pope Gregory the Great (see **Romantic Tales**, Type 933).

Whitley Stokes in *Irische Texte 3*, 312-3; R A S Macalister (1956), 284-7, 472-3; P S Dinneen (1908) *2*, 176-9; T F O'Rahilly (1946), 81-2.

FIACHU MUILLEATHAN Mythical king of Munster, regarded as contemporaneous with **Cormac mac Airt**.

Fiachu (later form, Fiachaidh) was one of the most famous ancestors claimed by the powerful Eoghanacht sept, and the best-known story of him occurs in texts from the 8th century onwards. According to this, he was the son of Eoghan, son of **Ailill Ólom**, and he was born posthumously. We read that, before the battle of Magh Mucramha in which he perished, Eoghan met a **druid** at Druim Díl (Drumdeel, near Clonmel in Co Tipperary). The latter had a daughter called Moncha and, realising that Eoghan would be slain, this druid told her to sleep with the warrior so that the future kings of Munster might descend from himself. After the death of Eoghan, and when her time came to give birth, Moncha was with her father by the river Suir at Raphae (Knockgraffon, Co Tipperary). The druid told her that if the child were born on that day he would be the chief jester of Ireland, but if she delayed the birth until the following day he would be the most powerful king in the country. She therefore went into the river and sat on a stone to delay the baby's coming. Next day the baby was born, but Moncha died from her efforts. Due to the forced delaying of the birth, the head of the baby Fiachu was widened out against the stone, and he thus was given the sobriquet Muinleathan or Muilleathan ('broad-crowned'). He was also known as Fear Dá Liach ('man of two sorrows'), on account of the deaths of his father and mother. The posthumous birth of Fiachu parallels that of Cormac mac Airt, but in the case of Fiachu it fulfilled a specific political purpose, for the druid Díl was said to have been of the Creacraighe, a sept of Ossory. It is likely that the borrowing from the Cormac context was done in or around the 7th century by the Creacraighe themselves, for they used the story to claim special privilege from the Eoghanacht. One variant, which discredits this Creacraighe claim, states that the druid reared two girls who were very alike in appearance. One of them was his own daughter and the other was the daughter of Eoghan. He pretended that Eoghan's daughter was his, and in this way sent her to her own father and claimed that her baby was his own descendant.

Other accounts of Fiachu are closely intertwined with the lore of Cormac (q.v.), but they are obviously Munster inventions. He helps Cormac at the battle of Crionna, and then triumphs over him in the battle of Drom Damhghaire when the high-king invades Munster. An account of Fiachu's death is found in a late source. According to this, a son of **Tadhg mac Céin**, called Connla, was a fosterling of Cormac, and he fell sick from leprosy at **Tara**. Cormac told him that the only possible cure would be for him to bathe himself in the blood of a king. Connla therefore went south to the court of Fiachu, who was his relative, at Raphae. He was warmly received there. One day he and Fiachu went swimming in the Suir at Áth Aiseal (Athassel), and when the opportunity arose he drove his spear through Fiachu in the water. The dying Fiachu showed his nobility by ordering his retainers not to put Connla to death.

Máirín O'Daly (1975), 14, 50-1, 64-5; Whitley Stokes in *Irische Texte 3*, 306-9; P S Dinneen (1908) *2*, 272-5, 322-5; F J Byrne (1973), 67.

FIANNA CYCLE A large corpus of stories relating to the band of warriors led by the mythical **Fionn mac Cumhaill**. The stories, the first of which appear in 8th-century texts, have been very popular in both literature and folklore for over a thousand years.

The word 'fianna' was used in early times for young hunter-warriors. Such groups of young men were a social reality in many early societies, as it was part of a warrior's training to live for a period in the wilderness in order to learn how to hunt and fight. The singular of 'fianna' was 'fian', a cognate of the Latin 'vēnatio' ('hunting') and of the word which appears in English as 'win'. Originally, it had no connection with the name 'Fionn', but when the Leinstermen used Fionn as a symbol of their efforts in the 5th-6th centuries to regain the Boyne valley from their Uí Néill foes, it is apparent that a Leinster version of the hunter-warrior cult got especially connected with Fionn. Thus in narrative Fionn came to be regarded as a great 'féinnidh', or leader of a troop of fianna.

The early mediaeval stories of Fionn show the influence of the life of such young men. As well as being a seer and warrior, we find him described as a great hunter, and much of the terminology associated with that occupation is connected with him (see **Dearg**, **Oisín**, **Oscar**). Very much in accord with the mentality which one would expect to find in such youth-cults, Fionn and his comrades are represented in the early literature as great feuders and womanisers. One early text, in fact, claims that the youthful Fionn had 'a woman in waiting for him in every region near him' and that these women were 'good to support the fianna'. The socially disruptive actions of Fionn and his companions in the earlier literature is intelligible when seen in that context of youthful fancy, and the early sources are in fact at pains to stress that fianna were distinct from the bands called 'díbheargaigh', who were groups of tribeless and desperate men. Yet an aura of youthful rebellion survived within the lore of Fionn and his comrades, and in time became one of the most fertile themes in the whole corpus of stories concerning them.

41. FIANNA *Prehistoric Irish model of boar, a favourite quarry of the Fianna.*

By mediaeval times, the only fianna who were really important in the narrative lore were the celebrated band of Fionn. A further development, which portrayed an unsteady reconciliation between

42. FIANNA *Native Irish red deer.*

the Leinster Fionn and the great high-kings of Uí Néill lore, **Conn Céadchathach** and his grandson **Cormac mac Airt**, led to the band becoming known as 'the Fianna of Ireland'. They were portrayed as a kind of volunteer army led by Fionn, which served the high-king and which was basically divided between the influences of two great families - that of Fionn (called the 'clanna Baoiscne') and of **Goll mac Morna** (called the 'clanna Morna'). The theme of this rather enigmatic force gave mediaeval writers many opportunities to employ their fancy. Some descriptions echo what would have been the real material life of early fianna groups. We read of how Fionn and his men hunted deer and wild pigs to provide food for themselves and how they cooked the meat on spits or at sites called 'fulachta fian', ancient cooking pits the remains of which survive in many parts of Ireland. These pits consist of a wooden trough connected to a stream, and the method of cooking was to place the meat there in water, which was brought to the boil with heated stones. The erection of hunting-booths with brace and ridge-pole is also described, as is the covering of the floor with heather, rushes, and foliage to lie on. Several texts mention a type of hummed refrain, called the 'dord fiann', made so as to call to their comrades for assistance when in danger. It was produced by drawing the lips together, and sometimes was accompanied by the clashing of spearshafts.

A more military perspective gradually came to the fore in the writers' musings on Fionn and his Fianna. An 11th-century text claims that the high-king Cormac appointed thrice fifty chiefs of the Fianna, with Fionn as the chief-of-staff. When a volunteer was accepted into the Fianna, his family undertook not to avenge him if he died in that service, and likewise they were not held responsible for his acts while he was in that force. To be accepted was no easy matter, for the applicant must be a poet and also a supreme athlete. One test was for the applicant to stand in a hole in the ground and ward off a spear-cast from each of nine warriors, another was to race through the forest pursued by many warriors without upsetting his hair or cracking a twig under his foot, yet another was at high speed to jump over a branch as high as his forehead and bend under another as low as his knee, and he must also be able to draw a thorn from his foot without slackening speed.

Various numerical fancies were used to describe the organisation of the Fianna, which force was sometimes said to consist of three great battalions and other times of seven. More consistent was the relative importance accorded to the personnel. A 12th-century account states that the five leading warriors were Fionn, **Lughaidh Lágha**, **Oscar**, **Goll**, and **Caoilte**. The pre-eminence of a half-dozen or so heroes was a recurrent feature of the Fianna lore, Lughaidh Lágha often being replaced by his son **Mac Lughach**. The storied **Oisín** and the swashbuckling young warrior **Diarmaid ua Duibhne** also figured among the elite group, while Goll's brother **Conán Maol** was the anti-hero of the tradition. A theme, which was probably suggested by the imagery of Caoilte (q.v.) as a great runner, was borrowed from folklore and became very popular in the literature from the 11th century onwards. This involved some marvellous helpers who come to assist Fionn in performing difficult tasks. Thus we read in 12th-century texts of three Norwegian princes who enter the service of Fionn, having in their possession a marvellous hound which coughs up gold and ale as desired; and also of helpers from several foreign countries who drain a troublesome lake for Fionn. We read further of a member of the Fianna called Leargan, who was so swift a runner that he could herd the deer as others did the cows.

Sources from the following centuries add much to the fanciful traits of individual members of the Fianna. We read of how Fionn (q.v.) was assisted by a group of strangers with a variety of great skills and thus succeeded in rescuing children who had been kidnapped by a giant. Some of the descriptions are quite humorous. Thus a man called Daolghus was the tallest member of the Fianna, and Mac Méin was the smallest, a sharp-tongued female messenger called Deardubha was the worst person in the Fianna, and Fionn's fire-attendant was the slowest worker. Fionn's most interesting retainer was the dwarf Cnú Dearóil, whom the hero had found outside the otherworld dwelling of Slievenamon. Cnú was but four fistfuls in height, and he and his similarly diminutive wife used to shelter from the rain under Fionn's cloak. A 15th-century writer with a taste for the exotic presents the Fianna as a type of incongruous society - including in it a deaf warrior who hears everything, a warrior with a wooden leg who can outrun all, a blind man who never made an inaccurate spear-cast, a woman whom Fionn had but who was dead by night and alive by day, and a warrior who on alternate years was a woman and a man.

Some mediaeval sources postulate that, long before Fionn was born, there had been great contests for power between his father Cumhall and Goll mac Morna. This was an extension of the account of the birth of Fionn (q.v.), which had his father defeated and slain by Goll at the battle of Cnucha (Castleknock, Co Dublin). All sources, however, agree that the golden age of the Fianna began with Fionn's accession to the leadership. A text written in the 10th century lists ten great battles fought by the Fianna under his command, and later sources attribute many more to him. Actual accounts of only a small number of these battles survive, however, and it is unlikely that there were many more such accounts. Already in the 8th or 9th century, a story was being told of a fierce battle fought against Fothadh Airgtheach, brother of **Fothadh Canainne**, at Ollarbha (Larne, Co Antrim), and the later literature claims that only six hundred of the Fianna warriors survived it. In the 10th or 11th century, another account of a battle in the north-east of the country was gaining currency. According to this, Fionn had left two Connacht princes, students of his called Art and Eoghan, to guard the shore at Tráigh Rudhraighe (Dundrum Bay, Co Down). These princes were accompanied by four hundred warriors and the same number of servants and, as night fell, they saw a huge fleet of Norse ships approach. The Norsemen, led by kings called Conus and Conmhaol, came ashore and were immediately attacked by the Connacht princes and their small force. Meanwhile, Fionn was sleeping in his camp, and he had a vision of two grey seals drinking from his breast. His poet, Fearghus Fíonbhéil, explained that this indicated that the Connacht princes were in danger, and Fionn rushed to that place. He found all the Norsemen slain and the two brave princes themselves mortally wounded.

The name of this strand, Tráigh Rudhraighe, was pseudo-etymologised as having the element 'ruadh' ('red'), and this allowed for a standard convention concerning a great slaughter to be attached to it. This convention had places before a great battle being named with the element 'fionn' ('white'), and afterwards with 'dearg' ('crimson'). So a writer from west Munster, who knew this story of Tráigh Rudhraighe, decided to compose another story on the same pattern, but situated on the 'white strand' best known to him i.e. Fionntráigh (Ventry, Co Kerry). From several mentions of this story in 12th-century texts, we know that it was already in existence by then, but the earliest full recension to survive is from the 15th century. It tells of how Dáire Donn, 'king of the world', sailed to Ireland with a massive fleet and, guided by a renegade member of the Fianna, anchored off Ventry. Fionn had sentries posted on all the major shores of Ireland, and the sentry at Ventry was one Conn Crithir. This Conn immediately attacked the invaders, and was assisted by three mysterious women who loved him and engaged their magic in his favour. Soon after, a strong man of the Fianna called Taistealach arrived and overcame the champion wrestler of Dáire. Conn sent Taistealach to alert the Fianna, and on his way he told a group of the otherworld people **Tuatha Dé Danann**, who hastened to the place to hold off the invaders until Fionn could muster his forces. The first great leader of the Fianna to enter the fray was Oscar, who slew whole companies of the foe and routed the French king, who raced demented from the field. A great warrior called Dolar Durba came ashore, performing wonderful tricks with a hurley and ball, and he was attacked by a young Ulster prince who came to assist the Fianna. All day and all night long they fought, and in the morning they were both found dead on the shore. The incessant fighting led to a great depletion in the ranks of the Fianna, and eventually Fionn decided on one great battle against the invaders. The fighting was atrocious, but gradually the Fianna gained the upper hand. The Norse king was slain by an Ulster warrior of the Rudhraighe clan, Conmhaol son of Dáire was slain by Goll mac Morna, and Fionn beheaded Dáire himself in a tremendous tussle. When only one of the invaders remained alive, he took to the sea but was followed by a young student of Fionn called Caol. Both sank to the bottom of the ocean in deadly combat, and the story ends with Caol's young wife lamenting him in verse.

There are echoes in that text from the epic called *Táin Bó Cuailnge* in the **Ulster Cycle**, and also from the story of the king **Suibhne** who went mad, and it is obvious that the writer or writers of the story did not scruple about borrowing material from any source to hand. A similar attitude prevailed in the composition of most late mediaeval and post-mediaeval stories of the Fianna. Few of the texts are of significant artistic value, but their combined effect and the manner in which the themes were continually developed makes them more than worthy of notice. Furthermore, their neat combinations of adventure and melodrama led to their easy absorption into popular culture, and versions of many of these literary tales have circulated widely in the Gaelic folklore of both Ireland and Scotland. They can be divided formally into two classes - richly ornamented prose narratives to be read aloud, and lays or versified texts which were recited in a chanting voice. In themes and in imagery both classes are similar to each other, but whereas a lay tends to concentrate on one dramatic episode the prose-texts have more scope and can pile episodes on each other.

The starting point for this new development in the tradition was the long 12th-century compendium called *Agallamh na Seanórach* (the Colloquy of the Old Men), in which the Fianna survivors, Caoilte and Oisín, tell many stories to St **Patrick**. This text contains many stories of hunts, conflicts, and adventures, with some of them retold in verse. Most of these narratives were the invention of the text's writer, even though they contain many earlier motifs and themes. The same types of setting are found in all the subsequent literary tales, whether in prose or verse. A favourite theme was the simmering rivalry between the Baoiscne and Morna clans, which is sometimes described as breaking out at feasts when the warriors become drunk and boastful. This is best exemplified in a prose story written in the 15th or 16th century. It describes how Fionn held a feast at his headquarters of Almhu (the hill of Allen, Co Kildare), during which Goll showed extraordinary generosity towards the poets who entertained them. Noticing that Goll was bestowing wealth from his Scandinavian tribute, Fionn grew jealous and claimed that the exacting of such tribute should be his own prerogative. Goll explained how, long ago, he had been driven from Ireland by Fionn's father Cumhall, and how he had conquered Scandinavia and thus earned the tribute. He further recalled that at a later stage he had rescued Fionn from captivity in Scandinavia. Tempers became frayed, and when Fionn was reminded of how Goll had slain his father a fierce conflict broke out between the two clans. Fionn lost twelve hundred men and women in the fighting, and Goll lost eleven men and fifty women. The poet Fearghus Fíonbhéil, however, got them to desist, and it was agreed that the question of compensation for injuries should be decided by the judges of the high-king Cormac. The celebrated judge **Fíothal** made a ruling which was accepted by all, according to which the Baoiscne clan were exempted from payment because of their great losses in the fight and the Morna clan were exempted because it was they who had been first attacked.

Several lays tell of how an otherworld visitor, usually either **Aonghus** or **Manannán**, comes in disguise to the Fianna to cause some problem or other for them or to teach them a lesson. This theme was a rather spontaneous one, and was an innovation in the lore. Older origins can be postulated for the many stories which tell of the Fianna being trapped in a sinister otherworld dwelling, for this situation seems to be a development in narrative from visits to the world of the dead made by Fionn's prototype, the seer **Find**. An 11th-century story tells of how Fionn (q.v.) and a few companions were forced to fight all night long in a sinister dwelling, and later writers revelled in such fancies. Thus, we read of how three savage witches trapped a group of the Fianna in the hill of Céis Chorainn (Keshcorran, Co Sligo), but they were released by the great Goll, who slew the three witches. Another story tells of how the Fianna were hunting in the Galway area when they were invited to lodge in his dwelling by one Eochaidh Beag Dearg, a hostile lord of the **Tuatha Dé**

Danann. The cantankerous **Conán Maol** insisted that himself and fourteen others only should go to the dwelling. When they reached there, these fifteen found themselves surrounded by hundreds of hostile warriors. Fionn learned of their danger through chewing his thumb of knowledge and, accompanied by his son Aodh Beag, quietly went to the place and joined them. Two huge assassins entered, but they were in turn overcome by Conán in cumbersome combats, and Conán also slew a horrendous hag. When morning came, the seventeen Fianna warriors took the field, but they were hopelessly outnumbered, and all seemed lost when the seven battalions of the Fianna arrived and slaughtered the whole army of Eochaidh Beag Dearg.

These stories of entrapment are each entitled 'Bruidhean', a word which meant a hostel and which came to have sinister connotations (see also **Conaire**). The most dramatic such Fianna story is called *Bruidhean Chaorthainn*, and tells of how a Scandinavian king called Colgán invaded Ireland but was defeated and slain by the Fianna in a great battle. Míodhach, son of Colgán, surrendered to Fionn and was well treated, being given land at the Shannon estuary, but he secretly plotted revenge. After several years, he connived with 'the king of the world', called Sinsear, and it was arranged that a massive invasion force would come to Ireland when Míodhach had trapped the Fianna leaders in his mansion. This mansion was built by three magicians, and Fionn and his companions were invited to a feast there. While there, they found themselves stuck to the ground, and when Fionn chewed his thumb he realised the treachery that had been arranged. Unable to escape, he told his companions to strike up their special hum, the 'dord Fiann'. Oisín, who had not come to the feast, grew suspicious, and sent two Fianna warriors to investigate. Realising what was afoot, these two - one of whom was Fionn's son Fiachna - fought bravely against the foe but were vastly outnumbered and slain. Just as Fiachna fell, the great warrior **Diarmaid ua Duibhne** arrived on the scene. Diarmaid beheaded Míodhach, and then stood guard over the mansion to protect the Fianna captives. However, the troublesome Conán Maol, who was within, was ravenously hungry, so Diarmaid had to go and forcibly take sumptuous food and drink from the very hands of the king of the world, who was feasting in another mansion nearby. He next slew the three magicians, and rubbed their blood to the captive Fianna warriors, which enabled them to rise from the floor. There was not enough blood left to free Conán, so he had to be pulled from the floor, leaving behind him a slice of skin from his poll to his buttocks. All the Fianna then assembled, and in a frightful battle the invaders were completely overthrown, Oscar beheading the king of the world himself.

Many lays tell of a great single warrior coming to Ireland and challenging the warriors of the Fianna to single combat. The basic structure of these lays has Fionn and his men being shamed by the rampant stranger, but the latter is eventually overcome by one of the Fianna. Goll is the champion in some cases. but more usually it is the mighty Oscar. A prose-text from the 16th century gives a humorous twist to this, telling of how an ungainly man, called the Giolla Deacair ('Difficult Servant'), once came to the Fianna as they hunted at Cnoc Áine (Knockainey, Co Limerick). This stranger had an ill-tempered and frightfully ugly horse, which Conán Maol foolishly mounted. He could not get the horse to budge, and so fourteen others of the Fianna also mounted the horse. With the fifteen on the nag's back, the Giolla Deacair raced away at great speed, followed by the animal. They were chased by Fionn and his men all the way to Dingle Bay, where they took to the water and disappeared. Fionn, with Diarmaid and some others, had to travel overseas to search for their comrades and, with the aid of two marvellous helpers whom they met, they managed to locate the Giolla Deacair in a wondrous foreign clime. The culprit said that his real name was Abharthach mac Ildathaigh, the most powerful magician in the world. He offered compensation to Fionn, but the latter forgave him all. Conán, however, was vengeful, and demanded that fourteen of the finest women in that country should come with him to Ireland on the nag's back, with Abharthach's own wife tied to its tail. This was agreed, but as soon as they reached Cnoc Áine all the strangers disappeared into thin air.

A quite original little story was written around the year 1600. This tells of how a stranger came from overseas to the Fianna at Binn Éadair (Howth, Co Dublin) and demanded that they set a man to race against him, the wager being the mastery of Ireland. His name was Caol an Iarainn ('Slender Fellow of the Iron'), and the perplexed Fionn set out for Tara to find the great runner Caoilte. As he passed through a forest, he met a huge ugly man with a grey cloak, who moved extremely slowly but claimed that he alone could defeat Caol. After some persuasion, Fionn agreed to let this stranger race for the Fianna. The course was to be from Binn Éadair to Sliabh Luachra (in south Kerry) and back, and when they set out Caol surged ahead. The grey-cloaked churl behaved very strangely, stopping for huge feeds and, at some stages, even retracing his steps to collect pieces of his torn garment. However, as the end of the race approached he moved like the wind, and easily defeated Caol. The piqued Caol drew his sword, but the churl threw a handful of meal and berries at him, which knocked his head off. The churl then replaced his head on the shoulders, but back to front, and thus Caol had to return to his own country. Then the wind and the sun lit up the face of the churl, and Fionn realised that it was none other than Manannán (q.v.) in disguise, who had come to assist them in their dire straits.

Some writer in or about the 11th-century noticed that the annalistic record had the fictional high-king **Cairbre Lifeachair**, son of Cormac, being slain by the Fotharta, a sub-sept of Leinster, at the battle of Gabhra (Gowra, Co Meath). Since the reign of this Cairbre was understood to coincide with the latter part of Fionn's career, the writer considered this a good opportunity to describe how the Fianna finally met their end. He accordingly invented the idea that that battle was a great clash between them and Cairbre, and that in it the high-king was slain by the great Oscar. The idea developed rapidly, and a 14th-century redaction of it has a dispute over hunting-rights as the cause of the battle. We must presume that the general setting was after the death of Fionn (q.v.), but this redaction states quite anachronistically that the great leader had gone on a pilgrimage to Rome when the dispute began. At any rate, Cairbre is described as mustering a mighty force from both Ireland and abroad, and the Fianna as fighting bravely in the battle though utterly outnumbered. Oscar, as usual, is in the leading role. Cairbre casts a deadly spear at him but, mortally wounded as he is, he manages to slay the high-king and then flings himself against the crack regiment of the foe before being himself destroyed. We read that 'until both sea-sand and stars are counted, one third of a third of those whom Oscar, son of Oisín, slew may not be reckoned'. The day is won by the Fianna, but they themselves have been decimated and, of all their leaders, only Caoilte and Oisín survive. An earlier, though now lost, version of this story must have been the basis in the 12th-century for the composition of *Agallamh na Seanórach*, which tells of how these two old heroes live on after the battle to meet St **Patrick**.

Variants of many of the Fianna stories, and motifs from them, are still found in the folklore of Irish-speaking areas. The chanting of Fianna lays, however, no longer survives in Ireland, though versions of several of these lays can still be heard in the western islands of Scotland. The Fianna tradition had a strong influence on world literature and culture in an indirect way, through the highly inaccurate reproductions of Scottish lays by James Macpherson in the late 18th-century. The works of Macpherson were translated into many languages, and were well-known to writers, philosophers, artists, and composers of music in Europe and America. For further material, see the individual entries on Caoilte, Céadach, Conán Maol, Diarmaid ua Duibhne, Feardhomhain, Fionn mac Cumhaill, Goll mac Morna, Mac Lughach, Oisín, and Oscar.

[Tradition of 'fianna'] Kuno Meyer (1910), v-xvi; Richard Sharpe in *Ériu 30*, 75-92; Kim McCone in *Ériu 35*, 1-30; J F Nagy (1985), 41-79, 240-55.

[Anthologies concerning Fionn's Fianna] Meyer (1910); Whitley Stokes (1900); Dubhglas de hÍde in *Lia Fáil 1*, 79-107; Nessa Ní Shéaghdha *1-2* (1942) and *3* (1945); Eoin Mac Néill (1908); Gerard Murphy (1933); Pádraig Ó Siochfhradha (1941).

[General discussion and references] Seán Ó Súilleabháin (1942), 588-97; Cormac Ó Cadhlaigh (1947); James MacKillop (1986), 69-266; Bo Almqvist / Séamas Ó Catháin / Pádraig Ó Héalaí eds (1987), 1-264; Dáithí Ó hÓgáin (1988), 27-51, 72-80, 139-50, 192-310.

FIND Name of an ancient personification of wisdom, many vestiges of whom are found in the early literature. In archaic Old Irish, the form of the name would have been 'Vind-', and this is cognate with Celtic 'Vindos'.

The name contains a root which exists in several Indo-European languages in the sense of wisdom, illumination, or discovery, for instance Latin 'vid-' and Germanic 'find-'. Among the Continental Celts, 'Vindobōna' occurred frequently as a placename, and the first element here can be taken as a personal name since 'bōna' (meaning a cluster of houses) was often employed in that sense. A Celtic deity called Vindonnus is indeed attested on the Continent, and it is reasonable to assume that this was a lengthened form of Vindos, a divine personification of wisdom. The first record of the name in Ireland is provided by Ptolemy's geography, which dates from the 2nd century AD but which may be based on quite earlier sources. This is the designation 'buvinda', a transliteration of archaic Irish 'bóu-vinda', for the river now known as the Boyne. The lore of wisdom associated with this river, and the river's perennial association with the wise seer Find (see **Bóinn** and **Fionn mac Cumhaill**) strongly suggests that its name originally referred to a mystical cow belonging to the personification of wisdom.

To the Gaelic people when they first arrived in Ireland - sometime around the year 500 BC - the Boyne valley was the most striking area of the country. Not only was it large and luscious, but it also contained a great number of ancient monuments left by earlier peoples. Whether or not some such peoples still survived at the time, all the evidence shows that Gaelic culture rationalised these ancient monuments - especially mounds and burial-chambers - by locating their own deities in them. In the development of this culture of the spiritual environment, the seers would have played the leading role, and so a figure who personalised the cult of the seers would have been of primary importance. In this way, the character 'Vind-' would have been intimately associated with the artefacts and the surroundings of the area, and especially with the river which flowed through the valley. The waters of that river would have been viewed as, not only the life-giving force to the surrounding countryside, but also the mystical stream of wisdom which was distributed through the seers. Thus the Boyne was the land **goddess** postulated in the form of a cow yielding nourishing milk, and whose consort was the archetypal seer. It is curious that Find does not figure among the divine race called the **Tuatha Dé Danann** by the mediaeval writers, but the reason for this must be that as a typical and representative seer he was usually imagined as a human person. His name does, nevertheless, appear in the mythical parts of genealogies, and the literature has mention of three characters whose designation reflects a divine triplication of him (see **Finn Eamhna**).

Lacking any narrative records from so early a period, the lore concerning this archetypal seer must be investigated through what survives concerning his avatars - characters such as **Find File**, **Morann**, and especially the celebrated **Fionn mac Cumhaill**. A study of these suggests that certain ideas were basic to the image of Find and were expressed in a number of standard ways. Firstly, knowledge was believed to be got from the dead ancestors, an idea which gave immediate relevance to grave-mounds, cairns, and such places. When ritually understood, this meant a great individual seer seeking out a wise predecessor, and there are several indications that this was expressed in a narrative concerning a wise youth called Find communicating with an old and dead namesake, in other words with a variant of himself. It is likely that a direct survival of the designation for this namesake is found in **Fionntan**, the antediluvian seer of mediaeval literature. His name (earlier, Fintan) can best be explained as deriving from a Celtic 'Vindo-senos' (literally 'old Find'), and there are parallels to this in fossilised names which survive in mediaeval Welsh literature viz. 'Gwyn hen' and 'Henwen'.

The youth of Find was sometimes expressed in imagery of a divine child who symbolised wisdom. True knowledge was understood in early times as being inspirational rather than gradually acquired, and such a child was symbolical of fullness in the beginning. Lore seems to have been current concerning the baby Find emerging from mystical waters, physically mature already in some striking ways, such as having grown hair which was bright in colour in accord with his name, and speaking in verse. He was already fully possessed of wisdom, the word for which ('fios') has the same root as his own name, and the babyish habit of thumb-sucking was for him a means of promoting his wisdom. The various images of Find - baby, young man, and old ancestor - made sense in the mystical understanding by seers of their craft, which penetrated into future, present, and past (see **Poets**). The mystical sense of wisdom involved the ability to experience different aspects of reality, and there are therefore several indications that metamorphosis was a basic element in early Irish seer rituals. This should be seen as a form of shamanism. Residues of it in narrative, deriving directly from lore concerning Find, are found in accounts of how such characters as **Fionntan** and **Mongán** went about in the forms of different animals and thereby acquired extra knowledge.

A study also suggests that the cult of Find was influenced in or about the 2nd century BC by the adoption of a new deity in the Boyne valley, namely **Nuadhu**. Accordingly, the wisdom-giving waters of the Boyne were said to contain a special salmon sacred to Nuadhu, and this deity was placed in the role of Find's old namesake as a bestower of knowledge. He was thus called Nuadhu 'Find-éces' (literally 'Find-seer'), and came to be regarded as an ancestor of Find. In line with this synchronism, the catching and eating of a marvellous salmon was mythically portrayed as a way in which Find acquired wisdom. At some stage also, a narrative which had Nuadhu being displaced by a young rival was adapted to the Find context, making the archetypal seer not just seek knowledge from his ancestor, but actually outmanoeuvre him. Probably through the Nuadhu influence, also, a tendency grew to apply appellations proper to the more imposing deity, the **Daghdha**, to Find's ancestor. This is clearest in the case of the designation **Ruadh Ró-fheasa** which was given to the salmon.

Some centuries later than Nuadhu, the cult of yet another introduced deity, **Lugh**, caused further developments in the Find image. This cult had Lugh defeating his tyrant grandfather, and when it was superimposed onto the existing lore of Find it transformed the contest with the wise predecessor into one of physical combat. Thus Find was well on his way to being portrayed as a martial champion, a process which came to final fruition in the context of his great avatar **Fionn mac Cumhaill**.

Julius Pokorny (1959), 1125-6; Alfred Holder (1896) 3, 328-50; Émile Thevenot (1968), 110-2; K H Schmidt in *Zeitschrift für celtische Philologie 26*, 295-6; Gerard Murphy (1953), lxxviii-lxxxiii; Dáithí Ó hÓgáin (1988), 3-26, 323-6.

FIND FILE Mythical king of Leinster who is mentioned in early sources. His sobriquet means 'poet'.

He is obviously an emanation from the ancient personification of wisdom in the Boyne valley, **Find**. However, this Find File was said to have had his residence at Ailleann (Knockaulin, Co Kildare), the largest hill-top fort in Ireland and residence of Leinster kings down to the 7th century AD. The form of that placename may have originally been Aillfhind, with a meaning such as

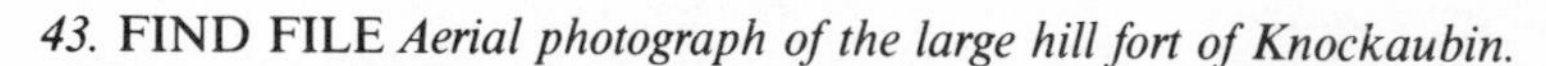

43. FIND FILE *Aerial photograph of the large hill fort of Knockaubin.*

'cliff of Find', but it is in any case likely to have become associated with a character called Find due to an extension of the Boyne valley culture. This would have occurred after the Leinstermen got control of the Boyne valley in or about the 3rd century (see **Cathaoir Mór** and **Tara**), and accordingly expropriated the lore of Find. That Find File is such a borrowing is underlined by the attribu tion to him of a father called Ros Ruadh, demonstrably a variant of the appellation **Ruadh Ró-fheasa**, an ancestor figure who was portrayed as giving wisdom to Find at the Boyne. Find File was said to have been one of three brothers, which might well be an echo of a divine triplication of Finn as found also in accounts of the three **Finn Eamhna**.

The actual context which led to the borrowing of the Find cult to the fortress of Knockaulin is difficult to ascertain, but it might have had to do with ritual installation of the Leinster kings at that site. The genealogies are perhaps reflecting some early reality when they claim that one of the brothers of Find File was a certain Cairbre Nia Fear, king of Tara. The name of this Cairbre seems to be a vestige of lore from the actual Leinster control of Tara in the 3rd-4th centuries (see **Cormac mac Airt**), and the format of the genealogies suggests that chief among the Leinster septs which held Tara in that period were the Uí Gharrchon. After the loss of the Boyne valley, this was also the sept which ruled Leinster to the end of the 5th century, and at that time Knockaulin was in the heart of their territory. They were uprooted and driven east into the Wicklow mountains at the beginning of the 6th century, and this may well account for the 'freezing' of the lore concerning Find File. Henceforth the front line against the dominent Uí Néill was held for the Leinstermen by a sept to the west of them, the Uí Fáilghe, and it is very significant that through this latter sept another emanation from the ancient Find flourished and underwent intense development in narrative. This was **Fionn mac Cumhaill**.

Some short poems on the mythical history of Leinster are attributed to Find File. The genealogists fancifully named as his third brother a character from the **Ulster Cycle**, the Connacht king Ailill mac Máta (for whom, see **Meadhbh**).

Kuno Meyer *HB* (1912) and (1914), 9-14; T F O'Rahilly (1946), 179; Edward Gwynn (1903), 46-9 and (1906), 80-5; Dáithí Ó hÓgáin (1988), 28-9.

FINN EAMHNA Triplet sons of **Eochaidh Feidhleach**, their individual names being given as Breas, Nár, and Lothar.

These characters are a confused echo in mediaeval literature from the ancient triplication of the mythic **Find**. Within the **Ulster Cycle**, they were given a new role as residents of the Ulster court at Eamhain Mhacha and were made sons of the **Tara** king Eochaidh Feidhleach. Because the word 'eamhain' could mean twins, they came to be regarded as triplets, born together to Eochaidh's queen Cloithfhionn. When she became estranged from her husband, we are told, she took them with her to Eamhain Mhacha, where she and the Ulster king **Conchobhar mac Neasa** continually urged them to oppose their father. Eventually they gathered their forces to mount an offensive against Eochaidh, and they went south to Cruachain (Rathcroghan in Co Roscommon) where their sister Clothra then reigned as queen of Connacht. She, however, refused to join them and tried to dissuade them from the undertaking, going so far as to make sexual offers to them, but all to no purpose. Her two druids also tried to dissuade them, prophesying disaster, but they were killed by the angry triplets.

When they arrived at Tara, Eochaidh sent his own druid Glúincheann to offer them two thirds of his kingdom, but they refused. Eochaidh then fasted against them, and next morning fierce battle was joined at Comar (near Navan in Co Meath). During the battle Lothar flung a stone at his father, and 'no stronger shot was made ever since'. It struck Eochaidh in the chest, laying him unconscious. Then three great warriors who were commanders of Eochaidh's army, but who had until then been restrained by Eochaidh, took the field. These were **Conall Cearnach**, **Ceat mac Mághach**, and Raon mac Roicheadail, and they routed the army of the Finn. They followed the three Finn themselves to Connacht and slew them there. Eochaidh was disconsolate when he saw the heads of his three sons. He directed that the heads be buried with their bodies, and with himself, at Cruachain. He then died from sorrow, and his instructions were carried out.

The treble imagery of the Finn was extended imaginatively by claiming that all three together were fathers of the hero **Lughaidh Riabhdhearg**, having begotten him on their sister Clothra on the night before the battle of Comar.

Whitley Stokes in *Irische Texte 3*, 332-3;

T F O'Rahilly (1946), 486; M E Dobbs in *Revue Celtique 43*, 277-342; Kuno Meyer in *Anecdota from Irish Manuscripts 5*, 17-8; Joseph O'Neill in *Ériu 2*, 174-5.

FINNBHEARA Leader of the Connacht **fairies** according to folklore. He was said to preside over an otherworld community in Cnoc Meadha (Knockmaa, some miles to the southwest of Tuam, Co Galway).

The name is a corruption of Findbharr (later, Fionnbharr), a designation with mythical origins (see **Barra**). The origin of Finnbheara was probably an epithetical 'findbharr' (literally 'fair top') to describe the summit of Knockmaa or a cairn on it, and this term would easily have been reinterpreted as the name of an otherworld being resident there. There is mention of the **Tuatha Dé Danann** chieftain Findbharr of Cnoc Meadha in the 12th-century **Fianna** text *Agallamh na Seanórach*, and he occurs again in the 15th-century *Feis Tighe Chonáin*, where he is an otherworld rival of **Fionn mac Cumhaill** for the hand of a lady. The Finnbheara of folklore is represented broadly in the same vein, several oral legends telling of how he enticed beautiful young women away into his preternatural realm. It is therefore probable that this Fianna text had a strong influence on the development of the character in folklore.

Several other narratives were attached to Finnbheara. As a fairy chieftain, he was said to lead his host in contention with rival otherworld groups. In this and in several other aspects, his imagery seems to have been coloured by that of the personage **Donn**, lore of whom was current from the late Middle Ages in Limerick and Clare. Thus a popular legend told of how, like Donn, Finnbheara came one night to a blackmsith to have his horse shod before a great battle. In Finnbheara's case some details are added, for his horse was three-legged and next day the blacksmith was rewarded by having cash blown to him on the wind. Finnbheara and his followers engaged each year in a hurling match against the fairies of other provinces, and when they won the crops of Connacht bloomed. Accounts were current also of how he invited humans into his palace in Knockmaa for feasts. These feasts were variously considered as ruses to entice people away into the fairy realm, or as entertainment offered in good faith by Finnbheara. Like Donn, he is often portrayed as the benefactor of local inhabitants. He once appeared in order to heal a sick woman, and on another occasion assisted the popular local landlord Hacket when the latter could find no suitable jockey for his horse in a race. Finnbheara himself appeared and took the mount, winning easily before vanishing again.

Whitley Stokes (1900), 140-2; Maud Joynt (1936), 49-56; Lilian Duncan in *Ériu 11*, 193-4; T F O'Rahilly (1926), 58; William Neilson (1845) *2*, 56-9; Lady Wilde (1888), 42-5, 259-63; Domhnall Ó Fotharta (1892), 33-5; Douglas Hyde (1910), 86-91; W Y Evans Wentz (1911), 42, 122; Seán Ó Súilleabháin (1942), 452-3, 495-6; Máire MacNeill (1962), 593.

FIONÁN CAM Saint of the early 7th century, founder of a monastery at Cionn Eitigh (Kinnitty, Co Offaly).

He was of the Corca Dhuibhne sept of Kerry, and his mother's name is given as Becnat. We read in a mediaeval text that she was bathing after sunset in Loch Léin (the greater Lake of Killarney) and that a golden salmon impregnated her there and thus Fionán was conceived. His epithet 'cam' meant squint-eyed. One old tradition claimed that he had been the first person to bring wheat to Ireland, having conveyed it hither from Leatha (Latium in Italy) in his shoe. There are several recensions of his biography, the fullest being a late version in Irish. According to this, his mother conceived by dreaming that a golden fish entered her mouth, and during her pregnancy no rain or snow fell on her. The young Fionán soon showed great knowledge and miraculous powers, impressing St **Bréanainn**, who directed him to leave Kerry and go north and build a church where he would meet a herd of wild boars. He therefore set out, and in this manner made Kinnitty the site of his foundation. The rest of the biography describes miracles performed by Fionán, particularly by way of healing sick and injured people and animals, and several of these are borrowed from the accounts of other saints. A special tradition has him banishing a plague from Uíbh Ráthach (the south-western part of Co Kerry). He became somewhat confused with his namesake, St Fionán Lobhar (i.e. 'the Leper'), who also lived in the Killarney area. His feastday is April 7, but it was celebrated in Kerry on March 16.

J F Kenney (1929), 421-2; Whitley Stokes (1905), 112-5, 423; Charles Plummer (1910) *2*, 87-95; W W Heist (1965), 153-60; R A S Macalister in *Zeitschrift für celtische Philologie 2*, 545-65; Cecile O'Rahilly

(1952), 81, 162; John O'Hanlon (1875) *4*, 57-72.

FIONN MAC CUMHAILL A celebrated hero in Irish literature and folklore. Stories concerning him are continuous in the literature for well over a thousand years. In the earliest texts his name occurs in the Old Irish form Find, in Middle Irish it is written Finn, and in Modern Irish Fionn. This latter form, which has been current for many centuries, is for convenience sake the one adopted here.

Fionn mac Cumhaill is always portrayed as a great warrior-seer. He can be viewed as an emanation of the archaic seer **Find**, or indeed as a continuation in tradition of that personage. This Find was archetypal in the cult of wisdom in the Boyne valley, and the Leinstermen adopted lore of him into their own tradition when they gained control of that prime area in the 3rd or 4th century. A leading Leinster sept, the Uí Gharrchon, associated the archetypal seer with their great centre at Ailleann (Knockaulin, Co Kildare), calling him **Find File**. Another sept, the Uí Fáilghe, inhabited a large territory in the west of the province (encompassing large parts of present-day Cos Kildare, Offaly, and Laois). This Uí Fáilghe sept also borrowed the lore of Find from the Boyne valley and centred it on a hill in the heart of their territory called Almhu (the Hill of Allen in Co Kildare), which apparently was a sacred site. They called the personage Find son of Cumhall.

The Leinstermen were driven from the Boyne valley by the ascendant Uí Néill sept of **Niall Naoighiallach** in the 5th century, and by the beginning of the 6th century the Uí Gharrchon had been routed. The Uí Fáilghe then assumed the leadership of Leinster and for some years engaged in a determined but futile struggle against the Uí Néill. All the indications are that in this struggle they used the imagery of Find as a symbol of their efforts to regain possession of the Boyne Valley and that, as part of this, Fionn was portrayed as having been a great war leader. The cult of war was particularly stressed in the case of young trainee-warriors known as **Fianna**, and thus Fionn was fancifully said to have been the leader of a mythical Fianna band long ago. This context explains how Fionn mac Cumhaill is at one with the ancient seer **Find** of the Boyne valley, and also with the fighting and hunting life of young men whose base is said to have been in the Uí Fáilghe territory. This composite character of the warrior-seer, originating in the early 6th century, underwent rapid narrative development in the following generations and, reflecting the abiding hostility of the Leinstermen to the Uí Néill, provided an increasingly dramatic corpus of stories.

Already in the 7th century, the Leinster genealogists were at work finding a place for Fionn in their tracts. They described him as a descendant of **Nuadhu**, and invented martial sounding names for his immediate ancestors. His father Cumhall was said to have been son of Tréanmhór (literally 'strong and big'), son of Sualt ('wholesome'), son of Ealtan ('having troops'), son of Baoiscne ('stalwart'). Various attempts have been made to explain the name of his father, Cumhall, but none seem satisfactory. It may well have been associated with the ancient Find of the Boyne valley before the Leinstermen borrowed the lore, and there are indications that its original form was 'Umhall', but beyond that it is a puzzle. There is a possibility that it referred to a 'visit' ('amhall') made by Find (q.v.) to the realm of the ancestors in search of knowledge.

A number of stories concerning Fionn mac Cumhaill are found in texts dating from the 8th century. Some of these are of Leinster provenance, and the others - from east Munster - show by the nomenclature employed in them that they are adaptations from Leinster. These attest to the fact that lore of the young hunter-fighters had given rise to an identifiable band of invented warriors as companions of Fionn. Principal among these are **Caoilte** and **Oisín**, both of which (q.v.) may originally have been nicknames for Fionn himself.

The dual function of Fionn as fighter and seer are brought out in a story which tells of how he had a woman of the Luaighne sept as lover, but she lay with a warrior of his band called Cairbre. Fionn's jester Lomhna saw them and, when he let Fionn know, Cairbre killed him. When Fionn found the decapitated body he put his thumb into his mouth and uttered a rhetoric proclaiming that this was Lomhna. He set out in pursuit of Cairbre, and found him in an empty house cooking fish, with Lomhna's head on a spike by the fire. The head was complaining that it had been given nothing to eat, and was threatening Cairbre with the destruction which Fionn would bring on him. At that Fionn attacked Cairbre and slew him. Apart from the Fianna (q.v.) context of fighting over a woman, this account stresses three important aspects of Fionn's power of wisdom. Firstly, he places his thumb in his mouth in order to gain knowledge, a trait inherited from the image of the ancient Find (q.v.) as a child seer. Secondly, he puts the knowledge gained by him into an obscure rhetoric, which was the standard custom of inspired **poets**. Thirdly, the head of a dead man speaks in his presence. This seems to have been a combination in the Fionn-context of two different early factors - one being the idea that Find gained information from the dead ancestors, and the other the general custom of fêting the heads of dead warriors (see **Conall Cearnach** and **Fearghal mac Maoldúin**).

The same themes recur in other texts of the period, for instance, in a Munster adaptation of the lore. This describes how his Fianna abducted women from Dún Iascaigh (Cahir, Co Tipperary), and Fionn kept one of the women for himself. She desired one of his servants, called Derg Corra, but he rejected her. Nevertheless he was banished by a jealous Fionn at her instigation. Some time later, Fionn met with a strange and mystical figure in the forest and, to discover who it was, put his thumb in his mouth. He was illumined by his wisdom and sang a rhetoric stating that it was Derg Corra. This strange servant (see **Dearg**) had the attributes of a deer-deity, and thus seems to reflect some hunting-lore current among Fianna bands. The general plot employed in this story is the international one known to scholars as 'Potiphar's Wife' (see **Romantic Tales**, Type 870C), the occurrence of which shows how the narratives concerning Fionn were being developed at the time. Deer lore also lies behind the name of Oisín (q.v.), who was regarded as Fionn's son and in relation to whom another well-known plot was borrowed (see **Romantic Tales**, Type 873). The language of this text concerning Oisín seems to belong to the 8th century, but it may be slightly later than that. Nevertheless, the fact that Fionn is portrayed in it as an elderly man with a grown-up son again shows how comprehensive the narratives had become by that time. The story describes how Fionn, having searched for a whole year throughout Ireland for Oisín, found the son cooking a pig in a lonely place. Fionn struck him and Oisín seized his weapons, but then they recognised each other, argued in verse, and were reconciled.

An 8th-century text which seems to be a composite between Leinster and Munster lore brings Fionn into contact with another famous 'fianna' leader of early myth, **Fothadh Canainne**. We read that Fionn carried off a woman called Badhamair from Dún Iascaigh, but a Leinster warrior called Cuirreach Life decapitated Badhamair. Fionn beheaded Cuirreach in revenge, but this led to conflict with the half-brother of that man, who was Fothadh. After some time, they made peace with each other, and Fionn invited Fothadh to an ale-feast. Fothadh, however, said that he would not drink ale 'unless it be in the company of white faces', and accordingly Fionn went to Dá Chích Anann (the hills called the Two Paps, near Killarney), and slew the husband of Fothadh's sister with a spear-cast there. He brought the head of this man to the feast, but the episode caused hostility between Fionn and Fothadh to be renewed with great ferocity. An account from around the same time goes further and puts Fionn into the context of mythical Munster history by having him track down and slay one Fearcheas, the man who had killed **Lughaidh mac Con**.

This type of lore is quite crude and savage -no doubt reflecting the life of young warriors of the time, but the greater stress remained on his aspect as a poet-seer. In the 8th century a story was invented to rationalise the strange power which he had of putting his thumb in his mouth to gain knowledge. According to this, when he and his men were on the banks of the river Suir cooking a pig, an otherworld being called Cúldubh came from Sídh ar Feimhean (the cairn on top of Slievenamon, a mountain in east Tipperary) and snatched the pig from them. Fionn followed him, and as he entered the cairn threw his spear at Cúldubh and killed him. A lady who had been distributing drink inside the cairn tried to close the door, but Fionn inserted his thumb between the door and the post to keep it open. The thumb was hurt, and Fionn put it into his mouth. Since it had been inside the otherworld dwelling, however, it had got the power of wisdom, and so, as soon as it was in his mouth, he began to sing a rhetoric concerning Cúldubh. This method of killing an otherworld foe with a spear-cast as the foe enters his dwelling recurs in several stories of Fionn, and in some of these the episode is said to have happened at Samhain (the November feast - see **Time**). Samhain was the festival of the dead, and this complex is probably an echo of the ancient cult of **Find** who got knowledge from the ancestors. The actual killing of the otherworld foe can be traced to the influence of the **Lugh** myth on the cult before Find was transformed into Fionn mac Cumhaill.

When put to creative use in the early Middle Ages, vestiges of Find's contact with the ancestors led to dramatic accounts of visits by Fionn mac

Cumhaill to otherworld dwellings. Perhaps the most striking early example of this was a story, current in the 9th century but now lost, which described an adventure of Fionn in Dearc Fhearna. This was the great prehistoric cavern at Dunmore in Co Kilkenny, which was described as one of the 'three dark places of Ireland'. Such otherworld dwellings visited by him could be either bright and inspiring or dark and threatening. Another development was the attribution to him, in place of rhetorics, of mystical nature-poetry which can be taken to reflect the inspiration of the seer at one with his environment. Yet another, and more planned, development is instanced by 8th-century engravings on a stone-cross at Drumhallagh in north Donegal. These show a figure with thumb in mouth, sitting over an engraving of a bishop with a crozier in his hand. This suggests that the Church was using the image of either Find or Fionn, as a great ancient prophet, to its own advantage by claiming that he had foretold the coming of St **Patrick** 'the Adze-Head'. A later mediaeval text is probably echoing this when it claims that Fionn once sat on the rock of Cashel in Co Tipperary, put his thumb into his mouth, and foretold the coming of that great saint. A more spontaneous development was the attribution to Fionn of a 'tooth of knowledge' with which he chewed his thumb - this was a natural transference of the source of his wisdom due to the idea of chewing.

44. FIONN MAC CUMHAILL *Detail from a slab at Drumhallagh, Co. Donegal, with thumb-in-mouth figure duplicated.*

A series of texts written from the 10th to the 12th century, when taken together, amount to a kind of biography of Fionn mac Cumhaill, preserving many ancient elements and adding new adventures and situations to the lore. There are some minor contradictions between these texts, but an outline of his life and actions which became generally accepted can be drawn from them. The material from all the texts, taken together, will be arranged here in as logical a pattern as the sources permit.

Fionn, we read, was of the Uí Thairsigh, a sub-sept to the Uí Fáilghe, who inhabited a place called Glaise Bolgain. This place is unidentified, but there are indications that it was in the vicinity of Almhu (the Hill of Allen), and we can assume that this hill was a cult centre in the Uí Fáilghe territory and that special responsibility for it rested with the Uí Thairsigh. His mother was Muirne, daughter of a druid called Tadhg mac Nuadhat who lived in a white mansion on Almhu. A warrior called Cumhall sought Muirne as wife, but this was refused by her father, and then Cumhall abducted her. Tadhg went to the high-king **Conn Céadchathach** for assistance and, as a result, the abductor had to fight a battle against Conn's forces at Cnucha (Castleknock, Co Dublin). Nine hours before the battle Fionn was begotten, and Cumhall was defeated and slain at Cnucha. The aggrieved Tadhg threatened to kill his daughter before she gave birth, but she and the child were protected by Cumhall's sister Bodhmhall, who lived with her husband Fiacail Fí at Teamhair Mhairge (a peak of the Slievemargy hills between Cos Laois and Kilkenny). The basic themes of the Fionn literature are here set out. Fionn, as the Uí Fáilghe, is in basic hostility to the royal Connachta sept of Conn; and his grandfather Tadhg mac Nuadhat is - as a vestige of **Find** lore - a tyrant developed from both **Nuadhu** and **Balar**. Imagery from the latter figure is clear from accounts of how, when Fionn grew up, he demanded combat or possession of Almhu from Tadhg, and the latter abandoned the place to him. Almhu is through the whole tradition described as Fionn's special fortress, but these mediaeval accounts of how he obtained it were not in the mainstream of the lore.

There are indications that, as a reflex of ancient lore concerning Find and the river Boyne, an early narrative described the baby Fionn as a great swimmer. Special connections with water and sea are found in the related birth-stories of the other wonder-children, **Mongán**, **Morann**, and **Noíne**, and - as we shall see - various narratives tell of great feats performed by Fionn in water. These feats are connected with his name in such a way as to suggest that involvement with water was an important and basic theme in his tradition. Similar to Morann, a birth-story of the Ulster king **Conchobhar mac Neasa** has the child falling into water immediately after birth. We read that Conchobhar was born with a worm in each hand, and this is parallelled in folklore accounts of Fionn's birth, according to which he was thrown into the sea on the orders of his grandfather, but emerged holding an eel in his hands. It seems plausible to suggest that this episode concerning Conchobhar was taken from an existing story of Fionn. One late mediaeval text, in fact, seems to echo such a story by having the child Fionn strangle a dangerous stoat. The caul on the head of the child Morann (q.v.) is also relevant, for when Morann is thrown into the sea the monstrous caul is reduced to a collar about his neck. The Fianna lore had a marked tendency towards diffusion of motifs and having them recur in different contexts, and it could well be that the basis for all of these portrayals was a narrative image of the child **Find** emerging from the Boyne river with the spirit of wisdom in his head. Frequent terms for Fionn's wisdom in the early literature were 'imbas' (a compound of 'fios' and meaning 'full knowledge') and the enigmatic 'teinm laéda' (which probably meant 'chant of fire'). The paradoxical image of fire in water would well suit his mystical knowledge, and that this should be in the head of the child-seer accords well with the portrayal of inspiration in early Irish rhetoric (see **Poets**). It is clear that, right through the tradition, Fionn's shining hair reflects both his name and his wisdom.

The fullest mediaeval account of Fionn's youth is entitled *Macgnímartha Find*. It describes how Cumhall, a warrior of the Uí Thairsigh, was outnumbered by the forces of Conn at Cnucha, and was slain by a great fighter called **Goll mac Morna**. This Goll (q.v.) was also an emanation from the image of Balar, and when the child Fionn was born Muirne had to take herself and it into hiding from him. She gave the child into the safe keeping of Bodhmhall, described as a nurse of young fianna. He was reared for six years on Sliabh Bladhma (Slieve Bloom in Co Laois), and we read that his first hunt was when he brought down a duck on a lake with a dart. He went travelling for a while with a group of poets, and a disease struck him so that he became mangy and was thus called 'Demne the Bald'. This is probably an echo of some kind of poetic or druidic tonsure. The name Demne is unclear, but it may be a corruption of 'daimhne' (meaning 'little stag') and thus reflect the Fianna context of hunting. At any rate it functions narratively to stress an event by which he is claimed to have got his real name. We read that he went on several occasions to the plain of the Liffey (i.e. the Curragh of Kildare) and overcame all the youths there at hurling. On the final occasion they were swimming and tried to drown him, but he drenched nine of them in the water. After his departure, the local chieftain was told by the boys that the stranger was fair-haired ('fionn'), and he remarked that this was the proper name for Demne.

The heroic youth had by this time grown so agile that he could outrun deer, and thus did the hunting for his two female guardians. They, however, advised him to leave the area for fear of his father's enemies, the family of Morna, and he went to west Munster. No chieftain would keep him in his service there for fear of the sons of Morna, and so he went east and met a smith at Cuilleann (Cullen, Co Tipperary). He became the lover of the daughter of this man, and the latter made two great javelins for him with which he killed a ferocious wild pig. Then he went to Connacht in search of his father's brother Criomhall, and on the way met and slew one of the warriors who had wounded his father at the battle of Cnucha. Criomhall was lying low in a forest with the remnants of Cumhall's band and, after a brief visit to him, Fionn went towards the Boyne valley to learn the craft of poetry. Now follows the best known of all the legends of Fionn.

Rather illogically, in view of the events which the text has already described, the hero is again called Demne and stated to be a mere seven years old, when he meets on the banks of the Boyne with a seer called Finnéigeas. This Finnéigeas (whose name means simply 'Fionn the Seer', and who thus can be seen as a variant of the old **Find**) had been for seven years seeking to catch the salmon of knowledge in that river. He had just then caught it, and entrusted it to the visitor for cooking, warning him not to eat it. As he cooked it, however, Fionn burned his thumb and put it to his mouth, thus getting the gift of wisdom. When he heard this, Finnéigeas said that the lad should be called, not Demne, but Fionn. This is clearly a folk narrative which the author has inserted into his text, but it has been changed somewhat to suit the Leinster genealogical lore. Elsewhere in the literature, the old seer is called Nuadhu Finnéigeas, and the author of this text has omitted some other details besides.

The story is very popular in folklore of both Ireland and Scotland. The folk versions portray the opponent as a one-eyed figure who intends to kill the boy Fionn, but when the latter gets the knowledge he realises this and kills the cyclopean figure. This is in agreement with the dramatic theme of the tyrant-grandfather which had long before permeated the lore from the **Lugh** context. The author of this text seems to have omitted it because he thought it inappropriate to the image of Nuadhu which the genealogies had as a respected ancestor of the Leinstermen. The story itself is another rationalisation of the motif of Fionn's thumb of knowledge, and can hardly be older in origin than the 9th or 10th century. It uses motifs from an international narrative plot (see **Wonder Tales**, Type 673), but its closest correspondent is a mediaeval Icelandic account of Sigurd the dragon-slayer, who accidentally burns his thumb while cooking the heart of a dragon and, realising that his companion intends to kill him, takes pre-emptive action. The relationship between the stories concerning Fionn and Sigurd is extremely complicated, but it is likely that the images of both heroes were perceived to be similar and that their lore influenced each other due to Norse-Irish contacts in or about the 10th century. The imagery of the Boyne salmon was long associated with Fionn due to the influence of Nuadhu (q.v.), but the international wonder-tale plot was probably attached to him from Sigurd, while Sigurd got his thumb and the slaying of his opponent from Fionn.

After this episode, the mediaeval text states - again rather incongruously - that Fionn went to study poetry with a warrior called **Ceithearn mac Fiontain** (another echo of the old **Find**). He accompanied Ceithearn when the latter went to woo a beautiful otherworld maiden at Sídh Éile (the hill of Croghan in Co Offaly) at November, but the venture was abandoned when one of their men was slain by an otherworld agency. The author was here dealing with some tradition which he did not clearly understand, but he repeats the theme in the event which follows. This has Fionn meeting with the warrior Fiacail, who gave him a javelin and told him to go to the Paps of Anu (in Co Kerry) and sit down between these two mountain peaks in the following November. He cast his javelin at an otherworld man who entered the dwelling there, and then went to Sídh Éile and seized a woman to hold as hostage for the return of the javelin. Having recovered it, he was told by Fiacail that the otherworld warrior he had slain had been the killer of Ceithearn's man.

Fionn then went with Fiacail to join a Fianna-band at Inbhear Colptha (the Boyne estuary), and while there he was placed on sentry duty at their camp for the night. He heard a shriek from the north and, going to Sliabh Slángha (Donard Mountain in Co Down) he saw three horned otherworld women who fled into the dwelling there. He snatched the brooch of one of them, and she begged him to return it, but the text breaks off here. It is obvious that the author has been telling different versions of one basic story i.e. of how Fionn slew with a spear-cast an otherworld warrior who came to do some harm to mortals. This, as suggested above, seems to have had its ultimate roots in the motif of the one-eyed destructive Balar who was slain by Lugh. When adopted into the Fionn context, that motif had become split into two basic recensions - the foe as a one-eyed fearsome warrior and the foe as a fiery otherworld foe. That this division occurred in the Fionn lore around the 6th or 7th century is suggested by the development of the character who in mediaeval times became known as **Goll mac Morna**.

A well-written 12th-century text gives the most dramatic version of the motif, showing clearly how the archetypal foe had been doubled and synchronised into the developing tradition of Fionn. This tells of how Fionn, at the age of ten, went to the court of the high-king **Conn Céadchathach** at Tara for the November-feast. The king was desolate, for every year on that night the citadel was burned down by an otherworld being called Aillén who came playing magical music to lull everybody to sleep. Fionn offered to stand guard, and he was given a spear by one Fiacha (apparently a variant of the previous Fiacail). When he heard the magical harp-music, he stayed awake by pressing the spear-point to his forehead, and then jumped up to face the fiery being. Aillén released a blaze from his mouth, but Fionn quenched it with his cloak and put the burner to flight. Fionn followed him to Sliabh Fuaid (the Fews Mountain in Co Armagh) and, as Aillén entered the hilltop cairn there Fionn cast his spear at him and slew him. Fionn then returned to Tara with the head of Aillén, and so grateful was the high-king to him that he installed him as head of all the Fianna of Ireland. The slayer of Fionn's father, Goll mac Morna, accepted this with good grace, and the three battalions of the high-king's soldiers put their hands in the hand of Fionn as a token of their loyalty.

The synchronisation and pseudo-historicising had thus proceeded quite far. Fionn mac Cumhaill, the archetypal hero of the Leinstermen in their struggle against the expanding sept of Conn, had now become the commander of Conn's own army. The dramatic potential of the old hostilities was remembered, however, and so, right through the tradition of Fionn, a poorly concealed friction continued between Fionn and Conn's heirs, as did open rivalry between Fionn and Goll. Indeed, it became conventional to regard the Fianna as comprised of two different groups - one the Baoiscne clan of Fionn and the other the Morna clan of Goll - and several stories are based on periodic breaches between these two. Friction with Conn's grandson, the celebrated high-king **Cormac mac Airt**, became endemic to the career of Fionn, who was regarded as a sort of alternative king, and so echoes from imagery of the **goddess** of sovereignty came into play. Since the goddess could be alternately beautiful and hideous, this competition between Cormac and Fionn gave rise to the idea that Cormac had a beautiful daughter called Gráinne (which actually meant literally 'the ugly one'). We read in 10th-century texts that Fionn wooed and married Gráinne, but she hated him and loved instead a young man called Diarmaid, with whom she eloped. As a result of this dispute, Fionn was banished for a while by Cormac. The story survives in full only in a later recension, but its origins seem to have lain in a confusion between Fianna lore of abduction and the goddess imagery (see **Diarmaid ua Duibhne**). One of the 10th-century texts goes on to relate how Fionn wooed a second daughter of Cormac, called Ailbhe. In the courtship, Fionn used his gift of enigmatic speech and engaged in a riddle-contest with the maiden - a theme which is related to a common **Romantic Tale** (Type 875). This marriage was a happy one, and we read that as a result of his union with Ailbhe some marvellous things happened to Fionn - including the appearance of a white and purple spot on his breast and his hair taking on a colour of gold (another echo from the imagery of his name).

An extremely rich lore grew up concerning the adult life of Fionn, some of it contradictory, and which will be dealt with presently. Accounts which purport to tell of how he met with his death were already current in the 9th century. The Luaighne sept of Tara, anciently mercenaries of the Connachta - Uí Néill, were always portrayed as special enemies of his, and they play a large part in stories of his demise. We read that it was prophesied to him that, if he drank from a horn, he would die, and so he always drank from goblets. However, he once took a drink from a spring at a place called Adharca Iuchbha (literally 'the horns of Iuchbha') and, when he put his thumb into his mouth and chewed it he realised that his death was near. Then he proceeded to the Boyne river, to an area controlled by the Luaighne. His foes gathered about him there and, in a fierce struggle, slew him. They brought his head with them and, when they began to cook fish, the head spoke and asked for a morsel. This was the learned tradition. An alternative account, based on folklore, was already current in the 11th century, and was still common until recent times in oral tradition. According to this he had once been challenged by an otherworld woman to leap backwards and forwards across either the Boyne river or from one cliff to another in Luachair Deaghadh (south-east Kerry). The woman enjoined on him to do this jump once every year, and when he grew old and attempted it he fell and was killed. It is interesting to note that the two locations mentioned in the context of Fionn's death were regarded as enemy territory for him in the early literature. The Boyne area was so regarded because of the control of it by the Connachta - Uí Néill and their Luaighne subordinates. In the case of the Luachair area of Kerry, this belonged to the western branch of the Eoghanacht sept, rivals of the eastern Eoghanacht of Cashel who had borrowed the Fionn imagery from Leinster.

The delineation and development of Fionn's character continued apace through the Middle Ages. Apart from wisdom, bravery, and good looks, the quality most attributed to him was generosity, and some quite creative images were used to illustrate this. We read that, if the leaves were gold and the waves silver, Fionn would have given them all away; and so hospitable was he that a troublesome man, whom everybody would avoid, would be invited by Fionn to stay in his house as long as he lived. There were varying accounts of his family. We have mentioned his marriages to Gráinne and Ailbhe, but other sources have him marrying Smirnat (daughter of **Fothadh Canainne**), Luchar (sister of the same Fothadh), and Bearrach Bhreac (foster-sister of **Goll mac Morna**), Maighnis (sister of the same Goll), Scoithfhionn, Daolach, a Scottish princess called Áine, and otherworld women called Scáthach, Sadhbh, and Blái Dheirg. His children are not consistently ascribed to definite wives, but they included the sons Raighne, Iollann, Caoince, Faolán, Aodh Beag, Fearghus, Faobhar, Dáire Dearg, and the famous Oisín, while the daughters mentioned are named Grian, Aoi, Samhaoir, Caon, and the Lughaidh who became the mother of **Mac Lughach**.

Various other members of his Baoiscne clan are mentioned, and we are left in no doubt that they were a hardy and efficient fighting force. A lay from the 13th century describes how, at a feast in Tara once, the high-king Cormac insulted Fionn and told him that he would make him pass under the fork of the cauldron. An argument broke out, and the Morna clan sided with Cormac. Fionn and his clan left, and sixteen of them decided to make a foray against Tara as revenge for the insult. They accordingly drove away a thousand head of cattle, but the mustered forces of Cormac soon caught up with them. The mere sixteen men turned about, made a vicious charge at Cormac's army, and took the king's son **Cairbre Lifeachair** as a hostage. Fionn's son, Faolán, would accept no ransom except that Cormac himself pass under the fork of the cauldron. Cormac had no choice but to comply, but to spare the high-king embarrassment Fionn himself graciously did so also.

The greatest compendium of mediaeval lore concerning Fionn is entitled *Agallamh na Seanórach* ('the Colloquy of the Old Men'). Written in the 12th century, and added to in two later versions, it relays scores of stories about the hero and his Fianna troop, placing them in the mouths of Oisín and Caoilte when they were claimed to have lived on and met St Patrick (see **Fianna**). Among these stories, the relations of Fionn with the otherworld continued to evoke most interest. Accounts of his visits to such places usually have the otherworld as a bright and shining place inside some hilltop cairn or other. A common format is to have him and his men out hunting in the countryside and, on chasing a fast deer or pig, finding themselves in an otherworld place, where they are entertained to a great feast. One story has him, with five companions, spending a whole year in the cairn on Slievenamon, and engaging in many otherworld battles in support of their hosts there.

Visits of Fionn and his men to supernatural dwellings prompted some mediaeval writer to compose an allegory based on the situation. The earliest surviving text of this allegory is a rather confused one dating from around the 15th century, but there is no doubt but that it was composed several centuries earlier. It gained great popularity, enough to influence a Norse story of Thor in the 13th century, and it is still current in the folklore of the Irish language. It tells of how Fionn and five of his men were benighted while hunting, and they came to a strange house. They found there an old man, a beautiful young woman, and a ram. A meal was served up to them but, before they could eat, the ram butted the table, knocking all the food on the floor. One by one, Fionn and each of his men tried to tie the ram to the wall, but failed. Finally, the old man did so without any bother. They ate, and then went to bed. During the night, Fionn tried to go to the room of the young woman, but she rejected him, saying that 'you had me once, and you will not have me again'. Puzzled by this strange household, Fionn sought explanations from the old man before they left next morning. He was told that the ram was the world, the old man was age which subdues all, and the beautiful lady was youth. The oral versions state that, on their departure, the lady gave a special gift to each of the warriors.

There is a sinister side to the otherworld also. The hostility of Dearg to Fionn, as instanced above in the story of Derg Corra, recurs in accounts concerning the daughter of that personage. A poem from about the 15th century tells how, when Fionn was once drinking with his comrades and their wives in his dwelling on the hill of Allen, a strange woman arrived and challenged the ladies present to put on her cloak. She explained that only if a woman were pure would it cover her completely. Most of the ladies present failed the test miserably, and none quite succeeded. At that the stranger revealed that she was the daughter of Dearg, and had once been the mistress of Fionn. She had come to create unrest among the Fianna. Fionn cursed her and ordered her to leave immediately. There was an old tradition concerning Fionn and this otherworld lover, who was in reality hostile to him. She probably was also the unnamed otherworld lady who - according to late mediaeval sources - the hero met one day by the shore of a magical lake near Sliabh gCuillinn (Slieve Gullion in Co Armagh). She sadly proclaimed that her bracelet had fallen into the lake, and inveigled Fionn into diving for it. When in the water, he was transformed into an old man, and was hardly recognisable to his comrades when they found him. They then besieged the hill-top cairn where Cuilleann, father of the malicious lady, dwelt. Cuilleann was forced to give a rejuvenating drink to Fionn, but the hair of the hero remained grey.

A story told in texts from the 11th century describes how a Munster prince presented him with a fine black racehorse, and Fionn set out on a long gallop with this horse, accompanied by Caoilte and Oisín on their mounts, until he reached a hillock called Bairneach (south of Killarney). They found a strange house in a glen there and entered, but were set upon within by monstrous people and had to stay fighting all through the night. With the coming of morn their attackers and the house faded from view. The idea of Fionn and his men being trapped in sinister otherworld palaces became very popular with the post-mediaeval writers, who composed several texts on this theme (see **Fianna**). Its culmination was in the popular folk account of how the Fianna escaped from hell (see **Oisín**).

The most colourful text concerning a visit to the otherworld has Fionn going into the mysterious fortress of a certain Conán at Ceann Sléibhe (possibly the headland of that name in west Kerry). This is entitled *Feis Tighe Chonáin*, was written in the 14th or 15th century by a quite imaginative author, and in it Fionn tells several of his own adventures to his otherworld host. Having conceived a desire for Conán's daughter Findearbh, he was eventually allowed to sleep with her, and a marriage was arranged for a month hence. However, when Fionn and his company arrived for the wedding, they were fiercely attacked by a large contingent led by Findearbh's otherworld wooer Fionnbharr. Conán and his people fought bravely to defend their guests, but the slaughter was massive, and the text mentions no more of the wedding.

Fionn is invariably portrayed as a great hunter of deer and wild pigs, and we read that he used to sit on hilltops to direct the chase. This led to lore concerning his hounds, many of which are mentioned, but the most famous being Bran and Sceolaing. Several texts in the mediaeval literature tell a story of how he acquired this great set of hounds. We read that the king of the Dál nAraidhe (in Cos Antrim and Down) desired Fionn's aunt Uirne as wife and, when the warrior **Lughaidh Lágha** guaranteed that she would be well treated, Fionn agreed to the marriage. However, Uirne was magically turned into a hound by the king's first wife, and as a result Lughaidh Lágha went and slew the king. Uirne regained her own shape and became the wife of Lughaidh. She bore him triplets, but at the same lying-in brought forth two pups also. These were therefore the cousins of Fionn, and they became his great hunting-dogs. It is clear that some author had been reflecting rather fancifully on the hound-lore associated with **Lughaidh mac Con**. The image of Bran was particularly developed. It was a massive hound, with its head as high as Fionn's own shoulder. It had two white sides, a purplish haunch, four bluish feet, and a fierce eye in its shapely head. It and Fionn used to make great noise together at feasts, and whenever the Fianna were hungry Bran would go into the forest and bring their meal to them. Fionn loved the hound with exceptional intensity, and a late mediaeval writer saw the potential here for pathos. We read that Bran was yelping impatiently once when the quarry was being risen, and Fionn angrily struck it on the head with the leash. The offended Bran stared at its master with tear-filled eyes, then wrenched itself free, and raced to a lake where it drowned itself. Every time afterwards that Fionn heard the baying of a hunting-hound, his heart was near to breaking.

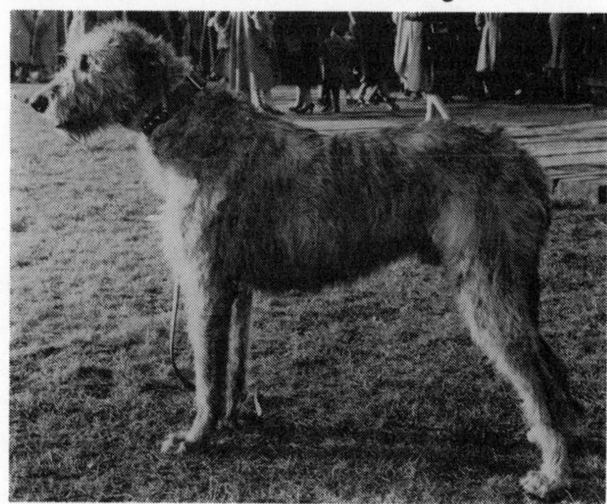

45. FIONN MAC CUMHAILL *Photograph of modern Irish wolfhound.*

Many battles were said to have been fought and won by Fionn, but the number of them actually described is less. These, as well as his military strategies and his household retainers, are discussed in the entry **Fianna**. A very fertile idea which grew up in the mediaeval lore - probably due to the imagery of the great runner **Caoilte** - was that of helpers who assist Fionn in the achievement of difficult tasks. Thus we read in the 12th-century Colloquy of how a lake burst forth on Sliabh Bladhma (Slieve Bloom in Co Laois) and was spreading out to cover all Leinster. Fionn, however, managed to avert that catastrophe through the help of magicians and female warriors from India, Germany, England and France, who sucked up all the water. Such motifs were obviously borrowed from general folklore plots concerning marvellous helpers with incredible abilities (see **Wonder Tales**, Type 513), and they became a frequent aspect of stories concerning the Fianna (q.v.).

In a text from the 15th century or thereabouts, we read of how Fionn was hunting one day when he was approached by eleven strange youths, who said that they were searching for a worthy master. They explained that they each had a great ability - which were respectively answering questions, kindling fires, serving at table, dividing wealth, listening, strength, tracking, running, shooting, climbing, and stealing. Fionn took them into his employ, and brought them with him to Dublin. The king of that place asked Fionn to protect his wife who was about to give birth, for she had already borne seven babies and they had all been taken away by a giant at night. Fionn undertook this task, and told his helpers to use their special skills to serve a meal for the household and to stand guard. However, the giant came and put his hand through the roof. The strong helper tore the limb away from its body, but the giant put in the other hand and took the baby away. Fionn, with his tracker and other helpers, followed on by land and sea. They came to an island, the lord of which challenged them to race against his daughter for her hand. If she won the race they would lose their heads, but Fionn's fast runner defeated her and thereby won the beautiful princess for Fionn. Resuming their quest for the stolen baby, they came to a great cliff in the sea. The climber scaled this cliff and saw the giant sleeping there with all of the children of the king and queen of Dublin, as well as two fine pups. He told this to Fionn, who instructed him to bring the thief on his back to the cliff-top, and in this way the children were recovered by Fionn. The giant, however, followed on, but he was beheaded by Fionn, and all returned happily to Dublin. The pups became the two great hounds of Fionn, namely Bran and Sceolaing.

This story, versions of which have been very popular in folklore, has a complicated history. A narrative was current in mediaeval times in either Ireland or Wales, concerning how a baby was stolen by a giant hand coming through the roof, and this narrative had attached to itself the well-known Celtic motif of animals who are congenital with humans. The independent Irish story of how Bran and Sceolaing were born also became attached to this, and so Fionn was brought into the story. He in turn caused the plot to be much lengthened by the inclusion of folk plots concerning extraordinary helpers (**Wonder Tales**, Types 513 and 653, both of which are embedded in this developed story).

The dramatic scenario of Fionn opposing a giant proved very productive in later Irish folklore. Such accounts usually have Fionn triumphing through wile, and several folklore plots were borrowed to illustrate this. The most frequent account - collected all over Ireland and also in Scotland and the Isle of Man - can hardly be more than a few centuries old. It describes how a giant visits Fionn's house intending to engage him in combat, but the clever Fionn jumps into the cradle and pretends to be the baby. As he waits for the 'father' to come home, the giant plays with the 'baby', who wastes no time in biting off the visiter's finger. When told by Fionn's wife that the Fianna children are born with sharp teeth, the giant imagines that Fionn himself must be a horrific fighter and flees in dread. This is a Gaelic ecotype of an international narrative plot (see **Humorous Tales**, Type 1149)..

A more recent stratum of lore, particularly strong in the English language, has Fionn himself portrayed as a giant. Elements of this grew from the tendency towards hyperbole in Gaelic narrative, and also from the custom of associating various landmarks with Fionn. The mediaeval literature already has mention of 'Suí Finn' as the name of a mountain top, the notion being that he sat there to observe the hunt. Variants of this placename occur all over Ireland for hilltops and mountain ledges, and folk fancy increases the size of Fionn to suit the elevations. Similarly, boulders are said to have been stones thrown by Fionn in contest with giants, great flagstones his griddle, and even level hilltops his table. Quite comical is the claim that the island known as Ireland's Eye off the Dublin coast is a sod torn from the ground by him in Co Wicklow, thereby causing the larger lake to spring up at Glendalough; and this is more

46. FIONN MAC CUMHAILL *Cairn on a hill-top called 'Suí Finn' or Fionn's seat in north Co. Wicklow.*

47. FIONN MAC CUMHAILL *Fionn and his harper, from an Irish school-book.*

than matched by another claim that the Isle of Man is a sod flung by him from the site of Lough Neagh in a contest with an English giant.

It is clear that, having held the stage in many centuries of storytelling, Fionn has come to represent all aspects of the human psyche, positive and negative, traditional and innovatory, serious and humorous. He has figured prominently also in 20th-century creative literature, most notably in James Joyce's *Finnegans Wake* and Flann O'Brien's *At Swim-Two-Birds*.

[Early sources] M A O'Brien (1962), 22-3, 45, 99; Kuno Meyer (1903) and (1906), 30-1 and (1910), xvi-xxii, 1-3, 18-27 and (1912), 87-8 and in *Zeitschrift für celtische Philologie 8*, 105, 117-8 and in *Revue Celtique 25*, 344-9; D A Binchy in *Ériu 11*, 48-9, 58-61; Vernam Hull in *Speculum 16*, 322-33 and in *Zeitschrift für celtische Philologie 30*, 17-20; Máirín O'Daly (1975), 82-8.

[Biographical sources] Edward Gwynn (1906), 72-7; Kuno Meyer (1885), 72-6 and (1910), xxii-xxxi, 46-51, 94-9 and in *Revue Celtique 5*, 195-204 and in *Zeitschrift für celtische Philologie 1*, 458-65; W M Hennessy in *Revue Celtique 2*, 86-93; Rudolf Thurneysen in *Zeitschrift für celtische Philologie 13*, 251-82; Vernam Hull in *ibid 18*, 422-4; Hull / J R Reinard in *Speculum 11*, 42-58; Whitley Stokes (1900) and in *Revue Celtique 7*, 289-307; L-C Stern in *ibid 13*, 12-22; Gerard Murphy (1953), 103-4.

[General literary sources] Meyer (1910); Eoin Mac Néill (1908); Gerard Murphy (1933); Neil Ross (1939). See also **Fianna Cycle**.

[Folklore] Dáithí Ó hÓgáin (1988), 275-310, 342-6.

[Discussions] Reidar Christiansen (1931); Cormac Ó Cadhlaigh (1947); Murphy (1953); J F Nagy (1985); James MacKillop (1986); Ó hÓgáin (1988).

FIONNACHTA High-king of Ireland from 674 to 695 AD. An alternative, poetic, form of his name was Fíonsneachta (literally, 'snow of wine') and it was often accompanied by the epithet Fleadhach ('bountiful').

His father was called Dúnchadh and, though a brother of the high-kings Bláthmhac and **Diarmaid mac Aodha Sláine**, was not prominent in political life. Fanciful lore therefore grew up to explain how Fionnachta became high-king. It was said that he was a poor man, and that he and his wife had but one ox and one cow between them. The king of Fir Rois (a sept inhabiting parts of Monaghan, Armagh, and Louth) was benighted in a storm and took shelter at the hut of Fionnachta. The latter killed the ox and cow in order to feed the king and his company, and out of gratitude that king later presented him with a large herd of cattle, pigs, and sheep, and many other riches besides. This account may be based on a folklore plot (see **Religious Tales**, Type 750B).

One day, as Fionnachta was on his way to a banquet, he met the young St **Adhamhnán**, who was travelling as a poor scholar. Adhamhnán ran out of the horse's way, and let fall a pitcher of milk which he was carrying on his back. The pitcher was smashed and, seeing this, Fionnachta offered to pay for its cost and brought Adhamhnán and his five fellow-students with him to the banquet. The tutor of Adhamhnán then prophesied that Fionnachta would one day be high-king of Ireland and that Adhamhnán would be his advisor until insulted by him. The prophecy was verified, though in a less than honourable manner, when Fionnachta fought a battle against his own cousin Ceannfhaolaidh to gain the throne.

After Fionnachta remitted the **bóraimhe** tribute to St **Moling** on behalf of the Leinstermen, Adhamhnán quarrelled with his decision because he regarded it as an insult to the supremacy of their Uí Néill sept, and thus the second part of the prophecy was fulfilled. Under pressure from Adhamhnán, Fionnachta changed his mind and vainly tried to capture Moling, who cursed him as a result. We read that this curse led to Fionnachta being treacherously slain by close relatives who were rivals for the kingship. He and his son Breasal were in a tent at Greallach Dolaidh (Girley, near Kells in Co Meath), when they were attacked and beheaded.

John O'Donovan (1860), 70-85, 94-7; Whitley Stokes in *Revue Celtique 13*, 98-117; R A S Macalister (1956), 382-3; S H O'Grady (1892) *1*, 402-6; P S Dinneen (1908) *3*, 138-41.

FIONNCHÚ (earlier, Findchú) Saint who died c664 AD, founder of a monastery at Brí Gobhann (Brigown, now Mitchelstown, Co Cork). The name means 'fair-haired hero' - it was sometimes written as Findchua and is anglicised as Fanahan.

He was noted for his self-mortification in order to save souls from hell, and an apparently early source places emphasis on this. We read that, when a corpse was brought to his church, he used to spend the night in the mortuary with it, suspending himself from the wall by an iron sickle in each armpit. By this sacrificial practice he prevented the devil from approaching and taking the soul of the dead person.

The legend of Fionnchú developed greatly through the Middle Ages, and a biography in Irish from the 11th or 12th century adds much imagery which makes him more of a romantic hero than of a conventional saint. According to this biography he was son of an Ulsterman called Findlugh, who was banished after plotting against the high-king of Ireland. Findlugh had got a girl called Iodhnait pregnant, and this girl was looked after by the Munster king. Once, when she sought a drink of ale from some brewers and was refused, the child in her womb spoke a rhetoric and caused the vats to burst. When the child was born he was baptised by St **Ailbhe**, and when he reached seven years of age he was noticed by the visiting Ulster saint **Comhghall**, who took him with him to his celebrated monastery of Bangor (in Co Down). When he was guarding the monastery's meadow one day, the king of Ulster placed his horses there and refused to move them, but Fionnchú turned the horses into stones and caused the angry king to sink to his knees into the ground. He restored both king and horses when Comhghall begged him to do so. He became a close friend and confidant of Comhghall and, when the latter died, he succeeded him as abbot.

Having spent seven years in the abbacy of Bangor, Fionnchú returned to the south and was given a site for a new monastery by the king of Munster. Seven smiths came to assist him in the building, and hence the place was known as Brí Gobhann, which meant 'the hillock of the smiths'. They made seven iron sickles for him, and he hung himself on these for seven years so as to ensure a place in heaven for himself. From his monastery of Brigown, this biography claims, he sallied forth on several occasions to assist those in need of military support. He helped Seachnasach, king of **Tara**, to repel foreign marauders; helped Nuadhu, king of Leinster, against the Uí Chinsealaigh sept which was challenging him; helped the Munstermen to rout an invading Ulster army and an attempted invasion by the royal Uí Néill sept of Tara; and helped the Connachtmen against another foreign set of raiders. On each occasion he first offered peace to the aggressors, and only when the offer was rejected did he play his role of 'cathaighe conghalach' ('valiant warrior'). In that role, he led the fighting men into battle, brandishing his crozier, emitting fire from his mouth, and causing the foe to shrink and to lose their vigour. The text rather fancifully derives his name from his great martial competence, stating that he fought like a hound ('cú') in a battle on behalf of his mother's sept, the Ciarraighe. Finally, he went to Rome to repent of the battles he had fought, dying there within a year.

The artificial character of this biography is obvious. For instance, the bursting of the ale-vats is borrowed from the lore concerning the satirist **Aithirne**, and a Leinster king called 'old Nuadhu Éigeas' is anachronistically borrowed from the mythology of that province (see **Nuadhu**). Nevertheless, the account is rich in adventure, and variants of it survived in the folklore of the Mitchelstown district. Fionnchú's feastday is November 25.

J F Kenney (1929), 457-8; Whitley Stokes (1905), 246 and (1890), 84-98; John O'Donovan (1864), 316-9; IFC 128:133, 407:332-3, 556:142-9/155-6, 947:148-51.

FIONNTAN Mythical seer in Irish literary tradition. He is described as son of Bóchna or Bóchra, who does not appear as a character. The patronymic really meant 'sea', and originally must have reflected an aspect of myth concerning seers. The name Fionntan (earlier, Fintan) is probably derived from a Celtic compound Vindo-senos, which would have meant 'old Find'. This suggests that Fionntan was a variant in ancient lore of the great mythical seer **Find**.

Fionntan was portrayed as a seer who had lived for hundreds of years and who thus had detailed knowledge of past events. The writers of pseudo-history interpreted 'Bóchna' as the name of his mother and claimed that his father's name had been Labhraidh. Fionntan, they said, had come to Ireland with the lady **Cessair** and her group of settlers forty days before the Deluge described in the Bible. There were fifty women and three men in the group, and Fionntan took Cessair as wife. When the two other men died, all the women came to him, but he fled from them. A poem put into his mouth tells of how the flood came and he alone survived it. He was hidden in the earth at Tul Tuinne (Tounthinna, the hill over the river Shannon near Portroe in Co Tipperary), and remained there until the inundation had passed away.

One text, accepting the pseudo-historical setting for him, nevertheless embodies some genuine mythic elements. This has him in conversation with a hawk from Acaill (Achill, Co Mayo) and gives him the opportunity to tell his story in detail. He was fifteen years of age when the Deluge came, and lived for five and a half thousand years thereafter. During that period, he had gone through transformations - first as a one-eyed salmon, then as an eagle, and then a falcon, before reassuming his own shape. In their conversation, the hawk tells that it too is very old, and has witnessed all the major events of the country's history, such as the various reputed settlements, the battles of Moytirra (see **Mythological Cycle**), the deeds of **Cú Chulainn**, the reigns of **Conn Céadchathach** and many other kings, until the coming of Christianity. This text also introduces a new motif into the lore of Fionntan, claiming that he had once met a strange man who offered him a branch of fruit, and that when he ate this fruit he was rejuvenated. Another text tells that, at the time of the Crucifixion, a stranger called Trefuilngid came from abroad and persuaded Fionntan to become a Christian. The stranger relayed to him a vast quantity of knowledge concerning the history and geography of the country. As a result of these encounters, Fionntan was replete with the ancient lore of Ireland.

It is clear that these texts have confused the original notion, which was that Fionntan himself had, through his longevity and wanderings in various shapes, acquired all the information. He could thus boast concerning Ireland that 'I am knowledgeable in its feasts and in its cattle-raids, in its destructions and its courtships, in all that has been done'. This statement is, in fact, a synopsis of what the poets and learned men of early Ireland should know, and it underlines Fionntan's role as a mythical projection of such sages. One text has him dramatically fulfilling this role by coming to the historical high-king **Diarmaid mac Cearrbheoil** and answering all the questions put to him by the king and his assembly at **Tara**. The basic myth involved is how the great seer gained much of his wisdom through transforming himself into the forms of various animals (see **Find**).

The format of the Fionntan story which survives, however, has him recast fully in the terms of reference of mediaeval culture, as a Christian witness to Ireland's pagan past. The account of his meeting with the high-king has him describing the proper procedures for the ruling of Ireland, and then states that he went to Dún Tulcha (at Kenmare Bay in Co Kerry). Worn out by age, he prepared for death and received the Sacraments from a bishop called Earc. The text states that the place of his burial was unknown, but that some people considered that he had been carried away to some secret place to await the final Resurrection.

R A S Macalister (1939), 166-229; Kuno Meyer in *Anecdota from Irish Manuscripts 1*, 24-39; R I Best in *Ériu 4*, 121-37; Edward Gwynn (1903), 2-5 and (1913), 236-9 and (1924), 256-7; Joseph Vendryes (1953), 4-6, 36-7; Douglas Hyde in *The Celtic Review 10*, 138-4 ; W M Hennessy / D H Kelly (1875), 6-11, 98-9, 248-75; Láimhbheartach Mac Cionnaith (1938), 202-4.

FÍOTHAL (also, Fítheal) Fictional judge at the court of the celebrated high-king **Cormac mac Airt**.

The name meant literally 'calf', and there are some indications that the character originated in the same context of Fianna hunting-lore as **Oisín** and **Oscar**. A 14th-century poem states that Fíothal was one of two brothers of **Fionn mac Cumhaill**, and claims that this was an old tradition. The other brother of Fionn named in the poem is Féinnidh (which meant 'Fianna-leader'), and it is therefore likely that this tradition was an echo of an ancient triplication of Fionn, the hero with a strong residue of ritual and myth. Fionn (q.v.) was in one text given the name 'Demne', which probably meant 'little stag', and in meaning this would approximate to the name Fíothal. It therefore seems that Fíothal was adopted into the context of Cormac from Fianna lore when these two hostile sagas were being synchronised with each other in or about the 8th century. This situation may be reflected in one text, in which a young man called Socht, son of Fíothal, is claimed to have been a hostage at the court of Cormac (q.v.) at the same time as Fíothal himself was a judge there. In the later mediaeval literature, Fíothal is represented as an arbitrator in disputes between the Fianna generally, as well as between Fionn and Cormac. Several collections of wise maxims were assembled and claimed to have been instructions given by him.

The 17th century historian Seathrún **Céitinn** relates a story of Fíothal which he apparently had from some written source. This describes how Fíothal, when dying, gave four advices to his son Flaithrí viz. not to rear a king's son, not to tell a dangerous secret to his wife, not to promote the son of a slave, and not to entrust his wealth to the keeping of his sister. After Fíothal died, Flaithrí decided to test the advices. He therefore promoted the son of one of his servants, and that young man grew extremely rich; and Flaithrí also entrusted a portion of his own treasures to his sister. He then took the son of Cormac as a pupil, and soon after left the boy with a swineherd in the forest with instructions to hide him away until summoned. Returning home, he affected great dejection and, on being pressed by his wife concerning this, he at length told her that he had killed his royal pupil and bound her to secrecy in the matter. Immediately, however, she informed the authorities, and Flaithrí was seized. The young man whom he had promoted was one of his strongest accusers, wishing for an opportunity to gain Flaithrí's property at a low price. Flaithrí called on his sister to go bail for him, but she denied that he had ever entrusted money to her. Realising the dire straits he was in, he called for a private conversation with Cormac, and told the king where the prince was. He was therefore allowed to send word to the swineherd, and the prince was released. He then explained to Cormac that he had been testing the advices of Fíothal and had found them to be good.

This story is based on a common folklore plot, but its details represent a rather rare variety (see **Romantic Tales**, Types 910 and 911). Miscellaneous mentions of advices against telling a secret to one's wife and promoting a slave in 9th and 10th-century texts suggest that the plot was known in Ireland by that time; and at some stage in the interval it got attached to Fíothal. There probably was a tendency to consider the name of this judge as synonymous with his profession, and one source even situates him at the 5th-century court of the high-king **Laoghaire**.

Eoin Mac Néill (1908), 18; Gerard Murphy (1933), 104-5, 110-1, 132-7 and (1953), 108, 371; Nessa Ní Shéaghdha / Máire Ní Mhuirgheasa (1941), 38-9; Whitley Stokes in *Irische Texte 3*, 199-202; R M Smith in *Revue Celtique 45*, 1-92 and 47, 30-8; P S Dinneen (1908) *2*, 338-43; Áine Ní Chróinin in *Éigse 3*, 67-8; D A Binchy (1978), 1654.

FIR BOLG A people who, according to the mediaeval historians, occupied Ireland in ancient times.

The designation, which means 'Bolg'-men, entails the Celtic population-name found in Britain and north-western Europe under the form Belgae. It is apparent that a group of early Celtic settlers in Ireland were called Bolga or such. The genealogists of early mediaeval times often designated septs by prefacing 'fir' (i.e. men) to their name, hence these ancient inhabitants came to be known as Fir Bolg. What the narrative literature tells of this population-group is, however, mere conjecture and phantasy. They were claimed to have been descendants of Semeon, grandson of **Neimheadh**, who left Ireland and went to Greece. His progeny increased till they were numbered in thousands, but they were enslaved by the Greeks, being made to carry loads of clay onto bare rocks in order to turn the barren landscape into a fruitful plain. They carried this clay in bags ('boilg'), hence the fanciful derivation of their name as 'bag-men'. An alternative notion was that the Greek king gave them to inhabit a territory full of venomous reptiles and that, as protection against these creatures, they carried about with them bags of Irish clay. Eventually they left Greece and set sail for Ireland.

When they arrived, their five leaders divided the country among them from the vantage-point of Uisneach (Ushnagh in Co Westmeath) which was regarded as the exact centre of the country. Thus the writers of pseudo-history explained the origin of the division of Ireland into five provinces - the word 'cúige' (i.e. a fifth) is still used for a province, even though since mediaeval times there have been only four. The idea of the Fir Bolg was used, not only for aetiological explanation, but also for the synchronising of data. Thus we are told that, properly speaking, the descendants of Semeon who came into Ireland were in three sections. These were the Fir Bolg proper, the Gaileoin, and the Fir Domhnann. As in the case of the first section, fanciful etymologies were used to explain the designations of the other two. The Gaileoin, we are told, were named from 'the javelins of wounding' ('gai leoin') with which they dug the clay in Greece; while the Fir Domhnann were named from the deepness ('domhaine') of the clay when it was heaped onto the rocks. In reality, Gaileoin was an alternative name for the Laighin (Leinstermen - see **Labhraidh**), and the Fir Domhnann were a group settled in various parts of Ireland whose name is cognate with the Celtic Dumnonii of Britain and western Europe. Whatever the relationships between these various Celtic groups in antiquity, to the mediaeval historians little of distinguishing characteristics survived except for their names, and so they were imagined as having been one extended tribe.

The Fir Bolg, it was claimed, were in possession of Ireland for thirty-seven years, until the coming of the **Tuatha Dé Danann**, who conquered them at the first battle of Moytirra (see **Mythological Cycle**). Some mediaeval historians claimed that, after this battle, the Fir Bolg settled in islands off the Scottish coast. Much later, presumably, the Fir Bolg were driven from these islands by the **Picts** and they returned to Ireland. They entered the service of the **Tara** king Cairbre Nia Fear and gave him sureties, but later rebelled against him and their four leaders, the sons of Umhor, were slain by four great warriors - **Cú Chulainn**, **Ceat mac Maghach**, **Conall Cearnach**, and Ros mac Deadha. The historians continued in this fanciful vein, eventually assimilating the Fir Bolg fully to the **Érainn**, which was the designation of the general body of non-dominant septs in early mediaeval Ireland.

R A S Macalister (1940), 144-9 and (1941), 1-111; A G Van Hamel in *Zeitschrift für celtische Philologie 10*, 160-3, 186-90; Toirdhealbhach Ó Raithbheartaigh (1932), 53-92, 101-31.

FITZGERALD, GEARÓID IARLA (1338-1398) 3rd Earl of Desmond, leader of the Munster branch of the Geraldines, the most powerful Norman family in late mediaeval Ireland. The surname was gaelicised as Mac Gearailt. He succeeded to the Earldom in 1358, and served two periods as Chief Justiciar for Ireland. Popularly known as Gearóid Iarla ('Gerald the Earl'), he was a leading example of the gaelicisation of the Norman lords, and was a noted composer of love poetry in the Irish language. The annals state that 'Ireland was full of the fame of his wisdom'.

Lough Gur in Co Limerick, where he had a castle, was at the centre of the earldom of Desmond (from Deasmhumhain i.e. 'south Munster'), and nearby is Knockainey (in Irish the 'Cnoc', or hill, of Áine). This **Áine** was in Gaelic tradition the goddess of Munster sovereignty, and as such was described in an early text as the mate of **Ailill Ólom**, mythical king of the royal Eoghanacht sept. The Geraldines, as the new Norman overlords of Munster, were not slow to expropriate such symbolism to themselves. Thus we find the professional poet Gofraidh Fionn Ó Dálaigh, who was in the employ of the Geraldines in the 14th century, referring to Gerald's father, Maurice the 1st Earl, as 'Áine's king' and to Gerald himself as 'the son of Áine's knight'. It is striking to find this idea embedded in a story which was current in the recent folklore of the Knockainey area. According to this, Maurice was walking one day by the shore of Lough Gur when he saw the beautiful otherworld woman Áine bathing. He seized her cloak, which act magically put her into his power, and then lay with her. In this way Gearóid Iarla was conceived, and when he was born Áine appeared at the castle of the Earl to present the child to him. This story is in reality a conflation of two distinct traditions - the Gaelic one whereby the Munster king lies with Áine, and a Continental legend which tells of how certain great families had a

48. FITZGERALD, GEARÓID IARLA
Lough Gur, Co. Limerick, where Gearóid Iarla sleeps.

swan-maiden ancestress. The conflation must reflect actual policy of the Geraldines themselves, who wished to place their Norman heritage within a Gaelic framework.

Another Continental legend which became applied to Gearóid Iarla was that which told of a 'swan-knight' and was quite popular in French, German, and English literature of the late Middle Ages. This tells of a knight who appears in a boat accompanied by a swan, marries a lady, but goes away with the swan again when she breaks a taboo by asking about his identity. In the folklore of Gearóid Iarla, it takes the form of a taboo which Áine puts on Maurice not to show surprise at anything his son does. When Gearóid grows up, he shows his magical agility by leaping into a bottle and out of it again, and the father shows astonishment. At that Gearóid leaves the castle, enters the water of the nearby Camogue river, and swims away in the form of a goose. An old saying in Irish refers to how island-geese never return to the same habitat, and since an island on Lough Gur was known as Gearóid's Island, the proverb was claimed to refer to this episode. The story, however, contradicts the mass of the folklore concerning Gearóid Iarla, which accords with history in having him succeed to the earldom and gain fame in that position. It must have been attracted to him because of its similarity to the Áine-story, not earlier than the 16th century, for it was at that time that the most celebrated motif concerning Gearóid gained currency. This was that he had not really died, but had disappeared from this world in a mysterious manner.

This motif is closely connected with the political fortunes of the great Desmond family in the generations after the death of Gearóid, their most famous and popular earl. During the 15th century, the rulers of England grew increasingly nervous of the growing power of the Desmond earls, who ruled Munster like kings. The Geraldines, however, were astute, and despite continued provocation and even judicial assassination, they managed to maintain their position. Their prestige was high throughout Europe, and a leading family of Florentine magnates, the Gherardini, claimed relationship with them and kept in close contact with them. Tension mounted in the early decades of the 16th century, with anti-Geraldine rumours being circulated in England to the effect that they were plotting to invade that country and seize power there. The other major branch of the Geraldine family, that of **Kildare**, were much to the fore at this time, but they were decimated by the English after a failed rebellion in 1534. In the year 1558 the 14th Earl of Desmond succeeded to the title. His name was Gerald, the first of the name in his line since the celebrated Gearóid Iarla. He was, however, deprived by the English of his vast family estates and himself kept in captivity in London for long periods. He was allowed to return home to Lough Gur in 1573, but immediately began to take a defiant pro-Irish stance and within a few years had joined his cousin in rebellion.

Hopes ran high, and messianic prophecies were circulated to bolster the Geraldine campaign. Remnants of these prophecies in later folklore show that the new Gearóid Iarla was being portrayed as embodying the great Geraldine spirit of his ancestral namesake. From their contacts in Florence, they would have heard the lore of the messianic Emperor Frederick II, who had died in 1250 but who was claimed to be alive and waiting to return, and there are several indications that legends of that Emperor became embroiled in the minds of the Geraldine supporters with the hoped-for return of their fortunes through the agency of a Gearóid Iarla. Thus popular fancy began to claim that the Gearóid Iarla of olden times had not died at all, but had disappeared mysteriously from one of his castles and was waiting to return at the hour of the family's greatest need. In line with the image of Frederick also, Gearóid was said to have been a great scholar who dabbled in magic, and so one particular legend grew up to explain how he had disappeared. It was said that, in his castle at Lough Gur, he had a secret room in which he used to perform magic spells. His wife grew curious, and asked to be allowed to witness a performance. He warned her not to utter a sound while the magic was in progress, no matter what she saw. Then he began to assume different shapes, one of them so frightful that she screamed. The taboo was broken, and the whole castle sank to the bottom of the lake, bringing with it Gearóid and all his household. He therefore was said to dwell underneath the water, enchanted until the opportune time for him to return and restore all as before.

The central messianic legend was of greater import. Versions of this are found throughout Europe concerning different great figures of history, but in Gearóid's case it seems to have been a direct borrowing from Frederick. It is said that a man was passing by Lough Gur one night, when he saw a light in the side of a hill there. He went to investigate, and found the entrance to a cavern, in which he saw an army of knights and horses all asleep. There was a beautiful sword on the floor, and as the man began to draw it from its scabbard the army began to awaken. Finally its leader, Gearóid Iarla, asked in a loud voice had the time come yet, but the man took fright and ran away. The army fell to slumbering again, and the entrance to the cavern could not be found later.

The second Earl Gerald of Desmond, in history, was not a very competent military man, and by 1583 his cause was completely lost and he himself treacherously slain. The sequel to this disastrous rebellion was the devastation of Munster by the Elizabethan armies, so that an annalist felt obliged to state that 'the lowing of a cow or the voice of a ploughman could scarcely be heard from Dunquin to Cashel'. The great affection for the Geraldine family, however, lived on, as did the hope that one of them would free the country. There are repeated references to this mystical belief in literature and social documents from the 17th to the 19th centuries, and the legends of Gearóid's enchantment and of his sleeping army are still told. An alternative telling claims that the enchanted earl rides around Lough Gur on midsummer night once every seven years. He is mounted on a fine white stallion shod with silver shoes, and when these shoes wear down he will return. Variants of this corpus of lore have been told for several centuries also concerning the Earls of Kildare (q.v.) and concerning the O'Neills and O'Donnells in Ulster and a chieftain called Dónall **Ó Donnchú** at the Lakes of Killarney. It is clear that in these cases the corpus has been borrowed from the lore of the Desmond Earl.

Munster folklore has assimilated other legends of magic and the otherworld to the context of Gearóid Iarla also. Two such legends of Continental origin concern his magical practices. According to one, he, with his kinsman Black David FitzGerald and Dónall Ó Donnchú, learned magic from the devil at a secret school. The devil demanded as payment that one of them should stay with him, but they each told him to 'take the man behind me' and he ended up with nothing but the shadow of Dónall. The other legend tells of how Gearóid was riding from his residence at Castleisland in Co Kerry one day, and as he passed through the town a magician looked through a window and put a spell on him. As a result, the Earl and his horse were sinking into the ground,

49. FITZGERALD, GEARÓID IARLA *16th-century woodcut, believed to represent the Earl of Desmond who was killed in 1583.*

but Gearóid quickly used his own magic to put a pair of horns growing on the head of his assailant. The latter could not withdraw his head through the window because of the horns, and Gearóid would not remove the horns until the other spell was also withdrawn. Several stories tell of Gearóid's appearances, such as visiting a blacksmith late at night to have his horse shod (see **Donn**), or meeting a benighted horse-dealer and inviting him into his castle under the lake to discuss a sale with him. Gearóid is also reputed to protect the environment at Lough Gur, and other stories tell of how he caused the horse of some local tyrant to bolt, with serious or even fatal injury to its rider, after the latter had planned to drain the lake or forbid access to it by local people.

Gearóid Mac Niocaill in *Studia Hibernica 3*, 7-59; Láimhbheartach Mac Cionnaith (1938), 201-6; David Fitzgerald in *Revue Celtique 4*, 186-99; Pádraig Ó Siochfhradha (1932), 42-4, 53-4; Dáithí Ó hÓgáin (1985), 78-86, 141-57, 329-30, 335-7 and in *Béaloideas 42-44*, 213-308 and in *Scríobh 4*, 234-59.

FLANN MAC LÓNÁIN A chief-poet of Ireland, whose death is put down to 918 or 920 AD. He was known as Flann Aidhne, which indicates that he was a native of Aidhne, an area in south Galway and north Clare.

Little is known concerning him. Possibly due to his skill in storytelling, a source from near to his own time relates an adventure concerning himself and a dramatic character from ancient lore. We read that Flann and his subordinate poets were once in an empty house, very hungry, when an ugly giant came to them with a cudgel in one hand and a bullock in the other. In return for the promise of a milking-cow, he killed and divided the bullock among them and then departed. A year later, he returned with five other giants to demand the cow which had been promised. Mac Lónáin demanded to know his name, and he said that he was Fiodhbhadhach ('forest-man'). Flann recited a poem describing the situation, and the stranger then said that this recitation was the 'cow' which he had come for. He revealed that he was none other than **Aonghus**, the 'Mac Óg'.

One source gives to Flann the reputation of surliness and greed. We read that, after his death, his harper offended another poet, Mac Liag, by praising his great knowledge to the detriment of the latter. Flann, the harper said, could name all the places to be seen from Sliabh nEachtga (Slieve Aughty in south Galway). Mac Liag said that he would have the harper hanged by the morning, but Flann appeared at dawn and proved by a poem that he knew all the lore in question. This story is obviously of a type with the discovery of the *Táin* epic by **Seanchán** and the proof of the antiquarian knowledge of **Mongán**. Another late mediaeval source develops this notion by stating that Flann was murdered and was buried in Tulach Mochaimhe (near Terryglass in north Tipperary), but he arose on the day after to recite a poem on himself and the other five people interred with him.

Osborn Bergin in *Anecdota from Irish Manuscripts 1*, 45-50; Edward Gwynn (1913), 532-3; J G O'Keeffe in *Irish Texts 1*, 22-4; Colm Ó Lochlainn in *Éigse 4*, 42-5.

FLANNÁN Saint of the 7th century, abbot of the monastery of Cill Dalua (Killaloe, Co Clare). The name is a diminutive of Flann (literally, 'red') which was a common name in early Ireland.

His biography, in Latin, dates from the 12th century. In it, we are told that Flannán was son of Toirdhealbhach, a king of the sept called Dál gCais in that area. His biography describes how he was educated by a St Bláthmet and then by St Dalua, founder of the Killaloe monastery. He decided to become a monk, and soon showed his miraculous power. When sent once to work at a mill, he remained at his task overnight, and his fingers emitted light after he had breathed on them. Dalua was so impressed by the young man that he resigned from the abbacy and persuaded Flannán to succeed him. Flannán then went to Rome to be consecrated by the Pope, and on his journey crossed the sea on a rock which miraculously floated for him. On his return he delivered so effective a sermon to his congregation that his father Toirdhealbhach, who was listening, decided to give up his throne and become a monk. The king thus quietly departed for the monastery of Lismore (in Co Waterford) where he was accepted by St Colmán, who was the abbot there.

Several of Flannán's adventures concern how he overcame robbers and brought them to repentance. For instance, the meat of oxen which they steal cannot be cooked and turns rotten before the robbers' eyes. We further read that, on one occasion, he turned into stone a group of jesters who threatened to satirise him. During his episcopate the crops grew copiously and the sea was full of fish, the trees full of fruit, and the poor were generously cared for. This is a borrowing of the conventional description of the **kingship** of a good ruler. Flannán's relics were kept at Killaloe, where they were much venerated. His feastday is December 18.

J F Kenney (1929), 404-5; S Malone (1902).

FLIODHAIS (earlier, Flidais) Mythical lady, apparently a goddess of deer and cattle. In origin, her name is likely to have referred to liquid, and in particular to milk. She is sometimes given the epithet 'foltchaoin', which means 'soft-haired'.

Some accounts have her as one of the Tuatha Dé Danann (see **Mythological Cycle**), among whom she is said to have had four daughters, but her husband is not named. Elsewhere she is described as wife of king Adhamair who, curiously, was identified through her name as 'Adhamair Fliodhais'. Through this husband she was mother of another king, Nia Seaghamain. The latter's name is explained fancifully as 'warrior of deer-treasure', and we are told that during his reign 'cows and does were milked together every day'. It was his mother who bestowed this benefit on his reign, for she was the tamer of deer. Thus her herd of both wild and domesticated animals was known as 'buar Fliodhais' ('buar' meaning cattle). She is apparently a version of an original mother-goddess and her name may well have been an alternative designation for such a personage (see also the associations of the **Mór-Ríoghain** and of **Brighid** with cattle and of **Oisín's** mother Blaí Dheirg with deer).

Doubtlessly because of her role as patron of cattle she was brought into association with **Fearghus mac Róich**, who had equine connections, and became his consort. We are told that she alone could satisfy his sexual appetite, whereas when she was absent he required no less than seven women. One of the tales of the **Ulster Cycle** told of how Fearghus wooed and won her. Here she is described as wife of Ailill Fionn, king of the Gamhanra sept (in present-day Co Mayo). When at the court of queen **Meadhbh**, the satiric poet **Bricriu** arranged for **Fearghus** and her to meet. They fell in love with each other, and accordingly began to plot against Ailill Fionn. The latter, suspecting treachery, made captives of Fearghus and his men when they came to feast at the fortress of Fliodhais. She, however, plied her husband with drink, knowing that he would release Fearghus through his noble nature when his senses were fuddled. Once free, Fearghus joined Meadhbh's forces in an attack on his rival. Ailill Fionn fought bravely against vastly superior odds. When all his men had fallen, he asked a smith called Ceartan to allow him to escape in that smith's boat but Ceartan refused, whereupon Ailill Fionn beheaded him with a sling-shot as he sailed away. Fighting alone against his foes, Ailill was slain; and Fliodhais together with her herd of wonderful cattle became the possession of Fearghus. The most prized beast among her herd was a cow called the Maol ('hornless one'), one milking of which would be full nourishment for three hundred men and their families. Fliodhais remained the wife of Fearghus until she died in his company long after in Ulster.

This story, which portrays both Fearghus and Fliodhais in an untypically treacherous light, was composed in the 9th or 10th century, and it remained popular in manuscripts for a long time. Because of its association with the area, versions of the story have been popular in the folklore of north-west Mayo in recent centuries. These versions, however, have altered the name of Ailill Fionn to Dónall Dualbhuí and that of Fliodhais to Muinchinn. Dónall, whose sobriquet means 'yellow-tressed', was in fact stated to have been father of Ailill Fionn in the manuscripts, some of which have him slain in single combat by Fearghus. The easier memorability of his name accounts for why he was substituted for Ailill Fionn in the oral lore. He is described as a great warrior who ruled the Erris peninsula, and it is said that his wife Muinchinn owned a wonderful white cow. The folklore claims that she colluded with Fearghus when the latter came from Ulster to visit the area, and Ceartan is described as a giant. Dónall drowned him by holing the boat with a sling-shot; and regarding the contest between Dónall and Fearghus we are told that Muinchinn secretly exchanged the swords of the two champions in their scabbards, leaving Fearghus with the magical weapon of Dónall. Thus Fearghus slew the cheated Dónall, and took his wife and all his property. On crossing a river, however, Fearghus thought to himself that he could not trust a woman who had betrayed her husband, so he drowned her there. That river, which flows out of Carrowmore lake, is thus called the Munchin after her. It is also claimed that as Fearghus with two other warriors were driving the cattle away from

Erris, a giant killed the three of them with holly-darts shot from a bow.

R A S Macalister (1941), 122-3, 132-3 and (1956), 282-3; M A O'Brien (1962), 362; Rudolf Thuerneysen (1921), 319-20; Edward Gwynn (1924), 70-5; Ernst Windisch in *Irische Texte 2 (2)*, 206-23 and *3*, 294-5; Donald MacKinnon in *Celtic Review 1-4*, passim; Margaret Dobbs in *Ériu 8*, 133-52; P S Dinneen (1908) *2*, 176-9; Ordnance Survey Letters - Mayo (1838) *1*, 13-4, 157-8, 170, 397; Liam Mac Coisdealbha in *Béaloideas 13*, 206-8; Alan Bruford (1969), 97, 265.

FOMHÓIRE Malign supernatural race in the **Mythological Cycle**. Their designation (earlier, Fomóiri) meant 'underworld-phantoms', but from a confusion of the element 'mór' (phantom) with 'muir' (sea) they came to be regarded as sea-pirates.

The Fomhóire were the opponents of the divine **Tuatha Dé Danann** in the Irish version of the Indo-European myth of a great struggle between a divine race and a demonic one. The surviving text which describes this - the so-called 'second' battle of Moytirra (see **Mythological Cycle**) - has the Fomhóire living in regions to the north of Ireland such as Scandinavia and the Hebrides. This is obviously a reflex from the Viking raids on mediaeval Ireland, and prior to this portrayal the Fomhóire were apparently regarded as underwater spirits, and ultimately as spirits residing in the nether regions of the earth. Such an origin is echoed in the Moytirra text, in which some of them are associated with the soil and with agricultural skill. This text, based on an 8th-century account but with a good deal of material added by the 11th-century redactor, gives the earliest detailed account of the Fomhóire. They are not described as being particularly monstrous, for the adaptation of the **Lugh** myth to the tradition had made a more salutary portrayal of them possible. Lugh's mother Eithliu (variously Eithne) was daughter of the tyrant **Balar**, and the motif of a hostile maternal line meant that both she and Balar had to be portrayed as Fomhóire in the context of the great mythic battle. The surviving text has the Tuatha Dé arranging the marriage between Lugh's parents Cian and Eithne as an attempt at rapprochement with the Fomhóire, but the authentic plot had Cian gaining access to the maiden against her father's wishes and as a result Lugh (q.v.) being born.

The idea of love and marriage between the two races necessitated the conceit that not all the Fomhóire were ugly and repulsive, a conceit which is found also in the description of the birth of **Breas** in the same text. His father Ealatha is of the Fomhóire and is extraordinarily handsome. Breas was installed as their king by the Tuatha Dé, partly as a diplomatic gesture to the Fomhóire, and he was given a Tuatha Dé wife (see **Brighid**). When he connived with the Fomhóire in imposing tribute on Ireland and refused to entertain his subjects with the generosity of a king, the Tuatha Dé demanded that he resign. He went to the territories of the Fomhóire and arranged with two of their leaders, Balar and Inneach, to invade Ireland. They gathered a mighty force from the whole region between Scandinavia and Ireland, but in the battle of Moytirra they were defeated by the Tuatha Dé, with Balar being slain by Lugh. The poet of the Fomhóire, Lóch Leathghlas, was given quarter by Lugh, as also was Breas. The price which Breas paid for his life was agricultural advice, thus echoing the underground origins of his race.

The other source for descriptions of the Fomhóire is the mediaeval pseudo-historical compilation, *Lebor Gabála*. Here they are given a generally repulsive portrayal. In the time of **Parthalán**, we are told, they were led by one Cichol Gricenchos and they had 'single arms and single legs'. Parthalán and his people fought for a whole week with them and nobody was slain 'because it was a magic battle'. These are echoes of the great mythic contest described as the battle of Moytirra, and it is clear that the Fomhóire and their deeds all derive from that contest. The pseudo-historians, aware of the chronological difficulty of having the Fomhóire already in Ireland when the various pioneering groups arrived, stressed that they were not settlers but mere sea-raiders. Accordingly, when **Neimheadh's** people had settled in Ireland they were oppressed by these Fomhóire, who had a fortress on Tor-Inis (Tory Island off the Donegal coast). This location was apparently chosen due to an early redaction of the Tuatha Dé versus Fomhóire clash which had the Fomhóire leaders residing in a great tower (Old Irish, 'tor' - see **Mythological Cycle**). We read that at the time of Neimheadh the Fomhóire were led by two kings, Conand and Morc, who had a great fleet and who demanded an exhorbitant tribute - namely, two-thirds of the progeny and wheat and milk which Neimheadh's people had. The latter attacked the

Fomhóire fortress on Tor-Inis and slew Conand, but Morc arrived with a huge fleet and, after a horrific contest, the survivors of Neimheadh's people withdrew and left Ireland. It is clear that in this account the pseudo-historians were making use of echoes from the clash between the Tuatha Dé and their Fomhóire oppressors.

In post-mediaeval literature the designation 'fomhóire' was applied in general to any strange grotesque beings required in the plot of narratives. Gradually the designation - in its later form 'fomhórach' - came to be used as a common noun to describe a huge and ugly enemy, so that a 'fomhórach' was in the late literature the usual counterpart of the 'fathach' or giant of folklore.

E A Gray (1982): R A S Macalister (1939), 270-1 and (1940), 10-5, 122-5 134-43; RIA Dictionary - s.v. 'fomóir', 'fomórda'.

FOTHADH CANAINNE Mythical warrior in early Irish literature. He is described as leader of a band of warriors ('fianna') in Connacht.

It has been suggested that 'Fothadh' was the name of an ancestor deity and is cognate with the designation Votadīnī for a Celtic people in Britain. In Irish genealogies Fothadh is an ancestor of the Uaithne sept of north-east Limerick and the adjoining part of Tipperary, but he also has been intruded into Leinster genealogies and it seems that he was originally connected with several septs, probably of the south Connacht area. Typical of a Celtic deity, he was often triplicated, giving rise to the characters Fothadh Canainne, Fothadh Cairptheach, and Fothadh Airgtheach. These are described as three brothers, sons of a warrior called Mac Nia and his wife Fuinche, but this is learned invention. A clue to their real identity is afforded by the according to them of nicknames such as 'Óendé', 'Clóendé', and 'Tróendé', all of which contain the word 'dia' which signifies a god. The trio were included in the lists of kings of Ireland drawn up by the mediaeval pseudo-historians, it being claimed that they ruled together for a year until Fothadh Airgtheach slew Fothadh Cairptheach and was himself slain by **Caoilte** in a great battle at Magh Linne (Moylinny, Co Antrim).

The sobriquet Canainne is a genitive, and an attested earlier form of it was Canann. It may be that this was a corruption of 'Danann' (see **Danu**) which would mean that Fothadh was anciently considered a consort of the land-goddess. Some references add weight to this, for Fothadh Canainne is mentioned as having been the mate of the **Cailleach Bhéarra**, who was very much of a kind with Danu. In literary narrative, he is described as a great warrior and leader of a fierce band of fighters. In this context he is connected with the most famous of all 'fianna' leaders, **Fionn mac Cumhaill**. We read in a 9th-century text that he was half-brother to Cuirreach Life, who was slain in a feud with Fionn. This brought Fothadh and Fionn into conflict with each other, but a truce was arranged and Fionn invited his opponent to an ale-feast. Fothadh stated that he was under **'geis'** not to attend a banquet except in the company of 'white faces', meaning heads of the dead, whereupon Fionn went and slew Téite, sister of Fothadh, along with her husband. This caused undying hostility between Fothadh and Fionn, and a huge number of warriors were killed in their feud. There may be an echo of Fothadh's original role as an ancestor-deity in this strange custom attributed to him of drinking with the dead.

His own death came about, according to the early literature, as the result of a love-affair with the wife of a Munster 'fianna' leader called Ailill Flann Beag. She eloped with him, but this led to a great battle at a place called Féic (apparently near Millstreet, Co Cork) in which Fothadh was defeated and beheaded. After his death, the head recited a poem to the woman describing the battle.

The later literature has a character named Fathadh Canann as a member of Fionn's troop. One genealogical source preserves the tradition that he was a king, and states with great fancy that 'he obtained the government of the whole world from the rising to the setting sun, and he took hostages of the streams, the birds, and the languages'.

T F O'Rahilly (1946), 6, 10-11, 34; M A O'Brien (1962), 99, 264, 656; R A S Macalister (1956), 340-3; Myles Dillon in *Celtica 5*, 73; M C Dobbs in *Revue Celtique 47*, 302 and 48, 211; Whitley Stokes in *Irische Texte 3*, 376-9; Kuno Meyer (1910), xv, 4-17 and in *Zeitschrift für celtische Philologie 7*, 299; Vernam Hull in *ibid 20*, 400-4; John O'Donovan (1849), 4-7; Gerard Murphy (1953), 363-4.

FRAOCH (earlier, Froech) Mythical Connacht hero in the **Ulster Cycle**. His father's name was Idath (later given as Fiodhach), and his mother was the otherworld lady Bé Find, sister of **Bóinn**.

A prose-text dating from the 8th century, *Táin Bó Fraích*, combines what seem in essence to be two different stories. The first of these can be taken as the original narrative of the hero, a narrative which had been developed a century or so earlier based on placenames. These were Dubhlinn Froích ('the heathery dark pool'), which was fancifully interpreted as a pool where a man named Froech was drowned; and Carn Froích ('the heathery cairn'), interpreted as the cairn where the same man was buried. According to the narrative, this Froech or Fraoch was a supremely handsome youth, and his mother brought twelve red-eared white cows to him from the otherworld. Fionnabhair, daughter of queen **Meadhbh** and king Ailill mac Máta, fell in love with him on his repute. Hearing this, he went to the Connacht capital of Cruachain (Rathcroghan, Co Roscommon), and was warmly welcomed there. Time passed by, and eventually he got an opportunity to meet Fionnabhair as she washed her hands by a river. She refused to elope with him, but gave him as token a thumb-ring which she had received as a present from her father. Fraoch then went and spoke to Ailill, who demanded all his wealth, including the twelve wonderful cows, as bridal-price for the girl. Fraoch refused and, fearing that he would take Fionnabhair away without permission, Ailill planned treachery against him. He invited the young man to go swimming in the river Dubhlinn, and when Fraoch was in the water Ailill looked in his wallet and saw the thumb-ring there. He flung it into the river, and a salmon consumed it, but Fraoch killed the salmon and hid it under the bank. Ailill then asked him to bring berries from a rowan-tree which grew on the far side of the river, knowing that a water-monster dwelt there. In midstream the monster attacked Fraoch, who called for his sword. Fionnabhair dived in and brought the sword to him despite the opposition of her father, who even threw a javelin in her direction. Fraoch slew the monster and, on his return from the water, his mother and a group of otherworld women came wailing there and took him into an otherworld dwelling which, like the royal court, was also at Cruachain. There he was quickly healed of his wounds, and Ailill visited the dwelling and invited him to a feast at the royal court. Fraoch sent a servant to find the salmon which he had hidden, and when Ailill demanded the ring of his daughter it was presented on a dish with the cooked salmon. Ailill then consented to the marriage, and Fraoch for his part agreed to bring his herd of cows to Cruachain.

This account has obviously been readjusted to suit the context of Meadhbh's court as described in the Ulster Cycle. The original narrative must have told of how the hero was drowned, or was slain by the monster, in the pool. Such a death of Fraoch is indeed described in the Cycle's main text, *Táin Bó Cuailgne*. There he goes to oppose **Cú Chulainn** in the water, the two warriors wrestle, and Fraoch is drowned. This is, however, a dislocation of the tradition of Fraoch's death, making it fit in with the tragic deaths of several other young warriors in single combat with the great Cú Chulainn. The motif of the ring in the fish's belly is a borrowing from early mediaeval lore (see **Wonder Tales**, Type 736A), and was no doubt included by the author for extra dramatic effect.

The second story follows in *Táin Bó Fraích* as if tacked onto the first. It describes how, on his return home to collect his herd, Fraoch found that the cattle had been stolen - together with his wife (rather inappropriately in view of the preceding account) and his three sons. He set out in search of them, and was joined by **Conall Cearnach** in the quest. Arriving at the Alpine mountains they found a great fortress there, where the captives were being held. They persuaded a woman-servant, who was of Irish descent, to leave the door of the fortress open for them at night, and thus they took the fortress and Fraoch rescued his family and cattle. Returning home, he joined Meadhbh and Ailill on the great cattle-raid of Cooley (see **Ulster Cycle**). The story, in fact, is little more than an 8th-century improvisation to fill out the details of the preparations for that great cattle-raid and, like the account of Fraoch's death at the hands of Cú Chulainn, is very much a secondary development due to the borrowing of Fraoch into the Ulster Cycle.

There were different versions of the Fraoch narratives, for an 11th-century verse-text does not bring Fraoch and Conall so far overseas on their quest, but they go rather to an otherworld dwelling of **Donn** in Scotland. Again, around the 13th century, a new prose version was compiled. This unites themes from the earlier literature by having Bóinn put prohibitions (see **'geis'**) on Fraoch against having a woman in his household, fighting Cú Chulainn, swimming between November and May, and pledging his arms. This text may well preserve some material from the original story - prior to Ulster Cycle influence. Fraoch's lover here is not Fionnabhair, but Treabhlann, a grand-daughter of the otherworld king **Aonghus**; and the girl's guardian is one Cairbre mac Rosa Ruaidh, who forbids her to go with Fraoch. Treabhlann is tricked by the otherworld lord **Midhir** into believing that Fraoch is dead, and as a result she dies from grief.

A 14th-century poem retells the first story, and this may also in some ways reflect the original plot, even though it accepts the Ulster Cycle context. According to it, Meadhbh also loved Fraoch and, when he preferred her daughter, she planned treachery by sending him to bring her some rowan-branches guarded by the water-monster. When he was attacked by the creature, Fionnabhair threw a knife to him and he slew it with the knife. But so badly wounded was he that he himself expired. Fionnabhair, it is implied, died from grief, and some placenames are derived from the adventure. This poem passed into oral tradition in Scotland and remained popular there for many centuries.

[*Táin Bó Fraích*] Wolfgang Meid (1974).

[Combat with Cú Chulainn] Cecile O'Rahilly (1976), 26-7.

[Ring in salmon] James Carney (1955), 37-47.

[Other versions] Carney in *Celtica 2*, 154-94; Kuno Meyer in *Zeitschrift für celtische Philologie 3*, 166-75; Neil Ross (1939), 198-207, 249-53. Cf. Edward Gwynn (1913), 356-65.

[Late folklore] J F Campbell (1872), 29-33.

FURSA Saint of the 7th century AD.

The mediaeval biographies of him state that he was the son of a Munster prince called Fionntan and that his mother was daughter of Aodh Fionn, king of Breifne (in Co Cavan). When Fursa came of age he decided to be a monk, and went to a monastery which had been founded by **Bréanainn** on an island on Loch nOirbsean (Lough Corrib in Co Galway). On the advice of Bréanainn, he settled at Ráth Mat, which became known as Cill Fhursa (near Headford). This settlement grew into a monastery, and some time later Fursa decided to go on a visit to his father, who had now become a local king in Munster. While sojourning in his native place, a sudden illness seized Fursa, and in the course of this illness he had a great vision. Three angels brought him to a hilltop, and when he looked down he saw the world with four fires dangling above it. One of the angels explained that these fires were falsehood, covetousness, discord, and cruelty. Gradually the fires grew together into one great conflagration, and a group of devils then assailed Fursa with false accusations. He was protected by the angels, who divided the flames before him to let him pass through. As he did so, however, the devils thrust towards him a man whom he had known in life and some of whose clothes Fursa had received when he died. For thus receiving the clothes of one who had died in sin, Fursa was burned on his shoulder and face, and these scars remained on him after he awoke and recovered from his illness.

Following on the vision, Fursa reduplicated his efforts at praying and preaching and, exactly a year from that day, an angel appeared to him and instructed him to continue his work in Ireland for twelve years. When that period was concluded, he crossed the sea to England and began to preach there. He was well received by king Sigbert of East Anglia, and from there proceeded to the Continent, where he was supported by the Frankish king Clovis II. After many years of missionary success, he died in or about the year 648 and was buried at Peronne.

The celebrated vision of Fursa seems to derive from an experience which the saint himself had. The earliest account of it is given by the English historian Bede in the year 731. Bede was told of the vision by an old monk who had heard it from a man who had it from Fursa's own mouth. It was a cold day when Fursa had recounted it to that man, but the saint had nevertheless sweated profusely from the recollection of it. The vision became widely known in mediaeval Latin literature, and it was very likely the source which suggested to Dante the plot of his *Divina Comedia*. No doubt due to Fursa's image as a visionary, a text in Irish from around the 9th century attributes a series of pessimistic prophecies to him concerning the social life of the future.

A mediaeval glossarian tells a fanciful anecdote concerning Fursa and his friend, St Maighniu. When Fursa once visited Maighniu at the latter's monastery (Kilmainham in Dublin) they, out of affection for each other, decided to exchange their ailments. Fursa thus transferred his headaches and piles to Maighniu, whereas the latter gave to Fursa a reptile which was in him. This reptile had a violent appetite, and in order to abate it Fursa had to eat three portions of bacon each morning. Later, when he was abroad, a bishop censured him for his voraciousness, whereupon the saint caused the reptile to enter the bishop's throat.

The bishop then understood, and Fursa recalled the reptile to himself. This anecdote is in fact an adaptation of an international folklore plot (see **Animal Tales**, Type 285B).

In disagreement with his Munster pedigree, one tradition claimed that Fursa was of the Conaille sept of Muirtheimhne (in Co Louth), but this appears to have been a secondary development. His feastday is January 16.

J F Kenney (1929), 500-3; Charles Plummer (1896) *1*, 163-8; W W Heist (1965), 37-55; Johannes Bollandus / Godefridus Henschenius (Paris, 1863), January, *2*, 401-8; Whitley Stokes (1905), 44-7, 190, 424 and in *Revue Celtique 25*, 385-404; Kuno Meyer in *Zeitschrift für celtische Philologie 9*, 168; John O'Hanlon (1875) *1*, 222-86; IFC 132:139.

[re Dante] see C S Boswell (1908).

G

'GEIS' A term often used in Irish literature to imply a magical demand or prohibition placed on a celebrated personage. The word itself has been variously explained. One theory relates it to 'guidhe', meaning request or prayer, while another theory is that in origin it meant 'happening' or 'destined occurrence'. It frequently occurs in its plural 'gessa' (later, 'geasa').

The idea seems to have been central to ancient Irish ritual of **kingship**, the king being a sacred person whose function it was to maintain equilibrium in the society and in the environment. The life of such a person would be hedged about by magic, and he therefore had to always make the correct decisions relative to his function. The phenomenon of 'geis' specified what his approach should be. The concept of 'geis' probably originated from an idea that the **goddess** of sovereignty imposed certain conditions on her kingly spouse, and it is significant that the early literature focusses in particular on the varieties of 'geis' associated with kings of the great cultic centre, **Tara**. From this, it spread to the contexts of great heroes also, and is instanced in the cases of **Cú Chulainn** and **Fionn mac Cumhaill**, among others. In all events, the result of acting contrary to 'geis' is the social destruction and the personal death of the individual.

Probably as a reflex from the image of female sovereignty, the imposition of 'geis' was represented in love-stories as being a special privilege of women (see, for instance **Deirdre**, and Gráinne in the entry on **Diarmaid ua Duibhne**). In the later romances and in folklore such conditions became known as 'heavy geasa of magic', and they were much employed as a device to set a plot in motion. A hero may lose to a hag at chess or cards, and as her prize she imposes 'geasa' on him to perform some seemingly impossible task.

RIA Dictionary s.v. 'geis'; J R Reinhard (1933); Philip O'Leary in *Celtica 20*, 85-107; David Greene in Hans Bekker-Nielsen ed (1977), 9-19; E P Hamp in *Ériu 32*, 161-2.

GHOSTS The native attitude to the dead in Ireland was that they formed a sort of otherworld community, and this tradition has survived into recent folklore in the context of the **fairies**. A good deal of lore, in fact, has an interchangeable situation between fairy dwellings and the graveyards where the dead are buried. As is clear from the fairy lore, members of the otherworld community were imagined to live lives which were broadly parallel to those led by the human community, and they sometimes entered the human world for quite natural reasons, such as trading or seeking assistance. There was also a strong and ancient tradition which had the dead highly respected as preservers of ancient learning and, under certain conditions, they bestowed special types of knowledge on the world of the living (see **Find**, **Seanchán**, **Poets**, and **Fairies**).

Although there are accounts in the mediaeval literature of warriors, after their own death, indirectly exacting vengeance on enemies (see **Conchobhar mac Neasa** and **Maolodhrán**), there seems to have been no generalised lore in early Ireland which had dead people gratuitously returning to cause terror or destruction. The hostility which the early literature sometimes describes as existing between the inhabitants of tumuli or cairns on one side and human heroes on the other is basically of the same type as competition between leading personalities in the ordinary world. In early mediaeval times, the Church made November 2 the feast of All Souls and, since this came two nights after the ancient Celtic festival of Samhain (see **Time**), much of the ideas concerning the community of the dead was switched to the new date. In a broader sense, the Christian religion gave rise to certain distinctive types of lore of its own concerning the dead. These can be divided into two categories. One concerns well-intentioned dead people, such as those who try to assist relatives who are in either physical or spiritual need, or those who are in Purgatory and who return to seek assistance for themselves in their plight. The other category concerns dead people who, through having led a bad life, have become evil spirits and maliciously return to do harm to the living. Finally, Irish folklore has many examples of ghosts of a type which were borrowed from the folklore of other countries in the post-mediaeval period.

There are some accounts in the mediaeval literature of saints returning to protect their monasteries and monastic communities, for instance **Seanán** and **Ciarán** of Clonmacnoise who stabbed the wrongdoers with their staffs. The hagiographical texts also give several examples of how the saints could effect the release of souls from Purgatory through the power of prayer. This, of course, would have been a point much stressed by clergymen down through the ages, but it is far more common for such revenants in folklore to seek, not prayer, but the settlement of some debt they have left unpaid. A legend found in many parts of Ireland, as well as abroad, tells of how a man was once inadvertently locked into a church and, finding no way out, he decided to bed down there till morning. At midnight a priest came out onto the altar and indicated that he required somebody to be a server at his Mass. The man willingly undertook the task, and after Mass was over he was thanked earnestly by the priest, who explained that he had been coming from Purgatory every night for a long time. He had left one Mass unsaid in life and could not celebrate it until he got somebody to assist him, but now was free to enter heaven.

It was said that revenants from Purgatory looked pale and wan, and had thin legs. They could not speak until spoken to by a human, and the proper form of address to use was 'in God's name, what is troubling you?' Such a soul might return to seek assistance to their own house or to that of a friend, but stories also tell of souls encountered in quite unexpected places. Purgatory was usually understood as a great fiery flagstone or a cold and miserable lake, but some souls could endure their suffering in lonely parts of the earthly landscape - such as in the bark of a tree, beneath a leaf, or between foam and a river. One story tells of a horseman who heard a loud laugh from one such location and enquired who was there. A voice explained that it was a suffering soul which had just heard the news that a baby had been born, a baby who would grow up to be a priest and who would read a Mass which would gain the soul's release from Purgatory. On hearing this, the horseman was struck by the magnitude of his own sins and jumped from his horse, begging forgiveness from God. All his sins were wiped away between the saddle and the ground. Variants of this have a suffering soul offering to share its Mass with another and thus halve their respective terms, and God is so touched by this charity that He forgives both immediately.

A particularly poignant tradition concerns the souls of unbaptised children, who anxiously seek baptism, without which they cannot enter heaven. It was customary to bury such babies on the perimeter of a graveyard, in a special little graveyard, or even in a boundary fence between two townlands. Being unbaptised their souls were said to inhabit limbo, which in Irish folklore was said to be situated at Sruth Orthuláin (probably the river Jordan). A story which was quite popular around the country describes how a priest notices twelve lights in the sky one night, and realises that these are the souls of the children born to a poor woman who was held in low regard. All of them had different fathers, and all had died young. The priest understood that they had appeared to him this night in order to let him know that their mother was very ill and needed a priest. He therefore went and prepared the woman for death, and as he left her hovel he noticed that one of the lights was dimmer than the rest. Realising that that light represented the only one of the children who had died without baptism, he recited the prayers of that Sacrament and immediately the light shone as strongly as the rest, before they all disappeared.

A story which can hardly be more than a few centuries old was current in several parts of the country. This tells of how a man meets with a pipe-smoking stranger one day, and they fall into conversation. The stranger offers him a puff of the pipe, and the man gratefully accepts it. On handing back the pipe, he prays God's blessing on the stranger. The latter, very pleased, explains that he is a soul from purgatory, and that he has now been released, for all that he required was that somebody should pray for his soul. This folk legend is told to explain the custom of saying a little prayer for the souls in Purgatory whenever one enjoys the comfort of smoking a pipe. An old saying in Irish claims that 'every ghost knows his own business', and some accounts tell of specific people who returned to give necessary financial advice to their relatives or dependents. They may also return to protect the helpless, for instance a dead mother warning the stepmother against illtreating her children. Several versions have been collected of a story which has a ghost saving a living person from some evil spirits which are abroad. A man who is benighted on his journey is told by the ghost to leave the road for a little while, and soon he notices some hostile beings passing by.

Such hostile beings can be in human or animal shape, but they are always regarded as evil spirits who intend to cause physical harm to people. They are either demons or damned souls, and more usually they appear as individuals which haunt some part of the countryside at night. A horseman or cart-man travelling by night, for instance, might suddenly notice a huge weight behind him, and on looking discover that a spirit is there. Such stories usually tell of how the man gets respite from the spirit when he promises to return to the same place on the following night. He brings a priest with him, and the priest makes a circle with blessed water around the man and then banishes the spirit. The spirit in this type of story is invariably that of a dead woman, and a common formula for the conversation has the priest first asking the spirit what made a devil of her. 'I committed murder,' she answers, but the priest says that this was not the reason. 'I murdered children,' she says, but the priest again states that this was not what made her a devil. Then she admits that she killed children for money, and the priest agrees that the sin of professional infanticide has demonised her. She is banished in a flash of fire.

A late mediaeval text describes a conversation between St **Colm Cille** and the devil, in which the evil one states in a semi-quatrain that the clergy deserve no respect because they preach for their own benefit. Challenging the saint to cap the verse, he says 'what is the semi-quatrain for this?' Colm answers in the same metre to the effect that the clergy's charity benefits those in need of it, and thus wins the debate. This is obviously a projection onto the spiritual realm of a practice of challenging each other common among **poets**. A similar stave-anecdote was popular among the Irish-speakers of Munster, and it appears to have been invented by some scholar acquainted with the Greek story of Oedipus and the sphinx. According to it, a certain lonely place was haunted by an evil spirit which was wont to confront late-night travellers, recite two lines about a candle and candlestick, and challenge them to 'put a semi-quatrain to that'. All failed the test, and were killed by the spirit, until one night a drunken poet was passing by. Three times he capped the verse for the spirit, which disappeared in a sheet of flame and was never again seen there.

Evil spirits were said to often appear in the form of animals, particluarly a black pig or a black dog, which nocturnal apparitions were identified with the devil himself. This type of lore was adopted from England in the 16th or 17th century and has now become general throughout the country. Although it is never expressly stated in Irish folklore, the idea is that such sinister animals could physically attack a sinner and take him away to hell. Their real function is to warn people against staying out too late at night drinking, card-playing, or otherwise misbehaving. Spirits were usually said to be encountered at intermediary places, such as a bridge, a crossroads, or a boundary fence. If confronted by some such apparition, the conventional advice was to recite a prayer and to make haste towards a stream or river, for it was believed that aggressive spirits could not cross running water. Other counsels were that one should not go out at night without some salt in one's pocket, some holy water, a hazel-stick, or a black-hafted knife, all of which were believed to give good protection against spirits. Regarding the knife, one was advised to 'plunge and not withdraw', the effect of this being that the spirit decomposed into an unpleasant substance resembling slime or jelly.

The idea that hidden treasure was guarded by spirits is probably quite old in Ireland, but it is expressed in folklore through imagery associated with later beliefs. For instance, men who go at night to dig up such treasure may be put to flight by the sudden appearance of spirits such as a savage bull, a massive dog, or a huge bird. There was also a belief, though not a very common one, that a human spirit could be a guardian of a hoard, such a spirit being that of a man killed and buried there long ago specifically for that purpose. Though this coincides with some archaeological discoveries, the actual folk belief may be of more recent origin. Definitely recent is the lore concerning the 'white lady', which is seen at night in the grounds of various castles and large houses. She is usually interpreted as being the ghost of a young woman who was once a resident of the particular building, and who committed suicide after being disappointed in love.

Other apparitions may be more formidable, such as the re-appearance at their former residences of notorious landlords or magistrates, often in the form of ferocious animals though unable to do further harm to mortals, and headless coaches which also are associated with big houses and power abused in former times. Because of a resemblance between these coaches and actual horse-drawn hearses, however, they were also interpreted as vehicles coming from the realm of the dead to bring people with them from this life. Thus, a nocturnal ghostly carriage either seen or heard was taken to be a sign that somebody in the locality would soon die. If the vehicle touched a person or spattered blood on him that was an indication that he would be taken away soon after, so people were advised that, on hearing the approach of such a vehicle, they should lie face downwards on the ground and turn their coat inside out so as to be unrecognisable. Other accounts of hauntings, such as the idea that phantom armies can be heard at the sites of famous battles, are folk fancies which arise naturally from contemplation of events of the past.

A curious story was told in connection with the popular love-song entitled 'Cailín Deas Crúite na mBó' ('the Pretty Milkmaid') which was sung to a beautiful and plaintive air. According to the story, a priest was going on a sick-call one night when he heard singing from behind a fence. He stood entranced by the air, and wondered who was singing it. So he went on tiptoes to the fence and looked into the field, only to discover that the beautiful notes were coming from the mouth of a massive black dog. Then the priest realised that the devil was using the song to delay him from tending to the person who was dying. How such a story got attached to the song is difficult to determine but it may have originated in an admonition to priests not to pay too much attention to love-songs.

A very distinctive body of lore centres on one particular spirit, which is called the 'púca'. This spirit appears in the form of a horse or a calf, and is wont to run in under the legs of a benighted person and carry him on nightmare rides. A legend was commonly told of a particular man who was thus terrorised by headlong gallops on cliff-tops for two successive nights. However, he got advice from a knowledgeable friend, and on the third night he was prepared for the púca. He had steel spurs attached to his boots, and when the spirit hoisted him onto its back he lacerated it mercilessly with the spurs. The púca begged to be let go, and the man complied on condition that the troublesome being would never again bother him. This story was told of several places, most notably of the aptly named Poll an Phúca (Poulaphouca, Co Wicklow). The name of this spirit is cognate with the English 'puck', and the being itself seems to have originated as a type of troublesome demon in Continental lore of the early Middle Ages. The snail was nicknamed in Irish 'the púca's spit', probably because its horns resembled the demonic image of the spirit-animal. The púca was said to either spit or defecate on wild fruit at the beginning of November, thus rendering it unsafe to eat such fruit from then onwards.

There is one other striking, though not very prominent, type of ghostly manifestation, called in Irish 'taise' and in English a fetch. This is the image of a living person seen in a place where the person is not present. It was a puzzling phenomenon, and was taken to presage some unfortunate event, such as an accident or drowning. Most frightening of all was for a person to meet one's own fetch, a circumstance which betokened certain death. Because of the widespread belief in ghosts, there were many humorous accounts of people who were over-nervous and prone to mistake ordinary things at night for some spirit or other.

J A MacCulloch (1911), 333-47; T P Cross (1952), 214-24; Seán Ó Súilleabháin (1942), 479-92 and in *Béaloideas 21*, 32-105, 210-29, 286-9, 298-300 and (1967), 86-9; Kevin Danaher (1964), 108-13; Patrick Byrne (n.d.); John J Dunne (1977); Dáithí Ó hÓgáin (1982), 369-73; Jennifer Westwood (1987), 176-80; Anne O'Connor in *Sinsear 1*, 33-41; Patricia Lysaght in *ibid*, 43-59; Bróna Nic Amhlaoibh (1977); Seán Garvey / Barry O'Reilly (1986); Deasún Breatnach (1990).

GLAS GHOIBHNEANN Famous cow in Irish folklore, which was said to have been a marvellous milker. Her name means literally 'the grey of Goibhniu', but it is often corrupted into various forms, such as Glas Ghoibhleann and Glas Ghoibhneach.

Goibhniu was a mythical smith, probably in origin a Celtic god of smithcraft, but a special cow is not connected with him in the literature. The strength of the Glas Ghoibhneann lore throughout Ireland and in western Scotland, however, suggests some antiquity in her legend. Furthermore, in folk recensions of the myth of **Lugh** and **Balar** in Ulster, she occurs as a cow owned by this same Goibhniu; and in the lore of southwest Munster she is the cow owned by Goibhniu's folk counterpart Goibhleann. The legend told of her all over

Ireland describes how she filled with milk every pail put under her by her unnamed owner. However, a jealous woman claimed that she had a vessel which the Glas could not fill, and accordingly she brought a sieve and began to milk the great cow. The Glas yielded a continuous stream of milk, enough to fill a lake, but it all ran through the sieve. Eventually, she became exhausted by the effort and died.

Variant accounts of the Glas state that she was a fairy cow which came in from the sea to a poor family, and that she yielded a great supply of milk for them and produced several calves. One day, however, a member of the family struck her with a spancel, and then she mysteriously disappeared, never to return. This may be related to ordinary fairy lore, but it contains echoes also of ancient tradition of a cow-goddess (see **Bóinn**). It is likely that such a great cow was connected with the smith Goibhniu in early Irish lore, and that this particular story of her nigh-inexhaustible milk and her death was a narrative which was invented at some stage on the basis of ancient myth. Since variants of the story are found also in Wales and in England, its origins must go back to early mediaeval times at least.

Séamus Ó Duilearga (1948), 257-9, 429; Seán Ó Súilleabháin (1942), 497; T P Cross (1952), Motifs B109.4.3 and D1652.3; Jennifer Westwood (1987), 254, 314-6.

GOBÁN SAOR Famous craftsman of Irish legend, concerning whom a number of anecdotes were told throughout the country.

The name seems to be a hypocoristic form of **Goibhniu**, the ancient god of smithcraft, while the sobriquet Saor means 'artificer'. There are indications that Goibhniu, and his Welsh counterparts Gofannon and Gwydion, were regarded as expert craftsmen generally, and Gobán could thus have functioned as an alternative form of the deity's name from an early period. One 9th-century religious poem refers to God, the constructor of the firmament, as 'Gobán', making it clear that such an appellation was appropriate to a master builder. An account from a century or so later claims that Gobán Saor was the son of a certain Tuirbhe who, by throwing a hatchet against it, stopped the tide from coming any further than Tráigh Thuirbhe (Turvey strand, near Lusk in Co Dublin). We read that Tuirbhe was one of the followers of **Lugh**, which puts him into the same cultural ambit as Goibhniu (see **Tuatha Dé Danann**). His story occurs in the **place-lore**, a quite unreliable source, but the allusion may echo the designation 'Gobán Saor' for Goibhniu.

'Gobán' also came into use as a personal name, and the fact that it was borne by several monks caused the mediaeval writers to confuse the imagery of the great craftsman Goibhniu with the monastic context. Thus we read in a biography of **Abán** that a distinguished wright called Gobán lived in the same neighbourhood as that saint. This wright charged high prices to the monks for his services and was blinded through their reproaches, but Abán caused his sight to be restored to him while he constructed a monastery. In the biography of **Maodhóg**, we are told that Gobán was a member of that saint's community and that, after his hand had been blessed by Maodhóg, he built a church with wondrous carvings in it. The accounts of **Moling** tell of a 'famous artificer', called Gobán Saor, who built an oratory of timber for the saint. Gobán's wife insisted that he demand as payment for this the fill of the oratory of rye-grain. Moling promised this, provided that Gobán could invert the oratory so that it could be filled. The saint thus thought to outwit the wright, but so skillful was Gobán that he succeeded in inverting it without the least damage. The Uí Dheagha sept (of Co Kilkenny) contributed all their corn to its filling and the triumphant Gobán took away his grain, only to find it turned into a heap of maggots on the morrow. It is noticeable that all of these three hagiographical accounts associate Gobán with south Leinster locations, and it therefore seems that lore of this particular avatar of Goibhniu originated in that area.

If so, it soon began to spread. Folklore shows that it has lost the definite identity of the master craftsman by applying the definite article to his name and calling him 'an Gobán Saor'. What seems to be an echo of his original identity with Goibhniu is the folk belief that the Gobán was 'the only true smith who ever lived', but he is mainly featured in folklore as a great builder and carpenter. Several old monasteries, and particularly round towers, in different parts of the country are said to have been erected by him, and one common folk legend shows that the old tension between a pagan deity and Christian saints, though transformed, has not disappeared. The Gobán Saor, we are told, was once building a monastery but, when it was almost completed, the monks tried to lower his wages. He refused to renegotiate the arrangement, but they waited until he was on top of the building and then removed all ladders and scaffolding. They said that they would not allow him to descend unless he agreed to their proposal. The clever Gobán, however, began to throw down stone after stone of the building, saying that this was as easy a way as any to descend safely to the ground, whereupon the monks relented and agreed to pay the full wages. That this legend is a development of the hagiographical accounts is obvious, but it adds the creative ingredient of quick wit attributed to the Gobán.

In the biography of Moling, the Gobán's wife is called Ruaidhseach, and she is there portrayed as a shrewd and calculating woman. The best-known of all the legends concerning him can be seen to be a further development on this theme. This, told in folklore throughout Ireland and Gaelic Scotland, relates how the Gobán and his son were once engaged on building a great castle for a king in foreign parts. They worked for seven years on the castle, and when it was nearing completion the wily king planned to put them to death, lest they might build an equally fine residence for somebody else. The Gobán, suspecting the king's intentions, said that he could not build the final turret without a tool which he had inadvertently left behind him at home. This tool, he said, was called 'crooked and straight'. The king, unwilling to allow the Gobán or his son to depart, sent his own son to Ireland for it, but the name of the supposed tool was in fact a coded message and when the Gobán's wife heard it she knew that her menfolk were in danger. She told the foreign prince that it was in a deep trunk and, when he bent into the trunk to fetch it, she caught his two legs and threw him in. She locked the prince in the trunk, and then sent a message to the foreign king that, if he wished to see his son again, he had better allow her husband and son home. The king had no choice but to comply. The central motif of this legend - the outwitting of the selfish magnate by a builder who seeks an imaginary tool - was told in connection with various great buildings in western Europe.

When the theme of a clever wife became a major theme in stories of the Gobán Saor, imagery was attracted to that context from a folktale which described a clever peasant girl (see **Romantic Tales**, Type 875). The plot of this folktale was not, however, applied to the Gobán's own wife, whose reputation was sufficiently established, but to his daughter-in-law. We are told that, when his wife was due to give birth, the Gobán was away on business, and she was accompanied by another pregnant woman. The Gobán's wife gave birth to a baby girl, while the other woman had a boy. Knowing that the Gobán desired a son very much, they exchanged the babies. Time passed, and as the boy grew up the Gobán noticed, to his disappointment, that his 'son' had inherited little of his own skill and intelligence. Eventually the Gobán decided that the boy must marry a clever girl who would be able to look after his affairs for him, and so he sent him to the market with a sheep and instructions to bring back 'the skin and its worth'. The boy was non-plussed, but at the market he met a girl who advised him to sell the sheep to a butcher and then ask for the discarded hide. He did this, and when he returned home, the Gobán sent an invitation to that girl to come visit them. She must come neither dressed nor undressed, neither on the road nor off the road, neither by day nor by night. She cleverly fulfilled these conditions, and the Gobán arranged that she marry his boy.

The daughter-in-law proved to be as resourceful as the Gobán hoped. One day, he and his 'son' were on a long journey, and he asked the young man to shorten the road for him. The son did not know how to do this, and similarly failed when asked the same question on a second journey. Before they set out on a third journey, however, he consulted his wife, and she said that he should tell a story to the old man as they travelled. He did so, and this 'shortening of the road' pleased the Gobán very much. The master tradesman himself was full of quick wit, and some storytellers state that he came to understand the trick which had been played on him and realised that the girl was in reality his daughter. The origin of various tricks of the trade concerning building and carpentry were attributed to him. For instance, on seeing his son trying unsuccessfully to build a straight wall, he invented the plumb-line for the purpose, and he similarly invented a rule-cord for cutting straight pieces of timber. On one occasion, he came upon some poor men building a house which they could not complete because the three pieces of timber which they had for joists were too short. The Gobán showed them how to make a cross-joist with these timbers, which held the roof as well as beams of the proper length would. It was also said that he invented the method of placing 'a stone in and a stone out and a stone across' to ensure a solid structure in buildings. So deft and accurate was he that he could drive nails into the top of a high building without any climbing. He would throw a nail into the air, throw the hammer after it so that it would strike the nail into the proper place, and then catch the hammer again before it reached the ground.

50. GOBÁN SAOR *Restoration of Holy Cross Abbey in Co. Tipperary.*

Many of the mediaeval craftsmen had their own trademarks, which they left on buildings as testimony to their skill. At Holy Cross Abbey in Co Tipperary, several examples of such trademarks left by artisans can be seen. They belong to the reconstruction phase of the Abbey's history in the 15th century, and one of the most striking and enigmatic of these is a carving in stone of a cat with two tails. The identity of the craftsman or craftsmen who used this symbol is not known, but in popular tradition it became attributed to the Gobán Saor. A legend tells of how he once came to Holy Cross Abbey when a team of workmen were busy there. He joined in the work, but he was not invited to dinner with the rest. He asked the foreman what should he be doing while the others ate, and was jeeringly told that he could make a cat with two tails if he wished. He did just that, and when the builders returned they found that carving there, but the Gobán had departed. This association with the Tipperary area led to another striking connection. Some miles to the east of Holy Cross is a large bog, in the centre of which is a small 'island' of good grassy land. This, called Derrynaflan, was the site of an early monastic settlement, and a grave marked by stones there is claimed to be where the Gobán Saor is buried.

T F O'Rahilly (1946), 526; Whitley Stokes / John Strachan (1903) *2*, 294; Edward Gwynn (1924), 226-7; Stokes in *Revue Celtique 16*, 76-7; Charles Plummer (1910) *1*, clxiii-clxiv and (1922) *1*, 10, 188, 233, 238; Stokes (1907), 26-41; George Petrie (1845), 380-7; Lady Wilde (1890), 224; Séamus Ó Duilearga (1948), 263-6, 430-1; Lady Gregory (1926), 27-32; Patrick Kennedy (1866), 67-9; Seán Ó Súilleabháin (1942), 496-7.

GODDESSES The literature has many accounts of otherworld ladies which can be taken to echo ancient myth. Its accounts are quite diffuse both in the names given to these ladies and to the themes concerning them, but certain underlying presumptions are clear.

Regarding the names, most of these were originally descriptions of aspects of particular localities and thus attributes of the otherworld women associated with these localities. Examples of this are **Áine**, **Aoibheall**, **Clíona**, and Grian (literally 'sun', the name of a goddess of east Limerick in ancient times). A few instances suggest a more basic system of appellations, such as **Brighid** ('the exalted one') or **Mór-Ríoghain** ('phantom-queen'), while the name **Danu** is attested from many parts of Europe and is patently of primitive Celtic, or even of Indo-European, derivation. The confusion is best explained by postulating that Danu was the original name for an earth-goddess and that local variations of her cult, abroad and in Ireland, gave rise to a variety of other names which could equally be applied to a patroness of agriculture and of productivity. Other aspects of these otherworld ladies, such as the tendency towards triplication and their ability to appear in different shapes, were associated with Celtic deities from antiquity.

The agricultural imagery is especially pronounced in the cases of Danu, Brighid, and **Macha**, but it occurs to some degree or other in the contexts of the others also. The idea of fertility and of food-production means that a goddess could be regarded as synonymous with the soil, but this naturally was extended to other aspects of the physical environment, such as rivers and mountains. Practically all Irish rivers have feminine names, the most famous and perhaps the earliest such designation being **Bóinn**. The identification with mountain-tops is best instanced by the peaks called Dá Chích Dhanann ('the two paps of Danu') in Co Kerry. Being guarantor of food, the goddess would be inherently involved with social life and this would be expressed ritually. As an echo of this, Irish literature at all stages stresses the symbolic unity of a king with an otherworld lady. Such ladies are a metaphor for the land, sometimes very directly so, as when the three leaders of the fanciful Gaelic invasion (see **Míl**) gain the kingship of Ireland by an agreement with three ladies of the **Tuatha Dé Danann**. The names of the three ladies - Éire, Banba, and Fódla - are very relevant, for each is a name for the country. The latter two are used repeatedly by poets to refer to Ireland, whereas the first is the term used for the country both in literature and in ordinary speech. Its earlier form was Ériu, which seems to be from a Celtic Īveriu, meaning 'land', and a further derivative **Érainn** was used to refer to the bulk of the population of Ireland.

In the literature of the **Mythological Cycle**, Éire is given a pivotal position as a woman of the Tuatha Dé beloved by the **Fomhóire** leader and thereby the mother of **Breas**, who is an adept at agriculture. Her importance is further underlined in a mediaeval text (see **Kingship**), which describes a vision of her as 'the sovereignty of Ireland' giving a drink to each successive king of the country. The drink-image is embedded in the name of a goddess of sovereignty associated in ancient times with **Tara**, but who in the literature was transferred to the role of queen of Connacht - this was **Meadhbh**, whose name meant 'she who intoxicates'. Éire the otherworld lady represents Ireland in bad times and in good. Thus she can appear either as an ugly hag or a beautiful maiden. In the legend of the great king **Niall Naoi-ghiallach**, ancestor of the royal Uí Néill sept, she is transformed by his kiss from the ugly form into the beautiful one. This symbolises the reign of the proper king when misfortune is banished from Ireland and the whole country prospers. Through mediaeval times, the poets used the conceit that their patron kings and chieftains were spouses of the country or of a particular territory. This theme maintained its popularity as a poetic convention down to the 19th century, with Ireland (called Éire, Banba, or Fódla) appearing in visions to poets and telling them that she has been deprived of her spouse and has been defiled and degraded by the English overlords.

Since the goddess represented the land, the forces of nature, and life in general, the king as her mate imposed social order on these things. This myth, of course, involved mutual obligations, and Irish literature shows that kingship was surrounded by many kinds of magical conditions (see **'geis'**) The mediaeval writers tended to make indiscriminate use of débris from early ritual but, despite some dislocation, the idea of mutual obligations shows clearly in the account of the Ulster goddess Macha (q.v.), of the conditions which she imposes on her husband, and of the dire consequences to the Ulster kingdom when she is abused. On the other hand, Macha shows her social power by forcing three suitors to build the rampart of the Ulster capital, which is called Eamhain Mhacha. This involves portrayals of her as being sexually attractive and as a warrioress. The sexual attraction is stressed in particular in the story of the otherworld lady **Éadaoin**, wife of the king of Ireland. It is also found in the story of Eibhliu, who was abducted by **Eochaidh mac Maireadha** and from whom Sliabh Eibhlinne (Slieve Felim on the Limerick-Tipperary border) was reputedly named. The various ladies in mediaeval literature called Eithne, though not all explicitly stated to be of the otherworld, should be included also in this context. The war-function of the goddess is most clearly expressed in the accounts of the Mór-Ríoghain (q.v.), and this is obviously an extension of the role of the land-goddess into that of protector of her territory.

The writers of the mediaeval **place-lore** made some quite spontaneous narratives out of the theme of goddesses at war. We read, for instance, of the royal lady Tailtiu of the **Fir Bolg** who, after the defeat of her people by the Tuatha Dé, was forced to clear forest-covered plains and died from exhaustion as a result. Further otherworld ladies described as having been held in captivity were Tea and Carman, both of them - like Tailtiu - patronesses of great assemblies in early Ireland. It may be that such subjection was a mythic theme, reflecting control of the powers of nature, but it is more likely to have been a mere extension of the war-lore. The uncertain fortunes of war are instanced also in the case of the great god called the **Daghdha**, who was himself for a time subjected to servile captivity. The important point is that, whether triumphant like Macha or defeated like Tailtiu, the goddess is very powerful in terms of the landscape. Her aspect as patroness of animals is most clearly expressed in the traditions of **Brighid** and **Fliodhais**. Through an extension of agricultural symbolism into the realm of artistic production, Brighid functioned as a patroness of poets - a process also evidenced, in a more general context, by the role of the Tuatha Dé Danann (q.v.).

Since the general welfare of the environment was, according to ritual, dependent on the relations between the reigning king and the earth-goddess, this is a recurrent theme in the biographical accounts of kings. The mediaeval literature has otherworld women coming to become the wives or paramours of kings, while even human queens have their portrayal influenced to some extent by ancient myths of goddesses. In folklore, too, the goddess lore has survived. Several otherworld ladies - such as Áine, Aoibheall, or Clíona - have become fairy-queens, while the imagery of a prodigious worker is still current in legends of the famous hag called the **Cailleach Bhéarra**.

T F O'Rahilly in *Ériu 14*, 1-28; Proinsias Mac Cana (1970), 84-95; M-L Sjoestedt (1982), 37-51; Anne Ross (1967), 265-301.

GODS A large number of characters who occur in mediaeval Irish literature have vestiges of divine attributes, but not many personages are overtly divine. Analysis of what constitutes divinity in such cases is complicated by the nature of the literature itself, since practically all the texts were written by Christians and much of them by clerics. Given this, the general lack of attempts at demonising the mythical characters is much to the writers' credit, but there is no guarantee that the lore is being set by them in its proper context. Consequently, it is difficult to decide whether the rather amorphous character of much of the mythological material is due to such a quality being inherent in Celtic tradition, or to deliberate debunking by the writers, or indeed to imperfect knowledge of the lore on the part of the writers.

Some things are, however, clear, one of the most important being that the **Daghdha** (literally, 'good god') was an ancient patron of agricultural wealth and had a central role in the pre-Christian religion of Ireland. There are several indications that his role had quite a broad scope, and that other personages such as **Dáire**, **Dearg**, **Donn**, and **Eochaidh** originated as descriptions of specific aspects of his character. It is possible to distinguish a different stratum of divinities, who appear to have originated as patron personages of particular crafts in the ancient Celtic world. The cult of one great personage was in Ireland from several centuries BC, although he is never given divine status. This was **Find**, or **Fionn mac Cumhaill** as he came to be known. Originally a personification of wisdom, the basic ideas in his cult made it easier to envisage him as an earthly seer, and so from the beginning of Irish literature he is thus regarded. A study of his tradition suggests that he predated the deity **Nuadhu**, whose associate was **Aonghus** and around whom the lore of the divine **Tuatha Dé Danann** beings developed. It is probable that such patrons as **Dian Céacht**, **Goibhniu**, and **Oghma** were borrowed from Celtic lore abroad and assimilated to the otherworld community presided over by Nuadhu in the early centuries AD. All indications are that the cult and lore of the great **Lugh** were introduced in connection with the harvest festival.

It is obvious from such a brief listing that the gods known to early Irish tradition were assorted from various sources and that they delineated various ideas. The mediaeval writers, already faced with some confusion, adopted an approach towards the material which suited Christian beliefs and which also helped to put some coherent structure onto the lore of such personages i.e. they portrayed them as characters of ancient times. That the writers were not altogether successful in their purpose is obvious from the remaining contradictions, but the pseudo-historical scheme did help tp dramatise the lore. It allowed for the ancient gods to be portrayed primarily as great martial heroes, and this guaranteed that their imagery long outlived their relevance in Irish storytelling.

Proinsias Mac Cana (1970), 11-73; Myles Dillon / Nora Chadwick (1973), 173-201; M-L Sjoestedt (1982), 11-36, 52-61; E A Gray (1982), 117-32.

GOIBHNIU Mythical smith of the **Tuatha Dé Danann**. The name is a simple derivative of 'gobha' (modern, 'gabha'), the word for a smith, and his Welsh counterpart was the similarly mythical craftsman Gofannon.

There is no doubt that Goibhniu originally represented a deity. 'The science of Goibhniu', by which is meant smithcraft, is referred to in some early Irish charms which appeal to him for his protection. Generally, however, he is listed among the leading artisans of the Tuatha Dé, for whom he fashions spears to be used in the second battle of Moytirra. During the preparations for that battle (see **Mythological Cycle**), Ruadhán son of **Breas** went to spy on the Tuatha Dé and, noticing that Goibhniu was manufacturing such wonderful spears, attempted to kill him. He wounded Goibhniu with a newly-made spear, but the smith managed to turn it back against Ruadhán and drove it through his body.

An aura of wonder surrounded Goibhniu and his craft. We read that so marvellous was his skill that no spear made by him would miss its target and nobody who was pierced by it could survive. One tradition of special significance is that he held a great ale-feast ('fled Goibnenn') for the Tuatha Dé, and all who partook of this feast were preserved from age and decay. Such a role for Goibhniu has the mark of antiquity, for in Greek myth also a smith, Hephaistos, served drink to the gods. The importance of Goibhniu is underlined by the fact that his character has survived in tradition. In folklore he is called Goibhleann, and is reputed to have been the owner of a marvellous cow - see **Glas Ghoibhneann** - whose milk yield was nigh inexhaustible. He was said to have had a forge or smelting-furnace in different parts of the country, but lore of this was particularly strong in the Beare peninsula in Co Cork. This again is significant, for there was a distinct tendency to situate deities in the south-west corner of Ireland (see **Balar**, **Donn**, and **Cailleach Bhéarra**). He is said to have had his forge on the tiny island called Aolbhach (i.e. Crow Island), at the tip of the Reen promontory in Beare. A giant who lived in Beare once demanded that Goibhleann make a perfect razor for him. This Goibhleann did, using the blood of rats in the tempering of the steel, and so keen was the razor that with one dash it shaved off both beard and epidermis from the giant, without in any way causing pain. On this island, too, it is said, Goibhleann kept his marvellous cow, and when she desired to taste the grass of the mainland she jumped back and forth over the sixty feet chasm without any bother. It was also said that Goibhleann buried his treasure on the island, killing his servant so that the **ghost** would ever after protect it.

Oral versions of the Lugh myth survived in the north and west of Ireland, and in these Goibhleann figures as the smith who befriends the hero and forges a great spear for him. This is doubtlessly an echo from manuscript versions of the second battle of Moytirra, but it is interesting to note that - as usual in folklore - he is in these versions also accompanied by his cow. Lore of him had a permanence and vibrancy of its own, and it is probable that one of the most celebrated characters in Irish folklore, the **Gobán Saor**, was in origin an emanation from Goibhniu.

[Literature] H A de Jubainville (1903), 174-5; Whitley Stokes / John Strachan (1903) *1*, 248; T F O'Rahilly (1946), 525-7; Lilian Duncan in *Ériu 11*, 188; Stokes (1900), 177, 189, 327; D A Binchy in *Ériu 20*, 2, E A Gray (1982), 42-3, 50-1, 56-7, 125.

[Folklore] Jeremiah Curtin (1894), 1-34; Ordnance Survey Letters - Cavan and Leitrim (1836), 16-7; Timothy O'Sullivan in *Bèaloideas 6*, 168; IFC 51:9-17. See also **Lugh**.

GOLL MAC MORNA Leading rival of the hero **Fionn mac Cumhaill** in the cycle of stories concerning the **Fianna**. Goll himself was a heroic character and a great warrior, and the leader of the Morna clan.

The origins of Goll mac Morna lie in the early lore concerning Fionn who, under the influence of the **Lugh** myth, was portrayed as being opposed by a fiery one-eyed foe. Designations given to this foe were Aodh ('fire') and Goll ('one-eyed'), and it is significant that the mediaeval literature gives Aodh as the real name of Goll mac Morna, the latter resulting - we are told - from his loss of an eye at the battle of Cnucha, in which he slew Fionn's father. In the synchronisation of the traditions about Fionn which was taking place in the 10th-12th century, this archetypal foe called Goll was made into the leader of those troops serving Cormac mac Airt who were hostile to the Leinster interest. The Luaighne sept, who had played this part in the earlier texts, thus had their function largely taken over by the Morna clan, who were reputed to be of Connacht origin.

The character called Goll had by this time become detached in narrative from the fiery otherworld foe of Fionn. We read, therefore, that when leadership of the Fianna was given to Fionn (q.v.) after he had slain the mysterious burner of Tara, Goll nobly accepted this and pledged his loyalty to the son of the man he had slain. The magnanimity of Goll continues in the succeeding literature, and he is described as exposing himself to many great dangers to protect Fionn and the Fianna. However, dramatic clashes between his clan and Fionn's Baoiscne clan are mentioned in several texts, and it was such a clash which brought about his tragic death. Various reasons are given for this final quarrel. One is that he had a dispute with Fionn over a pig, and another is that the champion's portion was denied to him at a feast by a relative of Fionn called Caireall (for this ancient warrior's prerogative, see **Conall Cearnach**). Yet another tradition had it that Fionn's daughter was married to Goll and that Fionn, in some unexplained way, caused her death.

Whatever the cause, the result was that Goll and his clan went on a trail of destruction against Fionn's people. The Baoiscne clan counter-attacked, and the sore pressed Goll crossed into Connacht and determined to hold the fords of the river Shannon. Hearing Fionn snoring on the other side of the river one night, Fionn crossed quietly and stood over his foe with drawn sword. He generously allowed Goll to reach for his weapons, and at that very moment a large force of Goll's men came on the scene. Goll repaid the debt of generosity to Fionn by allowing him to depart, and actually escorting him back across the river. The war continued to go against him, and eventually Goll had to stand alone against his foes on a promontory on the west coast. A long poem describes a conversation which he had with his wife, the only remaining one of his supporters, on that occasion. In it is described his great martial career, including conquests abroad as well as many victories at home. He pleaded with his wife to leave him for her own safety, but she refused, saying that no other man would be so kind to her. Eventually, worn out by hunger and fatigue, he was beheaded by one of Fionn's men who swam onto the promontory.

It is clear that there was a strong effort by some Connacht writers in the late Middle Ages to make Goll the real hero of the Fianna cycle, and they almost succeeded. The incendiary imagery of Fionn's ancient foe had not entirely left him, however. One poem states that, during his final war, his clan burned to death a large number of women, hounds, and youths in Fionn's fortress of Almhu (the hill of Allen, Co Kildare). Other sources have this reflect somewhat less on Goll by attributing the savage act to his brother Garadh. We read that this Garadh, being rather advanced in years, was one day left by Fionn in charge of the women of the Fianna while the other warriors went to hunt. The women teased and mocked Garadh concerning his age, however, and in a fit of rage he locked them into the palace and burned them all. Since this would be an obvious cause of great conflict, there is a tendency in folklore to make it the grounds for the final split between Fionn and Goll. The destrucive element also survived in accounts of another brother of Goll, the mischievous **Conán Maol**.

Toirdhealbhach Ó Raithbheartaigh (1932), 94-8; Kuno Meyer in *Revue Celtique 2*, 90-2 and *5*, 198, Whitley Stokes (1900), 56-62, 73-80, 132, 144-5, 183-7, 204-6, 219-20; Eoin Mac Néill (1908), 7-14, 17, 22-4, 60-1, 86-92; R I Best / M A O'Brien (1965), 978-88; Neil Ross (1939), 60-8; Dáithí Ó hÓgáin (1988), 159-66, 294-5, 359.

[Garadh mac Morna] Whitley Stokes (1900), 38-41; E J Gwynn in *Ériu 1*, 13-37; J S Brewer / W Bullen (1871), 7-8; Ó hÓgáin (1988), 154, 165, 359.

GUAIRE King of Connacht from 655 until his death in 666 AD, and who was celebrated for his generosity.

He was often referred to as Guaire Aidhne, since he belonged to the southern branch of the Uí Fiachrach sept, which inhabited the territory of Aidhne in east Galway. His royal fortress was Durlas (just east of the town of Kinvara). It was said that in his youth he was stingy and inhospitable, and when the saint **Colm Cille** visited the province of Connacht he was told about him. Colm went to him and explained that man comes into the world without possessions and leaves it in a similar manner. Furthermore, the world's wealth comes from God, and He is not grateful to those who ignore the poor. Guaire paid attention to the sermon and changed his ways, so that he became the most generous man in Ireland. Hence he was known as Guaire 'an oinigh' (i.e. of the hospitality).

Notwithstanding his genial temperament, Guaire is portrayed as a wily and ambitious man who was typical of his time. We read in one text that, when he became leader of the southern Uí Fiachrach, he was not satisfied until he took the kingship of the whole province from the bishop **Ceallach** and later allowed his supporters to slay that holy man. Later, when the brother of Ceallach, Cú Choingeilt, became king of the northern Uí Fiachrach (in the Sligo-Mayo area), the contention was renewed. The fighting continued until Guaire was surrounded and besieged at Durlas by the army of his rival, and to make peace he gave his daughter Geilghéis in marriage to Cú Choingeilt. He plotted treachery, however, and had Cú Choingeilt slain at a feast given in his honour at Durlas. The attribution of these crimes to Guaire is quite unhistorical, for Ceallach lived over a hundred years before his time, and such deliberate treachery was not a trait usually associated with him.

The major trait of Guaire, generosity, is stressed in another story which describes his military manoeuverings. Incensed at his cattle-raiding, the high-king **Diarmaid mac Aodha Sláine** launched an offensive against Connacht, and Guaire sent the cleric **Cumaine Fada** to arrange a day's respite before battle. Cumaine met with the high-king on a raft in the middle of the river Shannon. Diarmaid agreed, believing God to be on his side, and in the battle of Carn Chonaill (Ballyconnell, near Gort in Co Galway) he inflicted a crushing defeat on Guaire. The latter fled from the battle with his servant and reached a small convent where a lone nun dwelt. She looked after him, and Guaire caught a salmon in a nearby stream and cooked it. He lamented that this night he had to be satisfied with a salmon for a meal, whereas on other nights he had two bullocks for his retinue. Finally, Guaire decided to go and surrender to Diarmaid. In token of submission, he took Diarmaid's sword between his teeth, and the high-king decided to test his generosity by sending a leper to beg from him during the ceremony. Guaire immediately threw his darts to the leper, and threw his shield to another man with a similar ailment, and a golden brooch to yet another. One of Diarmaid's men took the brooch from the leper, and on hearing this Guaire gave him his belt of gold. This again was taken from the leper, and Guaire - who was still prostrate with the sword between his teeth - wept bitter tears because he had nothing else to give. He began to take off his shirt, but Diarmaid intervened and told him to arise. The high-king said that Guaire need not suffer humiliation before him, since he was already subject to a better king - the God of heaven and earth. Then Diarmaid prostrated himself before Guaire, and brought him with him to the assembly of Tailtiu (Teltown, Co Meath).

Guaire brought a large bag of money with him to Tailtiu in order to distribute it among the poor there. Diarmaid had ordered that nobody should beg from him at Tailtiu, but after three days Guaire complained that he would die if none of the poor were to seek his assistance. On hearing this, Diarmaid revoked his order regarding begging, adding a bag of his own to that of Guaire. Then Guaire began to give with both of his hands to all and sundry, so that from the giving his arms grew longer than before. Other accounts state that his right arm was longer by half than his left, because that was the one he most used in giving to the poor.

An in-tale in this text explains that Guaire was destined to lose the battle against Diarmaid because of an earlier event. According to this, he had dealt ungenerously with St Cáimín of Inis Cealtra (Holy Island in Lough Derg on the river Shannon), and as a result the saint had fasted for three days against him, praying that he might be weak against his foes. Guaire went with Cumaine Fada to be reconciled to Cáimín, and peace was made between them, but Cáimín said that he could not offset the coming defeat, as 'my throw has been cast and I cannot stop it now'. On that occasion, Cumaine and Cáimín asked Guaire what was his chief desire, and Guaire replied figuratively that he wished that Cáimín's chapel be filled with gold and silver, so that he could use it as alms. Cáimín then said that he wished that every kind of disease come on himself for love of God, and Cumaine Fada desired that the chapel be full of books which would help scholars to teach the Christian faith. The three wishes were granted, Guaire in time becoming so wealthy that he could be continually giving alms.

Guaire had a brother called Marbhán, who was a saint, a prophet, and a poet, and who continually gave good advice to him. This Marbhán seems to have been a fictional character derived from the lore concerning Cumaine Fada (see **Seanchán**). He is described as choosing to live the life of a swineherd, so that the solitude of such a life would help him achieve greater holiness. Guaire asked him once why he preferred to live in the wilderness, and received a long answer which extolled the beauties of wild nature. Impressed by this, Guaire stated that he would give up all his kingdom if he could but live like that. The fame of Guaire's generosity caused him to be brought into association with the extortions of poets, and a writer in or about the 11th century combined various elements of traditional lore in order to make him host to the ravenous company of the chief-poet **Seanchán**. For a long time, Guaire acceded to the increasingly dificult demands of the poets, and was in danger of total impoverishment when Marbhán intervened to fend off Seanchán (q.v.) and his coterie. Further adventures concerning Guaire are found in the story of **Cano mac Gartnáin** and in the biography of St **Maodhóg**.

Several separate anecdotes were told of him. We read that one Aonna, successor to **Ciarán** of Clonmacnoise, was the confessor of Guaire. It happened once that a widow's son was arrested while trespassing in the royal garden. The widow was ordered to pay heavy compensation or, failing that, the young man was to be executed. She went to Aonna for help, and he gave her a quatrain of poetry to recite in the presence of Guaire. The quatrain was a reminder of death and hell-fire, and when Guaire heard it from the widow he immediately released her son. Some time later, a fine horse belonging to Aonna was killed by a farmer, and Aonna demanded high compensation. The farmer went to Guaire for help, and Guaire gave him a quatrain to say. The quatrain accused Aonna of unjustly seeking compensation, and when Aonna heard it he felt compelled to accept no more than a single cow.

Another anecdote told of how St Colmán mac Duach, the bishop of Guaire's territory, spent Lent in the wilderness of Boirinn (the Burren area of north Clare). He was accompanied by a single clerk, and they fasted for a long time. After Mass on Easter Sunday, they sat to table, but there was no food. At the same time, Guaire was in his dwelling sitting down to a huge meal, and he wished that some holy man in need should have such food. Immediately, his great bowl rose into the air, carried by angelic hands, and went to Colmán in the wilderness. Guaire followed on and, after they had eaten, he brought Colmán and the clerk with him to his dwelling at Durlas, where he presented them with three score milking-cows. Variants of this story in the later mediaeval literature add the detail that Guaire and his men followed the departing vessels on horseback, and that Colmán miraculously stuck their horses to the ground outside his hermitage until he had eaten his meal. They also state that the road between Durlas and Boirinn was since known as 'Bóthar na Mias' (literally, the road of the dishes). The anecdote remains popular in the folklore of east Galway to the present day.

Even after his death, Guaire's generosity was manifest. As he was being brought to the monastery of Clonmacnoise for burial, a beggar approached the corpse. Though dead, Guaire stretched out his hand and threw a fistful of sand at the poor man. Immediately it touched him it became gold, and this was the final act of charity done by Guaire.

[Colm Cille] Andrew O'Kelleher / Gertrude Schoepperle (1918), 138-41.

[Ceallach] Kathleen Mulchrone (1933).

[Diarmaid] Whitley Stokes in *Zeitschrift für celtische Philologie 3*, 203-19.

[Right hand longer] P S Dinneen (1908) *3*, 64-5; S H O'Grady (1898) 1, 400.

[Cáimín] Stokes (1890), 303-4; J F Kenney (1929), 386. Cf. O'Kelleher / Schoepperle, 60-3, 136-7.

[Marbhán] Kuno Meyer in *Zeitschrift für celtische Philologie 3*, 455-7; Maud Joynt (1941), 13-40.

[Aonna] Meyer in *Archiv für celtische Lexikographie 3*, 1-2.

[Colmán] J G O'Keeffe in *Ériu 1*, 43-7; J F Kenney (1929), 456; P S Dinneen (1908) *3*, 64-7 (where Mac Duach is corrupted to 'Mochua').

[Colmán and Guaire in folklore] W J Thoms (1834), 42; Patrick Kennedy in *Dublin University Magazine 41*, 503; IFC 381:104-6, S36:222-3, S48:66-7, S96:298-302.

[Death] Meyer in *Zeitschrift für celtische Philologie 3*, 218.

[General] O'Grady (1892) *1*, 396-401 and *2*, 497-8; Cormac Ó Cadhlaigh (1939).

H

HORSES Because of their social, economic and military importance, horses are the animals on which most emphasis is placed in Irish literature and folklore. The mediaeval pseudo-historians were accurately reflecting the status of the horse in their culture when they ascribed its introduction to the god **Lugh**, but archaeology shows that horses had in fact been part of life in the country long before either the cult of Lugh or the Celts themselves arrived here.

The Celtic people, however, were noted in Europe for their fine horsemanship, and their goddess of horses Epona was adopted as patroness by the Roman cavalry. Although the name is different, it is clear that some of the lore of the Celtic horse-goddess survived in Ireland under the guise of **Macha**. In the mediaeval literature, both heroes and saints have their faithful horses, and folklore stresses the very close contact between horse and man by some curious traditions. We are told that horses once had speech, and for that reason one should always speak to a horse as if it were a Christian. Equine nature is said to be very closely akin to human, and one quite candid story told that Noah had forgotten to bring a stallion into the ark with him and that one of his sons had to perform its function. As a result, horses have a human ancestor, and they share several ribs with humans. Yet it is also said that the equine species have a certain animosity towards the human one, and that horses would kill people except for a fortunate quirk of their eyesight. For, to the convex eye of a horse, humans look several times bigger and stronger than they are, and we are told that this saves us from being savaged.

A common tendency in human thought is to express the social importance of things by attributing a spiritual significance to them. Accordingly, much lore represents horses as being very close to the otherworld. They can, for instance, see **ghosts** which remain unseen to the human eye, and many accounts tell of a horse stopping at a particular place and not moving despite the efforts of its rider or driver. If one looks forward between the two ears of the horse, it is claimed that the spirit or shade which has caused it to halt can be seen. Perhaps the origin of such ideas is in the very keen sense of smell which horses have and which causes them to notice many more things than humans do. Because of its crucial value for agriculture and transport, the owner of a horse tended to be himself quite nervous for its welfare, and thus beliefs abounded concerning many unexpected dangers which might lie in the animal's way. Often when the owner would come to the stable in the morning he would find the horse in a lather of sweat, and this was explained as the result of it being stolen overnight by some neighbour who rode with the **fairies**. These otherworld beings themselves were thought to be a danger to horses, as they might wish to abduct a fine one. From this arose the custom of tying a red ribbon or a piece of hazel to the horse, or of spitting on it, for all these things repelled the fairies. Moreover, it was said that the horse itself sneezed in order to keep these beings out of reach. One of the greatest dangers to the animal's welfare was believed to be the evil eye of some begrudging person, and to prevent this the Sign of the Cross was frequently made over the horse.

One type of horse was well able to defend itself, if tradition be credited. This was the 'true mare' ('fíorláir'), defined as the seventh filly foal born to its dam without any colt being born in the interval. No evil force could interfere with such a mare, and whoever was riding it was secure from all harm. If a racehorse, the true mare could never be bested. It was further believed that where the true mare fell to the ground at its birth a shamrock grew. This shamrock had four leaves and was known as the 'seamair Mhuire' (Mary's Clover). It was considered to have curative and protective powers and was a favourite talisman. Most horses have some luck attached to them, according to folklore. People liked to allow a horse to trample a little on seeds when sown, as this would cause them to sprout well, and the horse's halter was believed to bring good luck and should always be retained when the animal was sold. The horseshoe, of course, was believed to bring good luck, but this probably relates to its container shape rather than to its specific association with this animal.

Not all horses, however, were considered lucky. A foal born at Whitsuntide was held to have a vicious nature, and a white horse was generally considered an unlucky thing to see. A horse with four white feet was difficult to sell, as animals with this colouring were popularly believed to be of intractable disposition. There was much speculation, and many different maxims, concerning the best colour for a horse, but a white mark in the forehead was usually considered a good sign. A detailed system of evaluating good traits in a horse has been popular in Ireland for several centuries. According to this the perfect horse should have 'three traits of a bull - bold walk, strong neck, and hard forehead; three traits of a hare - bright eye, lively ear, and swift run; three traits of a woman - broad breast, slender waist, and short back'. The close relationship of equine and human is underlined by other parallels in beliefs concerning both, such as the idea that a foal born with a caul will be a great racehorse, and the rule that a mare in foal should never be put under a hearse or brought near to a corpse (see **Human Life**). The basic reason for such parallellism is no doubt that for many people their very livelihood depended on having a horse, and the horse was often a human's sole companion on long journeys.

This close relationship between man and beast led to the notion that the ideal rider was one who appeared to be part of the same being as his mount. Expert horsemen, of course, were held in high regard, and their trade could be quite a lucrative one, especially for those who could handle wild or vicious stallions. Some individuals had this skill, which seems to have been due to a combination of courage and manipulation of the horse's keen sense of smell. Various substances with odour either pleasant or odious to the animal could be used to calm it, halt it firmly on the road, or drive it wild. One of the favourite items used to calm a horse was the substance found in a foal's mouth after its birth, but it was usually complemented by a variety of medical oils. The explanation given to the folk, however, was that a savage horse could be tamed by whispering into its ear a special secret word. The most celebrated of these horse-whisperers was a Corkman called James Sullivan who flourished in the early 19th century. He met with astounding success, rendering tame and ridable even killer horses. In the year 1810 he performed his greatest feat when he so quietened a notorious stallion on the Curragh of Kildare that the animal actually took part in a race and won on the occasion. Lore of his native area claims that, having tamed a horse, he could with a word make it lie on its back with its four hooves in the air, so that a glass filled with drink could be balanced on each hoof.

A common folk legend told of a strange horse which came from a lake and was captured by a man. This water-horse became an invaluable worker or racer, and the man profited much by it. One day, however, he struck the horse, with the result that it raced away again into the water. Some versions tell that the man was soon after drowned in the lake, and that pieces of his body were seen floating on the water as if he had been eaten by the horse. This legend, found also in parts of Britain and in Scandinavia, was already known in Ireland in mediaeval times. The account of how the hero **Cú Chulainn** got his two great chariot-horses is a variant of it, and other variants are found in the literature concerning the saints **Bréanainn**, **Féichín**, **Maodhóg**, and **Ruadhán**.

Dáithí Ó hÓgáin in *Bėaloideas 45-47*, 199-243 and (1985), 279-80; Brian Ó Cuív in *Celtica 2*, 30-63 and *17*, 113-22; M F Cox (1897); Annaba Nic Ghiolla Pheadair (1988).

HUMAN LIFE The most immediate of all experiences, life itself, is naturally the subject of speculation in the culture of all peoples. The worldwide tendency to regard three points of human living as being particularly important is well represented by Irish tradition. These points are birth, coming of age, and death. In Irish literary biographies, whether of kings, heroes, or saints, special descriptions are given of these three crucial stages. In the folk custom and belief of Ireland, coming of age is generally replaced by marriage as the intermediate stage in the life of a person, and indeed there was a feeling that marriage was the only true introduction to adulthood.

The birth of children was a matter of great social importance, and as usual in such cases this was expressed in mystical terms. For example, it was said that sterility could be overcome if the childless couple slept on top of a dolmen, popularly regarded as the type of bed used by the great lovers Gráinne and **Diarmaid ua Duibhne**. The importance of fertility was underlined by fear of circumstances which might prevent it. It was believed, for instance, that conception would be prevented if an enemy tied a knot in a handkerchief at the time of marriage, and no child would be born to the couple until the malicious knot was untied. Pregnancy brought its own dangers. It was commonly believed that a woman with child should avoid meeting a hare, for if that animal crossed her path the child would be born with a cleft palate, known as a 'hare-lip'. The woman could prevent this if, when she saw a hare, she tore the hem of her skirt, thus transferring the blemish from the child to it. A pregnant woman should never enter a graveyard for, if she stepped over a grave, the child would be born with a twisted foot. When it came to birth itself, forms of the custom known to scholars as 'couvade' were practised in Ireland as in other parts of the world. This involved an attempt by the father to take some of the birth-pangs away from his wife. Accordingly, he would often give his waistcoat or some other item of his clothing to his wife to wear in the belief that this would transfer the pains, or he might engage in strenuous work in the belief that this would relieve her of some of the physical exertion. The time of birth could be regarded as indicative of the future life of the child. Thus a child born at midnight was likely to have some special talents, such as extraordinary intelligence or even the ability to see otherworld beings.

51. HUMAN LIFE *An Irish wedding party of the 19th century.*

Since marriage was the point when one adopted full social responsibility, many superstitions centred on the actual wedding itself. Some days of the week, especially Monday and Friday, were and still are considered unlucky as wedding-days (see **Time**). The colour green was believed to be an unlucky colour for a bride to wear, and it was also considered an ill omen for a glass or cup to be broken on the wedding-day or if rain fell before the ceremony. There were certain practices which were reputed to bring good luck to the couple - throwing something after them as they left the church, for instance, or throwing coins into the air over their heads. It was customary in some places in the 19th century for all the men on horseback, with their wives behind them, to race from the church to the house of the newly-weds. This was known as 'the race for the bottle', the prize being a bottle of whiskey placed on a wall near the house. Socially, of course, marriage arrangements depended to a greater or less extent on class. Those who were in possession of land or in business tended to make matches for their offspring with economic prospects in view, while love-matches were more common among the landless and the poor.

Folklore does not, in its concentration on the major points of life, exclude everyday matters. The human body being the immediate organ of life, much ordinary lore was current concerning it and its functions. Individual parts of the body were believed to display traits of the person. The eyes, for instance, were considered to be the mirror of the soul and thus by their expression revealed a person's mentality. Much hair on the body betokened strength, a split in the front teeth was a sign of a good singing voice, while a large forehead indicated intelligence. Much attention was focussed on abnormalities, whether real or imagined. Lunacy was considered to result from water on the brain which caused softness, and people with this affliction were believed to be extraordinarily agile at running or jumping. A simpleton was referred to as 'duine le Dia' (meaning one specially selected by God), and was believed to have a paradoxical kind of intelligence which could show in unexpected ways. On the other hand, certain people were believed to have an evil eye, usually through their envious disposition but sometimes as an in-born trait for which they were not personally responsible. Those reputed to have such an eye were the cause of great anxiety, and they were often imagined to be staring peculiarly at a child or a farm animal, it being thought that as a result of this the health of child or animal would wither away.

Speculation concerning the observable physical traits of persons is inevitable, but neither was the question of the soul ignored. It was believed to be immortal, a point of teaching which the druids are reported to have had long before the coming of Christianity. The common folk idea that dead people could reappear in the form of an animal such as a bird or a hare may well be a survival of quite ancient and pre-Christian belief in reincarnation, but it is difficult to be sure of this. Little attempt was made generally to envisage the soul in concrete form, apart from a rather vague idea that it was akin to a little creature within the person. An international legend, common enough in Munster, describes how a butterfly was seen to emerge from the mouth of a sleeping man, and when it returned to its source the man awoke and related that he had dreamt of the very things over which the onlooker had observed the butterfly to hover. Another fancy, referred to in the mediaeval literature and still found in folklore, is that each person has a 'salmon of life' within the body, and that over-exertion could cause this little fish to be ejected, resulting in death if it were not immediately replaced.

Birds also were associated with the duration of life, but in an external role. A raven hovering over the house was an indication that a sick person was in danger of death, and the departure of the crows from trees on a family farm betokened a death in the family also. A sinister bird, described as large but of an unspecified kind, was believed to lay its wings over the bed of a sleeping person, thereby causing a nightmare. Sleep, an experience described as 'brother' to death, had much fanciful lore associated with it, in which lore it was thought to give a kind of access to the otherworld. Many people regarded dreams as being of great import, thinking that messages from dead relatives could be received through them, and that something which happened in a dream was a premonition of the future. The soul had precedence over the body in sleep as in death. It was said, for instance, that a sleepwalker could walk on water with as little difficulty as on land, but if awoken he or she would drown. A common belief was that a certain duration of life had been allotted to each person, as if his or her death in particular circumstances could not be avoided. A curious idea, found in the early literature and surviving still in folklore, is that a certain sod is destined to be the spot on which a particular person will die. A prophet or wise companion of the person, or even an otherworld voice, may reveal to him how his destiny is connected with the sod, and the fulfilment of this in an unexpected way was the theme of many a dramatic narrative.

When the final illness approached, relatives of a sick person were usually more tense and inclined to take special note of things that otherwise would go unnoticed. Special attention might be paid to a bird perching on the window-sill, a dog howling at night, a picture which might chance to fall, or some strange sound heard outside, for any of these things could be taken as portents of death. As the old or ill person died, doors and windows would be opened to ease the passage of the soul; and after death the curtains were drawn, the clock stopped, the mirrors turned to the wall, and any pet animals in the house put out. These customs may have originated in an idea that the soul could pass into some other object after death, but if so no memory of such a rationale survives. There was definitely some amount of fear of the dead, and several customs illustrate this clearly. For example, round-about ways were taken by the funeral procession to the graveyard, and in some places the coffin was carried around the graveyard a few times before burial. The obvious reason for this was to put astray the ghost of the departed lest it should return to interfere in the affairs of those still alive. This did not contradict a sincere affection for the dead person, but the social role was considered to properly end at death. The most important way of showing concern both for and at the dead was the custom of waking. The wakes were great social occasions for, as well as the lamenting of the dead person by keening women, there were several less desolate practices. At the wake stories were told, songs were sung, music and games were played, and there might even be dancing. The corpse was often given its own hand of cards in a card-game, and the smoking-pipe was extended to it as to all the living adults present. In these and other ways efforts were made to show that the dead person was held in honour and affection, and that the friendly memories remained even though he or she was no more. An element of uneasiness, of course, is quite compatible with respect, and so ancient ideas according to which the departed ancestors might still wish to interfere in affairs could survive in the realm of folk custom and belief.

There is no doubt but that ideas which are, when taken philosophically, incompatible with Christian teaching on the afterlife did survive. The people themselves seldom noticed the contradiction, but the clergy did, and for centuries strenuous ecclesiastical efforts were made to abolish the customs associated with wakes. Keening of the dead was considered a denial of the promise of heaven, and the robust nature of many of the wake-games was considered disrespectful to the deceased. Nevertheless, most people, though very devout in their religious beliefs and practices, would feel hurt and aggrieved if they thought that they would not be 'waked properly' when they died. Until recently, the wake was the great backdrop against which the value of an individual to the community could be judged.

Seán Ó Súilleabháin (1942), 177-250 and (1961) and (1967), 39-55; W G Wood-Martin (1902) 1, 285-340 and 2, 26-45; Breandán Ó Madagáin ed (1978); Caoimhín Ó Danachair (1978), 22-4, 26-7.

[The soul visualised] Bo Almqvist in *Sinsear 1*, 1-22; RIA Dictionary s.v. 'bratán'; P S Dinneen (1927) s.v. 'bradán'.

[Sod of death] Maura Carney in *Arv 13*, 173-9; Whitley Stokes CTS (1905), 31; S H O'Grady (1892) *1*, 393; Barry O'Reilly (1985).

HUMOROUS TALES A great variety of stories of this nature are found in Ireland, and the best-known of them correspond to type-numbers listed in the Aarne-Thompson catalogue of international folktales. There the different genre of humorous tales are grouped together under headings such as 'Tales of the Stupid Ogre', 'Jokes and Anecdotes', 'Formula Tales', and 'Unclassified Tales'. Examples of Irish versions of the different kinds of humorous tales will, however, in this entry be discussed together. These stories are usually short, but there is a strong tendency in Ireland to string a number of them together and thus to create somewhat longer units.

The outwitting of a giant, devil, or hag, was a very popular theme in Irish storytelling, and narratives based on this usually involved a combined usage of ruses from different tale-types. For instance, the smart hero fools the giant as to his strength by pretending to squeeze a stone with his hand whereas it is in fact a piece of cheese (Type 1060), by pretending to cast a stone a long distance when in fact it is a bird which he throws (Type 1062), and in an eating contest with the giant slips food into a concealed bag (Type 1088). A very popular story, which is often the culmination of such contests, describes how a giant with murderous intent is tricked into killing his own offspring (Type 1119). The hero, while sleeping in the giant's house, exchanges places with the giant's children in bed, who are thus slain in the darkness. This folktale has been known in Ireland for a long time, as its plot occurs in a mediaeval text which tells of how the warrior **Conall Cearnach** turned the tables on a murderous host.

A very widespread account, frequently a mere episode in longer narratives, describes how a man escapes from a ferocious one-eyed giant by blinding him with a hot iron (Type 1137). Its earliest occurrence in Irish storytelling would seem to date from mediaeval times in the context of **Fionn mac Cumhaill** gaining wisdom from eating a special salmon (see **Wonder Tales**, Type 673). In that case, it would have been borrowed from the Polyphemus story of Greek literature as a development of an indigenous Irish tradition which had the hero slaying a fiery one-eyed foe. Of less antiquity was the borrowing and reshaping of Type 1149 to the context of Fionn. According to this, a giant visits Ireland to fight against Fionn, but the hero pretends to be a baby in the cradle, and Fionn's wife tells the visitor that this is their child. The giant plays with the 'baby', which bites off his finger, and the giant flees, thinking that if the baby is so fierce then Fionn himself must be a quite horrific warrior.

Type 1186 originated on the Continent in the Middle Ages, but appears not to have been introduced into Ireland until recent centuries. It is a satiric story against social tyrants, and the butt of it in Ireland is a bailiff who meets the devil while engaged in his work. They journey together and hear a woman curse a pig by saying 'may the devil take you!' The bailiff tells the devil to take the pig, but the evil one says that the woman did not wish it with her whole heart. Similarly, when another woman curses a child, the devil does not take it for the same reason. When a third woman sees the bailiff approach, however, she curses him 'to the devil', and the evil one seizes his companion. The bailiff protests in vain that the woman did not mean it with her whole heart.

Stories concerning the defeat of misers have been very popular in Irish tradition. These are grouped together under Type 1305. One of Aesop's Fables describes how a miser is desolate when his gold is stolen from him, but is advised to comfort himself by imagining that he still has it, as he did not intend to spend it anyhow. In or about the 18th century, this gave rise to a special Irish ecotype concerning the magnate **Damer**. A similar story seems to have developed independently in Ireland at a much earlier stage. Common in folklore, it tells of how, when he nears his end, a miser wishes to take all his gold with him on his departure from this life. He therefore orders that it be melted down so that he can drink it as liquid, but a trickster gives melted butter to him instead and he dies deceived. That a variant of this was known for many centuries is suggested by an account in a mediaeval text which has the greedy satirist **Cridhinbhéal** dying after he has eaten pieces of gold.

Stupid persons are the butts of many of these folktales. Some such stories, which are still popular in folklore, were used in or about the 15th century by the author of a long text on the fools **Comhdhán** and **Conall Clogach**. The stories include fools thinking that they themselves are dead (Type 1313), fools taking fright without good reason (Type 1321), robbers being put to flight from their den by an unwitting fool (Type 1527), and a fool swatting a fly on a person's head, with fatal or near-fatal consequences (Type 1586A). Type 1600 is told of Conall Clogach in the text, and scores of versions concerning other fools have been collected from recent folklore. These tell of a stupid fellow who sees the body of a murdered landlord's agent being buried in an unmarked grave and, on being questioned by the police, he points out the place. The fool's relatives, who have been involved in the murder, have anticipated this and have substituted the body of a billy-goat for the agent. On the grave being opened, the fool enquires 'had the agent horns?', and the exasperated police give up their investigation.

One of the most popular of all stories in Irish folklore tells of how a boy is apprenticed to a master thief and soon shows his skills at that profession (Type 1525). He steals a fine horse by disguising himself as an old woman selling liquor and making the grooms drunk. Then he steals sheep by leaving a good shoe on the road and its match further on, so that the shepherd leaves his herd to collect the shoes. Finally, he steals the sheet from under a rich couple in bed by creating diversions which cause them to briefly leave the bed. He asks his master to teach him the trick of escaping from the gallows, and when the old thief gives a demonstration the clever youngster kicks a box away from underneath him and leaves him to hang. He then marries the old thief's wife and acquires all his loot.

Type 1533 which has a clever man carving a goose or deer to his own advantage, occurs in a 17th-century text (see **Feidhlimidh mac Criomhthainn**). In later folklore, it is usually told of some poet who composes a quatrain to describe his method of carving. Several varieties of Type 1535 have been collected from Irish folklore. The most common pattern tells of how a poor man triumphs over his rich and selfish brother. The latter kills the poor brother's cow, but the poor man has some money concealed in the hide to fool him. Thinking to benefit in the same way, the rich fellow kills all his own cattle, but gains nothing. The enraged rich man puts his brother into a sack with the intention of flinging him over a cliff, but the poor man tells a dishonest cattle-dealer that he is going to heaven and gets him to exchange places. The dealer trades his herd of cattle for this 'privilege', and later the poor man tells his brother that he found the cattle in the sea. The brother jumps over the cliff in search of more cattle and is drowned.

Known to Irish literature since the 13th or 14th century is Type 1590, which describes how, while on another's property, a rogue swears that he owns the land he is standing on, having secretly put some of his own soil into his boots. Versions of this, excluding the moral dishonesty, occur in texts concerning **Colm Cille** and **Mongán**. A very popular story in Irish folklore concerns an honest but unexpected gain (Type 1649). It tells of a man who dreams of a treasure hidden near a certain bridge, and on going there is disappointed to find nothing. However, he meets a stranger who tells him that he has dreamt that it is near the man's own house, and on his return home he finds the treasure. Another man also gets rich in an even more unexpected way (Type 1653). This man has an extremely foolish wife, and in desperation decides to leave her. As he departs his house, she begs to be allowed to follow him, and he tells her to 'pull the door after her' and come. She obeys him literally, pulling the door from its hinges and carrying it on her back. When night-time comes, they climb a tree and use the door to sleep on. It so happens that a band of robbers gather under that tree to divide their loot, and the foolish woman is so frightened that she cannot remain still above them. Eventually, the door slips and bangs all the robbers on the head, knocking them out, so all their treasure falls to the man, giving him reason to be grateful to his wife.

Type 1739 is a hilarious tale, found widely abroad but not as common as might be expected in Ireland. It tells of how a cow's urine is substituted for that of a sick man, with the result that the doctor tells the man he is going to give birth to a calf. The man falls asleep and dreams that he has so given birth, and on seeing a calf when he awakes believes that this is his offspring. In later folklore, the story has been collected only from south Connacht and Munster, but it was known to the Ulster author of an 18th-century story concerning **Conán Maol**. Bizarre surroundings and happenings are the full subject matter of Type 1930, which has a rogue describe a strange land to which he claims he has been. Prevalent among the strange sights described are landscapes made up of delicious foods and animals which behave uncharacteristically, such marvels being often described in the form of 'lying songs'. It is obvious that a version of such a humorous narrative was known to the mediaeval author who described the comic vision of **Anéra mac Conglinne**.

A series of formulaic tales and catch-tales were told for and by children. Especially popular in this category were a description of how a pancake rolled out through the door of a house and was pursued by several different animals until eaten by the fox (Type 2025), of how a pig refused to go over a stile and the roundabout way in which its owner had to engage the help of several animals and objects to compel it to do so (Type 2030), and narratives which tease the listeners into asking questions which are saucily answered (Types 2200 and 2204). Finally, the international Type 2400 tells of how a rogue is offered as much land as he can cover with an ox-hide, and he encloses a large area by cutting the hide into thin strips. The story is told in Ireland only in the context of the saints **Brighid** and **Colm Cille**, and in it the trick-motif has been changed into a mantle which miraculously spreads. This Irish ecotype originated in the late Middle Ages in the context of St Brighid (q.v.)

Antti Aarne / Stith Thompson (1961), 346-539; Seán Ó Súilleabháin / R Th Christiansen (1967), 196-343; Ó Súilleabháin (1942), 579-88, 640-9 and (1973), 22-4.

I

ÍDE (earlier, Íte) Saint who died c570 AD, foundress of a convent at the place which became known as Cill Íde (Killeedy, Co Limerick). She was also known as Mo-Íde, hence the form Míde for her name.

Next to **Brighid**, she is the most famous woman saint of Ireland; and some motifs similar to those of Brighid got attached to her cult. For instance, the chamber in which she slept seemed to outsiders to be ablaze. Three recensions of her life exist in Latin, and it is thought that these may incorporate some material from a very early biography. It seems certain that she was a native of the Déise area (Co Waterford), and the accounts of her claim that she was daughter of one Ceannfhaolaidh, a man of noble lineage. We read that a young nobleman wished to marry her, and her father strongly opposed her desire to devote her life to Christ until an angel appeared to him in a vision and rebuked him. She founded a church in the Déise territory but, following the angel's directions, she went to Uí Chonaill Gabhra (west Limerick) and settled there at Cluain Chreadhail, which accordingly became known as Cill Íde. It is claimed that her first name was Deirdre, and that she became known as 'Íte' because of her thirst ('íota') for holiness. Several miracles are related of her, including healing ailments and having souls released from Purgatory. She is represented as a particularly compassionate saint - one of her achievements, for instance, was to obtain pardon from a local king for a murderer on condition that he repent.

Íde was reputed to have been a great counsellor and educator. Among her pupils, it was claimed, was the celebrated **Bréanainn**, and she was referred to as 'the foster-mother of the saints of Ireland'. It is likely that her convent did in fact devote itself to the teaching of young boys, and her care and kindness for them caused her to be imagined as a nurse suitable for the Christ-child himself. Accordingly, a 10th-century source relates a touching story of her. We read that, for a long time, she endured without complaint a huge beetle which gnawed away at her side. When her nuns saw this beetle follow her from her cell, they killed it, but Íde was displeased, saying that the beetle was her fosterling. Christ was so touched by this that he came as an infant to her, and Íde was so happy with this visit that she composed a beautiful little poem beginning 'little Jesus is nursed by me in my little hermitage, though a cleric have much wealth all is false but little Jesus'.

Several legends of Íde are still current in the folklore of west Limerick. Some are borrowed from the lore of Brighid (q.v.) - for example the miraculously spreading cloak and the man who had horse's ears but was made normal by the saint. As was natural in the rural community of west Limerick, she was popularly valued as a patroness of agriculture, and it is locally claimed that she was the owner of the famous cow called the **Glas Ghoibhneann**. It was also said that she took pity on a poor farmer whose seed was being destroyed by sparrows and banished all these birds into a nearby pond until his crop had been harvested. According to another legend, she provided a good catch for some penurious fishermen on the river Shannon. An unflattering tradition concerning the village of Tournafulla has it that some ill-natured fellows there set dogs at her donkey as she passed through one day. The donkey took fright and, while jumping across two rivers which meet there, it landed on a rock and left its hoofmarks on it. Another legend has it that a whitethorn tree at Killeedy grew from a thorn which she plucked from the donkey's hoof - all the thorns on that tree were turned downwards and were therefore innocuous.

Íde's feastday is January 15.

J F Kenney (1929), 389-90; Whitley Stokes (1905), 42-5, 182-3; Gerard Murphy (1962), 26-9, 183-4; Charles Plummer (1910) *2*, 116-30; John O'Hanlon (1875) *1*, 200-17; Nioclás Breathnach in *The Irish Press* 17/1/1978, 8; IFC 629:409-14, 947:385-8, S493-S497: passim.

J

JAMES II (1633-1701) King of England from 1685 until his deposition three years later by his daughter Mary and her husband **William of Orange**. He fled to France and in 1689, with the support of the French king Louis XIV, landed in Ireland. He raised a large but ill-equipped army, and was defeated by William in the Battle of the Boyne in 1690.

52. JAMES II *Portrait of King James in full regalia.*

Although he had shown courage while fighting on land and at sea earlier in his career, his performance at the Boyne was a disaster, fleeing needlessly and leaving his army leaderless. He raced to Dublin, and from there to Wexford and Kinsale, where he had first landed a year before. He sailed for France, publicly putting the blame for his defeat on the Irish who risked all for him and were left at home suffering the consequences of their naivety. His disdain for the Irish people was reciprocated, and he was remembered for the cowardice and cynicism he had shown. The traditional saying in Irish was that 'James had one English shoe and one Irish shoe when he lost Ireland', and he is always remembered by the nickname 'Séamas an chaca' (literally, James of the dung). At the Boyne, he had been completely outmanoeuvred by William and was little more than a spectator while he remained there. His Irish followers claimed that he was preoccupied, not with fighting, but with a bout of diarrhoea, and hence the nickname. Early in the battle, William had been wounded by a haphazard cannon-ball, but not seriously. Several of the Jacobites believed that he had been killed, and such a rumour spread to Dublin and even to Paris. There were other accounts also. One claimed that James' son, the Duke of Berwick, attacked and slew a small group of enemy officers, believing William himself to be among them and not willing to miss 'a splendid opportunity for putting an end to this war'. Another account, perhaps more reliable, had it that a gunner in the Jacobite army had William well within his sight and range for a moment, but James forbade him to shoot and William was thus spared. This latter story survived in folklore, which has James beseeching the gunner not to 'make a widow of my daughter'.

A contemporary report says that James entered Dublin 'in a manner stunned'. An apocryphal story soon spread which had him being asked by Lady Tyrconnell, the wife of his chief-of-staff, what he would like to eat, and the king replying that, after such a breakfast, he had little stomach for a dinner. The idea of this encounter with Lady Tyrconnell later gave rise to a legend which is still well known. According to this, she had been the first woman whom he met as he hurried into Dublin on his sweat-drenched horse. She sought news of the battle from him, and was told that the Irish had run away. The lady quickly retorted that his majesty had won the race. That James really was very nervous in his flight is clear from the report of a man who gave him a change of horses at Enniscorthy and noticed that he was riding with his pistols at full cock.

It is said, however, that James left one small benefit in Ireland, for it was believed that his blood could cure the skin disease scrofula commonly known as 'king's evil'. Folk anecdotes were current which told of how he spilled a drop of his blood either accidentally or deliberately and thereby healed people suffering from the ailment. The ability to cure this was the test of a true king, and the strong likelihood is that in the context of James the motif first became popular when he was held in high regard before the debacle at the Boyne. That, even more than his deposition, was the great turning-point of his career. As one Irish folklore account states: 'The people liked James well enough before he ran, they didn't like him after that!' See also Patrick **Sarsfield**.

Richard Bagwell *3* (1916), 260-308; P B Ellis (1976), 62-5, 122-30, 144-9; Lady Gregory (1926), 47-8, 55; Dubhglas de hÍde (1933), 146; Tomás Ó Concheanainn in *Éigse 14*, 225, 236; S H Bell (1956), 19; M R Toynbee in *Folk-lore 61*, 1-14; Ordnance Survey Letters - Wicklow (1839), 251-2; IFC 794:489-92, 924:489-95.

K

KILDARE, EARL OF The personage who stands immediately behind this designation in the folklore of Leinster and south Ulster was probably Gerald FitzGerald (1525-1586), the 11th Earl of Kildare. His stature was no doubt increased by the far greater fame of his grandfather and father, both bearers of the same name and, like him, known to the people as 'Gearóid Iarla'.

53. KILDARE, EARL OF
Kilkea Castle, where the Earl of Kildare had his magic room.

After the overthrow of his father and relatives in 1537, and while still a boy, he was protected by the native Irish chieftains and then spirited away to the friends and associates of his family in Florence. He was pardoned by Queen Mary in 1553 and was allowed to return to Ireland. His return was greeted with great delight and expectation in Ireland, where the people - according to a contemporary English report - were 'so affectionate to this house that they would sooner a Geraldine come among them than God'. Although he disappointed such hopes, it is clear that suitable legends became attached to him at the time. These legends were borrowed from the lore of the Earl of Desmond (see Gearóid Iarla **FitzGerald**) and applied to this other namesake. So we are told that the Earl of Kildare once engaged in magical practices in a secret room in Kilkea Castle but that, when one spell went wrong, he became enchanted and since sleeps in a hidden cavern somewhere in Co Kildare. Every seven years he rides around the flat plain of the Curragh on a horse with silver shoes, and when these shoes are worn out he will return to free Ireland. Since the 18th century at least, the motif of the sleeping army of the Earl of Kildare is also found in connection with a location further north - the rath of Hacklim near Ardee in Co Louth. The reason for this migration seems to have been the incidental occurrence of the name Gearóid in several local toponymics in that area.

Edmund Curtis (1936), 168; John O'Donovan (1848-1851), 1530-1; Walter Fitzgerald in *Journal of the Kildare Archaeological Society 3*, 13; Diarmaid Mac Íomhair in *County Louth Archaeological Journal 14*, 68-81; Dáithí Ó hÓgáin in *Béaloideas 42-44*, 219-20, 230, 245, 255-6, 283-97.

KINGSHIP The king (Irish, 'rí') was the most important personage in early and mediaeval society, and many beliefs and rituals attaching to his office seem to echo a role of 'priest-king' in more archaic times.

The echoes include the idea of truth ('fír') which was the quality of a good king, and falsehood ('gó') which attended a bad one. This has parallels in Sanskrit literature, and may be taken as an Indo-European system of valuation. One early Irish text states the position with a mystical flavour: 'Truth in a ruler is as bright as the foam cast up by a mighty wave of the sea, as the sheen of a swan's covering in the sun, as the colour of snow on a mountain. A ruler's truth is an effort which overpowers armies. It brings milk into the world, it brings corn and mast.' A general illustration of the belief is found in the references to the sacred prohibitions (see **'geis'**) which attended the office of kingship. These prohibitions show that the king, as mediator between supernatural powers and his community, was a power-

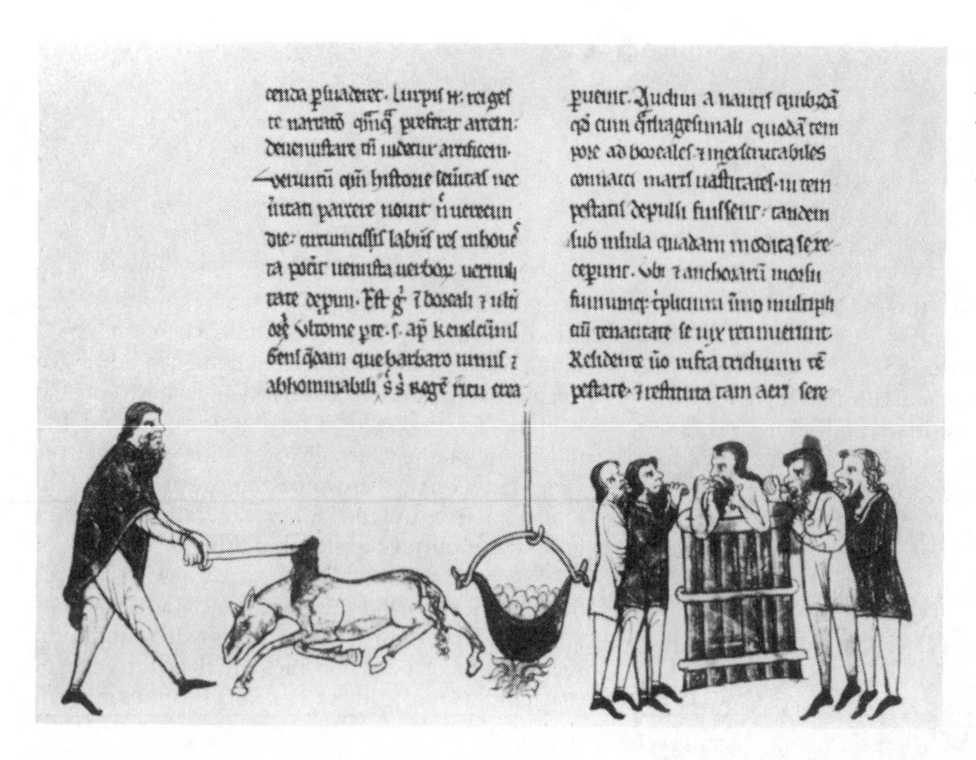

54. KINGSHIP
Inauguration of an Irish King, from a 12th-century Norman manuscript.

point, and that social equilibrium depended on his observing the often difficult demands placed on him by the supernatural powers which bestow prosperity.

The clearest expression of these concepts was in the context of the ritual kingship of **Tara**, which in mediaeval times was extended to entail the high-kingship of Ireland. The myth of king **Conaire** states that two steeds of one colour, never before harnessed, were placed under a chariot and that they could only be controlled by the man who was destined to be king. A special mantle fitted only the true king, whose selection had further to be ratified by a vision of seers. When the chariot was driven by that man, two flagstones at Tara would open before it to allow it through, and the upright stone called the Lia Fáil screeched against its axle. The strange prohibitions on Conaire (q.v.) are also illustrative of the sacred nature of kingship. Especially relevant is the way in which he must accord with the movements of the sun - he must not be in bed at sunrise, must not cross a particular plain after sunset, and must not go to sea on the Monday after the Bealtaine feast (see **Time**). The sacred prohibitions actually fulfilled a social purpose, for they tempered the authority conferred on the king with reminders that he was himself subject to rules and could lose office if general welfare did not result from his rule. It was held that, if he suffered a blemish, the king must resign, and presumably in archaic culture he would be sacrificed if his reign did not bring prosperity.

Sovereignty was posited as a gift proffered by the **goddess**, a gift of herself to the king who was thus her mystical spouse. She symbolically offered a drink, as in the mediaeval account of her appearance in the company of the god **Lugh** who gives a long list of future Tara kings to **Conn Céadchathach**. She is in fact the land-goddess, and the theme of her marriage to the proper ruler of a territory is a perennial one in Irish tradition. Under differing names, she may be the tutelary spirit of a particular area or of the whole country - the latter theme surviving as a patriotic convention in poetry down to recent times. It is likely that the whole complex of imagery and lore pertaining to kingship in Ireland should be regarded as residue of ancient rituals which accompanied the installation of kings, rituals which would have lauded their authority while reminding them of their responsibilities. That these responsibilities were broad-based is suggested by the frequent allusions in the literature to the good king as one who shows fierceness towards the strong and gentility towards the weak, a convention which in real life may have been honoured more in its breach than in its observance.

Many echoes from the goddess of sovereignty survive also in folk legends of great kings and rulers. However, in the narratives derived from, or influenced by, international folktales, the figure of king is rather based on the European feudal model (see **Romantic Tales** and **Wonder Tales**).

Myles Dillon (1969); D A Binchy (1970); F J Byrne (1973), 7-69; Josef Baudiš in *Ériu 7*, 101-7; Rudolf Thurneysen in *Zeitschrift für celtische Philologie 20*, 213-27; Calvert Watkins in *Ériu 30*, 181-98; Marilyn Geriets in *Celtica 20*, 29-52.

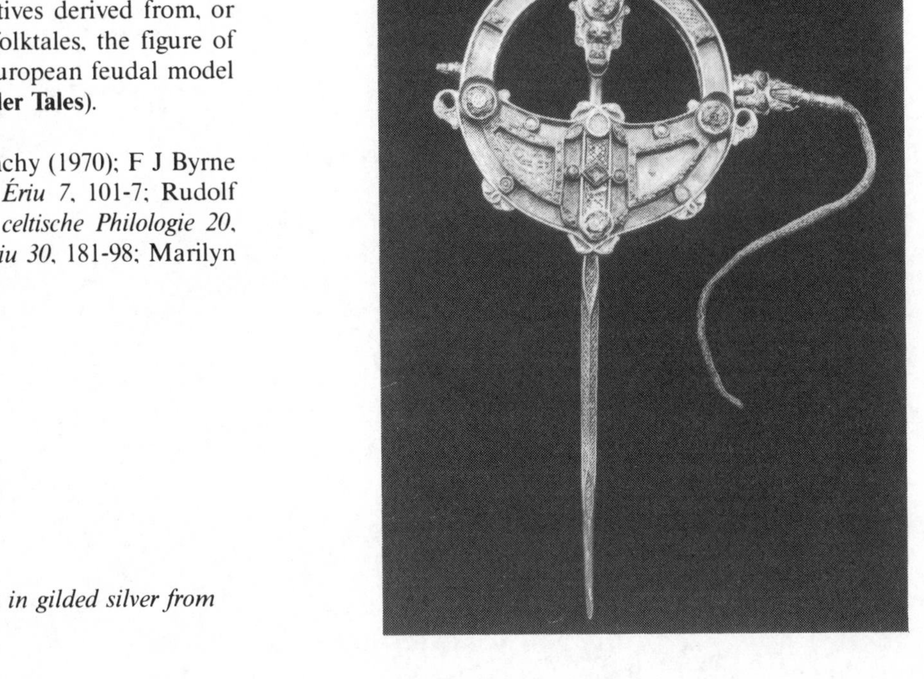

55. KINGSHIP *'Tara' Brooch in gilded silver from the 8th century.*

L

LABHRAIDH Mythical king and ancestor of the Leinster people (who were called Laighin, later Laighnigh). His name is accompanied by the sobriquet Loingseach ('exiled one'), and alternately Moen (later Maon, meaning 'dumb') or Lorc ('fierce'). His legend is the oldest tradition that the Leinstermen had concerning themselves, and it is believed to contain a memory of how they first came to Ireland around the 2nd century BC.

An invasion by Labhraidh at the head of his Leinstermen is referred to in a few poetic fragments which may be dated as early as the 6th century AD. One such fragment states that he destroyed by burning a fortress at Dinn Ríg (the moat of Burgage, south of Leighlinbridge in Co Carlow), and that he slew his foe **Cobhthach** there. A full account is given in a 9th-century text, and here his conquest is for political reasons represented as a return to his rightful inheritance. Laoghaire Lorc, we are told, was king of Ireland, and he had a brother called Cobhthach who wasted away from jealousy of him. Laoghaire went to visit the ailing Cobhthach, who feigned death. When Laoghaire reclined over him in mourning, the imposter stabbed him through the heart and killed him. Cobhthach then caused Ailill Áine, son of Laoghaire and king of Leinster, to be poisoned, and he himself usurped the kingdom. Ailill had a young son who never spoke and was therefore called Moen. One day on the playing-field Moen was struck on the shin by a hurley, and he cried out: 'I am hurt!' 'The Dumb speaks' ('labhraidh Moen'), said the other hurlers, and so that phrase became his name. When the usurper Cobhthach soon after asked his men of art who was the most generous nobleman in Ireland, in anticipation of praise for himself, they answered that Labhraidh Moen was. Overcome with jealousy, Cobhthach banished the youngster from the country, along with the poet **Feircheirdne** and the harper Craiftine who had praised him.

The banished trio betook themselves to Munster, to a people called the Fir Morca, whose king Scoriath gave them refuge. This king had a daughter called Moriath who was closely guarded by her mother, but who nevertheless fell in love with Labhraidh. One night while a feast was in progress Craiftine played magic music on his harp so that the mother slept, and then Labhraidh went to the girl. When the mother awoke, she heard her daughter heave the sigh of a married woman and realised what had happened. Labhraidh admitted his role, and was accepted by King Scoriath and promised help to gain his inheritance. They went on a hosting together to a strong fortress of Cobhthach at Dinn Ríg. Having failed to capture it, they resorted to a trick. Craiftine played sleep-music on the rampart while the besiegers covered their ears and, with the defenders overcome by sleep, Dinn Ríg was taken by storm. Labhraidh then sent a cordial invitation to Cobhthach to visit him, and for this purpose commenced the building at Dinn Ríg of a great banqueting-hall. It was all of iron and took a year to complete. None of the builders spoke a word of their work, and we read that from this a proverb grew up to the effect that 'every Leinsterman has his own secret'. When all was ready, Cobhthach came with a great entourage, but he refused to enter the hall unless Labhraidh's mother and jester should go before him. On Labhraidh's instructions, the door was fastened with a great chain and thrice fifty bellows were blown until the building was red-hot. Labhraidh then realised that his own mother was within, but she exhorted him to gain his vengeance at all costs, and Cobhthach with all his followers was destroyed.

This account is clearly inflated and, to some extent, a distortion of the original tradition. The designation 'Fir Morca' (i.e. men of Morca) for the allies of Labhraidh, and the locating of that sept in Munster, are curious features, for the text itself states that Labhraidh was banished from Ireland. In fact, an appendage to the text states that the hero was called Labhraidh 'Loingseach' after he left the country, established a kingdom near Muir nIocht (the English Channel), and 'brought back two thousand two hundred foreigners with broad lances (co laighnibh) in their hands, from which they are called Laighin'. It may therefore be that Fir Morca is a corruption of an earlier 'Armorica', and that this designation is an echo of Leinster origins, be these in Armorica (i.e. Brittany) or somewhere in the island of Britain. It is at any rate clear that there was ancient lore of how Leinstermen destroyed a fortress through a conflagration, for that is reflected also in the early saga of **Conaire**.

A later mediaeval tract gives a version of the story which is further expanded. This states that the young Moen was made by Cobhthach to eat a piece of the hearts of his father and grandfather and to drink a goblet of their blood. This, we are told, was why he became dumb. When banished he went to Armenia and became a famous champion of the king of that land. He could not refrain from speaking out in praise of the beautiful music played by Craiftine, and thus his handicap was overcome. Returning to Ireland with a fleet of three hundred ships, he landed at the Boyne estuary, marched to Dinn Ríg, and slew Cobhthach there. One man at Dinn Ríg asked another the question 'does the exile speak?' and got the answer 'labhraidh' (i.e. 'he speaks'). There were therefore varying descriptions of how the hero first spoke, and this shows that the acquisition of his name reflects some basic idea which had become confused with the passing of time. There may have been a faint memory of difficulties felt by the Leinstermen in mastering the Gaelic variant of the Celtic language which they encountered in Ireland. Alternately, or perhaps in addition to that, the king's eponymous speaking could refer to enunciation in formal or rhetorical language. The further epithet 'lorc' connected with his name has the general meaning of fierce or voracious, but it is also taken to be synonymous with 'moen' or dumb. Thus the general imagery connected with Labhraidh concerns an abnormality or blemish of some kind.

This imagery invited personal drama, and a less learned and more personal type of folktale was attached to Labhraidh in or about the 10th century. This (see **Religious Tales**, Type 782) was told of king Midas in Greek myth and had wide circulation in mediaeval Europe, but Labhraidh seems to owe the motif to the Welsh versions concerning king March ap Meirchion. It suited the context of Labhraidh, not only because of the notion of blemish, but also because of the stress placed in that context on magical music and on unexpected speech. So Labhraidh was said to have had horse's ears and, to preserve the secret, he had every barber who cut his hair put to death. When a widow's son was appointed to the task, the alarmed mother beseeched Labhraidh to spare him and promised that he would not reveal whatever he discovered. This was agreed, but the young man grew sick and pined for three years with the burden of the secret. A **druid** advised him to go to a crossroads, to turn to his right, and to tell the secret to the first tree he met. He did this, and soon recovered his health. The tree in question was a willow, and Craiftine afterwards used the timber of that very tree to make a new harp. When that harp was played, the sound came from it as the words 'Labhraidh Lorc has the two ears of a horse'. Hearing this, Labhraidh was stricken with remorse for having put his barbers to death, and he uncovered his ears for all to see his blemish.

The story of how Labhraidh triumphed over Cobhthach, and that concerning his ears, were retold in the 17th century by Seathrún **Céitinn** in his very influential history. Only the story of the horse's ears, however, survived in oral tradition. Versions of it have been collected from the folklore of many parts of Ireland in this century. In some areas it has undergone a further development, which brings the great mythical Leinster king into contact with the principal holy woman of that province, St **Brighid**. The literary biographies of Brighid described how she, by a miracle, gave eyes to a certain flat-faced man, and this episode provided the opportunity for a new twist to the story of Labhraidh's ears. So we are told - quite anachronistically - that Labhraidh was so depressed by his blemish that he went to seek consolation from the saint. He sorrowfully laid his head in her lap, and she blessed him. 'I see no blemish,' she said. He stood up and felt his head, and to his great delight found that he had ordinary human ears.

[Leinster origins] M A O'Brien (1962), 1-9, 334-5; T F O'Rahilly (1946), 101-20; F J Byrne (1973), 130-6; A P Smyth (1982), 7-12.

[Dinn Ríg] Whitley Stokes in *Zeitschrift für celtische Philologie 3*, 1-14 and in *Revue Celtique 20*, 429-33; Myles Dillon (1946), 4-9; Heinrich Wagner in *Ériu 28*, 1-16.

[Céitinn's telling] P S Dinneen (1908) 2, 160-75.

[Horse's ears] Brian Ó Cúiv in *Éigse 11*, 167-87; Máirtín Ó Briain in *Béaloideas 53*, 11-74. See also

Edward Gwynn (1913), 334-7.

[Brighid and Labhraidh] Pádraig Ó Milléadha in *Béaloideas 6*, 75; H M Roe in *ibid 11*, 189; Ó Briain, *op cit*, 52-7. See Dáithí Ó hÓgáin (1985), 24-5, 324.

LAOGHAIRE (earlier, Lóiguire) High-king of Ireland, who died c 461 AD, son of **Niall Naoighiallach**.

There is uncertainty concerning the length of his reign, traditional accounts claiming it to have lasted thirty-five years, but it is not likely to have extended to more than seven years. The question depends on the floruit of his father Niall, which is unsettled. All sources agree that the national saint **Patrick** began his mission in the fourth or fifth year of Laoghaire's reign. The saint's 7th-century biographer Muirchú gives a dramatic account of the meeting of the two. Laoghaire, he says, was a 'great king' and a 'fierce pagan' who had heard prophecies from his druids that such a missioner would come, and the expected event materialised when Laoghaire was in **Tara** performing his royal function of lighting a fire at Easter. Nobody was allowed to kindle a fire before the king on that night, but Patrick had lit his Paschal fire at Slane, and Laoghaire thus set out with his soldiers and **druids** to arrest him. Astounded by the saint's miraculous power, however, Laoghaire submitted and was converted to Christianity. The other 7th-century biographer of Patrick, Tíreachán, gives a more accurate historical account, stating clearly that Laoghaire did not accept the Christian faith. He has the king declaring that his father Niall would not allow this, but had ordered that Laoghaire be buried on the ridges of Tara, facing south against the Leinster royal graves at Maistiu (Mullaghmast, Co Kildare) 'because such is the fierceness of our hatred'. Tíreachán also mentions how two daughters of Laoghaire wished to follow Patrick, but the druids who reared them in Connacht tried to prevent them from doing so. The maidens came to the saint at a well near Cruachu (Rathcroghan, Co Roscommon), and were instructed and baptised by him there. They then demanded to see the face of Christ and died soon afterwards.

The subsequent texts repeat the claim that Laoghaire submitted to Patrick and adopted the new faith; and one 11th-century source - stressing his supposed conversion - states that the mythic hero **Cú Chulainn** appeared to him while he disputed with the saint and exhorted him to become a Christian. The mediaeval literature also gives a dramatic account of his death. We read that he was captured by the Leinstermen in an attempt to collect the **bóraimhe** tribute, and in order to be released he swore by the elements not to seek that tribute again. However, some time later he tried to re-impose the bóraimhe. It had been prophesied to him that he would die between Ireland and Scotland, and for this reason he always avoided travelling on the sea. There were, however, two hills in Leinster, one called Éire (Ireland) and the other called Alba (Scotland); and, as he moved south on a campaign against the Leinstermen, he was slain at Greallach Dá Phil (near Mullacash in Co Kildare), between these two hills.

Such ambiguous prophecies were quite popular as a narrative device to heighten the drama in accounts of the deaths of kings. The motif of being buried facing the foe was also a favourite narrative device, but it may encapsulate a burial custom in the cult of warriors. In the case of his father Niall (q.v.), we read that the dead body of the warrior-king was held aloft by his followers when going into battle.

James Carney (1973), 8-13; Ludwig Bieler (1979), 74-7, 84-99, 106-9, 127-45; Kathleen Mulchrone (1939), 26-37; Whitley Stokes (1887), 562-7 and in *Revue Celtique 13*, 52-3; R A S Macalister (1956), 352-5, 530-1; R I Best / Osborn Bergin (1929), 278-87.

LAOGHAIRE BUADHACH Fictional warrior in the **Ulster Cycle**. The sobriquet means 'victorious', and his father's name is given as Connadh Buídhe.

Laoghaire is, in several texts, enumerated among the leading warriors at the court of king **Conchobhar mac Neasa**. In particular he is featured as contending with **Cú Chulainn** and **Conall Cearnach** for precedence at the feast of Bricriu (q.v.) The only other noteworthy account concerns his death, which is described in an 11th-century text. According to this, Mughain, wife of Conchobhar, cohabited with one of the king's poets, Aodh. When Aodh was sentenced to death by the angry Conchobhar, he asked that the mode of execution be drowning. Each lake to which he was taken, however, Aodh sang a spell against it which caused it to dry up (see **Poets**). There was a lake, called Loch Laí, in front of Laoghaire's house, and the poet's spell could not affect this, so he was brought there to be drowned. Incensed that a poet should be thus killed in his lake, Laoghaire rushed out of the house with sword in hand. He struck the crown of his head against the door-lintel and his brains were spattered all over his cloak. Nevertheless, the dying Laoghaire slew thirty of the executioners before he himself expired, and the poet went free.

George Henderson (1899); Cormac Ó Cadhlaigh (1956), 476; Kuno Meyer (1906), 22-3; Myles Dillon in *Ériu 11*, 47-8, 51.

LAOGHAIRE MAC CRIOMHTHAINN A young prince, son of a fictional king of Connacht called Criomhthann Cas and subject of a romance written in or about the 14th century.

We read that Criomhthann Cas held an assembly by the shore of Éanloch (Lough Nen in Co Roscommon, near Athlone). They saw a finely-dressed stranger approach through the mist. This stranger said that his name was Fiachna and that he was of the 'sídhe' (otherworld beings). His wife had been taken from him by a 'sídhe' lord called Eochaidh, whom he had subsequently slain, but the woman had been taken by Eochaidh's nephew Goll, who lived in a fortress at Magh Meall ('the Pleasant Plain'). Fiachna had thus come to recruit warriors to assist him in battle against this Goll. Laoghaire agreed to go with him and was accompanied by fifty other young men. They dived into the lake after Fiachna and soon arrived in the otherworld. With their help, Fiachna defeated his foes and regained his wife. Fiachna's daughter married Laoghaire, and fifty other maidens of the otherworld became the wives of his companions. At the end of a year Laoghaire expressed the desire to visit his homeland, and Fiachna warned him to bring horses for his company to ride, and not to dismount. On their return, they met the assembled Connachtmen. King Criomhthann begged his son to stay, but to no avail, and Laoghaire returned to the otherworld and was not seen again.

The warning against touching natural land when returning from the otherworld was an international motif found in other Irish stories also (see **Wonder Tales**, Type 470).

S H O'Grady (1892) *1*, 256-7.

LEPRECHAUN Diminutive otherworld man in Irish folklore who is said to be the guardian of hidden treasure, envisaged as a crock of gold. He is invariably a solitary being, although he is sometimes claimed to be the shoemaker of the **fairies**.

Only one story of the leprechaun is general in Irish lore. This describes how a man catches him and holds him firmly in his hand, demanding to know where his crock of gold is. If the man keeps his eyes firmly on the leprechaun, the little fellow must tell. However, he manages to deflect the captor's attention from him by warning that a ferocious beast is approaching, and when the man looks again the leprechaun is gone. Other more spontaneous accounts claim that the leprechaun is sometimes glimpsed as he flits through woody surroundings, or else as he sits on a toadstool smoking his pipe, but such descriptions are intended only for children. In Ulster lore he has to an extent become assimilated to the brownie lore, which seems to have arrived from Scotland in the 17th century. These accounts have him, or a brownie, coming secretly at night to do farmwork and housework for people to whom he is well disposed, but he leaves in a huff when a suit of clothes is left as a present for him. In Munster, the leprechaun is sometimes said to present people with a 'sparán na scillinge' ('purse of the shilling'), which never becomes empty. However, those in receipt of this marvellous gift invariably misuse it, and find that its contents change to dust.

The designation leprechaun (Irish 'luprachán') was in fact used for the being only in the north Leinster area. In east Leinster the word was 'loimreachán' and in south Leinster 'lúracán', in Ulster 'luchramán', in Connacht 'lúracán', and in Munster the series 'luchragán', 'lurgadán' and 'clúracán'. All of these designations are suggestive of his traits - echoing terms such as 'luch' (mouse), 'lúth' (agility), 'lurga' (ankle), and 'lom' (sparse). He was believed to be small, speedy, large-footed, and rarely seen, and it is thus obvious that the basic designation was modified in accordance with folk imagination. The original term, attested in the early literature, was 'luchorpán', meaning literally 'little body'. In the 8th-century text on **Fearghus mac Léide** we read of a community of such diminutive beings, and they are represented as possessors of magical skill. When Fearghus seizes three of them they bestow great swimming prowess on him as a condition for their release. Subsequent literary sources also make them bestowers of magical objects, such as a mantle or pair of silver-bronze shoes which enable a person to travel in water without drowning. These are Irish adaptations of international motifs concerning objects which provide for magical travel or magical finance. It is therefore obvious that the designation 'luchorpán' was invented in Ireland when lore of dwarf-communities was adopted from abroad by Irish writers, and that the solitary leprechaun of folklore is a post-mediaeval development from the literature.

James Carney (1955), 103-10; D A Binchy in *Ériu 16*, 36-8, 41-2; Diarmaid Ó Giolláin in *Béaloideas 50*, 126-50 and *52*, 75-150.

[Magical objects] See Stith Thompson (1955-1958), Motifs D1455, D1470, D1520.

LÍ BAN A mermaid who is featured in a fantastic story composed in the 12th or 13th century. The name means literally 'beauty of women'.

She is described as daughter of **Eochaidh mac Maireadha**, who with most of his family was drowned when Lough Neagh burst forth in Ulster. She survived the inundation, being confined in her bower which - though the lake rose all around it - the water did not enter. She expressed the wish to be turned into a salmon, and this happened accordingly. Her lap-dog became an otter, and for a full three hundred years she roamed the seas. It so happened that St **Comhghall** of the monastery of Beannchar (Bangor, Co Down) sent one of his monks, called Beoán, on a message to Rome. As Beoán was sailing thither, he heard Lí Ban singing in the water, and met her. She told him of her life, and promised to meet him a year hence at Inbhear Ollarbha (Larne, Co Antrim). When that time came, she was caught in the fishing net of a monk called Fearghus, and many people came to marvel at her. A dispute arose between Fearghus and Beoán over which of them should have charge of her, and the monks fasted so as to gain inspiration from God concerning the matter. An angel told one of them that two stags would come from the grave of her sister Airiu, and that the stags should be yoked to her chariot and they would bring her to the correct place. All happened accordingly, and Lí Ban was brought to a church, where the clerics gave her the choice of dying immediately and gaining heaven, or of tarrying for a further three hundred years. She chose the former, and was baptised by Comhghall and christened Muirghein ('sea-birth') or Muirgheilt ('sea-prodigy').

This fanciful story makes use of the common motif in mediaeval Irish literature of a personage marvellously living on from the remote pagan past so as to encounter the Christian missionaries. In this case it was probably borrowed from the lore of **Patrick**, for the additional motif of the stags settling a dispute derives from a legend of the death of that saint (q.v.).

S H O'Grady (1892) *1*, 234-7 and *2*, 484-5; R I Best / Osborn Bergin (1929), 96-100.

LIADHAIN Poetess of the 7th century who reputedly belonged to the Corca Dhuibhne sept of west Munster. A tragic love-story concerning her is told in a text of prose and verse which was put together in the 10th century.

According to this, Liadhain went on a circuit to Connacht and met there a poet called Cuirithir mac Dobharchon, who proposed to her. She refused to abandon her circuit, but told him to come south for her to her home in Munster. When Cuirithir did this and arrived outside her house, he met there the wise fool **Comhdhán** and asked him to go inside and tell Liadhain 'by your wit' that her lover was outside. Comhdhán entered and recited verses, stating that 'the son of the beast that stays at night under pools' was waiting for her. By this she understood that Mac Dobharchon (literally, 'son of the otter') was outside, and she went with him. She, however, was 'under the spiritual direction' of St **Cumaine Fada** - which probably means that she had become a nun - and the saint forbade the two lovers to cohabit. After pleading, Cumaine agreed to let them spend one night together, but placed a clerical student between them in bed. Having been sent away by Cumaine, Cuirithir became a monk and went on pilgrimage to the territory of the Déise (in Co Waterford). Hearing soon after that Liadhain was coming from the west to visit him, he went away across the sea in a coracle. Liadhain came to the flagstone on which he was wont to pray, and stayed on it sorrowfully until she died and was buried underneath.

Kuno Meyer (1902); Gerard Murphy (1962), 82-5, 208-11.

LIR Mythical or fictional chieftain, one of the **Tuatha Dé Danann**.

This character does not seem to have belonged to ancient tradition. He occurs in sources from the 12th century onwards, being referred to as Lir of Sídh Fionnachaidh (the cairn on Deadman's Hill in Co Armagh). This is probably due to learned speculation which connected that placename with descriptions of the sea as the white field ('fionn-achadh') of **Manannán**. Since Manannán was 'the son of the sea' ('mac Lir'), it would be natural for scholars to imagine his personalised father as associated with a placename like Fionnachadh. The only real narrative concerning him is in a text written in or about the 15th century, which is entitled *Oidheadh Chlainne Lir* (the Tragic Fate of the Children of Lir).

This tells of how, after their defeat by the Gaelic people, the Tuatha Dé chose Bodhbh Dearg as their new king. Lir of Sídh Fionnachaidh was offended by this choice, but Bodhbh offered him one of his foster-daughters in marriage and so effected a reconciliation. This maiden was Aobh, and she bore him two sets of twins. The first set was a boy called Aodh and a girl called Fionnghuala. The second set was the boys Fiachra and Conn, in the bearing of whom she died. Lir was despondent, but Bodhbh gave him as second wife Aoife, the sister of Aobh. Aoife at first loved her four step-children, but she grew jealous of Lir's affection for them and began to plot their destruction. Accordingly, she took them with her one day, ostensibly on a visit to Bodhbh, but in reality with the intent of killing them. She could not get herself to ply the sword on them, however, and instead struck them with a magic wand and turned them into swans at Loch Dairbhreach (Lake Derravarragh in Co Westmeath). Fionnghuala besought Aoife to fix a term for their transformation, and Aoife said that it would last until a noblewoman from the south would marry a nobleman from the north.

When Bodhbh discovered what had been done, he changed Aoife into a demon, in which form she must wander through the air forever. For three hundred years, however, the four swans remained on Loch Dairbhreach, conversing with the Tuatha Dé who came to see them by day and singing beautiful music for these visitors by night. Then they flew away to Sruth na Maoile (the Sea of Moyle between Ireland and Scotland), where they spent a further three hundred years in cold and misery. After this, they spent three hundred years off Iorras Domhnann (Erris, Co Mayo), where they endured even greater misery. At the end of that time, they flew home to their father's dwelling of Sídh Fionnachaidh, but found the place empty and deserted. Returning to the west, they alighted on Inis Gluaire (Inishglory, an island in the bay of Erris). They met there the Christian missionary St Mochaomhóg, who treated them with great kindness and they attended his religious services. Not long after, the Connacht king Lairgnéan married Deoch, the daughter of the king of Munster. Deoch desired the three wonderful swans as a wedding-present, and Lairgnéan came to seize them. But their period of enchantment was now at an end, and they turned into three withered old men and an old woman. The saint baptised them and they died happily and were buried together.

This story is well-constructed and well-told, but it does not predate its text by very long. It is based on a migratory legend, known as 'the Knight of the Swan', which reached Ireland from either Britain or France at the end of the Middle Ages. A late 14th-century version of the legend in English literature, in fact, has several children turned into swans by a jealous stepmother, and thus may represent the prototype known to the Irish author. That author also shows acquaintance with the earlier story of mad **Suibhne**, the style of which he echoes at several points. It is a curious fact that the text *Oidheadh Chlainne Lir* had little influence on folklore, but the story is well-known nowadays from the many schoolbook retellings in the last hundred years.

[Editions] Eugene O'Curry in *Atlantis 4*, 113-57; Seán Ua Ceallaigh (1927), 42-64.

[Knight of the Swan] Léon Gautier (1897), 77-81; Thomas Cramer (1971), 68-123; W H French / C B Hale (1964), 859-73. See also Gearóid Iarla **FitzGerald**.

[Suibhne connections] James Carney (1955), 153-8.

LUGH Mythical hero, originally a Celtic deity. His name is usually accompanied by the sobriquet Lámhfhada ('long-armed'), the idea being not of a physically long limb but that his weapons had long range. He was adept at the use of the javelin and the sling. Lugh was also known as 'Samhildánach', meaning 'the one who possesses all the arts'.

Writing of the Gauls, Julius Caesar stated that they most worshipped a god whom he equated with the Roman Mercurius. 'They declare him the inventor of all arts, the guide for every road and journey, and they deem him to have the greatest influence for all money-making and commerce'. All the evidence points to Lugh (Celtic 'Lugus') as the deity in question. Sanctuaries with dedications to this personage have been discovered throughout

56. LUGH *Horse-swimming race at the festival of Lugh.*

Gaulish territories, and the Celtic placename Lugudūnon ('fortress of Lugus') survives in many forms, for example Lyon, Laon, Lauzun, Laudun, Loudon, and Leiden. Many scholars have argued that his name connects him with light and is cognate with the Latin word 'lux'; but it seems more likely that the proper derivation is from a Celtic word 'lugio', meaning an oath. Lugus would thus have originally been a patron of sworn contracts, a function which accords well with the description given by Caesar of the chief Gaulish god. He was also the focus of a harvest cult, for other Classical writers attest to a great festival at Lyon on the first day of August. The celebration of such a festival has been current in Ireland since very early times, being called in Irish Lughnasadh (see **Time**) and thus providing a direct link between the mythology of the Continental Celts and the insular tradition of Ireland.

Mediaeval Welsh literature has some echoes from the deity, such as the character Lleu, who was given the sobriquet Llawgyffes ('accurate arm'), but clear and definitive lore concerning him is extant only in Irish sources. His cult appears to have been introduced into Ireland, directly from Gaul or via Britain, around the time of Christ, and perhaps by refugees from the devastation caused by the Roman armies. The cult soon replaced earlier harvest lore and became the nexus of one of the four cardinal points of the Irish year. A glossary compiled in the 9th century, which embodies much ancient lore, explains Lughnasadh as 'an assembly held by him (i.e. Lugh) at the beginning of harvest each year', and another early source identifies this assembly as the great fair of Tailtiu (Teltown in Co Meath). The origins of various communal activities relating to festive celebrations were also attributed to him - such as ball-games, horse-racing, and 'ficheall' (the Irish form of chess).

Irish tradition at all stages represents Lugh as slaying his maternal grandfather, who was a tyrant. This must derive, together with the harvest lore, from the cult of Lugus among the Continental Celts, as it conforms to a myth-pattern which was prevalent among the ancient peoples of the Mediterranean. The pattern was known in Greek myth (Perseus), in Latin redactions of Persian myth (Cyros), and in ancient Babylonian culture (the Sargon inscription). It is feasible to assume that the Celts of antiquity borrowed it from the crop-cultivating peoples of the eastern Mediterranean area and applied it to their own harvest-god. Irish tradition describes Lugh's defeated grandfather as possessing a destructive eye, and this can be taken as a symbol of the blazing sun which wanes with the end of summer and the ripening of a new harvest.

The fullest description of Lugh is found in an 11th-century Irish text *Cath Maige Tuired* ('the Battle of Moytirra'). The text incorporates material written down several centuries earlier, and it describes the events surrounding what became known as the second battle of Moytirra (see **Mythological**

Cycle). It tells of the relations between the divine race, **Tuatha Dé Danann**, and the demonic race known as **Fomhóire**. In an attempt to establish peace between the two races, we are told, one of the Fomhóire leaders called **Balar** gave his daughter Eithne to a young man of the Tuatha Dé called Cian, 'and she bore him the child of accomplishment, that is Lugh'. Time passed by, and when the Tuatha Dé king **Nuadhu** lost an arm in battle he was deposed by his people on account of the blemish. They gave the throne to a Fomhóire prince called **Breas**, but the reign of Breas became a period of great oppression. Smarting under this, the Tuatha Dé restored Nuadhu, who had been fitted with a silver arm. The Fomhóire then gathered a massive force in the northern zones of the world and, under the leadership of Balar, prepared to invade Ireland. The Tuatha Dé were at **Tara** planning the defence when their doorkeeper saw a handsome young warrior approaching. The newcomer announced himself as Lugh, and was told by the doorkeeper that he could not enter the citadel without having an art. Lugh said that he was a builder, but the doorkeeper replied that they already had a builder and did not require another. Lugh said that he was a smith, but got a similar reply. Likewise when he said that he was a champion, harper, warrior, poet, historian, magician, physician, cupbearer, and brazier. Then Lugh said: 'Ask the king if he has one man who is skilled in all these arts, and if he has I will not enter Tara.' The doorkeeper told the king that a stranger had arrived who was 'the man of every single art', and Nuadhu commanded that he be allowed to enter, 'because a man like that has never yet come into this fortress'. When he entered, Lugh performed a prodigious feat by throwing a great flagstone over the wall of the building, and then he played magical music on the harp. Nuadhu decided to give him command of the Tuatha Dé in their hour of need, and Lugh inspected their forces, determining which particular skill each of the leaders possessed. When battle was joined with the Fomhóire on the plain of Moytirra (in Co Sligo), Lugh slipped away from his bodyguard and circled around the warriors, 'on one foot and with one eye closed', while he chanted a spell. This was a magical device used by **poets** to weaken the foe. Horrific slaughter ensued, and Lugh came face to face with his Fomhóire grandfather. This fearsome warrior, Balar, had a destructive eye which was never opened except on a field of battle. Four men would raise the lid of the eye, and the host on which it gazed would be destroyed by its poison. 'The lid was raised from Balar's eye. Then Lugh cast a sling-stone at him, which drove the eye through his head, and it was gazing on his own host. He fell on top of the Fomhóire army, so that thrice nine of them died under his side.' The Fomhóire were routed, but Lugh spared the life of Breas in return for advice on ploughing, sowing, and reaping the harvest.

In this narrative, the combat between Lugh and his tyrant grandfather has been inserted into the context of a struggle between two supernatural races (see **Mythological Cycle**). Perhaps the harvest imagery of Breas was the reason why this was the context chosen for the Lugh myth after its introduction into Ireland, but it is at any rate clear that the combination of the two plots caused some difficulties and the text of *Cath Maige Tuired* - even after several centuries of development - still betrays some disparate elements. The motif that Lugh is predestined to slay Balar is not brought out clearly; the time of the battle is given as Samhain (the November feast) rather than Lughnasadh (August); and we are not told if Lugh continued to lead the Tuatha Dé. Despite the glorious role assigned to him, he was clearly an interloper, but in time he was made to fit more comfortably into the Tuatha Dé company. References from about the 10th century state that, after the death of Nuadhu, he was installed as their king by the Tuatha Dé at the hill of Tailtiu and that he reigned as king of Ireland for forty years. An 11th-century text describes him as lord of the otherworld, living in a house of gold and silver and attended by the goddess of sovereignty (see **Kingship**). He is called 'an Scál' (the Phantom), is seated on a throne, and 'never was there seen in Tara one as wonderful as he'. In a poem written a century later Lugh is said to have been reared in Eamhain Abhlach, a beautiful wooded realm full of apple-trees and cognate with the Avalon of Celtic myth which was adopted into Arthurian literature.

One mediaeval writer, perhaps echoing some earlier tradition, states that Lugh had as wives two sisters called Buí and Nás. Buí was buried at Cnoghbha (Knowth in Co Meath) and Nás at the place which is claimed to be called after her (Naas, Co Kildare). The latter is pseudo-lore, for the word (and placename) 'nás' actually meant a fair or assembly, but all of this may be an echo of early importance of Lughnasadh celebrations at these places. The same writer states significantly that it was in memory of these two wives that Lugh instituted the fair of Tailtiu which, as suggested above, seems to have been the earliest great centre of his cult. Already by the 8th century Lugh was being regarded as the otherworld father of **Cú Chulainn**, and it is clear that a broad mosaic of folklore concerning him was circulating in mediaeval Ireland. One source applies the epithet 'leathshuanach' (i.e. side-mantled) to him and explains it by claiming that 'a red colour used to be on him from sunset till morning', while another states that he had a beautiful shirt of red-gold texture. Several placenames derive from his name or were interpreted as such, while the frequent personal name Lughaidh originated as a compound of Lugh. The hero himself was sometimes referred to through his patronymic as Lugh mac Céin, but was more often called Lugh mac Eithleann - from Eithliu, an early form of his mother's name Eithne. A poem from the 14th century refers to his coming to Tara and ascribes marvellous acrobatic skills to him on that occasion. These included prodigious jumping and swimming, as well as 'leaping on a bubble without bursting it'. He exemplified the process by which art and skill were extended into the realm of mystery and magic, and therefore was a prototype for several picaresque characters in later lore, such as the **Gobán Saor**, the **Ceithearnach Caoilriabhach**, and Cearbhall **Ó Dálaigh**.

The attempts of mediaeval writers to synchronise the multiple vestiges of earlier mythology led to great confusion in names and characters. For instance, there was an enigmatic reference in the *Cath Maige Tuired* text to how Lugh procured weapons for the battle from the 'trí dé Danann' (i.e. three gods of **Danu**). Some literary sources state that the father of this trio was called Tuirill, but others have Breas as their father. Yet other sources confuse Breas with Balar, with the result that Lugh is represented as gaining a singular victory over both in the battle of Moytirra. A surveyor of the literature in the 10th century could speculate that three brothers, whose father had been killed by Lugh, would seek vengeance by killing Lugh's own father Cian. According to the story thus invented, Cian went in the shape of a lap-dog to Brugh na Bóinne (the tumulus of Newgrange in Co Meath) and was killed there by the sons of Tuirill (later, Tuireann), who were called Brian, Iuchair, and Iucharba. The story soon became popular with writers. One version states that the three brothers were in turn slain by Lugh on the Isle of Man, but others state that Lugh was satisfied with compensation. The wergild he demanded was seven precious things which were extremely difficult to obtain and which included a mighty javelin. An expanded version of the story was written in the 14th century, according to which Lugh deliberately made the compensation difficult out of a spirit of malice. When the three brothers, having fulfilled the conditions, returned sick and weary from their exertions, their father beseeched Lugh to lend his mantle to them. This mantle had the magical property of healing all illness, but Lugh refused the request and let them die.

Despite its attractive plot - apparently suggested by the episode of Jason's fleece in Greek literature - and despite its frequent inclusion in manuscript compilations, this literary fabrication concerning the sons of Tuirill enjoyed no great popularity in oral storytelling. Another story from the mediaeval literature describes the death of Lugh as taking place at Uisneach (the hill of Ushnagh in Co Westmeath, also the venue of great assemblies in ancient times). He had, we are told, slain a certain Cearmaid 'through jealousy concerning his wife' and, in retaliation, the three sons of Cearmaid attacked Lugh at Uisneach. One of them thrust a spear into his foot, and Lugh retreated into a lake and was drowned there. This account has no warrant other than to fancifully explain the placename Loch Lughbhorta, and it was obviously suggested by the story of the sons of Tuirill.

Folklore attests that the presentation of Lugh depended on one great story from start to finish i.e. his triumph over Balar. Several versions of this have been collected from the oral tradition in recent times in Irish-speaking areas in the west and north-west. The occurrence of the story in the folklore of these areas undoubtedly owes something to manuscripts. There are many references to the epic in literature, and even some literary retellings, and there is little doubt that more of such written records did exist but have been lost. Sligo and Mayo readers of the literature would note that the battle was fought at Moytirra in their own area and would thus be inclined to memorise the story. In Donegal, the placename Dún Lúiche (Dunlewy at the foot of Mount Errigal) was popularly associated with Lugh because of its phonemic similarity to his name, and this appears to be the main reason why the story thrived in the folklore of that region. That these oral tellings have an integrity of their own, however, is illustrated by the fact that they give clearest expression to the basic motif i.e. that Lugh is the prophesied youth who will slay his tyrant grandfather. They differ from each other in the order and arrangement of the plot, but their underlying pattern is as follows:-

Balar was a one-eyed tyrant who lived on Tory Island off the Donegal coast. He had one daughter called Eithne, of whom it was foretold that, if she gave birth to a son, that child would kill its grandfather. Balar therefore kept the girl locked away in a tower so that no man could gain access to her. However, a young man called Cian had intercourse with her, and as a result he was seized and put to death by the tyrant. When she gave birth, the enraged Balar ordered that she and the child be set adrift in a boat. This was done, but they survived through the kindness of a smith called Goibhleann (see **Goibhniu**). When the child Lugh was growing to manhood, Goibhleann made a great spear for him. It happened that Balar coveted a marvellous cow, called the **Glas Ghoibhneann**, which belonged to the smith. He took the cow and brought it with him to Tory, but Goibhleann succeeded in having himself accepted into Balar's service and contrived to gain possession of the cow's halter. The cow broke out of its byre on the island and swam after the halter all the way back to the mainland. Balar vowed to destroy Ireland in revenge for this, and on his campaign of devastation came to the forge of Goibhleann. His one eye was full of poison, and it destroyed all on which it gazed. Finding himself confronted by Lugh, Balar removed the covering from his eye, but Lugh threw the spear and blinded him. Before being decapitated, Balar said that if his severed head were put on top of Lugh's own, then all the power of Balar would pass to Lugh. Suspecting treachery, Lugh placed the head on a large rock, and a drop of poison fell from it and dashed the rock to pieces.

The theme of Goibhleann and his marvellous cow was introduced into these oral versions because of the occurrence of that character, under his earlier form Goibhniu (q.v.), in the literary accounts of the Moytirra battle. A retelling of the Moytirra story from around the 15th century has Goibhniu busy in his forge during the battle. When Balar begins to uncover the eye Goibhniu uses his tongs to fling to Lugh the heavy slingstone with which he will slay the tyrant. The episode of the poisonous drop, not referred to in the earliest sources, occurs in the literature from late mediaeval times onwards. It was claimed that Balar was chased by Lugh all the way from Moytirra to Carn Uí Néit (Mizen Head in Co Cork), where the beheading took place. Literary sources can thus be seen to lie behind definite aspects of the recent oral tradition concerning Lugh. The retention in them of a purer form of the plot of the tyrant-grandfather myth shows, nevertheless, that these folklore versions reflect a time when the cult of Lugh was still vibrant in the oral stream.

[Origin] Heinrich Wagner in *Zeitschrift für celtische Philologie 31*, 22-5; Alfred Holder *2* (1896), 308-46; Émile Thevenot (1968), 72-96; T F O'Rahilly (1946), 58-61, 310-7; T G E Powell (1958), 120-7; Máire MacNeill (1962), 1-11.

[Lleu in Wales] W J Gruffydd (1928), 60-4.

[9th-century glossary] Kuno Meyer in *Anecdota from Irish Manuscripts 4*, 66-7.

[Tailtiu and sports] R A S Macalister (1941), 116-9, 128-9, 134-5; MacNeill, *op cit*, 320-1.

[Mediterranean myth] Otto Rank (1914), 12-44; P Saintyves in P-L Couchoud ed (1928), 229-72; Gruffydd, *op cit*, 350-75; Alexander Krappe (1927) 1-43.

[Moytirra] E A Gray (1982); Macalister, *op cit*, 118-21.

[Mediaeval lore] A G Van Hamel (1933), 41; Macalister, *op cit*, 120-1; Eleanor Knott (1957), 55; Gray, *op cit*, 62; Edward Gwynn (1913), 48-53, 122-3; Osborn Bergin (1970), 76-9.

[Lugh and Cú Chulainn] Van Hamel, *op cit*, 5, 30; Cecile O'Rahilly (1976), 64-5, 70.

[Name derivatives] MacNeill, *op cit*, 9; T F O'Rahilly, *op cit*, 120.

[Tuirill] Macalister, *op cit*, 128-31, 134-7; Rudolf Thurneysen in *Zeitschrift für celtische Philologie 12*, 239-50; R J O'Duffy (1888).

[Cearmaid] Macalister, *op cit*, 130-1; Gwynn (1924), 278-9; Bergin in *Medieval Studies for G S Loomis* (1927), 399-406.

[Moytirra in folklore] John O'Donovan (1848-51), 18-21; William Larminie (1893), 1-9, 241-5;

Jeremiah Curtin (1894), 283-311; Gruffydd, *op cit*, 65-76; Séamus Ó Searcaigh (1908), 3-7, 61; Seosamh Laoide (1913), 63-5; Elizabeth Andrews (1913), 73-6; Seán Ó Súilleabháin / R T Christiansen (1967), Type 934C; Sean O'Sullivan (1974), 17-22, 167; *Bentley's Miscellany 2*, 527-32; *An Gaodhal 12*, 78-81; Éamonn Ó Tuathail in *Béaloideas 3*, 128-9; Ordnance Survey Letters - Donegal (1835), 46-51, 81-97, 129-30 and Mayo 2 (1838), 41-2, 110-2; IFC Catalogue (numerous versions).

[General] Gray, *op cit*, 126-7; MacNeill, *op cit*, 3-11; Macalister, *op cit*, 116-37; T F O'Rahilly, *op cit*, 308-17.

LUGHAIDH LÁGHA Fictional warrior of Munster, brother of **Ailill Ólom**. His sobriquet (earlier, Lágae) was fancifully explained to refer to a great 'hand-spear' which he had.

Lughaidh Lágha was a faithful supporter of **Lughaidh mac Con** when Ailill acted treacherously towards the latter. He accompanied this namesake of his in exile to Scotland, and fought tremendously at his side on their triumphant return. He it was who slew the high-king **Art** in the battle of Magh Mucramha (in east Galway). When Lughaidh mac Con later abdicated as high-king in favour of **Cormac mac Airt**, Lughaidh Lágha refused to return to Munster with his friend but instead determined to serve the son of the man he had slain.

The mediaeval literature thus envisaged him as a great warrior at the court of Cormac - in fact, one of the five greatest warriors that Ireland had ever seen, the others being **Lugh**, **Cú Chulainn**, **Conall Cearnach**, and **Fionn mac Cumhaill**. He figures prominently in some late mediaeval stories concerning the latter, being described as the protector and husband of Fionn's aunt Uirne, and the opponent of **Goll mac Morna** in a brawl which broke out at a great banquet held by Cormac. After this brawl, he returned to his own area of Eatharlach (Aherlow, Co Tipperary), a point which echoes an alternative earlier tradition that he did not remain at Cormac's court, but settled at Eatharlach. This is the situation described in the 9th-century text *Cath Crinna*, which has Cormac mac Airt (q.v.) enlisting his support for a battle against the Ulstermen. Again, Lughaidh Lágha fought magnificently in that battle and, before returning to Munster, managed to survive a treacherous effort by Cormac to gain revenge for his father's death.

Though dramatised as a separate character by the mediaeval writers, it is clear that Lughaidh Lágha was originally an emanation from the Munsterised Lughaidh mac Con (q.v.).

T F O'Rahilly (1946), 61, 202; Máirín O'Daly (1975), 11-2, 40-1, 52-61; Whitley Stokes (1900), 163; Gerard Murphy (1953), 103-4; Pádraig Ó Siochfhradha (1941), 146-50; S H O'Grady (1892) *1*, 320-5 and *2*, 478, 490-3. See also **Mac Lughach**.

LUGHAIDH LÁMHDHEARG Fictional king of Ireland situated in prehistory.

The mediaeval writers tell little of this king, except that he ruled for seven years. His sobriquet means 'red-handed', indicating his prowess in battle, and was no doubt added to the name Lughaidh for alliterative effect. In accordance with the notion that ancient Ireland was sometimes divided into two halves (see **Conn Céadchathach**), we are told that a certain Conaing Beag-Eaglach ruled in the north and Eochaidh Uaircheas in the south. Lughaidh Lámhdhearg slew the latter in battle and reigned in the south until he fell at the hands of Conaing. The idea of a southern king called Lughaidh was probably suggested by the tradition of the Munster hero **Lughaidh mac Con**. The attractive alliteration of the name Lughaidh Lámhdhearg gave rise also to other incidental characters in the mediaeval literature with that name. A 17th century source gives a curious explanation for the epithet of this fictional king, stating that he was so called 'because he had a spot or mark on his hand'. This is a reflection of lore concerning heroes with a distinctive mark on their bodies (see **Ó Conchubhair**, Cathal Crobhdhearg; and **Ó Domhnaill**, Aodh Balldearg).

R A S Macalister (1956), 256-7; R I Best / M A O'Brien (1957), 480; Edward Gwynn (1913), 200-5, 512; P S Dinneen (1908) *2*, 144-5.

[Other warriors with the name] Cormac Ó Cadhlaigh (1956), 150, 228.

LUGHAIDH MAC CON Mythical leader of the **Érainn** people of Munster. His original name seems to have been simply 'mac Con', literally 'son of hound', but its true meaning would have been the figurative 'son of warrior'. Lughaidh was probably prefixed to his designation in order to give him a more normal name. A kindred character, Lughaidh mac Con Roí, occurs in the early literature, and the strong likelihood is that Lughaidh mac Con was a derivative in tradition of the celebrated **Cú Roí**.

The full appellation of Lughaidh mac Con may not have been applied to him until the 6th or 7th century, and indeed 'mac Con' survived as an alternative way of referring to him in the mediaeval literature. Writing in the 7th century, St **Patrick's** biographer Tíreachán relates how the saint revived a man who was long dead, having been slain by 'the warrior-band of Mac Con'. It is obvious from this that Tíreachán knew of a tradition concerning a great war-lord of that name, and he describes the episode as having taken place in Dichuil (an area in Co Mayo), far from Munster. Cú Roí was originally associated with the north midlands, and it is thus apparent that the character Mac Con - like Cú Roí - was transposed to Munster because of the prominent role played by Érainn septs in that southern province in the early literary period. An early emanation from him was a reputed character called Lughaidh Laíghde who, also like Cú Roí, was said to have been son of **Dáire**. This character is represented as one of seven brothers, also called Lughaidh. One day when hunting they met an ugly hag, who asked them to lie with her. Lughaidh Laíghde alone consented, and she became a beautiful young woman. She explained to him that she was sovereignty, and that the **kingship** of Ireland would be his. This is a borrowing of the motif of the dual aspects of sovereignty in the Uí Néill lore of **Niall Naoighiallach**, but it does suggest that the Érainn had a tradition about an ancient Tara king of theirs to whom the name Lughaidh had become applied. The second part of this character's name (earlier, Loígde) was the designation of an Érainn sept of Munster.

The mythical Érainn king was, however, most fully developed in the guise of Lughaidh mac Con. Already by the 8th century, finely dramatised accounts of his adventures were in circulation, accounts which reflect the conditions, not so much of prehistoric Tara as of early mediaeval Munster. These describe how he was of the Érainn people but, being the products of synchronising scholars, they make him son of the above-mentioned Lughaidh Laíghde. The synchronisers furthermore state that he was fostered by **Ailill Ólom**, mythical king of the dominant Munster sept, the Eoghanacht. This Ailill had seven sons, the leading son being Eoghan. When on a journey once, Eoghan and Lughaidh mac Con came upon an otherworld musician called Fear Fí at Eas Máighe (Caherass on the river Maigue in Co Limerick). They argued over which of them had first discovered the musician, and Ailill ruled in favour of Eoghan. The incensed Lughaidh complained of this and, when he was chided by Eoghan with being a vassal, he challenged his foster-brother to a battle.

When the armies were assembled at Ceann Abhradh (the Ballyhoura hills on the Cork-Limerick border) Ailill tried to trick Lughaidh by inviting him to a parley. Lughaidh attended, against the wishes of his people, but he brought seven hundred of his men with him. This troop determined not to flee, and accordingly they were fettered to each other. Ailill and Eoghan, however, slyly informed their ally Cairbre Músc that Lughaidh was making terms with them, and the enraged Cairbre gathered his own men and attacked the unsuspecting Lughaidh. The army of Lughaidh was completely overthrown, and he took to flight with the remainder. His jester Da Deara had the exact same appearance as himself and, in order to save his chief, Da Deara put on Lughaidh's diadem. The jester was thus slain, but the fleeing Lughaidh was recognised by the kingly white calves of his legs, and Cairbre Músc cast at him and lamed him. Lughaidh nevertheless managed to get away, and he went to Scotland as a refugee.

That this lore of Lughaidh mac Con was not very old in the 8th century is indicated by the fact that there were variant explanations of the battle of Ceann Abhradh. One was that Lughaidh mac Con and Ailill Ólom had only joined in the battle in support of opposite sides i.e. the three sons of **Conaire mac Mogha Lámha** who were giving battle to the killer of their father, Neimheadh mac Sraibhghind. The principal of these three sons was Cairbre Músc, and one version of the Ceann Abhradh story dispenses with the need for this other scenario by having Eoghan, rather than Cairbre Músc, wound Lughaidh. Yet another account has a warrior called Gnáthal (see **Art**) doing the wounding.

At any rate, after his flight to Scotland Lughaidh and his followers were welcomed by the Scottish king, who did not know who they were, and they were seven years in that country, during which time they won several battles for their benefactor. They did not reveal their identity, fearing that the king was an ally of the Irish high-king Art, who was a brother-in-law of Ailill Ólom. One day, when Lughaidh and the Scottish king were playing chess, an Irish poet arrived and gave news of events in Ireland. On hearing how his people in Munster were oppressed by Eoghan, Lughaidh knocked down a row of the king's chess pieces in anger. The king then realised who he was and decided to test him. He had dead mice placed as a meal before Lughaidh's followers, expecting that Lughaidh himself would not eat, but Lughaidh did eat and ordered his men to do likewise. 'They obey you!' said the king. 'I obey them too!' said Lughaidh. Then the king asked was he in fact Lughaidh. He replied truthfully and, much to his surprise, the Scottish king offered to help him with a host of Scots and Britons. Their ships stretched all the way from the Scottish to the Irish coast. Arriving in Ireland, Lughaidh swept all before him, and faced the combined forces of Art and Ailill Ólom at Magh Mucramha (the plain south-west of Athenry in Co Galway). Lughaidh tied his men together so that they would not flee, and hid half of the army in trenches. He won a great victory, with Art and the seven sons of Ailill being slain. He then advanced on Tara and took over the high-kingship, which he held for many years.

The immediate source of these accounts, however, was propaganda of the dominant Connachta - Uí Néill dynasties, and thus they show little of the point of view of the Érainn. So we read that, because he was a usurper, the reign of Lughaidh was a period of unfruitfulness and misery in the land. A son was posthumously born to Art, and when he - **Cormac mac Airt** - came to Tara and proved a judgement of Lughaidh wrong, Lughaidh had to resign the kingship and he returned to Munster. When he arrived at Ailill's dwelling, his foster-mother Sadhbh warned him against the vengeance of her husband. Nevertheless, he went to see Ailill, who embraced him and put his cheek to his. With this pretence, Ailill Ólom (q.v.) touched him with his poisonous tooth, and within three days half of Lughaidh's face had melted away. Ailill then sent one of his retainers, the Leinster seer Fearcheas mac Comáin, after Lughaidh. Fearcheas chanted a spell over his spear and cast it at Lughaidh at a waterfall on the Bandon river. Thus Lughaidh was slain.

The strange appellation 'mac Con' gave rise to attempts to interpret it. One mediaeval text claims that, when he was a baby in Ailill's fosterage, he crept to a bitch and was suckled by it, and hence was called 'son of a hound' by way of a nickname. In folklore, memory of him survived in the context of the myth of Cormac mac Airt (q.v.), which became a traditional oral story in the north and west of Ireland. Coincidentally, therefore, memory of his lore reverted to its original area, while he was forgotten in Munster. Some late tellings of the Cormac myth add a new motif to the image of Lughaidh. According to these he could never sleep, and when the young Cormac came to Tara Lughaidh told him that his reign had been miserable on that account. Cormac explained that the reason for this was that Lughaidh's father had been an otter, which had surprised his mother once when she had gone to bathe in the Boyne river. On Cormac's advice, Lughaidh went and lay on a raft in the Boyne, and his otter-father came and took him underneath. This is a borrowing from a migratory legend concerning a man who could not sleep because his father was a water-spirit (see **Moore**). The water-spirit was assimilated to the otter because of a folk-belief that otters (see **Animals**, Wild) kept their eyes open at night. The migratory legend got attached to Lughaidh because the 'hound' in his name ('cú') was taken to refer to an otter ('cu dobhráin', literally 'water-hound'), and because the misery of his reign could through it be rationalised into a personal ailment.

Ludwig Bieler (1979), 154-5; Kuno Meyer (1910), 28 and (1912), 75; T F O'Rahilly (1946), 77-9, 201-2; Whitley Stokes in *Irische Texte 3*, 322-23; Máirín O'Daly (1975), 9-11, 38-65, 74-93; Rudolf Thurneysen in *Zeitschrift für celtische Philologie 20*, 222; Myles Dillon in *Ériu 11*, 49 and 14, 154-65 and in *Publications of the Modern Language Association 60*, 340-5; Lucius Gwynn in *Ériu 6*, 136-7; Mícheál Ó Dúnlainge in *Irisleabhar na Gaedhilge 17* and *18*, passim.

[Lughaidh Laíghde] Stokes in *Irische Texte 3*, 316-23.

[Discussions] Dillon (1946),16-23; M E Dobbs in *Journal of the Royal Society of Antiquaries of Ireland 60*, 165-87.

[Folklore] A H Krappe in *Modern Language Review 24*, 200-4; Seán O'Sullivan (1966), 21-37; Éamonn Ó Tuathail (1934), 13; IFC 168:1-44, 169:822-31, 186:42-50, 289:376-93.

LUGHAIDH RIABHDHEARG Fictional king of Ireland whose reign was situated in prehistory.

An earlier form of his sobriquet was Reo-derg, meaning 'red-stripe', and it probably referred to a battle-wound. He occurs in several texts as a foster-son of **Cú Chulainn**, and obviously was one of the many characters invented to people the **Ulster Cycle** by the early mediaeval writers. The likelihood is that he was suggested by the character Lughaidh mac Con Roí, who was an echo in that cycle from the celebrated mythic hero of Munster **Lughaidh mac Con**. The character Lughaidh mac Con Roí was sometimes called 'mac trí chon' (i.e. son of three hounds) because of a divine triplication of his father **Cú Roí**. This suggested the idea that Lughaidh 'Reo-derg' had triple paternity, and so he was said to be 'mac na dTrí Finn Eamhna' (i.e. son of the three **Finn Eamhna**). This latter trio were seen by some writer as a tolerable alternative to the 'three hounds' in the context. The image of the red stripe provided the opportunity to rationalise the new character's triple paternity. Accordingly, it was said that the three Finn, in a fit of drunkenness, lay with their sister Clothra, and as a result Lughaidh was born. The child had red stripes, which divided his body into three parts. His head resembled Nár, one of the three Finn; his breast resembled Breas, another of them; and from his belt downwards he was like the third of the Finn, Lothar, Thus he had the sobriquet Riabh nDerg (later, Riabhdhearg) i.e. 'of the red stripes'. Some sources state that he had three stripes on his body, but others - computing for the three parts - give the number as two.

As a further development of his legend, it was claimed that he was reared by a certain Rumhal, king of Leinster, who was a brother to 'the Three Red-Heads' of that province (for whom, see **Conaire**). It was also claimed that these 'Red-Heads' slew Lughaidh Riabhdhearg - an idea speculatively derived from the image of three red stripes on his body, and probably also from the contrast between white ('fionn') as the colour of his three fathers and red as the colour of three slayers. This slaying motif seems to be what gave rise to the notion that Lughaidh Riabhdhearg was a king of Ireland. The three Red-Heads of Leinster were the slayers of king Conaire, and thus Lughaidh was made the successor of Conaire who was slain by the same trio. The claim that he had been a king of Ireland was known to a mediaeval interpolator of the text on the Wasting Sickness of Cú Chulainn, who describes how Cú Chulainn gave Lughaidh a series of advices on how to rule and how Lughaidh went to **Tara** for the royal election.

His death at the hands of the Three Red-Heads reads awkwardly in the Annals, for nowhere else are Conaire and Cú Chulainn regarded as contemporaries, and so a new narrative was invented in the 12th century based on imagery from the Wasting Sickness text. There the otherworld lady Fann and her sister came in the form of swans to woo Cú Chulainn. The new story therefore has Dearbhfhorgaill, daughter of the king of Norway, come with her handmaiden, both in the form of swans also to woo Cú Chulainn. In this case, however, that great warrior casts a stone at her. It lodges in her womb, and when Cú Chulainn sees her return to human shape he sucks it out. He rejects her love and instead bestows her on Lughaidh. The couple, we are told, were happy and had children. Then, during a winter-snow, the men-folk made pillars of the snow and, when they departed, the women went onto the pillars to compete concerning which of them could send their urine furthest through the snow. Dearbhfhorgaill was a reluctant competitor, but she won the game. Thereupon the other women were seized with jealousy, saying that if the men knew this they would desire only her. So these women knocked her eyes out and cut off her nose, ears, and hair. When Lughaidh returned to his house, accompanied by Cú Chulainn, he found his wife at the point of death. Lughaidh himself died from the shock, or according to some accounts threw himself on his sword. The infuriated Cú Chulainn overturned the house on top of the thrice fifty guilty women, killing them all.

The mediaeval literature variously gives twenty years, twenty-five years, and twenty-six years for Lughaidh's supposed reign. The motif of incest involved in his own birth was repeated in the tradition that he begat the future king **Criomhthann Nia Náir** on his own mother Clothra.

T F O'Rahilly (1946), 486-7; Whitley Stokes in *Irische Texte 3*, 333, 375; R A S Macalister (1956), 303-5; Myles Dillon (1953), 3, 8-11; A G Van Hamel (1933), 62; Carl Marstrander in *Ériu 5*, 201-18; Edward Gwynn (1924), 278-9; P S Dinneen (1908) *2*, 232-3; Cormac Ó Cadhlaigh (1956), 477.

M

MAC DHOMHNAILL, ALASDAIR (c1610-1647) Leading officer in the Confederate War in the 1640s. He was born on the island of Colonsay, off the west coast of Scotland, and his clan (anglicised in Ireland as MacDonnell and in Scotland as MacDonald) were chiefs of Antrim as well as of western Scotland. His father was a famous warrior called Colla Ciotach ('Colla the left-handed') and Alasdair himself was thus usually known as Alasdair Mac Colla. By the English he was called 'young Kolkitto'.

Lore concerning Alasdair's youth was very popular in western Scotland and in Antrim. It was said that, on the night of his birth, every sword rattled in its scabbard and every gunlock snapped. As a boy, he encountered a savage bull and slew it, and his father marvelled at his strength and determined to test it against his own. He therefore left his house one night, telling young Alasdair to protect it from possible attack by robbers. After some time, he returned, pretending to be a robber, and began to break the door in. The boy thrust a fork through the door and knocked an eye out of the head of the 'intruder'. It was also said that, when Alasdair was sent ploughing, he lost his patience and struck one of the horses with his fist. The horse fell dead immediately. The point of such extravagant stories is to underline that Alasdair was destined to be a great warrior, and this at least is in accord with history. While his father was being held hostage against his good behaviour, he joined the English army and was stationed at Coleraine, but on the outbreak of the 1641 rebellion in Ulster he promptly deserted and became one of the leaders of the Irish forces. It was said in Scotland that a plot had been hatched in the English army to murder him, and that with this intent he was invited to a feast at Dunluce castle in Co Antrim. A letter was despatched to his commanding officer to this effect, but the messenger, having been told that this officer was a tall dark man, mistook Alasdair for him. Alasdair pretended not to read the letter, but went to the feast and refused to surrender his sword, saying that it was 'in the bravest hand in Ireland'. His commanding officer asked jeeringly what was the next bravest hand, and Alasdair changed the sword into his left hand and said 'this one!' Since he was the only armed man present he walked unimpeded from the castle and joined the Irish. These narratives of his youth and early life show the clear influence of ordinary folktales.

Alasadair was a very successful military leader in both Ireland and Scotland, and he is believed to have originated as a military tactic what became known as the Highland Charge, which consisted of the firing of one volley followed immediately by a headlong charge at the foe. He and the Marquis of Montrose won seven successive battles in Scotland, but in 1645 they divided their forces and both were defeated. Alasdair fled to Ireland, and was assigned the command of a force of highlanders and Ulstermen in the Munster section of the Irish forces. This army, under the command of General Theobald Taaffe, was opposed by the Cromwellian forces under the notorious Murchadh Ó Briain, Earl of Inchiquin, whose incendiary tactics gave rise to a proverb in Irish to describe a frightened person as one who had 'seen Murchadh and his troop'. The two armies clashed at Knockanuss, near Mallow in Co Cork. Alasdair with his men charged the left flank of the enemy and swept all before them, but Taaffe's other lines gave way and Alasdair was surrounded and captured. There are different traditions concerning his fate. One states that he was slain as he rode to a hill-top to reconnoitre, another that he surrendered but was murdered in violation of safe conduct by an officer who was astounded to discover who his prisoner was.

Local Cork tradition has it that he was returning to the battlefield, having pursued his opponents a considerable distance, when he was made a prisoner. He was led off under a guard of five horsemen and, in crossing a stream, he leaned forward to allow his horse to drink. In doing so, an opening in his armour was revealed, and one of the guards stabbed him through the back. The place where this happened is pointed out as 'the Chieftain's Ford', but the tradition is an apocryphal one (see a similar motif in connection with Dónall Cam **Ó Súilleabháin**) and results from a confusion of Alasdair with that placename. Another Cork tradition states that, after the battle, his wife came on the battlefield and, finding so many other women lamenting there that she could not be heard, remarked, 'if I cannot lament him, I will dance for him!' A well-known slow air, entitled 'Caoineadh Alasdram' is said to have been composed as a lament for Alasdair, and a variant title for that air is 'Gol na mBan san Ár' ('the crying of the women at the massacre'). Alasdair was buried in a cemetery near Kanturk in Co Cork, and his great sword was preserved at Loughan Castle in Co Tipperary. This was said to have had a ball of ten pounds weight running along the back from the hilt to the point in an indented groove, so that when swung it struck home with terrible force.

Seosamh Laoide (1914); Gordon Mac Gill-Fhinnein (1966), 69-73; Marquis of Lorne (1898), 207-44; George Hill (1873), 61-114; James Buckley in *Journal of the Cork Historical and Archaeological Society* 5, 128-32; Dáithí Ó hÓgáin (1985), 171-4, 338.

[Folktale influences] See Antti Aarne / Stith Thompson (1961), Types 650A, 910K, 1559B.

MAC GIOLLA GHUNNA, CATHAL BUÍ (c1680-1756) Ulster poet celebrated in folklore for a wild and rakish life. He was a native of Co Fermanagh, and spent much of his life wandering around Leitrim, Cavan, and Armagh. He was of sallow complexion, hence the epithet 'buí' ('yellow').

His reputation in folklore derives largely from the themes of drinking and womanising which he connects with himself in his poems, many of which are of a penitential nature. One of the songs, in a more humorous vein, became very popular with Ulster and Connacht folksingers. This tells of how he once saw the dead body of a yellow bittern in winter-time, and he took it that the bird had died from thirst. This, he claimed, gave a license to himself to continue drinking, as he resembled that bird in both colour and mentality. Several humorous anecdotes were told of his rakish habits, the sentiment of which parallels the accounts found in Munster lore concerning the poet Eoghan Rua **Ó Súilleabháin**. We are told that when a certain priest heard a report that Cathal was visiting his parish, he spoke from the altar threatening seven curses on anybody who would give lodgings to such a notorious fellow. That very night, a poor woman came to the priest's door and begged shelter for the night. The priest allowed her to sleep in the kitchen, but when he arose next morning he found that she had departed, leaving only a note. The note was in the form of a quatrain, revealing that the 'old woman' had been Cathal in disguise and declaring that the priest's seven curses had now fallen on that clergyman himself. The priest looked frantically around his house and found that seven things were missing - his walking cane, riding-whip, horse, dog, overcoat, hat, and his servant-girl!

A very touching story was told concerning his death, and it seems to have developed as a kind of gloss on a striking line in one of his repentance poems. In this line he states that 'through the intercession of the Mother I will get pardon and release from my pain'. According to the folk-legend, which became widely known, he lay dying in a miserable shack, and a local priest refused to go to attend him because of his wild life. A kindly neighbour eventually persuaded the priest to go, and as he approached he noticed a strong light shining from the shack. Cathal had written his Confession on the wall with a piece of charcoal and, as the priest tended to the dying poet, he noticed that a very modest and demure woman was waiting on him. After the poet had died this woman disappeared, and the priest enquired in the neighbourhood as to who she might have been. He was told, however, that no woman would approach near to Cathal because of his reputation, from which the priest concluded that the strange lady had been the Virgin Mary who had come to succour the poor poet in his desolation.

Breandán Ó Buachalla (1975); IFC 1608:417-9, S929:218-9.

MAC LUGHACH Fictional grandson of **Fionn mac Cumhaill** in literature from the 12th century onwards. The designation means 'son of Lughaidh' and his own name is given as Gaoine.

One text says that he was the son of a warrior called Lughaidh Lághdha (a scribal mispelling for **Lughaidh Lágha**), hence his designation Mac Lughach. Some storyteller of the 11th century, however, decided to make Lughaidh the name of his mother and to connect popular motifs concerning incest-births to him. We accordingly read that Lughaidh was a daughter of Fionn, and that she was in fosterage with the otherworld people, the **Tuatha Dé Danann**. Her brother, called Dáire Dearg, visited her in the otherworld dwelling and she became pregnant by him. In this way Mac Lughach was born, and when he saw him Fionn was pleased and remarked that he thought the child wholesome ('gaíne'). While still a child, Mac Lughach killed a weasel, and when he was twelve years old he was given to rear to a great tutoress of young warriors called Mongfhionn. However, he was so rough with his fellow-students that they complained him to his grandfather, and Fionn then gave him a series of advices - telling him to be gentle towards women, servants, poets, and the common people. In various literary texts, Mac Lughach figures as one of the **Fianna** warriors who were closest to Fionn in the latter's great adventures.

Gerard Murphy (1933), 66-78 and (1953), 206; Whitley Stokes (1900), 16-8; Dáithí Ó hÓgáin (1988), 156-8, 360.

MAC NA MÍCHOMHAIRLE (literally, 'the Son of Ill Counsel'): Hero of a comical text written in the late 17th century, probably in Co Fermanagh.

The anonymous author calls himself Mac na Míchomhairle, and tells of his adventures in the first person. While walking about one day, he sees a strange house and enters it. Within he meets a 'gruagach' (otherworld wizard) accompanied by a beautiful daughter. The wizard invites him to stay the night and states that, if he takes part in a battle between otherworld armies next morning in Íle (Islay, off the Scottish coast) he may marry the beautiful maiden. She acts seductively towards Mac na Míchomhairle, and when they retire to sleep he tries three times to travel the short distance to her bed. Each time, however, he goes astray and mistakes ordinary household items and domestic animals for savage regions and fierce beasts. He is discovered by the wizard and the maiden as he flounders about, much to his embarrassment. Finally he falls asleep, but awakens on the side of a rath, with no house in sight.

The text is a prime example of the flowering of fanciful prose-literature in the south Ulster and north Leinster area from the 17th to the 19th century. It probably is indebted to a celebrated adventure of **Fionn mac Cumhaill** in an allegorical house. For a related story see **Conán Maol**.

Séamus Ó Ceithearnaigh (1955); Seosamh Watson (1979).

MAC SUIBHNE, MAOLMHUIRE Chieftain of the MacSweeney sept of north Donegal in the 16th and 17th centuries. He was a brave warrior and an astute politician, changing sides repeatedly in the wars of the time and living to an old age.

Because of his cynicism, the dark-haired Maolmhuire (anglicised Myles) gained a quite sinister reputation in folklore. The staff of knighthood was conferred on him by the English government for his services, and thus he was known to the folk as 'Maolmhuire an Bhata Bhuí' ('Myles of the Yellow Stick'). This staff was said to have secreted within it the devil himself in the form of a black beetle, and it was claimed that Maolmhuire greased it with butter every day to feed its formidable occupant. He quarrelled with members of the Boyle family, and a story was commonly told in Donegal concerning an adventure involving himself and a certain Feidhlimidh Cam Ó Baoill. According to this, Maolmhuire sent his servant to ask Feidhlimidh for the loan of a hound, but the latter claimed that he had no such animal. Knowing this to be untrue, Maolmhuire hatched a plot to gain revenge. He invited Feidhlimidh to a feast at his own dwelling in Doe, near Dungloe, and when the dupe had entered he had the iron doors locked. When Maolmhuire pointed out a thin loaf being hardened by the fireside, likening it to a hungry thief of the Boyles, Feidhlimidh realised what was happening. He flung the loaf into Maolmhuire's face, kicked open the doors, and ran out to where his servant was waiting with two horses. Closely pursued by Maolmhuire and his horsemen, they raced all the way to Derry, where they managed to board a ship and made their getaway. This was said to have been the longest and hardest chase ever in Co Donegal - the distance being fifty miles and including nine strands. In such a manner was Maolmhuire deprived of his quarry for the first time ever in his life. Folklore claims that he believed himself destined to die when thus overcome, so he lost all desire to live and soon expired.

Niall Ó Dónaill (1952), 97-9; Énri Ó Muirgheasa (1924), 26-9, 70-2; IFC.

MACHA Otherworld woman in the **Ulster Cycle**.

Several sources describe her as a goddess of war, grouping her with other such mythical ladies (see **Mór-Ríoghain**), but since her name signifies a pasture her basic image must have been that of a land-goddess. It is apparent that she represented sovereignty in the myths of the ancient Ulstermen, and their royal centre Eamhain Mhacha is called after her. Other important placenames containing her name in the same area were Magh Mhacha and Ard Mhacha (i.e. Armagh).

The mediaeval literature gives two separate accounts of Macha. According to one of these there were three kings - called Díthorba, Aodh, and Ciombaoth. They made an arrangement that they would alternate as kings of Ireland, each of them ruling for seven years at a time. When they had served three terms each Aodh died and his daughter, Macha 'the Red-haired', demanded his share for herself. She was refused, but through force of arms won her term. When Díthorba died she in turn refused the kingdom to his five sons. She routed them in battle and herself married the other king, Ciombaoth. After the wedding, she went to Connacht disguised as a leper and encountered the sons of Díthorba as they were cooking a pig. They shared their food with her, and one by one went into a wood to lie with her. She overcame each one, tied them up, and brought them back to Ulster, where she set them to building a fine rath for her. This account says that the rath became known as the 'Eo-muin' (i.e. Eamhain) of Macha, for to mark out its perimeter she used the clasp ('eo') which she wore about her neck ('muin').

The other story gives a different etymology for the placename. According to this, an Ulster farmer called Crunnchu (later, Crunn), who was a widower, was visited in his house one day by a beautiful young woman. She looked after the household cares for him, entered his bed, and brought him good fortune in all his dealings. She became pregnant by him, and when her time to give birth had almost come he went to attend the assembly of the Ulstermen. Her presence in his house was unknown to the Ulstermen, and she warned him not to mention her to any of them. At the assembly, the pair of chariot-horses belonging to king **Conchobhar mac Neasa** won all the races, and all present were loud in their praise of these horses. Crunnchu, however, boasted that he had a woman at home who could outrun them. Conchobhar had him arrested, and messengers were sent to bring the woman. She protested that she was pregnant, but when told that her husband would be killed if she did not race she consented. She outran the horses, but collapsed at the finish and gave birth to twins. Before she died, she put a curse on the Ulstermen that in the time of their greatest need every man of them would be struck down with the pains which she had suffered. The place, we are told, was thus called Eamhain Mhacha (i.e. 'the Twins of Macha'). In this way is explained the strange debility which struck the Ulster warriors at the crisis of the cattle-raid of Cooley (see **Ulster Cycle**). This debility was called the 'ces noidhen' (difficulty of childbearing), but in time it was altered to 'ces noindhen' (difficulty of nine), which was taken to mean that the debility lasted for nine half-days. Some scholars have interpreted the story as an echo of couvade practices, through which men tried to transfer the pangs of childbirth from their wives onto themselves. Others have seen it as a survival of some ancient fertility ritual. The most likely explanation, however, seems to be that the otherworld woman can drain away the strength of warriors and leave them as weak as a woman in childbed.

57. MACHA *Engraving of the Gaulish horse-goddess Epona.*

The strong suggestion is that Macha, as the Ulster goddess of sovereignty, had a close association with horses, as had the patron of Ulster kingship, **Fearghus mac Róich**. It is significant that the great horse of **Cú Chulainn** was called 'the

Grey of Macha'. The racing-motif would originally have symbolised a struggle for the kingship (see **Goddess**), and Conchobhar is indeed referred to as 'the king of Macha'. In his high-handed treatment of Crunnchu, there is a hint that Conchobhar was an unsuitable king, and this could well be related to the ritual myth of his taking of the throne from Fearghus (q.v.). The hostility shown by Macha towards the Ulstermen would thus be a rationalisation of how the sovereignty passed out of their hands when the fort of Eamhain Macha was taken by the Connachta in the 4th or 5th century (see **Ulster Cycle**). In order to dramatise the tradition, a plot concerning the violation of his wife's secrecy by a husband was borrowed - probably from the floating folklore of early mediaeval times.

The story of the building of Eamhain Mhacha was retold by the historian **Céitinn** in the 17th century, but she is not named as a character in the late folklore. The motif of her racing was, however, attractive enough to create echoes in some oral narratives. In Co Galway it is said that a race against a horse was run by the mother of Cú Chulainn before his birth; while Co Clare lore tells that a lord of Inchiquin had an otherworld wife who left him after he boasted of her beauty at a race-meeting (see **Fairies**).

[Name] Edward Gwynn (1924), 124-31; Whitley Stokes in *Revue Celtique 16*, 45; Eoin Mac Néill / R A S Macalister (1916), 74.

[Macha 'the Red-haired'] R I Best / Osborn Bergin /M A O'Brien (1954), 79-85.

[Macha and horses] Rudolf Thurneysen in *Zeitschrift für celtische Philologie 12*, 251-4; Vernam Hull in *Celtica 8*, 1-42; Best / O'Brien (1956), 467-8.

['King of Macha'] Edmund Hogan (1892), 32; Cecile O'Rahilly (1976), 117-8.

[Céitinn's telling] P S Dinneen (1908) *2*, 152-7.

[Late folklore] Alan Bruford (1969), 94.

[General] Thurneysen (1921), 359-63; P L Henry (1978), 28-39.

MAINE (plural, Mainí) The name of seven fictional sons of Connacht queen **Meadhbh** and her husband Ailill mac Máta.

The name Maine was common enough in early Ireland, but the idea of it being shared by seven brothers is obviously a literary fabrication. We are told that Meadhbh once asked a druid which of her children would kill her enemy, the Ulster king **Conchobhar mac Neasa**. The druid answered that the child was not yet born unless those born be renamed, and he then explained that Conchobhar would fall by one called Maine. She therefore gave that name to all the seven sons whom she had borne to Ailill, and these became better known by the name Maine than by their own proper names - which, we are told, were Feidhlim, Cairbre, Eochaidh, Fearghus, Sin, Ceat, and Dáire. Her plan did not have the desired result, however, for the prophecy referred to a different Conchobhar, who was a son of Arthur from Britain. This Conchobhar was killed by one of the seven, called Maine Andaí, whose proper name was Eochaidh. The ambiguous prophecy, as we have it, is somewhat confused. Its original form may have been that Conchobhar would be killed on one of the seven days of the week (genitive form, 'sechtmaine') which Meadhbh misunderstood to be a killing by one of seven men called Maine ('secht Maine').

A dramatic story was invented concerning the personage of Maine Mórghor (properly Sin). This told of how he went to court Fearbh, daughter of an Ulsterman called Gearg, accompanied by a troop of thrice fifty men. The mischievous **Bricriu** remarked that they would spend but one day in Ulster. They were well received by Gearg, but as they were being entertained a great wind blew and this was interpreted by the druid of Maine Mórghor as a bad portent. Meanwhile, an otherworld woman appeared to Conchobhar mac Neasa and told him that Maine was in his province. Conchobhar set out with a band of **Fomhóire** mercenaries and attacked the dwelling of Gearg, who defended his visitors well but was slain. The otherworld woman also appeared to Meadhbh and told her that her son was being attacked. The fighting continued in Gearg's dwelling, and Maine Mórghor was slain. All of Conchobhar's men also died, except for himself and his servant Brod. He got reinforcements just in time before Meadhbh arrived, and her force was routed. Meadhbh herself was hurried away by her bodyguards, and Conchobhar plundered the dwelling of Gearg, taking away all its treasures.

Stories in which the Mainí figure generally have them as extensions of the interests of their mother. One account, for instance, tells of a rich hostelier called Reaghamhain who lived in Corca Morua (north Co Clare). This Reaghamhain had a great herd of cattle, and seven daughters who were in love with the Mainí. As Meadhbh was preparing for the cattle-raid of Cooley (see **Ulster Cycle**), she found the burden of feeding her great army quite heavy and decided to send her sons to seek cattle from Reaghamhain. The Mainí met the girls, who stole away with them bringing a large number of cattle, sheep, and pigs. Reaghamhain and his men followed, and caught up with them as they forded a river. The Mainí sent the girls on with the cattle to their mother's court at Cruachain, while they themselves held the ford by erecting a fence of briars and blackthorns. Meadhbh and Ailill came with a strong force to relieve them, and Reaghamhain agreed to give his daughters to the Mainí in return for his herd. The girls, however, were allowed to take seven-times twenty cows with them to help feed Meadhbh's army.

Another story of a cattle-raid was probably suggested by the preceding. According to this, Ailill and Meadhbh sent a message to Eochaidh Beag mac Cairbre, king of Cliu (an area in east Limerick), asking him to visit them. Before Eochaidh Beag set out, a woman came to him in a vision and warned him not to go without a retinue. When he awoke next morning he found fifty fine steeds and riders' clothes for his men outside his dwelling. He was royally received at Cruachain, and agreed to Ailill's request for provision of a large number of cattle. On his way home, however, he and most of his men were killed by marauders. The otherworld woman apparently blamed Ailill for this, and sought vengeance against him. Soon after, he had a vision in which she and a warrior instructed him to seek cattle from Dartaid, daughter of Eochaidh Beag, who loved Ailill's son Órlámh. Accordingly, Órlámh set out with a troop and was welcomed by Dartaid, who agreed to go with him and to bring all her cows. The strange warrior and lady appeared also to a Munster champion called Corb Cliach and told him that Connachtmen were taking cattle from his territory. Corb attacked Órlámh's troop, and in the ensuing fight Drataid and most of the troop were slain. Órlámh, who survived with a mere nine men, was probably understood to be one of the Mainí, although his is not one of their proper names in other sources. In *Táin Bó Cuailnge* (see **Ulster Cycle**), where he is killed by **Cú Chulainn**, he is described as son of both Ailill and Meadhbh.

Other mentions of the Mainí include the encounter of Cú Chulainn with Maine Athramhail (also known as Maine Andaí, and properly Feidhlim), whom he spares, in the *Táin*; and the slaying by **Conall Cearnach** of Maine Mo-Eipirt (properly Eochaidh) after the latter had wounded the dying Cú Chulainn. We are told that Maine Andaí was slain by **Ceithearn mac Fionntain**, and that Maine Máthramhail (properly Cairbre) fell in combat with Furbaidhe in an attempt to avenge his mother's death (see **Meadhbh**). Furbaidhe also fell in that fight.

Kuno Meyer in *Anecdota from Irish Manuscripts 5*, 21-2; Joseph O'Neill in *Ériu 2*, 184-5; Eleanor Knott (1936), 12; Ernst Windisch in *Irische Texte 2(2)*, 185-205, 224-38; Whitley Stokes in *Irische Texte 3*, 382-3; Cecile O'Rahilly (1976), 27-8, 48-9, 304; Meyer in *Zeitschrift für celtische Philologie 9*, 175.

MANANNÁN Otherworld lord and mythical mariner. The earlier form of the name was Manandan, and the patronymic 'mac Lir' is usually added.

The Isle of Man was known to the Romans as Mona, and the same designation was used for Anglesey and for an island off the coast of Scotland (probably Aran). All three of these islands are to the east of Ireland and, since the otherworld was often understood to be a mystical isle in the eastern world, any of them could anciently be imagined as otherworld realms. The Old Irish form of the toponymic was Mana, with the genitive Manand. The name of a personage Manandan (meaning 'he of Mana') was thus a simple derivative of the toponymic itself.

Some literary sources claim that Oirbsiu was an earlier name for Manannán. A character called Oirbsiu was the reputed ancestor of the Conmhaicne sept which had settled in Connacht but which was of Leinster origin. It thus appears that the lore of Manannán originated with the Leinstermen, and that it was they who coined the name Manannán for the divine personage associated by them with an eastern isle. By them, and later by the rest of the people of Ireland, Manannán came to be regarded as the deity who ruled the otherworld. The faraway island which was the realm of this deity, when not specifically understood to be Mana, was known as Magh Meall ('the Pleasant Plain'), Tír Tairngire ('the Land of Promise'), or as Eamhain Abhlach ('the Region of Apples'). The fertile lore concerning the otherworld ensured that the character Manannán underwent rapid dramatic development, probably in the early centuries AD. Welsh storytellers adopted him from the Irish and portrayed him as a master craftsman and trickster. They called him Manawydan fab Llyr, which was a close parallel to the Irish - the element 'Manand' being replaced by 'Manawyd', since Manaw was the Welsh name for the Isle of Man.

Being a divine personage, and situated on an island, Manannán was naturally envisaged as having a special connection with the sea. For this reason he was known as 'mac Lir', which was a way of describing one who is accustomed to the water and which meant literally 'son of the sea'. Thus the ocean was poetically claimed to be his domain, it being to him 'solid earth' and 'a flowery plain' and its fish being his calves and lambs. He was described as driving his chariot over the waters, the waves were his horses, and he was accordingly 'the rider of the maned sea'. He had one particular horse which was called 'Enbharr' (literally 'water-foam'), and one kenning for the waves was 'the locks of Manannán's wife'. Sometimes he himself was identified with the waves, and one text has him travelling in the following manner: 'For the space of nine waves he would be submerged in the sea, but he would rise on the crest of the tenth without wetting chest or breast.' The most humanising account is in a 9th-century glossary. Here he is described as 'a celebrated merchant who was in the Isle of Man', and furthermore as a great mariner who 'knew by studying the heavens when there would be fine weather and when there would be bad weather'.

A text from the 8th century has him coming from the Isle of Man to beget the hero-king **Mongán**, and another from the same period has his wife Fann coming to seek the love of **Cú Chulainn**. In both these cases he is presented as a spiritual being, who appears and disappears at various places as he wills. A 12th-century account has him visiting **Cormac mac Airt** and bringing members of that king's family away to the happy otherworld called Tír Tairngire. He is described as finely clad and carrying on his shoulder a branch with three golden apples. The apples touching each other made delightful music which would soothe to sleep all those who were sick or wounded. The parallel is obvious here between this 'Region of Apples' and its cognate, the Avalon of Arthurian Romance, which was derived from Celtic sources.

Manannán was not numbered among the divine community, **Tuatha Dé Danann**, in the earlier literature, but by the 10th or 11th century he was being treated as one of them. We read in a late mediaeval text that, after their defeat by the Gaelic people, he came from his overseas domain to the Tuatha Dé and advised them to take up residence in the mounds and hillocks and lonely places of Ireland. He appointed a special 'sídh' (cairn-dwelling) to each of the Tuatha Dé nobles, and presented three great gifts to them. The first of these gifts was the 'féth fiadha' (literally, 'art of semblance'), understood as a cloak of concealment through which they could make themselves invisible. The second gift was the feast of **Goibhniu**, the celebration of which warded off age and death from their kings; and the third was 'the pigs of Manannán', which swine would come alive again after being hunted and killed. Then he made a circuit of the Tuatha Dé dwellings. A great feast was prepared for him by Ealcmhar (i.e. **Nuadhu**) at Brugh na Bóinne (the Newgrange tumulus in Co Meath), and the Brugh was freshly strewn with rushes before him as a welcome. Manannán disliked Ealcmhar, however, and he encouraged **Aonghus** to displace his host as lord of the Brugh and provided a charm which compelled Ealcmhar to depart. The same text also states that Manannán brought Aonghus on a trip to India, where they got two wonderful cows - a speckled one which Manannán kept afterwards on his domain in Eamhain Abhlach, and a dun cow which Aonghus kept at Brugh na Bóinne. The text also relates the story of the maiden **Eithne**, who lives alternately in Eamhain Abhlach and Brugh na Bóinne, and for whom the milk of these two cows is full nourishment.

The attribution of wonderful weapons and accoutrements to Manannán seems to have been commonplace. References are made to a great shield, as well as a valuable knife and shirt, which had once been his property but which came into the possession of the hero **Fionn mac Cumhaill**. In the post-mediaeval stories of Fionn, indeed, Manannán is treated as a deus ex machina. A 15th-century lay has him coming disguised as a warrior with a sword through his head, and inciting strife among the Fianna due to his hatred for them, but elsewhere he is friendly. In one late prose-text, for instance, he helps them on a foreign adventure by carrying them in his wonderful boat. His image in the late literature is generally that of a friendly trickster, such as in two colourful texts which have him disguised as the **Ceithearnach Caoilriabhach** and a grey-cloaked churl (see **Fianna**).

Of special interest is a ballad from the Isle of Man, dating from around the end of the 15th century. Here we are told that rent in the form of rushes was paid to him by the inhabitants of the island. This - taken along with the mediaeval Irish reference to the strewing of rushes for him at Brugh na Bóinne - suggests that these wild plants, with their aquatic associations, were considered sacred to him. It also reveals that there was a permanence in the folklore concerning Manannán through the centuries. The same Manx ballad claims that Manannán was the first owner of the Isle, which is described as 'Ellan Sheeant' (literally, 'otherworld island'), and he was able to conceal it from passing ships by use of a magic mist. This is undoubtedly connected with his power of 'féth fiadha', but the specific ability to remove territories from the human domain was also attributed to him. The sea, for which he was a metaphor, had a painfully obvious tendency to conceal islands and to flood the mainland. Thus a play on the territorial name Umhall (the Owles in Co Mayo) caused a mediaeval writer to imagine that Manannán had once, by his magic, surrounded that whole area with a cliff of brass ('umha').

The association of inundations with Manannán has a long tradition attaching to it. For instance, the sources which give Oirbsiu as another name for him state that he died and was buried in Connacht, and that a lake burst forth over his grave. This was given as the origin-legend of Lough Corrib, which according to it was originally known as Loch nOirbsen. As mentioned above, this memory of the name Oirbsiu is a remnant of the lore which belonged to the Conmhaicne, a Leinster sept which had settled in Connacht. The fact that the legend associates Manannán with water is, of course, significant, and in all probability the name Loch nOirbsen was given to this lake by the Conmhaicne themselves. The tendency to associate inland waters with Manannán continued, and in the late folklore several lakes were said to have got their names from daughters of his. These included Lough Sheelin in Co Cavan; Lakes Ennell, Owel and Derravaragh in Co Westmeath; as well as Loughmonoge and Lake Glina in Co Mayo. In line with this also is a folk legend from west Galway which describes another daughter as going boating in the bay of Kilkieran. A storm arose, and she was in danger of being drowned until Manannán came to her assistance. He, through his magic, caused an island to appear there and she was thus enabled to reach land. The island is called Mana. A folk legend from north Donegal puts him in the role of an exasperated parent. Three sons of his resided at the mouth of Strathbreaga bay, and they persisted in bickering with each other. The enraged Manannán refused to restrain the tide for them at that bay, and it burst in and drowned the three near Malin.

Other aspects of his ancient portrayal also had their echoes in late folklore. In Co Mayo it was said that he was a famous magician and resided at the castle of Mannin, in the parish of Bekan; while west Galway lore claimed that he was a learned wizard to whom young men were sent to be educated. Furthermore, accounts have been collected from the folklore of the northwestern parts of the country which repeat the notions that the sea-waves are his horses and that storms are caused by his anger.

[Names] Heinrich Wagner in *Zeitschrift für celtische Philologie 33*, 4 and *38*, 4; Rachel Bromwich (1961), 428, 441-3; Joseph Vendryes in *Études Celtiques 6*, 247-51.

[Oirbsiu] Whitley Stokes in *Revue Celtique 16*, 276-7 and in *Irische Texte 3*, 356-7; R A S Macalister (1941), 128-9; Wagner in *Ériu 28*, 12.

[Manawydan fab Llyr] Ifor Williams (1930), 49-65.

[Sea-imagery] A G Van Hamel (1941), 13-6; Myles Dillon (1953), 26-9; Kuno Meyer (1900), 79-80 and (1912), 78; Edward Gwynn (1913), 274-5.

[Golden apples] Van Hamel, *op cit*, 9; Stokes in *Irische Texte 3*, 193; Patrick O'Fihelly (1911), 7.

[Friendship with Aonghus] Lilian Duncan in *Ériu 11*, 184-225.

[Weapons and accoutrements] Eoin Mac Néill (1904), 21-2, 35.

[Sword through head] Gerald Murphy (1933), 240-6.

[Helping the Fianna] Máirín Ní Mhuirgheasa (1954), 146-8.

[Manx ballad] R L Thomson in *Études Celtiques 9*, 521-31.

[Umhall] Gwynn (1924), 274-5.

[Folklore] Ordnance Survey Letters - Meath (1836), 91 and Westmeath (1837) *2*, 302 and Mayo (1838) *2*, 395, 398; IFC 57:124, 202:105, 1395:538, S1119:363-4; Séamus Ó Duilearga in *Béaloideas 6*, 298; Wagner in *Zeitschrift für celtische Philologie 38*, 15; J A MacCulloch (1911), 87.

[General] Vendryes, *op cit*, 239-54; Gustav Lemacher in *Ar Aghaidh* 10/1945, 3.

MAODHÓG Saint who died c626 AD, founder of monasteries at Fearna (Ferns, Co Wexford), Drom Leathan (Drumlane, Co Cavan), and Ross Inbhir (Rossinver, Co Leitrim). His real name was Aodh (earlier, Aed) or its diminutive Aodán, and Maodhóg (earlier, Mo-Aedoc) is a hypocoristic form. It is sometimes anglicised as Mogue.

The several mediaeval accounts of his life are based on a biography compiled in Irish in or about the 9th century, but not now surviving. We read that Maodhóg was the son of a Connacht king and that, before his conception, a star was seen to enter the mouth of his mother. When the child was growing up he was given by his father as a hostage to the high-king Ainmhire at **Tara**. He so impressed Ainmhire that he was allowed to return to his parents, and he would accept his freedom only on condition that the other hostages were released also. Maodhóg was educated by ecclesiastics, and he soon showed his ability to work miracles. He once took pity on starving wolves, allowed them to take sheep from his father's fold, and then miraculously replaced the sheep. He was accompanied and protected by angels, and even succeeded in restoring to life a boy who had been drowned in Lough Erne. He and St Molaise were youthful friends, and when they were praying once at the foot of two trees, the trees fell away from each other. By this they understood that God willed them to part, and Molaise went north to build a monastery at Damh-inis (the island of Devenish on Lough Erne) while Maodhóg went south to the territory of the Uí Chinsealaigh sept (south-east Leinster).

We read that from there Maodhóg went to Wales to study under St David and was given holy orders by him. In that country he performed several other miracles, avoiding an assassination attempt by the servant of a jealous monk, cutting a new road through a forest by driving his ox-cart through it, and restoring the features of a flat-faced man. On his return to Ireland, he founded the monastery of Ferns in the Uí Chinsealaigh territory, and episodes are relayed which stress the importance of the saint in the political affairs of the area. When the Uí Chinsealaigh people took refuge from an invading army at his monastic site, he prevented that army from taking the sept's cattle by drawing a line with his crozier around the herd. A sole soldier who crossed that line was immediately struck dead. On another occasion the Uí Chinsealaigh themselves were on a plundering expedition, and their king gave alms to Maodhóg. The king was overcome by sickness, and dreamed that he had been saved from hell by the alms he had given. The king of all Leinster, **Brandubh**, was also indebted to Maodhóg when he clashed with the high-king Aodh mac Ainmhireach. It so happened that the high-king's son Cumascach came on a visit to Brandubh and insisted on sleeping with Brandubh's wife. The Leinstermen were so inflamed at this that they slew Cumascach, and the high-king came with a great army seeking vengeance. Maodhóg prayed earnestly for the success of Brandubh in the ensuing battle, with the result that the Leinstermen triumphed and the high-king was slain. Brandubh was later assassinated by a man named Saran. He was revived by Maodhóg, but he expressed a preference for the afterlife, and was allowed to return there when he had received the Last Sacraments from the saint.

Some of the legends refer to ordinary ecclesiastical matters. We read that Maodhóg was once bringing a team of oxen to a community of nuns, but he gave one of the oxen to a leper on the way. The nuns were angry because they could not plough with only one animal, but an ox came from the sea to do the work for them. Maodhóg went to Britain to visit the dying St David, but wished to return quickly to Ireland for an urgent appointment. On David's instructions, he went to the sea-shore and there found a wild animal (probably a sea-**horse**) which he mounted and which brought him across the sea to Ferns. This motif of miraculous travel occurs in several contexts in the accounts of Maodhóg. When directed by an angel to go to see the ailing king **Guaire** in Connacht, Lough Derg dried up before him so that his chariot crossed it like a plain. He crossed a swamp in similar fashion, and when he arrived he healed Guaire of the sickness. On another occasion, Maodhóg was teaching a student when a golden ladder descended by his side. He went up the ladder and disappeared. When he returned, he told the student that St **Colm Cille** had died and that he had gone to pay his respects to Colm in heaven.

When Maodhóg himself died, some of his miraculous power reputedly remained at Ferns, people being continually cured of ailments by his relics. Nobody could ever after him sleep in his bed without being overcome by weakness, and even his successor as abbot of Ferns, St **Moling**, failed in this test. One of the Irish accounts, of late mediaeval date, has detailed descriptions of the tributes due from northern septs to the monasteries at Drumlane and Rossinver. The division of the saint's labours into two specific areas (Wexford and Cavan-Leitrim) seems somewhat awkward, and it could be that traditions of two different saints called Maodhóg became confused in the early Middle Ages.

Fragments of Maodhóg's biography survived in the oral traditions of the two areas with which he was associated. In Cavan, it was said that the saint was born on a little island on Templeport Lough and was in danger of death. So as to ensure baptism, the baby was put sitting on a stone, and the stone floated across to the shore of the lake where a priest was waiting. The feastday of Maodhóg is January 31.

J F Kenney (1929), 448-9; Whitley Stokes (1905), 54-5; Charles Plummer (1910) *2*, 141-63, 295-311 and (1922) *1*, 183-290; W W Heist (1965), 234-47; John O'Hanlon (1875) *1*, 521-80; Ordnance Survey Letters - Cavan and Leitrim (1836), 19-20; IFC 54:89, 655:187-99, 948:220-1/229-32, 972:517-8.

MAOL DÚIN Fictional character in a text which was written in the 9th century.

He is described as posthumous son of a warrior of Árainn (the Aran islands in Co Galway) called Ailill Ochair Ágha. His mother was a nun, and when he was born she gave him to a queen to be reared along with three princes. As he grew up he excelled his fellows in all things, and one of the three grew jealous of him and teased him with not knowing his parentage. Surprised by this, he went to the queen and insisted that she tell him the truth concerning his background. She told him who his father was, and some time later he discovered that his father had been killed by the Laíghis sept. Intent on vengeance, he sought advice from the **druids**, who told him to go by sea to attack the Laíghis. A druid from Corca Moruadh (Corcomroe in Co Clare) told him the day on which to begin building his boat, and instructed him to take seventeen men on the enterprise. However, his three foster-brothers swam on board also. Reaching two small islands by night, they heard the men of the Laíghis feasting there, and one of them was boasting that he had slain Ailill. As Maol Dúin and his followers prepared to attack, a storm arose and carried their boat out to sea. When morning came they found themselves far from land, and Maol Dúin reproached his foster-brothers for violating the druid's counsel and thereby bringing them into these straits.

Thus begins their voyage into the unknown. They come across many islands, which surpass each other in fantasy born of the author's imagination and interspersed with details from Irish myth and from mediaeval bestiaries. In the latter context, Maol Dúin and his companions have encounters with massive ants and birds, demon horses, and a monstrous cat which guards treasure. They come to an island of women, who become their lovers in an ageless realm, but eventually Maol Dúin's men prevail on him to set out for home. As they leave, his own lover throws a ball of thread from the land to Maol Dúin, and when he seizes it she draws the boat back to the shore. This happens three times and finally, when one of the crew catches the thread, Maol Dúin's poet Diúran cuts off the man's hand and thus they escape. There are some elements which derive from native Irish lore of the otherworld, such as an island of apple-trees with beautiful golden apples (see **Manannán**), and wondrous pigs which disappear underground at night. On another island they come to a lake which restores youth to those who bathe in it, and which also restores health to the sick and injured. They also come to an island surrounded by a revolving wall of fire, which wall has one open doorway. Each time this doorway passes them they catch a glimpse of all within - handsome people with beautiful clothes drinking ale from goblets of gold, with wondrous music being played for them.

The narrative has some interesting twists which show the originality of its author. On one occasion, for instance, Maol Dúin and his men behold a silver pillar rising from the sea with a great silver net attached to it. Their boat goes through a mesh of this net, and the poet Diúran takes a piece of it with him, vowing to lay it on the altar at Armagh. This connection with the great cathedral of Armagh was inserted by the author as a pseudo-authentication of his story. The passage with most general relevance to literature concerns how they come to an island where an old Irish monk has settled. He explains that he is the sole survivor of fifteen disciples of St Bréanainn of Biorra (Birr, Co Offaly). This account was one of the sources used by another early mediaeval writer, who described a celebrated voyage by the namesake of this saint, **Bréanainn** of Clonfert. The old monk whom Maol Dúin meets is covered completely by his overgrown hair, and a parallel passage in the text describes another elderly Irish pilgrim clothed by his own hair. He had come there floating on a sod which miraculously grew to become an island.

The account of Maol Dúin's birth and youth is an oblique instance of a plot which was very popular in Irish storytelling (see **Romantic Tales**, Type 873), while the theme of the fantastic voyage is borrowed from the earlier story of **Bran mac Feabhail**.

A G Van Hamel (1941), 20-77; H P A Oskamp (1970); Myles Dillon (1948), 124-31.

MAOL FHOTHARTAIGH (earlier, Mael Fothartaig) Leinster hero of the 7th century AD. He was the son of the king of that province, Rónán mac Colmáin, who died around the year 624.

At some time in the 8th or 9th century a story came to be told concerning both of these men. It probably was invented by a genealogist who knew the Greek myth of Phaedra and Hippolytus, which it resembles. The composer did not scruple to alter chronology, and he made Maol Fhothartaigh and his father contemporaneous with the king of Dál nAraidhe, Eochaidh Iarlaithe, who in fact died in the year 665. The fullest surviving text of the story dates from the 10th century, and in it Rónán is claimed to have been son of a certain Aodh rather than of Colmán.

We read of how Rónán was married to a Munster lady called Eithne, and Maol Fhothartaigh was their son. The boy was much loved by the Leinster people and was the darling of the girls and women. His mother died, and some time later Maol Fhothartaigh encouraged his father to remarry. Rónán suggested the daughter of Eochaidh Iarlaithe, but was advised against it by Maol Fhothartaigh, who said that she was a skittish girl. Nevertheless, Rónán went to her father's court at Dún Sobhairce (Dunseverick, Co Antrim) and brought her home as his wife. The new queen (who is not named) lusted after Maol Fhothartaigh and sent her maid to solicit him. In order to entice him, the maid herself slept with the hero, but he refused to go to the queen and instead departed for Scotland, accompanied by fifty warriors, so as to avoid her. After some time, the men of Leinster insisted that Rónán bring his son back from Scotland. So Maol Fhothartaigh returned, and again the queen forced her maid to solicit him. He sought advice from his friend Conghal, who promised him to set things right in exchange for the two great hunting-hounds of Maol Fhothartaigh. Conghal sent a message to the queen that Maol Fhothartaigh would meet her, but when she came to the appointed place Conghal himself was there instead. He reprimanded her severely and beat her with a horse-whip, but she vowed vengeance on him. 'I will bring a gush of blood to your mouth!' she said.

That night Rónán was praising his son, who had not yet returned home from herding cattle in the wilderness, but the dishevelled queen said that Maol Fhothartaigh had tried to force his attentions on her. Rónán angrily accused her of lying, but she retorted that she would prove that it was true. Soon Maol Fhothartaigh entered and began to dry his legs by the fire. He recited a semi-quatrain about the cold weather, and she answered it, saying that it was cold for a man without his lover. Rónán took this to be an invitation by Maol Fhothartaigh and a rejection by her of the invitation, so in a rage he told one of his warriors called Aodán to drive a spear into his son. The spear transfixed Maol Fhothartaigh to the seat. As Conghal rose in surprise, his heart was pierced by a second thrust from Aodán, who further slew Maol Fhothartaigh's jester Mac Glas. Too late, Rónán realised his mistake.

In revenge, Conghal's brother went to Dún Sobhairce, lured the queen's father Eochaidh from his palace, and slew him and his wife and son. He then brought their heads to Leinster and flung them at the queen, who in desolation fell on her own knife. The two sons of Maol Fhothartaigh pursued Aodán and slaughtered him, and the men of Leinster rose against Rónán. The king, frantic with sorrow for having slain Maol Fhothartaigh and perplexed by the rebellion of his subjects, died of a broken heart.

For references to other occurrences in Irish literature of this plot of the lustful and treacherous stepmother, see **Romantic Tales**, Type 870C.

David Greene (1955), 1-15; Myles Dillon (1946), 42-8.

MAOLODHRÁN (earlier, Maelodrán) Leinster hero of the 7th century AD, concerning whom some anecdotes are found in the literature of the 9th-10th century. He was a son or grandson of a certain Dioma Crón, and belonged to the sept called Dál Messin Corb which inhabited the area of south-west Wicklow.

The annals record that in the year 650 Maolodhrán slew Dúnchadh and Conall, two sons of the high-king Bláthmhac, at a mill. Bláthmhac shared the high-kingship with his brother **Diarmaid mac Aodha Sláine** and they were grandsons of the famous **Diarmaid mac Cearrbheoil**. The Maolodhrán-stories substitute this latter high-king for Bláthmhac and, for dramatic effect, increase the number of slain sons to three - rather uninventively calling the third son by the name Maolodhar. We read that the three once went plundering in Leinster and came across Maolodhrán. They attacked and wounded him. The servant of Maolodhrán came to the rescue with the hero's horse, but was slain, and then Maolodhrán called his horse and mounted it. The three attackers fled before him and took refuge in a mill-pond. Maolodhrán told an old woman who was working at the mill to turn the wheel, which she did and the three were crushed to death.

We read that the high-king Diarmaid demanded that the Leinstermen hand Maolodhrán over to him on account of this, but his demand was rejected. He brought his army to Loch Gobhar (Logore, Co Meath) seeking vengeance, and encamped on an island in that lake. Maolodhrán managed to sneak in to the island at night and met the king as the latter went to relieve himself. Although he had been Maolodhrán's fosterer, Diarmaid did not recognise him in the dark, and asked him for some grass. Maolodhrán gave him a fistful of nettles and thistles, and when the king stung himself with these he realised that his companion was no friend. Maolodhrán threatened to behead him, but spared him when Diarmaid agreed to forego vegeance for his sons. After that Maolodhrán became Diarmaid's champion.

Another set of anecdotes tells of Maolodhrán's relations with his neighbouring sept of Uí Mháil (Imaal in south Wicklow). It is claimed that he slew large numbers of these in local warfare, but nevertheless had as wife the daughter of the Uí Mháil king, Aitheachda. Once, when this wife visited her own people, she was persuaded to betray Maolodhrán to them, and accordingly pointed out the bothy to which she and her husband retired by dropping pieces of phosphorescent timber behind her as she went with him. Soon the bothy was surrounded by men of the Uí Mháil and, realising this, Maolodhrán called out to them to allow their sister to escape. He himself then left the bothy wearing his wife's cowl, and in the darkness they slew their own sister in mistake for him. Maolodhrán counter-attacked so fiercely that he forced the Uí Mháil to make peace with him.

Aitheachda, however, plotted treachery, and he got the opportunity when Maolodhrán was visiting his house and taking a bath there. One of Aitheachda's men blinded the hero with embers used for heating the water, and then Aitheachda himself delivered the death-blow with Maolodhrán's own lance. This was a devastating weapon which could kill thirty men with a single thrust. It used to be left on the roadside, resting on a fork, and if anybody passed without leaving something for it, it would spring at that passer-by and kill him. Following his death, Maolodhrán was buried in Gleann Dá Loch (Glendalough, Co Wicklow), and then Aitheachda took the wife whom he then had, and also took the spear. Exactly a year later, Aitheachda was looking at this spear on a bridge, and the woman remarked that 'if ever a man was avenged after death, it is most likely that Maolodhrán will be!' At that the dead hero appeared, grabbed the lance, and slew Aitheachda with it.

These were obviously popular legends which circulated among Maolodhrán's sept in early mediaeval times, and in them he has the typical image of an accomplished and resourceful folk hero who can only be slain through treachery. The lore of the special lance seems to have been derived from some ritual concerning war. It is called the 'carr' (i.e. spear) of Bealach Duirghein (apparently Ballynabarny Gap), and we read that 'as long as it was covered and pointing south' the Leinstermen would not conquer their enemies to the north. Ballynabarny Gap was in Maolodhrán's territory, and thus the great spear would have become associated with him. It is surprising that these legends did not survive into later tradition, but the explanation for this must be that the setting was too local and the influence of the Dál Messin Corb too slight in the life of mediaeval Leinster.

Kuno Meyer (1894), 70-81; David Greene (1975), 45-56; Paul Walsh in *The Irish Book Lover 28*, 74-80; Edward Gwynn (1906), 64-5; Whitley Stokes in

Revue Celtique 15, 305-6; Gearóid Mac Eoin in *Ériu 15*, 60-64; C G Buttimer in *Ériu 19*, 128-32.

MARTIN, ST The cult of the great 4th-century saint, Martin of Tours, seems to have come to Ireland with the introduction of Christianity, and he was much venerated in the early Irish church. The influence of his biography, written by Sulpicius Severus, is evident in several early texts in hiberno-Latin and Irish. In the mediaeval literature, he is claimed to have been the maternal uncle of St **Patrick**, and his grave at Tours is said to have been discovered by **Colm Cille**. He is also referred to, quite anachronistically, as a friend of St **Seanán**. As if to underline the importance placed on St Martin by the early missionaries to Ireland, the literature makes much of a copy of the gospels written by that saint and variously claims that it was presented by him to Patrick, Colm, and Seanán.

Martin's feastday, November 11, was the final festival before the full onset of winter, and it was customary in different parts of western Europe to slaughter a bullock or fowl for a great meal. An Irish text from about the 11th century claims that this was begun by Patrick. We read that he was given the monastic tonsure by Martin, and that as a result of this he made it his custom to present a pig to monks and nuns on the eve of the saint's feast. The practice of killing a duck or hen on St Martin's Eve continued in most parts of Ireland until the beginning of the present century. The Sign of the Cross was made with the blood of the slaughtered fowl on the door and in different parts of the kitchen while a prayer was addressed to the saint. This was believed to ensure good fortune during the ensuing winter.

There was a general belief in Ireland that no wheels should be turned on St Martin's Day, and it was especially important that no milling should be done. The explanation given for this was the unhistorical one that the saint had been a miller and that he had been accidentally crushed to death by his mill-wheel. This lore probably developed from the fact that the grinding of corn was due to begin at that time of year, but it was delayed out of reverence for Martinmas and in order to obtain the saint's blessing on the work. One fairly common folk account of Martin had him throwing a fistful of dough into the fireplace in the house of a stingy man, thereby causing a green tree to grow in the fire; while another claims that he caused the first mice and cats to come into the world (see **Animals**, Wild). Both of these legend-types were borrowed to him from folklore concerning **Christ**, thereby showing how prestigious was Martin's memory in the folk mind. The saint was sometimes said to appear and take an animal away from people who failed to honour him at his feast, and in the south-east of the country he was said to be seen riding a white horse on the sea as a warning to fishermen to refrain from work at Martinmas.

J F Kenney (1929), 158-60, 810; Whitley Stokes (1887), xv, 8-9, 510, 560-1, 608 and (1890), 2, 7, 27, 62, 74; Andrew O'Kelleher / Gertrude Schoepperle (1918), 96-7, 114-5, 258-61; Seán Ó Súilleabháin in W E Richmond ed (1957), 252-61; Kevin Danaher (1972), 230-2; IFC Catalogue.

MEADHBH (earlier, Medb) Mythical queen of Connacht and a leading character in the **Ulster Cycle**.

The name originally meant 'one who intoxicates' and was used to denote the goddess of sovereignty. Early Irish sources often symbolised the gaining of **kingship** as drinking ale proffered by an otherworld woman. A character called Meadhbh Leathdhearg was associated with **Tara**, and a fortress there was called Ráth Mheadhbha after her. Her epithet means 'half-red' and probably referred to the bloody contests for the Tara kingship. She is represented as having had several husbands, a typical role for a personification of sovereignty, and one mediaeval text gives a typical description of her role: 'Great indeed was the strength and power of that Meadhbh over the men of Ireland, for it was she who would not allow a king in Tara unless he had her as wife.' The text further describes her as 'a shrewd and wise woman, being fierce and merciless'.

That description would be appropriate also to her namesake, Meadhbh of Cruachain (i.e. Rathcroghan in Co Roscommon). This queen of the province of Connacht was also said to have had several husbands, and the literature invariably portrays her as a great manipulator of men and an adept at power and intrigue. Moreover, she is said to have been reared at Tara, and there is little doubt but that Meadhbh of Tara and Meadhbh of Cruachain were one and the same personage. Symbolising the Tara kingship, the power-struggle between the Connachta sept which ruled there and the Ulstermen of the north brought her cult into contact with that of the mythical Ulster king

Fearghus mac Róich. This power-struggle of the 4th and 5th centuries is reflected in *Táin Bó Cuailnge*, an epic which was first assembled around the year 600 AD, when the name of the Connachta sept had become synonymous with the western province (see **Ulster Cycle**). Thus tradition came to situate Meadhbh's power centre at Cruachain. Regarding her husbands, one recension of the Tain has her boasting: 'I never was without one man in the shadow of another', and she attempts to gain the great bull of Cooley (see **Donn Cuailgne**) by offering its owner 'the friendship of my thighs'. One early account states that Fearghus deserted his native province out of lust for her.

It is clear that the dramatic potential of portraying her as a sex-object was recognised from an early date, and that she quickly developed from a symbol of sovereignty into an attractive and cunning woman. We are told that her husbands, in consecutive order, were **Conchobhar mac Neasa**, Tinne mac Connrach, Eochaidh Dála, and Ailill mac Máta. She left Conchobhar after a short time of marriage 'due to pride of mind', and returned to Tara. Later, we are told, Conchobhar visited Tara and violated her while she bathed in the river Boyne. Then one Fiodhach mac Féig came to woo her, but he was intercepted and slain by Tinne mac Connrach, king of Connacht. Meadhbh's father, the high-king **Eochaidh Feidhleach**, banished Tinne to the wilderness and installed Meadhbh as queen of Connacht in Cruachain. Eventually she took Tinne as husband, but he was killed by Conchobhar (q.v.) in a battle at the Boyne. Meadhbh was rescued from that battle and taken back to Connacht by Eochaidh Dála, whom she then allowed to be king of the province on condition that he marry her. Ailill mac Máta was a mere child when he was first brought to Meadhbh's court, but he grew up to be a fine champion and she deserted Eochaidh Dála for him. He is the husband who figures in the *Táin* epic.

In the surviving recensions of the *Táin*, the whole series of events is portrayed as being caused by the pride and scheming of Meadhbh, and this is the result of the increased dramatisation of her personality. She seeks the bull of Cooley in order to have her wealth equal that of her husband, she schemes to enlist the support of Fearghus and other powerful allies in her attack on Ulster, and she unremittingly plots to destroy the young Cú Chulainn who stands in the way of her ambitions. Moreover, she insists on herself being the leader of her assembled armies and belittles Ailill, whom she sees as having less determination than herself. One account shows him as a frustrated husband as he views her relationship with Fearghus. One day, we are told, he noticed the shaking of a hazel-branch near the royal court, and on going to investigate found Fearghus and Meadhbh engaged in sexual intercourse. He took the sword from Fearghus' scabbard and put a timber one in its place, vowing not to return the weapon until the final great battle of the cattle-raid. When this latter conflict was over, Ailill took his revenge on Fearghus (q.v.) by having him slain by a javelin-cast when Fearghus was cavorting in a lake with Meadhbh. The jealous way in which Meadhbh guarded her power is demonstrated by one reaction which is ascribed to her in the *Táin*. When she reviewed her troops and noticed the impressive troops of the Gaileoin sept, she feared that their prestige would so grow on the campaign as to outshine her own Connacht contingent and perhaps threaten her power. She therefore decided to have them slaughtered and was only dissuaded by the indignant objections of Fearghus. She then decided to have the Gaileoin warriors divided and dispersed among her forces. The Gaileoin were a Leinster sept, and this passage is an echo of ancient hostility between the Connachta axis and the Leinstermen.

Meadhbh's confrontations with Cú Chulainn, of course, had the attractions of high drama. In the initial stages of the cattle-raid she affected to be dismissive of his ability, but she was soon brought to view him more seriously. She slyly invited him to come unarmed to parley with her and, when on his charioteer's advice he did not fall for the trick, she prevailed upon his friend **Fear Diadh** to oppose him in single combat. This she did by making Fear Diadh drunk with ale, promising him her daughter Fionnabhair as wife, and taunting him with cowardice. Cú Chulainn, who frustrated all her schemes, increased her hatred for him by humiliating her whenever they came face to face. At one stage during the campaign he shot a pet-bird from her shoulder, and later came upon her when she was alone and menstruating. She begged him to spare her, and he did so, 'not being a killer of women'. Eventually Meadhbh had her revenge. She had the children of Cailitín trained in magic and sent them to kill Cú Chulainn (q.v.), which by an ingenious manipulation of circumstances they succeeded in doing.

The portrayal of Meadhbh in the *Táin* whetted the appetite of mediaeval audiences, and accordingly more narratives were composed. We are told that she would only take a husband on three conditions - that he be without stinginess, without fear, and without jealousy. There is obviously some echo here also of her original function as goddess of sovereignty, but this echo again was dramatised. On account of her lax moral standards, her husbands could not allow themselves the luxury of jealousy, and so, until his patience finally snaps, Ailill is portrayed as extraordinarily tolerant of her affair with Fearghus. The condition of tolerance, however, did not apply to herself. When **Conall Cearnach** was exhausted from his horrific campaigns against her men, that great Ulster warrior made peace with her and went to recuperate to her court at Cruachain. He spent a year there, and meanwhile Meadhbh had noticed that her husband Ailill was keeping company with one of her ladies-in-waiting. She was overcome by jealousy, and prevailed upon Conall to slay Ailill, which he did by a quiet javelin-cast. Meadhbh, however, treacherously announced to the Connachtmen that Conall was the culprit and so encompassed his death also.

Her own death is described in an 11th century text. There we are told that she killed her sister Clothra, who had preceded her as queen at Cruachain. Clothra had resided on an island in Lough Ree (on the river Shannon) but had been slain by Meadhbh there. A baby boy was delivered by putting swords through her side after her death, and he was called Furbaidhe (literally, 'the cut one'). Meadhbh herself went to live on that island and used to bathe every morning at a spring there. Once, when a great assembly was being held on the shores of the lake, the youth Furbaidhe saw a beautiful woman on the island going to bathe. He enquired who she was, and was told that she was his mother's sister. He had been eating cheese, and on hearing this he put a hard lump of cheese in his sling and shot it with such accuracy and force that it struck her on the forehead and killed her. This, like many of the accounts of Meadhbh in the mediaeval literature, was a rather spontaneous composition with no tradition behind it. Furbaidhe in a different account, indeed, was son of another sister of Meadhbh, called Eithne. In both cases his father is claimed to have been Conchobhar mac Neasa, but in this other account he is said to have been cut from his mother Eithne after she was drowned in a stream. The writers were obviously dealing with a jumble of names and were arranging them in narrative order by use of whatever motifs suggested themselves. Meadhbh's husband, Ailill, for instance, was rather awkwardly claimed to have been a grandson of another of her sisters, Éile.

Meadhbh appears in a background role in several stories of the Ulster Cycle, such as the Feast of **Bricriu**, the Intoxication of the Ulstermen (see **Cú Chulainn**), and the Adventure of **Neara**. Though symbolising basic traits of the ancient goddess of sovereignty and war-goddess, her character as a power-hungry virago was very much the creation of the mediaeval literati. Apart from some onomastic recollections, she does not figure at all in the later folklore.

[Name and sovereignty] Tomás Ó Máille in *Zeitschrift für celtische Philologie 17*, 129-46; T F O'Rahilly in *Ériu 14*, 15-7; P L Henry (1978), 17-25.

[Part in Táin] Cecile O'Rahilly (1976) and (1970), passim.

[Sexuality] Cecile O'Rahilly (1976), 32-3 and (1970), 3; Kuno Meyer in *Zeitschrift für celtische Philologie 8*, 305 and in *Anecdota from Irish Manuscripts 5*, 17-22; Ó Máille, *op cit*, 130-9; Joseph O'Neill in *Ériu 2*, 176-85; Donald MacKinnon in *Celtic Review 1*, 226-9.

[Gaileoin contingent] Cecile O'Rahilly (1976) 5-6.

[Encounters with Cú Chulainn] Cecile O'Rahilly (1976) 29, 31, 72, 123 and (1970), 35, 133-4.

[Slaying of Ailill] Meyer in *Zeitschrift für celtische Philologie 1*, 102-11.

[Her Death] Vernam Hull in *Speculum 13*, 52-61.

MIDHIR Mythical chieftain of the **Tuatha Dé Danann**. The name apparently had an original meaning such as 'judge'.

Midhir is represented as lord of the otherworld dwelling of Brí Léith (now called Slieve Golry, near Ardagh in Co Longford). He was the foster-father of **Aonghus**, whom he counselled on how to gain possession of Brugh na Bóinne (the Newgrange tumulus), and was lover and husband of **Éadaoin**. Some sources make him a brother of the **Daghdha**, and others claim that he was the father of **Macha**. One source makes him the father of Bláthnaid who was stolen, along with magical cows and a cauldron, by the celebrated warrior **Cú**

Roí. It was further claimed that three cranes belonging to him were stolen from Brí Léith by the satirist **Aithirne**.

M A O'Brien in *Celtica 3*, 173-4; J A MacCulloch (1911), 83-4; T F O'Rahilly (1946), 290, 293. See **Éadaoin**.

MÍL Fictional ancestor of the Irish people. His full name is given as Míl Easpáine and is an invention of the historians, patterned on the Latin term 'mīles Hispāniae' (soldier of Spain). Though it is possible that there was a character called Míl in genuine Celtic mythology, the idea of such a Spanish ancestor developed from the fanciful derivation of the Latin word for Ireland, Hibernia, from Ibēria or Hibēria.

The account of Míl and his imagined relatives is given in the *Lebor Gabála* ('Book of Invasions'), a text composed and developed in early mediaeval Ireland which purported to tell the ancient history of the country. This text was based on Biblical chronology, and used many details from the early 7th century writings of Isidorus of Seville. A few elements from Classical literature and from native Irish myth were also utilised. In it, the ultimate origin of the Irish people is put down to Scythia. The people of that area, we are told, were descendants of Noah's son Japheth; and the first important person among them was Fénius the Ancient, who was one of those leaders of different nationalities who went to build the tower of Babel. Fénius was a great linguist and, when the languages were separated at Babel, he alone retained knowledge of them all. His grandson was Gaedheal Glas who, we are told, fashioned the Irish language ('Gaedhilg') out of the whole seventy-two tongues then in existence. Gaedheal and his people lived in Egypt, where they were friendly with the captive Israelites. One recension of the text, in fact, states that Moses saved the life of the infant Gaedheal who had been stung by a serpent. From the green ('glas') mark left by the bite, we are told, Gaedheal got his epithet. Moses cured him by touching the affected part with his rod, and then pronounced that the descendants of Gaedheal would forever be safe from serpents and would dwell in a land where no such creatures existed.

In the time of Sru, grandson of Gaedheal, these people were persecuted in Egypt, and they left in four ships and returned to Scythia. They clashed with their old relatives, the inhabitants of that place, and, after several generations of turbulence there, they were driven out and became seafarers. They suffered much hardship in the Caspian Sea for seven years, but eventually their druid Caicher found a remedy for the music of the mermaids ('murdhuchu') which was bringing lethargy on them. The remedy was to melt wax in their ears, and by virtue of this they sailed far west into the Mediterranean and took Spain by force. Their king at that time, Breoghan, built a great tower at Brigantia (i.e. Braganza) to protect their territory; and on one clear winter evening Íth, son of Breoghan, saw Ireland from that tower.

Míl is now introduced into the narrative. He is said to have been a son of Breoghan's son Bile, and his proper name was Golamh. When he grew up, he became curious concerning his relatives in Scythia and went there. He was welcomed by the Scythian king, who gave him his daughter Seang as wife and made him an army commander. Míl was so successful that the king grew jealous and plotted to kill him; but Míl acted first, slaying the king and sailing away from that country with his followers in sixty ships. He arrived in Egypt, where he got land from the Pharaoh and was again made an army commander. His first wife having died in Scythia, he remarried - this time the bride was Scota, daughter of the Pharaoh. Remembering that the druid Caicher had prophesied that his people would settle in Ireland, he left Egypt after some time and set sail westwards. He was, however, interrupted on his journey by tidings that enemies were threatening Spain, and so returned to that country, where he gained the victory in several battles. He had by this time no less than thirty-two sons. Twenty-four of these were born of his affairs in Spain before he left for Scythia, two more - **Donn** and Aireach - were children of Seang, and the other six - **Éibhear**, **Amhairghin Glúngheal**, Ír, Colptha, Érannan, and **Éireamhóin** - were the offspring of Scota. These eight named sons were given importance as leaders of their people into Ireland.

All of this marvellous jumble is the result of liberal, and at times contradictory, speculation on the nomenclature applied to Ireland and the Irish people. Along with the Spanish connection of Míl (Hibēria versus Hibernia), we have pseudo-learned attempts to explain several other words. 'Féni', upon which was invented the character Fénius, was the designation used for themselves by the dominant Connachta sept (see **Conn Céadchathach**) in the early mediaeval period.

Gaedheal simply signified an Irish person, the word (earlier Goidel, later Gael) being in origin a borrowing from the Welsh word for an Irishman, 'Gwyddel'. Scōta was the Latin word for an Irishwoman; it was, in fact, on the basis of a fabricated connection between Scōti ('Irish people') and Scythia that the latter region was associated with the ancestors of the Irish. Éibhear (earlier, Éber) was forged out of Ēberus, a hiberno-Latin form of Hibernus ('an Irishman'); while Ír is a variant of Éire ('Ireland'), as also is the first element in 'Éireamhóin' and 'Érannan'.

Míl himself never reached Ireland. He died in Spain of an unspecified cause, and it was left to his sons to come and take the country. But in the meantime his uncle Íth, who had seen Ireland across the sea, decided to go and investigate with thrice fifty warriors. They disembarked and went to Aileach (near Derry) where the triumvirate of **Tuatha Dé Danann** kings had convened to divide the treasures of Ireland between them. Íth counselled them on how the division should be made, but they were suspicious of his intentions and had him slain as he returned to his ship. His followers brought the body back to Spain, and his nine brothers joined with the eight sons of Míl on an expedition to take Ireland from the Tuatha Dé. As they approached the country from the south-west, one of Míl's sons, Érannan, went up on the mast of his ship to reconnoitre and he fell and was drowned. Another son, Ír, rowed ahead of his fellows and his oar broke. He fell backwards into the sea and was drowned also. Finally, they landed at Inbhear Scéine (Kenmare Bay in Co Kerry) and Amhairghin (q.v.) was the first of them to set his foot on the soil of Ireland.

They defeated a Tuatha Dé force at Sliabh Mis (a mountain south of Tralee), and there they met the lady Banba, who asked them that her name be henceforth on the country. This was granted, and they made similar promises to the lady Fódla at Éibhlinne (Slieve Felim in Co Limerick) and to the lady Ériu (i.e. Éire) at Uisneach (Ushnagh, Co Westmeath). Thus these three **goddesses** were made by the pseudo-historians to sanction the takeover by the sons of Míl. At Tara the invaders met with the three Tuatha Dé kings. These were Mac Cuill, Mac Céacht, and Mac Gréine, and one recension of the text states that they were the husbands of the three goddesses. In order to trick the sons of Míl, these three kings sought a truce, asking that they be allowed to hold the country for a mere three days more and that the sons of Míl retire nine waves from the shore for that period. Amhairghin, who played the role of negotiator for his brothers, agreed to this. When the conditions were fulfilled, however, the druids of the Tuatha Dé sang spells against them, causing a storm which swept them far out to sea. Amhairghin then spoke a verse which calmed the waters. In a fit of anger, Donn (q.v.) threatened to put all who were in Ireland to the sword, but the wind rose against his ship and drowned him and his brother Aireach off the south-west coast. This meant that only four sons of Míl were left alive. Éireamhóin, who assumed the leadership, decided to sail with thirty ships right-handwise around Ireland, and they landed at the Boyne estuary. Colptha was the first to step ashore - hence, it was claimed, the estuary was known as Inbhear Colptha. They routed the Tuatha Dé at the battle of Tailtiu (Teltown, Co Meath), after which all Ireland was in their possession. They divided it into two parts, with Éireamhóin ruling in the north and Éibhear in the south. Colptha is not mentioned again, but contention soon broke out between the other three sons of Míl (for which see **Éireamhóin**, **Éibhear**, and **Amhairghin**).

The *Lebor Gabála* account of how the sons of Míl took Ireland was a literary fabrication, but it was accepted as conventional history by poets and scholars down until the 19th century.

R A S Macalister (1939), 1-165 and (1956), 1-175; P S Dinneen (1908) *2*, 2-109; H A de Jubainville (1903), 123-48; C-J Guyonvarc'h in *Ogam 19*, 265-6; T F O'Rahilly (1946), 195-9; A G Van Hamel in *Zeitschrift für celtische Philologie 10*, 167-81.

MIS A young woman who is featured in a literary romance of the post-mediaeval period.

Her name is fancifully derived from the mountain called Sliabh Mis, south-west of Tralee in Co Kerry. According to the mediaeval **place-lore**, she was a sister of **Eochaidh mac Maireadha**, and her husband, called Coemgen, gave her possession of that mountain as bride-price. Some later writer - probably of the 15th or 16th century - considered that she would be good material for a different story, and so composed a romance about her. The text of this is lost, but it is referred to in several poems. A late literary retelling from the 18th century does, however, survive, and it is apparent that this contains the basic structure of the romance. We read that Mis was the daughter of Dáire Donn, leader of the invasion which was defeated by the

Fianna at Fionntráigh (Ventry, Co Kerry). Finding her father's dead body on the battlefield, she began to drink the blood from his wounds and as a result became demented. She fled to Sliabh Mis and lived alone there for a very long time, and killed every animal or human being which came that way. The Munster king, **Feidhlimidh mac Criomhthainn**, offered a great reward to anybody who could capture her alive. At length the king's harper, Dubh Rois, went to Sliabh Mis and began to play his music there. She came and recalled that her father had had such an instrument, and on seeing gold and silver with Dubh Rois recalled also that her father had had such objects. On seeing the harper's private parts, she remarked that she did not recall her father having these. Dubh Rois then invited her to sexual intercourse, which helped greatly to calm her wildness. He stayed with her for two months, cleaning her and teaching her how to cook, and in this way she regained her reason and grew beautiful again. He then took her with him to his home and married her. Later, when Dubh Rois was attacked and killed by hostile warriors, she lamented him in verse.

This story is a curious one, not least for the anachronism which brings the pseudo-historical battle of Ventry into the same period as the 9th-century Feidhlimidh. It is best explained by postulating that the author of the romance was not a very learned man, but that he was acquainted with certain aspects of ancient tradition. These aspects would have included the lady Mis of mediaeval place-lore, and also the imagery of the **goddess** of sovereignty, an ugly hag who becomes a beautiful young lady through intercourse with a particular hero.

Edward Gwynn (1913), 240-1; T F O'Rahilly in *Celtica 1*, 382-4; Brian Ó Cuív in *ibid 2*, 325-33.

MOCHAOI (earlier, Mochoe) Saint and abbot of the monastery of Naondroim (Nendrum, on the island of Inish Mahee, Co Down). He probably lived in the latter 6th century AD.

No biography survives, but one striking little story is told of him in mediaeval texts. We read that he once went into the forest to collect timber to build a church, and while there a beautiful bird sang three strains for him. He thought that he was listening for a brief while only, but each strain in fact lasted fifty years. When he returned to the monastery he found that nobody there knew him and an oratory had been erected in memory of him. This is a version of a narrative plot (see **Wonder Tales**, Type 471A) which was very common in mediaeval European lore concerning saints.

Whitley Stokes (1905), 158-9; John O'Donovan (1864), 176-7.

MOCHUDA Saint who died c637 AD, abbot of Raithean (Rahan, Co Offaly), and founder of the monastery of Lios Mór (Lismore, Co Waterford).

A biography of him was compiled at Lismore in or about the 11th century, and from this are derived the various texts concerning him in Latin and Irish. His real name was Cárthach, and he belonged to the Ciarraighe Luachra sept (in Co Kerry). We read that a ball of fire descended from heaven onto his mother's head before his birth, and that he was reared by a bishop who gave him the nickname 'mochuda' out of fondness for him (i.e. 'mo chuidigh', meaning 'my loved one'). He built his first church near the place where he was born, by the river Maine. While abbot of Rahan he performed many miracles, healing the sick, raising the dead, and banishing demons. On one occasion an angel appeared to him and told him that the king of the Ciarraighe Luachra was at the point of death. The angel provided a fiery chariot, in which he travelled south in an instant and administered the Sacraments to the dying man. We further read that Mochuda was the most handsome man of his time, and that thirty maidens fell madly in love with him. He prayed that their love might be turned into a spiritual one, and accordingly they became nuns.

So great was the monastery of Rahan under his direction that the other abbots of Ireland grew jealous of him and prevailed on the high-king Bláthmhac to expel him from that place. When Bláthmhac came with his brother **Diarmaid mac Aodha Sláine** and a strong army, Mochuda sent one of his monks to confront them. This monk was Constantinus, a foreign pilgrim who had settled at Rahan and was a prodigious worker. Constantinus, by his rugged and threatening mien, twice got respite for Mochuda, but on the third occasion of Bláthmhac's approach he was absent, and the aggressors gained entrance. Diarmaid relented when he came face to face with Mochuda himself, but Bláthmhac - supported by the rival abbots - drove the saint and his monks out of their dwellings. One of the monks had gout, and his foot touched that of Bláthmhac, transferring the disease to the king. The departing Mochuda, for his part, cursed Bláthmhac and the abbots who had so illtreated him and his community. As they passed by the cemetery, a dead monk rose from his grave and seized Mochuda's foot, begging to be allowed to go with them, but the saint told him to stay and await the final resurrection there. Going south, the monks were welcomed by the king of Munster, Fáilbhe Fionn. When they reached the territory of the Déise (in Co Waterford), a flooded river dried up for long enough to allow them to pass through, and they settled at Lismore and founded the great monastery there.

This account reflects the actual resentment of the midland monasteries to the influence of monks from Munster in the 7th and 8th centuries, but the kernel of historical fact is, of course, much elaborated by imagery borrowed from the Bible and by literary creativity. Mochuda's feastday is May 14.

J F Kenney (1929), 451-3; Charles Plummer (1910) *1*, 170-99 and (1922) *1*, 291-311; Patrick Power (1914), xxvi-xxxi, 74-147, 178-95; John O'Hanlon (1875) *5*, 240-76; IFC 176:48-9, 245:363-5.

MOLING Saint who died c697 AD, founder of the monastery called Teach Moling (St Mullins, Co Carlow).

Anecdotes concerning him were in circulation soon after his death, and some of these are recorded in an early 9th-century text. His name at first, we are told, was Dairchill. 'Moling' signified 'the holy leaper', and these anecdotes claim that an old woman gave him the name when she saw him jump over a river in Luachair (Co Kerry). An account is given of how the devil once came to him disguised as Christ, and sought his assistance. Moling advised him to genuflect, but the evil one protested that he could not do so because his knees were backwards.

The biographies of the saint, in Latin and Irish, are all of late mediaeval date, and in them we read that a farmer of Luachair made the sister of his wife pregnant and she - called Eamhnait - fled for fear of her sister's vengeance. Helpless and caught in a snowdrift, she gave birth to her baby. She intended to kill the baby, but a dove came down from heaven and protected it. Some monks of the community of St **Bréanainn** noticed angels at the place, and they came and took mother and child to their monastery. When the child came of age, he began to go about seeking alms for all the monks. Once he was confronted on his travels by evil spectres, who spoke in verse to him, but he replied in rhyme to all that they said. He then sprang away from them, and in three leaps had gone completely from their presence.

Soon after, he went to visit St **Maodhóg** and spent some time with him. He decided to found his own monastery at Ros Broic and was assisted in his work by the celebrated tradesman called **Gobán Saor**. The great yew-tree of Ros Broic had fallen, and Moling sought and obtained this as material for the building, which became known as his 'house' (Teach Moling). He performed several miracles and gained a great reputation among the Leinster people, in whose territory he had settled. So high was his standing that the Leinstermen sought his assistance in their disputes with the joint high-kings **Diarmaid mac Aodha Sláine** and his brother Bláthmhac. These high-kings plotted treachery against him, but he avoided their ambushes by going in disguise, and eventually succeeded in having the Rye Water (between Co Meath and Co Kildare) established as the northen boundary of Leinster. Where he sat down to arrange the treaty with the joint high-kings became known as his 'seat', Suidhe Moling.

Later, however, **Fionnachta** became high-king and sought to extract the traditional tribute called **bóraimhe** from the Leinstermen. Moling then decided to go to **Tara** and seek remission of the tribute, and in the discussions played a trick on Fionnachta. He sought respite in the payment 'until Luan', and the high-king assented, believing that 'Luan' referred to the following Monday. Moling, however, explained that it actually referred to the Last Day, and through this use of verbal ambiguity achieved his purpose. We read that, on the same occasion, he raised from the dead a son of Fionnachta who had just expired. St **Adhamhnán**, however, who was of the royal Uí Néill sept, was much incensed at Moling's ruse concerning the tribute, and he prevailed on Fionnachta to send a group of men after the departing Moling. A mist fell on the pursuers and, through the miraculous power of Moling, they repeatedly mistook each other for him, and in this way a large number of them were slain by their fellows.

Several other anecdotes concerning Moling are found in the mediaeval literature. According to one of these, he had a friend called Maol Dobharchon, who was an exceedingly generous man. This Maol once claimed that he would have done all in his power to save Christ from the Crucifixion and, to test him, Moling set his cowl in a brake of thorns and told him to suppose that that was Christ. Maol cut his fingers trying to retrieve it, and thus proved his sincerity. We read that Moling was once captured by nine robbers, who challenged him to make a stanza for each of them. He did so and, as a result, was allowed to go unmolested. Yet another anecdote states that he had a pet fly which used to buzz musically for him, but a wren killed the fly. Moling then cursed the wren, and as a result a fox killed and ate it.

Moling was generally portrayed in the manner of a seer-poet. Many verse compositions were ascribed to him, and he was said to have been one of the four chief prophets of Ireland. Several placenames in Leinster indicate churches founded by him, but the actual founders may have been his disciples rather than himself. One tradition had it that he succeeded St **Maodhóg** as abbot of the monastery of Fearna (Ferns, Co Wexford). His feastday is June 17.

J F Kenney (1929), 461-3; Whitley Stokes (1905), 150-7 and (1907) and in *Revue Celtique 13*, 44-7, 98-117 and in *Anecdota from Irish Manuscripts 2*, 20-41; Charles Plummer (1910) *2*, 190-205 and (1922) *1*, 187-9, 244, 275-9; W W Heist (1965), 353-6; Kuno Meyer in *Revue Celtique 14*, 188-94; Vernam Hull in *Zeitschrift für celtische Philologie 18*, 90-9; John O'Hanlon (1875) *6*, 691-724.

MOLUA Saint who died c605 AD. His original name was Lughaidh, of which Molua was a hypocoristic form.

Three mediaeval biographies in Latin survive, and they seem to derive from a text written in or about the 9th century. According to these accounts, he was son of one Cárthach of the Uí Fidhgheinte sept (of east Limerick), and his mother was called Sochla. One imaginative source claims that he was a foundling, having been discovered in a brake of rushes by **Comhghall** as that saint was travelling in the territory of the Uí Fidhgheinte; but this contradicts the general tradition, which had Molua being reared diligently by his parents, along with two elder brothers. He spent much of his youth herding cattle and sheep, and showed his miraculous power on several occasions. Once his father found him asleep in a field, with an angel in white garments watching over him. When Comhghall visited Munster, he at once noticed Molua's holiness, and accordingly the youngster went north to be educated at the monastery of that saint at Bangor. He joined the community there, and soon showed his miraculous power by handling fire, being untouched by water though lying in the sea as penance, and lighting a candle with his breath. Molua prayed to God for intellectual prowess and, when reproached by Comhghall for this, he replied that he desired it so as to promote the divine will.

Having learned much from Comhghall, he left Bangor and, accompanied by a few companions, founded the monastery of Droim Sneachta (Drumsna, Co Monaghan), which became celebrated for its learning. He banished a great monster from a nearby lake, and restored to life a boy who had died from the terror of it (see **Saints**). After some time, Molua left that place also and went about founding several other houses along the boundary of the provinces of Leinster and Munster. This is undoubtedly an effort by the hagiographers to account for different dedications to a saint or saints called Lughaidh. We read that he eventually settled at Bealach Mór (Kyle, near Borris-in-Ossory, Co Laois) and founded there the monastery which became known as Cluain Fhearta Molua. He is described as exercising discipline over his monks by a combination of kindness, patience, and humour, and his method of teaching was one which was inspired by its gentle motto: 'A little here, and a little there!' His rule divided the monastic day into three parts - one part for prayer, the second for study, and the third for labour.

Many of the miracles attributed to Molua involve healing the sick and inspiring vocations to the religious life, and his human sympathy is repeatedly stressed. There is, however, no absence of drama. We read that on one occasion he resorted to a trick to secure the release of a captive from the high-king. Miraculously transforming some corn-seed into gold, he used this to ransom the captive, but when the man was free the gold returned to its former state. He died while returning to Cluain Fhearta Molua after a visit to St Crónán at Ros Cré (Roscrea, Co Tipperary). The Leinster and Munster people argued over which of them should have his body for burial, but an angel appeared and directed that it be placed on a wagon drawn by two unbroken oxen. This was done, and the body was brought by the oxen to his own monastery to be buried. This account of the oxen is in fact a direct borrowing from an early biography of St **Patrick**.

A mediaeval text in Irish has an angel announce that no saint ever got a greater welcome in heaven than he did; and we further read of how a bird was heard to lament him, because 'that Molua never killed a bird or any other living thing'. The memory of Molua survives in his native area, where a holy well at Emlygrennan, near Kilfinane in Co Limerick, is dedicated to him. At the site of his monastery in Kyle, Co Laois, a large stone is pointed out as having been yielded to him by a druid after the saint had used it as an altar for the Eucharist. The stone has five circular cavities, which are claimed to have been made by the saint's head, knee and elbows as he prayed. The feastday of Molua is August 4.

J F Kenney (1929), 398-9; W W Heist (1965), 131-45, 382-8; Charles Plummer (1910) *2*, 206-15; Whitley Stokes (1905), 180-3; John O'Hanlon (1875) *8*, 39-70; IFC 296:434-5, 1376:60.

MONGÁN Prince of the sept called Dál nAraidhe (in south Antrim and north Down). He was son of **Fiachna mac Baodáin**, the powerful king of Dál nAraidhe who was killed in battle in 626 AD. Mongán himself, according to the annals, was slain, in the year 624, by a Britain called Artur ap Bicoir.

The kings of the Dál nAraidhe and other north-eastern septs were great patrons of the **poets** and learned storytellers, and it is from this context that the extraordinary lore concerning Mongán grew. The name Mongán means 'hairy fellow', and its application to a person would suggest that he was born with a significant amount of hair already grown. A corpus of narratives was associated with a mythic seer who was portrayed as having been born with full-grown hair. It is evident that this symbolic child-seer was in effect **Find** (who became known as **Fionn mac Cumhaill**). Given this significance of his name, grateful poets would have been glad to compare Mongán to Fionn, and through such a conceit some ancient imagery of Fionn got attached to the Dál nAraidhe prince.

A reflection of the transformations anciently associated with the seer Find is found in an 8th-century account of Mongán. This describes him as visiting otherworld dwellings and gaining knowledge of secret lore there, and it also attributes to him the ability to travel in the forms of a wolf, deer, salmon, seal and swan. Such elaborate and unrealistic praise must have had an element of humour in it, and further play on the name Mongán made a connection between him and the sea-deity **Manannán**. This connection was attractive to the eulogists because the root of Mongán's name, 'moing' (i.e. mane), was a poetic kenning for the sea, and it may also have been assisted by vestiges of water imagery in the cult of Find (q.v.). Thus the conceit that Manannán was a symbolic father of Mongán was added to that of his identity with Find. Both conceits must have been employed in a poem or rhetoric composed for the prince during his own lifetime. The surviving literary texts, however, belong to the 8th century, and by this time the material had been developed into pseudo-biographical narratives.

One such narrative describes how Fiachna went to Scotland to the assistance of his ally Aodán mac Gabhráin, who was at war with the Saxons. During his absence, a handsome stranger came to visit his queen at his palace in Magh Line (Moylinny, Co Antrim). The stranger told her that Fiachna was in great danger, but that he himself would protect the king if she consented to lie with him. In order to save her husband, she lay with the stranger, who was Manannán. The latter left for Scotland and appeared between the two armies. He went to Fiachna and explained what had happened, and then slew a huge warrior of the Saxon army. This encouraged Fiachna and Aodán, and they routed the enemy host. Fiachna's queen (whose name is given in one version as 'Caíntigern' i.e. Caointighearn) gave birth to a son, and this baby was Mongán. The narrative has been influenced by the motif of a childless queen fertilised by a sea-spirit, which was the origin-legend of the Merovingian dynasty of the Franks. The 8th-century writer of the Mongán text, or his source, had very likely read in the Frankish chronicles an account of how the semi-mythical king Merovech had been conceived in this way, and considered it suitable for the development of the Mongán lore.

Another narrative in the 8th-century literature has sprung from the conceit concerning Find. According to this, in his palace at Magh Line, Mongán was once listening to a story being told by the importunate poet Forgoll (see **Dallán Forgaill**). This was a story about the hero Fothadh Airgtheach, whom Forgoll claimed had been slain at Dubhthair Laighean (the Duffrey in Co Wexford). Mongán contradicted him and, angered by this, Forgoll threatened to satirise him and refused all compensation except an offer of Mongán's wife Breothighearn, who was to be given to him within three days if Mongán could not prove the poet's statement to be incorrect. The evening of the third day arrived and Mongán still had not acquired the necessary proof. The queen was disconsolate, but Mongán said that he could hear the feet of a helper passing through rivers as he came to them all the way from the south-west of the country. Night arrived, and just when the poet was demanding his prize a man vaulted over the ramparts and arrived in the centre of the palace. The newcomer was the Fianna warrior **Caoilte**, and he stated that he had been present when Fothadh Airgtheach was slain on the Ollarbha (the Larne river in Co Antrim). He told where the grave was, and all was found as he had said. During the conversation, Caoilte called Mongán by the name 'Find', and the text states that 'Mongán was Find, though he would not let it be told'. The author of this text must have been somewhat confused regarding the nature of his sources, for he takes Mongán's identity with Find, not as a poetic conceit, but as a concrete fact. Undoubtedly he does this purely in order to present an interesting narrative, but that he should do so at all indicates the strength of the tradition that the mythic seer Find could take on different forms in different generations.

Visits to the otherworld are to the fore in this literature. One account tells of how Mongán sent a poor scholar on an errand to three otherworld dwellings in Ulster, instructing him to collect from them a bag of silver, another of gold, and a precious jewel. The scholar did as he was told, and was received into each dwelling with great hospitality. In the third, he asked for the key to a marvellous chamber there and found the jewel. On his return to Mongán, he was allowed to keep the silver for his efforts. Another account has Mongán's wife - here called Findthighearn - asking for a description of her husband's adventures. He sought and obtained a respite of seven years before he would answer her request, and at the end of that time the couple were caught in a great hailstorm and found shelter in a strange and beautiful house. It had a roof of bronze, a pleasant bower over the windows, and it contained marvellous tapestries and jewels. Seven handsome men were there, and seven vats of ale. Mongán became intoxicated with the ale, and he recited a 'buile' (i.e. frenzied vision) to his wife. Although they spent but one night in the house they considered it a full year. It was obviously a dream-visit, for the text states that they found themselves at home in Mongán's palace 'when they awoke'. The text, unfortunately, does not give the words of Mongán's recitation, although it claims that in it he told of his adventures.

In or around the 11th century a fanciful story was written concerning Mongán's youth. It tells of how his father, Fiachna mac Baodáin, engaged **Eochaidh Éigeas** as his professional poet, but Eochaidh made it a condition that the young Mongán should not be allowed to contend with him. Egged on by his companions, however, Mongán disguised himself and, with three other youths, contrived to meet Eochaidh on three occasions and asked questions concerning ancient edifices. Each time Eochaidh's ignorance was displayed and Mongán showed his superior knowledge. The enraged poet cursed his tormentor, and as a result Mongán had no royal issue. This story is an early example of a motif which is common in Irish folklore concerning **poets** - a visiting master is outwitted by a smart youngster or neophyte in the art. Another mediaeval tradition has Mongán encountering the famous saint **Colm Cille** and being converted to Christianity by him. This lays much stress on Mongán's magical powers - he walks on water, frequents otherworld dwellings in raths and on sea-islands, and goes in the form of whatever animal he chooses. By showing him visions of hell and heaven, the saint persuades him to renounce magic and accept Christianty.

In actual history, Mongán's father, Fiachna mac Baodáin (q.v.), was slain in battle against his own cousin, Fiachna mac Deamháin, in the year 626. This is, however, much distorted in a long narrative of Mongán which was compiled in the 14th century. It gives a somewhat altered account of his birth and - in contradiction of the annals - has him surviving his father. Also in contrast with the records, this text makes Mongán become king of Ulster. It tells of Fiachna being on a visit to Scandinavia when the king of that country, called Eolgarg, fell sick. The leeches stated that the meat of a white-eared cow was the only cure, and a hag who owned such a cow gave it on Fiachna's surety. Fiachna then returned home and was installed as king of Ulster. A year later, the hag came to Fiachna's palace and demanded the payment which Eolgarg, when healed, had refused to her. Fiachna accordingly invaded Scandinavia, but Eolgarg released a flock of venomous sheep against his army and he could make no headway. Then Manannán approached and offered to overcome the sheep if he be allowed to spend one night with Fiachna's queen. This was agreed, and Manannán took a fierce dog from his cloak, which killed the sheep. Fiachna conquered Scandinavia and compensated the hag, but on his return to Ireland he found his queen pregnant, and thus Mongán was born a son of Manannán. On the same night that he was born, the wife of Fiachna mac Deamháin gave birth to a girl, who was called Dubh Lacha and was betrothed as a child to Mongán. Manannán took Mongán with him to Tír Tairngire (the Land of Promise) and reared him there.

Mongán's father, Fiachna 'the Fair', was slain in battle by Fiachna mac Deamháin called 'the Black', and when Mongán was sixteen years old he was brought to Ireland by Manannán. Peace was made with Fiachna 'the Black', who gave half of the Ulster kingdom to Mongán, as well as Dubh Lacha in marriage. Manannán, however, came again and, disguised as a cleric, encouraged Mongán to avenge his father. He therefore slew Fiachna 'the Black' and became sole king of Ulster. On a visit to Leinster, Mongán was given a herd of red-eared white cows by the king of that province, **Brandubh**. In return, however, Brandubh demanded his wife, Dubh Lacha, and Mongán had in honour to agree. Dubh Lacha obtained a promise from Brandubh not to lie with her for a year. Mongán had a servant, called Mac an Daimh, who was coaeval with himself, and the wife of this servant had gone with Dubh Lacha. Thus Mac an Daimh also was pining for his wife and he prevailed on his master to take action. Mongán got two sods, one from Scotland and one from Ireland, and stood on these inside a basket, which the servant carried on his back to Leinster. Brandubh's druids were confused by the sods and did not realise that the king of Ulster was approaching. Coming to Leinster, Mongán and his servant met the monk Tiobraide with another cleric, and Mongán magically created a river and caused the monks to be carried downstream. Then he took onto himself and Mac an Daimh the shapes of the monks, and thus arrived at the court of Brandubh. Pretending to be the confessors of Dubh Lacha and her maid, they made themselves known to the two ladies and secretly took them to bed. Meanwhile, the real Tiobraide returned with a group of monks, but Mongán told the doorkeepers that the man outside was Mongán himself in disguise. Tiobraide was attacked, his men slain, and he himself forced to flee. By the time that Brandubh understood the trick which had been played on him, Mongán and his servant had made their getaway.

Once more Mongán visited his wife, but on the third occasion Brandubh had soldiers waiting for his approach and he had to turn back. When the year had passed, preparations were made for the wedding between Brandubh and Dubh Lacha. Mongán, however, came in disguise and, with a magic wand, gave to a hag called Cuimne the appearance of a beautiful princess of Munster. He also put a love-charm onto her cheek, and thus when Brandubh saw her he was completely captivated and agreed to exchange her for Dubh Lacha. During the night, Mongán and Mac an Daimh departed secretly on two swift horses, bringing their wives with them, and when morning came Brandubh found to his dismay that his sleeping partner was a shrivelled hag.

This narrative combines Mongán's magical abilities with some ordinary narrative devices from folklore, particularly tricks connected with disguise. Two notable instances of borrowed folk motifs are the trick of the two sods under Mongán's feet (see **Humorous Tales**, Type 1590) and the love-spot put in a woman's cheek (see **Diarmaid ua Duibhne**).

A striking description of Mongán's death is given in one annalistic source. We read that once, when he and his mother were walking on the strand, she picked up a beautiful coloured stone and showed it to him. He shocked her by saying that his death would come by that stone. To prevent this, she took it in a boat and cast it into the sea far from the shore, but unknown to her it was carried back to the strand by the tide. Later, when a great fleet of Britons attacked his territory, Mongán defeated them and, through his magnanimity, allowed them to depart in safety. One of them, however, picked up the destined stone from the sand and shot it at Mongán. It struck him in the head and, as he fell dying, he told his mother that he would come alive again in exactly a year's time and that she should open his grave for him then. It was, however, a leap-year, and so she came a day too late to the appointed task. She found the body warm and sweating, with blood coming from his nose, for he had been trying to come from the grave. This curious story was obviously a development from the earlier mystical imagery associated with the hero.

[Early stories] Kuno Meyer / Alfred Nutt (1895-7) 1, 16-7, 24-8; Séamus Mac Mathúna (1985), 54-6, 101-7; Vernam Hull in *Zeitschrift für celtische Philologie 18*, 414-9; M A O'Brien (1962), 282-4.

[Mediaeval stories] Eleanor Knott in *Ériu 8*, 155-60;

Paul Grosjean in *Analecta Bollandiana 45*, 75-83; Andrew O'Kelleher / Gertrude Schoepperle (1918), 78-83, 168-9; Meyer in *Zeitschrift für celtische Philologie 2*, 313-20; Séamus Ó Duilearga in *ibid 17*, 347-70; S H O'Grady (1892) *1*, 391-2 and *2*, 497.

[General] James Carney (1955), 280-95; Proinsias Mac Cana in *Ériu 23*, 102-42.

MONINNE (earlier, Monennai) Saint of the late 5th and early 6th centuries AD. She belonged to the Conaille sept of Muirtheimhne (north Louth).

Her biographies are in Latin and date from the 11th and 12th centuries, but they contain some elements which seem to be quite early, perhaps deriving from some material committed to writing in the 8th century. We read that her real name was Darerca and that her father was called Mochta and her mother Coman. The biographies further state that she was converted by St **Patrick** himself and that she received the veil at his hands. Nine other nuns followed her, one of them a widow, whose son was adopted by Moninne. They were guided by bishop Iobhar of Beag-Éire (Beggery Island in Wexford harbour), who was an associate of St **Brighid**, and then went to Brighid herself at Kildare. There Moninne impressed everybody by her selfless charity to the poor. Settling afterwards at Ard Conais (apparently in the Wicklow mountains), her community increased to fifty nuns. On a visit to Kildare once, Moninne was presented by Brighid with a silver vessel, but due to her unselfishness she did not take the gift with her but hid it in Brighid's convent. When it was later discovered there, Brighid ordered that it be cast into the river Liffey, but it flowed against the stream and was found in stagnant water near Moninne's dwelling.

The saint next went to her native territory and founded a convent at Fochaird (Faughart, Co Louth), followed by a larger one at Cill Shléibhe (Killeavy, at the foot of Slieve Gullion in Co Armagh). Apart from her charity, she practised great austerities, especially fasting, and we read that angels visited her and consulted with her each night. One tradition gives her original name as Sárbhile, and tells an interesting little story concerning how it was changed. We read that a dumb poet fasted against her in order to persuade her to get his speech for him. She consented, and as he began to talk the first babbling words he uttered were 'nin-nin!' As a result, the poet himself became known as Ninine, and the saint as Moninne. The year 517 is given as the date of her death, and her feastday is July 6.

Some saints with similar names were traditionally remembered in Scotland and England, and mediaeval writers attached to the convent of Burton-upon-Trent (in Staffordshire) claimed that Moninne was identical with their own foundress Modwenna. This inspired a fanciful literature which described Moninne as leaving Killeavy and founding churches at seven different locations in Scotland, before settling at Burton.

J F Kenney (1929), 366-71; W W Heist (1965), 83-95; Anne O'Sullivan (1983), 1688-9; Whitley Stokes (1905), 166-7; John O'Hanlon (1875) *7*, 79-93.

MOORE A young nobleman of that surname from Moorestown in the Dingle peninsula of Co Kerry who, it is said, could never sleep. No first name is given for him.

According to the legend, he entertained a travelling scholar in his mansion, and as they sat up late at night discussing affairs he confided his secret to the scholar. The latter said that he had once read that the offspring of spirits could not sleep, and on hearing this Moore went to his mother and demanded to know how he had been conceived. She admitted that her husband had not been his father, but that she had gone swimming in the sea one day and that she had fainted in the water. She said that as a result of this she had become pregnant, and Moore then realised that his real father had been a sea-spirit. Next day, he mounted his horse and rode into the sea, and was never seen again.

A variant of this story is found in the folklore of coastal areas of Connacht and west Ulster concerning **Lughaidh mac Con**, the opponent of **Cormac mac Airt**, and some commentators regard it as a survival in oral tradition of some early Irish myth. It is, however, more likely that it was a family legend which the Moores, an Anglo-Norman family, brought with them to Ireland after the Norman invasion. Another version of it is told in a 13th-century French lay of a character called Tydorel. This also contains the insomnia motif, which was probably added in mediaeval France to the basic plot of the legend i.e. that a sea-being can be the father of a mortal man. This basic plot was attached to Merovech, the founder of the pre-mediaeval Merovingian dynasty, and from that source it was adopted into Irish literature and appears in the birth-stories of **Mongán** and **Breas**.

All of these have associations with the sea, and a fanciful etymology would equally allow the Moore family (de Múr) to claim affinity to the sea ('mer' in French and 'muir' in Irish). That family has been settled in Kerry since the 14th century, and the legend could easily have been borrowed in the interval by sailors of the west coast and put in the new context of Lughaidh mac Con.

Kenneth Jackson *SB* (1938), 77-9, 92-3; Seán O'Sullivan (1966), 21-37; A H Krappe in *Modern Language Review 24*, 200-4; Barbara Hillers in Bo Almqvist ed (1988), 19-28.

MÓR MUMHAN (literally, 'Mór of Munster') Mythical woman, an emanation from ancient tradition, 'Mór' being originally a designation of the land-goddess (see **Mór-Ríoghain**).

There are several indications that Mugha or Mughain was the name of a goddess associated with the **Érainn** people. Since the Érainn were represented as having a special connection with Munster, her name was taken to be identical with that of the province, 'Mumha' or 'Mumhain'. The adjective 'mór' (meaning 'large') was often combined with the name of the province, and this seems to have been the reason why Mór became associated with Munster in particular.

The territorial **goddesses** were symbolically portrayed as the mates of reigning kings, and in one late mediaeval text this 'Mór of Munster' figures clearly in such a role. The text attempts to historicise her, but the function of a goddess is nevertheless clear. We read that Mór Mumhan was the daughter of Aodh Beannáin and that she was being sought by various kings. She went mad and wandered through Ireland for two years in a distracted state. Coming to the royal Munster stronghold of Cashel, she lay with the king of the province, Fínghein mac Aodha, and he put aside his wife in favour of her. When Fínghein died, she went to the new king **Cathal mac Fionghuine**. Mór's sister was later taken captive, and the sons of Aodh Beannáin declared war on the sons of Cathal for failing to give her proper protection. The celebrated king Cathal mac Fionghuine has been mistakenly substituted here by the writer for Cathal mac Aodha, who succeeded Fínghein as king of the province in the year 619 AD. The story is therefore a late fantasy based on earlier references to kingship.

The element Mughain has survived in petrified form in some placenames - such as townlands called Fiodh Mughaine (Fithmoone) and Cluain Mughna (Clonmona) in north Tipperary, Bealach Mughna (Ballaghmoon in Co Carlow), and Cill Mughaine (Kilmoone in Co Cork). Memory of an actual personage called Mór is, however, preserved in the case of one toponymic only - Tigh Mhóire ('the House of Mór'), situated in the parish of Dunquin in west Kerry. A series of stories concerning her are current in that area, and it is clear from their sentiment that they are not more than a few centuries old. They do, however, preserve within them some snatches of ancient tradition. For instance, the phrase in local speech which describes the breadth of Ireland as being from Tigh Mhóire to Domhnach Diagh (Donaghadee, Co Down) is in accord with similar statements in the early literature (see **Caoilte**). The oral lore of Kerry transformed the latter placename rather awkwardly into a character called Donncha Daoi, who is made out to have been the husband of Mór. We are told that this couple lived somewhere in the centre of Ireland but that Mór henpecked Donncha and he left her and went as far away from her as possible, thus leaving all Ireland between them.

Their three sons and one daughter went with the mother, but in time these all met with misery, referred to proverbially as 'íde chlainne Móire' ('the misfortune of Mór's children'). The two elder boys went overseas and became champions of a foreign king, for whom they slew giants and conquered foes. The youngest boy set out to find them, and all three got permission from the king to return home on holiday. They overstayed their time at home, however, and a strange ship soon arrived to collect them. There was nobody on board save a great black cat, and they went onto the ship to examine it. No sooner had they done so than the cat (who was the foreign king in magical disguise) had the sails raised, and the ship carried them away forever. The daughter married a stranger who continually beat her, and Mór herself grew lonely and desolate living on her own. Finally she decided to go to see her husband Donncha. She set out, and from a local hill-top called Mám Clasach saw a wide expanse of countryside. 'Ireland is indeed long and wide!' she said. She felt the need to urinate there and thus created the streams which are on Mám. She then returned to her house and went no further. Such humorous aetiological lore has not lost the aura of myth, and several local proverbial sayings refer to her doings as if she embodied the human state generally.

Thus 'íde chlainne Móire' is a cursing allusion, 'leaghadh mhúin Mhóire' ('the evaporation of Mór's urine') refers to the non-permanent nature of things, and ostentation is censured by the phrase 'cailín aige Mór agus Mór ag iarraidh déirce' ('Mór had a servant-girl while she herself begged').

Proinsias Mac Cana in *Études Celtiques 7*, 76-114 and 8, 64-5; T P O'Nolan in *Proceedings of the Royal Irish Academy 30*, Part C, 261-82; Gearóid Mac Eoin in *Zeitschrift für celtische Philologie 36*, 63-82; F J Byrne (1973), 204-7.

[Folklore] Pádraig Ó Siochfhradha in *An Claidheamh Soluis* 30/7/1910, 2-4 and (1938), 75-6; T C Croker (1829), 74-80; Patrick Kennedy (1866), 287-8; Jeremiah Curtin (1894), xli-xliii, 35-7; Seosamh Laoide (1915), 19; IFC, many references.

MORANN Mythical judge who was celebrated for his wisdom. His name is derived from 'Mór-Fhind', meaning 'great Find', and accordingly he would be an emanation from the archetypal wise seer of ancient tradition, **Find**.

He occurs in the mediaeval pseudo-historical writings, being portrayed as son of the usurper king **Cairbre Catcheann** who had banished the nobles from Ireland, but the motifs concerning him obviously belong to earlier tradition. We read that two sons were born to Cairbre with cauls on their heads, and that Cairbre regarded them as monstrous births and had them drowned. The third child was Morann, and he also had a caul. When Cairbre's soldiers threw him into the sea, however, a great wave arose and broke the caul. The soldiers saw the child's face on the top of the wave, and he spoke to them, saying 'rough is the billow!'. Then he spoke again, asking them to lift him up. They pitied him, and left him near the dwelling of a smith called Maon, and this smith found him and took him home to his wife. The smith called for a candle to examine the child, and the infant remarked 'bright is the candle!' Later, it happened that Cairbre was at the house of the smith drinking ale, and the child jumped into his lap. The soldiers asked him how much he would pay for that child, and Cairbre said that he would give the child's weight in gold and silver. At that, they told him that it was his own son.

His father therefore took Morann with him and reared him. Morann became chief-judge of Ireland and, when Cairbre died, he decided that the only male survivor of the nobility, Fearadhach Fionn, should be recalled from Scotland to take the throne. He therefore sent his son to summon Fearadhach, quoting a long list of advices concerning how a king should rule properly. These advices predate the mediaeval literature, probably originating in the 7th century AD from maxims used by the actual legal schools of early Ireland. It is thus easy to understand why they should be fancifully attributed to a character with the name of the archetypal seer Find. One early legal tract, in fact, in deriving the name of the great judge from 'mór' and 'find', explains the latter word as indicating how his decisions were full of wisdom ('fios'). This well suits the lore of that archaic seer-figure. The ordinary designation of the judge was 'Morann mac Maoin', that is his father being 'Maon' (earlier 'Moen') which means 'dumb'. This latter, curiously, was also a name given to the mythical founder of the Leinster kingship **Labhraidh**, and so it is apparent that Morann - like **Find File** and **Fionn mac Cumhaill** - originated in the Leinsterised version of the Find lore. The reason why the mediaeval writers associated him with Cairbre seems to be that the story of his threatened youth resembles that of the threatened youth of Fearadhach (see **Cairbre Catcheann**).

Both early and late sources tell of the 'sín' or 'iodh' of Morann. This was the remnant of his caul, which remained around his neck, and if ever he was beginning to give a wrong judgement it would tighten on him and thus lead him to revise his decision. A development of this states that he used to place it on the neck of an accused person, and that it would choke the guilty but spare the innocent. The pseudo-historians also said that Morann was the first person in Ireland to believe in the Christian God 'through examination of the elements and through his own clear understanding'. This appears to be an echo from Christian didactic which put the image of the ancient seer Find to its own use (see **Fionn mac Cumhaill**). The mediaeval literature also relates a story of how Morann discovered his wife dallying with his servant. He turned the servant into a speckled calf, and the wife said that she was sick and desired the meat of that calf. Approaching the calf with a sword, Morann enquired of it what the sword feared. The calf replied 'stone', and a question-and-answer session commenced viz. the stone feared fire, the fire water, the water wind, the wind hills, the hills boars, the boars hounds, and the hounds feared bad unrepentant women. When asked what a woman fears, the calf answered that it did not know. Morann then said that he would not slay his wife, because other men did not slay their unfaithful wives. This plot is in fact borrowed from folklore (see **Humorous Tales**, Types 2010-2044). Despite his status in the old literature, however, no lore of Morann survives in oral tradition.

Fergus Kelly (1976); E J Gwynn in *Ériu 13*, 41-4, 47-52; John O'Donovan (1865) *1*, 24-5; D A Binchy (1978), 1654-5; Myles Dillon in *Ériu 11*, 43-4; Whitley Stokes in *Irische Texte 3*, 188-90; Rudolf Thurneysen in *Zeitschrift für celtische Philologie 11*, 56-106 and *12*, 271-8 and *20*, 192-8; P S Dinneen (1908) *2*, 236-7 and *3*, 34-5.

MÓR-RÍOGHAIN (earlier, Mórrígu) Goddess of war. Her name was taken to mean 'great queen', but the more likely meaning was 'phantom-queen'. She is identified with similar personages such as Badhbh, Neamhain, and **Macha**, whose names function as alternative appellations for her (see **Goddesses**).

It is clear that the Mór-Ríoghain is an emanation from the earth-goddess, her battle-context reflecting contests for land in the material world. Several sources give her proper name as Anu, this being the leading goddess of the Irish Celts (see **Danu**). Just as there were hills called the 'Paps of Anu' at Killarney in Co Kerry, so the Mór-Ríoghain was also identified with the landscape by having two hillocks as her Paps ('dá chích na Mórrígna') near Newgrange in Co Meath. Her name occurs in several other toponymics, and further association of her with the landscape is evidenced by the term 'fulacht na Mór-Ríoghna' (i.e. the Mór-Ríoghain's hearth) for some ancient cooking-sites. As often with Irish divinities, she is represented as one of a triad of sisters. This triad are the active spirits of war, as in the account of the first battle of Moytirra, fought between the **Fir Bolg** and the **Tuatha Dé Danann** - where they, of course, take the side of the latter, 'the people of the goddess Danu'. Named as 'Badhbh and Macha and Mórrígu', they stand on the hill of **Tara** and fling magical showers and masses of fire and blood onto the Fir Bolg. The triad thus have the function, not specifically of encouraging war, but of encouraging their own people to victory.

This is clear in the tradition that the Mór-Ríoghain was in fact the wife of the **Daghdha**, who was a sort of over-all deity in the Irish pantheon. One early account has her sharing his exalted status, and that in a very significant context. Before the second battle of Moytirra, we are told, the Daghdha had a tryst with her at the river Unshin (in Co Sligo). She was washing there, with a foot on either side of the river, and he copulated with her in that position. She informed him where the enemy host of the **Fomhóire** would land, and promised that she would terrify the Fomhóire king, Inneach, by draining away his valour and 'the blood from his heart'. She also told the Daghdha to summon the poets of Ireland to her, and she directed these to sing spells against the foe. In the later text describing this battle, we are told that the Mór-Ríoghain, along with Badhbh and Macha, undertook to bring 'hailstones and fierce showers' down upon the Fomhóire, and to fling javelins and flails against them. These are clear illustrations of her combined functions as goddess of fertility and of war, protectress of her people's general interests.

It was, however, specifically in the role of war-goddess that she was cast by tradition. Encountered often by a riverside, she portended slaughter. One 8th-century text has the mythical warrior **Fothadh Canainne** say of the Mór-Ríoghain that 'it is she who has egged us on' and that 'horrible is her hateful laughing' which strikes terror into the hearts of men. The true warrior is one who is not overcome by fear and who is therefore on good terms with her. It was for this reason that she became attached to the developing lore of the hero **Cú Chulainn** in early mediaeval Ireland. We are told that, as a boy, he went to rescue king **Conchobhar mac Neasa** from a battlefield, and that he heard there 'the war-goddess crying from among the corpses' and encouraging him to great deeds. Here she is called the Badhbh, one of her alternative appellations. Cú Chulainn encountered her under her own name and in a more direct manner when he was single-handedly contending with the forces of **Meadhbh**. She approached him in the form of a beautiful young woman and stated that she had fallen in love with him on hearing his fame. She offered him her help, but he answered that he was not seeking a woman's torso, and she then threatened to encumber him when he was fighting. Accordingly, when he was locked in combat with a great warrior called Lóch, she came in the form of an eel and coiled herself around his feet. He fell, but arose again and struck the eel, breaking its ribs. Then she took the form of a grey wolf, and drove a herd of cattle against him, but he knocked an eye out of her head with a sling-shot. Finally, she became a red hornless heifer and led the cattle in a stampede towards him, but he cast a stone at her and broke her leg. He succeeded in slaying his opponent Lóch but, when he was exhausted from the fighting, she came to him again - this time in the guise of an old crone milking a cow with three teats. He asked her for a drink, and she gave him a drink from each teat, with the result that the three wounds which he had inflicted on her were healed.

Elsewhere in the **Ulster Cycle**, the war-goddess is called Neamhain and Bé Néit, as well as Badhbh. These three shrieked over Meadhbh's army, leading to great confusion and causing many of the soldiers to die of fright, and thus their portrayal is as protectresses of Ulster. Indeed, the Badhbh appeared to the great brown bull (see **Donn Cuailnge**) and told him that he must move with his heifers to new pastures in order to avoid capture by Meadhbh's men. She was in the form of a bird perching on a pillar-stone when she thus addressed the bull. The war-goddess in the Ulster Cycle is several times brought into association with cattle, no doubt because of the high profile of cattle-raiding in the practice of war. She is said, for instance, to have stolen a cow from Connacht and driven it to Cooley to be mated to the great brown bull there. As she brought it back, Cú Chulainn intercepted her. She was coloured red and was riding in a one-horse chariot, with a huge man walking beside and driving the cow. Thinking that she was stealing a cow from Ulster, Cú Chulainn challenged her, but she and her retinue disappeared. All that remained was a dark bird on a branch near him. In this shape the Mór-Ríoghain spoke to him and explained that the calf born of that cow would be coeval with himself and would give rise to the war of *Táin Bó Cuailnge* (see **Ulster Cycle**). Although the theme of this calf and its connection with Cú Chulainn is inconsistent with the ordinary sequence of the Cycle, it is clear that the narrative has as its theme the stirring up of war by the Mór-Ríoghain. When Cú Chulainn boasted to her of the feats he would perform, she threatened to discommode him in the manner described above. There is some ambiguity in her image here, for she and the hero are quite hostile to each other, even though she does promise him that she will be 'a shelter at your death'. No doubt due to the influence of these accounts, she occurs in the context of cattle in a rather puerile mediaeval story, which tells of how she stole away a fierce bull from the herd of a cattle-drover of **Tara** called Buchat. The latter's wife Odhras followed her to the rath of Cruachain (in Co Roscommon), but fell asleep there. Whereupon the Mór-Ríoghain came and chanted powerful spells over the woman, turning her into a river which thus was called by the name Odhras.

Several sources state that the Mór-Ríoghain's double Neamhain was the wife of Nét, who is described as 'the god of battle with the pagan Irish'. Other names for her given in these sources are Macha and Fea, but that which most frequently occurs is Badhbh. This was the ordinary word for a scaldcrow, a favourite form taken by the war-goddess as she hovered over the clash of contending armies. The image was a development from the reality of such ugly carrion-birds haunting the battlefields, and there is some evidence that it was of great antiquity among the Celts. The compound 'Cathubodŭae' appears in a slightly defaced Gaulish inscription, this being cognate with the Irish 'Badhbh Chatha' (i.e. the scaldcrow of battle). The image is repulsive, and accordingly there was a tendency to view her as a personage who exulted in slaughter for its own sake. One mediaeval gloss describes her 'fruit-crop' as 'the heads of men that have been slain', and she has little of the function of protectress in the account of the death of the mythical warrior **Cormac Conn Loingeas**. There the prophecy is made: 'The red-mouthed Badhbh will shriek around the house, for corpses she will be solicitous.' Another description of a battle - this a historical one between the men of Leinster and the men of Ossory in the year 870 AD - has equally sinister imagery: 'Great indeed was the din and tumult that occurred between them then, and the Badhbh raised her head between them, and there was massive killing between them.'

Such portrayals of perennial hostility to humans had their effect even on the relationship between the war-goddess and Cú Chulainn. Thus, in the account of his death which was compiled at the end of the Middle Ages, the name Badhbh is given to one of the demonic children of Cailitín who plotted the hero's destruction. Taking the shape of a carrion-crow ('feannóg'), this Badhbh tries to entice him into a magical ambush and, failing in this, she goes to him disguised as one of his serving-ladies to summon him to what will be his doom. When he is dying, this Badhbh again assumes the form of a crow and alights shrieking on the pillar to which he has tied himself, thus showing that his life is at an end. That the older tradition had not completely disappeared is shown by the action attributed to a being with the name of the Mór-Ríoghain on the same occasion. As Cú Chulainn sets forth on his doomed journey, he finds that she has disconnected his chariot on the night before in order to discourage him from his venture.

The dual aspects of the war-goddess persisted in the literature, but most stress was on her negative side. She was the 'red vehement Badhbh' who was joyful when human women are sorrowful at the slaughter of their men-folk. One late mediaeval text describes the 'grey-haired Mórrígu' as shrieking triumphantly over fighting soldiers, and appearing as 'a lean hag, speedily leaping over the points of their weapons and shields'. Such descriptions make her synonymous with the horror and panic of battle, a view which is surely as basic as her appearance in the form of a scaldcrow. Horrible as she is, however, she still tends to favour one side in a battle and helps that side to achieve victory. A 10th-century description of another historical battle, in which king **Fearghal mac Maoldúin** was defeated by the Leinstermen in 722 AD, also has dramatic mention of the war-goddess in a partisan context. She is called 'the red-mouthed and sharp-faced Badhbh' and is said to have raised an exultant shriek over the decapitated head of Fearghal.

One particular type of portrayal of the war-goddess became conventional in the literature. An 8th-century text, already referred to, has the Mór-Ríoghain as a horrible woman who strikes terror into the hearts of men. The text further states that 'horrible are the huge entrails... many are the spoils that she washes'. This recurs in several other accounts. By 'spoils' is meant weapons, even parts of bodies, but more usually the blood-soaked clothes of warriors is to be understood. The word used for the spoils is 'fadhbh' (earlier, 'fodhbh') which is an obvious phonemic parallel to 'badhbh' (earlier, 'bodhbh'). Although apparently unrelated, a stylistic connection was made between the two words within the over-all context of war. Before his death, Cú Chulainn is described as meeting the Badhbh as a beautiful young woman at a ford 'lamenting and moaning, washing in cold water purple hacked wounded spoils'. Again, before he died, Cormac Conn Loingeas met the Badhbh by a riverside. She was a red woman, and when she lowered her hand the water became red with gore and blood. She was washing his spoils, thereby portending disaster for him. This imagery was readily applied to battles fought in the late Middle Ages. A near-contemporaneous account of the battle of Corcomroe Abbey in Co Clare, fought in the year 1317, has Donnchadh Ó Briain meeting such a being on his way to oppose his kinsman Toirdhealbhach. She is described as a hideous hag and is washing mangled heads and limbs by the shore of a lake. He asks her who she is, and discovers that she is the protecting 'badhbh' of his opponents. She foretells the slaughter of Donnchadh and of his army, a prophecy which is fulfilled. The same hag is said to have taken Toirdhealbhach's part again in the following year, when he was contending with a Norman army under Richard de Clare. As he and his army crossed a river, de Clare saw 'a sharp and bare-mouthed badhbh' washing armour and rich robes from which red blood poured into the water. She stated that de Clare and his followers would soon be slaughtered, and this prophecy was also fulfilled.

The war-goddess as such does not occur in later folklore, but her influence is to be noted in the popular tradition of the **banshee**, whose crying is heard at night as a portent of death. In several counties in the south-east of Ireland, the banshee is in fact known by the appellation 'badhbh'. See also **Mór Mumhan**.

[Derivation of names] RIA Dictionary s.v. 'morrigu', 'badb', 'fodb'; W M Hennessy in *Revue Celtique 1*, 32-5.

[Associations with land] Edward Gwynn (1906), 18-9, 62-3; Hennessy, *op cit*, 54-5; A G Van Hamel (1933), 37.

[Mythic synchronisations] E A Gray (1982), 118, 128-30; R A S Macalister (1941), 122-3, 160-1, 188-9.

[First Moytirra battle] Joseph Frazer in *Ériu 8*, 29-48.

[Second Moytirra battle] Gray, *op cit*, 44-5, 64-5, 70-3; Brian Ó Cuív (1945), 20, 26-7.

[Fothadh Canainne] Kuno Meyer (1910), 16-7.

[Cú Chulainn] Cecile O'Rahilly (1976), 7, 16, 30, 57-64, 107, 118, 121; Ernst Windisch in *Irische Texte 2(2)*, 239-54; R I Best / M A O'Brien (1956), 443, 450; A G Van Hamel (1933), 89-91, 95-6, 113.

[Odhras] Gwynn (1924), 196-201.

[Cormac Conn Loingeas] Whitley Stokes in *Revue Celtique 21*, 156-9.

['Fruit-crop'] Hennessy, *op cit*, 36.

[Historical battles] Hennessy, *op cit*, 40; John O'Donovan (1842), 198-9; Pádraig Ó Riain (1978), 8; S H O'Grady (1929) *1*, 104-5, 140-1.

[General] Hennessy, *op cit*, 32-55; P L Henry in *Études Celtiques 8*, 407-11.

MUIRCHEARTACH MAC EARCA High-king of Ireland, whose reign belonged to the period from roughly 513 to 534 AD. He won several battles against the Leinstermen, and his fame in the annals caused several accounts of him to be written in mediaeval times.

An 11th-century poem tells of how the Scottish king Eochu carried off the young Muireadhach, grandson of **Niall Naoi-ghiallach**, to serve him, and how Muireadhach slew Eochu and brought back to Ireland with him a maiden called Earc, daughter of Loarn. It was said that Muireadhach was slain by his father's swineherd through jealousy of Earc, but that Earc revived him by placing an herb in his mouth as she had seen a weasel do for its dead mate. Another account also mentions how Earc eloped with Muireadhach and states that Muircheartach was the eldest son of their union. Muircheartach was expelled from Ireland for killing some jesters, and he was later expelled from Scotland also after he slew his grandfather Loarn. He went to the land of the Britons and became king over it, and eventually he came to Ireland accompanied by his cousin, the cleric Cairneach.

There was some basis for this in the annals, for one Loarn was there said to have crossed from Ireland to Scotland in the 5th century, and from 'cinél Loairn' (his descendants) is apparently derived the name of the district Lorne in Argyll. Muircheartach succeeded his father Muireadhach as king of Aileach (the area in the south of Ulster) at the end of the 5th century, but the designation of him by his mother's name ('mac Earca') is puzzling. Earc (earlier, Erc) might have been the name of some goddess and 'mac Earca' would thus have been a title rather than a name, but it is also quite possible that Muircheartach's mother was in fact called Earc. Cairneach (known in British records as Carantoc) was definitely historical. The mediaeval Irish literature describes him as son of a British king called Saran and makes his mother Babona a sister of Earc, but this connection between him and Muircheartach may have arisen from a verse which was attributed to him and which prophesied the latter's death.

The death of Muircheartach is the subject of a saga composed in or about the 11th century. It describes how, when he was high-king, he had his palace at Cleiteach (near Newgrange in Co Meath), and his wife was Duaibhseach, daughter of the king of Connacht. When hunting alone one day, he met a beautiful lady. She told him that her name was Sín, and she agreed to become his paramour on condition that he expel his wife and children from the palace. This was done, and Duaibhseach went to complain to Cairneach. The cleric cursed the dwelling of Muircheartach, and dug a grave for him there in anticipation of his death. Soon after, Cairneach met a Munster troop coming to negotiate with the king, and he supervised a treaty between the two sides. Because he had cursed him, however, Muircheartach ordered Cairneach to stay far away from his dwelling forthwith. To demonstrate her magical power, Sín entertained Muircheartach and his Munster guests by creating illusions of men fighting, by making wine from water, and by turning the fern into swine. Next morning, the king felt that his strength was leaving him. Sín made of the stones blue men and goat-headed men on the lawn before Brugh na Bóinne (the Newgrange tumulus), and Muircheartach himself went to fight these. All day long he slaughtered them, and then returned to his residence, where he was given more of Sín's food and drink. On the following morning he was further weakened, and again Sín created illusions of battalions of soldiers to oppose him.

Cairneach, knowing of the king's dilemma, sent three clerics to assist him. They found him hacking at stones and sods and stalks, and on their advice he made the Sign of the Cross and the dementia left him. They told him that his death was near and instructed him to build a church there. He did this, and then was shriven and prepared for death by the clerics. Returning to Sín, however, he was again beguiled by her. She brought a storm and a great snowfall, and when he fell asleep he dreamed that a host of demons were coming for him. He also dreamed that he was in a foundering ship and that a griffin came and carried him to her nest, where he was burned to death. He sent a message to the three clerics, and they explained that the ship was his kingship and that the griffin was the lady Sín. Finally he imagined that the demons were attacking his palace and slaughtering his people. He went to oppose them and found the place in conflagration. To escape the fire, he went into a great cask of wine, and he died there from the dual effects of drowning and burning. Next day the clerics brought his body to the river Boyne nearby and washed it. Cairneach came there and lamented him, as also did the queen Duaibhseach. She died from grief for him, and she and Muircheartach were buried together. Sín came to the clerics and explained that this was her revenge on the high-king for the death of her family in the battle of Cearb (Assey, Co Meath), in which Muircheartach had decimated the old septs of **Tara**. She was shriven by the clerics, and died from grief at what she had done.

Although this story makes use of memories of the struggle between the Connachta - Uí Néill and the remnants of the older septs of the Boyne valley (see **Érainn**), its central point is concerned with a later issue. This was the struggle between the Christian and pagan world-views in the 6th century, as seen through the eyes of the mediaeval writer. It is significant that the cleric Cairneach curses the high-king when the latter departs from the Christian ethic, and that this curse becomes a reality, thereby underlying the superior power of the Church. A similar situation applied in the saga of another high-king, **Diarmaid mac Cearrbheoil**, whose dramatic death was described as having three enigmatic aspects. This triple-death motif was borrowed from the Diarmaid context into that of Muircheartach, apparently by 9th-century writers or storytellers, and thus was embedded in the sources which the later mediaeval writer was using.

Lil Nic Dhonnchadha (1964); A G Van Hamel (1932), 40-1; Láimhbheartach Mac Cionnaith (1938), 217-20; L P Ó Caithnia (1984), 103-4, 116; Eoin Mac Néill in *Archivium Hibernicum 2*, 70; R A S Macalister (1956), 360-3, 532-5;

MURCHADH MAC BRIAIN (c970-1014) Eldest son of the high-king **Brian Boru** and the leader of Brian's army at the battle of Clontarf, in which he and his father were both slain.

The earliest account of that battle stresses the great heroism of Murchadh, fighting with a sword in each hand, for he was 'the last man in Ireland to have equal dexterity in each hand' and also 'the last man to be the equal of a hundred'. We read that he led a charge which broke the enemy ranks and then, swinging his two swords, he beheaded the Norse leader Sigurd. He and a Norse warrior called the son of Elbric then came to grips with each other, and so fierce was the combat between them that Murchadh's sword became red-hot and its handle melted. It burned his hand and he had to throw the sword aside. Knocking his opponent to the ground, he grabbed the Norseman's sword and stabbed him, but was himself stabbed with a knife in the stomach. He beheaded his opponent, but he himself was mortally wounded and died at sunrise on the following morning. When Brian got news that the standard of Murchadh had fallen, he was heartbroken and remarked that 'Ireland has now fallen with it!'

The only one of Brian's sons to survive the pyrrhic victory was Donnchadh. This, according to the text, was in accordance with the prophecy given to Brian (q.v.) by the otherworld lady **Aoibheall** to the effect that his successor would be the first of his sons whom he saw on the day of the battle. The apparent meaning of this was that Brian first noticed Donnchadh in the battle, but a later mediaeval text tells a fanciful story to explain it. According to this, when Brian received the prediction from Aoibheall he sent for Murchadh, who began to dress to go into his father's presence. Donnchadh, however, went straight to his father and so, much to the latter's disappointment, was the one destined to succeed. This story, echoing the Biblical account of Abraham's sons, must have derived from some dispute as to primacy among Brian's descendants.

The Aoibheall-theme also prompted the inclusion of another account into the narrative of the battle of Clontarf. According to this, a friend of Murchadh called Dúnlaing Ó hArtagáin arrived late just as the battle-lines were drawn. He explained that he had been detained in an otherworld dwelling but that he had foregone the beautiful life there out of loyalty to Murchadh. While in the otherworld, he had discovered that he himself, as well as Brian, Murchadh and other members of the royal family would be slain on that day. Dúnlaing then went into the battle and, fighting magnificently, was slain. A much later redaction has Dúnlaing bringing Murchadh from the thick of the battle to meet Aoibheall, and she confirms the prophecy for them. The theme of this Dúnlaing seems to have been invented by the subsept of Brian's people who bore the surname Ó hArtagáin (anglicised Hartigan), with the distinct purpose of increasing their prestige among the O'Briens.

Murchadh's reputation for heroism continued in the literature. A 13th-century poem credits him with overcoming and slaying a horrific 'red woman' who came with a large fleet and strong magical powers to destroy Ireland. Some writers of romances also found his personality suitable for their purpose. One such romance, written in the 17th century, tells of how, after following a magical stag and hound, Murchadh meets a hermit who is cutting wood. The hermit invites him to his castle, where Murchadh shows some untoward interest in his host's wife. The hermit explains the great difficulties which he has had in procuring his stag, hound, and woman, and describes how he had won back the woman when she had been abducted from him. Night comes, and Murchadh goes to sleep, but when he awakes in the morning the castle and all its occupants have disappeared. Versions of this story, sometimes ornamented, have been collected from the folklore of Ulster and Connacht, as well as from Scotland. Similarly, a romance written in or about the same time tells of a great adventure which Murchadh has in an underwater land where he recovers a magic cauldron stolen by a servant and rescues a maiden from a giant. Several versions of these romances circulated in folklore, and some oral storytellers introduced the heroic name Murchadh mac Briain at will into narratives of great deeds.

J H Todd (1867), clxxv-clxxxviii, 168-97, 336-7; A J Goedheer (1938), 47-8, 58-9, 67-71; Douglas Hyde *GF* (1899), 4-49; Alan Bruford (1969), 136-43 and in *Éigse 12*, 301-26.

MYTHOLOGICAL CYCLE A collective term applied to the stories in Irish literature which describe the doings of otherworld characters. The basis for the cycle is ancient Celtic myth, and many of the characters are Irish manifestations of a Celtic pantheon of divine beings.

The central story of the cycle was concerned with a battle between two supernatural groups. This theme is found in other Indo-European sources - such as the conflict between the Devas and Asuras in Vedic literature, between the Aesir and Vanir in Norse, and between Zeus' family and the Titans in Greek. In Irish myth this conflict was between the divine **Tuatha Dé Danann** and the demonic **Fomhóire** and, based on this ancient lore, an account of their struggle was written down in the 8th century AD. This account situated the battle between the two supernatural peoples at Magh Tuireadh (Moytirra, near Lough Arrow in Co Sligo). The original form of this toponymic seems to have been Magh Tuire, with the meaning 'Plain of the Pillar', and the myth was located there because some such edifice - dating from prehistoric times - was situated in that place. The original 8th-century text does not survive, but two different stories, each derived from it, are found in the mediaeval literature. Of these, the story called the 'Second Battle of Moytirra' reflects the earlier tradition more accurately, and the so-called 'First Battle of Moytirra' is in general a literary fabrication. Both stories, however, must be taken into account in order to understand the full tradition.

The 'first' battle was known by the title *Cath Muige Tuired Cunga* (the Battle of Moytirra of Cong). Cong lies between Lough Mask and Lough Corrib in Co Mayo. It abounds in cairns and other stone monuments, and thus it appeared to the mediaeval literati as a suitable place to be called 'the Plain of the Pillar', even though that name properly belonged to the place in Co Sligo. This story developed from the mediaeval pseudo-historical tract, *Lebor Gabála*, which claimed that the Tuatha Dé Danann were an ancient people who settled in Ireland and conquered a group of earlier inhabitants called the **Fir Bolg**. The idea of a clash between the Tuatha Dé and Fir Bolg necessitated a duplication of the battle of Moytirra - hence the notion of an earlier or 'first' battle. The text which purports to give a full description of this was composed in or about the 11th century, and goes as follows:-

The Fir Bolg were in possession of Ireland, and Eochaidh mac Eirc was their king. Eochaidh had a dream in which he saw a great flock of black birds coming from the ocean, and his poet explained that this was a fleet of ships carrying a thousand magical heroes. Thus the Tuatha Dé Danann, led by their king **Nuadhu**, arrived in Ireland. They broke and burned their boats, and encamped on a mountain in the north-east of the province of Connacht. The Fir Bolg sent one of their warriors, the huge Sreang, to parley with them, and he was confronted by **Breas** of the Tuatha Dé. Since both peoples were descended from **Neimheadh**, the two warriors spoke the same language. Breas demanded half of Ireland for his people, and Sreang was inclined to agree, but the assembly of the Fir Bolg at **Tara** refused this. The three sorceresses of the Tuatha Dé - Badhbh, **Macha**, and the **Mór-Ríoghain** - then sent magical showers of fiery rain against the Fir Bolg, causing great damage until the Fir Bolg sorcerers managed to counteract them. Nuadhu sent envoys to Eochaidh, offering the same terms as before, but again the Fir Bolg refused. A group of the Fir Bolg went and challenged the Tuatha Dé to a hurling-match, in which the Tuatha Dé players were slain. Then Eochaidh mac Eirc sent his poet to the Tuatha Dé nobles to arrange the conditions of the forthcoming battle. Each side built an entrenched fortress and prepared a well of healing for their wounded. Battle was joined at Cong, and on the first day the fighting went against the Tuatha Dé, but the Fir Bolg did not pursue their advantage. They returned to their own camp, and when king Eochaidh went to wash in their well next morning he was attacked by three warriors of the Tuatha Dé, who had come to spy. A young man suddenly appeared and protected the king. This unnamed stranger slew the three and was himself slain.

When the armies joined battle on that day, the position was reversed, with the Fir Bolg being driven across the field. On the third day the Tuatha Dé were led by the **Daghdha**, and in a furious combat the Fir Bolg were driven right back to their own camp. The fourth day of the battle was the most terrible of all, and the Tuatha Dé fixed pillars on the plain so that the foe could not escape their onslaught. For the Fir Bolg, however, Sreang was rampant, and with a tremendous sword-stroke he severed the right arm of Nuadhu from the shoulder. The Daghdha had the disabled king carried from the fray to be looked after by physicians. In the ongoing fighting, king Eochaidh was overcome by thirst and had to leave the field for a while to drink. The wizards of the Tuatha Dé caused all the streams and rivers to dry up before him until he came to Tráigh Eothaile (Beltra strand in Co Sligo). He was followed there by a trio of Tuatha Dé warriors, who slew him in fierce combat. On the final day of the battle, the great Sreang again came face to face with Nuadhu, but instead of contending they made peace, according to which Ireland was given to the Tuatha Dé and the Fir Bolg were allowed to keep the province of Connacht. Since Nuadhu was blemished he was disqualified from the **kingship** of the Tuatha Dé, and Breas was installed in his place. The text states that Breas died from a drink which he took while hunting seven years later. The missing arm of Nuadhu was then replaced, and he became king once more.

In this text, the original story of the Moytirra battle is quite distorted by pseudo-historical and antiquarian speculation. The account of the strange young warrior who saved Eochaidh from his three foes at the well, for instance, was invented on the basis of local landmarks called Carn an Aonfhir ('the cairn of the single champion') and Tulach an Trír ('the mound of the three'). The most distorting element, of course, is the general structure of the narrative which was drawn from the *Lebor Gabála*, but some basic traits unconnected with this come through clearly. The two contending races are described as not alien to each other but quite closely related, the Tuatha Dé are obviously masters in magic, and the loss of Nuadhu's arm is of great import. All of these traits occur also in the text on the 'second' battle of Moytirra. This, from the 11th century, is more directly based on the lost 8th century text, and it preserves much more accurately the original lore. Having briefly recounted the pseudo-historical material concerning the victory over the Fir Bolg and how Sreang had cut off the arm of Nuadhu in that battle, the text reverts to its 8th-century source. It relates the cause of the great battle of the Moytirra in Co Sligo, and describes - not without some embellishment of its own - the course of that conflict:-

The Tuatha Dé decided that, since Nuadhu had lost his arm and was thus blemished, the kingship should be taken from him. They conferred it on **Breas**, who was the son of a Tuatha Dé woman and whose father Ealatha was the king of the Fomhóire. In this way the Tuatha Dé hoped to cement friendship with the Fomhóire, and Breas for his part promised to give up the kingship if he misbehaved. Soon, however, with his connivance the Fomhóire began to oppress the Tuatha Dé. They imposed a tribute on every house from which smoke issued, and they forced **Oghma** to carry loads and forced the Daghdha to construct a great rampart around Breas' fortress. Both of these enslaved champions were kept in hunger and misery. When their poet **Cairbre mac Éadaoine** satirised Breas, the Tuatha Dé demanded that the oppressive king should resign. Breas agreed to this, but sought seven years respite, slyly planning to organise a great Fomhóire invasion. He soon quit the country, accompanied by his mother, and went to the northern regions of the world to enlist the support of his father. Ealatha was reluctant to assist him, because he had not ruled Ireland justly, but he directed him to two other Fomhóire magnates, **Balar** and Inneach. These two gathered a great invasion force, and they made a bridge of ships all the way from the Hebrides to Ireland.

Meanwhile, the physician **Dian Céacht** had replaced Nuadhu's severed limb with a silver arm which was 'as mobile as any hand', and the Tuatha Dé therefore reinstalled Nuadhu as their king. The restored monarch held a great banquet at Tara, during which a stranger arrived and demanded entry. This was **Lugh**, maternal grandson of the Fomhóire leader Balar but whose father Cian was of the Tuatha Dé. Lugh gained entry to the feast because he was the master of all arts and, impressed by his stupendous skills, Nuadhu decided to bestow the leadership on Lugh for thirteen days. Lugh accordingly made preparations for the impending clash with the Fomhóire, delegating functions to all the various craftsmen and magicians. For his part, the Daghdha (q.v.) held a tryst with the Mór-Ríoghain and enlisted her help, and then went to the Fomhóire camp in order to gain time for the Tuatha Dé in their preparations. He was mocked and humiliated there, and after he left the camp he encountered another strange woman, with whom he also had intercourse and who also promised magical assistance against the Fomhóire.

The battle was joined at Samhain (the November feast), and each of the Tuatha Dé scions played a special part in the effort. The slaughter was atrocious on both sides, and among those who fell was Nuadhu. Lugh (q.v.) rushed to the forefront of the Tuatha Dé, and began to chant a magical spell. He met and slew his tyrant-grandfather Balar, before the latter could use his destructive eye which had the power to lay low multitudes. The fighting went against the Fomhóire, who took to flight towards the sea. Their poet, Lóch Leathghlas, was spared by Lugh and promised in return that the Fomhóire would never again threaten Ireland and that Lugh's judgements would always be correct. Breas was also captured, and he promised that in Ireland the cows would always have milk and that a harvest of grain would be produced every season. These promises were rejected, however, and Lugh gave him quarter in return for advice on ploughing, sowing, and reaping. Then Lugh and the Daghdha and Oghma followed the Fomhóire to the banqueting-hall of Breas and his father Ealatha, and they recovered the harp of the Daghdha's musician which had been taken. The Daghdha played the three kinds of magical music, lulling the Fomhóire with the sleep-music so that the three could escape. The Daghdha also took away all the cattle which the Fomhóire had seized as tribute in Ireland. The Mór-Ríoghain then announced the great battle-victory to all parts of the country.

The elements of most antiquity in this text have to do with the otherworld clash of a divine race with a demonic one. The principal characters of the Tuatha Dé who are mentioned were all Celtic deities, as appropriate to the exalted atmosphere of such a survival from archaic narrative; and the gaining of agricultural benefits from the Fomhóire parallels a similar theme in the Vedic and Norse versions of the myth, where the defeated races represent the fertility of the soil. Since Nuadhu (q.v.) is central to the Irish story, it may be that it was as part of his cult that the myth was introduced into Ireland. If so, the other deities were soon added to the narrative so as to form a Tuatha Dé leadership. The separate myth of the contest of Lugh (q.v.) with Balar was apparently the latest of these additions, the probable reason for its inclusion being the corresponding agricultural theme. It is noticeable that the battle is claimed to have taken place at the November-feast, and not at Lughnasadh (August), which one would expect if Lugh had had an original part in the narrative. It is likely that Lugh and Balar were already involved in the story when the 8th-century scholar first committed it to writing, but the text as we have it has still not fully synchronised the varying elements, with the result that the role of Nuadhu is somewhat blurred and disjointed. It could indeed be argued that the text itself, which has Lugh as a newcomer into the Tuatha Dé host, reflects the actual history of the narrative.

The tradition of the great battle at Moytirra - with its descriptions of several Celtic deities in the guises of Tuatha Dé characters - is the principle connection between archaic myth and mediaeval lore concerning the otherworld community in Ireland. Other accounts of the 'second' battle, in mediaeval pseudo-history and in a post-mediaeval text, do not differ substantially from the plot given above. There are also echoes from the myth in the *Lebor Gabála* and in redactions of Nennius' *Historia Brittonum* - these echoes have a great tower on a small island in the sea being attacked by a race who inhabit Ireland and are being oppressed by the Fomhóire who live in that tower. The tower is called Tor Chonaing, and in one version the attackers are the people of **Neimheadh**, while in a later version the Tuatha Dé have been substituted for them. A variant, in the *Historia Brittonum*, has a great tower of glass being attacked by the sons of **Míl** when they reached Ireland. This line of tradition can be regarded as having sprung from the myth in its form prior to the work of the 8th-century writer. The idea of the taking of a Fomhóire tower ('tor') by the Tuatha Dé could well have been an early aspect of the myth. The genitive of this word was 'tuir', and as such was easily confused with 'tuir' or 'tuire', meaning 'pillar', a factor which might have given rise to the location of the great battle at the place called Magh Tuire.

There are a number of other texts which preserve, albeit in a confused form, traditions of the Celtic pantheon. For these, and further detail concerning the above materials, see the entries on Áine, Aonghus, Balar, Bóinn, Bran, Brighid, Breas, Cailleach Bhéarra, Cairbre mac Éadaoine, Clíona, Cridhinbhéal, Daghdha, Danu, Dian Céacht, Donn, Éadaoin, Eochaidh, Find, Fionntan, Fomhóire, Goddesses, Goibhniu, Lugh, Macha, Manannán, Midhir, Mór-Ríoghain, Neimheadh, Oghma, Tuatha Dé Danann.

['First' battle] Joseph Fraser in *Ériu 8*, 1-63.

['Second' battle] E A Gray (1982).

[References in *Lebor Gabála*] R A S Macalister (1941), 106-21, 168-73.

[Later version of 'second' battle] Brian Ó Cuív (1945).

[Tower motif] Macalister (1939), 249 and (1940), 122-5, 128-31, 138-43; A G Van Hamel (1932), 21-2.

[General] Ó Cuív in Myles Dillon ed (1968), 27-39; Gerard Murphy in *Éigse 7*, 191-8; Jan de Vries (1961), 148-56.

N

NEARA MAC NIADHAIN Character in the **Ulster Cycle**, who entered the otherworld at Cruachain (Rathcroghan in Co Roscommon).

The text concerning Neara (earlier, Nera) belongs to the 10th century. According to it, queen **Meadhbh** and her husband Ailill mac Máta were feasting in their court at Cruachain at Samhain (November), when Ailill promised to give his gold-hilted sword to the man who would go and place a withe on the leg of a captive who had been hanged on the preceding day. Neara undertook to do so, but the dead man spoke to him and asked to be carried on his back to where he could have a drink. Neara consented to this, but the captive refused to enter any house where a fire had not been raked or wetted or cleaned, and eventually a drink was found for him in a suitable house. When returning home, Neara saw Meadhbh's fortress being attacked and set on fire. He followed the attackers into the otherworld dwelling of Cruachain, where he was given a wife. She explained to him that the fire he had seen was an illusion, but that it would come to pass on the next November vigil, and she told him to warn Meadhbh and Ailill. He did this, and the Connacht warriors accordingly attacked and plundered the otherworld dwelling.

A year later, Neara returned to his wife. The otherworld inhabitants did not realise that it was Neara who had brought the attack on them, so he was welcomed, and his wife gave him a herd of cattle. However, the **Mór-Ríoghain** stole a heifer from him and brought it to be bulled by the great **Donn Cuailnge**. When the heifer was returned, it dropped a bull-calf, which Neara took with him from the otherworld dwelling a year later. When **Fearghus mac Róich** heard the young bull bellowing he prophesied that it would bring disaster. It fought Ailill's white bull, the Finnbheannach, and was slain. Whereupon Neara's otherworld wife and Meadhbh's herdsman both remarked that if the young bull's sire were present the result would have been different. Meadhbh then swore that she would not rest until she saw these two great bulls fighting. Thus the story is presented as a presage of the great cattle-raid of Cooley (see **Ulster Cycle**). Neara returned with his wife to the otherworld dwelling and remained there.

The corpse which speaks and gives information when carried on a man's back seems to have been a common motif in ancient times. It was also used by a mediaeval Irish cleric and made the basis for a quite different narrative, which became very popular in folklore (see **Religious Tales**, Type 764).

Kuno Meyer in *Revue Celtique 10*, 212-28; Séamus Ó Duilearga in Eoin Ua Riain ed (1940), 522-34; Alwyn Rees / Brinley Rees (1961), 298-303.

NÉIDHE MAC ADHNA (earlier, Néde mac Adnai) Fictional or semi-historical poet in early Ireland.

He engaged in a duel in rhetoric with the elder **Feircheirdne** for the office of chief-poet of Ireland. His father Adhna had held that post, but in the contest Néidhe was defeated and he accepted Feircheirdne as his superior. Another text describes a clash between him and his uncle Caier, king of Connacht. We read that Caier had no son and that he therefore adopted Néidhe as his own. The young man, however, plotted with Caier's wife against the king. She informed him that there was a magical prohibition (**'geis'**) on Caier not to give away a special knife which he had. Néidhe accordingly asked him for the knife, and when this was refused he satirised the king so that three blisters of shame arose on his face. This blemish disqualified Caier from holding the **kingship**, and so he went south to Dún Chearmna (near Kinsale, Co Cork) to hide his shame. Néidhe became king of Connacht in his stead, but after a year the poet repented of his action and went to visit his uncle. On seeing him, Caier died from shame. The slab underneath him began to heat and burst into flame, and a piece of it flew up and struck Néidhe in the eye, killing him.

Whitley Stokes CTS (1905); Kuno Meyer (1912), 68-60.

NEIMHEADH Mythical or fictional leader of an imagined ancient settlement in Ireland. The word Neimheadh (earlier, Nemed) was used in the sense of a sacred place or sacred person, and thus seems to have been a designation of a druid.

Neimheadh, it was claimed, arrived thirty years after the people of **Parthalán** had been wiped out by plague. He had a fleet of numerous ships, but on their journey they came across a tower of gold on the sea. Greedy for the gold, they went to take that tower, but the sea rose in a torrent and swept them all away but for one ship. This was Neimheadh's own, and on board with him were his wife Macha and his four sons and their wives, together with twenty others. After a year and a half wandering, they landed in Ireland. Neimheadh defeated the sea-pirates, the **Fomhóire**, in three battles, and he had four scions of that race build the fortress of Ráth Chinneich (somewhere in south Armagh). This they did in one day, and Neimheadh then slew them lest they build a better fortress for somebody else. He himself died from plague on the island of Ard Neimhidh (the Great Island in Cork harbour).

After his death, the Fomhóire oppressed his people, imposing a heavy tribute on them, and eventually Neimheadh's people rebelled and attacked the Fomhóire stronghold of Tor-Inis (Tory Island off the Donegal coast). They captured the tower ('tor') there, but Fomhóire reinforcements arrived and the sea went into flood. So frightful was the slaughter that only one ship of Neimheadh's people managed to get away. On board were thirty warriors, and they decided to leave Ireland completely. This account parallels their earlier effort to seize a tower at sea, and both episodes are an echo of the primordial clash between the **Tuatha Dé Danann** and the Fomhóire (see **Mythological Cycle**). In handling elements of ancient myth, the mediaeval scholars were more concerned with devising a chronological pseudo-history than with avoiding duplication in narrative. These scholars therefore claimed that later groups of settlers in Ireland were descended from Neimheadh's people. We read that one grandson of Neimheadh, called Semeon, went to Greece, where his progeny became the **Fir Bolg**. Another grandson, Beothach, died of plague in Ireland, but his progeny went into the northern parts of the world and became the **Tuatha Dé Danann**. A son of Neimheadh, Fearghus Leathdhearg, went to Britain and - the pseudo-historians claimed - from him and his son Briotan Maol were descended the Britonic people.

Neimheadh himself is probably drawn from genuine tradition. A different story has a personage of the same name being defeated in battle by three sons of **Conaire mac Mogha Lámha** and being buried also on the island of Ard Neimhidh. Given the druidic significance of his name, as well as the name of the goddess **Macha** attributed to his wife, it is likely that he originally belonged to the context of the divine pantheon known as Tuatha Dé Danann (q.v.).

RIA Dictionary s.v. 'neimed'; R S Macalister (1939), 249 and (1940), 115-206; T F O'Rahilly (1946), 75-6; A G Van Hamel in *Zeitschrift für celtische Philologie 10*, 155-60, 182-6.

NÍ MHÁILLE, GRÁINNE MHAOL (c1530-1603) Noblewoman of western Connacht who was famous for her involvement in piracy and intrigue. Her name in English was Grace O'Malley, and her nickname is given in English as Granuaile. Her father was the chieftain of the O'Malley sept of the Owles in Co Mayo, and she was first married to Dónall Ó Flaithearta of Connemara and later to Sir Richard Burke of Burrishoole on Clew Bay.

During her long and eventful career, Gráinne with her small fleet of ships raided along the west coast of Ireland and even as far away as Scotland, survived shifting alliances between Irish and English during the Elizabethan wars, was imprisoned for a while in Limerick and Dublin, and even went on a celebrated visit to Queen **Elizabeth I** in London. Much folklore concerning her and her battles and raids is still current in Connacht. In this she is represented as a formidable and resourceful woman, as indeed she was. One story describes how she gave birth to a son by her second marriage while on board her ship. A Turkish corsair attacked the ship on the very same day, and word of this was passed on to Gráinne by her men. Cursing their ineffectiveness, she jumped from the bed and went out on deck, carrying a brace of blunderbusses. She began to caper about to attract the attention of the Turks, and then emptied the blunderbusses at them, saying 'take this from unchurched hands!' Being thus given the advantage, her men triumphed over the foe. The son born to her on that occasion was Theobald Burke, known as Tioboid 'na long' (i.e. 'of the ships'). She was determined that he should grow up as brave a fighter as herself and it is said that, when he once showed a lack of courage, she remarked to him rather crudely: 'Are you trying to hide in my backside, where you came from?' Her efforts were successful, and Theobald grew up to be a very able soldier.

58. NÍ MHÁILLE, GRÁINNE MHAOL
18th-century representation of Gráinne Mhaol meeting Queen Elizabeth.

When married to Richard Burke, Gráinne operated from two strongholds on Clew Bay, one of them the castle of Carraig an Chabhlaigh (Fleetwood) on the mainland and the other being Clare Island. Various attempts to capture these strongholds by both English and rival Irish failed, and in July 1593 she sailed around the south coast of Ireland and of England and docked at London in order to submit to Elizabeth. Little detail survives of the actual interview between the two strong-willed women, but Gráinne impressed Elizabeth, who confirmed her in her lands and issued restraining orders on her major English enemy in Connacht, Sir Richard Bingham. Tradition fills in the gaps in detail by claiming that Gráinne entered the presence of Elizabeth barefoot and dressed as a Gaelic chieftain. Elizabeth held her hand high, but Gráinne was taller and held her hand higher still, and the two conversed in Latin. A lady-in-waiting noticed that Gráinne required a handkerchief, and one of cambric and lace was given to her. Having used it, Gráinne threw the fine handkerchief into the fire and, when Elizabeth remarked that she should have put it in her pocket, Gráinne expressed dismay at such a lack of cleanliness.

It is said that, on her return journey from England, Gráinne put in to port at Howth in Co Dublin. However, she found the gates of Howth Castle closed before her, as the lord was at dinner and would not be disturbed. In a fit of pique, Gráinne seized the son of that lord and took him captive with her to Connacht. She did not release him until Lord Howth went to her dwelling in Connacht and promised that his castle would henceforth be open to anyone who desired hospitality, an extra plate always being laid on his table for this purpose. There is a reference to such an event in the Annals for the 15th century, when the head of the Burkes of Connacht kidnapped the son of Lord Howth and released him for a nominal ransom, 'to keep the door of his court open at dinnertime'. The story obviously was switched to Gráinne because she was the wife of a successor of that Burke and because of her swashbuckling reputation.

Gráinne was also said to have had a great taste for gambling, her dwelling being a favourite resort for cardplayers and those addicted to dice. Because of her dramatic stature, she came to be regarded in literary tradition as a symbol of the Irish spirit, and the 18th-century Munster poet Seán Clárach Mac Domhnaill used her name for the metaphorical lady Ireland. In subsequent patriotic poetry in both Irish and English 'Gráinne Mhaol' or 'Granuaile' is the most common synonym for the country.

Anne Chambers (1979); Ordnance Survey Letters - Mayo (1838) *1*, 2-12 and *2*, 249-63; Risteard Ó Foghludha (1933), 85-7; IFC passim.

NÍ MHATHÚNA, MÁIRE RUA (c1615-1686) Noblewoman of Co Clare, daughter of the chieftain of the O'Mahony sept. She was married three times and was an astute protector of her lands in the district of Leamaneh, which she inherited from her second and best-known husband Conchubhar Ó Briain. In the period 1661 to 1663 she was put on trial for the murder twenty years earlier of a servant of an English settler, whose livestock she had been raiding, but she was not convicted.

59. NÍ MHATHÚNA, MÁIRE RUA *Contemporary portrait of Máire Rua.*

She married her first husband Dónall Ó Nialláin, who had extensive lands at Dysert O'Dea, but he died five years later, leaving her with four children. She married again within eight months - this time Conchubhar, for whom she gave birth to at least five more children. He was killed fighting against the Cromwellians in 1651. Two years later, she married a Cromwellian officer called John Cooper. In folklore she and her second husband have a sinister reputation which does not seem to accord with their actual characters. It is said that they waylaid and robbed travellers who passed by their castle at Leamaneh, and that they did not hesitate to hang from the castle-walls anybody who fell foul of them. Máire herself, with her flaming red hair, must have been quite a memorable person, but folklore is unfair to her when it claims that she had a dozen husbands. So lustful was she, we are told, that her maid-servants were in reality male lovers in disguise. It can hardly be doubted that such lore has been attached to her from similar notions concerning Queen **Elizabeth I**.

One very popular legend of her, however, is a special development in her own context. We are told that she had in the castle a ferocious stallion which nobody could ride, and that she was wont to challenge wayfarers to mount the animal and in this way bring about their death. Once a young man called Toirealach Ó Lochlainn took up the challenge. When he mounted the horse it tore savagely from its stable and raced from the castle towards the precipitous Cliffs of Moher nearby. Reaching these cliffs, Toirealach strained at the reins and for a moment horse and rider stood poised over the sea far below. The stallion's front feet made a strong impression on the cliff-face, but the rider pulled him away and they raced back towards the castle. Seeing them coming, Máire Rua ordered her servants to close a huge iron gate in their path. Toirealach was pulling so hard on the reins that he broke the stallion's jaw as it jumped the gate, and it crashed and was killed, but the rider survived, much to the chagrin of the malicious Máire Rua. The placename Leamaneh is in Irish 'Léim an Eich', meaning 'the stallion's leap', and there can be little doubt but that an old local tradition connected with the placename became confused with the memory of Máire Rua, thus giving rise to the story.

Máire MacNeill (1990); IFC.

NIALL FRASACH (717-778 AD) Son of **Fearghal mac Maoldúin**, and high-king of Ireland from the year 743 to 770.

His mother was Fearghal's queen, the daughter of a midland king, and we read that she was the gentlest woman in Ireland. She was barren for a long time, but conceived after a holy nun had prayed for her. Niall's epithet refers to a shower ('fras') which fell when he was born at his father's residence at Fathain (Fahan in north Donegal). This was developed in the literature, which claims that, at his birth, a shower of honey fell in Leinster and showers of silver and wheat fell at Fathain. We read that, as he grew up, he was remarkably polite and respectful to his father, and in this was a striking contrast to his elder brother **Aodh Allán**. As high-king he was extremely

60. NIALL FRASACH *Wall of the circular fort Grianán Aileach.*

generous, his subjects were happy, and there was plenty of 'fruit and produce and corn and milk'. One annalistic source has it that a great famine was in progress when he began his reign, and that he along with seven bishops fell on their knees and prayed earnestly to God for their people. Three showers then fell from heaven - one of silver, one of honey, and one of wheat which covered all the fields. This is clearly a development from the earlier motifs.

A story of an unusual kind is told of him in a text of the 11th-12th century. According to this, a young woman carrying a baby came to him at the great assembly of Tailtiu (Teltown, Co Meath) as he was watching the horse-racing there. She said that the baby was hers, but she did not know who the father was, for she had not been involved with a man. Niall thought for a while, and then enquired if she had dallied with another woman. She said that she had, and then the king explained that the other woman must have had intercourse with a man beforehand. In this way the baby's father was discovered. Just then, a phantom descended from the air amidst the assembly, causing everybody to flee. Niall stood his ground, and the phantom explained to him that he was a priest who had made a contract with a strange craftsman who had offered to do the woodwork on a house for him. The stranger had been a demon and, when he sought as payment that the priest bow to him, the former did so. He had thus unwittingly put himself into the power of demons, who carried him away and kept him for seven years. They had been passing through the air at that very moment, and when the demons felt the effect of the true judgement given by Niall they had fled in fear, leaving their captive free.

This story shows how the native ideal of true **kingship** was combined in the person of Niall with the ideal of Christian holiness. His reputation for piety was high, and another common designation for him was Niall Condail - the epithet here meaning 'prudent' or 'pure-minded'. It seems to have been well-deserved, for he resigned the throne in 770 and spent the remainder of his life as a monk at the monastery founded by **Colm Cille** in Iona.

John O'Donovan (1860), 20-33; Whitley Stokes in *Irische Texte 3*, 340-1, 416; R A S Macalister (1956), 384-7, 392-3; Denis Murphy (1896), 121; R I Best / M A O'Brien (1967) *5*, 1202-3; David Greene in *Saga och Sed* (1976), 30-7; Kuno Meyer in *Zeitschrift für celtische Philologie 8*, 102-3; P S Dinneen (1908) *3*, 144-5, 150-3; F J Byrne (1973), 156-7.

NIALL NAOI-GHIALLACH Historical king of **Tara**. The exact dates of his reign are unclear. Some sources date it from 379 to 405 AD, but there are reasons to believe that it was somewhat later. The true date of his death seems to have been around 454 AD. His real name was probably Nél (literally, 'cloud'), which was of mythical origin and would have been given to him for purposes of prestige. The change to Niall was probably due to the phonemic influence of 'giall' in his epithet. This epithet (earlier, Noigiallach) means 'having nine hostages', and reflects the power and success of his career. In mediaeval times, it was fancifully interpreted to mean that he had a hostage from each of the five provinces of Ireland, as well as one hostage each from the Scots, the Saxons, the Britons, and the Franks.

61. NIALL NAOI-GHIALLACH *Iron collar for hostages.*

Niall was leader of the predominant Connachta sept (see **Conn Céadchathach**) and was the first of a long dynasty who claimed to be high-kings of Ireland. They were known from him as Uí Néill ('descendants of Niall'), and were the most powerful family in the country for almost 600 years after his death. Niall was famous, or infamous, for his raiding abroad, and it may have been on one of his raids that the boy **Patrick** was seized in Britain and brought as a captive to Ireland. Niall was stated to be son of Eochu Muighmheadhon, whose sobriquet seems to mean 'lord of slaves'. That he preceded his son in such activity is strongly suggested by the description of Niall's own mother as a captive girl whom Eochu took in Britain and made his concubine. Her name confirms the authenticity of this tradition, for she is called Caireann (earlier, Cairenn), which is a hibernicisation of the Latin name Carina. Eochu may have been, as described in the literature, king of Tara, but if so he probably was the first of the Connachta sept to have gained control of that citadel.

The role of Niall in the political history of early Ireland was crucial, and knowledge of his biography would therefore be of great value, but the accounts which the literature gives of his birth and youth are fanciful. We read that he was the youngest of five sons of Eochu, the other four being born of the king's legal wife, Mongfhind. She wished to keep their full inheritance for her own sons, and so she reduced Caireann (also called Caireall) to slavery, compelling her to draw water from a well daily. Caireann's child was born in the open air as she lay beside her pail, and nobody dared care for her for fear of Mongfhind. Ravens were already gathering above the child when a **poet** called Torna came by and picked him up. Torna foresaw the future, and he took the infant Niall with him and reared him. When Niall was of age, Torna brought him to Tara. They met Caireann, and she was carrying water as usual. Niall told her to leave that task, and he brought her with him and clothed her in a purple robe.

Mongfhind called on Eochu to judge between all his five sons. He referred the matter to a druidic smith Síthcheann, who contrived to set fire to a forge in which the young men were working. Each of them emerged carrying some implements, but Niall had the anvil, and Síthcheann therefore proclaimed him the greatest. Then one day the five were together hunting in the forest, when they came upon a fearfully ugly hag at a well. She refused water to all but the one who would kiss her cheek. Niall embraced her and lay down with her on the grass. She immediately became a beautiful girl, and explained that she was sovereignty (see **kingship**). Under her instructions, he gave water to his brothers only on condition that they allow him to place his weapons higher than theirs in Tara. Niall related this at his father's court, and when the brothers publicly accepted his primacy, Síthcheann announced that Niall and his descendants would have dominion over Ireland.

A variant account has Mongfhind dreaming that her four sons were fighting - Brian in the form of a lion, Fiachra a greyhound, Ailill a beagle, and Fearghus a cur. Brian prevailed, and Síthcheann explained this to her as meaning that he would be the greatest of the four. When Eochu died, there was a struggle between these four and Niall for the succession. Seeing that Brian was not prevailing, Mongfhind persuaded the men of Ireland - by entreaty and by sorcery - to give the kingship to her own brother Criomhthann. When Criomhthann was away on his royal circuit, however, Mongfhind's four sons divided the kingdom amongst them and, on his return, Mongfhind proffered a poisoned drink to him. He compelled her to quaff first, which she did, and both of them died. Notwithstanding all her scheming, however, Niall was chosen as king. Brian became his champion in battle, seizing hostages and levying tribute for him. These accounts of Niall's youth show clearly the influence of popular narrative. As in usual in folklore, the socially weakest man triumphs over his fellows, and the oral motif of disenchantment by a kiss is deftly used in conjunction with the Irish literary theme of the goddess of sovereignty.

The folkloric and romantic elements predominate in the literature concerning Niall, and there is little by way of description of his actual reign or of his conquests. He is said to have gone to Letha (i.e. Brittany) and to Italy 'to seek a kingdom', but his real achievements abroad amounted to little more than raids on the west coast of Britain. His achievements at home were more significant, though these have been subsumed in accounts of three fictional personages who are each called **Colla**. These Collas, it was claimed, were cousins of Niall's grandfather Muireadhach Tíreach, and the tradition was that it was they who destroyed the northern citadel of Eamhain Mhacha (see **Ulster Cycle**) and seized the adjacent south Ulster territory of Airghialla. All the indications are that these actions were in fact carried out by Niall and his sons in the 5th century. Although he was reputed to be the high-king of Ireland, it is unlikely that Niall's power extended far into the south of the country, but this did not prevent the mediaeval writers from describing how he gained the overlordship of Munster also by a speedy invasion of that province.

The death of Niall was the subject of a saga which stressed his adventures overseas. We read that one Eochu, son of the Leinster king Éanna Cinsealach, was refused food at the house of Niall's poet Laidcheann. In anger, Eochu burned the poet's house and slew his son. Laidcheann satirised Leinster for this, so that that province was deprived of all growth and foliage for a year. Niall in retaliation invaded Leinster, and would not desist until Eochu was promised to him as a hostage. The Leinstermen tied Eochu to a stone pillar at Ath Fhadat (Ahade, Co Carlow), and Niall sent a troop of nine men to take him. When these men attempted to slay him, however, Eochu broke loose and wielded his chain against them. Some Leinstermen slew the nine, and as a result Niall came again into the province. Eochu was surrendered to him but when Laidcheann began again to satirise Leinster, the hostage slew the poet with a stone-throw. Eochu was then banished from Ireland for as long as Niall lived. Soon after this, Niall was on a campaign in Scotland and was invited to the dwelling of the king of that country who wished to submit to him. While sojourning there in the company of Pictish bards, he fell victim to an arrow shot at him by the exiled Eochu. A variant account locates the episode in the Alps, claiming that Niall had advanced that far in his conquests and that Eochu shot the arrow at him from long range across a valley. The Alps have clearly been substituted here for Alba i.e. Scotland, or in the early literature the whole island of Britain. Yet another tradition was that Niall was slain by Eochu in the English Channel ('muir nIocht') on the last of seven great expeditions abroad. Niall's men brought his body back to Ireland, triumphing in seven battles 'before his face after his death'. One account has them raising the body of the king aloft before the enemy in battle so as to ensure victory. He was buried at Ochann (Faughan hill, near Navan in Co Meath) and, on hearing news of the great king's demise, his faithful poet Torna fell dead from grief. Although these accounts date from several centuries after Niall's time, there is no special reason to reject their testimony that Niall was slain by a Leinster exile while raiding in Britain.

[Floruit] James Carney (1973), 7-13.

[Name] T F O'Rahilly (1946), 232-3.

[Birth and youth] Kuno Meyer in *Otia Merseiana 2*, 75-6; Whitley Stokes in *Revue Celtique 24*, 190-207; S H O'Grady (1892) *1*, 326-36; Maud Joynt in *Ériu 4*, 91-111.

[Disenchantment by kiss] Stith Thompson (1955-

1958), Motif D735. See also same motif in T P Cross (1952).

[Reign] O'Rahilly (1946), 222-5; Pól Breathnach in *Irisleabhar Muighe Nuadhat* 1932, 43-52 and *ibid* 1933, 34-41; Lambert McKenna (1918) *1*, 4-11.

[Death] Meyer in *Otia Merseiana 2*, 84-92; Edward Gwynn (1906), 36-41; Stokes in *Revue Celtique 15*, 295-7; M A O'Brien (1962), 122.

[General] R A S Macalister (1956), 342-9, 528-9; F J Byrne (1973), 70-86; O'Rahilly, *op cit*, 209-34; L P Ó Caithnia (1984), 118-9.

NÓINE A wonder-child described in early mediaeval Irish texts. His name and lore show signs of being confused memories of a more comprehensive tradition.

One account, found in the early Munster genealogies, describes how a druid told a king called Dáire mac Deadha that, if his daughter gave birth to a son, the king himself would die. Dáire accordingly watched her closely, but despite his efforts she conceived by Mac ind Óc (i.e. **Aonghus**). She was pregnant for nine years, and then the son was born. He had long locks and a curly beard, and uttered nine sayings immediately after his birth, following which Dáire died. It is clear that this plot derives from the **Lugh** myth of a prophesied wonder-child who will kill its tyrant grandfather. That Aonghus has been a spontaneous introduction into the account is evidenced by another version, which does not mention him but gives a few other details. According to this, Noíne's mother was Finghile, daughter of Dáire mac Deadha, to whom a druid had made the prophesy. One day the girl was playing on the seashore with the daughter of Noídhean mac Noímhaill, when a phantom came in from the sea and made her pregnant. When her child, called Noíndiu, was born Dáire died. The child gave nine audacious commands to its mother, and then itself died 'for it is not lawful for a son to argue with his mother'. The moralistic twist to the end of the story, and the child's own sudden death, we can take to be an addition, but in general this version seems to be nearer to the original story than the other.

The motif of the sea-spirit as father is probably borrowed from the birth-story of **Mongán**, but the location on the beach suggests a connection with seer-lore, and it echoes a similar location in the story of **Morann**, who also speaks immediately after birth when he is thrown into the water and survives. The motif of the hairy child is found also in the Mongán story, where it seems to be borrowed from lore of **Fionn mac Cumhaill**. The original form of the name must have been Noídhiu (genitive, Noídhean), meaning 'child', and indeed this occurs in the above text as a designation of another character. Because of a misinterpretation of the name, the number of statements uttered by the child was claimed to have been nine ('noí'). This number, of course, would be imagined as especially relevant to the idea of child-birth, and it is stressed by the claim that Noíne was nine years in his mother's womb. In the case of Fionn (q.v.), we read that he was conceived nine hours before his father's death. In fact, there is good reason to suspect that the child Noíne was originally identical with Fionn. In one text, his father's name is given as Umhall, the name also given to Fionn's father in some early sources; and his tyrant grandfather Dáire also occurs as an alternative name of Fionn's grandfather. Noíne seems therefore to have been an emanation from Fionn, and the original but lost story of him may actually have been an account of Fionn's birth.

Julius Pokorny in *Zeitschrift für celtische Philologie 12*, 331-3; Rudolf Thurneysen in *ibid 20*, 192-200; M A O'Brien (1962), 189, 288; Gerard Murphy (1953), lxxix.

NORSEMEN (or Vikings) The Scandinavian warriors who raided and settled in Ireland from the 8th to the 11th century, and in some scattered instances later still. The usual term for them in Irish is 'Lochlannaigh', but in the literature they were also referred to as 'Danair' and 'Gaill'. The latter term was the general one for foreign oppressors - it being, curiously, derived from the Latin word for the Gauls, who were like the Irish a Celtic people. In ordinary hiberno-English speech the Norse warriors were invariably remembered as 'the Danes'.

The greatest Irish victory over the Norsemen was gained by **Brian Boru** at the battle of Clontarf in the year 1014. A few generations later, a text entitled *Cogadh Gaedheal re Gallaibh* was written for his successors, and the description of the Norsemen given in that text became the standard one known to Irish literary and oral tradition. With much justification, the Norse were portrayed in the text as extremely oppressive. A precedent for the image of such raiders was already in Irish tradition viz. the oppression of the mythical race **Tuatha Dé Danann** by the sea-predators known as **Fomhóire**, and so the Norsemen were cast in the mould of the latter. The Fomhóire imposed heavy taxes on each household of the Tuatha Dé, and the Norsemen were claimed to have done likewise to the Irish. In addition they were described as ravaging the countryside, devastating churches, and seizing young men and women as slaves. They placed their stewards over every territory, quartered one of their soldiers in each house, and demanded the choice of the country's food produce.

This description in the *Cogadh* text gave rise to folk rationalisations of the oppressive power of the Norsemen and of its consequences. For instance, the text stated that they levied on the Irish each year 'an ounce of silver for every nose', and in folklore this is developed into a claim that they cut off the noses of those Irish people who would not pay taxes to them. A common motif concerning oppressors was introduced on a similar basis - we are told that their leaders demanded the right to sleep on the first night with any young bride of an Irishman. The harshness of the oppression became proverbial in expressions like 'as stubborn as a Dane' and 'as cruel as a Dane', and these Norsemen were said to have been rugged and savage in their habits. Adjectives derived from their appellations had similar nuances, such as 'danardha' (used in the sense 'fierce') and 'gallda' ('strong' or 'rough'). Special emphasis was placed on the colour of their hair, a distinction being made in the literature between fair-haired Norsemen ('fionn-Ghaill') and dark-haired ones ('dubh-Ghaill'). Both colours were considered extraordinary in mediaeval Ireland, when the conceit was that brown hair was the true mark of native descent. Similar ideas survive in folklore. Thus, whereas red hair was common enough in Ireland since early times, it is popularly supposed to be of Norse origin. Many Irish surnames are, of course, of Norse derivation, and according to folk speculation families with these surnames have certain notable traits. These include strong and rough hair, quick tempers, sharp intelligence, tall stature, and proud bearing.

The environment is fancifully held to contain much evidence from the Norse epoch. Though usually associated with the **fairies**, many of the raths which dot the countryside are claimed to have been constructed by these 'Danes', and prehistoric flints and arrow-heads found near raths are in such cases claimed to have been artefacts left by them. The tendency to assimilate the Norsemen to the fairies is instanced also in late mediaeval literary sources, which have the **Fianna** warriors engaged in battle with invading Viking armies as well as in conflict with the otherworld community. Several of the animals, too, were fancifully associated with the Norsemen. The weasels were said to have been their cats, the foxes their dogs, and they were reputed to have first brought hens to Ireland.

A curious belief, prevalent throughout the country, was that the inhabitants of Scandinavia never abandoned their claims to the land won by the sword in Ireland. According to this, they have preserved from generation to generation charters and legal documents made out to their ancestors, in the hope of one day returning to Ireland and reclaiming their many estates. In fact, the Norse settlements in Ireland - such as at Dublin, Wexford, Waterford, and Limerick - continued to flourish through the Middle Ages until fully assimilated into the native population. Disregarding this, one very popular and dramatic legend describes how, after the battle of Clontarf, only two Norsemen survived - an old man and his son. They were the only two people who knew the secret method which the Vikings had of making beer from wild heather. The old man refused to divulge the secret, but when threatened with torture he relented. He asked, however, that his son should first be killed, for he could not bear the shame of letting his son see him submit. The son was accordingly put to death, but then the old man refused to give the information and was himself slain. He had tricked the Irish and thus brought the secret to the grave with him. This story parallels a mediaeval Norse account of the Rhinegold and how the hero Hogni preserved the secret of where it is buried. Presumably the plot passed into Irish tradition of the Norsemen through that story being overheard, and partly understood, by some Irish person present at a Viking drinking-feast where the beer flowed freely. Perhaps the same ultimate source gave rise to the common idea that treasure was hidden somewhere in Ireland by the Norsemen, but that it has never been found.

J H Todd (1867), 40-53; Reidar Christiansen (1931) and in *Lochlann 2*, 137-64; Bo Almqvist (1975) and in *Arv 21*, 115-35; L-M Smith in *Ulster Folklife 25*, 103-12.

NUADHU Mythical king of the **Tuatha Dé Danann**. The meaning of the name (earlier, Nuadu) is unclear, but the most likely interpretation would be 'catcher'. A cognate in British Celtic was the name of the deity Nodons, to whom a temple was dedicated at Lydney in Gloucestershire. Several representations of dogs were found at the temple, which factor suggests that he was envisaged as a hunter, but in particular there was the figure of a man in the act of hooking a fish.

62. NUADHU *Pre-Christian statue of the god Nuadhu from Co. Armagh.*

In early Irish tradition Nuadhu was associated with the Boyne, being married to the eponymous goddess of the river, **Bóinn**. He was displaced through a trick from his residence at Brugh na Bóinne (the Newgrange tumulus) by the Mac Óg (i.e. **Aonghus**), and went to live at the nearby rath called Sídh Chleitigh. Since the Mac Óg is probably cognate with the British Celtic deity Maponos, and since both Nodons and Maponos were popular in northern England, it may well be that lore of the two deities reached Ireland at the same time. In the first battle of Moytirra (see **Mythological Cycle**) Nuadhu is described as the king of the Tuatha Dé who led them into Ireland, and it is therefore apparent that the myth - represented by that battle - of a struggle between the divine and demonic races was part of his cult.

The tradition concerning this battle has Nuadhu losing an arm and having to resign the kingship because of his blemish. The physician **Dian Céacht** magically made a silver arm for him, as good and manageable as any other arm, and as a result he was restored to the kingship. The import of this arm-motif is difficult to decipher, but it must reflect ancient lore. Similarly ancient must be the idea that the well at the source of the Boyne belonged to him. This well was said to have been in the Sídh (otherworld dwelling) of Nechtan. The origin of the name Nechtan is unclear, but it most probably contains an ancient word for water ('necht'). At any rate, it was from early times regarded as a pseudonym for Nuadhu, who was also known as Nuadhu Necht. Another well-known pseudonym for him was Elcmar (later, Ealcmhar) which meant 'the envious one'. This designation probably sprang from the triumph of the Mac Óg over him.

His association with water parallels the engraving connected with Nodons at Lydney. There is, indeed, a striking similarity between the hooked fish at Lydney and a mediaeval story which connects Nuadhu with a mystical salmon in the river Boyne. This salmon was claimed to have become a source of wisdom from eating nuts which fell from hazel-trees at the well of Nechtan. From the salmon the young **Fionn mac Cumhaill** gained knowledge in a striking account which has him tasting it by chance, whereas it was intended for an elderly seer called Finnéigeas. The full name of this seer is elsewhere given as Nuadhu Finneigéas, and the story was obviously suggested by the myth of how the youngster called Mac Óg got the dwelling of Newgrange from Nuadhu. The whole development can best be explained by supposing that the image of Nuadhu and his fish was super-imposed onto the earlier lore of Fionn's wisdom. Considering that Fionn (earlier, **Find**) was a cult figure at the river Boyne from a quite archaic period in the Celtic culture of Ireland, it is likely that the whole lore of Nuadhu was introduced into the region at some time in the final centuries BC.

A further development from this fusion was to make Nuadhu a maternal ancestor of Fionn. According to the mediaeval literature, when he came of age Fionn gained possession by force of Nuadhu's fortress on the hill of Almhu (Allen, Co Kildare). Some influence from the **Lugh** myth is involved here, but the basis must again be the contest between Nuadhu and the Mac Óg. Another result of the Fionn connection was the frequent designation of Nuadhu as 'Nuadhu Find', the epithet being interpreted to mean 'white'. We are accordingly told that Nuadhu whitened the walls of his fortress at Almhu with lime. He was regarded by the Leinstermen as their ancestor, and his removal from Sídh Chleitigh to Almhu was clearly part of the process by which the Leinstermen carried the cult of Fionn south with them when they were expelled from the Boyne valley by the Connachta (see **Fionn mac Cumhaill**). Further development of the Nuadhu lore is evidenced by the designation Nuadhu Find Feimhin (referring to the plain of Feimhean in Co Tipperary), and according to which he was claimed to reside in the cairn on Slievenamon. This resulted from the borrowing of Leinster ideology and lore by the ruling Eoghanacht sept in Munster during the 7th century, a factor which caused them also to claim descent from Nuadhu. The Eoghanacht were finding common cause with the Leinstermen in their opposition to the growing power of the Connachta - Uí Néill. This accounts for the pseudonym Mugh Nuadhat ('servant of Nuadhu'), given by the Eoghanacht to their ancestor **Eoghan Mór**, whom they represented as contending with the ancestor of the Connachta, **Conn Céadchathach**.

A more general designation is Nuadhu Find Fáil, which may derive from the early Boyne valley context, for the stone of Fál was the symbol of kingship at **Tara**. This stone was, according to tradition, brought to Ireland by the Tuatha Dé with Nuadhu as their king. They also brought a great 'sword of Nuadhu', from which no opponent could escape and no wound inflicted by which could be healed. It seems likely that originally Nuadhu's blemishing involved a sacrifice or an accident with his own weapon. No such account survives, but it may be that some type of curative water-symbolism was involved and that his arm was a metonym for a river. Mediaeval Irish literature had its own rationale for the blemish. According to it, Nuadhu's right arm was severed in combat between Nuadhu and the Fir Bolg warrior Sreang at the first battle of Moytirra. Other Tuatha Dé warriors intervened to save Nuadhu and he was carried from the field. He and Sreang resumed their combat in the battle next day. He asked Sreang to tie up his own right hand so as to ensure fair terms, but Sreang refused, and in order to prevent fatal injury to Nuadhu the Tuatha Dé offered the province of Connacht to Sreang and his Fir Bolg. **Breas** then became king of the Tuatha Dé, but after seven years Dian Céacht made the silver arm for Nuadhu and he was restored. Nuadhu gave authority over his army to the newcomer **Lugh** in the second battle of Moytirra, a battle in which he himself was slain by **Balar**. A post-mediaeval writer (probably 15th century) composed a romance the title of which claimed it to be the history of Nuadhu Find Feimhin. Here Nuadhu is represented as son of a Gaelic king of Ireland called Giallchadh who resides at Tara. Giallchadh is a widower, and he marries a young lady of his son's age. Egged on by her malicious maidservant, she makes sexual advances to Nuadhu, but he forcefully rejects her. Then she pretends to Giallchadh that his son has molested her, and Nuadhu has to flee before his father's army. He fights stupendously whenever confronted and takes refuge on the island of Gola (off the Donegal coast). There he encounters and overcomes a force of Norsemen who are coming to invade Ireland, and he sails away from the country. Meanwhile, his father's druid discovers the truth about the allegations against him but, on finding the remains of a Norse prince who resembles Nuadhu, it is presumed that the young hero is dead. Nuadhu gains several great victories abroad, and returns to Ireland at the head of a huge force. When he identifies himself, he is welcomed and inherits the kingship. The writer of this text had obviously read an account of the adventures of Eoghan Mór (q.v.), and he combined that with the 'Potiphar's Wife' plot which was quite popular in mediaeval Irish literature (see **Romantic Tales**, Type 870C). This comparatively late literary treatment of Nuadhu is somewhat strained, and Nuadhu was unknown in the post-mediaeval folklore.

T F O'Rahilly (1946), 278-81, 321-3, 467-8, 558; Anne Ross (1974), 230-3, 465; James Carey in *Zeitschrift für celtische Philologie 40*, 1-22; Joseph Frazer in *Ériu 8*, 46-7, 52-9; E A Gray (1982), 24-7, 32-3, 40-3, 60-1, 130-1; R A S Macalister (1941), 110-25; M A O'Brien (1962), 117, 120, 714-5; Kuno Meyer in *Anecdota from Irish Manuscripts 1*, 30.

[The name Nechtan] Jord Pinault in *Ogam 16*, 221-3; P K Ford in G J Larson (1974), 67-74.

[Late romance] Kate Müller-Lisowski in *Zeitschrift für celtische Philologie 13*, 195-250.

O

Ó CAOIMH, DÓNALL NA CÁSCA Outlaw who flourished in north-west Co Cork in the latter part of the 17th century and whose memory survives strongly in the lore of that area. The surname is anglicised as O'Keeffe, and Dónall was of noble stock, but the precise import of his nickname 'na Cásca' (literally 'of Easter') is unclear, unless it refers to his birth on an Easter Sunday.

He is represented as being forced into hiding by the victorious Williamites, and as carrying out repeated cattle-raids against them from his mountainous retreat near the town of Cullen. He also had a hide-out further south, a cave in the side of a huge cliff at Gortmore near Mallow. To gain access to this, one had to swim the river Blackwater and climb along the rock face. He had a lover called Máiréad Ní Cheallaigh (Margaret Kelly), who informed on him to a handsome English army officer. It was arranged that she would induce Dónall to a place where he could be captured, but Dónall, while embracing his loved one, found to his consternation that she had a letter in her bosom from the English officer. In a mad fit of anger, he ran her through with his sword. Several other accounts were current regarding his escapes and his marvellous horsemanship. For instance, when captured once, he secreted a sword inside his clothes and later used this to cut the ropes which bound him. It was also said that he escaped a pursuing band of cavalrymen by having his horse leap over a large precipice. We are told that his final betrayal was effected by a man who was in his close confidence. This man invited him to a meal in his house, at the same time apprising the soldiers of the situation. The man's wife, however, gave Dónall the hint during the meal by remarking 'caith fuar agus te' which means 'eat up both cold and warm', but sounds exactly the same as 'caith fuar agus teith' ('eat it cold and flee!') Dónall raced from the house, but he was shot down by the soldiers.

The stories concerning Dónall na Cásca are typical of outlaw-lore both in Ireland and abroad, which has recurring motifs such as marvellous escapes and betrayal by a woman or a close male confidant. The ambiguous hint concerning the food was common in such stories about different outlaws throughout Ireland, and the usual result is the escape rather than the capture of the fugitive.

Geoffrey Strachan (1904), 101-5; Anon in *The Shamrock 11*, 83; Dáithí Ó hÓgáin (1985), 179-81, 338; IFC.

Ó CONCHUBHAIR, CATHAL CROBHDHEARG (+1224) King of the province of Connacht from 1201 until his death. He succeeded his elder half-brother Ruairí Ó Conchubhair, who was the last native high-king of Ireland but had been deposed by the Norman invaders and reduced to the kingship of Connacht only. Cathal Crobhdhearg was an astute politician and managed to hold his lands in fealty to, but largely independent of, the kings who ruled from London.

His epithet Crobhdhearg means 'red-handed', and he did indeed have a red birthmark on his left hand, which he ordinarily kept covered with a glove. We know this from an inauguration ode composed for him by his professional poet. The poet makes it clear also that this red hand was taken as a messianic sign, and it is clear that Cathal had borrowed some of the imagery of the prophesied **Aodh Eangach** and was having it applied to himself. His Uí Chonchubhair (O'Connor) sept were of the same basic stock as the Uí Néill high-kings, but for a century and a half after the death of **Brian Boru** in 1014 the different leading families in Ireland had vied for the high-kingship. Thus, an Uí Néill prophecy in 1167 claimed that Aodh Eangach would destroy Cruachain (Rathcroghan, Co Roscommon), the ancient seat of Connacht kingship and headquarters of the Uí Chonchubhair. Now, Cathal's poet in 1201 turned this prophecy about, claiming that 'the red-handed one has come to Cruachain, I see the sign on his hand', and went on to describe how Ireland was becoming fruitful again because of this new **kingship** of Cathal.

A direct echo of Cathal's propaganda is found in an oral epical tale of his birth which survived until recently in the folklore of the western province. It tells of how the king of Connacht had no son by his wife, but that he got a girl called Gearróg Ní Mhóráin with child. The queen was very angry at this and she got a hag who was skilled in magic to set a charm to prevent the girl giving birth. The hag tied three intricate knots in a string and gave it to the queen, saying that the baby would not be born until these knots were removed. Gearróg was just beginning to give birth when the third knot was tied, and only the hand of the baby had emerged from its mother. Time passed, and mother and child remained in this critical situation. Then a wise man, who realised what had happened, went to the queen and told her that the girl had given birth. Believing him, the queen cursed the old hag and flung the string into the fire. It was burned, and immediately the child was born. This was Cathal, and his hand was red from the circumstances of his birth. As he grew up, he and his mother were repeatedly persecuted by the queen, but the clergy took him from one monastery to another to protect him from the hostile agents. Eventually, things got so bad that he and his mother had to flee the province altogether. They went to Leinster, where the young Cathal supported them both by doing servile work. To conceal his identity, he always wore a glove on his red hand. Yet he could not totally hide his nature, and his fellow-labourers often chided him, for as they applied themselves to their tasks, he was wont to be constantly talking of kings and wars and raiding. Then, when he was working at the harvest one day, a crier came by announcing that the Connacht king was dead, and that the council of the province had proclaimed that the fugitive Cathal, if he was still living, should be enthroned. Hearing this, Cathal threw away his glove and, revealing his red hand, said: 'goodbye to the sickle, now for the sword!' He and his mother then returned home and he was installed king. He never forgot how churchmen had protected him in his youth, and therefore as king became a great patron of the monasteries.

In actual fact, Cathal's father Toirdhealbhach was married three times and had children by each marriage. Cathal was a son of the second wife Dearbhfhorgaill, who married Toirdhealbhach in 1131 and who died in 1151. This must have been very close to Cathal's birth, and perhaps she died giving birth to him, although it might be that Cathal was in fact born of another woman outside wedlock. The high-king Ruairí was a son of Toirdhealbhach's first marriage, and Cathal had to contend with the family of this older stepbrother in order to gain and retain power, a factor which could lie behind the hostility of the stepmother in the folk story. His special patronisation of the monasteries is a historical fact, and the annals tell us that he actually died in the habit of a friar. Such elements, combined with Cathal's own messianic portrayal of his red hand, were at some stage - probably after his death - set within the plot structure of the Hercules myth, thus giving rise to the folk epic.

63. Ó CONCHUBHAIR, CATHAL CROBHDHEARG *Ballintober Abbey in Co. Mayo, founded by Cathal Crobhdhearg.*

E C Quiggin in Osborn Bergin / Carl Marstrander (1912), 167-77; John O'Donovan / C O O'Conor Don (1891), 80-92; O'Donovan (1848-51), 210-4; Brian Ó Cuív in *Celtica 19*, 31-54 and in *Ériu 34*, 157-74; Dáithí Ó hÓgáin (1985), 127-32, 333-4 and in *Léachtaí Cholm Cille 14*, 192-3.

O'CONNELL, DANIEL (1775-1847) Irish political leader and brilliant lawyer, who won Catholic Emancipation from the British Parliament in 1829. He organised huge public meetings in an attempt to have the Act of Union between Ireland and England repealed, one of which at **Tara** in 1843 was attended by close on half a million people. Born into a prosperous old Gaelic family who resided at Derrynane in Co Kerry, his name in Irish was Dónall Ó Conaill. Dubbed by the newspapers 'the Liberator', he was better known to the ordinary people as 'the Counsellor'.

A large number of anecdotes were told in folklore concerning Daniel in every part of Ireland. These centre chiefly on his skill as defence counsel in legal cases, but several also deal with his career as a Member of Parliament at Westminster. Sometimes his portrayal reaches epical proportions, as in a tradition that the mountains of his native area pealed out a thunderous echo at his birth. This birth, it was claimed, was God's reward to his parents for a good deed. It was said that they had once taken shelter from rain at a tumble-down church and, seeing how badly the place was in need of repair, they made a present of money to the local priest. The priest told the couple that they would have a baby son who would be the champion of Ireland. The ecclesiastical authorities were reticent about supporting Daniel at first, but as he became successful the Catholic clergy came to play a leading part in his organisation throughout the country and assisted him in fundraising. This close connection between him and the ecclesiastical world in reflected in folk legends of him. One tradition, for instance, claims that his cloak held a cure and that many people were healed of ailments by touching it - a direct borrowing from the Gospel account of how a woman was cured by touching the mantle of Christ.

64. O'CONNELL, DANIEL *Contemporary portrait of 'the Liberator'.*

Much ordinary narrative lore was also borrowed into his portrayal. For example, we are told that when he was a youngster, a very difficult law-case was in progress locally. The case involved a man who was suing another for the loss of an eye, whereas the eye had in fact been lost accidentally through being caught by a fish-hook. This had happened when the plaintiff was being saved from drowning by the other man, who had thrown the fishing-line to him. The judge was unable to decide on the case, but he chanced to overhear some children acting out the courtroom drama as they played. One little boy, Daniel, was acting the part of the judge, and he ruled that the plaintiff should be put back into the water, and if he could save himself without the help of the fishing-line, then he should be allowed damages against the other man. Realising that this was the correct verdict, the judge ruled accordingly, and the plaintiff dropped his case. This is in fact a version of an ordinary folktale, which has become attached to O'Connell.

Another such instance of a borrowed folktale concerns how a poor man emigrates to America, and before boarding the ship is given a meal of fried eggs by a certain woman. Years later, that man returns home, having become very rich, and the woman sues him for a large sum. She claims that if she had kept the eggs herself, they would have multiplied and she would now have a big chicken-farm. Daniel is engaged to argue the man's case for him, and he does so by producing peas in the courtroom and attempting to sow them in the wooden floor. When the judge demands an explanation of his behaviour, Daniel says that the peas would have the same chance of sprouting from the floor as the boiled eggs would have had of hatching out chickens. He thus wins the case. Yet another such story has Daniel defending a will against dishonest relatives of the deceased, who claimed that a later will had been prepared. Suspecting a trick, he asked one of these relatives was the will made while the dead man was still alive, and received the answer that it was 'while there was life in him'. The truth flashed across Daniel's mind, and he enquired 'was it the life that God put in him?' The imposter had to admit that it was not, but that a fly had been inserted into the dead man's mouth while his hand was guided to sign the will.

By his brilliant legal skills, the historical O'Connell often upset the odds in court cases. Particularly striking were his successes in bringing large numbers of people from the gallows, such as those charged in the Doneraile Conspiracy trial and the trials following the Carrickshock affray in Kilkenny. So, many folk traditions tell of ruses by which he successfully defended hopeless cases. One such has him going in disguise to the chief prosecution witness before a trial and getting that witness to lay a bet on the outcome. Then, at the trial, he has the witness disqualified by making him admit that he stands to gain personally from a conviction. Another story tells of Daniel discovering that a certain hanging judge once took bribes, namely a white horse and a barrel of red wine. When defending a man on a capital charge before this judge, Daniel creates ructions in the court by pretending to fall asleep and then crying out loudly. Asked by the judge to explain his behaviour, he says that he has had a nightmare, in which a white horse was being drowned in red wine. Fearing that Daniel will expose him, the judge hastily finds an excuse to dismiss the case. Other stories tell of him exposing perjurers and felon-setters, and there is evidence that some of such accounts derive from humorous anecdotes told by Daniel himself.

He had a fine taste for dramatic humour, as is clear from an actual occurrence when he laid a bet with some of his legal colleagues that he would defeat in vitriol a notorious scold. She was the proprietress of a huckster's stall opposite the Four Courts in Dublin and, having listened politely to a barrage of abuse from her, Daniel triumphed by himself using voluminous mathematical terms as nicknames for her, ending by calling her a 'porter-swiping similitude of the bisection of a vortex!' This was probably the episode which caused another common folktale to be attached to him. We are told that a foolish woman once sold the same cow to three different buyers at a market, and when she was arraigned for this she engaged Daniel as her defence-counsel. He advised her to feign madness, and to answer 'moo!' to every question put to her. She did so, and was acquitted by the judge as not being responsible for her actions. When Daniel sought his fee from her, however, she again answered 'moo!'. Another borrowing of a

65. O'CONNELL, DANIEL *Contemporary portrait of the fatal duel with d'Esterre.*

common folktale plot has Daniel being outwitted by his servant, who claims that geese have only one leg after he has eaten part of his master's dinner.

In 1815 O'Connell was challenged to a duel by a member of Dublin Corporation, Norcot d'Esterre, who foolishly wished to impress those in power. He had no choice but to go ahead with the duel, and in it he shot d'Esterre, who died two days later. Daniel was quite upset at the episode and pitied d'Esterre, but to the folk mind it was a great victory which readily fitted into a heroic pattern, and d'Esterre was popularly believed to have been an expert gunman hired by the authorities to kill O'Connell. Another great victory was his election to Parliament in 1828, and his re-election after being disqualified on account of being a Catholic. He was received at Westminster with no small degree of hostility, and a large number of people had gathered to observe him with derisive curiosity. This situation is put in a humorous form in a popular Irish folk legend, which tells of how, faced with a jeering crowd, Daniel was somewhat abashed and slipped on a banana-skin, falling heavily on his backside. The onlookers went wild with delight, but he slowly picked himself up, looked around with a gracious air, and then curtsied to the ground. 'Pavements of London,' he said, 'you are so polite, and you give good example, for you kiss the Irishman where the English ought to!'

The Parliament provided him with a great theatre in which to display his wit and cunning, his major achievement being Catholic Emancipation. Several anecdotes tell of how he upset protocol and had unnecessary rules changed by clever ruses, and in these he is always represented as taking advantage of pompous and quite dull-witted opponents. This is well in tune with what O'Connell actually remarked before he won the right to sit in Parliament: 'How cruel the Penal Laws are which exclude me from a fair trial with men whom I look on as so much my inferiors.' A folk account of how he gained Emancipation is a masterpiece in hilarity. We are told that, having failed for a long time to win support for his Bill, he finally decided on a ruse. He wrote the terms of it on a parchment and, procuring a fine cane with a spin-off top, hid it inside the top of that cane. When he was in his seat in Parliament, he nudged the Member next to him and handed him the cane. That member admired its fine silverwork, and Daniel whispered to him to pass it on to the next man to seek his opinion also. In this way the cane was passed right around the house, all admiring it for its style and craftsmanship. When it came back to Daniel, he stood up and asked did all present approve of this piece of handiwork, and the 'ayes' were unanimous. Then he screwed off the handle of the cane with a broad smile. 'Gentlemen,' he said, 'I congratulate you - we have Emancipation!'

In 1832, *The London Times* published an article in which a woman, who had in her youth been looked after by O'Connell and his family, claimed that Daniel was the father of her thirteen-year-old son. The newspaper further described alleged encounters between Daniel and this boy in the street. It was a crude attempt to damage O'Connell politically and had no basis in truth, but the idea was quickly seized on and promoted by his enemies. It imprinted itself on the Irish folk memory also, but there much of the damage was taken out of it by setting the allegation in a humorous setting. For instance, a version of a popular type of folk story (see **Romantic Tales**, Type 873) was adopted to the context, and accordingly it was said that Daniel happened to be in a certain place once when he met a very clever little boy and gave him some money. He told him that he would give more to him the next time they met. As soon as he turned his back, the boy jumped inside the fence, and raced up to where he would again meet Daniel. The latter had no choice but to fulfil his promise and, having parted with more money, asked the boy who his people were. 'They say that I am a son of Daniel O'Connell!' said the boy. Daniel enquired as to his age and, on reflection, remarked that that might well be true.

O'Connell once said that he could 'drive a coach and six' through any law passed by Parliament, and the folk view would concur with him in this. He always protested that he would use only peaceful means to achieve his objectives for Ireland, but he was not adverse to delivering strongly-worded speeches which could sound quite alarming to the authorities. A curious story came to be told of him in different parts of the country, which had him using a threat to back his demands. It was said that, when failing to get support from Parliament for a reasonable measure, he said that he could, if he wished, have all Ireland in rebellion within twenty-four hours. This was scoffed at, so to prove his point he returned to Ireland, gave a wisp of straw to each of four persons, and told them to do likewise. Within twenty-four hours every adult in Ireland had received a wisp, and thus Daniel showed that he could if he wished fulfil his boast. This story has no historical basis in the context of Daniel, but it is a reconstruction of an event which actually took place in 1832, when he was at the height of his power. This, called the week of the blessed turf, was an extraordinary surge of religious devotion when an outbreak of cholera was feared. A man in Charleville, Co Cork, was said to have been instructed by the Virgin Mary to give packages of ashes to his neighbours and to tell them to do likewise. Soon the ashes were replaced by pieces of turf, which were given by each person to four others, and during the following six days this continued and spread to most parts of the country, before quietly subsiding. Daniel was active in having measures taken against outbreaks of cholera at the time and, perhaps because of this, the event became linked to his name and to his career in Parliament.

The most popular and dramatic of all the legends concerning Daniel describes an attempt reputedly made by English politicians to poison him. We are told that he was invited to dinner by them, and that they had poison put in his drink. Before he drank, however, the servant-girl, who was from Ireland, spoke to him in Irish verse, warning him of the plot by remarking that 'there is pepper on your drink which would kill hundreds'. Daniel answered her in Irish, and also in verse, saying that his hosts themselves would drink it. Then, in feigned surprise, he stood up and said that he had seen a royal carriage pass by the window. Thinking that some very distinguished personage was coming to visit them, the others rose from the table to look through the window, and Daniel quietly switched the glasses around. When they returned, remarking that it had been but an ordinary carriage and chiding him for his mistake, Daniel proposed a toast, with devastating consequences for one of his would-be assassins. It is difficult to trace the origin of this story, but it resembles an account in the apocryphal 'Acts of the Holy Apostle Thomas'. Daniel may have known this early Christian text from his education in seminaries on the Continent, and it may be that a version of it was one of the many anecdotes which he delighted in telling. In this way it could easily have become attached to his own image.

As well as his large and lasting profile as a social leader, in his great brain and his gifted speech Daniel echoed the age-old archetypal image of the Irish **poets**. Yet his wit was not enough. He planned a huge public meeting at Clontarf - scene of the ancient triumph of **Brian Boru** - in October 1843, but this had to be abandoned when massive military forces were deployed against it. Following this, Daniel was imprisoned for a while on a charge of conspiracy, and he died a broken man at Genoa in May of 1847 as famine raged at home.

W J O'Neill Daunt (1848); Ríonach Uí Ógáin (1984); Caoimhín Ó Danachair in *Studia Hibernica 14*, 40-63; Dáithí Ó hÓgáin (1985), 99-119, 331-3.

[Alleged womanising] Denis Gwynn (1930).

[Folktale-plots] Antti Aarne / Stith Thompson (1961), Types 155, 785A, 821B, 873, 1585. See also Uí Ógáin, *op cit*, 332-5.

Ó DÁLAIGH, CEARBHALL A famous romantic poet in Irish folk tradition. From the late mediaeval period, the family called Ó Dálaigh (anglicised as O'Daly) had as their main profession the composition of poetry, and accordingly branches of them were under the patronage of different nobles throughout the country. Cearbhall was a favourite Christian name among them, and the great poet of that name in folklore is in reality a combination of several different historical characters.

It is apparent that all members of the O'Daly family are descended from a 13th-century poet from the Westmeath area called Aonghus Ó Dálaigh, who had seven sons. One of these was Cearbhall Fionn (the epithet meaning 'fair-haired'), and he was the ancestor of the branch which settled in Co Cork and became professional poets to the powerful MacCarthy sept. All indications are that this branch developed a family-legend which served as a kind of trademark for their craft, basing it on the figure of Cearbhall Fionn. Their MacCarthy patrons were sprung from the royal Eoghanacht dynasty of Munster, and the O'Dalys would have been well-acquainted with the myth of that dynasty concerning how **Conall Corc** by an unintentional act gained the kingship of Cashel. They also would have known well the mediaeval story of how the hero **Fionn mac Cumhaill** got the gift of wisdom and poetry by an unintentional act. On the basis of such stories, and of old metaphors which likened poetry to milk from a mystical cow, these O'Dalys of Munster invented an account of their own ancestor Cearbhall Fionn. The account became widespread in the folklore of Munster and Connacht and is still told today.

According to the Munster versions Cearbhall Ó Dálaigh was a little boy who was the servant of a farmer and whose work was to herd the cattle. Each evening, when he returned to the farmhouse, he was asked by his master had he seen anything strange during the day. He always replied truthfully that he had not, until one day he saw a cloud descend onto a clump of rushes and a brindle cow went and ate the rushes. When he told this in the evening, he was instructed to bring the first milk of that cow to his master. Cearbhall did diligently as he was told, but a drop of the milk spilled onto his finger, and thus he got the first taste of it. Immediately a great change came over him. His face became lustrous, and every word he spoke was in verse. Realising that the boy had got the drink intended for himself, the farmer ordered him to leave that place, and henceforth Cearbhall was a roving poet. Because of his first tasting the milk, he had not only genius at poetry, but also many kinds of magical powers. Connacht versions of the story claim that a black bull was in the cloud, and that he fertilised the cow, thereby giving the power to her beastings, but this is a later embellishment of the narrative.

It is probable that this family trade-legend developed in the 14th or early 15th century, and one can surmise that it was promoted especially by the various poets of the sept who were actually christened Cearbhall. Towards the end of the 15th century, a romance-text was composed in Connacht which featured a character of the name as its hero. Although no reference is made to the cow-story, this character is portrayed as a poet and harper with extraordinary powers. We read that Fearbhlaidh, daughter of the king of Scotland, saw the handsome young Cearbhall in a dream and fell in love with him. Her maidservant had her magically transported to Ireland to spend some time with him, and later he travelled to Scotland in a bardic company so that they could again meet. He put all the royal court to sleep with his magical music, except himself and Fearbhlaidh, so that he could dally with her. The Scottish king suspected that they were in love and had Cearbhall thrown into prison, but Fearbhlaidh visited the poet, changed clothes with him, and thus allowed him to escape. Tricked by sorcerers later, Cearbhall forgot his loved one and married another lady, but Fearbhlaidh came magically to the wedding-feast and wrote her name in her own blood on his harp. This brought back his memory, and the bride left him, complaining that he did not consummate the marriage. Finally, the Scottish king bribed some Irish visitors to tell Fearbhlaidh that Cearbhall had died in Ireland, and she died from a broken heart. These messengers then went to Ireland and told Cearbhall of her death, whereupon he laid his head on his harp and died. The author of this text identifies his Cearbhall with a poet of that name from north Clare who died in the year 1404, but it is obvious that he has confused several different people and one gets the impression that he had little historical information on any of them.

Another celebrated bearer of the magical name was a poet who lived at Pallis, in north Wexford, in the early 17th century. Some verses survive in which he and a fellow poet humorously discuss the question of whether he is or is not the Cearbhall Ó Dálaigh who excelled at poetry, music, athletics, tricks and 'eol amhra in ilgheasaibh' (literally, 'wondrous knowledge in all studies'). This Cearbhall from Wexford seems to have fallen in love with Eleanor Kavanagh, daughter of Sir Morgan Kavanagh (Murchadh Caomhánach) of Clonmullen Castle in Co Carlow. Two love-poems concerning her are attributed to him in manuscript, and perhaps he also composed lines of rhythmical prose for her on the pattern of the Fearbhlaidh story. From some such context has sprung a folk narrative which has been well-known throughout most of Ireland from at least the 18th century. This, which usually follows on the story of how the archetypal Cearbhall got the gift of poetry from the cow's milk, tells of how he married a young woman. During the wedding festivities, however, he heard mention of a more beautiful lady, and therefore pretended to be a sexual imbecile and did not consummate the marriage. The other lady was Eleanor, and she was at that time preparing for her own betrothal party. He cleverly took up employment with a shoemaker in her locality and, when she wished to have a special pair of shoes made for the occasion, he went to the castle to take her measure. By this means he and she fell in love, but there was no hope that her father would consent to this when a match was being arranged with a wealthy suitor. On the night of the betrothal party, Cearbhall came to the castle disguised as a beggarman, but he soon showed that he was an accomplished gleeman and entertainer. When he was asked to play music for the company, he played a magical air which put all to sleep and then persuaded Eleanor to elope with him. He turned his horse's shoes backwards so that they could not be tracked, and in this way they made their getaway. Differing endings are given to the story. Some versions claim that they were captured, and that Cearbhall was put on trial, but that by his learning and skill he convinced the court that he was a proper husband for Eleanor. Other versions, however, have both lovers dying tragically in a foreign country - for instance Cearbhall slips on a spear while performing a trick and Eleanor dies from heartbreak as a result. This theme of an unhappy ending is one of several features which parallel the romance of Cearbhall and Fearbhlaidh, and there can be no doubt but that the literary story is to some extent in the background of the folk legend.

A love-song with a very touching air which was popular since the 16th century had the title 'Eibhlín a Rún' (literally 'darling Evelyn'), it being addressed by its unknown composer to a young woman of that name. Because the first three syllables of the title sound very much like 'Eleanor' and because it suited the context, this song was incorporated into the folklore of Cearbhall and Eleanor Kavanagh. Other material also was added. In Munster the motif of a love-spot ('ball searc') was borrowed from another great story of elopement, that concerning **Diarmaid ua Duibhne** and Gráinne, and applied to Cearbhall. This development may have been assisted by speculation as to the poet's name. Cearbhall was an old Irish name, perhaps in origin meaning 'war-valour', but by folk etymology it could be taken to be 'car-bhall' (literally 'love-spot'). Thus we are told that Cearbhall Ó Dálaigh had a love-spot on his breast and that, when he came to take Eleanor's measure for the shoes, he allowed his shirt to open so that she would see it and thereby fall in love with him.

The Cearbhall Ó Dálaigh of folklore is a very colourful character. A mixture of verse and prose called the 'Seachrán' ('wandering') of Cearbhall was current since the 18th century, and this seems to have been based on some text composed by the Wexford man but now lost. Another tradition was that Cearbhall was a great composer of vision poetry and that he communed often with the otherworld. One by-product of this was a series of verses current in west Munster which described an attempt by the otherworld lady **Clíona** to entice him to become her lover and how he overcame her in verse and thus rebutted her. Because of this tradition of his contact with supernatural powers, Cearbhall was reputed to be quite reckless and fearless, and a story from Limerick describes how he met one night with the otherworld lord **Donn** and tried to follow the latter into his residence at Knockfierna. Coming to the summit of that mountain, Cearbhall saw the entrance to a cavern there and threw a stone in to discover how deep it was, but the stone was flung back at him, giving him a black eye and knocking him down the slope.

66. Ó DÁLAIGH, CEARBHALL *Mason's trademark of cat with two tails on the wall of house in Limerick City.*

Several humorous anecdotes concerning Cearbhall are common, some of them based on lore of the mythical crafstman, the **Gobán Saor**. Like the Gobán, he is said to have shown his skill as a sculptor by chiselling the figure of a cat with two tails while the other workers ate their dinner to which the unfortunate poet had not been invited. Again like the Gobán, he was a master shipbuilder, and could drive nails home by a throw of a hammer. Also a great trickster, a story popular in Connacht claimed that he had once cured a rich man after twelve doctors had failed to do so. In the sick-room, he made 'pills' by putting icing on excrement and then called in the doctors to test these pills. The patient, who had seen what Cearbhall had done, was convulsed with laughter when he saw the learned doctors eating the pills, and the merriment caused an internal boil to burst in his breast and thus he was healed. This anecdote has been borrowed from a 19th-century English translation of the adventures of the German trickster Till Eulenspiegel.

T F O'Rahilly in *Proceedings of the Royal Irish*

Academy 36, 100-2; Dáithí Ó hÓgáin (1982), 215-31, 242-64 and (1985), 234-6, 258-71, 345; Siobhán Ní Laoire (1986); J E Doan in *Éigse 18*, 1-24 and in *Béaloideas 50*, 54-89 and *51*, 11-30.

Ó DOMHNAILL, AODH 'BALLDEARG' A messianic name among the O'Donnell sept of Donegal. Prophecies concerning a leader of the sept who would bear this name were current since the 12th or 13th century, and they seem to be an adaptation of the O'Neill lore concerning **Aodh Eangach**. It was said that this leader would defeat the English oppressors and thereby give the O'Donnells great prestige in the country. The epithet Balldearg means 'red-spotted', the belief being that the prophesied O'Donnell champion would have such a mark on his body.

The O'Donnells were descended from the celebrated **Conall Gulban** and were therefore of the same royal stock as the O'Neills. Another claim to fame was that the celebrated saint **Colm Cille** had been of their family, and they carried the reputed psalter of that saint - called the 'Cathach' ('battler') - in front of their armies when going to war. All of this strengthened their reputation and self-confidence, and thus facilitated their belief in a great champion of theirs to come. Several of the O'Donnell chieftains were called Aodh and their poets could, as occasion permitted, identify any of these with the prophesied Balldearg. The Annals make it clear that a chieftain of the sept who died in 1537 had been identified with Aodh Eangach himself, and a spy reported to the English in 1593 that a prophecy was current that 'when two Hughs succeed each other as O'Donnells the last shall be a monarch of Ireland and banish all foreign conquerors'. The man of the moment in this case was the colourful young chieftain Aodh Rua ('Red Hugh'), who had been kidnapped on board a ship by the English in Lough Swilly but, after a dramatic escape from Dublin Castle, had succeeded his father (also named Aodh) as chieftain. With the Earl of Tyrone, Aodh Ó Néill, he led a rebellion against the Elizabethans which was very successful for nine years. His friend and biographer, Lughaidh Ó Cléirigh, called him 'a chosen one whom the prophets had foretold long before his birth' and makes it clear that Aodh Rua's supporters made copious use of such prophecies.

The Irish chieftains of the 16th century looked to Spain for help, and this was rationalised by the literati through use of the old lore of how the fictional **Míl** had first brought the Gaelic people to Ireland from that country. Therefore it was said that Spain would not allow the Irish to be destroyed in their hour of need. When a Spanish expeditionary force did come in the winter of 1601, it landed in the extreme south of Ireland, and Aodh Ó Néill and Aodh Rua Ó Domhnaill had to travel south in an attempt to relieve it from the English army, which was besieging it at Kinsale. The result was a drastic defeat for the Irish forces, after which Aodh Rua went to Spain to seek meaningful help. He died there in the following year, his followers suspecting that he had been poisoned by an English agent.

Several other leading members of the family resorted to Spain and, to the O'Donnells at home in Ireland, the prophecy of the coming Balldearg was now joined specifically to the idea that assistance would come to them from that country. Thus it was claimed that the long-awaited Balldearg would arrive in Ireland at the head of a strong army from Spain. In July 1690, four days after the Battle of the Boyne, an accomplished soldier of the family did land at Kinsale. He was also called Aodh Ó Domhnaill, and because he had the prophesied red spot on his body had the nickname Balldearg. He immediately attracted a large number of supporters, and fought skillfully. The machinations of king **James 11** and his officers, however, prevented him from being given the command of his Donegal people, and finding himself in an impossible situation he had little choice but to surrender to the forces of **William**. He returned to Spain, and died in 1704 with the rank of major-general.

67. Ó DOMHNAILL, AODH 'BALLDEARG' *Irish soldiers of the 16th century, drawn by Albrecht Dürer.*

The belief that a great Balldearg would come from Spain continued, and many versions of a story concerning this fanciful figure have been collected from the folklore of Donegal. The story is a loose combination of episodes from the lives of Aodh Rua and the later Aodh, and probably had its genesis among oral storytellers in the 18th century. We are told that the baby Balldearg was seized by a group of English soldiers who arrived in Donegal by ship. Noticing the red spot on his skin, the commanding officer of these soldiers determined to kill the baby but when the baby saw the naked sword it laughed, and the officer could not find it in his heart to do the foul deed. Therefore he took the little Balldearg with him to Dublin and reared him with his own two sons. The three boys grew up together and, when they were in their early teens, they stayed out late one starry night and each made a wish. The eldest wished that he had a cow for every star, the second preferred a horse for every star, but Balldearg wished for an army with himself at its head. Hearing this, the officer grew afraid and sent Balldearg north to Derry with a message for a fellow-officer. Growing suspicious, Balldearg opened the letter and saw that it bore instructions to kill him, so he boarded a ship at Lough Foyle and reached Spain as a stowaway. When the ship reached its destination he was imprisoned. However, horse-racing was in progress near the prison, and a fine black horse belonging to the king was bested by another animal. Balldearg said that if he were allowed to ride the horse the result would be different. He was therefore released and won a great race, after which he was accepted into the king's service. Having been sent to Ireland on a mission to buy horses, he returned to his native place, Portacran, where he learned that his father was dead. Sojourning a while with his mother, he tamed a fierce stallion which the family owned and which no man could ride, and then departed again for Spain with this horse. There he fought a fencing-duel in place of the son of the Spanish king, and the royal family were so grateful to him that he was made a divisional commander in the army. He was said to be waiting with this army for the opportune time to return to Ireland.

W M Hennessy / D H Kelly (1875), 150-1, 228-31, 352-3; A M Freeman (1944), 702-3; Bernard Burke (1884), 747-8; C P Meehan (1868), 98-9; Pól Breathnach / Colm O Lochlainn *1-2* (1948); Constantia Maxwell (1923), 91-4; T C Croker (1841), 85-96, 133-7; Martin Haverty (1860), 665-6, 765-6; Thomas Gilbert (1892), 151; Seosamh Maguidhir (1973), 47-53; Dáithí Ó hÓgáin (1985), 133-41, 334-5 and in *Léachtaí Cholm Cille 14*, 193.

[Motifs - child smiling at sword, treacherous letter] See Eleanor Knott (1936), 3; Stith Thompson (1955-1958), Motif K978.

Ó DOMHNAILL, MÁNAS (c1490-1563) Donegal chieftain, scholar and poet. He succeeded his father as leader of the O'Donnell sept in 1537, and five years later he compiled his celebrated biography of St **Colm Cille** at his castle near Lifford. He was twice married, his second wife being the sister of Gearóid Óg FitzGerald, Earl of Kildare. He joined with the O'Neills and the Geraldines in a combined effort against the English, but was defeated in battle and had no choice but to surrender to King Henry VIII in 1540. He was displaced as chieftain in 1555 by his son Calbhach, and seven years later he died and was buried at the Franciscan Monastery of Donegal.

His fame as a scholar survived in the folklore of Donegal, where several stave-anecdotes are related of him. The fact that he was a patron of the Franciscan monastery is reflected in a very popular account of a slight quarrell which he had with these friars. It is said that it was his wont to send a bullock to them regularly, but that on one occasion he declined to do this. The friars, for their part, used to present him with apples from their orchard, but they also ceased this practice. Mánas then composed a satiric quatrain, claiming that 'these Donegal friars plant their trees so plentifully, but no fruit grows on their tops until meat is applied to their roots!'

Most of the other folk accounts of Mánas involve verbal duels between him and his professional poet, Niall Mac an Bhaird. This Niall was a member of one of the leading poetic families in Ulster. The surname means literally 'Son of the Bard' and is anglicised as Ward. We are told that Niall was a very clever little boy and that Mánas noticed this and had him educated. When he grew up, Mánas gave a letter to him with directions to deliver it to the chieftain's rent-collector. Niall was lazy and, having travelled a short distance, decided to wait until the rent-collector came his way. When this happened, the collector read the letter and remarked to the poet that he ought to have come further to meet him, for Mánas had ordered in the letter that all the land travelled that day by Niall should be conferred on him. So the poet got no more than a townland in the Rosses which thus became known as his letter - 'Leitir Mhic an Bhaird'. This is the result of a folk etymology, for the word 'leitir' in this placename actually means a hillside. It appears that Mánas did really confer that land on the poet, and the folk memory is that Niall built a house there from wattles, sods, and straw. The poet was quick-witted and sharp-tongued. We are told that Mánas, exasperated by his smart answers, once threatened to hang him 'with the moonlight', to which Niall replied that he preferred that to being hanged with a withy. Then Mánas asked what would his last request be, and the poet said 'that you put your head into the noose with me!' On another occasion, Mánas came hurriedly to Niall's house, and so impatient was he that he did not dismount from his horse but rode directly into the doorway. He angrily demanded to know who was within, but received the clever answer from the poet: 'A man and a half and a half-horse!'

Anraí Mac Giolla Chomhaill (1981), 16-24; P A Breatnach in *Celtica 16*, 63-72; T F O'Rahilly (1921), 29, 77-9; Séamas Ó Catháin in *Béaloideas 53*, 75-86; Niall Ó Dónaill (1952), 100-2; Énrí Ó Muirgheasa (1924), 1-25 and in *Béaloideas 3*, 58-9; Dáithí Ó hÓgáin (1982), 6, 418; IFC passim.

Ó DONNCHÚ, DÓNALL NA nGEIMHLEACH Chieftain of the O'Donoghue sept of south Kerry. The agnomen 'na nGeimhleach' probably was intended to mean 'of the fetters', although an alternative form is 'na gCaoil-each' meaning 'of the slender steeds'.

The original personage behind the folklore seems to have been a 12th-century chieftain called Domhnall, grandson of that Donnchadh who gave its name to the sept. Hence he was known as 'Domhnall ua Donnchadha', which in modern form gives us the name Dónall Ó Donnchú. The idea that his spirit lived on after his death may have developed from some family cult associating

68. Ó DONNCHÚ, DÓNALL NA nGEIMHLEACH
Ross Castle, haunted by Dónall.

the O'Donoghues with the eponymous otherworld deity **Donn**. However, the corpus of legends attached to this shadowy figure was borrowed from the lore of Gearóid **FitzGerald**, Earl of Desmond, and so would postdate the great Desmond rebellion of the 16th century. The reason for this may have been the fact that the then chieftain of the O'Donoghues took part in the rebellion and was attainted as a result.

69. Ó DONNCHÚ, DÓNALL NA nGEIMHLEACH *Dónall appears on his white horse on May morning.*

The legends tell of how Dónall once engaged in magical practices in a secret room in Ross Castle at Killarney and how, when one spell went wrong, he became enchanted and since sleeps in a hidden cavern under Loch Léin (the greater Lake of Killarney). He is seen riding every May morning on the waters of the lake, his horse being shod with silver shoes, and when these are worn out he will return. Like the Earl of Desmond, he is said to have often appeared in order to protect local tenants from oppressive landlords. On one occasion he gave money to tenants to enable them to pay their exorbitant rents and, having given receipts, the landlord found to his dismay that the money turned to leaves. A fantastic legend has one of his O'Donoghue descendants laying a bet with an English lord on a hurling match. All looks lost for O'Donoghue, but Dónall appears on the field of play, takes part in the game, and his magnificent performance gains the victory for his team.

Tadhg Ó Donnchadha (1940), 531; Pádraig Ó Siochfhradha (1932), 44-52; Donncha Ó Cróinín in *Béaloideas 35-36*, 112-4, 358-9; Dáithí Ó hÓgáin (1982), 353-8 and (1985), 157-9, 337 and in *Béaloideas 42-44*, 221, 245-6, 253-4, 302-7.

Ó FÁILBHE, CLUASACH Character in a folk narrative of south-west Kerry, claimed to have been a native of the Ballinskelligs area.

He is said to have been a great sailor, and to have travelled with a sea-captain called the Ceannaí Fionn ('Fair-haired Merchant'). Together they set out to discover where the end of the sea is. Having encountered many wonders on the voyage, they reached a great wall of brass, and considered that their quest was over. They examined the wall, but when they tried to draw anchor again found that it was stuck at the bottom of the sea. Cluasach dived down to release it, but found himself in a fine city where a beautiful maiden invited him to stay with her. He agreed, but said that he first wished to return home to put his affairs in order. He therefore set sail again, but was followed by a great wave in which the beautiful lady swam. He threw a knife at the wave, knocking an eye from her head. However, a strange horseman came riding on the sea, stating that he was the lady's brother and warning the sailor to keep to his bargain. After a short visit home, Cluasach went to the sea-shore, was engulfed by a wave, and was seen no more. Before he departed, he said that he would send a burned sod to a local strand each May morning to show that he was alive, and such a sod was accordingly found there for a long time afterwards.

This is in fact a local variant of a story found in other parts of Ireland also, a story which combines two different legends. One of these legends concerned an attempt by a mermaid to entice away a fisherman into her world; and the other described how an otherworld being was injured by a man, who was later brought into the otherworld to recover the offending instrument. Both of these legends are found abroad also, but in Ireland they are usually told in combination as above. It is clear that at some stage in recent centuries a mariner of some repute, known as the Ceannaí Fionn, was made the main character in the story as told in Munster and Connacht. The south-west Kerry variant is a further elaboration of this which duplicates the character by introducing Cluasach. His surname, Ó Fáilbhe (anglicised Falvey), was a common one in that area, and he may in reality have been a noted local teller of the story who was converted by tradition into an actor within the narrative. Some influence from learned tradition is evident, for there are echoes of the type of sea-literature which concerned characters such as **Bran mac Feabhail**, **Manannán**, and **Maol Dúin**.

Domhnall Ua Murchadha (1939), 7-10; Séamus Ó Duilearga (1948), 259-63, 429-30.

[International legends] Stith Thompson (1955-1958), motif B81; Archer Taylor, (1927).

Ó hANLUAIN, RÉAMONN (+1681): Outlaw who had a successful career on the roads of Ulster and north Leinster for seven years before he was betrayed and murdered. He was the leader of a band of about fifty men, and their principal source of income was a 'black rent' which they levied on English planters and other well-to-do people. His name is anglicised as Redmond O'Hanlon.

A chapbook describing him and some other celebrated outlaws was written in the mid-18th century by a certain John Cosgrave, and this shows that most of the folklore concerning him was already current at that time. We read that Réamonn's mother had special dreams before his birth, and that he had a mark in the shape of 'T' on his breast when he was born. When he grew up, he was a master at disguise, 'sometimes appearing like an officer, sometimes like a country gentleman, sometimes like a footman, and could alter the tone of his voice at pleasure, so that the soldiers seldom knew him though he often gave them money to drink'. The chapbook describes how, disguised as an army officer, he once directed a party of soldiers in a search for himself, and on another occasion, when dressed like a country gentleman, he was given a bodyguard to protect him from himself! He led the bodyguard into a trap, so that they were disarmed and robbed by his men. We also read that, having been arrested once, he contrived to get the soldiers drunk in a tavern and completed his triumph by tying them all up neck and heels and taking their weapons. Another writer stressed his ubiquity: 'He was everwhere, in fact, for those whom he looked for, and nowhere for those who looked for him. That was the most curious thing about Redmond O'Hanlon - there was plenty of him where he could be spared, and the greatest possible scarcity where he was wanted.'

Cosgrave further describes how the leading highwayman in Munster, Richard Power, once set out to meet Réamonn, and put up at an inn near where he expected to find his great counterpart. Power noticed a rich gentleman there and contrived to meet him on the road the next day to rob him. The strange gentleman, however, exchanged pistol-shots with him and then took to sword-fencing. When both were exhausted, Power enquired as to the stranger's name and found that it was Réamonn himself. Later on, when Power was arrested in Munster, Réamonn travelled south in an attempt to rescue him from Clonmel jail. Dressed in fine clothes, he fell in with four soldiers who were escorting Power to his execution, plied them with liquor and then had his men seize them and tie them up. The hue and cry was raised for the escaped prisoner and his accomplices, and Réamonn himself 'assisted' the soldiers in the hunt, slipping away from them in the Bog of Allen when all was safe.

Whatever the basis for these legends, the historical Réamonn had a fine sense of showmanship. He proclaimed himself 'chief ranger of the mountains, surveyor-general of the high roads, lord-examiner of all travellers and high protector of his benefactors and contributors', and his reputation for both dignity and elusiveness was so great that he was referred to in French newspapers of the time as a Count. Since he accorded so well with the romantic image of highwaymen in 17th-18th century culture, it is natural that several standard folk accounts of outlaws should have become attached to him. For instance, it is said of him - as of many other Irish outlaws - that he could trick and frighten his opponents by pretending that he was accompanied by a large force of men, though in fact quite alone. Réamonn, we are told, did this by having heads of cabbage with hats on them set in the hedges at dusk when the soldiers could not see clearly.

One story told by Cosgrave was well-known in international robber-legends and is still widely popular concerning Réamonn. According to it, a merchant in Dundalk wished to have a large sum of money collected for him from Belfast, but nobody would undertake the task for fear of being accosted by Réamonn on the country roads. Eventually, an apparently dull-witted boy undertook to go and set out, mounted on a broken-down nag. On the way to Belfast, he met a gentleman on a beautiful horse, and they conversed for a while, the boy revealing the nature of his business and his time-table. He then went on, collected the money in Belfast, and on his return-journey met the same gentleman on the road. The gentleman said that he was Réamonn and demanded the money. The boy caught his saddle-bags and threw them into a tangle of briars, and the outlaw jumped off his horse to recover the bags. The boy jumped from his own nag and, mounting Réamonn's fine steed, set off for Dundalk at high speed. Réamonn found nothing of value in the saddle-bags, for the boy had hidden the money within his shirt, and the highwayman had nothing for his trouble but the loss of his quality horse. This legend, when set in the context of a popular outlaw like Réamonn, reflects the folk tendency to have great men sometimes outwitted by very ordinary people and is closely related to the popular psychology of hero-worship (see also Daniel **O'Connell** and Jonathan **Swift**).

It was said that Réamonn had a shirt made from flax which was plucked and scutched and spun and woven between sunrise and sunset and that, as a result, it could not be penetrated by any bullet except one fired from his own gun. However, he was betrayed by his foster-brother Art, whom he had set as a look-out while he slept in a hut near Eight-Mile-Bridge in Co Down. Eager to collect the large reward on the head of the famous outlaw, Art stole into the hut and shot Réamonn through the breast with his own blunderbuss.

T W Moody in *Proceedings of the Belfast Natural History and Philosophical Society 1*, 17-33; John Cosgrave (1776), 4-32; M J Murphy (1975), 55-7; Dáithí Ó hÓgáin (1985), 181-5, 338-9; IFC passim.

Ó NÉILL, EOGHAN RUA (1582-1649) Brilliant Irish military leader. Of the noble O'Neill family of Tyrone, he was taken to the Netherlands in his youth and became a distinguished officer in the Spanish army. He returned to Ireland in 1642 to take command of the Ulster army after the rebellion, and in 1646 scored a great victory over the Covenanter forces at Benburb. Despite his continuing success in very difficult circumstances, wrangling and petty jealousies prevented him from being appointed over-all commander of the Irish forces. In 1649 **Cromwell** arrived in Dublin with a huge army, and Eoghan Rua prepared his own under-equipped men to face the daunting challenge. He was struck down by illness, however, and died at Cloughouter in Co Cavan before he and Cromwell crossed swords. After his death his army was poorly led and was utterly defeated in 1651.

70. Ó NÉILL, EOGHAN RUA *A contemporary sketch of Eoghan Rua.*

The military skills of Eoghan Rua caused amazement to friend and foe alike, and he was loved by his followers on account of his concern for them and for the clever stratagems by which he kept casualties on his own side to a minimum. His son said of him that he would 'protract time and make a thousand wheels and turns to save the life of a single soldier'. A contemporary story had it that, noticing that one of his gunners was not performing well in a battle at Trim, he himself seized the weapon and showed him how to use it by shooting the enemy commander. Cavan town was his headquarters for a while, and a typical story from local folklore there describes a trick by which he got provisions for his army. He had only one bullock left, whereas the enemy had a large herd. He therefore took his bullock to a wood near to the foe's encampment and, by lighting some straw on its back, caused it to bawl. Attracted by this, the herd came across to where Eoghan's men were waiting, and were quickly driven to his camp.

He was known to the ordinary people as 'the General' or as 'Eoghan of the War', and many places of Ulster and Leinster were popularly pointed out as the scenes of his ambushes and triumphs. His death was one of the most momentous losses in Irish history, and the people refused to believe that it had come from natural causes. He apparently suffered from some form of cancer, and the most acute pain was in his knee. The illness first struck him at a banquet in Derry, when he was negotiating with the Parliamentarian commander Charles Coote. It was therefore suspected that he had been given poison on that occasion, but an alternate explanation arose from the boast of one of his Irish rivals called Plunkett. This man claimed that he himself had been responsible for Eoghan's death by sending him a pair of poisoned boots as a present. An account from late folklore brings both theories together in narrative form, by stating that a dance was organised in Eoghan's honour, and that a certain woman put poison in his shoes beforehand. He danced several times, and with the heat the poison worked itself up into his blood.

A poet lamenting Eoghan referred to him as 'the very David who would not allow Goliath to escape him', and a contemporary report shows that a messianic motif (see Gearóid Iarla **FitzGerald**) became associated with him. We read of his followers' belief that God had 'lulled him to sleep and snatched him away to some secret corner of the world to keep him there for future better purposes'.

Elizabeth O'Neill (1937); Denis Murphy (1897), 130-3; T S O'Cahan (1968), 375-7; Cecile O'Rahilly (1952), 23-7, 111-5; Seosamh Mag Uidhir (1977), 5, 62-4; Douglas Hyde / Breandán Ó Conaire (1985), 28-33; Dáithí Ó hÓgáin (1985), 169-70; IFC 924:420-5, S965:369-70.

Ó RATHAILLE, AOGÁN (c1670-1729) Leading 18th-century poet. He was born in the area of Sliabh Luachra, in south-east Kerry, and spent most of his life in the service of the noble MacCarthy family of west Munster. Aogán was the leading proponent of the type of vision-poem called 'aisling', in which the composer claims that an otherworld woman comes to him with a message that the Irish will yet triumph over their oppressors.

Aogán was very much an aristocratic poet in his sentiments, and depended on the noble families for support and sustenance, but the defeat of that interest left him in dejection and poverty. In folklore, therefore, he is portrayed as a man of inspired intellect and quick wit who is buffeted by life and by the indifference and cruelty of upstarts. Several anecdotes tell of how he composed witty verses to satirise and deflate such people, and his wit can be both humorous and biting. An example of the latter describes how one day he saw the son of an English settler desecrating a churchyard by cutting down a venerable old tree which grew there. The youth slipped and was hanged between the branches, and the poet spoke a stanza wishing that trees bore such fruit every day. The anecdotes are usually of a more benevolent and lighthearted nature, however. We are told that he once got lodgings in the house of a very stingy man and was given nothing but watery porridge to eat. He asked for a spoon, and was told that all he could have was a piece of shell to scrape the pot. His host then enquired as to who he was, wherupon he replied in verse that he was Aogán Ó Rathille from Sliabh Luachra who broke his shell in the bottom of the pot, and not due to the weight of the food.

As a typical poet, Aogán was said to have been able to show his immediate knowledge of any kind of situation. Thus, we are told that he once saw a group of men trying to build a bridge, but the arch continually collapsed despite their efforts. He spoke a quatrain stating that he had never yet seen a bridge without a prop, thereby instructing them that they should use wattles as a crossbeam. On another occasion, he had two pigs at the market and was tricked by a slick buyer who asked what was the price of 'that white pig there with the black pig'. Aogán named his price, to be told that he had thereby sold both pigs. At the next market, the poet was selling more pigs, and when asked his price by the same buyer he stated that all he was asking was one grain of corn with permission to double it for half an hour. The buyer agreed, and Aogán started on a long rhetoric which had the single grain increasing to sheafs and stacks and cornfields and parishes and counties until he was demanding all of Ireland as payment. The slick buyer was thus fored to settle for a reasonable price as a compromise.

The actual poetry of Aogán was of a very serious and heart-rending nature, but in folklore he is portrayed as a great trickster. One story has the daunting scholar Dean **Swift** going on a visit to Kerry to discover if the people of that area had any spark of intelligence. As he travelled in his carriage he noticed a bedraggled fellow driving some cattle along the road. The Dean stopped to ask for directions, and he was answered by the yokel in Latin, Greek, Hebrew, and archaic Irish.

Swift was so amazed by this that he turned on his heel and headed back for Dublin, remarking that if the tramps in Kerry were so knowledgeable the scholars of the place must be unrivalled in their learning. The man whom he had encountered was, of course, Aogán. This type of folk legend was conventional in the lore concerning Irish poets, with the visitor to an area always routed by a witty child or by the local sage in disguise. The plot was current in Ireland since mediaeval times (see **Mongán**). One story has Aogán exploiting folk ideas concerning the magical knowledge of poets. It is said that he was overtaken on his travels one night by a frightful downpour. When he was wringing wet he noticed a fine house, surrounded by tall trees, on the roadside, and went to ask for shelter there. His knock was answered by a surly man, who said that he would not admit a stranger to his house. Aogán looked up at the trees where the crows were cawing, and remarked: 'It is very strange that you do not know me, when even the crows recognise who I am.' He then told the man that he was Aogán Ó Rathaille the poet, and instructed him to listen carefully to the crows. The man did so, and it seemed to him as if they were cawing 'Aogán, Aogán, Aogán Ó Rathaille!' Needless to say, the poet was then admitted and treated hospitably.

P S Dinneen / Tadhg O'Donoghue (1911); Pádraig Ó Siochfhradha (1932), 261-5; Séamus Ó Duilearga (1948), 328-33, 441; Dáithí Ó hÓgáin (1982), 473 and (1985), 98-9, 230-3, 248-51, 344.

Ó RIAIN, ÉAMONN AN CHNOIC Outlaw of the late 16th and early 17th century, known in English as 'Ned of the Hill'. The tradition is that he was born at Knockmeoll Castle in Atshanbohy, in north Tipperary. It is said that he was of noble stock and was forced into outlawry at the time of the Williamite Wars. A proclamation, dated 1702, offered as reward for his capture £200, then a very large sum. He was treacherously slain by a close confidant some time later.

Éamonn was one of the most famous of the outlaws known as raparees (from the Irish 'rápaire', meaning a half-pike, which was a common weapon with them). A great deal of folklore concerning him was current until recently and this was enhanced by a very popular love-song known as 'Éamonn an Chnoic'. The song consists of a conversation between the young man Éamonn and his loved one, in which he seeks admission to her house on a cold and windy night. It is likely that the song predated the outlaw, and that his nickname was in reality borrowed from it. In the folk stories, the raparee Éamonn is portrayed as a high-minded man who dressed well and was a master marksman with his fine brace of pistols. We are told that he studied for the priesthood abroad but, on his return home for holidays, he intervened to prevent a cow being taken by a tax collector from a poor widow and in the resulting fracas the tax-man was killed. This meant that Éamonn had to take to the hills and woods as a fugitive, but he soon gathered a strong band of men and fought for the Jacobites in the war against **William of Orange**. Together with a noted raparee leader, Dónall Ó hÓgáin (known as 'Galloping Hogan') he attacked and destroyed an English convoy near Dundrum, in Co Tipperary.

Most accounts, however, portray him as on his own, mounted on a fine grey horse, evading search-parties of soldiers and when need be attacking them and putting them to flight. He was always gallant, robbing only from the rich and rendering assistance to the poor. One especially popular story tells of how he once met an English lady who had been robbed by some men claiming to be his followers, and how he indignantly chased and captured these men and then returned her money to the lady. Her husband was a senior army officer, and it was said that out of gratitude he did all he could to secure a pardon for the chivalrous outlaw. It was said that Éamonn often fell in with rich travellers on the road, and as often as not treated them well and did not deprive them of their wealth. Once he thus chatted with an English officer for a long while before revealing his identity. The officer feigned friendship and, taking Éamonn to a tavern for a drink, had him surrounded and captured by a company of soldiers. Éamonn, however, contrived to get the soldiers drunk, and in the confusion made his getaway, later slaying the treacherous officer with a well-directed shot.

Several conventional types of outlaw-legends were attached to him. For instance, a man tries to betray him by luring him to his house for a meal, but the man's wife hints to him to eat cold and flee (see Dónall na Cásca **Ó Caoimh**). In this case, the migratory motif has apparently been substituted for a real episode in which a certain Reuben Lee of Gurnaskehy tried to lure Éamonn into a trap, but the outlaw was warned by a relative who was also in the house. Another story has

71. Ó SÚILLEABHÁIN BÉARRA, DÓNALL CAM *Cattle-raid in Ireland, from a 16th-century woodcut.*

Éamonn being waylaid by a highwayman, and both fighting long and hard before he realises that his opponent is none other than Réamonn **Ó hAnluain**. This is borrowed from the account of the latter outlaw (q.v.) in an 18th-century book. Also borrowed from that source, where it is told of a highwayman called Richard Power, is an account of how Éamonn gives money to poor tenants to settle debts with their rapacious landlord, and then retakes the money from the tyrant and returns it to the tenants. This was a widespread legendary plot in the lore of outlaws in many countries. Yet another such story has Éamonn allowing himself to be taken so that a poor man can collect the reward for his capture, and then escaping again.

The typical heroic outlaw can only be overcome by foul and unfair means, and so it was with Éamonn in real life as in legend. We are told that he was sleeping at the house of a man called Dwyer whom he believed to be his friend, but who actually intended to collect the price on the outlaw's head. Éamonn dreamed that Dwyer was approaching him with a hatchet, but on starting up from his sleep he rejected such a suspicion. He fell asleep again, and the 'friend' really did behead him and brought the head to Clonmel to claim the reward. Tradition has it, however, that a pardon had just been procured by the English officer who was indebted to the outlaw for the courteous treatment of his wife, and that as a result the traitor got nothing for his efforts.

D J O'Sullivan in *Journal of the Irish Folk Song Society 24*, 36-60; Dáithí Ó hÓgáin (1985), 186-7, 290, 339, 346; John Cosgrave (9th edition - 1776), 14, 34-6.

Ó SÚILLEABHÁIN BÉARRA, DÓNALL CAM (1560-1618) Chieftain of the O'Sullivan sept of Beare in west Cork. He gained national fame due to the long march which he and his people accomplished in the winter of 1602-1603 in order to escape the rampant Elizabethan armies. He left Glengariff with a group of over a thousand men, women, and children, and they suffered continual attacks and terrible hardships as they travelled northwards for a fortnight. Eventually, Dónall and a remnant of his band reached the fortress of the O'Rourkes in Leitrim.

A strong folk memory of Dónall, in the form of epical legends, survives in west Munster. His nickname 'Cam' meant 'crooked', and folklore explains that, though a tall athletic man, he was slightly stooped and had bandy legs. We are told that he was very lazy as a youth, and that his parents could not get him to do any work. His mother's brother was the chieftain of the neighbouring O'Donovan sept of Carberry, and we are told that this uncle raided the O'Sullivan territory. As the raiders left the Beare peninsula, driving a huge herd and laden with booty, Dónall's mother chided him for lying at the fireside and not assisting his people to oppose the aggression. At that, the youth jumped up in anger and seized one of his father's swords. He wielded it so strongly that it broke, as did a second sword, but the third one was very strong and it held. Then he went to confront his uncle at the head of the raiders. O'Donovan had sworn not to rest until he laid his hand on the westernmost promontory of Beare, and Dónall now cut that hand off and slew his uncle. In order to fulfil the uncle's vow, he brought the hand and laid it on the point furthest west of the peninsula. The folk accounts are to an extent corroborated by annalistic entries, which state that, not the chieftain Diarmaid Ó Donnabháin, but his namesake son raided Beare in 1581 at the instigation of the English. Dónall, then twenty years of age, gathered fifty men and attacked the raiders, slaying hundreds of them and also their leader, who was his cousin.

After the defeat of the Irish forces at Kinsale in 1601, Dónall held out for a year against the overwhelming English forces and, after the accession of King James I, he visited England in the company of some other Irish leaders in an attempt to have his territories restored to him. The attempt failed, and he travelled in secret to Cork, from where he and his family sailed to Spain. On account of his extraordinary ability to elude enemies, folk tradition claimed that he had the power to make himself invisible. It was said that he had got this gift while sleeping one night in a hut by the seashore. A voice spoke to him in a dream and told him that he had been betrayed and that the hut was surrounded by English soldiers. However, the voice also said that there was an herb on the table, and that if he put that in his mouth he could not be seen. In this manner he went outside, slew the bewildered soldiers, and escaped.

When he arrived in Spain, Dónall was received with great honour by King Philip III, and folklore had its own way of dramatising this. It is said that he burst his way through the royal guard and entered the king's presence. Philip demanded an explanation for this behaviour, and Dónall said that his sword was his pass. There was a great slab of brass in the court, which no cham pion had ever been able to cut with a sword-stroke, and the king ordered Dónall to attempt this feat. Dónall gave a terrible look at all those present, and then rose himself into the air and brought his sword down onto the block with terrible force, splitting it in halves. His servant began to throw water on him, and when the king queried the reason for this, Dónall explained that he had worked himself into a frenzy in order to procure the necessary strength and that, unless cooled down, nobody present would be safe from him. Similar accounts were told of other Irish chieftains cutting great blocks with a sword-stroke to prove their prowess, and this plot seems to have been a conventional one in folk epic.

The historical Dónall Cam worked hard to get Spanish assistance for a new campaign in Ireland and, along with other Irish emigré leaders, his affairs in Spain were closely watched by English intelligence sources. This is reflected by folk accounts of various attempts to assassinate him, but it is claimed that his death resulted from the greed of his valet, who knew him to have money. When Dónall bent down to tie his shoe, his cloak rose, revealing a chink in his armour, and the valet stabbed him through it. Thus he was referred to as 'Dónall Cam who was killed by treachery in Spain'. The reality was hardly less dramatic, for Dónall was actually stabbed to death outside a church in Madrid. He had lent money to an English friend called John Bath, and this matter led to a violent quarrel between Bath and his nephew, Philip O'Sullivan Beare. Two of Dónall's retainers separated them, but Bath unexpectedly lunged at the unsuspecting chieftain and stabbed him fatally through the neck.

Domhnall Ó Súilleabháin (1940), 95-121; John O'Donovan (1848-1851), 1762-3; Matthew Kelly (1850), 118, 337-8; M J Byrne (1903), 208; R B Breatnach in *Éigse 7*, 162-81; Dáithí Ó hÓgáin (1985), 163-8, 338; IFC S274:199-201.

[Epical motifs] See Jan de Vries (1963), 65-6, 132, 214-5; Seosamh Laoide (1905), 55-7; IFC 924:405-7.

Ó SÚILLEABHÁIN, EOGHAN RUA (1748-1784) Poet who was celebrated in Munster lore for his wit and his bohemian lifestyle. He was born at Meentogues, east of Killarney in Co Kerry and spent much of his life as a part-time teacher and migrant labourer in different parts of Munster. Tradition claims that he was a great womaniser, and that to avoid one such involvement he entered the British Navy in or about the year 1776. Another, and perhaps more accurate, tradition, has it that he was press-ganged, and this is what he himself states in one of his poems. In 1782 he was present at a fierce sea-battle between the British and the French in the Caribbean, and composed a poem in English praising the victor Admiral Rodney. It is said that he thought to gain his freedom by this poem, but Rodney refused this. Eoghan persisted in his efforts to be released, blistering his shins with spearwort, and so terrible did his sores become that he was discharged. He returned to Ireland, but soon after was killed in an ale-house brawl caused by a satire which he had composed.

72. Ó SÚILLEABHÁIN, EOGHAN RUA *English portrayal of a press-gang at work.*

Eoghan Rua's poetry, although quite conventional in its themes, was extremely rich in its language and metre. As a result, this red-haired and rakish young man was popularly regarded as a wizard with words. Like all the Gaelic poets of his time, he was well-versed in traditional Irish literature, and seems to have got as good an education as possible in the unofficial 'hedge-schools' of the time. He had good English and some knowledge also of Latin, Greek, and perhaps a little Hebrew. By the folk, this proficiency in learning was expressed by the belief that Eoghan had perfect knowledge of 'seven languages' and that 'he had poetry and history and everything else at his disposal'. The many stories told of him have him use his fluency and quick wit to express folk sentiments, with which - considering his material circumstances - Eoghan must have been very much in accord. Thus we have him using his poetic skills to castigate stinginess, pomposity, and oppressive authority, the three main objects of popular odium. It is said that he was once engaged in sowing seed for a dogged and ruthless farmer, who refused to give him his dinner but told him to continue at the work. Eoghan did so, but he began to recite some verses in unison with his sowing. 'The first unit,' he said in Irish, 'may you, drill of the field, have neither fortune nor luck; the second unit, may you not grow copiously; the third unit, desolation and scattering on your progeny; the fourth unit, may a thunderbolt strike your house!' Hearing this, the farmer began to fear the poet's curse, and he begged Eoghan to come to dinner and to cease his versifying.

How poetry could so easily be composed by some, and yet was so difficult to others, was a puzzle to the folk, and so a story was told of how a simple man one day asked Eoghan how it was done. Eoghan said that it was just speech, and as they walked along the road together he picked up four observations made by the man and strung them together in a well-rhymed verse, thus proving that poetry was a natural and easy process. When occasion demanded, however, he would deliberately mystify his skill. He was very hungry once, and gained admittance to a wedding reception, but was put sitting with the tramps and was given nothing but sprats to eat. Picking up one of the sprats, he pretended to engage in a whispering conversation with it. This was soon noticed, and the host came to him and enquired as to what he was doing. Eoghan said that he was seeking information from the sprat regarding his brother's affairs overseas. The host asked him to make enquiries concerning his own brother, who also was abroad, and having whispered for a while Eoghan said that the sprat did not know but had revealed that the hake yonder might have some information. He was therefore brought to the hake, and after some further whispering, he said that the hake had directed him on to the cattle, as the man in question was known to have been herding abroad. Eoghan was therefore put sitting at the beef-table, where he ate ravenously and said that the host's brother was enjoying great fare in foreign climes. This is in fact an adaptation into the context of Eoghan of a common folktale concerning a trickster.

It is not clear whether or not there was a basis in truth for Eoghan's reputed amours, but folklore makes much of the theme, portraying him as a roguish and likeable gallant. It is said that he began early. When a mere seven years of age, he was late for school one day and faced a beating from the schoolmaster if he could not explain his delay. Little Eoghan then recited some polished octuplets describing how he had been detained watching two beautiful young women whom he had encountered on the road, and the master was so captivated by the description that he pardoned him. Having pursued the same line of interest in his adult life, Eoghan was once accosted in his travels by a little boy who answered everything in verse and he thus recognised the child as a son of his own. This is in fact an example of a narrative plot found in many different countries (see **Romantic Tales**, Type 873). Another account has a lover thrusting her crying child at Eoghan and demanding that he take care of it, whereupon he composes a lullaby for the baby promising it all the beautiful things which the mind of the poet could imagine.

A favourite type of anecdote has Eoghan contending with overbearing clergymen. According to one of these, a priest determined to criticise him publicly from the altar for his loose living. When all the congregation was assembled, the priest called out ominously: 'Is Eoghan Ó Súilleabháin here?' Receiving no reply, he called out again, to no avail, and then he shouted: 'Is Eoghan Rua here?' The poet answered from the body of the church: 'Yes, and may you not see the painter!' This was a clever reference to the meaning of his epithet 'rua' (i.e. red). On another occasion, Eoghan was mending his torn shoe on the side of the road when a portly priest passed by and remarked in a semi-quatrain that the poet was not much of a shoemaker. Filling in the metre, Eoghan referred to 'a priest with his head full of Latin and his belly dancing with punch!' We are told also that he was refused admittance to Mass once because he had no offering to make at the door, and was told to listen from the outside of the church. Eoghan sat on a heap of turf, and was later challenged by the priest for not properly attending Mass. He replied in a rolling metre that poverty was not what most hurt him nor to be underfoot always, but to have his dignity insulted, and that if God was like the Church he was just as well off sitting on the turf. Stung by Eoghan's theological sophistication, the priest relented. A humorous story of a type found in mediaeval European literature was also attached to Eoghan. According to this, he once offered to carry a priest on his back across a flooded river, on the condition that the priest hear his Confession simultaneously. Halfway through the water, Eoghan confessed some very serious sin, and the enraged priest shouted 'tá an diabhal thiar ort!' which can be translated as 'the devil is riding you!' 'Well, if so,' said Eoghan, 'he will not be for much longer!', and he flung the priest into the flood.

The anticlericalism attributed to Eoghan and to some other poets is very much a demand by the folk for charity and a rejection of authoritarianism. For instance, another story has him reprimanding a lazy priest who refused to rise from bed on a stormy night to attend to a sick woman. Eoghan's remark that 'she will have plenty of priests to accompany her on her journey to heaven without you' set the priest thinking and he lost no time in fulfilling his duty. Other quatrains attributed to him have him castigating various clergymen for their greed and their indifference to the poor, a theme of social protest which has a long history in European literature and popular sentiment. In fact, the portrayal of Eoghan Rua has all the psychological power of the 'sinner-saint' image, and this is very much in accord with the actual poetry composed by him. His life, compositions, and portrayal in folklore all share the paradox of a personality split in equal measure between its degrading physical surroundings and the soaring flights of its imagination. Such a paradox, of course, is of frequent occurrence in various milieux.

Two curious traditions are attached to the death of Eoghan Rua. According to one, after he had been struck on the head with a pair of tongs in the fatal brawl, he lay incapacitated for some time. It is said that a certain young woman, wishing to discover if he really was dying, came to his bed and took her clothes off, but Eoghan spoke a candid verse saying that his sexual powers were gone and she realised then that his death was near. Another tradition states that, when the Bishop of Kerry heard of his death, he remarked sadly: 'More distressful is his death than that of a hundred priests. A priest can be made if money is available for his education, but a poet like Eoghan Rua can never again be made!' Both traditions are apocryphal, and the saying attributed to the bishop has parallels in accounts of some famous Renaissance artists in Europe.

Pádraig Ua Duinnín (1901) and (1902); Daniel Corkery (1967), 184-221; Dáithí Ó hÓgáin (1982),

473 and (1985), 218-24, 243-56, 341-4 and in *Feasta* 1-2/1980, 8-12, 21-5.

[Folktale plot of trickster] Antti Aarne / Stith Thompson (1961), Type 1567C.

[Priest on back] See Johannis Pauli (1972) *1*, 330, 385.

[Saying of bishop] See Ernst Kris / Otto Kurz (1979), 50-1.

OGHAM The earliest form of writing in Irish. It is found in inscriptions on standing-stones in many different parts of the country, especially in the south, and also in areas of Irish settlement in Scotland, the Isle of Man, and Wales. Its use dates from the 4th or 5th century AD down to the 8th century.

73. OGHAM *Inscribed ogham-stone from Co. Kerry.*

Ogham is in reality a borrowing of the Latin alphabet, but istead of the standard symbols the letters are represented by a system of notches and grooves. The early literature refers to rhetorics and charms being written in ogham on timber, but the surviving evidence consists solely of standing stones with memorial inscriptions to the dead. The form of Irish in these is sometimes quite antique, with the longer Celtic word-endings. Thus, for instance, a name (in genitive form) in one inscription, 'Dalagni maqi Dali', would have been written 'Dalláin maic Daill' by the time that Irish literature began in the 6th-7th century. It is obvious that ogham was in reality an adaptation of the Latin alphabet by Irish poets or learned men before Christianity brought widespread knowledge of Latin letters to Ireland. The Celtic forms of the words may have been deliberate preservation of archaic language - it is likely that they were already obsolete when ogham was first used, surviving only in rhetorical speech of **poets**.

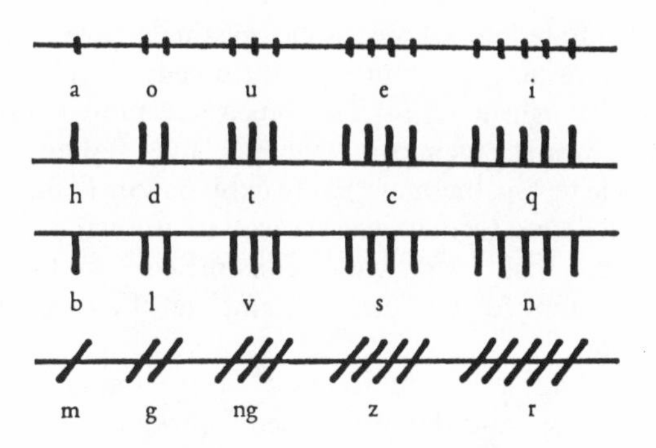

OGHAM *The alphabet in 'ogham' script.*

ᴀ	b	c	ꝺ	e	ꝼ	ᵹ	h	ı
a	b	c	d	e	f	g	h	i
l	m	n	o	p	ꞃ	ꞅ	ꞇ	u
l	m	n	o	p	r	s	t	u

OGHAM *The alphabet in Irish manuscript lettering.*

It is difficult to decide on the exact development of the word 'ogham', but the most likely theory is that the learned caste derived it from the name of the divinity associated with rhetoric, **Oghma**. As a system of writing, it was well-known to the scholars who adopted the standard Latin lettering system, and explanations of it are found in manuscripts down to recent times. This meant that the knowledge of ogham was never really lost. The general attitude to it in the literature and folklore is that it was a form of writing with quasi-magical significance, and this indeed is likely to have been the attitude which prevailed when some member of the learned caste devised this system to first commit words to visual form in Ireland.

R A S Macalister (1945-1949); George Calder (1917), 187-91, 272-99, 349-50, 373; Damien MacManus in *Ériu 37*, 1-31; Anthony Harvey in *Ériu 38*, 45-71.

OGHMA Mythical champion of the **Tuatha Dé Danann**, originally a deity.

The Latin writer Lucian described a Gaulish deity called Ogmios who personified eloquence and whose tongue was joined by mystical chains to the ears of his listeners. This is paralleled by an early reference to the Irish Oghma as 'a man most knowledgeable in speech and in poetry'. In line with this, he is claimed to have been son of a certain Ealadha, whose name meant 'art' or 'poetic composition'. To him was attributed the invention of the **ogham** script. The precise relation between the words 'Ogmios', 'Oghma' and 'ogham' are unclear, but the most likely explanation is that the appellative Ogmios was borrowed from the Gauls by the Irish Celts, who reconstructed it as Oghma and applied the deity's name to their magical script.

Oghma is said to have been brother of the **Daghdha**, and he was given sobriquets such as 'Grian-aineach' (i.e. 'sun-faced') and 'Grian-éces' (i.e. 'sun-poet'). He is represented as one of the chieftains of the Tuatha Dé. In the time of oppression during the reign of **Breas** he, with the Daghdha, was forced to do heavy manual labour, his task being to carry loads of firewood. Despite this humiliation, he continued to show his skill at arms, and was the principal champion of the Tuatha Dé as they prepared for the second battle of Moytirra (see **Mythological Cycle**). On the arrival of Lugh at the Tuatha Dé court, Oghma engaged in a contest with him throwing a flagstone over the side of the royal hall. One account states that he was slain in combat with one of the enemy leaders at the height of the battle, but alternately he is said to have survived the battle and to have shared the triumph with Lugh and the Daghdha.

T F O'Rahilly (1935), 41-2; H A de Jubainville (1903), 172-3; David Comyn (1902), 222; George Calder (1917), 187-8, 272-3; E A Gray (1982), 28-9, 32-3, 38-45, 52-3, 64-5, 68-71, 131.

OISÍN A leading character in the **Fianna Cycle**, son of the celebrated **Fionn mac Cumhaill**. His name (earlier, Oiséne) means 'little fawn', and was a common one in early Ireland. Its application to him, however, reflects the hunting imagery of the Fianna.

The character Oisín was already part of the Fianna lore by the early 9th century, for a text of that time has him quarrelling with Fionn (q.v.) and leaving his father for a long time. The text describes how they met in the wilderness while Oisín was cooking a pig, and they almost came to blows before they recognised each other. This is a version of a popular folklore plot (see **Romantic Tales**, Type 873). In line with the lore of hunting and of deer, a story was already current in the early Middle Ages concerning the birth of Oisín. According to this, his mother was called Blái Dheirg and she used to come to visit Fionn's band in the form of a doe. Later tradition claims that she was a beautiful girl who married Fionn but, when the hero was absent one day, a malicious wizard came and turned her into the shape of a deer. When Fionn returned she was gone, and he searched long and hard for her, but to no avail. She gave birth to his child in the wilderness while still in that shape. After several years, Fionn's hunting hounds found a handsome little boy in the forest, and when the boy said that he had been reared by a deer, Fionn realised that it was his son and called him Oisín. This seems to be a romanticised version of an older tradition which had Oisín's mother as an otherworld woman who deliberately took the form of a deer during a hunt in order to lure Fionn deep into the forest and seduce him there. Her name links her to **Dearg**, a divine figure often hostile to Fionn, and the likelihood is that she was in fact the daughter of Dearg, a lady who had a special grudge against the hero.

74. OISÍN *Fawn of the Irish red deer.*

The otherworld could be either friendly or hostile in Irish storytelling, but it is always quite mysterious. Thus the mediaeval lore found little difficulty in accepting the idea that Oisín's mother weas an otherworld lady, and did not trouble too much about whatever hostility she had towards Fionn. We read in a 12th-century text that Oisín, after the final defeat of the Fianna troop, sojourned for a while with his mother Blái Dheirg in the otherworld dwelling of Ocht Cleitigh (a rath near Newgrange in Co Meath). This text, called *Agallamh na Seanórach* (the Colloquy of the Old Men), fancifully describes how Oisín and **Caoilte** survived the demise of the rest of the Fianna warriors and lived on to meet the great missionary saint **Patrick**. Although most of the conversation in the text takes place between the saint and Caoilte, the subsequent literature puts Oisín clearly into the leading role. This was probably due to the fact that, since the early Middle Ages, Oisín was being patterned after the imagery of his father Fionn as a wise and knowledgeable poet. The Colloquy was the greatest mediaeval compilation of Fianna lore, using the format of Patrick's conversations with the survivors, and the learned Oisín therefore came to be regarded as the more suitable spokesman for the ancient memories.

The idea of Patrick thus meeting ancient Irish heroes and converting them posthumously to Christianity had been current for some time, and an earlier story had **Cú Chulainn** return from the dead and accept the new teachings. When it became attached to Oisín and to his memories of the Fianna, however, the idea gradually developed into dialogues of unprecedented drama and humour. From the 13th to the 18th centuries, new verses were continually being composed and put into the mouths of Patrick and Oisín as they argued the pros and cons of the warrior life of old and the monastic life of the saints. The earlier versions were obviously written by ecclesiastics, and these have Oisín being completely overcome by the rationale of Patrick's arguments. When the lay writers put their hands to composing such dialogues, however, they had Oisín pointing out several sanctimonious attitudes of the clergy and stressing that the generosity of the Fianna outdid the type of narrow moralism which was comically attributed to Patrick.

This tradition of a dialogue between Oisín and Patrick became the vehicle for many new adventures of the Fianna (q.v.) which were invented in the post-mediaeval period and told in the form of versified lays. Some older motifs, too, were adapted and set to the context of the great debate. For instance, an old story told of how Patrick (q.v.) had baptised the Munster king Aonghus and had inadvertently put his crozier through the neophyte's foot. In the 15th or 16th century, this story was switched from Aonghus to Oisín, who similarly suffered the pain and loss of blood patiently, believing it to be part of the ceremony. In order to rationalise the encounter of Patrick and Oisín, a whole complex of storytelling developed around the same time. According to this, Oisín had not been at the great battle of Gabhra in which the Fianna (q.v.) had been destroyed, but had departed from Ireland sometime before. It happened that the Fianna were hunting one day when they were visited by a beautiful lady who loved him and asked him to accompany her to the Land of Youth. He did so, but after some time there expressed the desire to pay a visit to his homeland. Although it seemed a short while to him, three hundred long years had passed, and the lady warned him not to set foot on the soil of Ireland. He arrived in Ireland on horseback, but found that the Fianna were all dead and gone. He met some men who had trouble lifting a load which seemed trifling to him. Without thinking, therefore, he leaped from the saddle to lift the load for them, but immediately on touching the ground he was changed into a very old man. While in that state, he was approached by Patrick and the celebrated dialogue began.

This story was widespread throughout the Gaelic world in recent centuries, although there is only one literary version of it, and that as late as the mid-18th century. The literary version calls the beautiful lady Niamh, has her and Oisín riding a fine white horse, and has Oisín accidentally falling from the horse when his saddle-girths break in an attempt to lift a large boulder. These seem to be colourful extras inserted into the story by the author of the literary text, Mícheál Coimín from Co Clare. Coimín must have got the story from the folklore of his time, for it is in fact a variant of an international narrative plot which was long known in Ireland (see **Wonder Tales**, Type 470).

The post-mediaeval folklore went on to tell of how Oisín was displeased with the type of food given to him by Patrick's housekeeper. He boasted that in the time of the Fianna he had seen a blackbird's egg larger than the joint of meat she was cooking, a rowan-berry larger than her chunk of butter, and an ivy-leaf larger than her cake. She refused to believe this, but Oisín was determined to prove his point. We are told that Patrick had a bitch which gave birth to a litter of pups, and Oisín selected the best one of them. He did this by fastening a sheepskin to a wall and throwing each of the pups at it, the best being the one which alone clung to the skin. When the pup grew up somewhat, Oisín took it with him to the forest. He found an old trumpet there and told his servant to blow it. Soon a huge blackbird approached, and the young hound was loosed against it and killed it. The hound became demented by its triumph, and so fierce was it that Oisín decided that it must be slain. Though failing of sight, he took a metal ball and accurately flung it into the hound's gullet, choking it. Oisín then procured a huge rowan-berry and ivy-leaf - relics from the lost epoch - and returned to Patrick's housekeeper to win the argument.

This story also was widespread throughout the Gaelic world, as was the idea that Oisín finally managed to persuade Patrick to ask God for the release of the dead Fianna (q.v.) from hell, where they were confined on account of their paganism. Munster storytellers added a clever touch to this, claiming that Oisín had asked only for the release of Fionn, and when this request was granted he declared that they were all 'fionn' (i.e. beloved) to him.

[Biographical] Kuno Meyer (1910), xviii, xxviii-xxx, 24-7 and in *Revue Celtique 6*, 186; R I Best / M A O'Brien (1957), 729; Whitley Stokes (1900), 2; Gerard Murphy (1953), xxi; Edward Gwynn (1913), 242-53; L-C Stern in *Zeitschrift für celtische Philologie 5*, 180.

[Colloquy] Stokes (1900), 2-9, 64-74, 220-4, 359-60; Dubhglas de hÍde in *Lia Fáil 1*, 79-107; Nessa Ní Shéaghdha (1945), 224-5.

[Debate with Patrick] Eoin Mac Néill (1908), 74-5; Gerard Murphy (1933), 168-73, 178-83, 204-15; Pádraig Ó Siochfhradha (1941), 227-40

[Folklore] Murphy (1953), xx; Ó Siochfhradha (1941), 213-26; Seán Ó Súilleabháin / R Th Christiansen (1967), 96-7; Cormac Ó Cadhlaigh (1947), 447-50.

[General] Dáithí Ó hÓgáin (1988), 49-50, 77-80, 117-8, 155-6, 241-55, 330, 340-1, 361 and in Bo Almqvist / Séamas Ó Catháin / Pádraig Ó Héalaí eds (1987), 233-4.

OLLAMH FÓDLA Fictional king of Ireland situated in prehistory. His name means 'high-poet of Fódla', Fódla being an alternative name for Ireland (see **Goddesses**).

The mediaeval writers claimed that he reigned for forty years, and that he instituted the Festival of **Tara** and constructed 'the Rampart of the High-Poets' (Múr na n-Ollamhan) at that royal centre. He died, we are told, a natural death within the rampart. A seventeenth-century writer, apparently quoting some lost source, gives a more detailed account of this king. According to this, Ollamh Fódla was so called because he was the leading man in the country for wisdom and knowledge and drafting laws. The Festival of Tara which he instituted was held every third year at Samhain (November), and at that session the laws were reviewed and the annals were put in order.

Some earlier writers give clues to the origin of this fictional king. One source states that his real name was Eochaidh, that he was 'a marvellous poet', and that he had as brother a wonderful wizard called Araidhe. It is further claimed that the Dál nAraidhe people of east Ulster were named from this Araidhe. Other texts, equally inventive, state that the Ulstermen (Ulaidh) got their name from him, giving for 'Ulaidh' the false etymology 'oll-leith' (i.e. the side of Ollamh). These references indicate that the personality whose image suggested this fictional king was the 6th-century Ulsterman **Eochaidh Rí-Éigeas**, known as 'the chief poet of Ireland'. The mediaeval writers did not scruple about using what were to them obscure names and titles to invent characters and so fill in the imagined ancient history.

R A S Macalister (1956), 232-5; P S Dinneen (1908) *2*, 130-5; Whitley Stokes in *Irische Texte 3*, 392-3; R I Best / M A O'Brien (1957), 477; James Carney in *Celtica 1*, 101.

OSCAR Leading warrior in the **Fianna Cycle**. His name has the element 'os' (meaning 'fawn'), and his origins obviously lay in the hunting lore of the Fianna. He is always described as the son of **Oisín**, and therefore grandson of the celebrated **Fionn mac Cumhaill**.

It might be that his name was originally an alternative one for Oisín. As a character, Oscar does not figure in the literature until the 11th century, but lore of him must have been in existence for some time previously. This occurrence is already a crucial one, as he is described as slaying with a spear-cast the high-king **Cairbre Lifeachair** in the battle of Gabhra, where the Fianna were finally overthrown. The succeeding literature is unstinting in the prestige which it accords to him. He is repeatedly portrayed as the hero who plays the foremost role in battle and who triumphs for the Fianna against strange warriors who come to seek single combat. His name in fact came to be used as a common noun 'oscar' to denote a champion, and a 13th-century text says of him that 'there never will be after Oscar a warrior of so many hardy triumphs, nor in his own time was there a man his match in battles'.

Later tradition has Oisín tell St **Patrick** of his son: 'If I saw Oscar and God, fighting hand to hand on yonder hill, if I saw Oscar laid low, then I would admit that God was a strong man!' Folklore has Oscar defeating the great **Goll mac Morna** in a wrestling contest and thus gaining general recognition as the strongest man of all the Fianna. Finally, when the dead Fianna warriors perform their most dramatic feat by breaking out of hell, it is Oscar who acts as their rearguard. He wields a great flail, which has an unbreakable thong, and thus keeps the demons at bay while each one of the Fianna go free through the gates of hell. This account of him is based on a general folklore plot (see **Wonder Tales**, Type 650A), which has an enormously strong man make a great flail and overcome the devils in hell with it.

For the great fighting feats of Oscar, see **Fianna Cycle**.

Ernst Windisch in *Irische Texte 1*, 158; Eoin Mac Néill (1908), 74; Pádraig Ó Siochfhradha (1941), 85; Gerard Murphy (1953), 50-1, 56, 116; Reidar Christiansen (1931), 17-9; Dáithí Ó hÓgáin (1988), 149-50, 156, 240, 248-51, 284-5, 361.

P

PARTHALÁN (also, Partholón) Leader of a fictional ancient settlement in Ireland.

He and his people were an invention of the early mediaeval historians. 'Parthalán' is an Irish adaptation of Bartholomaeus, a name which had been explained by St Jerome as 'son of him who stays the waters'. This explanation was repeated in the influential work of Isidorus of Seville in the 7th century. Since the historians based their chronology on the Biblical Deluge, they thus claimed that the first leader of a settlement in Ireland after that event was called Parthalán. This idea developed early, for Parthalán is mentioned in an account of Irish prehistory in the *Historia Brittonum* of Nennius, which was compiled in the early 9th century. The *Historia Brittonum* had as one of its sources a primitive text of the Irish pseudo-historical work called the *Lebor Gabála*.

According to the *Lebor Gabála*, Parthalán fled from Greece after slaying his father and mother in an attempt to take the kingship from his brother. He also lost his left eye in the episode, and bad fortune was destined to follow him on account of his kin-slaying. After seven years wandering, he reached Ireland accompanied by his wife and three sons and their wives. Various accounts are given of retainers whom he also brought with him. For instance, Beoil who made the first guest-house in Ireland, Bréa who instituted cooking and duelling, and Malaliach who was the first brewer, manufacturing ale from the fern. Furthermore, he brought with him four oxen, the first cattle in the country. The settlers found but one unforested area in Ireland, Sean-Mhagh nEalta (the plain on which the city of Dublin now stands), and so they set about levelling four other plains. Curiously, the accounts accept that the demonic **Fomhóire** race were already in Ireland, and these were encountered and defeated by Parthalán in the battle of Magh nÍotha (the plain of south Donegal). This conflict lasted for a week, but no combatant was slain, 'for it was a magic battle'. It was fought 'on single legs and with single arms and single eyes', and the account of it is obviously an echo of the great mythic contest between the otherworld powers (see **Mythological Cycle**).

Some personal drama was also infused into the narrative concerning Parthalán. Once, when he went hunting, he left his wife Dealgnat with his man-servant Topa at Magh-Inis (the estuary of the river Erne). Dealgnat seduced the servant, and they used Parthalán's own suction-tube to drink ale from his vat. When he returned and found the taste of their mouths on the tube, he realised what had happened and flew into a rage. One recension states that he killed the unfortunate Topa, whereas others have his wife's lapdog as the victim. This was the first adultery and the first jealousy ever in Ireland. Dealgnat, however, justified her actions with a quatrain to the following effect: 'Honey with a woman, milk with a cat, food with a generous person, meat with a boy, a wright where an edged tool is - one with one, great the risk!'

Having been thirty years in Ireland, Parthalán died on the primaeval plain of Sean-Mhagh nEalta. His people continued to inhabit the country for five hundred and twenty years. When they numbered over nine thousand, they were overtaken by a plague on that same plain and all perished there between two Mondays in May. A variant telling, however, had one survivor, the long-living **Tuán mac Cairill**.

R A S Macalister (1939), 249, 253-73 and (1940), 2-114; Kuno Meyer in *Zeitschrift für celtische Philologie 13*, 141-2; H A de Jubainville (1903), 16-25; T F O'Rahilly (1946), 475-6 A G Van Hamel in *Zeitschrift für celtische Philologie 10*, 152-5, 181-2.

PATRICK (Irish Pátraic, later Pádraig, from the Latin Patricius) The national saint, who flourished in the 5th century AD. The date of his mission was traditionally given as from the year 432 to 461, but a more likely dating is from 456 to 493. He was not the first Christian missionary in Ireland, but it is clear that he was the most influential and his efforts were very significant in the general change to Christianity.

Patrick was born somewhere in the west of Britain into a family of Romanised Celts, his

75. PATRICK *Iron bell, reputedly that of St. Patrick.*

father's name being Calpurnius. At the age of sixteen he was seized by an Irish raiding party - possibly led by **Niall Naoi-ghiallach** - and brought to Ireland as a slave. He was set to herding pigs and sheep in a lonely place, but after six years he escaped, travelling two hundred miles before he got a ship to bring him to the Continent. He studied there, was ordained to the priesthood, and after a long interval returned to Ireland to begin his mission. This much is clear from his own work, the *Confessio*, and in it he tells that, while on the Continent, he had a vision in which a man brought him letters containing 'the voice of the Irish' and beseeching him to 'come back and walk once more among us'. In the vision, he recognised the voices of people who lived beside the wood of Foclath (apparently in the parish of Meelick, Co Mayo), and it seems from this that he had spent at least part of his bondage in that area. The *Confessio* is very much a private document, and it is difficult to decipher much from it regarding the physical environment and actual events of his career. One other document survives from his hand, a letter written in condemnation of a north British prince called Coroticus who had seized some of Patrick's converts and taken them as captives.

The earliest surviving biographies of Patrick date from the second half of the 7th century. One of these was by Muirchú, who seems to have been a cleric from Armagh, and the other was by a bishop named Tíreachán, apparently a native of Tirawley in Co Sligo. In some respects both of these biographies draw from a common source, and it can therefore be assumed that a written account of Patrick had been compiled anterior to these works. There are some indications that that account contained information left by a disciple of Patrick himself, called Mochtae. Muirchú and Tíreachán, however, developed the material greatly and added much.

76. PATRICK *Map of Lough Derg, from the 17th century.*

Borrowing from the *Confessio*, Muirchú describes Patrick's youth, captivity, and escape, and then goes on to tell in very dramatic terms of the saint's mission to Christianise the country. We read that the **druids** of the high-king **Laoghaire**, son of Niall, had foretold in verse the coming of such a one, an 'adze-head' who would triumph over the old ways. Accordingly, Patrick arrived at Inbhear

Dé (Arklow), but then sailed north to Sliabh Mis (Slemish in Co Down) to redeem himself from the man who is described as having been his master when in slavery, Miliuc. The latter, hearing that the escaped slave was approaching, feared that Patrick might become his master and burned himself to death. On seeing the burnt-out pier, Patrick turned away in disappointment and sailed to Inbhear Colptha (the Boyne estuary). It was Easter-tide, and the custom was for the high-king to light a fire at **Tara** at that time. Anybody who lit a fire before Laoghaire did so would forfeit his life. Patrick, however, lit his own Easter fire at Sláine (Slane, Co Meath), and when Laoghaire saw this he rushed in anger, accompanied by his druids and soldiers, to confront the newcomer.

Patrick was ordered to explain his behaviour, and he immediately got into contention with the druids - one of whom, named Lochru, he caused to be raised into the air and to fall and dash his brains against a stone. Seeing this, Laoghaire and his men tried to seize the saint, but darkness fell and the ground shook, causing them to mistake each other for him. Following this, Laoghaire pretended to do reverence to Patrick and invited him to come to Tara. Patrick, however, suspected treachery. He blessed his eight companions, and they disappeared into the wilderness in the form of deer. On the following day, the saint with five of his companions entered Tara through closed doors as the royal household was feasting. He was invited to join in the feast, and a druid called Lucat Moel put a drop of poison into his drink. Patrick blessed the drink, which froze, and the drop fell out. A contest in wondrous feats between the saint and Lucat ensued. To show his power, the druid covered the plain with snow, but he could not remove it and Patrick had to do that for him. Similarly with a fog which the druid brought. Finally they agreed to a test of fire. A house was built, half of greenwood and half of dry wood. Lucat went into the green part, wearing the saint's chasuble, and Patrick's servant-boy Benignus went into the other part, wearing the druid's garb. The house was then set on fire, with the result that Lucat was burned to death while Benignus emerged unscathed. However, the druid's garment on Benignus was consumed, whereas Patrick's chasuble on Lucat was untouched. We read that Laoghaire was then converted, but Patrick told him that - on account of his previous opposition - none of his descendants would be kings.

Muirchú goes on to describe various events of Patrick's mission - including a claim that Coroticus, having made captives of some of the saint's converts, was turned into a fox. We read that a fierce tyrant in Ulster, called Mac Cuill (recte Mac Goill) tried to entrap the saint by having one of his men feign death and demanding that Patrick heal him. When the cover was removed from the face of the imposter, however, he was found to be really dead and had to be revived by the saint, whereupon Mac Cuill submitted to Patrick and sought baptism. As penance, Patrick ordered him to set himself adrift in a boat, and he did so and reached the Isle of Man, where he became a hermit. In an adventure at Droim Bó (near Downpatrick), Patrick rebuked pagans for building a rath on a Sunday, and as a result a storm came and destroyed their work. We also read that a powerful man named Dáire refused Patrick the hill of Droim Saileach (now Armagh), but instead gave him an inferior site for a monastery. One of Dáire's horses later died after grazing on this site, and as a result the magnate told his men to go and kill the saint. Immediately, however, Dáire himself was struck down with illness, and the men begged Patrick to come and heal him. The saint gave them blessed water, with which both Dáire and the horse were revived. The magnate then gave a bronze cauldron as a present to Patrick, who reacted only by saying 'grazacham'. Dáire ordered that the cauldron be taken back, and again Patrick spoke the same word. Finally, the magnate himself went with the cauldron and gave it to him, giving also the piece of land at Droim Saileach, which became Patrick's great centre of Ard Mhacha.

Other details in Muirchú's text include a conversation of Patrick with a pagan over whose grave a cross had inadvertently been placed. The dead man told him that the cross should rather have been placed next to him, on the grave of a man who had died a Christian. We also read that the saint was untouched by rain, and that he could light up the dark with his fingers, which glowed. Before he died, he obtained special requests from his companion angel Victor. These were that Armagh should be pre-eminent in the Irish church, and that all the Irish people should be judged by Patrick himself at the end of time. For twelve days after his death at Sabhall (Saulpatrick, Co Down) there was no darkness in that area. The angel had advised him regarding the manner of his burial, and his body was accordingly placed in a cart drawn by untamed oxen. They stopped at

Dún Leathghlaise (Downpatrick) in the territory of the Ulstermen, and he was buried there. The Ulstermen and the royal Uí Néill sept quarrelled over which of them should have the body, but an illusion of another pair of oxen drawing a cart was seen by the Uí Néill, and they therefore thought that they had the body for burial.

This biography by Muirchú had various sources. It is clear that he dramatised his account of the saint's coming to the court of the high-king with various imagery from Christian tradition - he himself compares Laoghaire to the Old Testament tyrant Nebuchadnezzar, the angel speaks to Patrick from a burning bush as God did to Moses, and the contest with the druids is modelled jointly on that of Moses with the Pharaoh's magicians and on the apocryphal account of St Peter's contest with Simon Magus. Other sources, too, can be identified. The account of Mac Cuill, called a 'Cyclops' in the text, contains a residue of ancient Irish myth concerning a one-eyed foe (see **Goll**), while the Dáire story contains echoes of the **Daghdha** and his cauldron of plenty. On the other hand, the puzzling word 'grazacham' may preserve an actual memory of Patrick's strange-sounding Latin or mixture of Latin and Irish (viz. 'gratias agam' - a non-idiomatic way of saying 'thank you'). The contest with Lucat Moel and the story of the burning hut is given also in shorter form by Tíreachán and must have been included in the common source used by both biographers. It is possible that Lucat was originally a Christian parody of **Lugh**.

Tíreachán gives a shorter and less ornamented account of the saint's coming to Tara, and states - more realistically - that Laoghaire (q.v.) refused conversion. This biography concentrates more on Patrick's activities in Tíreachán's native area of north Connacht, giving much detail of the saint's supposed itinerary. It also gives the first version of Patrick's famous retreat on the top of Cruachán Aigle (Croaghpatrick in Co Mayo). We read that the saint spent forty days and forty nights there, and that the birds were so numerous there that they were troublesome to him. Tíreachán represents the saint as climbing many mountains, another echo of the early stratum of lore which envisaged him on a par with Moses, who communicated with God on Mount Sinai. The Croaghpatrick story is given in a developed form in the third major work on the saint's life, entitled *Bethu Phátraic*, which was compiled mostly in Irish between the years 896 and 901. Here we are told that Patrick stayed at the top of the mountain for the duration of Lent. At the end of that time the peak was filled with black demonic birds, and Patrick banished them by ringing his bell. Angelic white birds then came and sang melodiously for him. He refused to leave the mountain or abandon his fast until God agreed to give him the right to judge all the Irish on the Last Day. This request is the genesis of the long tradition which makes Patrick a symbol of Irish integrity. A text from the same early period adds two further boons - that no other people should rule over Ireland forever, and that the country would be submerged by the sea seven years before the end of the world and thus be spared the final desolation.

The text *Bethu Phátraic* is in three parts, making use of the works of both Muirchú and Tíreachán, but adding much material concerning Munster, the province in the interest of which it was compiled. A whole new (and quite unhistorical) missionary tour of Munster by Patrick is described, particularly influential being an account of the baptism of the provincial king Aonghus mac Nadfraoich at Cashel. We read that Patrick inadvertently put the spike of his crozier through Aonghus' foot. When he noticed what he had done he asked why Aonghus had not complained, and Aonghus said that he thought that this was part of the rite. Patrick was so pleased at this piety that he ordained that none of Aonghus' descendants as kings should ever die of a wound. The text connects Patrick with various parts of Munster, and it thus represents a culmination of the process which turned the early missionary to the north midlands and south Ulster into a national saint who travelled the length and breadth of Ireland, singlehandedly converting the pagan people to Christianity. *Bethu Phátraic* also contains lore of the saint's youth which had developed since his time. We read that his mother was called Concess, and that she was a kinswoman of St **Martin**. He was baptised by a blind priest, but there was no water available and the priest made the Sign of the Cross with the infant's hand. Immediately a well sprang up from the ground and, when the priest washed his eyes in it, his sight was restored. We further read that Patrick, during his childhood, miraculously healed his sister who was on the point of death after an accident, restored his dead fosterfather to life, caused a wolf to return a stolen sheep, and made firewood from icicles, honey from water, and butter from snow.

Tíreachán gives a description of how Patrick

77. PATRICK *The towering Croaghpatrick in Co. Mayo.*

resuscitated a dead giant in order to baptise him, a motif borrowed from a 7th-century Latin biography of Pope Gregory, who is claimed to have revived the Emperor Trajan for that purpose. This idea of how Patrick could revive and posthumously convert great men of old was put to use by writers from the 11th century onwards, who represent him as gaining heaven for the dead **Cú Chulainn** and as meeting with the Fianna heroes **Caoilte** and **Oisín** who are claimed to have outlived their time. Beginning in the 12th century, several accounts were written of his dialogues with this latter duo, and the folklore concerning Oisín (q.v.) preserves many snatches of such. The mediaeval account of the death of the mythical Ulster king **Conchobhar mac Neasa** was also developed in folklore by having Patrick baptise his soul. The soul spoke to the saint from a bush, and this story was further applied to the celebrated high-king of Ireland, **Cormac mac Airt**.

Several versions of Patrick's biography were written by Anglo-Norman scholars in the Middle Ages. The most striking innovation in these is the notion that the saint banished snakes from Ireland. This motif first became attached to him in the 12th century, and various explanations of it have been suggested. Ireland was well-known for its lack of snakes from ancient times - the Greek writer Solinus referred to the fact over a century before Patrick was born. Early mediaeval writers, such as Isidorus and Bede, also mention it as a scientific fact and with no reference to any tradition involving Patrick. The connection with the saint seems to have been due to the fancy of the hagiographical writers, who had read in earlier biographies that Patrick had studied for some time on the island of Aralanensis (which was understood to be the island of Lérins off the south coast of France). The monastery on Lérins had been founded by St Honoratus, whose biography claimed that he had banished the snakes from that island, and so the Anglo-Norman writers considered the motif a suitable one to borrow into the Irish context of Patrick. The notion is far more popular in late written and pictorial sources than in folk tradition, which has not quite digested a scenario so unrealistic in environmental as well as practical terms.

A rich harvest of custom and lore concerning the saint does, however, survive in genuine folk tradition. He is said, for instance, to have banished monsters into lakes at several different locations throughout the country. This is in line with the general popularity of that motif in Irish hagiography, but the tradition that Patrick banished a monster into Loch Dearg (Lough Derg in Co Donegal) seems to date back as far as the 7th century and to have been the main factor which gave rise to the great annual pilgrimage to that place. The pilgrimage was a very celebrated one in mediaeval times, with people coming to participate from all over the country and many different parts of Europe. A cavern on the island in Lough Derg was said to have been the entrance to Purgatory, and penitents would have to endure the ordeal of spending one night in that cavern. The pilgrimage is still current, taking place on all the weekends between June 1 and August 15, during which the pilgrims spend three days praying and fasting in the environs of the modern church built on the island, as well as one whole night without sleep. Another great annual penitential exercise which survives from the Middle Ages is the climbing of Croaghpatrick (in Co Mayo). This is done barefoot on the first Sunday in August (see **Time**), and also attracts pilgrims from all over Ireland.

Patrick looms large in folk legend. Versions of the test of the burning hut have been collected from living lore all over the country, as have versions of the story of the cauldron given to him as a gift by the great pagan. The name of the druid, Lucat Moel, does not however survive in these oral versions, and Dáire's name has been changed to **Crom**. The strong likelihood, then, is that these two legends passed into folklore from a post-mediaeval reading of some of the biographical texts. The folk also invented some original legends of the great saint. For instance, we are told that, exhausted from preaching once, he decided to take a nap and warned his servant-boy to listen carefully to what he would say. Three times the exasperated Patrick cursed Ireland through his sleep, but each time the clever boy deflected the curse with a prayer - firstly onto the tops of the rushes, secondly onto the bullocks' horns, and thirdly onto the bottom of the furze. That is why these three things are ever since black. When he awoke, Patrick praised the boy for his alert responses, because, he said, 'you have saved Ireland'.

78. PATRICK *The fanciful portrait of St. Patrick - an engraving dated 1624.*

In the early biographies, Patrick is represented as placing blessings on some septs, and curses on others, thus reflecting the bias in the backgrounds of the writers. This tendency passed over into folklore, although in a somewhat more humorous vein. Thus residents of various localities tease their western neighbours by claiming that Patrick never visited the latter, being put off by the bleakness of their territory and the crudity of the inhabitants. Another common jibe has the residents of various areas accusing their neighbours of having been guilty of the heinous offence of stealing the saint's goat while he was busy with his spiritual duties. The same type of banter lies behind a legend which was quite popular by way of chiding innkeepers. It was said that Patrick once visited a tavern but was given short measure by the landlady. Offended by this, he pointed out to her that the devil, in the shape of an ugly beast, was hiding in her cellar and being fattened by her dishonesty. The terrified woman begged Patrick to banish the evil spirit, but he told her that she must do so herself by mending her ways. Some time later, when he visited that same tavern, he found her filling the glasses of all her customers so that the whiskey poured out over the brim. He praised this change in behaviour, and brought her to the cellar, where they found the devil in a miserable state. The evil spirit fled in a flash of fire at their approach, and Patrick ordained that, in memory of this, people should always take a drink of whiskey on his feastday.

This drink was called the 'pota Phádraig' ('Patrick's pot'), and is known in English as 'drowning the shamrock', for it was customary to place the shamrock in the drink. The custom of wearing a sprig of shamrock on one's coat on St Patrick's Day, March 17, does not seem to be very ancient, the first known mention of it dating from the year 1681. It was popularly explained that Patrick had used this little trefoil plant as a means of explaining the Trinity, there being three persons in one God just as they are three leafs on the one stem. It would scarcely have been difficult for the saint to explain the mystery of the Trinity in this way, as the ancient Irish were well acquainted with the triplication of deities in their own mythology (see **Goddesses**). Nevertheless, in recent centuries the shamrock has become in a very special way the symbol of Patrick and of his mission. It was customary in the 18th and 19th centuries for people to wear little crosses on their coats on the saint's feastday. These crosses were made from paper which was coloured green and red, and were pinned onto a white paper background and decorated with ribbons. In recent generations, their place has been taken by manufactured green and gold badges in the shape of a shamrock or a harp.

Another recent addition to the celebration of St Patrick's Day is the holding of great parades through towns, led by brass and pipe bands. This is an imported tradition, deriving from the practice in 18th-century north America of holding military parades on that day so as to impress the populace and to encourage the recruitment of Irishmen to the British and US armies. The custom, with its military function discarded, was adopted in Ireland in the 19th century; and colourful parades are now held on St Patrick's Day in most large towns in Ireland and in places where substantial numbers of Irish people have settled abroad. The national saint has become a symbol of affection for Irish culture and of the desire for national freedom. This is criticised by some influential people, who however ignore the fact that in their long history of misery and subjection the Irish people have regarded this, the most famous of the early missionaries, as their special spiritual champion.

[Patrick's writings] Ludwig Bieler *1-2* (1951); R P C Hanson (1983).

[Personal history] James Carney (1973); Hanson (1968); E A Thompson (1985).

[Muirchú] Bieler (1979), 1-35, 61-122, 193-213.

[Tíreachán] Bieler (1979) , 35-46, 122-63, 213-33.

[Other early texts] J P Migne in *Patrologiae Latinae 53*, 823-6; Bieler, (1979), 46-56, 164-92, 233-41; Whitley Stokes / John Strachan (1903) *2*, 354-8.

[Bethu Phátraic] Stokes (1887); Kathleen Mulchrone (1939).

[Other biographies] Bieler (1971); Stokes (1890), 1-19.

[Patrick and snakes] Dáithí Ó hÓgáin in *Béaloideas 51*, 95-6.

[Lough Derg] Shane Leslie (1932); Michael Haren / Yolande de Pontfarcy (1988); Alannah Hopkin (1989), 84-105; Ó hÓgáin in *Béaloideas 51*, 90-9.

[Croaghpatrick] Máire MacNeill (1962), 71-84, 686.

[St Patrick's Day] Kevin Danaher (1972), 58-66; Hopkin, *op cit*, 106-43.

[Folk legends] Ó hÓgáin (1985), 5-16, 323; MacNeill, *op cit*, 434-648; IFC, much material.

[General] D A Binchy in *Studia Hibernica 2*, 7-173; Bieler (1949); J F Kenney (1929), 165-70, 319-56, 812; John O'Hanlon (1875) *3*, 399-831.

PICTS (in Irish, Cruithin, Cruithnigh) An ancient people who inhabited parts of Scotland, and apparently also of Ireland. The designation Cruithin is an Irish adaptation of the Celtic word for them, Priteni. The Latin term Picti is a secondary designation (meaning 'painted people') and was used in relation to the Scottish branch of the people only. It is believed most likely that the Picts were a Celtic people, speaking a language more akin to British Celtic than to Irish.

It may be that the Picts were in Ireland prior to the coming of the Gaelic Celts, but in historical times they had become fully assimilated to the Gaelic people in language and culture. Nevertheless, memory survived of the fact that some septs had a Pictish origin. There is mention of 'Cruithnigh tuath Cruachan' (i.e. the 'Pictish' tribe of Croghan, in Co Roscommon) in an early genealogical tract, and there are also indications that tributary septs of Leinster such as the Loíghis and the Fotharta had Pictish origins. The most prominent sept which was reputed to have such origins was the Dál nAraidhe, who occupied parts of Cos Antrim and Down and to whom belonged the celebrated **Mongán**.

So little survived by way of tradition concerning the early history of Irish Picts that a story was fabricated which claimed that they had in fact been later arrivals than the Gaelic people. According to this, they landed at Inbhear Sláine (the mouth of the river Slaney at Wexford) and were welcomed by the Leinster king Criomhthann Sciathbhéal. This king was troubled by a group of Britons called Tuath Fiodhgha, who had poison-tipped weapons and thus were slaying many of his men. A druid of the Picts ('Cruithentuath'), called Drostan, advised that the milk of six score hornless white cows be poured onto the battlefield. This was done, and all of Criomhthann's wounded men lay in the milk and were immediately healed. The Tuath Fiodhgha were defeated, and the power of the Picts grew greatly. Cathluan was the name of their king, and he took over Scotland for them. The Gaelic king **Éireamhóin**, however, drove them out of Ireland. They had no women, and one of their leaders called Cruithne came to Ireland to seek wives from Éireamhóin. They were given the widows of the men who had been drowned in the initial attempts by the sons of **Míl** and their Gaelic people to land in Ireland. There was a condition attached to this arrangement, however, namely that the Picts would have women as their leaders henceforth.

This curious account contrasts with the pseudo-historians' claim that the Cruithin were of the same stock as the Gaelic people (see **Érainn**). Although the chronology involved in it is unrealistic, the account must in part be based on early tradition, such as the idea that the Picts practised a matrilineal system of inheritance. The boast that the Irish had imposed that system on the Picts in return for Irish wives was already current in the early 8th century, for it is mentioned by the Anglo-Saxon historian, Bede. It probably reflects politicking on the part of the Gaelic settlers in Scotland from the 5th century onwards. There is no indication that Irish Picts were involved in any of this. Indeed, all that was known of Pictish language and culture in early mediaeval Ireland pertained only to Scotland, and it may be doubted whether the Irish Cruithin were really Picts at all.

There was no post-mediaeval tradition concerning the Cruithin or Cruithnigh. In Scottish folklore, however, the Picts were said to have been a dwarf people who lived long ago and were great builders. Some of this Scottish lore influenced folk belief in the province of Ulster in recent centuries, so that the Picts are sometimes given a role comparable to that of the **fairies**. Flints discovered near raths in parts of Ulster are claimed to have been arrow-heads belonging to them and pieces of crockery their pipes. These 'Pechts' are described as having been a small sturdy people with long hair and large feet. So large were their feet, indeed, that they could shelter themselves from rain by standing on their heads. According to another humorous tradition they were very numerous. When building a fort, they would stand in a line and could bring the materials from a far distant source by handing them on from one to another without moving a step.

[General] T F O'Rahilly (1946), 341-84; F T Wainwright (1955).

[Septs associated with Cruithin] M A O'Brien (1962), 41, 153-4, 195, 375; O'Rahilly, *op cit*, 34-5; Kuno Meyer in *Zeitschrift für celtische Philologie 8*, 313.

[Mediaeval story] O'Rahilly, *op cit*, 342-6; R A S Macalister (1956), 175-85; Joseph Fraser in *Medieval Studies for G S Loomis* (1927), 407-12.

[Irish reference to Pictish language] Meyer (1912), 25.

[Folklore] Elizabeth Andrews (1913), 15-6, 27-31, 57-8; Katherine Briggs (1977), 322-3.

PLACE-LORE Great interest has always been shown by the Irish people in antiquities and in historical probing into the past of various localities and landmarks. In early Ireland, the discovery and preservation of such knowledge was the specific duty of the **poets**, who were the official men of learning, and this function continued to be associated with them until recent times.

The surviving texts of mediaeval date suggest that the learned men attained a far higher degree of accuracy in their preservation of genealogical lore than in place-lore proper. By the early Middle Ages, at any rate, the poets were finding it necessary to create new place-lore from the various stories known to them and to invent new stories where there was no suitable material to hand. So, from the 9th century onwards, we have a series of onomastic poems written in this manner, and by the early 12th century these poems were brought together into one great unit known as the *Dindshenchas*. There is no full surviving manuscript of this work, but in all there were nearly three hundred poems, many accompanied by a prose synopsis. Each poem has the heading of a particular placename, and it then relates a story which purports to explain the origin of that toponymic.

The writers of these poems drew on many sources for their material, including the **Mythological, Ulster**, and **Fianna Cycles**, stories of the ancient kings, and some local traditions, but many of the narratives are strained. Many more are fabricated, favourite devices being pseudo-etymologising and the invention of characters on the basis of existing placenames. To cite an example, the toponymic of Dublin (Dubhlinn) is explained by claiming that a poetess called Dubh was angry because her husband was consorting with another lady. As the latter was boating in the bay, Dubh sang a charm against her, causing her to be drowned. A retainer of the dead woman, however, made a sling-shot at Dubh, killing her so that she fell into the water, hence Dubhlinn ('the pool of Dubh'). The placename, in fact, meant simply 'black pool' - it has been generally superseded in Irish by the city's other designation Baile Átha Cliath, which means 'the town of the wattle-ford'.

A second recension of the *Dindshenchas* was compiled about a century later. This repeats many of the verse-texts, but its prose adds length to the stories and variety to the interpretations. Notwithstanding the mental efforts which went into the compilation of these works, a great deal of the material is still structured in the form of mere speculation, and most of the genuine narratives involved are adoptions of stories known from earlier texts. In the present volume, stories from the *Dindshenchas* are treated, as is the material found in other compilations, according to their subject-matter. In later mediaeval times, it was claimed that the 6th-century poet of king **Diarmaid mac Cearrbheoil**, called Amhairghin mac Amhalghaidh, had been the author of the *Dindshenchas*. This highly anachronistic claim sprang from the account of how the antediluvian **Fionntan** recited ancient lore at the court of Diarmaid.

Neither the texts of the *Dindshenchas*, or the many other miscellaneous items of place-lore in the literature, had much influence on the oral tradition. Yet folklore shows an enduring interest of its own in local lore, centring on matters such as historical happenings, supposed connections with **saints** and other celebrated personages, social and economic history, and accounts of **ghosts** and **fairies**. The folklore also displays some aspects which are entirely absent from the literature, such as humorous legends concerning places and humorous interpretations of their names. It is said, for instance, that the city of Limerick was once without a mayor, and it was decided to elect the first man who crossed the principal bridge there. The man who did so was a poor chimney-sweep called 'Seán na Scuab' (John of the Brushes) and he thus became mayor. A favourite nickname for the inhabitants of Kilkenny is the 'cats', and a story is told to explain why this is so. It is said that the soldiers of **Cromwell** once set two cats fighting by hanging them by their tails to a pole, and when the soldiers returned to see the fight the cats had eaten each other down to the tails. This story possibly originated in jibes directed by the victorious Cromwellians at the mid-17th century Kilkenny Parliament, which was notorious for its squabbling.

Satiric verses on towns are common. For example, an anecdote told of various places in Munster called Baile an Fhaoitigh (anglicised Ballyneety or Whitestown) have a beggarman passing through and being attacked by a fierce dog. The unfortunate man bent down to pick up a stone, but found that it was stuck to the ground. After he was badly bitten, he made a wry verse on the placename, saying that the stones were tied there and the dogs were loose ('clocha ceangailte agus madraí scaoilte'). Some late anecdotes claim to explain the meanings of placenames, giving hilarious etymologies - such as a beggarman complaining that the people of a Co Derry town were 'done giving' (hence Dungiven!), or St Patrick, having been struck by a stone, complaining of the 'wicked low' people who inhabited a town (Wicklow!) on the east coast.

[*Dindshenchas* texts] Edward Gwynn (1903), (1906),

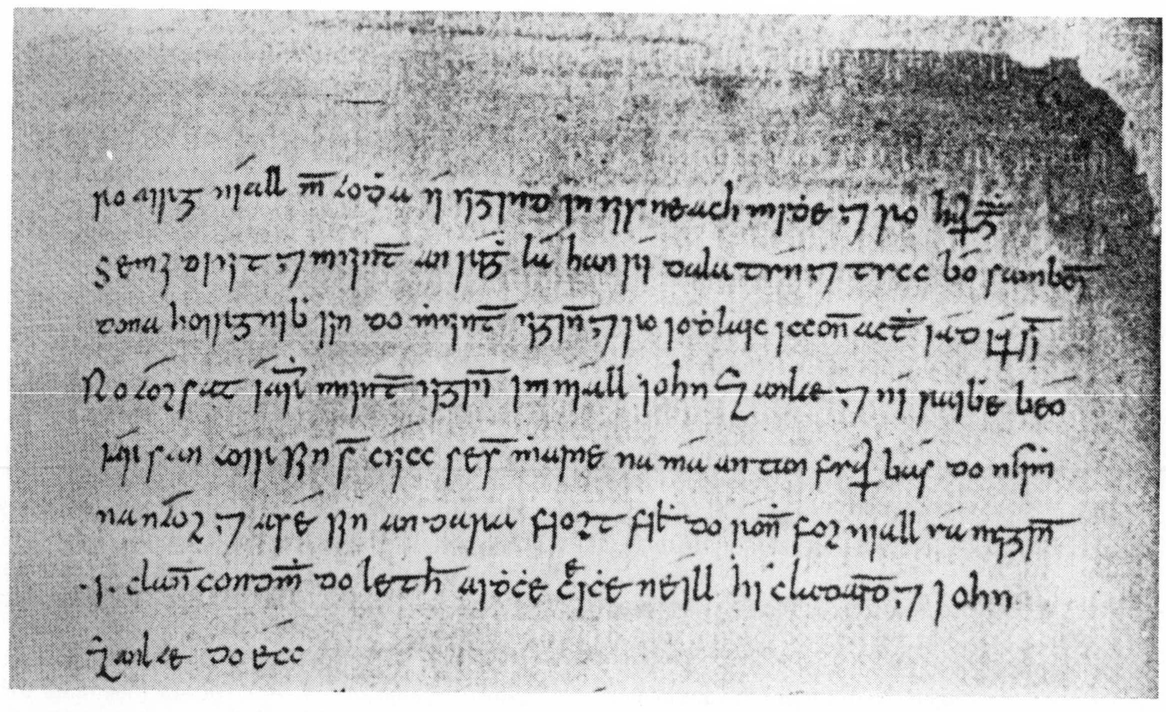

79. POETS *Account of the death of Sir John Stanley from the original manuscript.*

(1913), (1924), (1935); Whitley Stokes in *Revue Celtique 15* and *16* (passim).

[Dubhlinn] Gwynn (1913), 94-5; Stokes in *Revue Celtique 15*, 326-7.

[Seán na Scuab] Seán Ó Súilleabháin / R Th Christiansen (1967), Type 1383.

[Kilkenny cats] P M Egan (1884), 26-9.

[Other folklore] IFC passim.

POETS The word used for a poet, in Irish literature at all stages and in the spoken language, is 'file'. This word contains a Celtic root meaning to see, and all the evidence suggests that the Irish 'file' was originally a 'seer' who expressed his mystical insights in the form of rhetoric. Early literary sources indicate that learned rhetorical speech was known as 'béarla na bhfileadh' ('the language of the poets').

The mythical **Find** was the archetypal seer, and there can be little doubt but that his cult was developed by the poets or 'filid' (modern Irish, 'filí'). A single term, 'fios', is applied to the knowledge of Find and to that of the poets; and this knowledge is expressed in the same dimensions of antiquarianism, clairvoyance, and prophecy. Poets in both Irish literature and folklore often appear as repositories of knowledge concerning the past, as possessors of immediate insight into issues of the present, and as deliverers of prophecies regarding the future. It is impossible to make a clear distinction in the early sources between 'file' and 'druí', as both poets and **druids** tend to fulfil the same functions. The likely explanation for this is that the 'file' was really a variety of druid and that, after the triumph of Christianity, much of the druidic cult was preserved under the comparatively innocuous guise of poetry. The Christian literature itself exemplifies this process. We read, for instance, that St **Patrick** abolished pagan rituals, but that a 'file' called Dubhthach mac ua Lughair supported the saint. As a result, Patrick blessed the mouth of Dubhthach, who immediately began to compose inspired religious verse. Such a rapprochement between the two systems of learning was indeed reached in real history, and to it we owe the preservation of many of the rich secular stories which the monks and their students committed to writing. The native tradition of learning was, of course, an oral one, and memorisation of stories and traditions was an essential part of the poet's trade. He needed to be able to recite poetry and tales when called upon to do so by his royal and noble patrons, and the introduction of writing through the monasteries was therefore a much-valued asset to him.

Apart from the more strictly didactic texts, there is a similar or identical method of describing druids and poets in the early literature. One text - that which describes the verbal contest between the poets **Feircheirdne** and **Néidhe mac Adhna** - is especially enlightening in this regard. Both make many obscure references to ancient lore, Feircheirdne causes his younger opponent to sink somewhat into the ground through magic, and a colourful account is given of the paraphernalia associated with Feircheirdne as 'ollamh' (chief-poet). We read that his robe was of purple colour, adorned with gold and silver, and that it was decorated with bird-feathers and spangled with bronze. A golden branch was carried above him, and a special seat was allotted to him. Whether or not these details are accurate, there can be little doubt but that the poets cultivated much lore concerning themselves in order to add to their prestige. Thus, since earliest times, one encounters the conceit that the poet is a special and unique type of person. A compound of the word 'fios', written 'soas', is explained in the ancient laws as the property of the 'ollamh' and he displays it by 'making a verse without thinking'. Poetry being a verbal manifestation of mystical knowledge, it was a kind of genius within the poet himself, the most important element in his unique nature. This idea persisted into recent folklore. A true poet, we are told, can pour forth perfect verses without planning them, and he always fills in the rhyme when challenged with a half-quatrain. His is popularly regarded as one of the three gifts which must be born with a person and cannot be acquired by learning - the other two being a melodious voice and a generous heart.

Poetry always has an element of paradox, however, and it is not surprising to find that a contrary view concerning it existed side by side with the above. As well as being an inspired art, it was often referred to by poets themselves as being a trade or skill which had to be perfected by the practitioner. Metaphors for poetry abound in the literature, and many of these refer to it as the process of 'weaving' words, or 'spinning', 'cutting', 'shaping', 'rinsing', 'tying', or 'forging' them. A similar tendency is noticeable in folklore, which has developed anecdotes as glosses on the metaphors. So we are told that Eoghan Rua **Ó Súilleabháin** took special care when composing a song, because 'it will need to be good, as many the bad hand will have a go at it!' Similarly, it is said of the 19th-century Mayo poet Anthony Raftery that he once broke a shoemaker's scissors in anger and, when asked why he had done so, replied that it was retaliation, as the shoemaker had ruined his own trade by wrongly reciting one of his poems. Presumably anecdotes of this sort have been spontaneously springing up in oral narrative since earliest times. Poetry is regarded, in both literary and oral tradition, as 'the king of trades', and there has long been a tendency to regard poets as experts, not just in their specific profession, but in many other trades as well.

There is a remarkable continuity in the whole of this tradition. Although the physical circumstances changed, as did the matter and form of the verse, there are recognisable threads of imagery stretching from antique times down to recent centuries and in the surviving folk legends of the 'fili'. We read, even in sources concerning the Continental Celts, of the great emphasis placed on druidic schools, where students spent many years studying under some celebrated master. Such a system of druidic schools is referred to in Irish literature also, and it is parallelled by the mediaeval poetic schools, where the full training period reputedly was twenty-one years. The material to be studied by the apprentice 'file' consisted of ancient stories and legal issues, as well as problems of syntax and metre. There are also, however, echoes of more mysterious matters. Much of the contest between Feircheirdne and Néidhe, for instance, takes the form of riddles, and such enigmatic questions were associated with occult knowledge in many ancient cultures. We find in a 9th-century text that a professional poet called Cruitíne taught his pupils how to solve linguistic riddles, and several other accounts have poets showing their skill and contending with each other in such forms of speech. To be able to see into the hidden meaning of enigmatic statements is in these cases posited to be of equal importance as fluent and deft use of speech.

A late instance from folklore concerns the 18th-century Tipperary poet, Liam Ó hIfearnáin 'the Blind'. We are told that, on his way to a poetic assembly once, he approached a tree from the northern side, caught a squirrel in it, and took the little creature with him in his pocket. When asked by the assembled poets which direction he had come from, he replied: 'Do ghabhas anoir aniar inné, agus níor thug mé aon choiscéim ach aduaidh (i.e. 'I came from the east from the west yesterday, and the only step I took was from the north'). All were puzzled by this answer, but the learned Seán Clárach Mac Domhnaill enquired 'where is it?' He realised that Liam was referring to the squirrel, for the words of his first phrase, written another way, could have meant 'I caught the squirrel in an oak yesterday!' A quite popular folk legend, told of various versifiers, concerns how a neophyte comes to the poetic school or to the poetic assembly and, when a question is posed to test his skill, utters such a polished quatrain that he is admitted to be their superior by all present. This legend is of a type found in other cultures also concerning brilliant youngsters, and it is difficult to determine its antiquity in Ireland.

Though education and training could bring extra refinement of their skill, if tradition is to be credited Irish poets were born and not made. This idea was known to the learned men of long ago as it is to present-day storytellers. A text from the 10th century or thereabouts describes a child called Aí mac Ollamhan, the son of a druid. As the druid sits to a meal with his brother, the high-king Fiachna mac Dealbhaith, a great blast of wind is heard outside, and the druid states that this is a portent that his wife will give birth that night and the child will be of equal status with the king. Fiachna determines to prevent this but, immediately after its birth, the baby speaks a rhetoric naming the gift which it desires from the king. The astounded Fiachna complies. The name of this child means in fact 'Art son of Chief-Poet', and it is obvious that he is a personification of poetry. The anecdote must have been invented by some professional poet, probably as a teaching device for his students. The same motif occurs also in the birth-story of the judge **Morann** and in that of the seer-child **Noíne**, thus underlying the functional role of poetry relative to these other skills. Late folklore has various celebrated poets speaking immediately after their birth, or composing verse in the very early years of childhood, and thus astounding the watching adults.

Contradictory ideas can, however, abound in tradition. Thus it is said that many poets got their gifts of wisdom and fluency from otherworld sources as adults. A common folk legend - variants of which are told throughout the country - concerns how a man, not hitherto noted for his intellectual

80. POETS *Two aspects of a triple stone head from Co. Cavan.*

accomplishments, falls asleep one night by a fairy rath. He dreams that a beautiful woman comes to him and gives him inspiration, sometimes even offering him a book of wisdom, and when he wakes up he has the ability to compose verse without effort. This legend has a long pedigree, involving ideas of **goddesses** as bestowers of material and mental wellbeing and of the **fairies** as keepers of secret lore, but it owes much also to idioms employed by poets themselves. The image of the inspiring otherworld lady can be traced through different epochs in the history of Irish poetry. One early text, for instance, posits the queston 'what is poetry?' and gives the answer that it is a maiden which appears to the poet as he composes. She is 'multiformed multifaceted multimagical, a noble well-clasped maiden'. This is clearly a metaphysical argument. In post-mediaeval literature the poets often used an encounter with an otherworld lady as a stock-situation to introduce their material, which makes the image into a convention; while folklore has the poet actually gaining his art from such a lady, thereby turning it into a narrative legend. All expressions of the image can, in fact, be taken as survivals of lore of poet-seers such as **Find** gaining inspiration from otherworld beings, as in the shamanic rituals of archaic cultures generally.

Another system of metaphors, prevalent in both literature and folklore, concentrates on the anatomy of the poet. Most emphasis is on the tongue, which is claimed to be extraordinarily agile and sharp. One mediaeval source refers to a 'soft tuft' on the tongue of a poet, signifying praise, and another source of the same time refers to 'a bag of poison' on such a tongue signifying satire. This concretises the division of poetry into 'moladh agus aoir' (praise and satire), a division which reaches back into archaic Indo-European culture. It has remained the standard definition in Irish tradition, and a folk anecdote from Waterford expresses it succinctly. According to this, the poetess Máire Ní Dhonagáin was asked rather flippantly by a priest to make a verse for him. She replied ominously but metrically to the effect that 'there are two sides to my tongue, the gentle side and the rough side!' Equally important with the tongue is a mystical vein of poetry, which both literature and folklore claim is an essential part of the poet's physique. This is a particularly clear instance of the spontaneous process by which narrative tends to put abstract ideas into concrete form. It was fancied that the blood flowing through the vein ('féith') was the special pulse ('cuisle') of poetry. Folklore situated the vein in the back of the poet's head, and this probably encapsulates the mystical theory on which the belief is based. For that is the 'dark' part of one's body which the eyes cannot see, and extra insight is the unique quality of the poet. It was customary for 'filí' of old to lie in dark huts when they were composing, and they themselves used the image of 'darkness' for the much-lauded quality of obscurity in their verse. This idea of special 'seeing' was also the rationale used for the social fact that many poets were blind.

Literary and oral sources alike often presume that the composition of verse was due to a special activation within the poet's body. A general belief was that he was in a peculiar state of mental ferment as he composed - ecstatic, frenzied, mystically inspired, sometimes even intoxicated. Some folk traditions tell of particular poets who had abandoned composing, but resumed when moved to great sorrow or anger upon a special occasion. The poet's body was a general reservoir for genius, with the heart as the centre of both emotion and intellect. From it the blood pulsated through the special vein, causing words to spring from the lungs, be refined in the head, and fashioned by the tongue as they entered the world.

81. POETS *Irish chieftain being entertained by poet and harper from a 16th-century woodcut.*

Connected with the idea that poetry is an inborn capacity is that which regards it as a talent running in specific families. This latter idea was much magnified by the fact that, from the Middle Ages at least, some families predominated as professional poets - the most famous being the O'Dalys, the Wards, the Higgins and the Keoghs. Since the surname is retained through the male line, the belief developed also that poetry would leave the family for seven generations if it passed to a daughter rather than a son. There were in fact many women poets in both ancient and recent times, but few if any were considered to be of the first grade. This apparently has to do with social conventions which regarded certain occupations as being proper to one sex only, but it reflects also the worldwide notion that women have secret powers and can bring bad luck to men. In folklore, at any rate, a common type of legend tells of an old poet who, on his deathbed, speaks a semi-quatrain in the hope that his son will answer, but to his dismay it is the daughter who speaks with full and accurate metre.

Nowhere is the power of the poet more obvious than in the context of satire. The ancient Irish laws specified different kinds of satire and attributed magical effects to some. The poet maintained a high social position in Ireland down to the 17th century, being more or less on a par with the chieftain and the bishop, and his disapproval expressed in verse was much feared. It was believed that - if he were justified in his satire - he could raise three blisters of shame on a person's face, deprive that person of honour and reputation, and even cause his death. The annals record that in the year 1414 the English Viceroy, Sir John Stanley, died from the 'poison' of a satire made on him by an Irish poet whom he had wronged, and several similar instances could be cited from literature and lore. Sometimes the poets were said to contend fiercely with each other, and the effect could be devastating to both parties. Folk legends tell of how, with a verse, poets could cause storms, knock down trees, or in a less serious vein shave a person's head or cut off his eyebrows.

The powers of Irish poets were commented upon by several English writers of the 16th and 17th centuries, including Ben Jonson, Philip Sidney, and Shakespeare himself. Perhaps the most celebrated power was that of banishing rats. All over Ireland it was believed that poets had such power, and many folk accounts tell of a benighted person who encountered a huge drove of rats on the road moving from one place to another in accordance with the versified directions given by a poet. It was sometimes reported also that a poet would sent rats to eat the corn of those who had offended him, but the major emphasis is on the 'file' as a culture hero banishing pests and thus protecting his community. Other less widespread traditions claimed that poets could banish **ghosts** and even cure illnesses with their verse.

There is some divergence between the literature and the folklore with regard to the effect of poetic praise. Down to recent centuries, skilled literary eulogies were much valued and sometimes commissioned from poets at a high cost by chieftains and other prominent individuals, yet in popular lore there is a strong fear of one's name being mentioned at all in a poem. This seems to have been a side-effect from the time-honoured practice which poets had of composing mock-praises for those whom they wished to satirise but were constrained by law from so doing openly. Another folk belief which contradicts literary tradition holds that poetry is itself unlucky, and parents would thus discourage their children from making verses. This seems to have also been coloured by the strong tradition of satire, but its origin may be in the age-old idea that those with mystical power stand at a juncture between the physical and spiritual worlds and are thus themselves in some danger. Yet again in this instance paradox holds sway, for folklore equally represents people as envying poets for their art and wishing to emulate them.

82. POETS *Contemporary 18th-century portrait of the blind poet Foirdhealbhach Ó Cearbhalláin.*

Because of their quick wit and their dramatic role in society, folklore represents these men of art as being great entertainers and tricksters, and it is usual to meet with an element of humour even in the most serious legends concerning them. For individual poets, see the entries on Aithirne, Amhairghin Glúngheal, Amhairghin mac Éigit Salaigh, Bricriu, Comhdhán, Dallán Forgaill, Eochaidh Éigeas, Feidhlimidh mac Criomhthainn, Feircheirdne, Flann mac Lónáin, Néidhe mac Adhna, Rumann mac Colmáin, Seanchán, and Urard mac Coise; and the later poets Piaras **Feiritéar**, Cathal Buí **Mac Giolla Ghunna**, **Cearbhall Ó Dálaigh**, Mánas **Ó Domhnaill**, Aogán **Ó Rathaille**, and Eoghan Rua **Ó Súilleabháin**.

Liam Mac Mathúna in *Veröffentlichungen der keltischen Kommission 2*, 225-38; George Calder (1917); James Carney (1967); F N Robinson (1969); Osborn Bergin (1970); J E Caerwyn Williams (1971); P A Breatnach in *Proceedings of the Royal Irish Academy 83C*, 37-79; Pádraig Ó Fiannachta (1978); Dáithí Ó hÓgáin (1982) and (1985), 216-56 and in the following:- *Irish University Review* 1/1979, 44-61; *Léachtaí Cholm Cille 18*, 89-107; *Comhar* 2-3/1980, 7-8/1980.

R

RAGHALLACH King of Connacht from 622 to 649 AD. His father's name was Uadhu, hence he was usually known as Raghallach mac Uadhach. He belonged to the Uí Bhriúin sept, and gained the kingship of the province by slaying Colmán mac Cobhthaigh, who was head of the Uí Fiachrach and father of **Guaire**. This was at the battle of Ceann Bugha (Cambo, near Roscommon) in the year 622.

The genuine annalistic references to Raghallach are meagre, but a dramatic and pseudo-historical narrative concerning him was invented in mediaeval times. According to this, he had a nephew, the son of his elder brother, and he was extremely jealous of this nephew and fearful that he would take his crown. He therefore feigned sickness and, hearing that he was on the point of death, the nephew came to visit him. Not trusting Raghallach, the young man was accompanied by a strong troop. Raghallach, apparently at the point of death, bewailed the fact that the kinsman to whom he wished to bequeath the kingship did not trust him, so the nephew relented and went to him alone, whereupon Raghallach had his own men slay the unfortunate prince.

After this, Raghallach's wife, Muireann, questioned her **druid** as to the king's future, and was told that since he had slaughtered all his relations, he would fall by one of his own children. Hearing this, Raghallach ordered the queen to have slain any baby which might be born to her. Muireann gave birth to a daughter, whom she accordingly gave to her swineherd to kill, but the swineherd pitied the infant and left it at a cross outside the church of a holy woman. The baby was reared by this woman and, hearing of her beauty, Raghallach sent his men to seize and bring her to him. Neither he nor the queen knew who the girl was, but Muireann grew jealous of her husband's love for the young woman. In her jealousy, she swam across the river Shannon and fled to her former fosterling, the high-king **Diarmaid mac Aodha Sláine**. Meanwhile, Raghallach was so captivated by the girl that he insisted on continually gazing upon her face, even when they were in separate chariots.

When St **Féichín** heard of these events, he and several other saints went to rebuke the Connacht king for so rejecting his wife, but Raghallach ignored them and they fasted against him, praying that he would perish dishonourably before the following Bealtaine (i.e. May-feast - see **Time**). When that feast was near, Raghallach was hunting a wounded stag on an island. The stag escaped him and swam away, whereupon the king followed it alone in a boat. He came upon some churls who had killed the stag and had divided it among themselves. He quarrelled with them over this, and they slew him with their spades. One account states that Muireann died from jealousy of her daughter.

This dramatic lore of Raghallach's career is quite contrived, and it is noticeable that neither his nephew nor his daughter are named. The episode concerning his nephew is clearly borrowed from the Leinster story of **Cobhthach**, while that concerning the daughter is based on the well-known plot of a child who is prophesied to kill its tyrant grandfather (see **Balar** and **Romantic Tales**, Type 934). The annals make no reference to such events concerning Raghallach, merely recording his death as having taken place on a Sunday, and at the hands of one Maolbhrighde mac Mothlacháin. They describe him as sitting on a white horse when slain, and say that Muireann lamented him and that he was avenged by his son Cathal, who was in fact one of three sons of Raghallach. The narratives concerning the reputed nephew and daughter would seem to have been invented to discredit the Uí Chonchubhair (O'Connors), who were direct descendants of Raghallach.

[Annals] John O'Donovan (1848) 1, 258-61; Whitley Stokes in *Revue Celtique 17*, 188-9; Paul Walsh in *Journal of the Galway Archaeological and Historical Society 17*, 132.

[Narratives] S H O'Grady (1892) *1*, 394-6; P S Dinneen (1908) *3*, 130-5.

[General] F J Byrne (1973), 246-8.

RELIGIOUS TALES These folktales are mostly mediaeval in origin. They have spread throughout Europe, and versions of over half of the types listed in the Aarne-Thompson catalogue have been collected from Irish oral narrative. Some of them are exempla - tales told by the clergy of the Middle Ages to stress points of morality - and all are based in one way or another on ideas concerning the spiritual otherworld. The ordinary people, however, preserved them for their dramatic traits rather than for their didactic ones, and accordingly the adventurous side of them was developed. Moral points have slipped quietly into the background in these folktales, but they are still operational, and the result is a strange atmosphere, a weird kind of world in which typicalised beings act out the parts which are their very purpose and life-line.

They are not without humour, as illustrated by the very first such story listed, Type 750A. We are told of God guaranteeing to a certain man the fulfilment of three wishes, which are stupidly wasted. In Ireland, it is usually the man's wife who causes this, for instance she gets hungry and asks for sausages. This angers her husband very much, but to please her he wishes for the sausages and they appear. Realising that the wish has been wasted he remarks bitterly: 'May they stick to your nose!' This, of course, the sausages do, and two wishes are thus spent. In order to remove them from her nose, he has to use the third wish. The foolish wish of the woman may vary from version to version, but she always causes her husband's wishes to be expended in similar manner. Type 750B is an international tale which tells of how a holy man restores to life a cow which a peasant had generously killed in order to provide a meal for him. It does not survive in Irish folk tradition, but a story in the mediaeval literature concerning the high-king **Fionnachta** was probably based on it, and an ecotype of it is found in legends of saints (see **Déaglán**).

The miraculous is also featured in a very popular story which originated in western Europe and spread far and wide, gaining great popularity in Ireland (Type 753). It tells of a blacksmith who is visited one day by a stranger wishing to have his horse shod. The stranger says he will do the shoeing himself, but his method of work is very odd. He cuts off the horse's legs, puts on the shoes, and then puts the legs back on the horse. Soon after, an old woman comes to the forge, and the stranger tells her that he can rejuvenate her. He does this by throwing her into the furnace, from which she emerges as a beautiful young girl. Observing all of this, the blacksmith thinks it easy and determines to try it himself. He cuts the legs off a horse, but cannot replace them, and the unfortunate animal dies. Thinking that he had merely got some minor detail wrong, the smith determines to try the second trick. He calls his wife and throws her into the furnace, but she burns. The smith is desperate, but the stranger steps forward and miraculously restores both woman and horse to life. The stranger, who is **Christ**, rebukes the smith for his pride and irresponsibility.

A group of stories dealing with penances are listed together under Type 756, and these, on account of their dramatic range, were in great demand. We are told of a certain hermit (756A) who was so holy that, in order not to interrupt his prayers, meals were sent to him from heaven. In a fit of anger at continuous bad weather, however, the hermit criticises God, and the food no longer arrives. The hermit is desolate, but an angel appears and tells him that he must do penance by standing in a river until his staff blossoms. He is standing in the water for a long time, and a robber who is passing by enquires as to why he is doing this. The hermit tells his story and, on hearing it, the robber compares the hermit's one sin with the many he has himself committed. He is stricken with remorse and joins the hermit to do penance in the river. The robber's staff blossoms before that of the hermit, however, which serves as a lesson in humility to the latter.

Equally popular in Ireland was a macabre story which tells of how a youth offered his soul as surety to the devil's sister in a card-game and lost (Type 756B). In desperation, he went to seek advice from a certain Seán Bráthair (Friar John), who told him that he must go to hell and recover the bill of contract. Arriving in hell, he tells the devil that Friar John has directed him thither, and the devil makes it clear that the friar has great influence in that place. The youth is given back his contract, and before he leaves the devil brings him to see the fiery bed that is being prepared in hell for the friar. On his return home, the youth tells Friar John of this bed. The friar is alarmed, but thinks of a plan. He brings the youth to a mountain-top and, kneeling before him, directs him to slay him with an axe. As the blow is struck, a flash of lightning strikes the mountain-top, and when the youth looks again there is no sign of the friar. However, he sees a white dove flying to heaven, by which he understands that Friar John's soul has been saved.

A more pleasant type of story is Type 759B, which has been most copiously collected in Ireland, but which was current in other parts of western Europe also. This describes how a young man lives on the mountains herding cattle and sheep, and has no contact with the rest of the people. When he meets a villager, he is told that he must come to Mass in the village every Sunday. Arriving in the church, he puts his coat hanging on a sunbeam which is coming through the window. The priest notices the wild man and the coat which hangs miraculously but says nothing. On the second Sunday the same happens, but on the third Sunday the coat falls down. The priest approaches the stranger and asks why this is so. The nonplussed youth explains that he has done nothing new, except to listen to some uncharitable gossip which some of the congregation engaged in after the second Mass. Hearing this, the priest tells him to go back to the mountain and continue with his innocent life there alone, for human company is an occasion of sin for him.

Elements which appear in the secular literary story of **Neara mac Niadhain** gave rise to a religious tale (Type 764) which became quite popular in Irish folklore and spread also to Iceland. This tells of how a poor scholar on his travels meets with the corpse of a hanged man who asks to be carried on the scholar's back. They journey on in this manner until night falls. The dead man, however, refuses to enter a house where happiness reigns, and also a house where prayers are being said. Reaching a third house where a husband and wife are fighting, he tells the poor scholar that this is appropriate lodgings for them. The householder and his wife sleep apart, and during the night the scholar notices that his companion goes and sleeps with the woman. The travellers leave the house next morning, and as they part the dead man tells the scholar that a baby boy will be born to that woman in due course, that the boy will become a priest, and that all of the people blessed by that priest will belong to the dead man himself. The scholar then realises that his companion is none other than the devil. Years later, when the scholar is passing through the same place, he learns that the boy is to be ordained a priest in the local church. He rushes to the church, and succeeds in preventing the new priest from blessing the congregation. Then he privately tells the priest the horrible story of his conception. The distraught priest sets out for Rome to try to find a solution for his difficult situation, and has a very difficult ordeal imposed on him there. The ordeal may involve kissing horrid serpents which he meets on the road, crawling on his hands and knees to the North Pole and back, going naked through a great clump of thorns, or some other such excruciating experience. He succeeds, but so great is the effort that he dies. Beetles are seen to consume his body, since it belongs to the devil, but his soul goes to heaven in the form of a dove.

Type 774K tells of how St Peter once complained to **Christ** when a ship-full of sailors was drowned because one sinner was on board. Soon after, Peter gets stung by a bee and in anger destroys the whole hive, and Christ then points out to him that he has done the very thing for which he had criticised God. This story was already known in Ireland in the 16th century, for a variant of it occurs in a biography of **Colm Cille** from that time. Established in Ireland from the 10th century was Type 782, which tells of how a certain king had donkey's ears. Irish versions always substitute horse's ears, the earliest occurrence concerning a midland king called Eochaidh (which name contains the element 'each', meaning a horse). Soon, however, it got attached to the celebrated mythical Leinster king **Labhraidh**, and it is still told of him in folklore. St Peter is featured again in Type 785, which tells of how, when mutton is being divided, a companion of that saint eats the heart and then claims that the lamb had no heart. When Peter divides money between the company, the rogue confesses in order to get his share. Similar in plot though without a religious focus is Type 785A, which has a servant eating the leg of a goose and telling his master that geese have only one leg. Later they see geese standing on one leg in water, and the rascal cites this to prove his point, but the master says 'whoosh' and the geese put down both legs and fly away. This humorous tale is often told in Ireland as a legend concerning Jonathan **Swift** or Daniel **O'Connell**.

As if to underline the religious purpose of this genre of storytelling, an Irish variant of Type 844 contrasts the physical and spiritual realms. It tells of a king who seeks the shirt of the happiest man in his kingdom, believing that this shirt will bring happiness and good fortune to himself. He finds, however, that the happiest man has no shirt.

Antti Aarne / Stith Thompson (1961), 254-84; Seán Ó Súilleabháin / R Th Christiansen (1967), 145-65; Ó Súilleabháin (1942), 573-5, 629-40 and (1952) and (1973), 18-9; Pádraig Ó Héalaí in *Béaloideas 42-44*, 176-212.

ROMANTIC TALES Over one hundred and fifty international folktales are listed in the Aarne-Thompson catalogue under the heading 'Novelle (Romantic Tales)'. These have a mostly European provenance, and versions of over half of them have been collected from Irish folklore. The characters in Romantic Tales are usually of the ordinary human kind, but the things which happen to them are quite extraordinary though generally credible. Tricks, accidents, and coincidences are the guiding principles of these stories.

Type 851 concerns a princess who loves riddles and who offers to marry any man who will put a riddle to her which she cannot solve. On his way to the contest, a smart fellow sees twelve crows feeding on the carcass of a dead horse. He discovers that the horse has died as a result of eating poison, and decides that this will be a good subject for a riddle. He therefore asks the princess: 'What killed none and yet killed twelve?' The princess is puzzled, and asks for a day's respite to solve it. She hears that the questioner talks in his sleep, and so she goes in disguise to his bed at night. Realising who she is, he pretends to be asleep and says the answer. Next day, she boasts before the assembled court that she can solve the riddle, but as she begins to give the answer she notices that he has a personal item of clothing belonging to her in his hand. Realising that he is ready to expose her nocturnal conduct, she defers and agrees to marry him instead. Type 852 is somewhat similar, telling of a certain king who boasts that nobody can make him disbelieve a good story. He offers the hand of his daughter in marriage to any man who can disprove this, but the price of failure will be the man's head. Several ambitious young men attempt this, but all pay with their lives, until a smart fellow comes to the court and relates the most incredible things. The king listens carefully, agreeing all the time, until eventually the fellow attributes vulgar personal habits to the king himself and even questions the legality of his birth. At this, the king shouts out in anger that he is lying, and so the smart fellow gets the princess in marriage.

Type 870C, as listed in the Aarne-Thompson catalogue, is entitled 'Stepmother Makes Love to Stepson' and a quite confined variant is given. It seems proper to suggest that the plot and range of this type number should be extended to cover the well-known international tale told in the Bible of Joseph and the wife of the Pharaoh Potiphar. In that tale, a woman - often a stepmother - whose sexual advances to a young man have been rejected, gains revenge by falsely accusing him before her husband. Several versions of it occur in Irish literature from the 8th century onwards - these include stories concerning **Dearg**, **Conall Corc**, **Maol Fhothartaigh**, **Comhdhán**, and **Nuadhu**.

A celebrated and very ancient folktale tells of a hero who does not recognise a young man for his son (Type 873). It may have either of two endings - both recognising each other after a contest, or else the father kills the son and recognises him too late. This story, in its happier form, was already being told of the hero **Fionn mac Cumhaill** and his son **Oisín** in the 8th century, and in its tragic form concerning **Cú Chulainn** and his son **Conlaí** at around the same time. The opening of the literary tale concerning **Maol Dúin** also seems to be indebted to it, and the mediaeval account of the birth of **Breas** definitely is. Due to redactions of the literary tale, the Conlaí version survives in the folklore of Ulster and Connacht, while in Munster the folktale is told in the Fionn context. In these latter versions, however, some other son of Fionn besides Oisín is named as the young man, and sometimes the characters are Oisín and his son **Oscar**. The ending, as in the ancient text concerning Fionn, is always a happy one in these Munster variants, but it is clear that they derive from a re-adoption of the folktale in recent centuries. Humorous versions of the international folktale are also current in the south, being told of contests in wit between characters such as Eoghan Rua **Ó Súilleabháin** or Daniel **O'Connell** and their even more clever offspring.

Type 875 tells of an unmarried king who meets with a peasant girl and is amazed by her cleverness and smart answers. He decides to set some impossible tasks for her, and when she succeeds at them decides to marry her. The tasks may include such things as coming to his palace neither walking nor riding, neither on the road nor off the road, neither naked nor clad, neither by day nor by night. She achieves them by being half-mounted on a billy-goat, half on the verge of the road, dressed only in a net, and arriving at sunrise or sunset. After their marriage they are happy together for a while, but one day the king gives an unfair judgement in a dispute between two men. A mare belonging to one of the men has dropped a foal into a a cart belonging to the other, and the king awards the foal to the cartman. The queen, however, objects to this, and she is proved correct when the foal is set free and follows the mare. Embarrassed and angry at being contradicted, the king orders his wife to leave the palace. She prepares to go, but as a last request she asks that she be allowed to take with her the thing which is dearest to her in all the world. When the king assents, she takes him on her back, and they are reconciled. That this folktale was known in Ireland at an early date is suggested by the fact that variants of the first part of it are found in a 10th-century text on the encounter of **Fionn mac Cumhaill** with his sweetheart Ailbhe and in a slightly later text on the encounter between king **Feidhlimidh mac Criomhthainn** and a clever girl.

The story entitled 'the taming of the shrew', immortalised by Shakespeare in English literature, can in fact be traced to Continental folklore of the Middle Ages (Type 901). In Ireland, also, it has been quite popular. We are told of a certain rich man who has three daughters, two of them girls of gentle disposition while the third is shrewish in the extreme. A young man comes to ask for the hand of the shrew, and the pleasantly surprised father offers a large dowry with her. After the wedding the young man sets off for home on horseback with his bride. He forces the horse towards a large gate, and when the horse refuses he remarks 'that is once!' At the second effort the horse again refuses, and he says 'that is twice!', and when the horse acts similarly a third time he stabs it through the heart with a knife. When they reach his home, he similarly orders the dog to do an impossible task, and having enumerated each refusal he kills the dog also. Then he asks his bride to prepare tea, and when she angrily refuses he remarks in a chilling voice 'that is once!' She immediately obeys him, and it is later proved that neither of her two sisters are so obedient to their husbands.

Type 910B is somewhat less discriminatory against women. It tells of a married man who works for twenty years as a farmhand far from home. When that period is ended, he asks for payment, but the farmer refuses to give him anything except three advices. These are not to take a shortcut on his travels, not to spend the night in a house where a young woman is married to an old man, and not to do anything at night which he might regret in the morning. He sets out for home, ignores the first advice by taking a shortcut on his way, and barely escapes with his life when he falls among robbers. Then he ignores the second advice, and hears a young woman plotting with her lover to kill her husband and blame the traveller. He rushes from that place, and eventually reaches home. Arriving at night, he opens the door of his house and finds his wife sleeping in the same bed as a young man. He takes a hatchet to kill the young man, but then decides that he had better follow at least the third advice. Controlling his anger, he waits until morn, and when his wife awakes she welcomes him and proudly presents their son, who has in the time that he was absent grown into a young man. From that day forward he follows the advices, and through his prudence becomes in time a very rich man. A 12th-century Irish adaptation of the Classical story of Ulysses contains a version of the three advices given to the hero on his travels, which shows that some version of the folktale was already known in Ireland at that time. Some references in a text of the 8th-9th century suggest that a related story of advices was known in Ireland even earlier. This (Type 911) must have been more widespread in mediaeval Europe than the recorded instances suggest. It tells of how a man is advised not to confide secrets to his wife, not to accept a fosterson of higher social standing, not to trust an underling, and so on. It is told in Irish literature concerning the judge **Fiothal** and, apart from echoes of this, has not otherwise been noticed in Irish oral narrative.

Type 921 tells of clever answers given by a peasant boy to the questions put to him by a king or other exalted personage. For instance, he says that his mother is fowling, that his father is hunting but throws away what he catches, and that his sister is lamenting her former laugh. These three answers are discovered to mean that the mother is picking fleas, the father is delousing, and the sister is giving birth to a baby. Clever answers are again featured in Type 922, which tells of how a tyrannical king tries to entrap his bishop. He orders the bishop to come to his palace and answer three questions correctly, else he will lose his head. The bishop is perplexed, but his identical twin, who is a fool, offers to go in his place. The fool, dressed in episcopal garb, is mistaken by the king for his brother, and the questioning begins. The first two questions may vary, but are always successfully countered with trick-answers - for instance the king asking how many loads of sand on the seashore, and the fool replying 'one, if you had a cart large enough', and then the king asking how much he himself was worth and being told less than thirty pieces of silver, 'for Christ was sold for that amount and you are not half as good a man!' The third question and answer are standard -'what am I thinking?', with the fool replying 'you are thinking that I am the bishop, but I am not!' There are witnesses present, ensuring that the king cannot renege on his word, and thus the fool saves his brother's life. Irish folklore associates the story with a king of England and a bishop of Canterbury, having assimilated it to the conflict between Henry 11 and Thomas Becket.

Type 933 tells of a boy who is born of an incestuous union and who, after many trials, becomes Pope of Rome. Versions of this were told in mediaeval Irish literature concerning St **Cumaine Fada** and, in adaptations to a secular context, of **Fiachu Fear Mara** and **Mac Lughach**. The story survives in later Irish folklore in its international setting, having the boy become Pope. The idea that a person is destined to be killed in a certain way is the basis of the various kinds of stories listed under Type 934. In Irish folklore, the most common version concerns a boy for whom the prophecy is made that he will be killed by lightning on his seventh birthday. His father has an iron hut constructed underground, in which the unsuspecting boy is placed on his birthday. He escapes from the hut just in time before the lightning strikes it. A variant of this tale, also found internationally and common in Irish folklore, has a less happy ending, describing the death of a boy who is fated to drown at a certain age. That stories of this kind were current in mediaeval Ireland is evidenced by similar motifs in texts concerning **Fiachu Muilleathan** and **Mongán**. A very dramatic ecotype has for some reason declined in popularity since mediaeval times in Ireland as elsewhere. This concerns a man for whom a three-fold death - by wounding, drowning, and burning - is prophesied. This was known in Ireland as early as the 7th century and its appeal continued through the Middle Ages (see **Diarmaid mac Cearrbheoil** and **Muircheartach mac Earca**).

An international story of great antiquity is listed as Type 950. It concerns how the treasury of a king is robbed by the sons of the architect who built it and left one stone loose for this purpose. The story does not seem to have been in Ireland for very long, probably being borrowed in the post-mediaeval period from the Greek literary version in Herodotus' work. It has, nevertheless, become quite widespread and popular, though in a much altered form. We are told of how a man called the Barrscológ ('Leading Scholar') sends his three sons to be educated by Aristotle, and the great philosopher foretells that two of them will be beheaded and the third will get 'croch gheal Bhaile Átha Cliath' (which is interpreted to mean 'the definite gallows of Dublin'). They soon after are engaged to build a treasure-house for the Mayor of Dublin, and in so doing they leave a brick loose so that they can themselves raid the treasury later. The Mayor, however, has traps set for any prospective robbers, and when they enter the treasury at night two of them are caught in the traps. They tell their brother to behead them so that their bodies will not be recognised, and he thus escapes detection. Having unsuccessfully tried many ruses to discover who the escaped thief was, the exasperated Mayor proclaims that if the culprit comes forward he will give him his own daughter in marriage. The girl is called 'Croch' and she is fair-haired ('geal'), and in this unexpected way the prophecy is fulfilled.

A special story about a master-thief (Type 953) was very popular in northern and western Europe, and in Ireland the picaresque character was known as 'an Gadaí Dubh Ó Dubháin' (the Black Thief Dwan). A certain king is so impressed by the escapades of this thief that he sends out a challenge to him to steal a fine stallion from the royal stables. The Black Thief comes and, despite the close guard on the horse, almost succeeds, but is foiled and captured when bells on the horse's rug ring out. He is brought before the king, who triumphantly announces that the executioner is at hand, and jeeringly tells the thief that he is doomed unless he can describe a moment when he was nearer to death than now. The thief tells of some breath-taking escapes which he has effected, but to no avail, and finally states that he was once captured by a man-eating giant who ordered him to slaughter and prepare for dinner a captive baby. The thief had saved the baby by boiling a piglet in its place, and to convince the giant that it really was baby-meat he had cut off one of the infant's fingers and cooked it along with the piglet. When the king hears this he looks down at his own hand and realises that the thief had been his rescuer long ago. The Black Thief is forgiven and given the stallion as a present. Dishonesty is featured also in Type 978, which tells of how a young man finds himself among cheaters but is saved by the quick wit of a person who comes to his assistance. No examples of this folktale have been collected from Irish folklore, but a version of it was known to the 14th-century author of a story concerning a young man called Socht at the court of **Cormac mac Airt**.

Another popular story (Type 970) deserves the title of Romantic Tale in more senses than one. This, still popular in Irish folklore, describes how a youth and a girl love each other, but their parents oppose the match and both die of heartbreak. The vindictive parents have them buried at the furthest distance from each other in the graveyard, but a tree grows from each grave and the branches of both trees intertwine overhead. This folktale, found throughout Europe and Asia, was already known in Ireland in the 10th century, for it appears in the text from that period concerning the young man **Baile mac Buain** and his sweetheart Aillinn.

Antti Aarne / Stith Thompson (1961), 284-346; Seán Ó Súilleabháin / R Th Christiansen (1967), 165-96; Ó Súilleabháin (1942), 575-9, 622-8 and (1973), 19-21.

RUADH RÓ-FHEASA Name of an ancestral divinity in the genealogies of the Laighin (Leinstermen). It can be translated as 'the all-knowing red one', and is probably synonymous with other names such as **Dearg** and **Donn** for the father-god called the **Daghdha**.

His sobriquet 'Ró-fheasa', meaning literally 'of great knowledge', was adopted from the lore of the seer **Find**, who ritually obtained knowledge from an ancestor figure. In the Leinster genealogies, indeed, the character **Find File** is claimed to have been son of a personage with a curious name – viz. 'Find File mac Rosa Ruadh'. This patronymic was no more than a learned inversion of the designation Ruadh Ró-fheasa. The personage Ruadh was fully assimilated into the developing lore of Find, becoming associated like him with the Boyne river, and being invested with the power to appear in the form of a salmon there. Moreover, as Find became **Fionn mac Cumhaill** and was portrayed as fighting against an otherworld figure alternately called Aodh and **Goll**, these latter designations also were assigned to the Ruadh.

The final curious twist to the history of this personage occurred sometime in the 12th or 13th century, when due to folk etymology his name became confused with the place called Eas Ruadh, which means 'the red waterfall' (it is anglicised as Assaroe i.e. at Ballyshannon in Co Donegal). Thus we read of an ancient personage called Aodh who had been drowned at Assaroe, and of a wonderfully wise salmon which resided there called Goll Easa Ruaidh. The latter salmon surfaces in redactions of the story of **Fionntan** and in a very popular Irish folktale (see **Animals, Wild**).

Kuno Meyer (1912), 98; Whitley Stokes in *Irische Texte 3*, 356-7; T F O'Rahilly (1946), 318-20; M A O'Brien (1962), 21-3, 99.

RUADHÁN Saint who died c584 AD, founder of the monastery of Lothra (Lorrha, in north Co Tipperary). His name means 'red-haired man' and in modern form is rendered Ruán.

The several accounts given of him in Latin and Irish all derive from a lost biography, which was compiled in the 10th or 11th century. We read that he was son of one Fearghus Bearn of the royal Eoghanacht sept of Munster, and that he was educated by St Finnian of Cluain Ard (Clonard, Co Meath). When he went to Lorrha to found his monastery there, a fierce wild boar which had its lair in the hollow of a tree quitted the place so that he could have possession of it. He performed many miracles in different parts of Ireland, including finding their treasure for the people of Ros Éinne (in the Oriors area of south Armagh) who had forgotten where they had hidden it during a pestilence; healing the queen of Cualu (north Wicklow) who was afflicted by a dangerous blood-clot; and rescuing a ship caught in a whirlpool near Limerick. He had a wondrous tree at Lorrha, the sap of which provided full sustenance for all who tasted of it. The other saints of Ireland grew jealous of Ruadhán on account of this tree and of his holiness generally, but he reconciled them to him by entertaining them with a fine feast in Lorrha.

The most celebrated story of him concerned his conflict with the high-king **Diarmaid mac Cearrbheoil**, who seized a hostage from out of Ruadhán's sanctuary and was elaborately cursed by the saint as a result. The two were eventually reconciled, and Diarmaid returned the hostage to Ruadhán in return for thirty beautiful dark-grey **horses**. These had come to the saint from a river, and they defeated the king's own horses at racing. Soon after the king had acquired them, however, they raced away into the sea. Another legend has Ruadhán giving his own two chariot-horses as alms to lepers, and two stags coming from a wood to draw his chariot in their place. Several of the other miracles attributed to him involve healing the sick and raising from the dead people who were recently deceased. For a miracle concerning the restoration of sight to the blinded Eochaidh mac Maolughra, king of Munster, see the general entry under **Eochaidh mac Luchta**.

The feastday of Ruadhán is April 15.

J F Kenney (1929), 391-2; W W Heist (1965), 160-7; Charles Plummer (1910) *2*, 240-52 and (1922) *1*, 317-29; Paul Grosjean in *Analecta Bollandiana 49*, 100-1; John O'Hanlon (1875) *4*, 148-60.

RUMANN MAC COLMÁIN Poet who, according to the annals, died in 747 AD. One mediaeval source accords him high distinction by referring to 'the three poets of the world - Homer of the Greeks and Virgil of the Latins and Rumann of the Irish'.

A text from the 12th century or thereabouts tells a few anecdotes of him. We read that he was the chief-poet of Ireland and that he once went on a pilgrimage to the monastery of Raithean (Rahen, Co Offaly) while a famine raged. The people of that place did not wish to allow him to enter, and so they challenged him to state the number of timber planks which were being used in the building of an oratory there. Through his poetic genius, Rumann spoke a quatrain saying that there were ten hundred planks, which was the exact number. He was admitted to Raithean, and soon after he headed for Dublin, where the **Norsemen** asked him to make a poem. He demanded as payment 'one penny from every bad Viking and two pennies from every good Viking', whereupon they all paid the two pence each. They desired him to praise the sea, and in a frenzy he then recited a long descriptive poem in a new metre which he called 'laídh luascach' (literally 'see-saw lay'). Rumann then returned to the midlands and divided his fee among some monasteries and schools. We read that he died at Raithean and was buried there. It is clear that this account was influenced by oral tradition. Folklore made much of the magical knowledge of **poets**, and the trick by which he got double payment from the Norsemen seems an adaptation of some folktale concerning tricksters.

Kuno Meyer in *Otia Merseiana 2*, 76-83; Anne O'Sullivan (1983), 1588.

[Folktale plot of clever man] See Antti Aarne / Stith Thompson (1961), Types 1567-1569.

S

SAINTS From the 5th century onwards, considerable numbers of Irish people were turning to Christianity, and by the 8th century the new religion was general throughout the country. The intervening period is sometimes referred to as 'the age of the saints', and it is to that period that all of the saints who are celebrated in Irish hagiography belong.

The actual writing of the biographies began in the 7th century and continued well after the end of the Middle Ages. Latin and Irish are the languages of these texts, the Latin works being somewhat in the majority, and in the case of a number of saints several different biographical texts survive. The writers of Irish hagiography, like their counterparts abroad, drew on material from several different sources for their themes, plots, and imagery. Such sources included not only the Old and New Testaments, the Apocrypha, and biographies of Continental saints, but also Irish and Classical works of secular literature, as well as oral tradition from within the monasteries and from the populace in general. It is sometimes quite difficult to unravel the various strands of lore in the texts and to determine how much of the accounts have direct historical value, but it must always be borne in mind that many of the biographies were written with the definite purpose of advancing the prestige of particular paruchiae or monasteries. Thus the profile of an individual saint depended to a large extent on the interests of those who inherited his or her foundation, and the hagiographers did not hesitate to borrow, or even to fabricate, material for their purpose. This is not to say, however, that the hagiographers were men without taste or discrimination. The vast majority of them were monks, with varying degrees of learning, but usually with some theological sense and never devoid of piety. They could also, on occasion, give good insight into the human predicament and portray individual characters and personalities with some depth of feeling.

The biography of the saint, in Ireland as elsewhere, is basically a sacred version of the life-pattern of all heroic or celebrated people. Thus the saint's birth is accompanied by wonders and marvels, he or she shows special holiness and miraculous powers while still a youth, on coming of age the saint gains great triumphs against hostile forces and as a result of this is recognised and given authority, and extraordinary circumstances again attend his or her death. For reasons of history and authentication, however, the hagiographer had to garner and include in the text as much detail concerning the real life of the saint as possible; and, for reasons of interest and variety, he had to select good adventures from whatever sources were available. The success of the narrative, of course, depended on the quality of such adventures and of their presentation, and thus the hagiographers built up a rich store of motifs with which to punctuate their texts.

Particularly popular were accounts of healings, and in some cases the hagiographers did not scruple to have their saints going so far as to restore to life people who had recently died. The miraculous power of the saints could, of course, also strike down those who were persistently hostile to them or to those under their care, and their prophecies in both positive and negative senses were much in demand. As a spiritual champion, the saint always acts with extraordinary dedication and intensity, and so the hagiographers felt free to exaggerate greatly in descriptions of pious practices. Extraordinary self-mortification was a standard convention, at least in the literature (see **Caoimhghin**, **Íde**, and **Fionnchú**), while one writer teeters precariously between opposite feelings when trying to impress readers with the piety and chastity of St Scoithín. He describes that holy man as having 'two maidens with pointed breasts' in his bed with him each night 'so that the battle with the devil might be the greater for him'.

Fire and light were particularly popular as dramatic devices, no doubt because of standard Christian symbolism of the faith, but to an extent also because such imagery had already been associated with the sacred men of pre-Christian belief, the **druids**. We read of fiery manifestations, and lights seen in the sky, at the time of the births of saints. Sometimes the saint is described as surrounded by the mystical light of holiness, and he is generally impervious to fire. A particularly impressive image has the saint lighting candles by breathing on them, or even having his fingers emit light in the darkness like a torch. The person of the saint is generally untouched by rain or snow, no matter how exposed to the elements or severe the weather. His book, containing the sacred writings, was also impervious to wetting, and several legends tell of how such books were dropped into water but remained perfectly dry.

83. SAINTS *Illustration of a saint from a popular Irish book.*

Objects closely associated with the saint were often claimed to have miraculous power attached to them, for instance, the 'bachall' or crozier. This pastoral staff, if the hagiographers are to be credited, could raise the dead, drive back a flooding river, or divide the sea as Moses did in Exodus. It could also split rocks or cleave the ground, subdue wild animals, banish demons, or protect travellers. In some cases, the crozier was claimed to be able to attract and catch fish, discover treasure, produce fountains on dry land, and fly through the air and return to the saint when misplaced. It is clear that this staff was regarded in early Christian Ireland as the most characteristic implement of the missionary. The old literature tells us that croziers were enshrined in precious metals, and some such coverings are preserved in modern museums.

Almost as impressive was the saint's bell, many examples of which have also been preserved. The bell, being used to summon people to prayer and devotions, was seen as having a central function in the Christian life, and accordingly the hagiographers were keen to dramatise it. We read therefore of saints' bells which could raise the dead, protect the community from diseases and disasters, banish demons, repel enemies and cause them to be swallowed up by the ground. A common motif is for a bell to remain dumb until the place destined for the saint's settlement is reached, whereupon it rings out joyously of its own accord. Like the crozier, the bell could of its own accord return to its owner if mislaid or stolen. Many bells had names of their own, which were usually based on their colour, and the application of actual personalities to them was sometimes carried to the point of attributing human-like voices to them. In all of this, the hagiographers were merely developing

84. SAINTS *Ardagh chalice from the 8th century.*

in narrative terms the popular attitude to the special paraphernalia of churchmen in early Christian Ireland. Both croziers and bells were in fact ritually used in collecting ecclesiastical revenue, in cursing and excommunicating foes, and in the administration of solemn oaths.

A sense of genuine, if naive, spirituality was seldom far from the minds of the hagiographers. Thus they claim that various saints were in constant communication with angels, and concerning **Íde** we even read that an angel brought food to her every day. Although they could be quite partisan, the commitment of the hagiographers to particular foundations had a strong element of pious devotion, and so the fantastic powers of the saints were basically intended to show how goodness can pervade all reality. Nowhere is this more obvious than in the idea that the saints had a very special relationship with the animal world. We read again and again of how these holy men and women were sympathetic to all of God's creatures, and how these creatures were much attracted to the saints and assisted them in many ways. For instance, not only horses and oxen, but wild stags also, come of their own accord to work for the saint. The stags even allow their antlers to be used as book-rests when sacred study is in progress or prayers or hymns are being read. A charming account of St Colmán mac Duach (for whom, see **Guaire**) states that he had three pets - a cock, a mouse, and a fly. The cock used to crow for him at midnight to call him to prayer and, as Colmán then sang his psalms, the fly would walk along under each line of the psalter, pausing at a word each time that the saint did so. If the saint nodded off to sleep, the mouse would begin to nibble at his ear in order to awaken him so that he would continue with his office.

All creation was attracted to the saints - for example, the birds lamented St **Molua** after his death because he had never killed any living thing. The same Molua had a tame partridge, St Crónán had a tame stag, and Moling had a tame fox. Other saints had miscellaneous pets - such as cranes, wrens, robins, doves, crows, cats and flies. The swans on the Lakes of Killarney were wont to come at the call of **Cainneach**, and the swans on Lough Foyle came at the call of **Comhghall**. Swans were also helpful to St Columba of Terryglass, carrying him from place to place as he wished; and the same birds used to sing for St Colmán Eala and his monks as they worked. One of the animals portrayed as being closest to these Irish saints was, curiously, the wolf. For instance, **Caoimhghin** and **Maodhóg** fed starving wolves from their herds, and Molua is even claimed to have instituted a feast for the benefit of the wolves. It is apparent that some beliefs from pre-Christian Ireland are involved in this case, wolves being in some way imagined to be connected with human beings. The ritualistic king **Conaire**, for example, was said to have had seven wolves as hostages for an agreement that more than one calf a year would not be taken from each cattle-byre in Ireland.

St Colmán mac Luacháin had a standing covenant with wolves, according to his biography. We read that the wolves of the forest came to him and licked his shoes like domestic dogs, and that he said to them: 'Be here continually, and the day that my name is mentioned to you in intercession, you must not draw blood on anyone!' Of this same Colmán it was said that, when he was a child, he spent a whole day and night under the river Brosna (in Co Kerry) and, while he was there, the water-creatures came and ran races before him as a welcome. The image of the holy hermit surrounded by wild animals who behave with great docility towards him was borrowed into Irish tradition from the lore concerning the Desert Fathers of eastern Christendom, the cult of whom was predominant in the Church at the time that Ireland was converted to the new faith. The point of such stories is that holiness puts a person in a properly balanced relationship to the world. The 8th-century English cleric and scholar, Bede, summed up the philosophy when he wrote that 'the more faithfully man obeys the Creator, the more he will regain his lost empire over the creatures'. This type of portrayal of the saint at peace with the environment continued for some centuries in western Christendom, and it survived indefinitely in Ireland.

The fame of particular saints was spread and perpetuated through the Middle Ages by numerous dedications of local parishes to them. This is the major reason why the cults of individual saints are found over so widespread an area, but in tradition it was in turn explained by greatly exaggerating their journeying and travels. The lore of some saints was spread into places far beyond their actual fields of activity, such as **Bréanainn** and the lady-saints **Brighid** and **Moninne**, whose cults took root in parts of Britain and occasionally even further afield. The actual travels, from the 7th century onwards, of Irish missionaries in Britain and throughout much of Europe added much to this imagery of our peripatetic saints in the mediaeval literature.

Much of the literary imagery passed into the Irish folklore concerning saints, through the media of clerical preachers and of local scholars. This is evidenced on a widespread level in the case of the great national triad of **Patrick**, **Brighid**, and **Colm Cille**, and in more localised traditions concerning the other saints. Thus in folklore the saints are generally portrayed as thaumaturges, as ascetics, and as miraculous protectors of their communities, and some of the most dramatic stories from the literature are related of them. It is apparent, however, that the folklore preserves some legends in a more accurate form than the literature does. In a number of such cases, the folklore may be primary and the mediaeval literature may in fact have done no more than reflect tradition which had long been current in the oral stream. An example is the widespread folk legend, told of several saints, of how a great reptilic monster is banished into a lake (see **Colm Cille** and **Patrick**). We read of several such banishings in the hagiographical texts, but the folklore alone stresses that the monster is tricked by the saint into remaining in the water until 'Lá an Luain' (which actually means the Last Day although the monster takes it to mean the following Monday). This verbal trick, which is reflected in a different type of story concerning **Moling**, derives from an idea that the final judgement will take place on a Monday. Thus the oral emphasis on the Last Day in the contest between saint and monster underlines the basic source of the legend - the New Testament Apocalypse, which has a great dragon being released on the Last Day and then confined in a fiery lake.

Another legend, also widespread in folklore, describes how two saints argue over where the boundary between their jurisdictions should lie. They agree to start from their own dwellings and to begin walking towards each other at an arranged time, and that the boundary line will be drawn where they meet. One of them, however, cheats by setting out too soon, and when this is discovered he is punished by having the boundary drawn to the advantage of the other. The full plot of this legend is nowhere found in the literature, but that it was already in popular tradition in the 9th or 10th century is strongly suggested by the occurrence of such a contest between saints in the *Bethu Phátraic*, a tripartite text on Patrick (q.v.). A further legend, again told of several different holy men, describes how the saint as a boy was in service with a farmer, who ordered him to protect a newly-planted cornfield from the birds. When Sunday came, the youngster wished to go to Mass, and so he miraculously collected all the birds and confined them in a roofless barn while he was absent. This legend appears only once in the literature, in a late mediaeval biography of **Ailbhe**.

One folk legend, quite absent from the literature, represents the saint as the focal point of the whole human community. This was told in the oral tradition of **Barra**, **Mochuda**, **Bréanainn**, **Éinne**, and others, and whatever its origin it is well in keeping with the early Christian worldview. According to it, the holy man forgets his book when he leaves his monastery to conduct a religious service a good distance away. On reaching the arranged place, he remembers the book and remarks on it to the man who is standing nearest to him. Word is passed along the line, and so great is the multitude that they form an unbroken chain all the way back to the monastery. They therefore pass the book along from hand to hand until the saint receives it without moving from where he is standing.

There are individual entries in the present work on those saints who have especially developed lore attached to them. These are the great triad Patrick, Brighid, and Colm Cille, the great traveller Bréanainn, and the more localised saints Abán, Adhamhnán, Ailbhe, Barra, Bearach, Bearchán, Caillín, Cainneach, Caoimhghin, Ceallach, Ciarán of Cluain, Ciarán of Saighir, Comhghall, Déaglán, Éinne, Féichín, Fionán Cam, Fionnchú, Flannán, Fursa, Íde, Maodhóg, Mochaoi, Mochuda, Moling, Molua, Moninne, Ruadhán, and Seanán.

[Sources] J F Kenney (1929); R I Best (1942), 152-63; Rolf Baumgarten (1986), 576-98; T P Cross (1952), 510-6.

[General background] John Ryan (1931); N K Chadwick (1961).

[Texts on Patrick, Brighid, Colm Cille] see the entries on these saints.

[Compilations of hagiography] Whitley Stokes (1890) and (1905); Charles Plummer *1-2* (1910), *1-2* (1922), and (1925); W W Heist (1965); Anne O'Sullivan (1983), xiii-xiv, 1527-1708. See further Kenney, *op cit*.

[Discussions of hagiography and folklore] Hippolyte Delehaye (1907); John O'Hanlon *1-9* (1875); Plummer (1910) *1*, lxxxix-clxxxviii; Felim Ó Briain in Eoin Ua Riain ed (1940), 454-64; Dáithí Ó hÓgáin (1985), 4-61, 322-7 and in *Béaloideas 51*, 87-125.

SARSFIELD, PATRICK (1650-1693) Officer in the army of **James 11** and leading figure on the Irish side in the war of 1689-1691. He was born of a prosperous family at Lucan, Co Dublin, and was known in Irish as Pádraig Sáirséal. In his youth, he was sent to France to pursue a military career, in which he rapidly won promotion and later proved his worth again while in the service of King James in England.

85. SARSFIELD, PATRICK *Portrait of Sarsfield drawn after his death.*

Despite his reputation, Sarsfield was never allowed a position of real importance in the Jacobite army when the war came to Ireland. He was kept in the background at the Battle of the Boyne and, after the flight of James, had to assent to the authority of the inept commanders left behind. At the siege of Limerick a month later, however, he performed the feat for which his name survives in folk memory. Learning that a large consignment of provisions and heavy armaments was being brought to enable King **William** to batter down the walls of that city, he travelled by night with a troop of cavalry to intercept it. Evading the enemy patrols, he encountered the siege-train at Ballyneety, about fifteen miles south-east of the city. He had his men pile all the wagons together, and then the whole consignment was blown up in a tremendous explosion. The result of this action was that William did not have the means to take Limerick and had to abandon the siege.

Popular speculation held that Sarsfield fortuitously gained the information which he needed to get his men inside the enemy encampment at Ballyneety. As he and his troop rode through the night, one of their horses cast a shoe and its rider was told to stay behind the rest and walk it. This rider met a woman, who told him that she was married to one of the Williamite soldiers, and in the conversation let it be known that the password at the Ballyneety encampment was the name of Sarsfield himself. When Sarsfield was informed of this, he instructed some of his men to gain access to the camp by use of the password. When himself challenged by a sentry he shouted out triumphantly, 'Sarsfield is the word and Sarsfield is the man', thus giving the signal for attack. Popular lore also claimed that, on his return to Limerick, he confused the Williamite search-parties by having the shoes turned backwards on the horses of his cavalcade. The motif of an enemy soldier's wife telling the password seems to have been borrowed from the lore of how **Brian Boru** gained a great victory at Limerick; while the motif of the horseshoe-change was common, in Ireland and abroad, in folklore concerning outlaws and fugitives.

Following a second siege of Limerick by the Williamite general Godet de Ginkel a year later, Sarsfield surrendered, and he and his soldiers were allowed to depart for the Continent. This departure became known as 'the flight of the wild geese'. Sarsfield himself was slain at the battle of Landen in the Netherlands. It was claimed that, as he was being carried mortally wounded from the battlefield, he uttered 'Oh, that this were for Ireland!' His courage was recognised, not only by his Irish soldiers, but also by his opponents. In plays performed in London after the Williamite victory King James was depicted as a petulant coward, but Sarsfield was regarded as a hero of the Irish. In one scene, James is represented as saying in an aside: 'This fellow will make me brave in spite of myself!' The contrast between these two characters became a popular theme. It was widely reported that, after his surrender at Limerick, Sarsfield had remarked to some Williamite officers: 'As low as we now are, change but kings with us, and we will fight it over again with you'. One fanciful anecdote has James criticising the Irish to the French king, Louis XIV, in the presence of Sarsfield. The latter drew his sword to run James through, but was prevented from doing so by the intervention of their French host.

Alice Curtayne (1934); P B Ellis (1976), 144-51; J C Mac Erlean *3* (1917), 142-57; Richard Bagwell 3 (1916), 299; Tomás Ó Concheanainn (1981), 2-3, 69-70 and in *Éigse 14*, 215-36; Lady Gregory (1926), 46-51; Patrick Kennedy (1855), 71.

SEANÁN Saint who died c544 AD, founder of a monastery on Inis Cathaigh (Scattery Island in the mouth of the river Shannon). Seanán (earlier, Senán) must have been a nickname, for it meant 'old man'.

There are a few versions of his biography in Latin and one in Irish and, though differing somewhat in content, they all probably derive from a 9th or 10th century work. A sense of chronology is quite lacking in these accounts, Seanán being brought into contact with the 4th century **Martin of Tours**, as well as the 7th-century **Maodhóg**. We read that the birth of a great saint was foretold by **Patrick** to the Corca Baiscinn (of west Clare), and that a wizard of that sept identified the prophesied one as being in the womb of the wife of a peasant called Geirgreann. When Seanán was born his mother was clutching a stake of rowan, and that stake burst into foliage and grew into a celebrated tree. The saint showed his miraculous powers at an early age, and was sent to study under the monk Nothail of Cill na Manach (Kilnamanagh, Co Kilkenny). He later visited Maodhóg, and from there went to Martin of Tours, who presented him with a gospel and promised to be with him at his death.

We read that, on his return to Ireland, Seanán was numbered among the five leading monks of the country, and that he founded several island monasteries off the southwest coast. Coming to Scattery Island, he encountered and banished a great monster and settled there. The king of the Uí Fidhgheinte sept (of Co Limerick) claimed the island and sent his wizard to contend with Seanán, but both wizard and king perished in their attempts to expel him. The new king of that sept, Neachtan, submitted to the saint and was blessed by him, and thus Seanán's cult was advanced by that sept as well as by the Corca Baiscinn. Several conventional miracles are attributed to Seanán, such as the restoration to life of people who had died accidentally. One striking account has a maiden called Canair walking over the waves to Scattery Island, and insisting that women as well as men be allowed by Seanán to follow the monastic life there. After a long argument, the saint consented to this.

When the time of his death came, he ordained that his body be conferred on the nun's community at Cill Eochaille (apparently the convent on Scattery). Angels transported St Martin all the way to that place from France in order to give the last Sacraments to the dying Seanán, as the two saints had earlier arranged between them. An obscure praise-poem on him, entitled *Amra Senáin*, was fancifully attributed to the 6th-century poet **Dallán Forgaill**. Seanán's feastday is March 8.

J F Kenney (1929), 364-6; W W Heist (1965), 301-24; Whitley Stokes (1890), 54-74 and in *Zeitschrift für celtische Philologie 3*, 220-5; Charles Plummer in *ibid 10*, 1-35; John O'Hanlon (1875) *3*, 210-57; IFC 354:279-91, 1133:417-20.

SEANCHÁN (earlier, Senchán) Poet who flourished towards the end of the 6th and in the first half of the 7th century AD. The designation Seanchán was probably a nickname, since it means 'man of lore' and would describe his profession. It is usually accompanied by the enigmatic sobriquet Torpéist.

He wrote a genealogical text known as the *Cocangab Már* (i.e. 'Great Compilation'), mere fragments of which survive, but a later tract may be a paraphrase of it. The tract mentions, in a context which would be contemporaneous with the poet, one 'Senchán mac Uarchride' of the Araidh sept, and this is quite likely the poet himself. The Araidh dwelt in the area on the northern Tipperary-Limerick border and it can be inferred from several of the references to Seanchán Toirpéist in the mediaeval literature that he was a native of that area. His sphere of activity was, however, more wide-ranging. The literature claims that he was one of the **poets** present at the Convention of Drom Ceat (in Co Derry) in the year 575 and that he succeeded **Dallán Forgaill** as chief-poet of Ireland. It also represents him as a close associate of king **Guaire** who reigned in Connacht from 655 to 666. One, or both, of these attributions must be wrong. The real situation would appear to be that Seanchán was a younger colleague of Dallán Forgaill, who was still alive though probably quite old in the year 597. This would almost certainly rule out participation by Seanchán in a convention as early as 575, though it would suggest that he spent a period in Ulster, where Dallán flourished. On the other hand, Seanchán himself would be a very old man if he was among the entourage of Guaire as Connacht king, though he might well have frequented the Connacht court when Guaire was a youth and Guaire's father Colmán (+622) ruled.

The surviving fragments of *Cocangab Már* are verses on the genealogies of the Leinstermen, but no doubt the work had a much wider scope than that. The earliest occurrence of Seanchán in narrative dates from the late 9th century, in which we read that a poetess of the Uí Fidhgheinte (a sept of east Limerick) was missing for some time, having gone on a circuit of Ireland, Scotland, and Man. It happened that Seanchán with an entourage of fifty colleagues, attired in his professional garb (see **Poets**), set out in a boat to visit the Isle of Man. As they left, an extremely ugly man called to them from the shore to bring him with them. The brain of this man bulged through his forehead, emitting filthy fluid through his ears, and the rags on him were alive with lice. When he told Seanchán that he would be a more worthwhile companion than the haughty retinue of poets, Seanchán decided to risk letting him come along. On reaching the Isle of Man, they saw a tall old woman scavenging on the beach and they told her who they were. She challenged them to poetically answer a half-quatrain, and neither Seanchán nor his colleagues could do so. The monstrous stranger who had come with them did, however, answer, and gave poetical replies twice more in similar fashion. From the verses, Seanchán realised that the woman was none other than the missing Inghean Uí Dhulsaine. They took her back to Ireland with them, and on their return they noticed that a great transformation came over their monstrous companion. He became a handsome and beautifully attired young man, and then disappeared. He was the Spirit of Poetry.

A passage in this story purports to explain Seanchán's sobriquet. When the monstrous stranger came aboard the boat, the other poets shrunk from him, remarking to Seanchán 'a monster approaches you' (viz. 'tot-rorpai péist'). This is contrived, but the idea of a synthesis between ugliness and comeliness was well established in early Irish thought. It was strongly evidenced, for instance, in the concept of sovereignty (see **kingship**), and its extension to the context of poetry was easy, given the dialectic between praise and satire in the productions of poets (q.v.). It is possible that Seanchán taught some such allegory on the nature of poetry, and that echoes of it are preserved in this story. Several early Irish sources suggest that special poetic skill was learned in Alba, which earlier meant Britain but which came to mean in particular Scotland. An 11th-century source may preserve some original detail when it explains Seanchán's sobriquet by stating that, when he was in Alba, the spirit of poetry met him on his road and conversed with him in very obscure rhetoric. His interlocutor was in hideous guise, but this 'monster profited him' (viz. 'dorarba péist'). If Seanchán allegorically referred to poetry as sometimes having a horrid guise this in itself could explain the sobriquet, for a monster was denoted by words such as 'torathar' and 'péist'. Thus his designation might properly have been Seanchán Torphéiste (i.e. 'Seanchán of the Monster').

An even more striking and dramatic tradition was associated with this poet. According to it, he was the one who discovered the great epic called *Táin Bó Cuailgne* (see **Ulster Cycle**) after it had been lost to living memory. Earlier versions of the tradition had it that the text of the *Táin* had been taken to the Continent by a scholar from Armagh and had been left there by him in exchange for the 'Culmen' (i.e. the Etymologiae of Isidorus). Seanchán assembled the poets of Ireland to see if any of them knew the epic, but they could recall only a few fragments. He accordingly set out in search of the text. Coming to the grave of the hero **Fearghus mac Róich**, at Éanloch (Lough Nen in Co Roscommon), Seanchán's son Muirghein recited a poem over the grave and as a result the dead hero appeared to him and told the story of the *Táin* from start to finish. In or about the 11th century this account was developed and transformed, the discovery of the epic being set within the ambit of Seanchán's supposed patron, the Connacht king Guaire. The fullest recension of this dates from the 13th century and is entitled *Tromdámh Guaire*. It goes as follows:-

The chief-poet of Ireland, Dallán Forgaill, died as the result of unjustly satirising a king, and Seanchán Toirpéist became chief-poet in his place. Because of the fame of Guaire's generosity, Seanchán brought his retinue of poets and servants to visit that king. This retinue was infamous for its demands and its readiness to satirise if the demands were not met. Guaire - through the advice of his brother, the hermit Marbhán - satisfied all their eccentricities, no matter how difficult. To suit one demand, Marbhán had to have his pet white boar killed, and he swore vengeance for this. Seanchán himself became impossibly presumptuous and testy, demanding that the nobility of Connacht be excluded from a feast, and then found fault with Guaire's servants. The grandfather of the cook, he claimed, had horny nails, and the grandmother of the waitress had once touched a leper. Finally, when told that mice had eaten his egg, he satirised them, killing ten of the little creatures immediately with his words. On second thoughts, Seanchán decided that he should rather satirise the cats, since this would cause more mischief to his hosts. When the king of the cats, called Hirusán, felt the power of the satire he left his cave at Cnoghbha (Knowth, Co Meath) and seized Seanchán at Guaire's court. Slinging him over his back, the huge cat was taking him to the cave when intercepted by **Ciarán**, the saint of Clonmacnoise. Ciarán was working in his forge, and he flung a lump of molten metal at the cat and slew it. Seanchán's life was spared, but he was angry, for if he had died his poets would have had an excuse to satirise Guaire.

The aggrieved Marbhán began to put riddles to the poets in order to test their skill. They answered correctly, and then he demanded to hear the poetic croon. Declaring himself unsatisfied with their efforts, he went on to demand the 'choking croon' ('crónán snagach') To be unable to perform any of the poetic skills would make them obvious failures in their profession, and so Seanchán himself had to attempt to save their honour. He raised his beard on high and started to croon, but the staccato effect which Marbhán sought was atrociously difficult to achieve, and so Seanchán overstrained himself and one of his eyes jumped from his head with the effort and onto his cheek. Marbhán miraculously replaced it, and then demanded to hear a poetic story. What he asked for was 'Táin Bó Cuailnge'.

Neither Seanchán or any of his retinue knew this story, and so they had no choice but to go and seek it out or else retire from their profession in shame. They set out for Scotland, but nowhere there could it be found. Returning to Dublin, they met the saint **Caillín**. Seanchán and Caillín are here described as sons of the same mother, and so Caillín assembled the saints of Ireland to give their assistance. Marbhán relented slightly and told the poets that there was but one way to learn the story and, following his advice, they went to the grave of Fearghus mac Róich and fasted against him. As a result, the huge warrior Fearghus appeared and sat down to recite the *Táin* to them. St Ciarán wrote down the epic from the dictation, and Marbhán ordered the poets to return to their own territories and never again to assemble as a 'tromdhámh' (literally, burdensome company).

This recension has made several additions to the tradition of Seanchán's rediscovery of the *Táin*. It is in fact a humorous belittling of the poets and was clearly intended as a jibe at that profession by a pro-clerical writer. This writer made use of the lore of the Convention of Drom Ceat, held in 575 AD, and where - it was claimed - the extortions of the poets (q.v.) had been strictly curtailed. Descriptions in the literature of that convention stressed the rapaciousness of the poets and had Dallán Forgaill and Seanchán as leading participants. The plot involving Marbhán predates the actual text *Tromdámh Guaire*, having been borrowed from the mediaeval lore of Guaire (q.v.). This lore, centring on the idea of a very generous king, drew on a source which was also used in the biography of the British saint Kentigern. In that text, a jester demands mulberries in winter from the generous king Rhydderch. This is parallelled by a demand of blackberries in winter by Seanchán's daughter in *Tromdámh Guaire*, and a white boar belonging to Kentigern corresponds to Marbhán's pet animal. The source for both texts is now lost, but it was presumably in Latin and seems to have been a primitive account of the hermit-saint Kentigern. Marbhán would therefore have been modelled on Kentigern, though in origin he seems to have been derived from lore concerning the saint **Cumaine Fada**, who was claimed to have been a half-brother of Guaire. One source from the 10th-11th century has Seanchán contending with this Cumaine - the latter recites twelve lessons from the Gospel and Seanchán fails to repeat them until he has heard them three times, whereas Cumaine can repeat the poetical compositions of Seanchán immediately. An early poem on the death of Cumaine repeatedly refers to his corpse ('marbhán'), and this could well be what suggested a character called Marbhán as an opponent of Seanchán at Guaire's court.

It is possible, even probable, that Seanchán was the man who put the various elements of the *Táin* into a unified narrative (see **Ulster Cycle**); and in that case the tradition that he discovered, or caused to be discovered, the text of the epic would reach back to his own time. One can speculate that, just as a metaphoric reference by himself to the spirit of poetry gave rise to one narrative concerning him, so also he might have cultivated the conceit that he had got the *Táin* from the mouth of Fearghus himself. The seeking of inspiration from the dead was a fancy much associated with poets in early Irish tradition, and if Seanchán did indeed belong to the Araidh sept he would have regarded Fearghus as an ancestor of his own. It is noticeable that there are some elements common to the accounts of the spirit of poetry and the finding of the *Táin*. These include the quest-journey to Britain and the spiritual revelation.

The literature generally knew this poet only in the context of his adventures at Guaire's court. One example of this is the surviving text concerning **Cano mac Gartnáin**, which incorporates an account of Seanchán as a rapacious poet apparently predating the text of *Tromdámh Guaire*. We read that a third of Guaire's dwelling was allotted to him, but he schemed to eject Cano and thus get half of it. Among other things, he attempted to discommode Cano by causing his hunting party to be scattered through magic. Seanchán is described as a miserable little man wearing a woollen cloak, and with a poor appetite. He ate a mere quarter of a loaf each day, but his wife Brighid used to eat the other three quarters. The same text relates that he once composed a praise-poem for the high-king **Diarmaid mac Aodha Sláine**. As payment Diarmaid gave his servant a horse's fetter to bring to him. He then made another poem for the high-king and got a forked branch as reward, but he persisted and on a third occasion he got gold and silver, and on the fourth a fine steed. We further read that once, while passing through part of Guaire's territory, a drop of rain struck him on the forehead. An abscess grew on his forehead, and he demanded a large compensation from every settlement in the area as a result.

Echoes from the text *Tromdámh Guaire* survived in Scottish folklore, where 'cliar Sheanchain' (i.e. Seanchán's scholars) were described as a large wandering band of lazy, ill-mannered and demanding poets. His memory has faded from the living oral tradition of Ireland, but the literary texts seem to have guaranteed that he was well-known in the folklore of previous centuries.

M A O'Brien (1962), 19, 22, 386; Kuno Meyer (1912), xiii-xvii, 90-4 and (1914) *2*, 19-21 and in *Archiv für celtische Lexikographie 3*, 2-4 and in *Zeitschrift für celtische Philologie 12*, 378-9; Rudolf Thurneysen in *ibid 19*, 193-207; Owen Connellan (1860), 262-5; Ernst Windisch (1905), liii; D A Binchy (1963), 8-11; Maud Joynt (1941); P S Dinneen (1908) *3*, 80-1, 94-5.

[General] Cormac Ó Cadhlaigh (1939), 193-215; James Carney in *Ériu 22*, 68, 73-5 and (1955), 165-88; Seán Ó Coileáin in *Ériu 28*, 32-70.

[Folklore] C A Gordon in *Scottish Gaelic Studies 8*, 22-5; W J Watson in *The Celtic Review 4*, 80-8; Iain Mac Aonghuis in Seosamh Watson ed (1986), 103-4; Séamus Ó Duilearga in *Béaloideas 25*, 144; Dáithí Ó hÓgáin (1982), 291-2, 334.

SEVEN BISHOPS A common Irish folk legend describes how seven baby brothers were saved from drowning and grew up to each become a bishop, and accordingly seven churches were founded by them.

Variants of the story were told throughout Ireland. It was said that all seven were born at one birth and that their parents were poor and despaired of being able to support them. The father therefore put them into a sack and was bringing them to a river with the intention of drowning them, when he met a holy man who enquired as to what was in the sack. The father protested that they were pups, but the holy man saw through the lie and insisted that the children be given to him. He took them, and reared and educated them, so that each of the seven became a priest and eventually a bishop. This is based on an international folktale which tells of how a parent tried to kill his or her children, but was prevented by the other parent from doing so. Although scarcely more than a few centuries old, the Irish adaptation is often cited as biographical material for groups of local saints whose names survive in toponymics but concerning whom little else is known.

A special variant was developed in the area of south Kilkenny and south-east Tipperary due to a carving of seven episcopal figures on the famous high cross at Ahenny. The original significance of these figures is not known, but the folk speculated that they were the seven boys of the legend, and we are told that an aged cleric saved them from being drowned by their father and brought them to Rome for education. They became bishops, and on his death he directed them to return to Ireland and continue his religious work there. They were entertained at Grannagh castle by the great 16th-century Countess of Ormond, Margaret **Butler**, but she grew suspicious that they had gold in their luggage and sent some of her servants after them to kill them. They were accordingly beheaded at Áth na gCeann, on the Lismatigue river in Aghavillar, Co Kilkenny. Thus folklore explains this placename Áth na gCeann, which means literally the 'ford of the heads'. We are anachronistically told that they were buried at Ahenny and the high cross erected over them. The cross actually dates from the 8th century. It is sometimes said that only one of the bishops was buried there, and that other high crosses in the vicinity mark the graves of the other six.

Antti Aarne / Stith Thompson (1961), Type 765; Seán Ó Súilleabháin / R Th Christiansen (1967), Type 765B; Francoise Henry in *Béaloideas 15*, 257-60; William Carrigan (1905) *4*, 7.

SPECIAL POWERS All societies have speculated on whether the ordinary physical and mental limits of human existence could be transcended, and preserve accounts of some people who are reputed to have done so. In Irish literature, the portrayal of a lauded individual usually entailed a selection of some quite extraordinary powers, and the same is often true in folk legends. The telling of narratives about such heroes or heroines never failed to gain an audience, and no doubt many of the listeners secretly longed to themselves have similar abilities.

Apart from accounts of epical heroes, **saints**, and **poets**, folklore includes many types of people among those to whom special powers are credited. The leading profession in this regard for several centuries is the church, many priests being believed to have miraculous powers of healing. This was of course an extension into the social realm of the theology of spiritual healing, and folklore adds its own quality of concreteness to the belief. The custom was common until recently for people to ask their local priest to write some lines from John's Gospel in Latin on a piece of paper, and this was frequently worn about the neck in a little satchel to guarantee protection against illness, temptation, and misfortunes of every kind. Here we see the reputed power of a mysterious language, Latin, being added to the religious power of the priest. Several stories were told of how priests banished **ghosts**, and a particularly popular legend told of a priest temporarily bringing a dead landlord from hell so as to prove his power to that man's son and persuade the son to mend his ways. This legend seems to have sprung from religious arguments in Reformation England, where it was believed even by those opposed to Roman Catholicism that 'none can lay a spirit but a Popish priest'.

The untheological nature of folk belief is well exemplified by the belief that some priests had more power than others, and young priests were in greater demand than older men because of the idea that they would not yet have used up their spiritual energy. It was also held that silenced priests - men who had been deprived of their office by church authorities - had more power as healers than the ordinary clergymen. It is clear that, in social terms, lore of how priests could if necessary use their power made life more bearable. Accounts abounded of how cruel magistrates and wicked landlords were laid low by the well-deserved curse of a priest. A dramatic little legend, of a type current in Europe since mediaeval times, was employed as a good example of this. It tells of how a priest was once invited to a party by a group of disreputable landlords, and while there his hosts insisted that he join in the drunken merriment by singing a song. He consented, on condition that they all sing together, and then he struck up a lively hunting-song. During the singing, which became more and more boisterous, the priest slipped out, and the landlords were miraculously compelled to continue at the song until next day. By that time, they were near to death from their exertions, but a servant went for the priest to relieve them of their agony. The prototype of this story on the Continent tells of how dancers were thus compelled to dance to exhaustion by a priest whose instructions they had ignored.

A noticeable social type in 18th and 19th-century Ireland was the 'poor scholar', a man of some learning who travelled about in search of employment as a part-time schoolmaster. In the absence of an organised educational system for Catholics, such a scholar could eke out an existence by setting up a 'hedge-school' and charging a small fee to the parents who wished to send their children to him to be given a basic education. These scholars were often quite learned men for their time and circumstances. Several of them were poets, all had a good knowldge of English reading and writing and of mathematics, and a few had a good knowledge of Latin and Greek also. In folklore, they are represented as wise men who were consulted on matters relating to propitious movements of the stars and on the interpretation of prophecies. One popular legend tells of how a poor scholar was staying in a house one night and the householder asked him to interpret some lettering which was on a slab in the fireplace. The lettering, we are told, was in **ogham** script, and the scholar said that it meant that a treasure was hidden under the slab. Upon investigation this was found to be so.

Those credited in the folk mind with extraordinary powers usually come from very definite sectors of society. They may belong to specialist professions which were seen by the general populace as in some way secretive, such as clergymen, poets, scholars, and blacksmiths. The high standing of the latter has to do with the special value of iron implements in both war and peace, and as such must be of great antiquity. The smith was regarded as one of the wisest men in the community, and his forge was a great centre for social communication and for conversation. It was believed that the water in the trough of the forge, being impregnated with iron, held a cure for many ailments, and the smith himself was credited with the ability to curse an individual who offended him by turning the anvil against that person. The stone-mason was also regarded as a particularly skilled and knowledgeable person. As with the smith, this seems to derive from the material on which he worked, stone being a valuable commodity, and it is interesting to note that another method of cursing was to turn stones against a person. Professions, of course, tended to be hereditary, and some special powers were regarded as likewise running in families. The blood of the Cahills and Keoghs, for instance, was believed to cure the shingles if applied to the affected part of the body, and the blood of the Darcys could cure wildfire. Those with the surnames Cassidy, Gough, and Walsh were also sometimes claimed to have cures.

It was widely believed that people whose parents had, before their marriage, the same surname, had the gift of healing. Another idea was that a cure could only be handed on by a dying person to a member of the family who was of the opposite sex. A general assumption was that those who had extraordinary powers should not over-use them, as to do so might reduce the practitioner's own protective energy and leave himself or herself at risk. Noted healers were often of types which live on the periphery of ordinary social life, such as poor scholars, travelling poets, beggars or travelling people generally who pass through a community and on to the next. This meant that the person with such powers was an outsider and, in line with this, people who were in some way unusual within the community were often thought of as having special powers. These included people born posthumously or born out of wedlock, born on a Sunday or with a caul, twins, and in particular a seventh son of a seventh son. Red-haired people, constituting a small minority in the community, could also be considered to have extraordinary abilities.

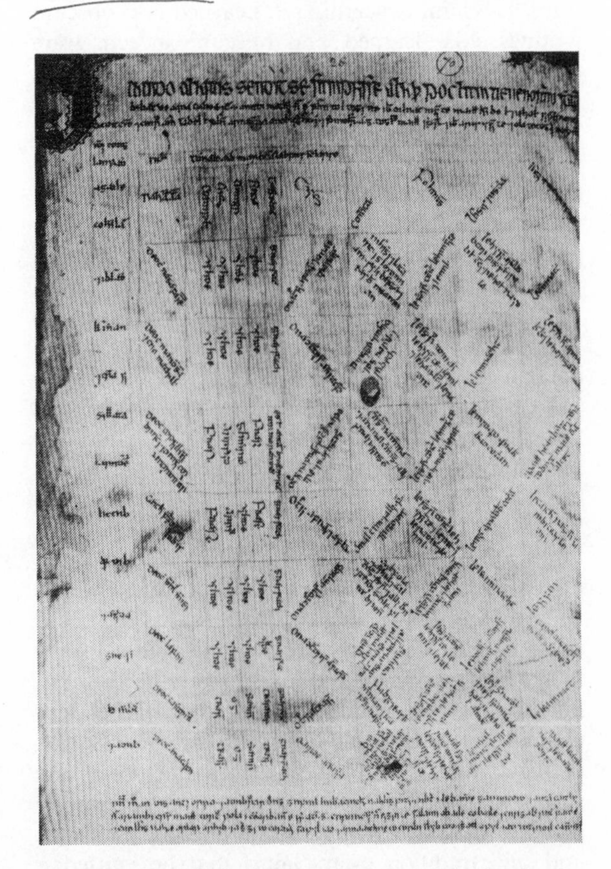

86. SPECIAL POWERS *A page from the book of Ó Laoi, reputedly of otherworld origin.*

Some people were reputed to have first obtained special powers when already in adult life. One of the most curious cases concerns the family of Lee, who were traditionally doctors and physicians. It is said that one of this family, Muircheartach Ó Laoi, was taken away by the **fairies** to an otherworld island off Galway Bay, and that he found a book there which was full of medical knowledge. He brought the book ashore with him, read it, and as a result became a great doctor. This character lived in the latter 17th century, and a contemporary account makes it clear that he himself claimed to have had the experience. The actual book in question is preserved in the Royal Irish Academy in Dublin, but on examination it proves to have been written in the 15th century, being a collection of many cures translated into Irish from Latin text-books. The book is colourfully decorated, and it was no doubt a combination of its contents and aspect which allowed Muircheartach to convincingly put forward his claim concerning it. Learned and obscure writings, like learned and obscure speech, were popularly regarded as containing magical power. A striking if alarming instance of this is a report from the year 1627 of how the beautifully illuminated Book of Durrow was being used by a farmer as a means of curing sick cattle. This farmer used to dip the book in water, which was then given to the cattle to drink, but fortunately the priceless manuscript was rescued from such usage.

Also in the 17th century, a man who lived in the Erris area of west Mayo was reputed to have amazing powers of prophecy. This was Brian Rua Ó Cearbháin, and he was said to have got his gift when he used whatever money he had to pay the rent due by a poor widow and thus prevented her eviction. The widow prayed earnestly that he might be rewarded, and on his way home from the landlord's office Brian began to feel tired and fell asleep in mountainous terrain. He dreamed that a voice told him to search the sleeve of his coat, and on awakening he did so and found a little mirror there. This mirror used to reflect future happenings for him and thus enable him to prophesy. Folklore claims that he foretold many of the great social, political, and technological developments of the succeeding centuries. Stories were told of how he could disclose where gold was hidden in the earth, and one tradition even claims that he caused a mysterious and unpiloted ship carrying gold sovereigns to dock off the Mayo coast so that a generous Ulsterman, who had sold cattle to him on credit, should not be kept waiting for his payment. The Mayo lore concerning Brian Rua is the most dramatic concerning a folk-prophet, but in greater or less degree other local prophets were highly regarded throughout the country.

Of the many women with no formal education who were reputed healers in different parts of Ireland in the 19th century, the two most celebrated were Moll Anthony who lived on the Curragh of Kildare and Biddy Early from Feakle in Co Clare. These women were said to travel with the **fairies** by night, and by this means were able to answer any question regarding an ailment put to them by those who came to seek their aid or advice. According to folklore, they seldom failed to cure either man or beast when their services were called upon. Although she died as recently as 1873, Biddy's fame spread through most of Munster and Connacht. People came from far and near to her, and found her to be a clairvoyant who could tell them the most private of things as well as a specialist in herbs. She apparently first got her powers after a bout of illness, and it was popularly supposed that during that illness she had been presented by the fairies with a special black bottle into which she looked to find information. As with folk-healers generally, she never used her power except for good purposes, but a humorous anecdote claims that an over-officious priest once came to upbraid her for dabbling in magical practices. She politely received him, but was not convinced that her healing contravened God's law. The priest left in some anger, but found that his horse would not budge for him and so he had to return rather shamefacedly to seek Biddy's help. She advised him to spit on the horse and bless it, whereupon it obeyed his commands as before.

Some people with magical powers were naturally treated with suspicion. A folk legend current in Ireland since mediaeval times tells of a showman with a cock who, to the amazement of his onlookers, has the bird effortlessly draw a large block of timber after it. One man, however, is carrying a bundle of hay, and in it is a four-leafed shamrock, which enables him to realise that the cock is in fact pulling a straw and that its owner is a hypnotist. In order to avoid discovery, the showman pays a large sum of money for the hay. Somewhat more eerie than sightshifting was the power employed by certain mowers, who could maintain a sharp edge on their scythes by inserting a black beetle into the handle, and most alarming of all was a type of man who could make any woman fall hopelessly in love with him by drying his hands in her apron.

T P Cross (1952), 119-210, Seán Ó Súilleabháin (1942), 304-15, 362-439 and (1967), 56-60, 76-80; W G Wood-Martin (1902) 2, 160-205; Kevin Danaher (1966), 81-7 and (1984), 98-123; Dáithí Ó hÓgáin (1985), 204-15, 271-89, 340, 345-6; Pádraig Ó Héalaí in *Léachtaí Cholm Cille 8*, 109-31; Micheál Ó Tiománaidhe (1906); Edmund Lenihan (1987); Pat Logan (1972); Caoimhín Ó Danachair (1978), 29-31.

[Book of Durrow] Liam de Paor in *Thomas Davis Lectures* (1967), 1-13.

[People compelled to dance] Stith Thompson (1955-1958), Motif C94.1.1; Michael Chesnutt in V J Newall ed (1980), 158-66.

[Cock and log] Joseph Szövérffy (1957), 151-5; Eleanor MacNicholas / Donncha Ó Dúlaing / Micheál Ross (1989).

SPORTS AND PASTIMES Some of the forms of recreation in Ireland had much tradition attached to them, storytelling putting particular emphasis on those who excelled in the different skills.

The literary stories repeatedly refer to the playing of a board-game termed 'fidhcheall', which was a form of what we call chess. It consisted of two sets of men pegged into position on a board, but the rules followed are not known. Another board-game frequently mentioned is 'bran dubh' (literally 'black raven'), and from at least the 12th century the game of backgammon (called 'táiplis' from French 'tables') was popular with the nobility. Apart from martial skills and athletics, the favourite pastime with young men is represented as playing hurley, involving a large number of players on each of two teams, each player having a hurley stick ('camán'). The game took the form of each team alternately defending a hole in the ground or a stick with both ends in the ground, into which the opposing team tried to drive a brass ball. The hunting of birds, deer, and pigs is a frequent activity in the literature, as is the racing of horses.

Feasting and storytelling were evening recreations for the nobility - ale and mead being the favourite drinks. Mediaeval lists typify the stories told as narratives of courtships, feastings, otherworld adventures, hostings, destructions, and cattle-raids. These stories were the business of the professional poets and their reciters, but other forms of entertainment were also in demand at banquets. Gleemen (usually called 'crosáin') seem to have had quite a rewarding profession, despite frequent clerical censure of some lewd performances which they proffered. They were skilled jugglers and acrobats and specialised in a humorous medley of verse and prose. This genre of composition, called after them 'crosánacht', was in recent centuries practised by the poets, and there can be little doubt but that the trickster-image of **poets** in later folklore owes much to these mediaeval entertainers (see **Anéra mac Conglinne** and **Ceithearnach Caoilriabhach**). No doubt the ordinary people had humbler versions of conviviality, although no clear accounts of these survive. With regard to storytelling, it can safely be taken that the narrative genres current among the ordinary folk in mediaeval times were of the same general nature as those found in more recent folklore. The literature, often the preserve of the higher orders of society, shows clearly the influences of oral legend and oral folktale, as referred to in many instances in this book.

There seems to have been no major change in the patterns of entertainment until the 15th and 16th centuries, when new sports were introduced due to the spread of English rule and influence. Two of these, cardplaying and dice, quickly became an addiction for many Irishmen. Elizabethan writers describe with shock and amazement how professional gamblers lay in wait for travellers on the roadside, and how some of these gamblers staked all their possessions - even their clothes and parts of their body - on games. The term used for such a gambler, 'cearrbhach', is cognate with the word for 'cut' and this may indicate that they specialised in the quick and hazardous game of cutting the deck. Clergymen of all denominations were strictly opposed to gambling, and through their censuring a legend was adopted from abroad, becoming very popular in Leinster and from there spreading to the other provinces. This told of how a dark stranger once appeared at a card-playing house and joined in a game. In the course of play, a card slipped from the table and, when one of the players stooped to pick it up he saw that in place of a foot the stranger had a cloven hoof. The devil, for it was he, disappeared in a flash of fire, having been foiled by a mere chance in his attempt to win the souls of the players. This cautionary tale had as its purpose to discourage people from cardplaying, and it was said that the evil one was not far away when this and other crazed forms of gambling were in progress.

On a lighter note, the playing of cards for small stakes - such as a goose or duck - became very popular in rural Ireland, variants of the five-card game being the most popular. It is interesting to note that oral narrative reflected social reality by substituting cards for chess in stories which involved wagers.

87. SPORTS AND PASTIMES *Hurlers from a 19th-century illustration.*

The 17th century brought some new and unsavoury forms of entertainment to the towns, such as bull-baiting, dog-fighting, and cock-fighting. In the countryside, hunting the fox with a pack of hounds became a favourite pastime with landlords. The latter also began to take an interest in hurling and reorganised it into teams of tenants who played on specially chosen fields. Alongside this, other more spontaneous forms of hurling survived, including whole parishes contending with each other to drive the ball past a boundary fence or ditch. From the more structured form of the game emerged both hockey and the great national game of hurling instituted by the Gaelic Athletic Association in 1884. That association also took under its care the Irish forms of football and handball, both of which had been played in primitive form for some centuries. Folklore told of many great hurlers of old, some of whom were so skilled that they could keep a ball in the air by repeatedly striking it while they disrobed and then dressed again, and others who could race around large buildings and strike the ball from all sides without allowing it to touch the ground. A common folk legend told of how some famous hurler was taken away by night by the **fairies** and how he goaled for an otherworld team before being returned to his bed.

Wrestling and boxing became popular from the 17th century onwards, and lore developed concerning great champions at these sports also. Several of such legends centre on Irish champions defeating English ones. For instance, Connacht lore told of how Tomás Láidir Ó Coisdealbha (Strong Thomas Costello) defeated a giant English wrestler who had come to Sligo to challenge all and sundry. The unfortunate visitor had his neck broken in the contest and died. The victor was also a great athlete, and was reputed to have outraced a horse on one occasion - a fanciful motif associated with great local athletes in other parts of the country also. Tomás was an epitome of the sort of man on which folk legend thrived - he was lithe and handsome, and was long remembered for his sad love-affair with Una MacDermott, to whom he composed a well-known love-song. Her rich parents would not allow the marriage, and so both pined away and died from heartbreak. They were buried on an island in Lough Key in Co Roscommon and a tree grew from each of their graves and entwined over the graveyard (see **Romantic Tales**, Type 970). The most famous of Irish boxers was a Dubliner, Dan Donnelly, who between the years 1814 and 1819 won three great fights against English champions. These were in actual fact long and brutal contests, but folklore has Donnelly winning them easily with a few tremendous blows. His greatest victory was gained on English soil, and it is said that King George 1V personally congratulated him on the occasion, stating that he was

88. SPORTS AND PASTIMES *Dan Donnelly, famous Irish boxer.*

the best man in Ireland. Donnelly answered that he was in fact 'the worst man in Ireland' but the 'best man in England'. This dialogue, repeated in lore of 19th-century athletes and jockeys, is a clear example of national grievances being expressed through sport.

A common formula in folktales is for the heroic company to make three thirds of the night - 'a third with drink, a third with music, and a third with slumber and deep sleep'. Music, song, and dance have all been extremely popular in the Ireland of recent centuries, but no great antiquity can be attributed to the surviving genres. Singing can be traced with some precision. It is apparent that early Irish songs were in fact chanted poems, of both popular and learned type, with the rhythm dependent on the words. Working songs, such as those sung by ploughmen and spinning-women, were popular until the 19th century, as were also chanted rhetorics in folk keening of the dead. All of these may be descendants of ancient Irish styles of singing. It is clear that such styles did not become calcified in form, for despite changes in prosody through the centuries the composition of poetry in Irish was usually intended for the singing voice. Precedence for the actual melody gradually developed under the influence of Latin, French, and English sources during the Middle Ages, and it can be shown that the very emotional love-songs in the Irish language derive their themes and imagery from the 'amour courtois' conventions which became popular in western Europe from the 13th to the 15th century. These songs describe love as a malady which can only be cured by its fulfilment, and they treat much of idyllic surroundings and of secrets and pacts between lovers. They became the favourite genre of song in Ireland, and so much attention was focussed on them that the post-mediaeval spread of international ballad-types had little influence on Ireland. With the strengthening of the English language in the 18th and 19th centuries, however, versions of these ballads from England and Scotland began to take root and in time became very popular.

The harp ('cruit' or 'cláirseach') is the musical instrument mentioned most frequently in the early and mediaeval literature, but there are also references to instruments the nature of which is less certain - such as a stringed 'tiompán' and a type of pipe called 'feadán'. Music was considered a highly artistic skill, and many stories referred to experts who could play three magical strains. These were 'goltraighe' which made listeners weep, 'geantraighe' which made them merry, and 'suantraighe' which brought on slumber. The harp had virtually disappeared by the 18th century, being replaced by combined pipes of a type which had long been popular among the ordinary people. The violin, known as a 'fiddle', was introduced to Ireland in the 17th century, and was the favourite instrument for dance-music until largely displaced by the accordian (known as 'mileoidín' or 'little melody') in the 19th century. Two words are used synonymously in Irish for dancing - 'damhsa' and 'rince'. Both are borrowings from English ('dance' and 'rink'), which suggests that Irish traditional dancing is not of native origin. Post-mediaeval accounts of 'rince an ghadraigh' (withy dance), 'rince fada' (long dance), and 'rince an chlaímh' (sword dance) make it clear that forms of group and processional dancing became popular, but in the 17th and 18th centuries these were displaced by jigs, reels, and hornpipes from Scotland and England. In the late 18th and early 19th centuries, professional dancing-masters toured the country teaching deportment to children, and they spread modified forms of quadrilles, from which are sprung the set-dances which have been popular now for several generations.

There was no formal drama in Gaelic Ireland, but plays were being staged in English in the towns since the 14th century. A form of folk drama called 'mumming' was adopted from England and became very popular in recent centuries in large parts of Ulster and Leinster. Performed in the Christmas season by local people travelling from house to house and suitably accoutred, these plays consisted of long speeches and supporting action by a mixture of saints, devils, and historical characters. More general and spontaneous pastimes included weight-throwing, skittles, and bowls, while divination games of a variety of types were in great demand, particularly by girls speculating as to whom they would marry. Speech-games such as riddles and tongue-twisters were family entertainment, and adults were much given to tracing genealogy and to discussions of linguistic usages and proverbs. Above all else, however, traditional Irish culture specialised in storytelling, and the variety and sophistication achieved in that skill is the basic subject of this book.

Anne Ross (1970), 93-109; Proinsias Mac Cana (1980); T P Cross (1952), 287-93; Eoin MacWhite in *Éigse* 5, 25-35; Alan Harrison (1979); RIA Dictionary s.v. 'crosán', 'crosánacht'; Edward

MacLysaght (1950), 128-65; Seán Ó Súilleabháin (1942), 652-99; Caoimhín Ó Danachair (1978), 41-3; Kevin Danaher / Patricia Lysaght in *Béaloideas 48-49*, 214-6; Art Ó Maolfabhail (1973); L P Ó Caithnia (1980) and *BCE* (1984); Dubhglas de hÍde (1909); Marcus MacEnery in *Éigse 4*, 133-46; Donal O'Sullivan (1974); Seán Ó Tuama (1960); Breandán Breathnach (1971); Alan Gailey (1969); Breandán Ó Madagáin in *Béaloideas 53*, 130-216; Dáithí Ó hÓgáin C (1982) and (1985), 289-305, 346-7; N J A Williams (1988).

SUIBHNE Fictional character in a story which was written in the 9th century and a full version of which is in the 12th-century text *Buile Shuibhne.* The name Suibhne was a common one in early Ireland.

The story describes him as a 7th-century king of the sept called Dál nAraidhe (who lived in south Antrim and north Down). One day, on hearing the bell of St Rónán who was building a church in his territory, Suibhne rushed in anger to expel the saint. His queen, Eorann, tried to restrain him and caught his cloak, whereupon he ran naked from his house and attacked the saint, flinging his psalter into a lake. He was dragging the unfortunate Rónán along when a messenger came to summon him to the assistance of the Ulster king Conghal Claon, in a battle against the high-king **Domhnall mac Aodha**. Suibhne went with the messenger, and Rónán cursed him for what he had done - praying that he would wander through the world naked, as he was when he abused a servant of God.

An otter came and restored Rónán's psalter as if it had never been in water, and then the saint went to try to make peace between the contending parties. As he blessed the armies, Suibhne was angered by the sprinkling of holy water on him and he speared one of Rónán's clerics to death. He made a second cast at the saint himself, but the spear broke against the saint's bell and its shaft flew into the air. Rónán cursed him again, praying that Suibhne might thus fly through the air and die of a spear-cast. When the battle was joined at Magh Rátha (Moira, Co Down), Suibhne looked up amid the horrid clamour and saw everything whirling about. He became deranged and fled from the battlefield. He raced far away and leaped onto a yew-tree, which he made his dwelling. A kinsman tried to restore him to his senses, but he fled again and perched on a tree in Tír Chonaill (Co Donegal). When the victorious army of the high-king encamped near there, Domhnall mac Aodha himself encountered the mad Suibhne, pitied him, and tried unsuccessfully to dissuade him from such a life. Suibhne fled once more and travelled through all Ireland until he came to Gleann Bolcáin (apparently at Rosharkin in Co Antrim), a place where the lunatics used to congregate and find solace. There a faithful friend and relative, Loingseachán, found his footprints near a river where he used to eat watercress, but failed to locate Suibhne himself. As Loingseachán slept in a hut one night, the madman came near, but he avoided him when awake.

Loingseachán succeeded in meeting him by disguising himself as a mill-hag who used to give food to Suibhne. The madman told him that he would go to see his wife Eorann. She had gone to live with another man, and Suibhne reproached her for doing this but, when she said that she would prefer to live with himself even in misery, he took pity on her and advised her to remain with the new lover. A crowd gathered as they spoke, and Suibhne once more fled to the wilderness and took up his abode in trees again. Loingseachán came to him a second time and pleaded with him to return to his stately comfortable life as king. When Suibhne asked for tidings of his kingdom, Loingseachán told him that his father, mother, brother, and daughter had died. As Suibhne lamented this loss of his family, Loingseachán told him that his son also was dead. The madman said that this news 'would bring a man to the earth, that a little son who used to say papa is cold and lifeless'. Overcome by grief, Suibhne fell from the tree, and Loingseachán tied him up and told him that his family were in fact alive. He took him back to the people of Dál nAraidhe and re-installed him as king.

One day, when alone in his palace, the old mill-hag mentioned to him his period of madness and persuaded him to jump as he had then done. She competed with him and both went away jumping into the wilderness, where Suibhne resumed his life of lunacy as before. Coming to Dún Sobhairce (Dunseverick, Co Antrim) he cleared the fortress there with a leap and, in attempting to emulate his feat, the hag fell from the cliff and was killed. Having travelled Ireland, Suibhne then went to Britain and met there a lunatic like himself, Alladhán, who had the nickname Fear Caille. Alladhán had been cursed into madness by his people after he insisted that they go into battle dressed in satin. The two lunatics stayed together for a year, until Alladhán decided to go and drown himself in a waterfall. Suibhne now returned to his own people. Coming to his house, he would not enter for fear of being captured there. Eorann protested that she was ashamed of his madness and said that, if he would not stay with her, she would prefer that he depart forever. Suibhne left, sadly bemoaning the fickleness of women.

Again he went flighting around Ireland, until he was caught out in a fearfully wet and cold night, and the misery of this caused his reason to return to him. Once more, therefore, he set out for his own territory of the Dál nAraidhe. His adventures were miraculously revealed to Rónán, and that saint prayed that he not be allowed to return to persecute the Church again. As Suibhne passed by Sliabh Fuaid (the Fews in Co Armagh) he was beset by horrendous phantoms who roared at him that he was a lunatic and sent him deliriously astray. Finally, when he was in Fiodh Gaibhle (Feegile, Co Laois) he became repentant for the bad deeds of his life. He met with **Moling** at Teach Moling (St Mullins, Co Carlow), and that holy man took pity on him and told him to return from his wanderings to the monastery each evening. He got supper there, and Moling wrote down his adventures. The saint's cook used to feed his supper to him by making a hole in cowdung with her foot and filling it with milk. The cook's husband grew jealous of her attention to the madman, and he ran him through with a spear. Swooning from the wound, Suibhne confessed his sins to Moling and was given the Last Sacraments. Moling led him by the hand to the door of the church, where he expired.

That this Suibhne was not a historical personage is strongly suggested by the fact that he does not appear in the genealogies of Dál nAraidhe, and neither is he mentioned in the earlier accounts of the battle of Magh Rátha, which was fought in 637 AD. Scholars accept that the story of his madness was borrowed from the British tradition of St Kentigern and the wild man called Lailoken. This Lailoken went mad as the result of a horrible vision which he saw in the sky during the battle of Arfderydd in 574 AD. This episode is doubled by an account that the wise man Merlin went mad due to grief for the slain at the same battle. Both are described as going to live in the woods, eating wild fruit and roots, and due to their madness they could make prophecies. Furthermore, Lailoken is described as being befriended by St Kentigern before he died. Merlin was known as Myrddin Wyllt, the second word being a mutated form of 'gwyllt' (meaning 'wild'). This corresponds to the designation 'Suibhne geilt' - the sobriquet here denotes him as a lunatic and is very likely a borrowing of the British word. The roles played by the saints Rónán and Moling are largely an innovation in the Irish story - the former saint providing a rationalisation of Suibhne's madness and the latter parallelling and developing the role of Kentigern. The celebrated St Moling (q.v.) was attracted to the context by his reputed ability at jumping and his encounter with phantoms. The text of *Buile Shuibhne* puts much nature poetry into the mouth of the madman, and this seems to be a reflection of similar verse attributed to Moling. The motif of a contest with a hostile hag was very popular in ordinary Irish folklore, and the curious episode of the mill-hag and her malificent influence on Suibhne was obviously derived from the oral tradition.

A 14th-century text in the **Fianna Cycle**, *Cath Finntrágha*, situates Gleann Bolcáin in west Kerry, apparently identifying it with the wild valley in Kilgobban Parish on the Dingle Peninsula. This place is known as Gleann na nGealt ('the Glen of the Lunatics'). It is difficult to say whether the valley already bore that name in the 15th century or whether the name became associated with it as a result of the *Cath Finntrágha* text. The latter proposition seems the more likely, for that text was very popular in manuscripts. Texts of the Suibhne story were less numerous, but were known to poets and scholars and in this way would have had their influence on the folk consciousness. At any rate, the imagery associated with Suibhne became part of the folklore concerning the west Kerry glen. In the popular lore of the past few centuries, it was said that lunatics from all over Ireland used to retire to that place, drink water from a well there, eat water-cress, and race wildly about.

J G O'Keeffe (1913); James Carney (1955), 129-53.

[Contest with hag] Rosemary Power in *Scottish Studies 28*, 69-89.

[Lailokin and Merlin] Basil Clarke (1973).

[Gleann na nGealt] Gearóid Mac Eoin in *Béaloideas 30*, 105-20; Pádraig Ó Siochradha (1939), 284-5; Kenneth Jackson in *Béaloideas 8*, 48-9; Dáithí Ó hÓgáin (1981), 29.

SUIBHNE MEANN High-king of Ireland from 615 to his death in 628 AD. His sobriquet (earlier, Mend) means 'dumb' and is likely to have referred to a speech defect.

Suibhne's father was called Fiachna and, though a descendant of the famous **Niall Naoighiallach**, was not prominent in political life. To explain how a son of this Fiachna could become high-king, a fanciful story is told in one annalistic source. According to it, Fiachna was ploughing one day when the thought struck him that he should rise in the world and contest the kingship. He lay with his wife while his mind was occupied by this thought, and the fire of ambition passed on to the child who was thereby conceived. This was Suibhne, and when he grew up he would not be satisfied until he was high-king. Another set of annals claims that his ambition was fed by his wife, who in conversation one day chided him for not seeking the leadership of the northern Uí Néill and leading them in battle. Next morning he armed himself, set out from home, and collected a strong force of warriors by overcoming them one by one in single combat.

Suibhne gained the throne by defeating the incumbent high-king Maol Cobha in the battle of Sliabh Bealgadáin (near Cong in Co Mayo), but was himself slain by the Ulster king Conghal Caoch at the battle of Tráigh Bréine (on the east shore of Lough Swilly in Co Donegal). Narrative tradition, however, claimed that he was murdered by Conghal, while engaged in a game of chess, at the instigation of **Domhnall mac Aodha**, brother of Maol Cobha.

John O'Donovan (1848), *1*, 246-7 and (1860), 16-9; S H O'Grady (1892) *1*, 390; R A S Macalister (1956), 374-7; Whitley Stokes in *Irische Texte 3*, 410-1, 423; P S Dinneen (1908) *3*, 116-9; Ruth Lehmann (1964), 10-11.

SWIFT, JONATHAN (1667-1745) Dean of St Patrick's Cathedral in Dublin from 1713, and one of the greatest of writers in the English language. Because of his satires against the English establishment, he became very popular with the ordinary Irish people, although he was of a different religion and also of a different outlook to most of them, and many anecdotes concerning him are told both in the English and Irish languages.

He had several traits of personality which helped to endear him to Irish popular lore, especially his honesty and quick wit, and his hot temper and often crude use of language added drama to his image. The anecdotes are all of a humorous nature, and centre on the relationship between himself and a supposed servant called Jack. The perennial theme is of a clever master being upstaged by his even cleverer servant, and this seems to derive from the actual social circle of the Dean himself. Contemporary accounts describe his tendency towards tomfoolery with those in his employment, and he even wrote a humorous tract entitled 'Instructions to Servants'. He became quite a celebrity, particularly among the young intelligentsia of Dublin, and it is clear that the humorous theme owes much of its origin to that context also. The anecdotes told in folklore, although echoing the social surroundings of the Dean, are however mostly adaptations of common humorous lore and of stories from jokebooks which circulated widely in the 18th and 19th centuries. Once the Dean became established in tradition as the archetypal clever and somewhat jolly master, any kind of narrative regarding clever servants could get attached to his name, and in order

89. SWIFT, JONATHAN *Contemporary portrait of Dean Swift.*

to make matters more definite and memorable the apocryphal Jack was invented.

One common story describes how he first took Jack into his employ. Three applicants answered his advertisement for a servant, and the learned clergyman decided to test their memories. He therefore told them to repeat after him the words 'Lamb of God, who takest away the sins of the world, have mercy on us' and to return to him a year later and repeat the sentence. The year passed, and at the appointed time the first two applicants came to the Dean and repeated the sentence. The third fellow, however, had altered the words to 'sheep of God' and, when the Dean queried this, he stated that what was a lamb a year ago would be fully grown by now. The Dean was amazed at his wit, and gave the position to him. This was the redoubtable Jack. The story itself is an example of a widespread humorous folktale. A variant tradition has the Dean question the applicants regarding their ability to drive a coach. One of them said that he could gallop a coach with six horses through a wood, and another said that he could drive the horses within an inch of a cliff-edge. Jack, however, said that he would prefer to drive carefully, and so got the job.

Other accounts also make use of material from popular international folklore plots. For instance, we are told that when Jack applied for the position, Swift put some rudimentary questions to him concerning ordinary work and was amazed at his stupidity. 'Can you do anything at all?' the Dean finally asked in desperation, and Jack said that he could not. The Dean then asked about Jack's family, and got saucy replies, and finally in exasperation ordered him out, saying that he would only employ him if he could come to work neither dressed nor undressed, neither walking nor riding, neither on the road nor off the road. Jack came next day clad only in a fishing-net, seated on a billy-goat so that he was half-walking and half-riding, and with one leg on the grass and the other on the road. Swift remarked that he was the smartest fellow he had ever seen, and took him on.

When employed Jack continues to show his cleverness. In order to teach him a lesson, Swift locks him into the kitchen with no meat and orders him to cook meat for a meal. Jack takes the leather from the Dean's walking-boots, cooks this, and serves it up as tripe. Swift is very pleased with the meal, but when he looks for his boots later he realises what has happened. He flies into a rage, and tells Jack that as punishment he will be allowed nothing to eat until he sees 'water running against a hill'. Then the Dean goes riding, with Jack running along behind the horse. When they stop to let the horse drink, Jack remarks that this is water running uphill. Another anecdote has Jack being reprimanded for not cleaning his master's boots. He replies that 'it's no use cleaning them, for they will be dirty again tomorrow', but Swift then denies him breakfast, saying that 'it's no use eating, for you will be hungry again tomorrow!' This has the Dean triumphing, and it can be compared to an account printed in the year 1789, according to which Swift made two servants go without breakfast because they had disputed over which of them should clean his boots. We know from contemporary sources that the Dean did really have a large pair of boots which attracted some attention when he went riding.

The most popular of all the stories concerning him tells of how one day he instructs Jack to cook a fine goose for him. Jack is hungry, and eats a leg of the goose before he serves it at table. When Swift queries this, Jack says that geese have only one leg. Later, when they go riding, they see a flock of wild geese with one leg under their wings, and Jack points this out as proof of his earlier assertion. Swift claps his hands and says 'whoosh', with the result that the geese put down both legs and fly away. Jack, however, counters this by asking why he had not said 'whoosh' to the cooked goose. This is a version of an international oral story, but was also found in jest-books, and it may have become attached to Swift from either such source. Fowl also figure in a hilarious folktale which became attached to him. According to this, Swift brought home a tramp to lunch one day, and Jack was displeased because he knew that he himself would get neither of the two chickens which had been cooked. He therefore suggested darkly to the visitor that the old Dean was accustomed to castrate his guests. The Dean liked to carve the chicken himself, and when he suddenly appeared in the doorway with a large knife the startled tramp took flight. Referring to the chickens, Swift called out that he was going to take only one, to which the fleeing guest retorted: 'No, I want the two of them myself!'

A direct connection can be made between the historical Swift and one story commonly told about him. This deals with the unfaithfulness of women, of the 'Ephesian Matron' type, and we know that Swift's young protegée William Dunkin wrote a version of such a story in verse for him and that the Dean read it 'with some glee'. It was no doubt due to its popularity within his circle that the Dean himself was made an actor in the narrative in folk tradition. We are told that, one day as they travelled in a fine coach, Jack and the Dean argued about the nature of women. Swift had a very chivalric attitude, claiming that women were angelic creatures and that but for them men would go about like wild beasts. Jack's attitude was somewhat more cynical, claiming that women were flippant and unreliable. As the debate heated up, they noticed a woman in a graveyard, weeping copiously over the grave of her dead husband. Jack, who was well-dressed, approached the woman and made a proposal of marriage to her, remarking that his chaplain was with him in the coach. She immediately accepted the proposal, much to the chagrin of the Dean who was thus proved wrong in his estimate of the fair sex.

Another adaptation of a folklore plot has Swift married, but when away from home he asks Jack to find a sleeping partner for him. Jack finds an ugly old woman, and is immediately dismissed from his service by the enraged Dean. When they return home, Swift's wife asks Jack how he had displeased his master, and Jack explains it by saying that 'the Dean sent me out to find a pullet and I brought an old hen'. The wife then asks Swift how did he expect poor Jack to be an expert on fowl, and he begins to explain, but thinks better of it and takes Jack back into his service. Another adaptation has the Dean reprimanding Jack for his rude manners and reverses roles so as to show him how to behave. 'You are a good boy', says Jack in the Dean's role, 'and here is money for you!' Yet another has Jack lazily indicating direction by pointing his foot, and when the Dean offers him a sovereign if he can do anything more lazy than that, Jack mutters 'Put it in my pocket for me!'

Although Dean Swift was a senior clergyman of the Established Church, many Roman Catholics believed that secretly he was more inclined to their way of thinking. Thus a humorous story grew up concerning his death and his supposed vacillation between the two religions. It was said that he told the Protestant minister who was attending him on his deathbed that he had a debt to pay to one particular man before he died. The minister kindly offered to bring this man to him so that the matter could be settled, and then Swift named a certain Catholic priest. Rather reluctantly, the minister did as requested of him, but he was outraged to see Swift confessing to the priest and preparing for death in the Catholic manner. 'If you recover you will pay for this!' shouted the minister, to which Swift cunningly replied: 'Well, then, you will be dismissed from your ministry, for it was you who brought the priest to me!'

Thomas Sheridan (1784); Patrick Kennedy (n.d.), 32-6; M L Jarrell in *Journal of American Folklore 77*, 99-117; Dáithí Ó hÓgáin (1985), 86-99, 330-1.

[Borrowed folktale-plots] Antti Aarne / Stith Thompson (1961), Types 785A, 875, 921, 1510, 1623, 1741, 1832E, 1832N, 1950.

T

TADHG MAC CÉIN Fictional Munster nobleman, whose father Cian was claimed to have been son of **Ailill Ólom**, the mythical Munster king.

The mediaeval literature represents Tadhg as the lord of Éile, in north Tipperary, and as an ally of **Cormac mac Airt** in the battle of Crionna (near Mellifont on the river Boyne). Cormac, however, tried to trick him out of the land which had been promised to him in lieu of that help. The wounded Tadhg was for a while helpless in the care of Cormac's leeches, who plotted to bring about his death. He managed to get word to his own doctors in Munster, however, and they came and cured him. When he returned home, Tadhg threatened war on Cormac, who thereupon consented to pay the agreed fee for his support at Crionna. The land comprised a substantial part of eastern Bréagha (in Co Meath), and the story was invented in order to rationalise the presence of a sept known as the Ciannachta (literally, 'descendants of Cian') there.

A sept to the south of the Ciannachta was known as Gaileanga, and early tradition claimed them also to be descendants of Tadhg. Already in the 8th century a story was in existence which rationalised this. We read that a son of Tadhg, called Cormac, was making a feast for his father, and had the meat of many kinds of animals prepared for it. He had no badger-meat, however, and so he went to a set and called the badgers out to him. When he guaranteed their safety under the protection of his father Tadhg, they came to him and he killed a large number of them for the feast. When Tadhg saw this meat, however, his heart shuddered, and he angrily rebuked his son, calling him Gaileang (derived here from 'gae lang' i.e. 'fouling of honour') and banishing him from his household. This strange story is apparently based on the survival of an ancient Celtic word 'tazgos' (meaning 'badger') in the form 'tadcc', thus giving rise to the personal name. This would mean that badgers were namesakes of Tadhg mac Céin and that it was taboo for him to eat them on that account.

The inference from the story of Tadhg and a badger-taboo is that a special corpus of heroic lore had developed concerning him. The only surviving long story, however, dates from the 14th century or thereabouts and is typical of the fanciful romances of that period. According to it, he was visiting the west of Munster when he and his company were set upon by raiders from a country called Fresen, which is described as being near to Spain. The raiders took away several of Tadhg's people, including his wife Lí Ban and his two brothers, and Tadhg himself barely managed to escape from them. The captives were taken overseas to Fresen, and the leader of the raiders, called Camthann, made Lí Ban his paramour. Tadhg's brothers, Eoghan and Airnealach, were put to menial tasks and given the worst of food. Only forty of Tadhg's men remained free, but they slew an equal number of the foe and captured one of them alive. This prisoner told them about the land of Fresen, and they constructed a large boat in order to travel there.

On their journey, they visited an island where there were huge sheep, and a pair of other islands with beautiful birds. When they ate the eggs of these birds, feathers sprouted on them, but the feathers fell off as soon as they bathed. Setting sail again they came to a frightfully stormy sea, but Tadhg urged his men to stand firm, and they survived this ordeal, coming eventually to a wondrous land where they met a beautiful and wise lady. She told them that she was **Cessair**, the first woman ever to reach Ireland, and she related that in this land lived all the people who had formerly dwelt in Ireland. They were in fact in the otherworld paradise, with luscious foliage, delightful climate, and dwellings of gold and marble. Among those whom they encountered there were **Conn Céadchathach** and his son Connla. They also met the otherworld lady **Clíona**, who gave them three musical birds and a goblet which had been found in the heart of a whale.

They spent a whole year in that land, thinking it but a day, and then set sail again. Reaching Fresen, Tadhg met his brother Eoghan, who was working as a ferryman. Eoghan told him that he and Airnealach had been conspiring with two

91. TARA *Aerial view of Tara.*

nephews of Camthann to overthrow that tyrant. He also related that Lí Ban had gained respite from Camthann until then, but that she now had perforce to marry the tyrant and the wedding was being prepared. Tadhg combined his forces with those of Camthann's nephews and decided to attack the feast, but the Fresener prisoner escaped and went to inform Camthann of their plans. Reaching the castle, he first met Airnealach there and, not recognising him, told his news. Airnealach beheaded him and went to welcome the attackers. In a frightful melée, Tadhg's men slaughtered the king's soldiers, and Tadhg himself engaged Camthann in his bed-chamber and beheaded him. He was then reunited with his wife. Installing the elder of Camthann's nephews, Eochaidh Armdhearg, as king, Tadhg set sail triumphantly for Ireland.

S H O'Grady (1892) 1, 319-26 and 2, 491-3; Kuno Meyer in *Zeitschrift für celtische Philologie 10*, 42; Alan Mac an Bhaird in *Ériu 31*, 150-5; Whitley Stokes in *Irische Texte 3*, 384-5 and (1862), xlii-xlv.

[Romance-text] O'Grady (1892) *1*, 342-59.

TARA (in Irish, Teamhair, earlier Temuir): The centre of the high-kingship in early mediaeval Ireland, it is situated a few miles north-west of Dunshaughlin in Co Meath. The anglicised form 'Tara' is based on the genitive 'Teamhrach'. The word itself meant 'spectacle', and the fine view of the centre of Ireland available from this vantage-point must have been the original reason for the importance attached to the place.

Archaeology has shown that Tara was an important burial site from the second millenium BC. After their arrival, probably around 500 BC, the Gaelic people adopted it to their own culture, and made it the centre of the cult of a sacred king. Much of the evidence for this was preserved in the myth of **Conaire**, a Tara king whose reign was described as propitious and hedged about by many magical conditions. The account of Conaire's death can be taken to reflect the manner in which the Laighin (Leinstermen) seized control of Tara in or around the 3rd century AD, and it may have been the Leinster kings who developed the idea of a special goddess of sovereignty called **Meadhbh** presiding over the site. A special 'feast of Tara' was celebrated - apparently at Samhain (i.e. November, see **Time**). This was anciently known as 'feis Temro', the word 'feis' having the basic meaning of sleeping with the goddess and the celebration was thus closely connected with the cult of **kingship**. All of this was highly prestigious to the Leinstermen, and the importance in which they held Tara as the most strategic point of the luscious Boyne valley is reflected in their mythic lore concerning **Fionn mac Cumhaill**.

The powerful 5th-century magnate **Niall Naoighiallach** displaced the Leinstermen and made Tara focus of the control wielded over the whole centre and west of Ireland by his Connachta sept. The descendants of Niall (the Uí Néill) became high-kings of all Ireland, and they put the cult of the sacral kingship of Tara to their own advantage. The principle tenet of their propaganda was based on one great figure who came to be regarded as the archetype of Irish kingship. This was **Cormac mac Airt**, the basic elements of whose myth seem to have been taken over by the Uí Néill from the lore of their Leinster predecessors at the site. By the early Middle Ages, they had developed the myth of Cormac to such a degree that the cultural landscape of Tara was explained by reference to it. Thus a striking neolithic tumulus on the site was re-interpreted as a mound on which Cormac kept his hostages, and the huge surrounding enclosure known as Ráth na Ríogh ('the rampart of the kings') was said to have been constructed by him. At the centre of the Ráth were two other structures which were claimed to have been Cormac's House and his royal assembly-seat. To the north is a long sunken rectangular area, which was interpreted as having been the site of Cormac's great banquet-hall called the Teach Miodhchuarta; and near this was an enclosure which was said to have belonged to his daughter Gráinne (for whom, see **Diarmaid ua Duibhne**). Among the other remains at Tara associated with the reign of the Uí Néill kings are a mound where Niall's son **Laoghaire** was buried, and a circle of banks and fosses reputed to have been the site of synods held by **Adhamhnán** and other saints.

The hill of Tara is central to most of the great drama in early Irish literature, but it was always regarded as a site of ancient rather than of contemporary glory. The Uí Néill dynasty continued to refer to themselves as 'kings of Tara' and the

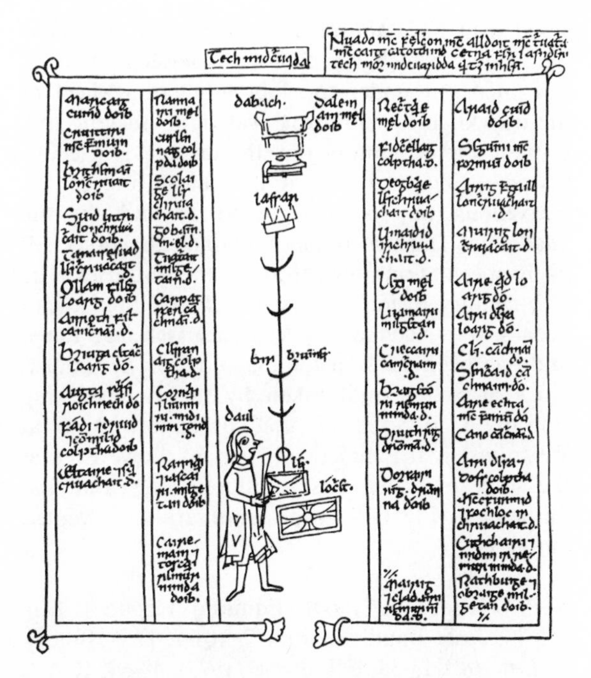

92. TARA *Plan of the Teach Miodhchuarta from a 12th-century manuscript.*

'feast of Tara' was apparently still celebrated at the inauguration of high-kings down to the 9th century. However, the prestige of the place in mediaeval culture was rather abstract. The actual site was overgrown and reclaimed by nature, and was the subject of speculation by poets and antiquaries. Thus the fiction grew up that Tara had been abandoned due to a curse placed on it by the 6th-century saint **Ruadhán**, and the ultimate alienation from the ancient cult was reached when an 11th-century scholar invented a new interpretation of its name. According to this, a lady called Tea was the wife of the pseudo-historical Gaelic leader **Éireamhóin**, and had come from Spain with him. She had seen in Spain a rampart around the grave of a lady of that country called Teiphe. On reaching Tara, Tea begged her husband to bestow the hill on her and, when he complied, she built a wall ('múr') around it in imitation of Teiphe's rampart. When she died, she was buried within that enclosure, hence - the writer fancifully argues - the placename Teamhair. Another object of great curiosity at Tara is the upright granite stone called the 'Lia Fáil', which nows stands on the mound known as Cormac's House but which formerly stood near the 'Mound of the Hostages'. This was the stone which symbolised **kingship**, and it screamed out under the foot or chariot-wheel of the true king. Its cultic role was quite ancient and, in their appreciation of this, the mediaeval pseudo-historians claimed that it had been one of the marvellous objects brought to Ireland by the **Tuatha Dé Danann**. It has remained the object of lively speculation down through the centuries. The 17th-century historian **Céitinn** believed that it had been sent to Scotland by **Muircheartach mac Earca** and had been used for the inauguration of Scottish kings at Scone until taken by the English king Edward I to serve as the coronation stone at Westminster. It is practically certain, however, that the stone at Scone was a different one, and that the ancient Lia Fáil is the landmark still pointed out at Tara.

S P Ó Ríordáin (1960); Edmund Hogan (1910), 629-30; Josef Baudis in *Ériu 7*, 101-7; D A Binchy in *Ériu 18*, 113-38; F J Byrne (1973), 48-69; R A S Macalister (1931); David Comyn (1902), 100-1, 206-9.

TIGHEARNMHAS Fictional king of Ireland situated in prehistory. His name means 'lordly'.

He is described as a descendant of **Éireamhon**, and is said to have slain Conmhaol, son of Éibhear, and to have won thrice nine battles in one year. It is further stated that, during his reign, the first gold-mine in Ireland was discovered in the territory of the Fotharta of the eastern Liffey (i.e. near Naas in Co Kildare). Tighearnmhas employed a wright called Iuchadán to make a brooch for him from the gold. Also attributed to Tighearnmhas were the making of the first goblets and silver vessels, and the first use of the colours purple, blue, and green on garments. He ordained that colours of garments be worn according to social status - one colour for bondsmen, two for peasants, three for paid warriors, four for lords, five for chieftains, six for learned men, and seven for royalty.

Tighearnmhas was said to have originated the worship of the idol Crom Cruach (see **Crom**) at Magh Sléacht (the plain at Tullyhaw in Co Cavan). He went to that place at Samhain (November) accompanied by the men of Ireland, but was overtaken by some unspecified disaster and died there along with three-fourths of his followers. He is clearly the invention of the mediaeval writers and, although his reign is ascribed to the pagan era, his sudden death was meant to signify the wrath of God against the sin of idolatry.

R A S Macalister (1956), 199-209, 432-7; Edward Gwynn (1913), 266-9 and (1924), 19-23; P S Dinneen (1908) *2*, 120-3.

TIME The basic Irish division of the year was into two parts, the summer half beginning at Bealtaine (May 1st) and the winter half at Samhain (November 1st). There were two further sub-divisions of almost equal importance, beginning at Imbolg (February 1st) and Lughnasa (August 1st), so that the year was divided into the standard four seasons. At each of these four junctures a festival was celebrated which involved an impressive amount of custom and lore. The festivals properly began at sunset on the day before the actual date, evincing the Celtic tendency to regard the night as preceding the day. Thus, for instance, Oíche Bhealtaine (literally, 'the night of May') actually referred to the last day of April, and similarly with Oíche Shamhna. The festival of Imbolg is better known to history as the feast of St **Brighid**, and the eve of the festival is known as Oíche Fhéil Bhrighide. There is no particular stress on the eve of Lughnasa, for the celebration of that is not tied to the actual first day of August. Having been strongly Christianised (see **Lugh** and **Patrick**), this festival of the harvest has since mediaeval times been celebrated on the Sunday nearest to that date.

The term Imbolg or 'Oímelg' occurs only in the early literature, and its meaning may be either 'parturition' or 'lactation'. Tradition shows clearly that this feast of Brighid was concerned with the birth of young animals and that it was originally under the tutelage of the goddess **Brighid**. Until recently, it was customary to invoke the protection of her namesake saint (q.v.) on farm animals at this time. The St Brighid's crosses were hung in the cow-byre, and the hope for general agricultural prosperity was expressed by leaving a piece of cloth outdoors overnight to gather dew. The cloth was called 'Brighid's mantle', and the saint was believed to touch it as she passed by. A general manner of communal celebration was engaged in at this as at several other festivals - the young people going from house to house in disguise, singing and playing music. On this particular feast they were usually led by a young girl representing the saint, and the boys were humorously accoutred as women.

The word Bealtaine (earlier, Beltine) originally meant 'bright fire', and it was a festival of crucial importance as it was the beginning of the good weather, of the sowing season, and also the time when the amount of the prospective milk-yield became clear. The mediaeval literature claims that it was on this festival that the Gaelic people had first come to Ireland (see **Míl**). The celebration of the May festival was of course common throughout Europe, but it had certain distinctive traits in Ireland. In former centuries, for instance, a great fire was lit by the various communities at this time, recalling the Irish name of the festival itself and no doubt deriving anciently from a desire to encourage the sun. Symbolising the desired prosperity, some greenery was brought into the house, and there are accounts from the 18th century which describe how young people dressed up in greenery and celebrated the coming of summer by open-air dancing. The May bush - usually a whitethorn - was cut and brought home, decorated with garlands and egg-shells, and set up near the dwelling house.

This being the beginning of summer, it was considered to foreshadow all of that season. Agriculture can be in many ways an unreliable affair, and so people were extremely careful to protect their prosperity. It was believed that some malicious neighbours might attempt to magically steal away one's good fortune, and this gave rise to several traditions and stories. For instance, a loan of salt should never be given to a neighbour who asked for it on May Eve, nor should a piece of the household fire be allowed to be brought outside of the house. Especially important was the dew in one's fields and the water in one's well, for it was believed that certain greedy individuals were keen to take a portion of these overnight, with the same magical effect. Two well-known international legends, appropriate to the context, were particularly associated with May Eve in Irish folklore. One of these tells of how a woman, regardless of how hard she worked at the churning, could not make butter, but eventually she was advised to put a piece of red-hot iron into the churn-dash. A neighbouring woman, who had put the harmful charm on the butter-milk, came screaming to the house, contorted in pain as if pierced by hot iron, and could only get relief by herself taking a hand at the churning and thereby undoing the charm. The other legend tells of how an old lady took the form of a hare and drank the milk from the neighbour's cows until discovered (see **Animals**, Wild).

Lughnasa (earlier, Lughnasadh) was the feast of **Lugh**, and its celebration marked the ripening of corn and the weaning of calves and lambs. In early Ireland several great fairs coincided with this festival, but since the Middle Ages its celebration on a Sunday meant that it was religious and recreational in character. Its original designation does not survive in popular tradition, that being now the common word in Irish ('Lúnasa') for the month of August. The festival is rather known as the Sunday of **Crom Dubh**, or in varying areas as Lammas Sunday, Garland Sunday, Bilberry Sunday, or Fraughan Sunday. Hill-top climbing for both prayers and for gathering bilberries was general throughout the country, as were assemblies at lakes and holy wells, and other favourite pastimes were horse-racing, horse-swimming, and games of hurling. The earlier commercial aspect of the festival was not completely lost, however, as fairs or markets were held on a day near to the Sunday at Ballycastle in Co Antrim, Muff in Co Cavan, Ennistymon in Co Clare, Killorglin in Co Kerry, and many other places.

The word Samhain meant 'the end of summer', and it was the festival which attracted most interest in Irish literature. Being the beginning of the dark season, it was especially associated with the dead and the otherworld. Many of the supernatural adventures of heroes in the early literature are said to have taken place at this time. Particularly striking in this context are the adventures of **Fionn mac Cumhaill**, and it is likely that his prototype, the seer **Find**, had a special association with Samhain. The dead ancestors were of great importance in Irish custom and belief, and this was the date of the festival of **Tara**, traditionally the ritual centre of kingship itself. Folklore places great emphasis on Oíche Shamhna (Halloween) as a time when **ghosts** are abroad and **fairies** are moving from their summer to their winter quarters. Due to the Church festivals of All Saints and All Souls on the first two days of November, much of the solemnity has gone from the attitude towards Halloween itself. There is, however, a clear remnant of native belief in the tradition - which survived until recently - of leaving the fire lighting and going to bed early on All Souls' Night, so that the family kitchen or parlour would be left to the dead ancestors who would again congregate there on that night.

The Christian festivals were very popular, though they never developed the same wealth of lore as the four great seasonal feasts. Christmas and Easter were of course the most important, and popular traditions associated with them were of the type general in Europe. Christmas, being dedicated to the birth of **Christ**, was a time of special mystery and deep human and religious feeling. Everybody became more devout, more charitable, and more good-humoured, and presents were exchanged according to people's means. Special emphasis was on the children - for instance, the youngest child in the household would light the Christmas candle. This was placed in the window to light the way for any poor travellers who, like Mary and Joseph long ago, might be seeking their way through the world in the darkness. The children were told that at the hour of midnight the cattle and donkeys received the power of speech for a while in remembrance of how the cow and donkey kept the infant Jesus warm, but it was unlucky to be near these animals at that time and so their speech was never heard. During the twelve days of Christmas, it was said, the doors of heaven were open, and anybody who died in that period passed over directly to eternal happiness.

Regarding Easter Sunday, it was said that, as it rose in the morning, the sun danced in joy at the Resurrection of Jesus. Many people therefore woke early and climbed onto some hilltop to watch the sun or went to a well to see its reflection quiver in the water. This belief was common in most parts of Europe since the Middle Ages, as was the custom of painting, rolling, and eating eggs. This latter probably arose, not from any ritual, but from the simple reality that the eating of eggs was forbidden during Lent and therefore a great number of them would have been stored up by Easter. Folk beliefs relative to the other important days in the Christian calendar were generally derived from biblical imagery. For instance, the Slaughter of the Innocents being commemorated on December 28 meant that that day was regarded as a sinister one. It was known as 'lá crosta na bliana' (forbidden day of the year), and no new enterprise was undertaken on it. Similarly, no carpentry or other work involving the driving of nails was carried out on Good Friday, because of Christ's crucifixion on that day. On the other hand, the Epiphany, known as Little Christmas or the Women's Christmas, was regarded as second only to Christmas Day itself in happiness and beauty. An old saying in Irish claimed that 'on the Night of the Three Kings wine is made of the water, silk of the rushes, and gold of the gravel'. Again, however, this was not observed by humans, and any toper who slyly went to drink water at midnight from the well was in danger of being turned into stone.

A European tradition which survived with particular vigour in Ireland was the lighting of bonfires at Midsummer, the festival of St John. Also very popular was the collecting of money and presents on St Stephen's Day by groups of disguised singers and dancers, a custom which has apparently been moving gradually northwards in Europe since mediaeval times, but which has not yet reached Scotland or most of Ulster. In Ireland the custom is associated with hunting the wren (see **Animals** etc, Wild). For some reason Whit Sunday is generally regarded as an unlucky day on which to be born, a belief which was especially strong in Leinster. If a child were born on this day, it was said that he was destined to be a killer, and in order to prevent this a worm was placed in the baby's hand, which was then closed tightly so that the destined killing was done and over. The question of destiny, of good luck and bad, has for the past two centuries been associated above all with New Year's Day, known in Irish as 'Lá Coille' ('Kalend-Day'). The Church has observed January 1 as the beginning of its year since the 16th century, and it has been the legal beginning since the reform of the Calendar in 1751. Since then, popular lore has taken that day as a kind of premonition of the coming year in terms of business, weather, and general welfare, and its eve is celebrated with a great family feast. This was called 'Oíche na Coda Móire' (the Night of the Large Portion), for to eat well on this night was regarded as a way of preventing scarcity and hunger during the ensuing year.

The seven-day week unit was introduced into Ireland by Christianity, and the names of all the weekdays in Irish derive from Latin or Church culture. Luan, Máirt, and Satharn come from 'Luna', 'Mars' and 'Saturn'; whereas Domhnach comes from 'Dominus', Céadaoin means 'first fast', Déardaoin means 'day between two fasts' and Aoine means simply 'fast'. Because of its association with the crucifixion, Friday was generally observed as a day of special prayer by the devout, and it was regarded as an unlucky day to embark on an undertaking, especially marriage. A direct echo from the Gospels is the expectation that if a storm began on a Friday it would subside on the following Sunday. Because of its initial position in the week, Monday was also considered a risky day to begin a new enterprise. Thus, if a deal had to be made, payment was held over until the following day or, if a grave had to be dug, the first sod was turned on the Sunday beforehand. People did, however, feel that Monday was a good day on which to give alms to the poor. Tuesday and Thursday were regarded as the most propitious days for business affairs.

Kevin Danaher (1972); Seán Ó Súilleabháin (1942), 316-64 and (1967), 61-75; Máire MacNeill (1962).

TOMÁS MÓR ('Big Thomas') Fanciful ancestor of the churls of Ireland in a satiric prose-text written in the early 17th century. The text is entitled *Pairlement Chloinne Tomáis* (the Parliament of Clan Thomas), and its author was from south Kerry or west Cork.

Tomás is described as the son of one Liobar 'the Rotten', of demonic descent. He was, we read, a contemporary of St **Patrick**, and was ugly and surly. When that saint banished the demons from the summit of Croaghpatrick, he allowed Tomás to remain, since his mother was of the human race. Patrick, however, ordained that his descendants should be ignorant and crude, of lowly status and with a taste for the roughest food and manners. Tomás had no fewer than twenty-four sons, and these spread throughout Ireland and had numerous progeny, to whom silly and rugged names are applied. Eventually, one of the sept, called Murchadh Ó Multuaiscirt, became very rich, and he convened an assembly of all the important men of the Clan Thomas to his dwelling at Clonmacnoise in Co Offaly. He told the assembly that he required their support in his courtship of the daughter of a Connacht chieftain, Maghnus Ó Madagáin, and they all set out for Connacht. Maghnus' counsellors advised him not to allow his blood to be sullied with that of Clan Thomas, but his avaricious wife insisted on such a wealthy alliance, and so the maiden was married off to Murchadh. The wedding-feast was held on Crom Dubh Sunday (see **Time**: Lughnasa), and at it a disgraceful brawl broke out, with various members of the Clan Thomas abusing each other and hacking at each other. Eventually Murchadh succeeded in quieting them, and he then made a great speech, advising the whole clan to get education for their children, to dress like the aristocracy, and to gain power in the country.

They accordingly rose in the world, and by the time of Queen **Elizabeth** they had amassed vast wealth. It so happened that a great warrior of the Clan, Cairbre Crom Ó Céirín, lived on the plain of Cashel in Co Tipperary, and he had a daughter called Seiligeán. There was a huge crop of wheat on that plain and, in order to have it harvested, he sent out a proclamation that the best reaper of Clan Thomas could have the hand of Seiligeán. Hundreds of aspirants assembled from all over Ireland and set to work. However, contention arose and the proceedings deteriorated into a brutal riot, leaving many dead and wounded by sickles, bill-hooks, and flails, and the beautiful plain of Cashel was turned into a quagmire. Eventually, Cairbre awarded his daughter to one Yellow Cathal Ó Breisleáin, who lived at Dún Eochair Máighe (Bruree, Co Limerick).

With the thinning out of the Irish aristocracy due to the Elizabethan Wars, the Clan Thomas began to take possession of much territory and even to marry into the upper class. In the time of King James 1 they had become so precocious that they decided to convene a great parliament of their own at Cros Uí Fhloinn (Crusline, a few miles north-east of Tralee in Co Kerry) under the chairmanship of a crude fellow named Seán Séideánach Ó Smutacháin (literally, 'Snorting John O'Flatnosed'). There they discussed their social position and their grievances, and rejoiced at the new county juries, which blamed the crimes of Clan Thomas on the nobles. Soon two horsemen approached, one of whom was the noble poet Muiris, son of Black David Fitzgerald, who had written a detailed account of the Clan. Two of the boors asked Muiris to settle a dispute between them. A sow belonging to one of them, Bearnard Ó Broic, had been attacked by a dog belonging to the other, called Tomás 'of the Trumpet'. The wife of the latter had seized the dog, and Bearnard aimed a blow of an axe at it but missed his target, killing his own pig and breaking the shin-bone of his wife. They were thus suing each other for damages. Muiris could not decide between them, and he departed, whereupon the two litigants laid hands on each other and this led to a general melée.

Clan Thomas reconvened at the same place thirteen years later. This time they had arranged rules of procedure, but their conversation and general behaviour was as vile as ever. Crude personal remarks soon led once more to a vicious brawl, and many of the Clan were maimed and worse, so that the parliamentary deliberations had to be interrupted to bury the dead. The statutes which they enacted related principally to agricultural and dietary matters, but they also decided to take noble surnames for themselves. An

Englishman approached, selling tobacco, and the leaders of Clan Thomas bargained with him for its purchase. They spoke execrable English, but were held in high estimation by their followers for their efforts. Then they all began to smoke the tobacco, but Tomás accused Bearnard of farting and recited a hideous quatrain on this. Bearnard left in high dudgeon, cursing the parliament and all its proceedings.

The author of this satire has not been personally identified. He was clearly a learned man, with some knowledge of foreign literature, and the savagery of his attack on the churls is derived from some such source. The theme of parliaments held by rustics and rogues was fashionable in the anti-peasant satires of late mediaeval Europe, but the immediate texts which suggested such material to this author were a 16th-century translation into English of Sebastian Brant's German work *Narrenschiff*, and an early 17th-century English work by Samuel Rowlands entitled *Martin Mark-All*. In writing *Pairlement Chloinne Tomáis*, the author seems to have intended not so much to ridicule the peasantry as to lampoon special trends which were developing in the socio-political life of his time. This, at any rate, is the drift of a poem by Muiris, son of David Fitzgerald, to which he refers laudingly and which was probably his immediate inspiration. The boorish characters described in the *Pairlement* could well have been caricatures of individuals of his own time known to the author. There are several indications that the leading target of the satire was the anglicising Black Thomas Butler (1532-1614), the tenth Earl of Ormond. The boisterous humour of the text, based largely on verbal profusion, over-rides its illogical social assumptions, and the literati of succeeding centuries looked to it as a rich source of humorous and abusive phraseology in more general contexts.

An addendum to the text was written around the year 1660. This describes how one of the Clan Thomas, Dónall Ó Plubarnáin, was knighted and became a magistrate, owing this to his great Protector, Oliver **Cromwell**. Dónall decided to convene a parliament near Mullingar in Co Westmeath, and scions of the Clan assembled there from all over Ireland. They discussed a curse which had been put on them long ago by the Pope because one of their number had slain a friar with his coulter. Through all their bickering and rowing they managed to agree to send a delegate to Rome in order to have this curse set aside, but he succeeded in having it removed from three millers only. On hearing this, the parliament of Sir Dónall enacted that all millers should be boycotted by the Clan Thomas. They then dispersed, bickering still and admitting that their misfortune arose from their treachery towards the nobility who would willingly help them in dire straits.

93. TOMÁS MÓR *Black Tom Butler, 10th Earl of Ormond, from a contemporary portrait.*

Several other works of social and personal satire composed within the following half-century made use of the setting and nomenclature from *Pairlement Chloinne Tomáis*. Accusations of rural boorishness, derived from the text, became a favourite stylistic device. Most notable of such works were two late 17th-century satires on the pretensions and intricacies of ecclesiastical life, entitled *Comhairle Mhic Clamha* and *Comhairle Comissarius na Cléire*.

[First and second texts with discussion] N J A Williams (1981).

[Fitzgerald poem] Williams (1979), 48-57.

[Derived works] Williams in *Éigse 15*, 126-30; Alan Harrison in ibid 15, 189-202; Máiréad Ní Ghráda in *Lia Fáil 1*, 49-78; P S Dinneen / Tadhg O'Donoghue (1911), 287-98.

[Satires on ecclesiastics] Seosamh Ó Dufaigh / B E Rainey (1981); Ó Dufaigh in *Studia Hibernica 10*, 70-83.

TUÁN MAC CAIRILL Fictional character who, in mediaeval Irish literature, is claimed to have lived for hundreds of years. He was apparently invented by a 9th-century writer on the pattern of the antediluvian survivor **Fionntan**.

We read that Tuán was a rich warrior who resided in the vicinity of St Finnian of Magh Bhile (Moville, near Newtownards in Co Down). He refused hospitality to the saint at their first encounter, but Finnian fasted against him and was then admitted to his house. When the saint enquired who he was, Tuán disclosed that he had lived for a long time, and that he had undergone many transformations. He was born son of Caireall, after Caireall's wife had eaten him when he was in the form of a salmon. Before that he had been in turn a stag, a boar, and an eagle for long periods. Originally he had been son of Starn, brother of **Parthalán** who led a group of people into Ireland in the very distant (and fictional) past. Growing old in his various shapes, and being renewed in others, Tuán had witnessed all the great events which had occurred between the coming of Parthalán and the coming of Christianity. and was also an expert on genealogy. Tuán relayed all this knowledge to Finnian, thereby preserving it for posterity.

John Carey in *Ériu 35*, 93-111; R A S Macalister (1933), 272-3; H A de Jubainville (1903), 25-35.

TUATHA DÉ DANANN The principle otherworld race in Irish literary myth. Their designation means 'the People of the Goddess Danu'. **Danu** was an ancient Celtic land-goddess, but it is not clear why her name in particular was chosen to refer to the otherworld race, who were often referred to in a shorter form as Tuatha Dé.

Groups of Celtic people, in their westward expansion, were apparently reaching Ireland as early as the 6th century BC, and these influxes of Celts continued until the early centuries AD. These groups must have brought with them whatever mythical and religious ideas which they had inherited in the Celtic areas of Europe. When they reached Ireland, they encountered many archaeological remains of much earlier settlements. Particularly noticeable were the passage-graves and tumuli of north Leinster and east Ulster, constructed by a specially advanced people in the 3rd millenium BC; but there were also cairns, dolmens, megaliths, and indeed pliable artefacts, surviving throughout the country, having been left behind by other ancient inhabitants. The incoming Celts must have been quite impressed by such remains and - in a conventional cultural reaction - tended to associate these non-natural aspects of the environment with mystical otherworld beings of old. The pantheon of such beings known to the Celts were their own deities, and in this way archaeological remains came to be associated with the characters and activities of Celtic mythology. Specific deities were said to have dwelt in noteworthy archaeological sites and to inhabit them still as spiritual beings, while the myth-patterns of Celtic lore were adapted to a geographical plane which was based on the occurrence of such sites in the landscape. Thus arose the Irish complex of imagery and story associated with the Tuatha Dé Danann.

The myth which gave a unified basis to the lore of the Tuatha Dé was that of a great battle (for which see **Mythological Cycle**). This myth, of Indo-European derivation, told of a primordial conflict between a divine race (which in Irish became known as the Tuatha Dé) and a demonic race (in Irish called the **Fomhóire**). It is likely that the myth was first introduced by a group of new Celtic immigrants from Britain in the 3rd or 2nd century BC (see **Nuadhu**), and, once situated on Irish soil, the plot of the myth allowed for various elements of the Celtic otherworld to be synchronised and for a logical Irish theogony to be constructed. This was further developed with the passing of time, the great battle being located at Moytirra in Co Sligo and a separate myth concerning **Lugh** being incorporated into it. Some other surviving elements of ancient Celtic lore were not overtly fitted into the Moytirra context, but were relayed as separate fragments of narrative under the general umbrella of the Tuatha Dé theme (see list at end of entry on **Mythological Cycle**).

When the early mediaeval writers set themselves the task of constructing a pseudo-history of Ireland, they enthusiastically put this mythological material to use. These writers being Christians, probably indeed monks, this part of their work had particular appeal for them, for the 'historicising' of the Tuatha Dé removed the remnants of pre-Christian religious belief from their general ambit. The culmination of the process was the long description of the Tuatha Dé given in the *Lebor Gabála* (Book of Invasions), which was assembled and expanded from the 8th century to the 12th. This book purported to tell the ancient history of Ireland, and its account became the standard source for later references to the Tuatha Dé. The gods and goddesses having been mythic patrons of arts and skills, the *Lebor Gabála* was following good precedence when it portrayed the Tuatha Dé as having among them many magical crafstmen. The division of the race into nobles and peasants, however, was probably not so much a mythic theme as a reflection of mediaeval Gaelic society. The *Lebor Gabála* tells us that only the nobles had these magical abilities, and elaborates by stating that 'gods were their men of art, non-gods their husbandmen'.

In typical mediaeval style, the Tuatha Dé are described as having been descendants of **Neimheadh** and as having sojourned in the northern parts of the world learning wizardry. The character who led them into Ireland, and their first king in the country, is stated to have been Nuadhu (q.v.), and he gained control of the whole country when the Tuatha Dé defeated the Fir Bolg at the so-called 'first' battle of Moytirra. Due to the loss of his arm in that battle, however, he was replaced for seven years by **Breas**, whose father was of the Fomhóire. When an arm made of silver was put on him, Nuadhu was restored to the kingship but was slain at the 'second' battle of Moytirra. He had given the command of his army to the newcomer Lugh in that battle, and now Lugh became king and reigned for forty years. After his death, the **Daghdha** became king and reigned for eighty years. Then Dealbhaeth reigned for ten years, and he was in turn succeeded by his son Fiacha. Finally three grandsons of the Daghdha - called Mac Cuill, Mac Céacht, and Mac Gréine - divided Ireland between them and married the three eponymous goddesses of the country called Banba, Fódla, and Éire. They ruled for twenty-nine years until the coming of the sons of **Míl**, who took the kingship for the Gaelic people.

The trio of Mac Cuill, Mac Céacht, and Mac Gréine reflect the tendency in early Irish myth to triplicate deities. This finds most striking expression in 'the three gods of Danu', called Trí Dé Danann, which designation parallels the name of the supernatural race itself. Indeed, the Tuatha Dé are called 'fir Trí nDéa' (i.e. 'men of the Three Gods') in the earliest surviving text of the Moytirra battle, where we are told that Lugh went to the three gods of Danu to provide him with weapons. It is, however, apparent that the original form of the phrase was the otherwise attested Trí Dé Dána (meaning 'three gods of art'). The *Lebor Gabála* states that the three were Brian, Iuchair, and Iucharba - sons of the goddess Danu - but three of the Tuatha Dé champions who played a leading part in the Moytirra battle were **Goibhniu** the blacksmith, Luchta the wright, and Créidhne the silversmith. These made weapons for Lugh and, although they are not expressly identified as such, it may be that they were the original 'three gods of art' who were alternately known as the three sons of Danu. Other leading characters of the Tuatha Dé mentioned in the *Lebor Gabála* were the physician **Dian Céacht**, the warrior **Oghma**, the poetess **Brighid**, and the satirist **Cridhinbhéal**.

An atmosphere of magic and mystery surrounds the Tuatha Dé in the *Lebor Gabála*. We read that they first came to Ireland in obscure clouds, landing on a mountain in the west of the country, and that they caused an eclipse of the sun which lasted for three days. They brought with them the Lia Fáil (Stone of Destiny) which cried out at **Tara** when touched by the rightful king, the great spear of Lugh which guaranteed victory to its wielder, the sword of Nuadhu from which no opponent escaped, and the cauldron of the Daghdha from which no company departed unsatisfied.

After their defeat by the Gaelic people led by the sons of Míl, the *Lebor Gabála* gives no further details, but a 12th-century writer tells that an agreement was reached whereby the Tuatha Dé left the upper half of the ground to the Gaelic people and they themselves went underground to live in the ancient barrows and cairns which dot the landscape. Thus mediaeval Irish Christianity explained the age-old belief which associated the deities with the prehistoric monuments, while at the same time demoting these deities to the level of the Fomhóire by claiming that their habitat was in the nether regions. Regarding the barrows and cairns, it was claimed that the Daghdha assigned to each of their chiefs one such dwelling - hence the idea, found throughout Irish literature, that the mystical Tuatha Dé live on side by side with the human inhabitants of Ireland. Another 12th-century writer, notwithstanding a strong antipathy to the subject which caused him to call the Tuatha Dé 'devils', puts the tradition in a nutshell when he states that they 'used to fight with men in bodily form, and used to show delights and mysteries to them, and people believed that they were immortal'. This synopsises the relationship, which is the general one in the literature, between the Tuatha Dé and the Gaelic people. One early source states that, as part of the war between them, the Tuatha Dé destroyed the corn and milk of the sons of Míl, but the Daghdha made restitution once the peace agreement was arranged.

The late mediaeval literature makes the Daghdha's son, Bodhbh Dearg, king of the Tuatha Dé, and gives to the sea-deity **Manannán** the function of dividing the ten principal otherworld dwellings among their chiefs. It is Manannán, too, who institutes the 'féth fiadha' (the probable meaning of which was 'cloak of concealment'), an obscure magical device which enabled the Tuatha Dé, when they so wished, to become invisible to the human world. He also arranged that they would have magical swine which returned to life after being killed so that the warriors could again hunt them. The variety of locations for the otherworld which is usual in human thought is evidenced by the tradition that, notwithstanding their dwelling in cairns and barrows, the Tuatha Dé are portrayed also as living in idyllic overseas realms such as Magh Meall ('the Delighftul Plain') or Eamhain Abhlach ('the Region of Apples'), which is cognate with Avalon, the version of the Celtic otherworld which surfaced later in Arthurian romance.

The later writers often confused the Tuatha Dé with the Fomhóire, and in post-mediaeval literature the Tuatha Dé are represented as having both salutary and demonic groups among them. They were thus suitable as powerful beings to be introduced into a variety of literary narratives. As well as being a vestige of the idea of a divine race, however, the Tuatha Dé were also a version of the ancient and far-flung notion of quasi-human communities living beside the human one. As such they are of the same stock as the **fairies** of ordinary folklore, and it is clear that Irish fairy lore owes much to them in its general themes.

[Archaeological remains] Michael Herity / George Eogan (1978).

[Moytirra] see references at **Mythological Cycle**.

[*Lebor Gabála* account] R A S Macalister (1941), 91-342 and (1956), 14-83 - especially (1941), 106-37 and (1956), 14-39. Cf. A G Van Hamel in *Zeitschrift für celtische Philologie 10*, 164-7, 190-3.

[Three gods] Kuno Meyer (1912), 83; E A Gray (1982), 44-5, 50-3; T F O'Rahilly (1946), 308-17.

[Tuatha Dé underground] J C Watson (1941), 1; Lilian Duncan in *Ériu 11*, 188.

[Writer on 'devils'] Myles Dillon (1953), 29. See also Toirdhealbhach Ó Raithbheartaigh (1932), 197-201.

[Daghdha makes peace with sons of Míl] Vernam Hull in *Zeitschrift für celtische Philologie 19*, 55-7.

[Ideas concerning otherworld] Cf. Myles Dillon / Nora Chadwick (1973), 182-92. See also **Manannán**.

TUATHAL TEACHTMHAR Mythical or historical king, who is reputed to have reigned in the 2nd century AD.

The name Tuathal is not a mythic one, being the Irish version of a postulated Celtic 'Teutovalos', meaning 'people's leader'. The sobriquet (earlier, Techtmar) has been variously explained, but the most likely meaning was 'possessing wealth'. Judging by the names, therefore, it seems quite possible that Tuathal Teachtmhar was a historical person, but the lore concerning him is definitely the result of propaganda invented by the Connachta (see **Conn Céadchathach**) who came to power at **Tara** in the 4th or 5th century AD. Whether he was in fact an early leader of this sept, or whether the sept expropriated his memory from some other group, he is represented in the genealogies as grandfather of Conn. The earliest surviving account of him is in a poem from the 9th century, according to which the descendants of **Ughaine** were oppressed by the subject-peoples ('aitheach-thuatha') of Ireland. A leader of these subject-peoples, Éilim mac Conrach, slew the king of Ughaine's line, who was called Fiachu, and usurped the kingship. A famine was visited on the country, for there was no harvest or fruit or fish. Then Fiachu's son, Tuathal, came to claim his heritage. He was joined by the brothers Fiachra Casán and Findmhall with six hundred men. Together they marched on Tara, and slew Éilim in the battle of Achall (at Skreen in Co Meath). Tuathal went on to win a large number of battles against the subject-peoples of all the provinces, and he then held an assembly of all the chieftains of the country at Tara and made them swear loyalty to his descendants.

These events are again referred to in a text which belongs to the 10th or 11th century. Here the assembly of chieftains which he held is called 'the Festival of Tara' i.e the ritual gathering which began a king's reign. He is also described as originator of a controversial and long-lasting tax on the Leinstermen, on account of a dishonourable act done on his daughters by their king, Eochaidh mac Eachach (see **bóraimhe**). Another mediaeval account of Tuathal tells that after the death of his father Fiachu the subject-peoples put to death all the descendants of Ughaine, except for the young Tuathal himself. His mother brought the youngster to Fiachra Casán, who commanded a hundred and fifty mercenaries in the service of the usurper Éilim. Fiachra took Tuathal into his corps, and one day the youngster went to the rath of Tara and sought admission. The usurper ordered that this be refused, but Tuathal announced that his father and grandfather had ruled at Tara. Éilim allowed him to enter then but, fearing the usurper's intentions, Fiachra spirited him out of the country. Later, when Tuathal returned to Ireland with a fleet, Fiachra took his corps to meet him at Rinn Ruamann (probably Wexford harbour), and together they fought and defeated Éilim at the battle of Achall. Still further information is given in other texts. These state that Tuathal's mother was called Eithne Imgheal, and that she was daughter of the king of Scotland. After her husband Fiachu was killed in his own house at Tara, we are told, she fled to her native country, where she gave birth to Tuathal. When he was twenty years old, he returned to Ireland with his mother and landed at Inbhear Domhnann (Malahide in Co Dublin). There they were joined by the 'díbhergaigh' (i.e. marauding outlaws) of the country, under their leader Fiachra Casán, who made him king. A 17th century source retells the story, with some variation. After Fiachu's death misfortune filled the country, and eventually the subject-peoples themselves sent messengers to Tuathal in Scotland. He was then twenty-five years of age, and when he returned with his mother and landed at Iorras Domhnann (Erris in Co Mayo) he was joined by the remnants of the nobility ('saorchlanna') who had been resisting and plundering the subject-peoples who ruled. These plunderers were led by Fiachra Casán and his brother (here called Fionnbhall), and they assisted Tuathal in defeating Éilim at Achall.

The idea that Tuathal ruled over all the provinces of Ireland is of course a fiction, for there was no high-king of the country in his time. The purpose of the fiction was to give a moral claim from immemorial tradition to the Connachta - Uí Néill overlordship, and the ancient division of Ireland into five parts was made to fit into the scheme. The fifth province was Midhe (meaning 'the middle'), and it was accordingly claimed that Tuathal had formed this province by taking pieces from each of the other four. This was explained by a false etymology for Midhe, viz. 'mede' (neck), and Tuathal was said to have 'cut off the neck of each province'. He was further said to have built four great fortresses, one in the territory expropriated from each province. These were Tlachtga (near Athboy in Co Meath) taken, in contradiction of all history and geography, from Munster; Uisneach (Ushnagh in Co Westmeath) taken from the western province, here anachronistically called Connacht; Tailtiu (Teltown in Co Meath), taken from Ulster; and Tara, taken from Leinster. Having ruled for thirty years, Tuathal was slain at Móin an Chatha (near Larne, Co Antrim), through an unspecified act of treachery by the Ulster king Mál mac Rochraidhe.

Tuathal Teachtmhar belongs solely to the literature of genealogy and pseudo-history, and no traditions of him are found in folklore.

T F O'Rahilly (1946), 154-70; C-J Guyonvarc'h in *Ogam 19*, 231-3; R A S Macalister (1956), 308-31, 484-5; Whitley Stokes in *Revue Celtique 13*, 36-43 and in *Irische Texte 3*, 332-3; D A Binchy (1978), 877; R I Best / O Bergin / M A O'Brien (1954), 250-1; Edward Gwynn (1906), 46-9, (1913), 473, and (1935), 179; P S Dinneen (1908) *2*, 238-59.

TURGESIUS (properly Thorgestr or Thorgils, in Irish Tuirgéis) Viking leader who raided Ireland in the mid-9th century. He was defeated and slain in 845 AD by Maoilsheachlainn (earlier, Mael Sechnaill), the king of Meath who in the following year became high-king of Ireland.

A detailed, and quite imaginative, account of him is given in the annals and historical tracts. We read that he came from Norway, and that he assumed the leadership of all the **Norsemen** of Ireland. He captured Armagh, the principal ecclesiastical centre, usurped the authority of the abbot there, and made himself the most powerful man in the north of the country. Gathering a great fleet on Lough Ree (on the river Shannon) he attacked and plundered the major monasteries of the midlands - including Clonmacnoise, where his wife Ota used to sit on the high-altar as if it were her throne and give pagan oracles.

Seeing one day the daughter of Maoilsheachlainn, Turgesius lusted after her and demanded her of her father. Maoilsheachlainn agreed to send the girl to him, at an island on Loch Uair (Lough Owel in Co Westmeath), accompanied by fifteen other maidens. At the appointed time, however, he sent with her fifteen beardless young men disguised in women's clothing and secretly carrying daggers. The aging Turgesius promised a woman to each of his fifteen Viking commanders, and he himself waited in his chamber for the daughter of Maoilsheachlainn. The fifteen young men wasted no time in slaughtering their hosts, and then they went and captured Turgesius. Maoilsheachlainn took him and drowned him in the lake. The drowning itself was a historical fact, but the story of the young men disguised as women is derived from Herodotus or some other Classical source. An elaboration of the story has Maoilsheachlainn, some time before, seeking advice from Turgesius concerning what should be done with some troublesome cormorants which had recently come to Ireland. Turgesius had recommended that their nests should be destroyed. Accordingly, after the drowning of the tyrant, Maoilsheachlainn put the advice to good purpose by telling the Irish to attack every Viking fortress in Ireland, and in this way the power of the raiders was broken.

The earliest version of this story concerning Turgesius dates from the 11th century, but it proved very attractive to later historians whether Norman, English, or Irish. In the 17th century, Seathrún **Céitinn** gives a much dramatised version of the story, having the girl and fifteen disguised youths being sent to Turgesius's headquarters in Dublin. They seize Turgesius there, and at the same time Maoilsheachlainn attacks with a strong force. All the Vikings are slain, except for Turgesius who is brought as a prisoner to Maoilsheachlainn's palace and from there to Loch Ainninn (Lough Ennell), rather than Lough Owel, where he is drowned. On hearing the news, the Norsemen are seized with dread throughout Ireland, race to their ships, and depart the country. The situating of the action in Dublin is the result of annalistic references to how Maoilsheachlainn defeated the Dublin Vikings and plundered their settlement in 849 - four years after the death of Turgesius.

The folklore of Westmeath claims that the tyrant had a fortress at Ballania, near Castlepollard, as well as a house on an island in Lough Lene nearby. To this house, by his command, was brought every new bride in Ireland so that Turgesius might have the opportunity of spending the first night with her. Folk accounts do not specify how he was seized by Maoilsheachlainn, but they are clear that he was shown no mercy. They describe him being bound in chains and then thrown into Lough Owel, while some storytellers elaborate further by stating that he was put into a barrel and rolled down a hillside into the water.

J H Todd (1867), xlii-lv, 12-5, 224-7; J J O'Meara (1982), 120-1; John O'Donovan (1848) *1*, 466-70; P S Dinneen (1908) *3*, 172-83; Raphael Holinshed (1586), 55-6; Meredith Hanmer (1633), 83-5; Edmund Campion (1633), 49-51; Sylvester O'Halloran (1778) *2*, 158-75; Patrick O'Kelly (1844), 207-11; Ordnance Survey Letters - Westmeath (1837), 69-76, 87-97.

[Story of disguised young men in Classical literature] see O'Meara, *op cit*, 136.

U

UGHAINE (earlier, Ugoine) Possibly a local chieftain in ancient times, Ughaine is portrayed as a prehistoric king of Ireland and ancestor of **Conn Céadchathach**. His name is usually accompanied by the epithet Mór ('great').

The mediaeval writers claimed that Ughaine had been a foster-child of the queen **Macha**. This Macha was killed by Reachtaidh Ríghdhearg who usurped the kingship of Ireland, but Ughaine slew him in turn and ruled at **Tara** for either thirty or forty years. During that time, he is reputed to have extended his dominion to cover Scotland and the Isle of Wight, and it was even claimed that he took the kingship of all Europe. A story which was known in the 10th century, but which has since been lost, was entitled 'the Hosting of Ughaine Mór to Italy', and it is clear that he was given a very fanciful reputation as a conqueror. This was apparently a projection onto him of lore associated with the historical king **Dáithí**. We are told, quite anachronistically, that Ughaine married the daughter of the king of the Franks. She, called Cessair, bore twenty-five children to him, and Ughaine divided Ireland between these in equal parts. Only two of his sons, however, had progeny. These two were Laoghaire Lorc (father of **Labhraidh**) and **Cobhthach Caol**.

Such pseudo-accuracy in attributing background detail to the débris of ancient tradition is further evidenced in an account of why he divided the country. The twenty-five children, when grown up, used to go on repeated circuits of Ireland, expecting to be lavishly fed and entertained everywhere. The nobles complained of this to Ughaine, with the result that each was given a separate area, without permission to seek provisions elsewhere. During the following three hundred years, it was claimed, these twenty-five units continued to be used for taxation and other administrative purposes.

It was said that Ughaine fell at the hands of his own brother Bodhbhcha at Teallach an Choscair (near Gormanstown in Co Meath). The fratricide, however, reigned for only a day and a half before being himself slain by his victim's son, Laoghaire Lorc.

R A S Macalister (1956), 267-75, 467; P S Dinneen (1908) *2*, 156-9; Proinsias Mac Cana (1980), 48, 59.

ULSTER CYCLE A large corpus of heroic tales in Irish literature, based on the Ulaidh, an ancient people from whom the province of Ulster got its name. The Ulaidh inhabited the eastern part of the province, and were a branch of the **Érainn** people. They called themselves Rudhraighe (which probably meant 'rightful occupiers'), and hence the literary sources often refer to them as Clann Rudhraighe. Dundrum Bay in Co Down got its ancient name, Loch Rudhraighe, from them; and the general body of legend concerning them came to be known as Rudhraigheacht. This tribal designation was early misinterpreted as having the element 'ruadh' (i.e. red), and hence the palace of the legendary king of the Ulaidh, **Conchobhar mac Neasa**, was called by mediaeval writers 'an Chraobhruadh' which means the red-branched or red-poled edifice. This (earlier, 'in chraebruad') might well have been a misunderstanding for an original term such as 'craeb ruda', which would have designated the Ulaidh as 'the rightfully occupying sept'. The mediaeval writers, at any rate, made sense of it by imagining the royal palace as a magnificent and richly ornamented house supported by 'posts of red yew', the focal point of the Ulster capital Eamhain Mhacha. From a loose rendering by translators of the texts into English, the Ulster Cycle itself is now often referred to as 'stories of the Red Branch knights'.

The mediaeval Irish writers, who made a fine art of fanciful derivation, claimed that the tribal designation Rudhraighe originated in a character of that name, who they said had been an early king of Ireland. Aware that the Ulaidh were a different people from the midland septs, who had become predominant, these writers made the fictional king Rudhraighe a descendant of Ír, who was a third and rather inconsequential son of **Míl**. In order to give support through detail to the existence of Rudhraighe, some writers described him as dying from a plague, while others had him slain by a phantom. Though some accounts tried to represent many generations of his descendants ruling Ireland (see, for example, **Breasal Bódhíobhadh** and **Ollamh Fódla**), the mediaeval historians generally had to concede that the ambit of the Ulaidh was confined to the northern part of the country. This localised power-sphere is in fact the situation postulated in all the stories of the Ulster Cycle.

The central, and structurally the basic, story in the cycle is *Táin Bó Cuailnge* (the Cattle Raid of Cooley). There are several recensions of this *Táin* epic, all presenting the same pattern of narrative. The earliest surviving recension dates from the 11th century, it being a conflation of two 9th-century texts with some extra material added by the compiler himself. The basic material which he used is believed to derive from a version of the narrative which was committed to writing as early as the 7th century. This narrative is taken to encapsulate many aspects of the culture of the ancient Ulaidh, portraying a warrior-aristocracy organised on the lines of a heroic society and providing an authentic picture from the inside of an Iron Age Celtic culture. The military-political situation described in the narrative was explained by a series of 'pre-tales' which were put together at a quite early date in support of the *Táin*. These 'pre-tales' also preserve fragments of myth and ritual from ancient tradition, and thus the general corpus evidences several details which can be compared with what Greek and Latin writers on the Continent attribute to the Celts known to them. The details include fighting from two-horse chariots, head-hunting for prestige, single combat between warriors while opposing armies stand by, the awarding of the best portion of meat to the greatest champion at a feast, and the general custom of cattle-raiding as a test of martial prowess. Lesser details in the *Táin*, such as clothes and dress, superstitions, and in some cases even phraseology, can also be matched with reports of the Continental Celts from Classical authors.

The first surviving recension of the *Táin* is somewhat disjointed; and the second surviving one, which dates from the 12th century, gives a better synthesis of the incidents. The following is the general pattern:-

The queen of Connacht, **Meadhbh**, and her husband Ailill mac Máta argued as to which of them had brought more wealth into their marriage. Meadhbh matched all of Ailill's boasts, except that he had a magnificent bull, called the Finnbheannach ('white-horned'), which had no equal in her herd. She was told, however, that there was as fine a bull in the possession of a farmer in Cooley (in Co Louth), which was the southern cantred of Ulster. Messengers were sent by her to seek a loan of that great brown bull - called the **Donn Cuailnge** - but they failed to secure it. Thereupon she gathered her army and decided to take it by force. As her great army set out, she sought a prophecy from a strange woman whom they met. The woman answered ominously: 'I see crimson, I see red!' In the forefront of Meadhbh's army was the exiled former king of Ulster, **Fearghus mac Róich** who, although thirsting for revenge against his usurper Conchobhar mac Neasa, delayed the progress of the host and sent warnings to the men of his native province. But the Ulstermen were stricken, in this the hour of their greatest need, by the magical debility which resulted from the curse which the lady **Macha** had put on them. Only the young **Cú Chulainn**, who was not a real Ulsterman - being from Muirtheimhne, on the southern border of the province - was exempt from this debility. Therefore he alone could go to face Meadhbh's Connachtmen and her assembled allies from other parts of Ireland. At Ard Cuillinn (now Crossakeel in Co Westmeath), he cut a sapling of oak with a single stroke and, using but one arm, one leg, and one eye made a hoop of it and wrote a message in **'ogham'** script. He fixed this on a stone pillar, and when the enemy approached Fearghus interpreted it to mean that the invading army should go no further until one of them could make a hoop in the same way. They circumvented that place, and next day Cú Chulainn found them near Cnoghbha (Knowth, Co Meath). He killed two warriors and their charioteers, and stuck the four heads on a tree-fork. When the army came upon this grisly sight, Fearghus stated that there was a magical prohibition (**'geis'**) against crossing that ford until one of them could remove the fork with one hand without dismounting from his chariot, because Cú Chulainn had placed it there in that manner.

Ailill asked Fearghus about Cú Chulainn (q.v.), and had described for him the youth-biography of this new Ulster hero. Next day the army went eastwards, devastating the countryside but harassed all the way by Cú Chulainn. Meadhbh grew worried as he continued his sorties, leaving hundreds dead, and she sought a parley with him. The only condition he would accept was that they should send a warrior to fight him each day and that the army should advance only while the combat lasted. Many such combats ensued, with Cú Chulainn always the victor, and since the progress of her army was thereby impossibly impeded Meadhbh reneged on the agreement. She marched north, and Cú Chulainn was sore pressed as her forces ravaged Ulster, with one contingent taking away the great brown bull of Cooley. Then the supernatural champion **Lugh** came from the otherworld to the assistance of the young warrior and held the front for him while he slept for three days and nights. When he awoke he learned that one hundred and fifty boys from Ulster had joined the fray and had killed three times their number of Meadhbh's men before being themselves overwhelmed and slain. He thus arose in a frenzy of anger, and as was his wont in such situations (see **Cú Chulainn**) his body became marvellously distorted. Mounting his chariot, which bristled with knives, hooks, and spears, he wrought havoc on the foe. In this, 'the great slaughter on the plain of Muirtheimhne', multitudes were killed and not a third of the foe escaped unscathed. The rampant Cú Chulainn sustained not a scratch, and next morning he appeared in all his splendour before the women and poets of Meadhbh's host. Struck by the beauty of his countenance and figure, the women climbed onto the soldiers' backs to behold him.

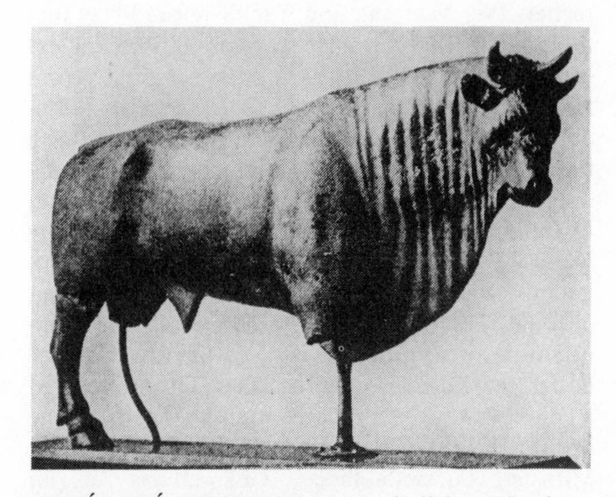

90. TÁIN BÓ CUAILNGE Bronze bull from Gaul.

Meadhbh then prevailed upon Fearghus to oppose Cú Chulainn. Since he was the young hero's former tutor, however, Fearghus brought no sword and the two reached a face-saving agreement according to which Cú Chulainn fled before Fearghus and Fearghus promised to yield to him in the final battle. Growing confident now, Meadhbh sent out parties of men to find and slay Cú Chulainn, but to no avail, as they all met with death at his hands. Finally, she tried to persuade a renowned warrior called **Fear Diadh** to oppose him. Fear Diadh was a foster-brother to Cú Chulainn. They had been trained in arms together and had faced many dangers together in former times, but Fear Diadh was one of the band of exiles who had defected from Ulster with Fearghus. He was reluctant to fight his friend, but Meadhbh insinuated that Cú Chulainn had claimed superiority over him and thus tricked him into the undertaking. In a harrowing scene, the two friends faced each other at a ford on the river Dee (Ardee in Co Louth). They fought heroically, but in the end Cú Chulainn shot his barbed javelin, the 'ga bolga', from his toes at his opponent and killed him. He lamented the death of his friend, and himself lay fainting from wounds on the ground.

Meanwhile, nine days of the crisis having passed, king Conchobhar and his Ulstermen recovered from their debility, and an advance party of their forces rescued Cú Chulainn and bore him away to a safe place. The Ulstermen fell furiously upon Meadhbh's army, and in the heat of battle Conchobhar came face to face with his old rival Fearghus. Loth to wreak havoc on his own province, Fearghus turned his rage against the hills and sheared three of these of their heads with his sword. Hearing the din of battle, Cú Chulainn himself rose from his sick-bed and rushed forth wielding his chariot as a weapon. Seeing him approach, Fearghus fulfilled his part of their agreement and led his company out of the battle. The men of Leinster and Munster followed them, and so Meadhbh's Connachtmen stood alone to face defeat by Conchobhar's Ulster forces. She appealed to Cú Chulainn to spare her army, and he consented. Crestfallen, they went westwards past Athlone into Connacht, and Fearghus remarked to Meadhbh that a drove of horses led by a mare could have no luck.

Not to be foiled, however, Meadhbh had the stolen brown bull despatched to her herd at her headquarters in Cruachain (Rathcroghan, Co Roscommon), and now the two bulls met. A ferocious contest ensued, and when night fell the noise of the Finnbheannach and the Donn Cuailgne was heard as they travelled all over Ireland goring and rending each other. In the morning, the brown was seen passing by Cruachain with the mangled carcass of its rival on its horns. The Donn Cuailgne then headed back to Ulster, scattering pieces of the dead bull at different places. On reaching its homeland, the heart burst within the great bull of Cooley and it expired.

The *Táin* thus ends, as it began, with the bulls, but they play little or no part in the main events of the story and it is indeed difficult to decipher how the several strands which run through the narrative became intertwined. The four basic themes can be enumerated as the rivalry between Fearghus and Conchobhar, the struggle between the Ulaidh and Connachta peoples, the contest between the bulls, and the heroic exploits of Cú Chulainn. The rivalry between Fearghus and Conchobhar has all the marks of a survival from ancient ritual concerning the Ulster kingship. Fearghus (q.v.) apparently was in origin a patron of that kingship, whose role was ritually taken over by the reigning king - in this case Conchobhar. The female personification of Ulster sovereignty was Macha (q.v.) who, like Fearghus, was closely associated with equine imagery. Sovereignty, however, became a precarious matter for the Ulaidh, and a protracted struggle between them and the Connachta must be the source of the great war in the *Táin* narrative. All indications are that the Connachta sept (see **Conn Céadchathach**) established themselves in the plain of Meath during the 4th century AD and caused the territory of the Ulaidh to the north of them to shrink rapidly. When the royal Ulster stronghold of Eamhain Mhacha fell to the Connachta, the focus of authority shifted to **Tara**, which the Connachta made their headquarters. Dramatised in personal terms, this meant that Fearghus went over to the side of Meadhbh, who was the female personification of Tara sovereignty and thus symbol of Connachta power. These Connachta had also extended their power across the river Shannon into the western province, which thereby became known by their name. This is the reason why the *Táin* narrative, as we have it, represents attacks on Ulster as emanating from the capital of the province of Connacht, Cruachain, and situates the power-base of Meadhbh there.

The title of the epic suggests that the theme of the bulls derives from cattle-raiding, a typical practice of great warrior-kings which is likely to have figured prominently in the warring between the Ulaidh and Connachta. The bull-lore itself, however, has a definite mythic background. The names of the two protagonists were designations of divine personages (see **Find** and **Donn**), and their contest exemplifies a tendency to view such deities as opposites to each other. One of the 'pre-tales' confirms this by describing how the two bulls had previously existed as rivals in other shapes (see **Donn Cuailgne**), and such transformations are typical of characters with divine traits in ancient Irish lore (see **Fionntan**, **Éadaoin**, **Mongán**, **Cú Roí**). The stallion imagery of Fearghus could well have given rise to an emphasis on great male animals within ancient Ulster lore, and it would have been natural to attribute divine traits to a pair of highly dramatised bulls. It has been suggested that the *Táin* contains evidence of a special bull-cult, but no other traces of such are found in Irish literature and that interpretation is hardly necessary to explain the contest of the Finnbheannach and the Donn Cuailnge.

These primitive elements - Fearghus deserting Ulster for Meadhbh, the warring, the bulls and their herds - were strung together in saga form, probably in the early 7th century. The kingdom of the Ulaidh was greatly shrunken at that time, but it had not lost memories of its earlier glory. The Dál Fiatach (who inhabited present-day Co Down) were the lineal descendants of the Ulaidh, but that honour was claimed also by the Dál nAraidhe and Dál Riata (of Co Antrim). There are several indications in the early literature that the kings of these septs were lavish patrons of poets and reciters (see **Mongán**), and it is therefore likely that the original *Táin* narrative was forged from ancient legends of the Ulaidh as a tribute paid by professional storytellers to these septs. Once its political and geographical outlines were fancifully fixed, the story underwent rapid development. It became popular, not just in the north, but also in the south of Ireland, no doubt due to a feeling of solidarity with the Ulaidh against the expansionist Connachta, whose chief branch in the 6th century had become known as Uí Néill (see **Niall Naoighiallach**). It is probable that, as literary romance has it, the Munster poet **Seanchán Toirpéist** played a significant role in developing the epic at the beginning of the 7th century. His contemporary in Munster, Luccreth moccu Chiara, has left an obscure poem which gives some insights into what the early form was. Luccreth calls his material 'seneolas' (i.e. old lore), probably intending by this the scattered legends of the ancient Ulaidh which in his own time had been assembled into a narrative unit. Fearghus mac Róich and his associates, the poem states, were proclaimed by Conchobhar, and they went to Tara, where Fearghus became the rival of Meadhbh's husband Ailill. War and cattle-raiding, apparently between the Ulaidh and the Connachta, are mentioned, and significantly a son of Fearghus plays a leading part. He, a fierce warrior called Fiacc, fights against his father.

How and when Cú Chulainn was introduced into these events is unclear, but it must have been at some stage when the narrative had assumed a stable form. It seems likely that he displaced the above-mentioned Fiacc, for in the *Táin* he is represented as a beloved foster-son of Fearghus who is nevertheless on the opposite side. It is significant that the native territory assigned to Cú Chulainn, Muirtheimhne, lies outside Ulster proper but is in the same general area as Cooley, to which the bull belonged. Being a sacred personification of war, and demonstrably a cult figure of some group in that area, the dramatic potential of Cú Chulainn (q.v.) was so great that he forced himself onto a story the title of which referred to Cooley. Moreover, a gradual development in his role can be deduced. The motif of the debility of the Ulstermen must have grown up in some way from the original fertility imagery which lies behind the legend of Macha (q.v.), and once this motif became part of the *Táin* narrative Cú Chulainn fitted well into the context as a dramatic substitute in the war. Further amplification can be traced. His boyhood deeds, for example, are described as an in-tale in the narrative, thus betraying that the passage is an insertion. Similarly, the sorrowful combat with Fear Diadh (q.v.) is a late inclusion, and the surviving recensions themselves clearly illustrate its development.

The final recension of the *Táin* was written in Modern Irish in the 15th century, and manuscript copies of this were being made until recent centuries. Yet the story of the great cattle-raid is hardly known at all in oral lore, and this may well have been the case since the end of the Middle Ages. It is a quite complex and involved story, with various levels of action, and is assembled very much as a literary rather than an oral unit. Episodes from it which have been collected from folklore, as well as some onomastic data in popular tradition referring to it, all derive from written sources in the not too remote background. The same is generally true of the whole Ulster Cycle. Stories from it, together with derived accounts, span the literature from the 8th to the 18th centuries, yet only a small selection from the narratives is found in the late folklore.

For the voluminous material of the Ulster Cycle, apart from *Táin Bó Cuailnge*, see the entries under the headings Aithirne, Amhairghin mac Éigit Salaigh, Bricriu, Cathbhadh, Cealtchair, Ceat mac Mághach, Ceithearn mac Fionntain, Conall Cearnach, Conchobhar mac Neasa, Conghal Cláiringneach, Conlaí, Cormac Conn Loingeas, Cú Chulainn, Cú Roí, Cúscraidh Meann Macha, Deirdre, Donn Cuailnge, Dubhthach Daol Uladh, Fear Diadh, Fearghus mac Léide, Fearghus mac Róich, Feircheirdne, Finn Eamhna, Fliodhais, Fraoch, Laoghaire Buadhach, Lughaidh Riabhdhearg, Macha, Maine, Meadhbh, Mór-Ríoghain, Neara mac Niadhain.

[Ulaidh] T F O'Rahilly (1946), 175-81, 341-52; F J Byrne (1973), 106-110.

[Craobhruadh] A G Van Hamel (1933), 20; Whitley Stokes in *Ériu 4*, 26-7 and *Irische Texte 2 (2)*, 135; Cecile O'Rahilly (1970), 131; Edward Gwynn (1924), 128, 130.

[Fictional king Rudhraighe] R A S Macalister (1956), 290-7, 490-1; M A O'Brien (1962), 269-86, 406-13.

[Surviving texts of *Táin*] Recension 1 = Cecile O'Rahilly (1976). Recension 2 = Cecile O'Rahilly (1970). Recension 3 = Rudolf Thurneysen in *Zeitschrift für celtische Philologie 8*, 524-54 + Max Nettlau in *Revue Celtique 14*, 254-66 and *15*, 62-78, 198-208. Fifteenth-century version = Cecile O'Rahilly (1961).

[Luccreth's poem]: Kuno Meyer in *Zeitschrift für celtische Philologie 8*, 305-7; James Carney in *Ériu 22*, 73-80.

[Discussion] K H Jackson (1964); David Greene in Myles Dillon ed (1968), 93-104; P L Henry (1978), 9-27.

[Folklore] Seán Ó Súilleabháin (1942), 597-9; Alan Bruford (1969), 93-105.

URARD MAC COISE (+990 AD) Poet who is represented in the mediaeval literature as an exemplar of his profession in its dealings with kings and nobility. He was the leading man of learning in Ireland in his time, and he died at the renowned monastery of Clonmacnoise. One text states that he was on pilgrimage when he died, and describes him as being extraordinarily charitable.

Another poet, Airbheartach mac Coise, is referred to in the annals as having been taken captive by the **Norsemen** and ransomed by **Brian Boru** at Scattery Island in the year 990. The correspondence in dates caused the two to be confused. The annals state that Airbheartach died in either 1015 or 1023. Due to the confusion, the late mediaeval writers thus felt it feasible to claim that Urard mac Coise, 'chief poet of Ireland', composed several verses on the high-kingship of Brian.

A rhetorical prose-text, known as 'the Stratagem of Urard mac Coise', seems to have been composed by the poet himself and is the basis for his portrayal in later tradition. This text tells of how Urard was despoiled by members of the northern Uí Néill sept, who carried off his wealth and destroyed his house. The poet went to **Tara** and, when asked to recite a story by the high-king Domhnall mac Muircheartaigh, he told of 'the destruction of the fort of Maol Milscothach'. It was in reality an allegory of his own misfortunes, and when Domhnall realised this he called for a judgement on the matter. The leading scholar of Clonmacnoise, called Flann, decreed full compensation to the poet, and it was decided that the chief poet should henceforth have equal honour-price with the king of Tara.

It is clear that Urard flourished at the court of the high-king, for he is associated with Domhnall's son and successor, Maoilsheachlainn, in a later story which is a kind of parody of the foregoing. We read that Maoilsheachlainn, due to his love of learning, bestowed the revenues of the kingship on Urard for one year. When the year had passed, Urard insisted on keeping the privilege permanently, whereupon the king challenged him to a combat on horseback. Maoilsheachlainn was the best horseman 'in those parts of Europe', and so he put on no armour and wielded only a headless staff for fear he might injure the poet. Urard, despite wearing full armour, was vanquished by the king.

Another fanciful story from the late mediaeval period tells of Mac Coise seeing one day on the shore of Loch Léibhinn (Loch Lene in Co Westmeath) a huge but beautiful woman weeping. He spoke to her, and she said that her sweetheart had been killed and had been buried at Clonmacnoise that very day. Going to that monastery, Mac Coise was told that nobody had been buried there for a quarter of a year. Soon after, however, a grave was being dug for a deceased monk, and the diggers found the newly-interred corpse of a huge man with a fearsome wound. They covered in the grave to discuss what to do, but when they dug again next day nothing could be found. This story is obviously a combination of belief in an otherworld community and of antiquarian speculation, but the special connection of **poets** with the otherworld is an old convention. Yet the atmosphere is that of pseudo-lore, and it is obvious that the writer was not serious in his description. We read in another story of Mac Coise shooting a swan on the Boyne. When he took it up, the swan became a woman, who explained to him that she had been put into that shape by demons. Mac Coise then brought her back to her people. Such accounts can be taken as narrative developments from the status of the poet Urard mac Coise as a reciter of ancient lore.

In the Annals, a curious little story is told of his later years. We read that he made his residence in Clonmacnoise, so that he could be near enough to the church to attend Mass every day. One night, however, an angel appeared to him and told him that his paces to and from the church would be measured by God in deciding the reward due to him. As a result of this information, Mac Coise went to live in a bog at a good distance from Clonmacnoise, and walked from there to the monastery each day.

M E Byrne in *Anecdota from Irish Manuscripts 2*, 42-76; Osborn Bergin in *Ériu 9*, 175-80; Denis Murphy (1896), 161-2; T F O'Rahilly in *Celtica 1*, 316-7; Colm Ó Lochlainn in *Éigse 3*, 208-18 and 4, 33-4; Kuno Meyer in *Zeitschrift für celtische Philologie 8*, 218-22, 559-60; J H Todd (1848), 208-11.

W

WEATHER This, of course, has always been a matter of immediate concern to people, farmers and others alike. So much depended on it in the economy of traditional society, and yet it could be very unreliable. So, great efforts were made to foresee what the weather had in store, or at least to see what was most likely to happen. In deciding on the type of weather to be expected, people used all the methods which had been worked out over many generations in order to grapple with the environment. These vary from the scientific approach and from experience to premonitions and some fantastic guesses.

The sky is the great vista whose mystery is ever-present, never diminishing, and so people observed it closely in the hope that it would reveal at least some of its secrets. Its change of colour is one obvious and interesting phenomenon. 'A reddening at night is the shepherd's delight,' we are told, 'and a reddening at morn is the shepherd's scorn!' But the distinctions could be more sophisticated, especially in winter. The old people took a red sky in the east to presage frost or even snow, while a red sky to the west meant that sunshine was imminent. If the redness was in the north, rain was coming, and if in the south there would be rain and strong wind. In spring-time, a red southern sky was taken as an indication of pleasant moist weather which would help the crops to grow. The size of the rainbow was calculated with great care. If only a small piece of it could be seen on the horizon, this was taken to mean plenty of more rain, and a rainbow in the east was considered even more ominous than a sky which was already clouded. Fishermen, however, were generally pleased with a fine rainbow high over the waves, for they took that to betoken a change for the better and a good fine period in the future.

The sun could itself be a great indicator. Bright rays emanating from it in the morning were referred to as 'cosa na gréine' ('the sun's feet'), and it was said that they were a sure sign that the evening would be fine. This was especially assured if intermittent winds blew during the morning. A close eye was kept to the moon also. If a white haze could be seen around it, and if this haze cleared from the north, very good weather was expected; but if it cleared from the south it meant the opposite. A red moon was an ominous thing, not just in the works of poets but also in the eyes of the unlettered. This red moon meant storms and the elements running wild. As for the stars, if these were perceived to be shining too brightly something was wrong also, and people - natural pessimists in the Irish climate - feared a sudden change for the worse. These folk readings of the weather chart were a mixture of observation, experience, and imagination. The same was true of the wind. If it blew from the north it would drive away the rain, but leave in its place some very harsh and cold weather, and if from the south the weather would be moist and good for farming. The east wind was dry and the west wind good for fishing as it stirred the waters. Regarding possible change in the weather, much notice was taken of fog. If it occurred as the moon was waning, this was taken to mean rain in the near future. If seen over a river, fog was considered a sign of good weather, but a cap of fog on a hill-top was not so good. This, of course, was a quite realistic interpretation, as was the idea that rain is imminent when 'distant hills are looking nigh'. But again complication could set in. For example, when fog rested on a high hill, but did not touch a lower hill adjacent to it, it meant that the rain would pass and fall somewhere else.

Things varied according to the time of day also. The Connemara people claimed that if a morning were so clear that they could see Mount Brandon far away in Kerry, that was a sign that the day would be very wet. If, however, they had that clear view in the evening, then fine weather would follow. Or at least the rain would fall overnight, for the rather tongue-in-cheek wish in Irish is: 'Báisteach ó Dhia chugainn is gan í a bheith fliuch, is cuid an lae amáirigh go dtite sí anocht!' ('May we get rain from God without it being wet, and may tomorrow's portion fall tonight!'). Frost is much feared by the countryman and the town-dweller alike. It is also quite unpredictable, especially on a night in late autumn. It is said that the great **Fionn mac Cumhaill** himself was fooled by it, for he once sold his shoes when he saw frost at night-fall. He thought that the morning would be fine, but he was wrong, and had to buy his shoes back again, no doubt at a higher price! Tradition holds that the frost is inevitably followed by rain, and its onset would be suspected if scattered raindrops were blown on the wind. Such a wind was likened to a fierce dog, ready to bite at anything which came in its way.

Leaving aside the elements, people very wisely observed what the other creatures around them were doing. Loud quacking of ducks was a proverbial sign of rain, and equally ominous was the sight of hens going to roost too early in the evening. Sea-gulls coming too far inland were taken to mean the same thing, as did the sudden appearance of an agitated flock of swallows. A crane could also be a good indicator - if this large bird moved up-river the weather would be dry, but the opposite was expected if it moved downwards. The curlew was well-known to 'whistle for rain', and the early arrival of wild geese meant that a prolonged and severe winter was in store. People also looked to domestic animals for some indications. Thus, if the dog suddenly took to eating grass and did not otherwise appear to be sick, this was taken as a sign of rain; and if the cat remained stubbornly near the fireplace, then cold and harsh weather could be expected. The goat was considered the most perceptive of all animals, being able even to see the wind. So, when the climate was about to take a turn for the worse, the goats wasted no time in going under a bush or fence, and would make every possible effort to reach the shelter of the farmyard. Something could also be learned from the bushes and trees. A quick withering of leaves in autumn was a very bad sign, being both physically and visually bleak. The old people used to say that a plentiful crop of haws indicated that a snowy winter was at hand, for providence would compensate the birds for whatever hardship was in store.

To the countryman, of course, the seasons are all important. Folklore has an intricate pattern of determining how these relate to each other, the general idea being that there is a balance in nature and that the effects of one season are cancelled out by the next. The farmers of old regarded the following as the most natural weather: - a foggy winter, a frosty spring, a variable summer, and a sunny autumn. The weather, of course, seldom behaves exactly as expected; but tradition claims that there is a very special way of knowing what variations are in store. According to this, each of the twelve days of Christmas represents a month of the following year. Whatever type of weather comes on the first day, so will January be, the second day gives a foretaste of February, the third a foretaste of March, and so on with the rest of the twelve days and the twelve months.

Seán Ó Súilleabháin (1942), 254-69; T S Ó Máille (1952) 1, 15-38; Énrí Ó Muirgheasa / Nollaig Ó hUrmoltaigh (1976), 123-33; Pádraig Ó Siochfhradha / Pádraig Ua Maoileoin (1984), 153-61.

WILLIAM OF ORANGE (1650-1702) Chief of state of the Netherlands who became King William 111 of England in 1689 after his father-in-law **James 11** was deposed. In Ireland, William is remembered for his resounding victory over James at the Battle of the Boyne on July 1st (according to the revised calendar July 11th) 1690.

94. WILLIAM OF ORANGE *King William at the Boyne, an idealised portrait.*

William had landed at Carrickfergus two and a half weeks before this, at the head of a fleet of some seven hundred ships and a huge and well-equipped army of Danes, Dutch, French, and Prussians. Folk tradition claims that he left the imprint of his foot on the quay there and that he signed his first warrant in his blood, using a sprig of hyssop for pen and saying that 'the first Orange warrant should not be written by anything made by the hand of man'. As he led his army southwards towards the Boyne, it is said that he plucked a spray of lily and wore it as his emblem, hence the Orange Lily. All of this is remembered by Irish loyalists on July 12th each year, when the victory at the Battle of the Boyne is celebrated with marches, music, and pageantry. William is represented on banners, dressed in colourful military regalia, brandishing his sword, and riding a fine white horse. He did indeed wear his full decorations in the battle - a factor which caused some worry to his supporters as it made him a conspicuous target - but this iconographic portrayal of him stems from a painting done by Benjamin West in 1771. In fact, the popular image of William belongs rather to the end of the 18th century than to the end of the 17th, for the founding of the Orange Order in 1795 made him into a figure who was a champion of all Protestant sections and an implacable opponent of 'Popery'. In fact, because of their opposition to James' supporter, Louis XIV of France, most of the Catholic powers of Europe had openly rejoiced at the victory of William; while, in a religious context, his triumph had negative results for Presbyterians as well as for Roman Catholics.

William showed great personal courage in the Battle of the Boyne, this being in stark contrast to the behaviour of James. He was wounded once in the shoulder, another shot struck the cap of his pistol, and yet another carried away the heel of his boot. Though suffering from an asthmatic attack, he rode tirelessly through the thick of the battle, personally looking to every section of his army, and refusing to retire to a safe vantage-point. He was admired for this even by his Jacobite opponents, and Patrick **Sarsfield** is reputed to have remarked later to some English officers, 'change but kings with us, and we will fight it over again with you'.

P B Ellis (1976), 56-121; Richard Bagwell *3* (1916), 294-9; S H Bell (1956), 12-9, 118-9; Lady Gregory (1926), 47-9.

WONDER TALES This is the folklore genre which has most attracted the attention of scholars, creative writers, and psycho-analysts. Several hundreds of such international folktales are listed in the Aarne-Thompson catalogue, where they are entitled 'Tales of Magic'. In the Ireland of recent centuries, they have been the most popular genre in oral narrative, and it is clear from the literature that a number of them have been current in the country for a very long time. There are good Irish reasons for this, for wonder tales are long, very stylised and open to ornamentation, and are quite bombastic in their content and form. All of these traits are particularly marked in the culture of the Irish language, which has taken to the wonder tales with special relish. They are sometimes referred to as 'fairy-tales', which is a rather inaccurate term, since fairies very rarely have a role in them. The world of the wonder tale is a fantastic one, full of strange beings and happenings, and is generally prefaced with the remark 'long ago'. That is, the events are said to have taken place in a context totally different from the ordinary experienced world, in reality a quite incredible world.

One of the most popular oral tales of all in Ireland, listed as Type 300, was also one of the most popular throughout much of the world. It tells of a beautiful princess who is being offered in sacrifice to a dragon (called in Irish 'ollphiast', or great worm). This dragon threatens to ravage her father's kingdom if the princess is not handed over to it. So, on the appointed day, the king sadly exposes his daughter on the beach, tied down in waiting for the dragon to come in from the sea. Just then, however, a widow's son arrives and fights the dragon, and in a prolonged and fierce contest slays it. The king and his people can only observe the combat at a distance, due to their fear of the terrible creature, and so they are not sure of the identity of the young hero. A false warrior pretends that he is the victor and, as the widow's son is a retiring sort of fellow, this warrior threatens the princess into going along with the deception. The unsuspecting king promises the girl in marriage to the false warrior, but on the day of the wedding the widow's son comes forward to tell the truth. The false warrior dismisses his claim, displaying the dragon's head as his trophy, but the true hero proves that he was the real dragon-slayer by producing the tongue of the fierce creature, which he had cut from its terrible maw.

Another wonder-tale has a young hero pitted against a giant who has kidnapped a princess and forced her to become his mistress (Type 302). Here again the hero is an insignificant youth, who has been kind to several creatures while on the quest for the girl. Discovering the giant's residence, he goes to visit the princess when the giant is away hunting, and she tells him that the giant has an external heart and can only be killed when that heart is destroyed. She does not know where it is located, but promises to try to discover it. When the giant returns to the house she tries in vain to inveigle the secret from him. Similarly on the second day, but on the third evening she has the threshold strewn with beautiful flowers and explains to the giant that she has done this to honour his heart, which she believes is situated there. The giant is touched by her tenderness and confides his secret to her. The heart is, he says, in an egg in a duck's belly in a well on an island in a lake. She informs the young man of this, and the creatures to whom he has been kind now come to his aid. A wolf carries him to the lakeside, a raven brings him to the island, and a salmon dives down into the well and picks up the egg as soon as the duck lays it. The youth then smashes the egg to pieces, and immediately the giant falls down dead in his residence. The youth is given the hand of the princess in marriage, and they live happily ever after. This story must have been known in Ireland for several centuries, for elements of it are used in an early mediaeval account of how the massive warrior **Cú Roí** was slain.

A story which was very popular in western Europe concerns the adventures of two young men who are twins (Type 303). In Ireland, they are called 'É the Salmon's Son' and 'Ó the Salmon's Son'. We are told of how an old fisherman catches a salmon, which speaks to him and asks that it be allowed back into the water. This he does, and the same thing happens on the second day. On the third day, however, the salmon tells him to bring it home and give it to his childless wife to eat. The fisherman does so, and as a result his wife becomes pregnant and gives birth to twin boys, who are given the names É and Ó. When they grow up, É tells his brother that he intends to go abroad to seek adventures, and so sets out, bringing with him his horse, hound, and hawk. He meets and marries a beautiful princess in a foreign land, and then sets out to subdue an evil hag who is ravaging that land. The hag, however, tricks him by feigning helplessness and fear of his animals. She pulls a long strand of hair from her head and begs him to tie the animals with it before they engage in conversation. When he does so, she strikes him with a magic wand and turns him into stone. His brother Ó at home notices blood on a flower, and from this realises that he is in trouble. So Ó sets out, with his own horse, hound, and hawk. Since they are identical twins, the princess mistakes Ó for her husband, and Ó learns from her what has happened. Going to the hag, he also ties his animals at her request, but uses a running knot, so that when she tries to enchant him the animals come to his assistance. He then slays her, and uses the magic wand to resuscitate his brother. É enquires as to how Ó learned of his fate, and is struck by jealousy when he learns of Ó's dealings with his wife. He therefore slays Ó, and returns to the princess. She remarks to him that he is much more affectionate than on the previous night, and from this he realises that his brother has not been unfaithful to him. So he uses the magic wand to resuscitate Ó, and providentially the princess has an equally beautiful sister, who becomes Ó's wife, and all ends happily.

Many versions have been collected from Irish folklore of a worldwide story concerning a youth rescuing a girl from enchantment (Type 313). The youth, in trying to effect the girl's release, gambles with the captor, but loses and is given several difficult tasks to perform as forfeit. The girl helps him to successfully carry out the tasks, and when they flee together she performs great feats of magic to keep the pursuers from catching up with them. She first throws back a comb, which turns into a forest to block the pursuers' path, then throws back a stone which turns into a mountain, and a piece of flint which becomes a great fire. They finally escape over a magic bridge, which folds up behind them and stops the pursuers for once and for all. The girl, however, has warned the youth not to kiss anybody when he gets home, for if he does he will forget her. When his dog rushes out to greet him he kisses the animal, thinking it no harm, but as a result he immediately forgets his lover. Time passes, and a marriage is arranged for him with another girl. As the wedding festivities begin, his true love appears on the scene with a magical ruse to jog his memory. She has two speaking birds, one a cock and the other a hen, which she sets talking. The whole conversation which passes between them follows word for word what the youth and herself had said to each other when they were together. In this way she succeeds in getting him to remember her, and they marry. This folktale has been current in Ireland for a long time, for several elements from it have been borrowed into the 10th-century literary story of **Éadaoin** and again into the somewhat later literary account of the high-king **Art**. The international folktale sometimes begins with a wounded eagle being cared for by the youth, who is magically plummeted into the world of the girl and her captor by precipitately opening a present given him in gratitude by the bird. Several Irish versions therefore explain the eagle's wounds by reference to a folktale concerning a war between birds and quadrupeds (see **Animal Tales**, Type 222).

The story of a magician and his pupil (Type 325) has been current in Europe from antiquity. It involves several transformations of the characters, and to this extent its plot seems to have effected the above-mentioned literary tale of **Éadaoin** as well as the account of the **Donn Cuailgne**. The folktale describes how a boy becomes apprenticed to a magician, and gains access to his master's secret book. He learns from the book how to transform himself into different shapes and, in order to help his impoverished father, turns himself into a horse which the father can sell at the market. When the magician discovers how his book has been used, he is livid with anger and attacks the pupil. In the course of their fight, they change themselves into several different shapes, and finally the pupil attempts to escape by becoming a grain of corn. At that, the magician changes himself into a cock and dives at the corn to swallow it, but the pupil becomes a fox and kills the cock, thus triumphing over his master. An equally popular folktale concerns another irrepressible youth. This fellow does not know what fear is and wishes to discover it. He spends three successive nights in a house haunted by a most boisterous ghost, and eventually the ghost speaks to him and thanks him, for the former was destined to remain there until a mortal should undergo that ordeal. Furthermore, the ghost tells him where a fine treasure is hidden, and the newly-rich youth decides to marry. He still has not discovered what fear is, but when his bride slips a live fish down his back he wakes up shivering. This is his first experience of fear! The context and the provenance of that story suggest that it originated in mediaeval Europe. Such an origin is even more definite in the case of another narrative which was popular in Ireland (Type 330). This tells of a blacksmith who sells his soul to the devil, and who then gets the opportunity to set the deal aside when guaranteed by an angel the fulfilment of any three wishes. He wishes for three foolish things - that anybody who plucks an apple from his tree, who sits on his chair, or who enters his bag, will stick thereto. When the devil comes at the appointed time to take his soul, he sticks the terrible visitor to the tree and so gains respite, and on the next occasion he gains further respite by using the chair-wish. When the devil comes for the third time, he plays on the pride of the evil one by saying that there is one feat impossible even to him, namely to escape from the blacksmith's bag. The devil angrily denies this, and to prove the point enters the bag. He gets stuck inside, however, and is subjected to a tremendous beating by the smith, so much so that he flees in terror, vowing never again to trouble the smith. When the smith dies, he is refused access to both heaven and hell because of his behaviour. Some storytellers say that he is thus fated to wander the earth continually, and that he is the strange light 'ignus fatuus' often seen at night and popularly called 'Jack of the Lantern' and 'Will of the Wisp'. Other storytellers, however, describe him throwing a deck of cards through the gates of heaven, and when told by St Peter to collect them he enters and claims successfully that nobody, once in, can be put out of heaven. In Munster, this roguish character is usually said to have been a shoemaker rather than a smith.

Type 332 originated from some literary source in mediaeval Europe, and has marked allegorical traits. It tells of a cautious man whose wife gives birth to a son, and who, wishing to avoid all conflict, rejects the offers of both God and the devil to be the child's godfather. However he accepts the offer made by death, believing the latter to be the most neutral possible patron. At the baptism, death gives the man a special present, the gift of healing, and so he becomes a famous doctor. Death says that if ever he himself is seen by the doctor at the head of a patient, then that patient must be allowed to die. After several years of successful healing, death appears at the head of a sick man, but the doctor slyly reverses the patient's position and thus tricks his benefactor. Death is angry, and soon afterwards demands the life of the doctor himself as compensation. However, the doctor again tricks him by gaining respite to say the 'Pater Noster', and then delaying recital of the prayer indefinitely. Death, however, is not fooled thrice. The doctor sees a little boy crying and, on enquiring the reason for this, is told by the boy that he will be cruelly beaten by his father if he fails to learn the words of the 'Pater Noster'. Overcome by sympathy for the child, the doctor teaches him the prayer, only to realise that in doing so he has recited it and that the little boy is death in disguise. Thus the doctor is taken away by death, an unhappy ending which is unusual in wonder tales and which reflects the unusual origin of this folk story.

Type 400 concerns a boy who is abandoned by his father and who on an island meets a girl who has been enchanted so that she becomes a swan while in water. By stealing her swan-cloak he disenchants her and they marry. On a visit home, an enemy puts him to sleep with a magic slumber-pin and, when he does not return to her, his wife thinks she is deserted. She recovers her swan-cloak and forgets him. Furnished with magic boots and assisted by a variety of animals, however, he arrives just in time before she is remarried, and they are reconciled and live happily ever after. Type 425 is in Ireland known by the title 'Cú Bán an tSléibhe' ('the White Hound of the Mountain'). It tells of a man who is put under a spell by a witch so that he becomes a hound by day and regains his own form by night only. His wife learns that she can disenchant him by burning his hide, but she does so too soon and as a result he is compelled to leave her. She follows him and, finding him in the power of the witch, decides on a plan to redeem him. She barters with the witch for one night along with him in exchange for a beautiful comb, gets a second night in exchange for a fine scissors, and a third night for her magical needle. On that third night she manages to disenchant him and win him back by a kiss.

Some quite dramatic material is found in Type 461, which has a prophecy being made to a king that a certain poor boy will marry his daughter. In order to be rid of him, the king gives the boy the extremely dangerous task of getting three hairs from the devil's beard. The boy sets out for hell, and on his way meets various people who wish to have difficult questions solved. These include a farmer who cannot understand why his well is bloody, a gardener who cannot understand why his apple-tree does not flourish, and a ferryman who does not know when he will be relieved of his magically-imposed work. Reaching hell, the boy secures the help of the devil's wife, and thereby succeeds in all his tasks. On his return home, the king is seized with envy and decides to emulate the boy's exploits. He sets out and, on reaching the river, has an oar handed to him by the ferryman, who by this means is released from his obligations. The king in his place must remain continually rowing.

A trip to the otherworld is featured also in a folktale which has a man fulfilling a promise to a dead friend or to a speaking skull (Type 470). On the way he sees some strange sights, such as a fat and a thin cow, a broad and a narrow road, a house of plenty and another of great dearth, and he has these sights explained to him by his friend. On his return home he finds that he has been many centuries absent. A variant of this international Type has a man visiting the land of the immortals and marrying its queen. She allows him to visit his home, but warns him not to get off his horse, but he breaks the prohibition, becomes old and dies. In Irish folklore this variant is always told of **Oisín**, but the fact that general versions of Type 470 have been known in Ireland for a very long time is evidenced by the use of the plot in the story of **Bran mac Feabhail** in 8th-century literature (see also **Laoghaire mac Criomhthainn**). Another narrative of the same kind is instanced by Type 471, which tells of two brothers who attempt to go thither, but neglect to cross the correct bridge and are turned into stone. Their younger brother crosses correctly, sees strange sights illustrative of religious truths, and returns home. A variant of this Type was very popular in mediaeval Europe, telling of a monk who listens to a bird singing and does not realise that centuries are passing as he does so. When the singing is over, the monk finds that all has changed around him, but is told that a monk had disappeared from that monastery without trace many years before. Versions of this story were told in the folklore of different parts of Ireland, and it occurs in a late mediaeval text concerning St **Mochaoi**.

One of the best-known folktales in Ireland is Type 503, which tells of a man with a hump who hears the **fairies** singing and dancing one night. Their tune was to the words 'Dé Luain, Dé Máirt' ('Monday, Tuesday'), and the man joined in, adding an extra day 'Dé Céadaoin' ('Wednesday'). The fairies were so pleased with this new rhythm that they took away the man's hump from him. He went home very pleased with himself and told his brother, who also was a hunchback. The brother went on the following night to the fairy dwelling, and he added all the rest of the weekdays to the words. He thereby ruined the melody, however, and in high dudgeon the fairies put the other hump on him also, leaving him with two. There are many Irish versions of the worldwide Cinderella story (Type 510), in which the heroine is called 'Cóitín Luachra' or 'Rushy Coat' and in which the supernatural helper is usually her dead mother returning in the form of a cat.

Equally popular in Ireland was Type 513, which tells of marvellous helpers who assist a young man in his attempt to recover a princess who has been stolen away by an enchantress. On his quest, the young man is joined one by one by the helpers. These include a fellow who is so strong that he can pull up trees, another so accurate that he can shoot the eye from a fly's head at a great distance, another who runs so fast that he has one leg tied up under his belt to prevent him from running away, another who can hear the grass growing, one who can blow strongly enough to drive a windmill, a great climber, and so on. By employing all their special skills, the young man manages to carry out a seemingly impossible task set by the enchantress, which is to bring water from the well at the world's end. The princess, however, states that she will marry the young man only if he or one of his retainers can defeat her in a race. She is a great runner, but proves no match for the fleet-footed helper, and so she marries her rescuer. In addition to the standard versions, this story has, since the Middle Ages, exerted a strong influence on the narratives concerning the celebrated **Fionn mac Cumhaill**. A story with certain similarities to it also exerted an influence on the Fionn-cycle in mediaeval times. The international form of this (Type 570) tells of a king who promises his daughter in marriage to any man who can herd all the rabbits in his kingdom, and of a youth who gets possession of a magic pipe with which he assembles the herd. This was adopted and adapted into the lore of Fionn's fleet-footed companion **Caoilte**, and it is not evidenced from Ireland outside of that context.

The lore of Fionn's grandson **Oscar** was influenced, in or about the 15th century, by Type 650, which related the adventures of a stupendously strong man. As well as this, the folktale survived independently in Irish oral tradition, telling of how the man was so strong that he used a tree as a walking-stick and performed several difficult tasks for his master, who feared him and wanted to be rid of him. Among the tasks were hauling a huge load of timber, threshing with a roof-beam as flail, and visiting hell and driving the devils out of that place. Somewhat earlier was the influence on the Fianna lore of Type 653, which describes four brothers with extraordinary skills. One of them can count the number of eggs in a bird's nest on a tree, another can steal the eggs, another can shoot them as they fall, and the fourth can sew the shells together again. A princess is kidnapped and taken to a high rock in a distant sea, and they set out to rescue her. The climber scales the rock and brings the others up with him, the thief steals her from the kidnapper, the marksman shoots the kidnapper with an arrow, and the handyman repairs their boat when it is in danger of sinking. Each then claims the princess as wife, but the question is undecided as to which of them best earned her. When told in the context of Fionn, the four assist him to recover a kidnapped baby, and the plot has obviously been attracted to that context by the earlier use there of the related folktale Type 513 above.

Type 655, which tells of how a man makes extraordinarily wise deductions, influenced Continental hagiography in mediaeval times, and it is in the context of saints only that it occurs in Ireland (see **Déaglán**). Wise men are fooled in Type 660. We are told of how three doctors test their skills on themselves, one removing his eyes, another his hand, and the third his heart. The organs are stolen overnight, and so they must find substitutes. The first doctor inserts a cat's eye in his own head, the second attaches a thief's hand to himself, and the third inserts a pig's heart. The result is that - much to their embarrassment, the substitute organs retain their natural propensities. That the story has been known in Ireland for some centuries is proved by the occurrence of the cat's eye motif in a literary text concerning the mythical physician **Dian Céacht**. Sight and cats figure prominently also in Irish versions of a story which compares the relative values of truth and falsehood (Type 613). According to this, a liar is judged to be more wise than a truthful man, and the liar demands that the other man pay the penalty of defeat by having his eyes knocked out. Later, the blind man overhears a nocturnal assembly of wild cats say where a bottle which could restore the sight of an afflicted princess is hidden. He gets the bottle, heals himself, and also heals the princess, for which he is given a large reward. On hearing how he learned the cure, the liar goes to the assembly of the cats to learn valuable information for himelf, but is noticed by them and they tear his eyes out.

Type 673 is a far-flung story concerning how a man learns the language of birds by eating the flesh of a white serpent which another person was cooking. This story does not occur in Ireland in its standard form, but a much altered ecotype is told concerning Fionn mac Cumhaill. This ecotype has been current since before the 12th century, but its relationship to the international pattern is an extremely complex problem (see the entry on Fionn and that on **Ó Dálaigh**, Cearbhall). The earliest instance of an occurrence in Irish literature of a catalogued wonder tale involves Type 736A, which describes how a ring is thrown into the sea but is recovered from the belly of a fish. This story was very popular in Christian literature, and that no doubt was the context from which it entered the 7th-century biography of St **Brighid**. Probably borrowed from that biography, it occurs again in the 8th-century account of the hero **Fraoch**, and it has survived in some Irish folk accounts of **Christ** and the saints.

Antti Aarne / Stith Thompson (1961), 88-254; Seán Ó Súilleabháin / R Th Christiansen (1967), 58-145; Ó Súilleabháin (1942), 559-73, 611-22; Christiansen (1959).

BOOKS AND TREATISES CITED

Aarne, Antti / Thompson, Stith *The Types of the Folktale* (Helsinki, 1961)

Almqvist, Bo *The Vikings in Irish Folk Tradition* (1975) - unpublished script in IFC *Crossing the Border: a Sampler of Irish Migratory Legends about the Supernatural* (Dublin, 1988) / Ó Catháin, Séamas / Ó Héalaí, Pádraig *The Heroic Process* (Dublin, 1987)

Anderson, Alan O / Anderson, Marjorie O Adomnan's *Life of Columba* (Edinburgh, 1961)

Andrews, Elizabeth *Ulster Folklore* (London, 1913)

Atkinson, Robert *The Passions and Homilies from Leabhar Breac* (Dublin, 1887)

Bagwell, Richard *Ireland under the Stuarts 1-3* (London, 1909-1916)

Baumgarten, Rolf *Bibliography of Irish Linguistics and Literature 1942-1971* (Dublin, 1986)

Bekker-Nielsen, Hans *Oral Tradition, Literary Tradition : a Symposium* (Odense, 1977)

Bell, Sam Hanna *Erin's Orange Lily* (London, 1956)

Bergin, Osborn *Irish Bardic Poetry* (Dublin, 1970 - ed D Greene / F Kelly) / Marstrander, Carl *Miscellany Presented to Kuno Meyer* (Halle, 1912)

Bernard, J H / Atkinson, Robert *The Irish Liber Hymnorum 1-2* (London, 1898)

Best, Richard I *Bibliography of Irish Philology and of Printed Irish Literature* (Dublin, 1913) *Bibliography of Irish Philology and Manuscript Literature Publications 1913-1941* (Dublin, 1942) / Bergin, Osborn *Lebor na hUidre* (Dublin, 1929) / Bergin, Osborn / O'Brien, Michael A *The Book of Leinster 1* (Dublin, 1954) / O'Brien, Michael A *The Book of Leinster 2-3* (Dublin, 1956-1957) / Lawlor, H J *The Martyrology of Tallaght* (London, 1931)

Bhreathnach, Áine *Damer in Irish Folk Tradition* (1972) - unpublished essay in IFC

Bieler, Ludwig *The Life and Legend of St Patrick* (Dublin, 1949) *Four Latin Lives of St Patrick* (Dublin, 1971) *The Patrician Texts in the Book of Armagh* (Dublin, 1979)

Binchy, Daniel A *Scéla Cano Meic Gartnáin* (Dublin, 1963) *Celtic and Anglo-Saxon Kingship* (Oxford, 1970) *Corpus Iuris Hibernici 1-6* (Dublin, 1978)

Bollandus, Johannes / Henschenius, Godefridus *Acta Sanctorum* (Paris, 1863)

Boswell, Charles S *An Irish Precursor of Dante* (London, 1908)

Breathnach, Breandán *Folkmusic and Dances of Ireland* (Dublin, 1971)

Breathnach, Pól / Ó Lochlainn, Colm *Beatha Aodha Ruaidh Uí Dhomhnaill 1-2* (Dublin, 1948-1957)

Breatnach, Deasún *An Púca* (1990) - unpublished thesis in Trinity College Dublin.

Briggs, Katharine A *A Dictionary of Fairies* (Middlesex, 1977) *The Vanishing People* (London, 1978)

Briody, Mícheál *Súil na Sióg le Slánú* (1977) - unpublished essay in IFC

Brewer, J S / Bullen, W *Calendar of the Carew Manuscripts 5* (London, 1871)

Bromwich, Rachel *Trioedd Ynys Prydain* (Cardiff, 1961)

Brown, Arthur C L *The Origin of the Grail Legend* (Cambridge, 1943)

Brown, Arthur / Foote, Peter *Early English and Norse Studies* (London, 1963)

Bruford, Alan *Gaelic Folk-Tales and Mediaeval Romances* (Dublin, 1969)

Bryan, Donough *The Great Earl of Kildare* (Dublin, 1933)

Burke, Bernard *The General Armory* (London, 1884)

Byrne, Francis J *Irish Kings and High-Kings* (London, 1973)

Byrne, Matthew J *Ireland under Elizabeth* (Dublin, 1903)

Byrne, Patrick *Irish Ghost Stories* (Dublin, n.d.)

Calder, George *Auraicept na n-Éces* (Edinburgh, 1917)

Campbell, John F *Leabhar na Féinne* (London, 1872)

Campion, Edmund *History of Ireland* (London, 1633)

Carney, James *Studies in Irish Literature and History* (Dublin, 1955) *The Poems of Bláthmhac son of Cú Brettan* (Dublin, 1964) *The Irish Bar-*

dic Poet (Dublin, 1967) *The Problem of St Patrick* (Dublin, 1973) - see Ó Ceithearnaigh, Séamus
Christiansen, Reidar Th *The Vikings and the Viking Wars in Irish and Gaelic Tradition* (Oslo, 1931) *The Migratory Legends* (Helsinki, 1958) *Studies in Irish and Scandinavian Folktales* (Copenhagen, 1959)
Clarke, Basil *Life of Merlin* (Cardiff, 1972)
Comyn, David *Forus Feasa ar Éirinn 1* (London, 1902)
Connellan, Owen *Imtheacht na Tromdháimhe* (Dublin, 1860)
Corkery, Daniel *The Hidden Ireland* (Dublin, 1967)
Cosgrave, John *Lives and Actions of the Most Notorious Irish Highwaymen, Tories and Rapparees* (Belfast, 1776 - 9th edition)
Couchoud, P-L *Congrés d'histoire du Christianisme* (Paris, 1928)
Cox, Michael F *Notes on the History of the Irish Horse* (Dublin, 1897)
Cramer, Thomas *Lohengrin* (Munich, 1971)
Croker, Thomas C *Legends of the Lakes* (London, 1829) *The Historical Songs of Ireland* (London, 1841)
Cross, Tom Peete *Motif-Index of Early Irish Literature* (Bloomington, 1952)
Cullen, Luke *'98 in Wicklow* (Wexford, 1938 - ed Myles V Ronan)
Curtayne, Alice *Patrick Sarsfield* (Dublin, 1934)
Curtin, Jeremiah *Hero-Tales of Ireland* (London, 1894)
Curtis, Edmund *A History of Mediaeval Ireland* (London, 1923) *A History of Ireland* (London, 1936)
Danaher, Kevin *Gentle Places and Simple Things* (Cork, 1964) *Irish Country People* (Cork, 1966) *The Year in Ireland* (Dublin, 1972) *That's How It Was* (Dublin, 1984) - see Ó Danachair, Caoimhín
Daunt, W J O'Neill *Personal Recollections of the late Daniel O'Connell 1-2* (London 1848)
Davis, Thomas see Thomas Davis Lectures
de hÍde, Dubhglas *Abhráin Ghrádha Chúige Connacht* (Dublin, 1909) *An Sgéaluidhe Gaedhealach* (Dublin, 1933) - see Hyde, Douglas
de Jubainville, H d'Arbois *The Irish Mythological Cycle* (Dublin, 1903 - trans R I Best)
de Vries, Jan *Keltische Religion* (Stuttgart, 1961) *Heroic Song and Heroic Legend* (London, 1963 - trans B J Timmer)
Dégh, Linda / Glassie, Henry / Joinas, F J *Folklore Today* (Bloomington, 1976)
Delehaye, Hippolyte *The Legends of the Saints* (London, 1907 - trans V M Crawford)
Dickson, Charles *The Life of Michael Dwyer* (Dublin, 1944)
Dillon, Myles *The Cycles of the Kings* (London, 1946) *Early Irish Literature* (Chicago, 1948) *Serglige Con Culainn* (Dublin, 1953) *Lebor na Cert* (Dublin, 1962) *Irish Sagas* (Cork, 1968) *The Archaism of Irish Tradition* (Chicago, 1969 - reprint from *Proceedings of the British Academy 33*) / Chadwick, Nora K *The Celtic Realms* (London, 1973)
Dinneen, Patrick S *Foras Feasa ar Éirinn 2-4* (London, 1908-1914) *An Irish-English Dictionary* (Dublin, 1927) / O'Donoghue, Tadhg *Dánta Aodhagáin Uí Rathaille* (London, 1911) - see Ua Duinnín, Pádraig
Dunne, John J *Haunted Ireland* (Belfast, 1977)
Edsman, Carl-Martin *Ignis Divinus* (Lund, 1949)
Egan, Patrick M *The Illustrated Guide to the City and County of Kilkenny* (Kilkenny, 1884)
Ellis, Peter Berresford *The Boyne Water* (London, 1976)
Evans, E Estyn *Irish Heritage* (Dundalk, 1942) *Irish Folk Ways* (London, 1957)
Evans, George Ewart / Thomson, David *The Leaping Hare* (London, 1974)
Evans, J Gwenogvryn *The White Book Mabinogion* (Pwllheli, 1907)
Festschrift Nikolaus Grass *sic* (Innsbruck, 1974)
FitzGerald, Brian *The Geraldines* (London, 1951)
Freeman, A Martin *Annála Connacht* (Dublin, 1944)
French W H / Hale, C B *Middle English Metrical Romances* (New York, 1964)
Gailey, Alan *Irish Folk Drama* (Cork, 1969) / Ó hÓgáin, Dáithí *Gold Under the Furze* (Dublin, 1985)
Garvey, Seán / O'Reilly, Barry *Legends of Hidden Treasure* (1986) - unpublished essay in IFC
Gaughan, J Anthony *The Knights of Glin* (Dublin, 1978)
Gautier, Léon *Bibliographie des Chansons de Geste* (Paris, 1897)
Gilbert, Thomas *A Jacobite Narrative of the War in Ireland* (Dublin, 1892)
Goedheer, Albertus J *Irish and Norse Traditions about the Battle of Clontarf* (Haarlem, 1938)
Grass, Nikolaus see Festschrift Nikolaus Grass
Gray, Elizabeth A *Cath Muige Tuired* (Dublin, 1982)
Greene, David *Fingal Rónáin and Other Stories* (Dublin, 1955

Gregory, Lady *The Kiltartan History Book* (London, 1926)
Gruffydd, W J *Math Vab Mathonwy* (Cardiff, 1928)
Gwynn, Edward J *The Metrical Dindshenchas 1-5* (Dublin, 1903, 1906, 1913, 1924, 1935)
Hanmer, Meredith *Chronicle of Ireland* (London, 1633)
Hardiman, James *Irish Minstrelsy 1-2* (London, 1831)
Haren, Michael / de Pontfarcy, Yolande *The Medieval Pilgrimage to St Patrick's Purgatory* (Enniskillen, 1988)
Hansen, R P C *The Life and Writings of the Historical St Patrick* (New York, 1983)
Harrison, Alan *An Chrosántacht* (Dublin, 1979)
Haverty, Martin *The History of Ireland* (Dublin, 1860)
Heist, W W *Vitae Sanctorum Hiberniae* (Brussels, 1965)
Henderson, George *Fled Bricrend* (London, 1899)
Hennessy, William M *The Annals of Loch Cé 1-2* (London, 1871) *Mesca Ulad* (Dublin, 1889) / Kelly, D H *The Book of Fenagh* (Dublin, 1875) / McCarthy, Bartholomew *Annals of Ulster 1-4* (London, 1887-1901)
Henry, Patrick *Saoithiúlacht na Sean-Ghaeilge* (Dublin, 1978)
Herity, Michael / Eogan, George *Ireland in Prehistory* (London, 1978)
Hill, George *The MacDonnells of Antrim* (Belfast, 1873)
Hogan, Edmund *Cath Ruis na Rígh for Bóinn* (Dublin, 1892) *The Irish Nennius and Homilies and Legends* (Dublin, 1895) *Onomasticon Goedelicum* (Dublin, 1910)
Holder, Alfred *Alt-Celtischer Sprachschatz 1-3* (Leipzig, 1896)
Holinshed, Raphael *Chronicles* (London, 1586)
Hopkin, Alannah *The Living Legend of St Patrick* (London, 1989)
Hughes, Kathleen *The Church in Early Irish Society* (London, 1966)
Hull, Vernam *Longes Mac n-Uislenn* (New York, 1949)
Hunt, B *Folk Tales of Breffny* (London, 1912)
Hyde, Douglas *A Literary History of Ireland* (London, 1899) *GF* i.e. *Giolla an Fhiugha* (London, 1899) *An Sgéaluidhe Gaedhealach* (Dublin, 1901) *Beside the Fire* (London, 1901) / Ó Conaire, Breandán *Amhráin Chúige Chonnacht* (Dublin, 1985) - see de hÍde, Dubhglas
Jackson, Kenneth *Cath Maighe Léna* (Dublin, 1938) *SB* i.e. *Scéalta ón mBlascaod* (Dublin, 1938) *The Oldest Irish Tradition* (Cambridge, 1964)
Jónsson, Gudhni *Konunga sögur* 2 (Reykjavík, 1957)
Joynt, Maud *Feis Tighe Chonáin* (Dublin, 1936) *Tromdámh Guaire* (Dublin, 1941)
Kelly, Fergus *Audacht Morainn* (Dublin, 1976)
Kelly, Matthew *Historicae Catholicae Iberniae Compendium* (Dublin, 1850)
Kenney, James F *The Sources for the Early History of Ireland : Ecclesiastical* (New York, 1929)
Kennedy, Patrick *Legends of Mount Leinster* (Dublin, 1855) *The Fireside Stories of Ireland* (Dublin, 1870)
Knott, Eleanor *Togail Bruidne Da Derga* (Dublin, 1936) *Irish Classical Poetry* (Dublin, 1957)
Krappe, Alexander H *Balor with the Evil Eye* (Columbia, 1927)
Kris, Ernst / Kurz, Otto Legend, *Myth and Magic in the Image of the Artist* (New Haven, 1979)
Kurth, Godefroid *Histoire Poétique des Mérovingiens* (Paris, 1893)
Laoide, Seosamh *Sgéaluidhe Oirghiall* (Dublin, 1905) *Cruach Chonaill* (Dublin, 1913) *Alasdair Mac Colla* (Dublin, 1914) *Réalta de'n Spéir* (Dublin, 1915)
Larminie, William *West Irish Folk-tales and Romances* (London, 1893)
Larson, Gerald J *Myth in Indo-European Antiquity* (Berkeley, 1974)
le Roux, Françoise / Guyonvarc'h, Christian-J *Les Druides* (Ouest-France, 1986)
Lehmann, Ruth *Fled Dúin na nGéd* (Dublin, 1964)
Lenihan, Edmund *In Search of Biddy Early* (Cork, 1987)
Leslie, Shane *Saint Patrick's Purgatory* (London, 1932)
Logan, Pat *Making the Cure* (Dublin, 1972)
Loomis, Gertrude Schoepperle see Studies for G S Loomis
Lorne, Marquis of *Adventures in Legend* (Westminster, 1898)
Lot, Ferdinand see Mélanges a Ferdinand Lot
Lysaght, Patricia *The Banshee* (Dublin, 1986)
Mac Airt, Seán *Leabhar Branach* (Dublin, 1944) *The Annals of Inisfallen* (Dublin, 1951)
Mac Cana, Proinsias *Celtic Mythology* (London, 1970) *The Learned Tales of Medieval Ireland* (Dublin, 1980)
Mac Cárthaigh, Críostóir *Midwife to the Fairies* (1988) - unpublished thesis in IFC
Mac Cionnaith, Láimhbheartach *Díoghluim Dána* (Dublin, 1938) - see McKenna, Lambert
Mac Gill-Fhinnein, Gordon *Gàidhlig Uidhist a Deas*

(Dublin, 1966)

Mac Giolla Chomhaill, Anraí *Beatha Cholm Cille* (Dublin, 1981)

Mac Giolla Eáin, Eoin *Dánta, Amhráin is Caointe Sheathrúin Céitinn* (Dublin, 1900) - see MacErlean, John C

Mac Giollarnáth, Seán *Loinnir Mac Leabhair agus Scéalta Gaiscidh Eile* (Dublin, 1936) *Annála Beaga ó Iorras Aithneach* (Dublin, 1941)

Mac Mathúna, Séamus *Immram Brain* (Tübingen, 1985)

Mac Néill, Eoin *Eachtra Lomnochtáin* (Dublin, 1904) *Duanaire Finn 1* (Dublin, 1908) / Macalister, R S *Leabhar Gabhála* (Dublin, 1916)

Mac Philib, Seamas *Iarlaisí* (1980) - unpublished thesis in IFC

Macalister, R A Stewart *Latin and Irish Lives of Ciarán* (Dublin, 1921) *Lebor Gabála Érenn 1-5* (Dublin, 1938-1941, 1956) *Corpus Inscriptionum Insularum Celticarum 1-2* (Dublin, 1945-1949)

MacCulloch, John A *The Religion of the Ancient Celts* (Edinburgh, 1911)

MacErlean, John C *Duanaire Dháibhidh Uí Bhruadair 3* (London, 1917) - see Mac Giolla Eáin, Eoin

MacKillop, James *Fionn Mac Cumhaill:Celtic Myth in English Literature* (New York, 1986)

MacLysaght, Edward *Irish Life in the Seventeenth Century* (Dublin, 1969)

MacManus, Dermot *The Middle Kingdom* (London, 1959)

MacManus, Seamus *Heavy Hangs the Golden Grain* (Dublin, 1951)

MacNeill, Máire *The Festival of Lughnasa* (Oxford, 1962) *Máire Rua: Lady of Leamaneh* (Whitegate, 1990)

MacNicholas, Eleanor / Ó Dúlaing, Donncha / Ross, Mícheál *The Four-leafed Shamrock and the Cock* (1989) - unpublished essay in IFC

MacSweeney, Patrick M *Caithréim Conghail Cláiringhnigh* (London, 1904)

McKenna, Lambert *Iomarbhágh na bhFileadh 1-2* (London, 1918-1920) - see Mac Cionnaith, Láimhbheartach

MacNamara, Martin *The Apocrypha in the Irish Church* (Dublin, 1975)

Maguidhir, Seosamh *Maith Thú, a Mhicí* (Monaghan, 1973) *Pádraig Mac a Liondain* (Dublin, 1977)

Malone S *Life of St Flannan* (Dublin, 1902)

Maxwell, Constantia *Irish History from Contemporary Sources* (London, 1923)

Meehan, C P *Fate and Fortunes of Tyrone and Tyrconnel* (Dublin, 1868)

Meid, Wolfgang *Táin Bó Fraích* (Dublin, 1974)

Mélanges a Ferdinand Lot *Mélanges d'histoire du Moyen Age offerts à M Ferdinand Lot* (Paris, 1925)

Mercier, Vivian *The Irish Comic Tradition* (Oxford, 1962)

Meyer, Kuno *Cath Finntrágha* (Oxford, 1885) *Aislinge Meic Conglinne* (London, 1892) *Hibernica Minora* (Oxford, 1894) *Liadain and Curithir* (London, 1902) *Four Old-Irish Songs of Summer and Winter* (London, 1903) *The Death-Tales of the Ulster Heroes* (Dublin, 1906) *The Instructions of King Cormac Mac Airt* (Dublin, 1909) *Fianaigecht* (Dublin, 1910) *Sanas Cormaic* (Halle, 1912) *HB* i.e. *Hail Brigit* (Dublin, 1912) *Über die älteste Irische Dichtung 1-2* (Berlin, 1914) / Nutt, Alfred *The Voyage of Bran 1-2* (London, 1895-1897)

Mulchrone, Kathleen *Caithréim Cellaig* (Dublin, 1933) *Bethu Phátraic* (Dublin, 1939)

Murphy, Denis *The Annals of Clonmacnoise* (Dublin, 1896) *Cromwell in Ireland* (Dublin, 1897)

Murphy, Gerard *Duanaire Finn 2-3* (London, 1933-1953) *Early Irish Lyrics* (Oxford, 1962)

Murphy, Michael J *Now You're Talking...* (Belfast, 1975)

Nagy, Joseph Falaky *The Wisdom of the Outlaw* (Berkeley, 1985)

Neilson, William *An Introduction to the Irish Language 1-3* (Achill, 1845)

Newall, Venetia J *Folklore Studies in the Twentieth Century* (London, 1980)

Ní Chléirigh, Meadhbh *Eachtra na gCuradh* (Dublin, 1941) *Coimheasgar na gCuradh* (Dublin, 1942)

Ní Chróinín, Áine *Beatha Chríost* (Dublin, 1952) - see O'Sullivan, Anne

Ní Laoire, Siobhán *Bás Cearbhaill agus Farbhlaidhe* (Dublin, 1986)

Ní Mhuirgheasa, Máire *Imtheacht an Dá Nonbhar agus Tóraidheacht Taise Taoibhghile* (Dublin, 1954) / Ó Ceithearnaigh, Séamus *Sgéalta Rómánsuíochta* (Dublin, 1952)

Ní Shéaghdha, Nessa *Agallamh na Seanórach 1-2* (Dublin, 1942), *3* (Dublin, 1945) *Tóruigheacht Dhiarmada agus Ghráinne* (Dublin, 1967) / Ní Mhuirgheasa *Trí Bruidhne* (Dublin, 1941)

Nic Amhlaoibh, Bróna *Sprid an Tobac* (1977) - unpublished essay in IFC

Nic Dhonnchadha, Lil *Aided Muirchertaig meic*

Erca (Dublin, 1964)

Nic Ghiolla Pheadair, Annaba *Irish Water Horse Beliefs* (1988) - unpublished essay in IFC

Nolan, William / McGrath, T G *Tipperary:History and Society* (Dublin, 1985)

Ó Buachalla, Breandán *Cathal Buí* (Dublin, 1975)

Ó Cadhlaigh, Cormac *Cormac Mac Airt* (Dublin, 1927) *Guaire an Oinigh* (Dublin, 1939) *An Fhiannuidheacht* (Dublin, 1947) *Diarmaid Mac Chearbhaill* (Dublin, 1950) *An Rúraíocht* (Dublin, 1956)

Ó Caithnia, Liam P *Scéal na hIomána* (Dublin, 1980) *Apalóga na bhFilí* (Dublin, 1984) *BCE* i.e. *Báirí Cos in Éirinn* (Dublin, 1984)

Ó Cathain, Séamas *The Bedside Book of Irish Folklore* (Dublin, 1980) *Irish Life and Lore* (Dublin, 1982) *Uair an Chloig Cois Teallaigh* (Dublin, 1985)

Ó Cathasaigh, Tomás *The Heroic Biography of Cormac Mac Airt* (Dublin, 1977)

Ó Ceithearnaigh, Séamus *Siabhradh Mhic na Míochomhairle* (Dublin, 1955) - see Carney, James

Ó Concheanainn, Tomás *Nua-Dhuanaire 3* (Dublin, 1981)

Ó Corráin, Donncha / Maguire, Fidelma *Gaelic Personal Names* (Dublin, 1981)

Ó Cuív, Brian *Cath Muighe Tuireadh* (Dublin, 1945)

Ó Danachair, Caoimhín *A Bibliography of Irish Ethnology and Folk Tradition* (Dublin, 1978) - see Danaher, Kevin

Ó Domhnaill, Maoghnus *Beatha Mhuire* (Dublin, 1940)

Ó Dónaill, Niall *Na Glúnta Rosannacha* (Dublin, 1952)

Ó Donnchadha, Tadhg *An Leabhar Muimhneach* (Dublin, 1940)

Ó Duilearga, Séamus *Leabhar Sheáin Í Chonaill* (Dublin, 1948) / Ó hÓgáin, Dáithí *Leabhar Stiofáin Uí Ealaoire* (Dublin, 1981)

Ó Dufaigh, Seosamh / Rainey, Brian E *Comhairle Mhic Clamha* (Lille, 1981)

Ó Fiannachta, Pádraig *An Barántas* (Maynooth, 1978)

Ó Foghludha, Risteard *Seán Clárach* (Dublin, 1933) *Cois na Cora* (Dublin, 1937) *Cois Caoin-Reathaighe* (Dublin, 1946) *Éigse na Máighe* (Dublin, 1952)

Ó Fotharta, Domhnall *Siamsa an Gheimhridh* (Dublin, 1892)

Ó Gallchobhair, Tomás *Gadaidhe Géar na Geamh-Oidhche* (Maynooth, 1915)

Ó hAodha, Donncha *Bethu Brigte* (Dublin, 1978)

Ó hEochaidh, Seán / Ní Néill, Máire / Ó Catháin, Séamas *Síscealta ó Thír Chonaill* (Dublin, 1977)

Ó hÓgáin, Dáithí *Duanaire Osraíoch* (Dublin, 1980) *Duanaire Thiobraid Árann* (Dublin, 1981) *An File* (Dublin, 1982) *C* i.e. *Cardplaying in Irish Tradition* (1982) - unpublished script in IFC *The Hero in Irish Folk History* (Dublin, 1985) *Fionn Mac Cumhaill* (Dublin, 1988)

Ó Laoghaire, Diarmaid *Ár bPaidreacha Dúchais* (Dublin, 1975)

Ó Luaighnigh, Liam *Dánta Aindréis Mhic Cruitín* (Ennis, 1935)

Ó Madagáin, Breandán *Gnéithe den Chaointeoireacht* (Dublin, 1978)

Ó Máille, Tomás S *Sean-fhocla Chonnacht 1-2* (Dublin, 1952)

Ó Maolfabhail, Art *Camán : Two Thousand Years of Hurling in Ireland* (Dundalk, 1973)

Ó Maonaigh, Cainneach *Smaointe Beatha Chríost* (Dublin, 1944)

Ó Muirgheasa, Énrí *Oidhche Áirneáil* (Dublin, 1924) *Dhá Chéad de Cheoltaibh Uladh* (Dublin, 1934) / Ó hUrmoltaigh, Nollaig *Seanfhocail Uladh* (Dublin, 1976)

Ó Murchú, Liam P *Cúirt an Mheon-Oíche* (Dublin, 1982)

Ó Nuanain, P *Glendalough* (Wicklow, 1936)

Ó Raithbheartaigh, Toirdhealbhach *Genealogical Tracts* (Dublin, 1932)

Ó Rathile, Tomás *Laoithe Cumainn* (Cork, 1925) *Dánta Grádha* (Cork, 1926) - see O'Rahilly, Thomas F

Ó Riain, Pádraig *Cath Almaine* (Dublin, 1978)

Ó Riordáin, Seán P *Tara : the Monuments on the Hill* (Dundalk, 1982)

Ó Searcaigh, Séamus *Cloich Cheann-Fhaolaidh* (Derry, 1908)

Ó Searcaigh, Séamus *Beatha Cholm Cille* (Dublin, 1967)

Ó Siochfhradha, Pádraig *An Seanchaidhe Muimhneach* (Dublin, 1932) *Triocha-Céad Chorca Dhuibhne* (Dublin, 1938) *Laoithe na Féinne* (Dublin, 1941) / Ua Maoileoin, Pádraig *Seanfhocail na Mumhan* (Dublin, 1984)

Ó Súilleabháin, Domhnall *Seanchas na Deasmhumhan* (Dublin, 1940)

Ó Súilleabháin, Seán *A Handbook of Irish Folklore* (Dublin, 1942) *Scéalta Cráibhtheacha* (Dublin, 1952 = *Béaloideas 21*) *Caitheamh Aimsire ar Thórraimh* (Dublin, 1961 - trans *Irish Wake Amusements*, Cork, 1967) *Irish Folk Custom and Belief* (Dublin, 1967) *Storytelling in Irish Tradition* (Cork, 1973) / Christiansen, Reidar Th *The*

Types of the Irish Folktale (Helsinki, 1967) - see O'Sullivan, Sean

Ó Súilleabháin, Seán C *Lá Fhéile Bríde* (Dublin, 1977)

Ó Tiománaidhe, Mícheál *Targaireacht Bhriain Ruaidh Uí Chearbháin* (Dublin, 1906)

Ó Tuama, Seán *An Grá in Amhráin na nDaoine* (Dublin, 1960)

Ó Tuathail, Éamonn *Sgéalta Mhuintir Luinigh* (Dublin, 1933) *Seanchas Ghleann Ghaibhle* (Dublin, 1934 - appendix to *Béaloideas 4*)

O'Brien, Michael A *Corpus Genealogiarum Hiberniae* (Dublin, 1962)

O'Curry, Eugene *Lectures on the Manuscript Materials of Ancient Irish History* (Dublin, 1855) *Manners and Customs of the Ancient Irish 1-3* (London, 1873)

O'Daly, Máirín *Cath Maige Mucrama* (Dublin, 1975)

O'Donovan, John *The Genealogies, Tribes and Customs of Hy-Fiachrach* (Dublin, 1844) *The Banquet of Dún na nGédh and the Battle of Magh Rath* (Dublin, 1842) *Annála Ríoghachta Éireann 1-7* (Dublin, 1848-1851) *Miscellany of the Celtic Society* (Dublin, 1849) *Three Fragments by Dubhaltach Mac Firbhisigh* (Dublin, 1860) *The Martyrology of Donegal* (Dublin, 1864) / O'Conor Don, C O *The O'Conors of Connaught* (Dublin, 1891)

O'Duffy, Richard J *Oidhe Chloinne Tuireann* (Dublin, 1888)

O'Dwyer, Peter *Mary : a History of Devotion in Ireland* (Dublin, 1988)

O'Fihelly, Patrick *Mil na mBeach* (Dublin, 1911)

O'Grady, Standish Hayes *Silva Gadelica 1-2* (London, 1892) *Caithréim Thoirdhealbhaigh 1-2* (London, 1929)

O'Halloran, Sylvester *The History and Antiquities of Ireland 1-3* (Dublin, 1778)

O'Hanlon, John *Lives of the Irish Saints 1-9* (Dublin, 1875ff)

O'Kearney, Nicholas *The Prophecies of St Columbkille* (Dublin, 1856)

O'Keeffe, James G *Buile Suibhne* (London, 1913)

O'Kelleher, Andrew / Schoepperle, Gertrude *Betha Colaim Chille* (Illinois, 1918)

O'Kelly, Patrick *The History of Ireland by the Abbé Mac-Geoghagan* (Dublin, 1844)

O'Meara, John J *The History and Topography of Ireland : Gerald of Wales* (Middlesex, 1982) *The Voyage of Saint Brendan* (Dublin, 1978)

O'Neill, Elizabeth *Owen Roe O'Neill* (Dublin, 1937)

O'Reilly, Barry *Two Irish Legends of Fate* (1985) - unpublished essay in IFC

O'Rahilly, Cecile *Tóruigheacht Gruaidhe Griansholus* (London, 1924) *Five Seventeenth-Century Political Poems* (Dublin, 1952) *Cath Finntrágha* (Dublin, 1962) *The Stowe Version of Táin Bó Cuailnge* (Dublin, 1961) *Táin Bó Cuailnge from the Book of Leinster* (Dublin, 1970) *Táin Bó Cuailnge : Recension 1* (Dublin, 1976)

O'Rahilly, Thomas F *Dánfhocail* (Dublin, 1921) *The Goidels and their Predecessors* (Oxford, 1935) *Early Irish History and Mythology* (Dublin, 1946) - see Ó Rathile, Tomás

O'Sullivan, Anne *The Book of Leinster 6* (Dublin, 1983) - see Ní Chróinín, Áine

O'Sullivan, Donal *Carolan 1-2* (London, 1958) *Irish Folk Music, Song and Dance* (Cork, 1974)

O'Sullivan, Sean *Folktales of Ireland* (London, 1966) *The Folklore of Ireland* (London, 1974) *Legends from Ireland* (London, 1977) - see Ó Súilleabháin, Seán

Oskamp, H P A *The Voyage of Máel Dúin* (Groningen, 1970)

Owens, Cóilín *Family Chronicles : Maria Edgeworth's Castle Rackrent* (Dublin, 1987)

Partridge, Angela *Caoineadh na dTrí Muire* (Dublin, 1983)

Pauli, Johannis *Schimpf und Ernst 1* (New York, 1972)

Petrie, George *The Ecclesiastical Architecture of Ireland* (Dublin, 1845)

Piggott, Stuart *The Druids* (London, 1968)

Plummer, Charles *Vitae Sanctorum Hiberniae 1-2* (Oxford, 1910) *Bethada Náem nÉrenn 1-2* (Oxford, 1922) *Miscellanea Hagiographica Hibernica* (Brussels, 1925)

Pokorny, Julius *Indogermanisches Etymologisches Wörterbuch* (Bern, 1959)

Powell, T G E *The Celts* (London, 1958)

Power, Patrick *Lives of Ss Declan and Mochuda* (London, 1914)

Rank, Otto *The Myth of the Birth of the Hero* (New York, 1914)

RIA Dictionary *Contributions to a Dictionary of the Irish Language* (Royal Irish Academy : Dublin, 1913-1975)

Reinhard, John R *The Survival of Geis in Medieval Romance* (Halle, 1933)

Richmond, W Edson *Studies in Folklore* (Bloomington, 1957)

Robinson, Fred Norris *Satirists and Enchanters in Early Irish Literature* (New York, 1969 - originally in D G Lyon / G F Moore eds, *Studies in the History of Religions*, New York

1912)
Roider, Ulrike *De Chophur in Da Muccida* (Innsbruck, 1979)
Ross, Anne *Everyday Life of the Pagan Celts* (London, 1970) *Pagan Celtic Britain* (London, 1974)
Ross, Neil *Heroic Poetry from the Book of the Dean of Lismore* (Edinburgh, 1939)
Ryan, John *Irish Monasticism* (Dublin, 1931) - see Ua Riain, Eoin
Shaw, Francis *The Dream of Oengus* (Dublin, 1934)
Sheridan, Thomas *The Life of the Reverend Dr Jonathan Swift* (London, 1784)
Sjoestedt, Marie-Louise *Gods and Heroes of the Celts* - trans Myles Dillon (Berkeley, 1982)
Smyth, Alfred P *Celtic Leinster* (Dublin, 1982)
Stokes, Whitley *The Calendar of Óengus* (Dublin, 1880) *The Tripartite Life of Patrick 1-2* (London, 1887) *Lives of the Saints from the Book of Lismore* (Oxford, 1890) *The Bodleian Dinnshenchas* (London, 1892) *Acallamh na Senórach* (Leipzig, 1900 = *Irische Texte 4*) *Félire Óengusso Céli Dé* (London, 1905) *CTS* i.e. *The Colloquy of the Two Sages* (Paris, 1905) *The Birth and Life of St Moling* (London, 1907) / Strachan, John *Thesaurus Palaeohibernicus 1-2* (Cambridge, 1901-1903)
Strachan, Geoffrey *Irish Fairy Tales* (London, 1904)
Studies for G S Loomis *Medieval Studies in Memory of Gertrude Schoepperle Loomis* (Paris, 1927)
Szövérrfy, Joseph *Irisches Erzählgut im Abendland* (Berlin, 1957) *Some Stages of the St Columba Traditions in the Middle Ages* (Boston, 1988)
Taylor, Archer *The Black Ox* (Helsinki, 1927)
Thevenot, Émile *Divinités et Sanctuaires de la Gaule* (Paris, 1968)
Thomas Davis Lectures *Great Books of Ireland* (Thomas Davis Lectures, Radio Telefís Éireann : Dublin, 1967)
Thompson, E A *Who Was Saint Patrick?* (Suffolk, 1985)
Thompson, Stith *Motif-Index of Folk-Literature 1-6* (Bloomington, 1955-1958)
Thoms, William J *Lays and Legends of Ireland* (London, 1834)
Thomson, David *The People of the Sea* (London, 1965)
Thurneysen, Rudolf *Die irische Helden- und Königsage* (Halle, 1921) *Scéla Mucce Meic Dathó* (Dublin, 1935)
Todd, James Henthorpe *The Irish Version of the Historia Britonum of Nennius* (Dublin, 1848) *The War of the Gaedhil with the Gaill* (Dublin, 1867)
Ua Ceallaigh, Seán *Trí Truagha na Scéaluigheachta* (Dublin, 1927) *Rudhraigheacht* (Dublin, 1935)
Ua Duinnín, Pádraig *Amhráin Eoghain Ruaidh Uí Shúilleabháin* (Dublin, 1901) *Beatha Eoghain Ruaidh Uí Shúilleabháin* (Dublin, 1902) *Dánta Phiarais Feiritéir* (Dublin, 1903)
Ua Murchadha, Domhnall *Sean-Aimsireacht* (Dublin, 1939)
Ua Riain, Eoin *Féil-sgríbhinn Eoin Mhic Néill* (Dublin, 1940) - see Ryan, John
Uí Ógáin, Ríonach *An Rí gan Choróin* (Dublin, 1984)
Van Hamel, A G *Lebor Bretnach* (Dublin, 1932) *Compert Con Culainn* (Dublin, 1933)
Vendryes, Joseph *Airne Fíngein* (Dublin, 1953)
Wainright, F T *The Problem of the Picts* (Edinburgh, 1955)
Walker, Joseph Cooper *Historical Memoirs of the Irish Bards* (Dublin, 1786)
Watson, J Carmichael *Mesca Uladh* (Dublin, 1941)
Watson, Seosamh *Mac na Míchomhairle* (Dublin, 1979) *Féilscribhinn Thomáis de Bhaldraithe* (Dublin, 1986)
Wentz, W Y Evans *The Fairy Faith in Celtic Countries* (London, 1911)
Westwood, Jennifer *Albion:a Guide to Legendary Britain* (London, 1987)
Wilde, Lady *Ancient Legends of Ireland* (London, 1888)
Williams, Ifor *Pedeir Keinc y Mabinogi* (Cardiff, 1930)
Williams, J E Caerwyn *The Court Poet in Medieval Ireland* (London, 1971)
Williams, Nicholas J A *Dánta Mhuiris Mhic Dháibhí Dhuibh Mhic Gearailt* (Dublin, 1979) *The Poems of Giolla Brighde Mac Con Midhe* (Dublin, 1980) *Pairlement Chloinne Tomáis* (Dublin, 1981) *Cniogaide Cnagaide* (Dublin, 1988)
Windisch, Ernst *Die altirische Heldensage Táin Bó Cúailgne* (Leipzig, 1905)
Wood, Herbert *The Chronicle of Ireland 1584-1608* (Dublin, 1933)
Wood-Martin, W G *Traces of the Elder Faiths of Ireland 1-2* (London, 1902)

PERIODICALS CITED

('The' as an ordinary preface to several of the titles has been omitted here, but the Irish equivalent 'An' has been retained)

An Claidheamh Soluis (Dublin, 1899-1932)

An Gaodhal 1-23 (New York, 1884-1904)

An Lóchrann (Dublin, 1907-1931)

An Stoc (Dublin, 1923-1930)

Analecta Bollandiana (Brussels/Paris, 1882-)

Anecdota from Irish Manuscripts 1-5 (Halle, 1907-1913)

Anecdota Oxoniensia, Mediaeval and Modern Series, *1-15* (Oxford, 1882-1929)

Ar Aghaidh (Galway, 1931-1970)

Archiv für celtische Lexikographie 1-3 (Halle, 1898-1907)

Archivium Hibernicum (Maynooth, 1912-)

Arv (Stockholm, 1945-)

Atlantis 1-5 (Dublin, 1858-1870)

Béaloideas (Dublin, 1927-)

Bentley's Miscellany 1-64 (London, 1837-1868)

Celtic Review 1-10 (1904-1910)

Celtica (Dublin, 1946-)

Comhar (Dublin, 1938-)

Dublin Historical Record (Dublin, 1938-)

Dublin University Magazine 1-75 (Dublin, 1833-1870)

Edda (Oslo, 1913-)

Éigse (Dublin, 1939-)

Emania (Belfast, 1987-)

Ériu (Dublin, 1904-)

Études Celtiques (Paris, 1936-)

Feasta (Dublin, 1948-)

Folk-Lore (London, 1890-)

Galvia (Galway, 1954-)

Hermathena (Dublin, 1873-)

Irische Texte 1-4 (Leipzig, 1880-1909)

Irish Independent (Dublin, daily newspaper)

Irish Monthly 1-83 (Dublin, 1873-1954)

Irish Press (Dublin, daily newspaper)

Irish Rosary (Dublin, 1897-)

Irish Texts 1-5 (London, 1931-1934)

Irish University Review (Dublin, 1970-)

Irisleabhar Muighe Nuadhat (Maynooth, 1907-)

Irisleabhar na Gaedhilge 1-19 (Dublin, 1882-1909)

Journal of American Folklore (New York, 1888-)

Journal of the Cork Historical and Archaeological Society (Cork, 1892-)

Journal of the Galway Archaeological and Historical Society (Dublin, 1900-)

Journal of the Kildare Archaeological Society (Dublin, 1892-)

Journal of the Royal Society of Antiquaries of Ireland - originally, *Journal of the Kilkenny Archaeological Society* (Dublin, 1849-)

Léachtaí Cholm Cille (Maynooth, 1970-)

Lia Fáil 1-3 (Dublin, 1928-1930)

Lochlann (Oslo, 1958-)

Modern Language Review (Cambridge, 1906-)

New Ireland Review 1-32 (Dublin, 1894-1910)

Ogam (Rennes, 1948-)

Old Kilkenny Review, Ist Series, 1-25 (Kilkenny, 1946-1973)

Otia Merseiana 1-4 (Liverpool, 1899-1904)

Patrologiae Latinae 1-221 (Paris, 1844-1864)

Proceedings of the Belfast Natural History and Philosophical Society, 2nd Series (Belfast, 1935-)

Proceedings of the British Academy (London, 1903-)

Proceedings of the Royal Irish Academy (Dublin, 1836-)

Publications of the Modern Language Association of America (Wisconsin, 1884-)

Revue Celtique 1-55 (Paris, 1870-1934)

Saga och Sed (Uppsala, 1932-)

Scottish Gaelic Studies (Edinburgh, 1926-)

Scottish Studies (Edinburgh, 1957-)

Sinsear (Dublin, 1979-)

Speculum (Cambridge, Massachusetts, 1926-)

Studia Celtica (Cardiff, 1966-)

Studia Hibernica (Dublin, 1961-)

Studies (Dublin, 1912-)

Shamrock 1-34 (Dublin, 1867-1896)

Ulster Journal of Archaeology, 3rd Series (Belfast, 1938-)

Ulster Folklife (Belfast, 1955-)

Veröffentlichungen der keltischen Kommission (Vienna, 1981-)

Zeitschrift für celtische Philologie (Halle, 1896-)

REFERENCES TO MANUSCRIPTS

IFC Irish Folklore Collection in the Department of Irish Folklore, University College, Dublin

OSL Ordnance Survey Letters in the Placenames Commission, Dublin

RIA Gaelic collection in the Royal Irish Academy, Dublin

INDEX 1

(characters and personages in lore)

INDEX 2

(peoples, septs, groups, and families)

INDEX 3

(places, with locations in Ireland indicated generally by county)

INDEX 4
(general subjects)

NOTES

NOTES

NOTES